# A History of Latin America

SEVENTH EDITION

VOLUME 2
Independence to the Present

Benjamin Keen

Keith Haynes

*The College of Saint Rose*

Houghton Mifflin Company    Boston    New York

Publisher: Charles Hartford
Editor in Chief: Jean L. Woy
Senior Sponsoring Editor: Sally Constable
Development Editor: Leah R. Strauss
Senior Project Editor: Christina M. Horn
Senior Production/Design Coordinator: Jodi O'Rourke
Senior Designer: Henry Rachlin
Senior Manufacturing Coordinator: Marie Barnes
Senior Marketing Manager: Sandra McGuire

Volume 2 cover image: Araujo Yaponi, *Nuptial Dance*, Brazil, 20th century. © Superstock.

Printed in the U.S.A.

Library of Congress Control Number: 2002109494

ISBN: 0-618-31853-4

1 2 3 4 5 6 7 8 9-QUF-07 06 05 04 03

# CONTENTS

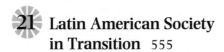
# Maps

# PREFACE

T HE SEVENTH EDITION of *A History of Latin America* has two major objectives. First, it seeks to make available to teachers and students of Latin American history a text based on the best recent scholarship, enriched with data and concepts drawn from the sister social sciences of economics, anthropology, and sociology. Because the book is a history of Latin American *civilization*, it devotes considerable space to the way of life adopted at each period of the region's history. To enable students to deepen their knowledge of Latin American history and culture on their own, it includes an updated bibliography, "Suggestions for Further Reading," limited to titles in English.

The second objective of this edition is to set Latin American history within a broad interpretive framework. This framework is the "dependency theory," the most influential theoretical model for social scientists concerned with understanding Latin America. Not all followers of the theory understand it in precisely the same way, but most probably agree with the definition of *dependency* offered by the Brazilian scholar Theotonio dos Santos: "A situation in which the economy of certain countries is conditioned by the development and expansion of another economy to which the former is subject."

Writers of the dependency school employ some standard terms that we use in this text: *neocolonialism, neoliberalism, center,* and *periphery. Neocolonialism* refers to the dependent condition of countries that enjoy formal political independence. *Neoliberalism* refers to the policies of privatization, austerity, and trade liberalization accepted willingly or unwillingly by the governments of dependent countries as a condition of approval of investment, loans, and debt relief by the International Monetary Fund and the World Bank. (The IMF and the World Bank prefer to give such policies the innocuous-sounding name of "structural adjustment programs.") The term *center* is applied to the dominant group of developed capitalist countries, and *periphery* to the underdeveloped or dependent countries.

Periodically, dependency theory has come under attack from scholars, mostly North American, who announce its "collapse." The most recent announcements of dependency theory's "collapse" have been linked to the seeming triumph of neoliberal ideology and its creation, the so-called global economy. Claiming that the neoliberal tide can lift all ships, including the countries of Latin America and the rest of the Third World, and pointing for proof in the case of Latin America to such macroeconomic indicators as increased exports (often based on intense exploitation of finite natural resources and subject to sudden changes in price and demand) and large inflows of foreign capital (often speculative and volatile), these critics argue that dependency theory was basically flawed and outmoded, that its analysis of Latin America's problems has lost all meaning in today's world.

Those who reject the dependency approach typically favor one of a number of alternative paradigms for explaining Latin America's historical struggle for development. Among these scholars, modernization theory informed and dominated discussions in the United States and Western Europe in the first decades following World War II. Drawing upon their own postwar national experiences, these theorists typically assumed that "underdevelopment" and "economic backwardness" were conditions common to all societies at one time in their evolution. The key to unlocking the mystery of development, for these scholars, was to study conditions in the "developed countries" in contrast to those in "tropical" or undeveloped areas. This produced a prescription for social, political, cultural, and economic change that sought to bring the developmental benefits of modernity to all. As a result of their studies, the modernizationists concluded that the undeveloped world suffered from a lack of personal freedom, excessive government regulation, highly politicized states, weak civil societies, a shortage of "entrepreneurial values," and the survival of powerful "antimodern" cultural traditions that stressed cooperative communal, rather than competitive individualistic, values.

For the modernization theorists, then, Latin America's "failure" to develop was largely a consequence of its own internal problems and its reluctance to open itself to the forces of modernity that allegedly emanated from Western Europe and the United States. Some authors even suggested that this "failure" was the product of a "distinct tradition" in Latin America, informed by a historical legacy of militarism, local political bosses (*caudillaje*), indigenous communalism, and insular Iberic Catholic culture. To combat these alleged deficiencies in the developmental experiences of Latin America, the modernizationists prescribed a bitter medicine that largely mirrored what recently have come to be known as neoliberal imperatives: dismantle state bureaucracies, reduce budget deficits, cut spending on social services, deregulate private business, privatize national resources, provide incentives to foreign investors, promote free trade, encourage entrepreneurial education, and reduce the political power of "antimodern" social sectors.

But a rapid glance at the results of over a decade of application of neoliberal therapy to Latin America's problems suggests that in all essential respects, the area's economic and social crisis has worsened and its dependency on the core capitalist powers has deepened. We draw upon a critical synthesis of these two intellectual traditions and emphasize both internal and external factors that have shaped Latin America's historical struggle for development. We expose the developmentalist myths that all countries have been equally "underdeveloped" in their historical past and that the "developed countries" achieved modernity by promoting personal freedom, free trade, and unfettered foreign direct investment. On the contrary, the text unambiguously shows that European and U.S. modernity was built upon a five-century legacy of brutal conquest, enslavement, exploitation, and unequal trade enforced alternately by military and market coercion. Moreover, unlike classical dependency theorists, who emphasized transnational social forces and institutional structures of power that seemingly rendered inconsequential all forms of popular resistance, this text documents the powerful role that internal class,

racial, gender, ethnic, and interest group struggles have played in shaping the region's development.

Unlike both classical dependency and modernizationist formulations, this text's "revised dependency" approach also draws upon recent feminist theorization that defines women as the "last colony," whose shared experiences, according to feminist scholars Christine Bose and Edna Acosta-Belén, include unwaged and low-wage labor, extreme poverty, and "structural subordination and dependency." But women, like colonial peoples more generally, have not been passive victims in the developmental process. They have been active in the spheres of both production and reproduction. As producers of material wealth in Latin America, women have played a significant, but largely neglected, historical role, working endless hours without pay in household activities that have been an essential source of private capital accumulation. For example, even an inefficient colonial workforce needed certain household services—shopping, cooking, cleaning, first aid, child-rearing, washing, elder care, and so on—in order to reproduce its labor on a daily basis. If poorly paid male workers in Latin America had had to purchase these services that women—wives and daughters—freely provided, they would have had to insist upon higher wages and employers would have had to pay these higher costs out of profits.

Historically, women were largely confined to the family household, where they were responsible for reproduction, rearing, nurturing, and educating the next generation of producers. Once "freed" from these constraints to seek employment in the marketplace, however, many working-class women became doubly exploited, first as poorly paid wage earners whose collective hard work outside the home produced great value that enriched their employers, and second as traditional unwaged household labor that sustained working-class families as the bedrock of classical capital accumulation. This text both highlights the transition of women's roles in Latin America and documents women's demand for state regulation of market activities to protect their developmental contributions in the vital areas of production and reproduction.

Like classical dependency writers who originally blamed global markets for Latin America's poverty and doubted the region's developmental potential in the absence of socialism, we conclude that market expansion has created economic growth at the expense of development. But unlike these classical dependency theorists, we stress the key role of popular social movements in taming markets, restraining inequities produced by their unregulated activities, and transforming them into agents of development. Contrary to modernizationists who argued that market expansion was key to development, this text shows that markets in and of themselves have been far less important than how they have been regulated. The specific nature of these regulations, in turn, has been shaped by historical struggles. In socialist Cuba, for example, the expansion of market activities since the collapse of the Soviet Union and its global trading partners has had a decidedly different developmental impact than it has had in neoliberal Argentina or Peru. Similarly, global markets have been regulated differently in Chile, Venezuela, and Brazil, with correspondingly different developmental impacts. Our text documents these conclusions in historical detail, but here we present a few telling facts that underline the general collapse of the neoliberal, modernizationist model and simultaneously reinforce the relevance of our revised dependency perspective.

First, since the early 1980s, when neoliberal orthodoxy emerged as the dominant paradigm for promoting development in Latin America, this region, in effect, has subsidized wealthy industrial nations. During this period, Latin American nations claimed smaller shares of the world's income as the U.S. share grew. According to the *Atlas of Global Inequality* compiled at the University of California at Santa Cruz, the national income of the United States as a percentage of the global mean average national income doubled between 1980 and 1999, while it declined for every single Latin American country, with two types of exceptions: those countries like Haiti and Honduras, whose national incomes in 1980 already ranked at the lowest level, and those like Panama, Colombia, and the Dominican Republic, whose rank remained unchanged. According to Mexican economic historian Carlos Marichal, since 1980 Mexico alone has paid almost $300 billion in foreign debt service on an original loan of $100 billion.

Second, poverty and inequality within each of the countries in the region either have remained stubbornly high or have grown. Recent estimates in 2002 suggest that more than 200 million Latin Americans live below the poverty line. Even the World Bank, a relentless and enthusiastic champion of neoliberalism, acknowledges that its prescription for national development has not solved the problem of poverty, which it conservatively estimated at affecting 159 million people in 1998, an increase over the 1987 figure of 148 million. Extreme poverty,

according to the Economic Commission on Latin America, grew even more steadily from 36 million people in 1980 to 74.5 million in 1995. Even more significant than this decade-long growth in poverty was the stark inequality that the World Bank reported in its *World Development Indicators* for 2002: on average, the poorest 20 percent of the region's population received only 3.5 percent of their country's income, while the richest 10 percent claimed 40 percent of their nation's wealth.

Third, the region is more dependent on foreigners than ever before in its history. External debt in 1980 almost doubled from $257.3 billion to $475.4 billion in 1990, and then it grew by another 70 percent to $813.4 billion in 1999. During the same period, debt service as a percentage of revenues from exports increased dramatically from 34.4 to 41.8 percent, which meant that out of every $1 earned in export sales, Latin America sent 42¢ to foreign bankers. Foreign export trade dependency also grew. From 1980 to 1990, Latin American exports grew at 4.3 percent per year, but they rose to 15 percent per year in the decade ending in 2000. Moreover, the export-oriented nature of neoliberal development strategies reinforced the region's traditional reliance on a few largely agricultural and mineral raw materials. With the exception of Mexico, all Latin American nations depended on one or two products for 40 percent of their export revenues. Reliance on foreign imports also increased faster than export growth, rising from an average annual rate of 2.1 percent in the 1980s to 17.3 percent in the 1990s. The resulting trade imbalances, combined with other hidden costs of trade, produced dramatically larger deficits in Latin America's current account balance, which skyrocketed from $1.1 billion in 1990 to $46.8 billion in 2000.

Fourth, unemployment, underemployment, and precarious, low-income "informal sector" employment all increased steadily throughout the region, making it virtually impossible for working families to subsist on a single income. Even the World Bank's conservative official estimates show that regional unemployment grew each year from a low of 6 percent in 1990 to a high of 9.2 percent in 1999. Moreover, neoliberal policies that increased unemployment forced women to enter the wage force at significantly higher rates, to prevent their families from falling below the poverty line. By 1995 women constituted 44.5 percent of the paid labor force. Women who were not heads of households contributed from 25 to 35 percent of household income. But the number of female heads of households also rose by 2 to 5 percent throughout the 1990s, and these women, according to a 1995 ECLA report, "experience higher rates of unemployment, lower numbers of hours worked, lower salaries and greater difficulties in entering the market than do male heads of household."

Fifth, political violence and disillusionment with democracy have grown dramatically, along with popular disrespect for politicians who preach electoral populism and practice neoliberal governance. According to a respected Chilean public opinion pollster, Latinobarómetro, popular support for democracy over the past five years has declined in every country except Mexico. In Argentina, it fell from 71 percent in 2000 to 58 percent in 2001; in Venezuela, support declined only modestly from 61 to 57 percent, in part due to the popularity of Hugo Chávez, the populist paratrooper elected to the presidency in 1998. More people now trust the military (39 percent) than political parties (19 percent), parliament (22 percent), or the judiciary (26 percent). Even more striking, the percentage of people who feel trust in their fellow citizens has fallen steadily in every country except Mexico and Nicaragua.

Sixth and finally, these changes were not the result of economic recession but occurred in the context of substantial economic growth largely fueled by the region's close ties to U.S. markets, which experienced a decade of unprecedented prosperity. With the exception of significant declines in 1994 and 1997, Latin America benefited from a decade of generally strong global economic expansion. After a comparatively anemic increase of 43 percent from 1980 to 1990, the region's average gross national product nearly doubled from 1990 to 2000. Perhaps the most striking of these facts is this: dramatic economic growth in the 1990s bequeathed a legacy of social inequality and political disenchantment.

Meanwhile, the deepening Latin American dependency has assumed a more sinister form. The drug traffic to the United States and Europe has virtually become the life support system of the economies of Bolivia, Colombia, and Peru, and its influence, as recent revelations show, has reached into the highest levels of officialdom in countries like Colombia and Mexico. Another symptom of growing dependency, directly linked to the impact of neoliberal policies on the Mexican economy, is the swelling flood of illegal immigrants seeking to cross the U.S.-Mexican border and the violence inherent in U.S. policies designed to prevent this immigration, such as Operation Gatekeeper. According to a study by the University of Houston, "Death at the Border," from 1993 to 1996 nearly 1,200 immigrants died while attempting to cross the U.S.-Mexican border. In the light of these and other compelling facts, it appears that dependency theory continues to have a large relevance for Latin America. It remains, in the words of Professor Peter Evans, "one of the primary lenses through which both Latin American and North American scholars analyze the interaction of classes and the state in the context of an increasingly internationalized economy."

A number of events provides compelling evidence of a crisis of the "global economy" project and the neoliberal theory on which it rests. An economic storm, beginning in the Far East in 1997, left the economies of Indonesia, South Korea, and other "Asian tigers" in ruins, spread to Russia, and deeply affected Latin America. Countries such as Brazil, Argentina, Chile, Venezuela, Mexico, and Colombia, which had commercial ties with Asian markets, suffered sharp declines in the prices of their raw material exports. Michel Camdessus, the IMF's managing director, himself described the situation as "the crisis of a system." The famed financier George Soros proclaimed "the crisis of global capitalism." The board of directors of the International Forum on Globalization drew its own conclusion: "After more than 50 years of this experiment, it is breaking down. Rather than leading to economic benefits for all people, it has brought the planet to the brink of environmental and social catastrophe. The experiment has failed" (*New York Times*, Nov. 24, 1998).

In the early twenty-first century, a growing popular movement in the region appeared to share this assessment. Argentina's economy, which never really recovered from the 1997 global crisis, unceremoniously collapsed in 2001, unleashing wage reductions of more than 20 percent, unemployment rates that approached 25 percent, unprecedented poverty, rapidly rising prices, and a torrent of general strikes, urban riots, and looting that forced a succession of presidents to resign. To stem the hemorrhaging, a new interim president, Eduardo Duhalde, denounced his predecessors' free-market policies and pledged to create a "new model" of development based on an "alliance between labor and domestic industries." Although less violent, Peruvians likewise protested the neoliberal reforms implemented by Alejandro Toledo, the nation's first president of indigenous descent, who received a Ph.D. in economics from Stanford University. General strikes and weekly protests against Toledo's efforts to privatize state companies led to rapidly deteriorating popular support, which, according to the Peruvian pollster *Apoyo*, plunged to less than 14 percent in 2003. Brazilians similarly endorsed a new strategy for development. The perennial candidate of the democratic socialist left, Lula da Silva, who had consistently resisted the neoliberal agenda during the 1990s, won a landslide victory in the 2002 presidential elections with 61 percent of the vote. In Ecuador in the same year, a coalition of workers, women, students, and indigenous peoples elected populist president Lucio Gutiérrez. In Venezuela, however, a popular movement joined forces with loyal soldiers to reverse a military coup organized and led by Pedro Carmona, wealthy businessman and president of the National Chamber of Commerce. Carmona had opposed the charismatic, democratically elected populist president, Hugo Chávez, whose efforts to redistribute national wealth alienated Venezuelan elites, international bankers, and the U.S. State Department alike.

A word about the organization of this text. In the book's planning, the decision was made to reject the approach that tries to cover the postindependence history of the twenty Latin American republics in detail, including mention of every general who ever passed through a presidential palace. Most teachers will agree that this approach discourages students by miring them in a bog of tedious facts. Accordingly, it was decided to limit coverage of the national period in the nineteenth century to Mexico, Argentina, Chile, and Brazil, whose history seemed to illustrate best the major issues and trends of the period. In addition to covering these four countries, the survey of the twentieth century broadened to include the central Andean area, with a special concentration on Peru, and Cuba, the scene of a socialist revolution with continental repercussions.

The Second Edition added a chapter on Central America, where a revolutionary storm, having toppled the U.S.-unsupported Somoza tyranny in Nicaragua, threatened the rickety structures of oligarchical and military rule in El Salvador and Guatemala. The Fourth Edition recognized the political and economic importance of the Bolivarian lands of Venezuela and Colombia by including a chapter on the modern history of those countries. The current Seventh Edition more fully integrates the discussion of the Andean and Central American regions, Cuba, and the Bolivian republics into the text's original layout. Chapters 9 and 10, for example, now examine these nations' nineteenth-century histories, along with those of Mexico, Argentina, Chile, and Peru. Because teachers rarely have time to cover all Latin American countries in their survey classes, this organization provides greater flexibility, without sacrificing historical continuity, as instructors select those nations upon which they wish their students to focus.

To accommodate alternative course configurations, *A History of Latin America* continues to be published in two volumes as well as in a complete version. Volume 1 includes Latin American history from ancient times to 1910, and Volume 2 covers Latin American history from independence to the present.

Last, the recent history of all the countries under discussion has been brought up to date, and the rest of the book has been thoroughly revised to reflect current scholarship, particularly the respective roles of race, class, and gender in the region's historical development. Special emphasis is placed on such topics as the impact of neoliberal economic policies and the gathering revolt against them, the effects of the North American Free Trade Agreement, the growing urgency of environmental issues, the heightened visibility of the women's movement, and the significance of popular culture.

The book has also benefited from the careful scrutiny of the Sixth Edition by colleagues who made valuable suggestions for revision:

Julia E. Rodriguez, University of New Hampshire
William Schell, Jr., Murray State University
Michael Snodgrass, Indiana University Purdue University–Indianapolis
Karen Sundwick, Southern Oregon University
Ernest S. Sweeney, Loyola Marymount University

Many but not all of these colleagues' suggestions were adopted; these individuals bear no responsibility for any remaining errors of fact or interpretation. We also want to acknowledge a special debt of gratitude to Professor Asunción Lavrín who graciously shared her photo archive on Latin American feminism. We wish to recall, too, the many students, graduate and undergraduate, who helped us to define our views on Latin American history through the give-and-take of classroom discussion and the reading and discussion of their papers and theses.

Benjamin Keen
Keith Haynes

# INTRODUCTION

# The Geographical Background of Latin American History

**L**ATIN AMERICA, a region of startling physical contrasts, stretches 7,000 miles southward from the Mexican-U.S. border to the tip of Tierra del Fuego on Cape Horn. The widest east-west point, across Peru and Brazil, spans 3,200 miles. This diverse geography has helped produce the distinctive development of each Latin American nation.

Latin America has two dominant physical characteristics: enormous mountains and vast river systems. The often snowcapped and sometimes volcanic mountain ranges—the three Sierra Madre ranges in Mexico and the 4,000-mile-long Andes in South America that make a western spine from Venezuela to Tierra del Fuego—form the backbone of the landmass. Nearly impassable for most of their length, these mountain ranges boast many peaks of over 22,000 feet. The mountains have presented a formidable barrier to trade and communications in Mexico and the nations of the southern continent. Not only do the mountain ranges separate nations from each other, but they divide regions within nations.

The enormous rivers most often lie in lightly populated areas. Three mammoth river systems (the Amazon, the Orinoco, and the Río de la Plata) spread over almost the entire South American continent east of the Andes. The size of the Amazon River Basin and the surrounding tropics—the largest such area in the world—has posed another impediment to the development of transportation and human settlement, although some rivers are navigable for long distances. Only with the advent of modern technology—railroads, telegraph, telephones, automobiles, and airplanes—has geographical isolation been partly overcome, a condition that has helped create markets and forge independent states.

Latin America encompasses five climatological regions: high mountains, tropical jungles, deserts, temperate coastal plains, and temperate highlands. The first three are sparsely populated, while the latter two tend to be densely inhabited. With the exception of the Maya, all the great ancient civilizations arose in the highlands of the Andes and Mexico.

The varied climate and topography of South America, Mexico, and Central America have helped produce this highly uneven distribution of population. Three notable examples—the gargantuan Amazonian region of mostly steamy tropical forests and savannah, the vast desert of Patagonia in southern Argentina, and the northern wastelands of Mexico—support few inhabitants. In contrast to these inhospitable regions, a thin strip along Brazil's coast, the plain along the Río de la Plata estuary in Argentina, and the central plateau of Mexico contain most of the people in these countries. Thus these nations are overpopulated and underpopulated at the same time.

In western South America the heaviest concentration of people is found on the inland plateaus. None of the major cities—Santiago, Chile; Lima, Peru; Quito, Ecuador; and Bogotá and Medellín, Colombia—are ports; there are few good natural harbors on the west coast. In contrast, in eastern South America the major cities—Buenos

The maps on these two pages form an overall picture of the natural geographical features of Latin America: Middle America (*above*), composed of Mexico, Central America, and the Caribbean region; and South America (*next page*).

Aires, Argentina; Montevideo, Uruguay; and São Paulo–Santos, Rio de Janeiro, Bahia, and Recife, Brazil—are situated on the Atlantic coast. The majority of people in Argentina, Brazil, and Uruguay reside on the coastal plains. Mexico City, Guadalajara, and Monterrey, Mexico's largest cities, are inland. Almost all these cities have a population of over 1 million, with Mexico City, the largest, having over 20 million.

The number of waterways and the amount of rainfall vary greatly from region to region. Mexico has no rivers of importance, while Brazil contains the huge Amazon network. Lack of rain and rivers for irrigation in large areas makes farming impossible. Barely 10 percent of Mexico's land is fertile enough to farm; rainfall is so uncertain in some cultivable areas that drought strikes often and for years at a time. Mexico, with too little water, contrasts with Brazil, with too much. Much of Brazil's vast territory, however, is equally uncultivable, as its tropical soils have high acidity and have proved infertile and incapable of sustaining agricultural crops.

On the other hand, Latin America has enormous natural resources for economic development. Mexico and Venezuela rank among the world's largest oil producers. Mexico may have the biggest petroleum reserves of any nation other than Saudi Arabia. Bolivia, Ecuador, Colombia, and Peru also produce oil. Over the centuries, Latin American nations have been leading sources of copper (Mexico and Chile), nitrate (Chile), silver (Peru and Mexico), gold (Brazil), diamonds (Brazil), and tin (Bolivia). Much of the world's coffee is grown on the fertile highlands of Central America, Colombia, and Brazil. Much of the world's cattle have been raised on the plains of northern Mexico, southern Brazil, and central Argentina. Argentina's immense plains, the Pampas, are among the planet's most fertile areas, yielding not only cattle but sheep and wheat as well. Over the past five centuries, the coastal plains of Brazil have produced enormous amounts of sugar. In addition, human ingenuity has converted geographical obstacles into assets. Some extensive river systems

Caribbean Sea

ATLANTIC OCEAN

*Orinoco R.*

GUIANA HIGHLANDS

Equator

*Negro R.*

*Amazon R.*

*Amazon R.*

*Xingu R.*

AMAZON BASIN

*Madeira R.*

*Tocantins R.*

*São Francisco R.*

BRAZILIAN
HIGHLANDS

PLATEAU OF
MATO GROSSO

ANDES MTS.

ATACAMA DESERT

GRAN CHACO

*Paraná R.*

*Paraguay R.*

*Uruguay R.*

Tropic of Capricorn

PACIFIC OCEAN

ANDES MOUNTAINS

*Saldo R.*

*Colorado R.*

PAMPAS

PATAGONIA

Falkland/Malvinas Is.

Tierra del Fuego

Cape Horn

0   250   500Km.
0   250   500Mi.

Legend:

Tropical rainforest

Tropical and subtropical
forest and scrub

Savannah grassland and
wooded savannah

Midlatitude forest

Steppe and prairie grassland

Desert and desert scrub

Highland

XV

have potential for hydroelectric power and provide water for irrigation as well, as has been done in Mexico's arid regions.

The historical record shows that the richness of Latin America's resources has had a significant impact on the economic and political development of Europe and North America. The gold and silver of its New World empire fueled Spain's wars and diplomacy in Europe for four hundred years. Many scholars trace the origins of the Industrial Revolution in such nations as Great Britain and the Netherlands to resources extracted from Latin America by its colonial masters, Spain and Portugal.

Latin America's resources have affected economic development elsewhere, but how these resources have been developed and by whom and in which ways has profoundly changed the history of the nations in this area. Geography has perhaps narrowed historical alternatives in Latin America, but the decisions of people determined its development. Going back to the colonization by Spain and Portugal, Latin America's history has been marked by exploitation of its peoples and its natural resources. Imperial Spain's policy to drain the lands it conquered of gold, silver, and other resources fixed the pattern for later exploiters. With European dominance came the decision to subjugate the indigenous peoples and often force them to labor under subhuman conditions in mines and on large estates, where many died. In the more recent era, there has been the decision to grow bananas on the coastal plains of Central America instead of corn or other staples of the local diet; this has made export profitable, usually for North American concerns, but this land use has left many, like the Guatemalans, without sufficient food. Meanwhile the uncontrolled expansion of capitalism in the area has led to an ecological crisis, reflected in massive deforestation, severe soil exhaustion, and growing agricultural and industrial pollution. These developments have contributed to rapid depletion of renewable resources, lack of clean water and air, and major epidemics of contagious diseases and other health problems.

The work that follows is a history of the development of Latin America's economy, politics, and society viewed primarily from the perspective of ordinary people, who were exploited and oppressed but who resisted and endured. It is the story of the events and forces that produced the alternatives from which Latin Americans created their world.

# PART TWO

# Latin America in the Nineteenth Century

*Coffee Plantation*, 1935, by Candido Portinari/Museo Nacional Bellas Artes, Rio de Janeiro, Brazil/Index/Bridgeman Art Library, London/New York.

**A**FTER WINNING THEIR INDEPENDENCE, the new Latin American states began a long, uphill struggle to achieve economic and political stability. They faced immense obstacles, for independence, as previously noted, was not accompanied by economic and social changes that could spur rapid progress—for example, no redistribution of land and income in favor of the lower classes took place. The large estate, generally operated using primitive methods and slave or peon labor, continued to dominate economic life. Far from diminishing, the influence of the landed aristocracy actually increased as a result of the leading military role it had played in the wars of independence and the passing of Spanish authority.

Economic life stagnated, for the anticipated large-scale influx of foreign capital did not materialize and the European demand for Latin American staples remained far below expectations. Free trade brought increased commercial activity to the coasts, but this increase was offset by the near destruction of some local craft industries by cheap, factory-made European goods. The sluggish pace of economic activity and the relative absence of interregional trade and true national markets encouraged local self-sufficiency, isolation, political instability, and even chaos.

As a result of these adverse factors, the period from about 1820 to about 1870 was for many Latin American countries an age of violence and of alternate dictatorship and revolution. Its symbol was the *caudillo* (strongman), whose power was always based on force, no matter what kind of constitution the country had. Usually the caudillo ruled with the aid of a coalition of lesser caudillos, each supreme in his region. Whatever their methods, the caudillos generally displayed some regard for republican ideology and institutions. Political parties, bearing such labels as "conservative" and "liberal," "unitarian" and "federalist," were active in most of the new states. Conservatism drew most of its support from the great landowners and their urban allies. Liberalism typically attracted provincial landowners, professional men, and other groups that had enjoyed little power in the past and were dissatisfied with the existing order. As a rule, conservatives sought to retain many of the social arrangements of the colonial era and favored a highly centralized government. Liberals, often inspired by the example of the United States, usually advocated a federal form of government, guarantees of individual rights, lay control of education, and an end to special privileges for the clergy and military. Neither party displayed much interest in the problems of the native peasantry and other lower-class groups.

Beginning in about 1870, the accelerating tempo of the Industrial Revolution in Europe stimulated more rapid change in the Latin American economy and politics. European capital flowed into the area and was used to create the facilities needed to expand and modernize production and trade. The pace and degree of economic progress of the various countries were very uneven and depended largely on their geographic position and natural resources.

Extreme one-sidedness was a feature of the new economic order. One or two products became the basis of each country's prosperity, making these commodities highly vulnerable to fluctuations in world demand and price. Meanwhile, other sectors of the economy remained stagnant or even declined through diversion of labor and land to other industries.

The late nineteenth-century expansion had two other characteristics: in the main, it took place within the framework of the hacienda system of land tenure and labor, and it was accompanied by a steady growth of foreign control over the natural and human-made resources of the region. Thus, by 1900 a new structure of dependency, or colonialism, had arisen, called neocolonialism, with Great Britain and later the United States replacing Spain and Portugal as the dominant powers in the area.

The new economic order demanded peace and continuity in government, and after 1870 political conditions in Latin America did, in fact, grow more stable. Old party lines dissolved as conservatives adopted the positivist dogma of science and progress, while liberals abandoned their concern with constitutional methods and civil liberties in favor of an interest in material prosperity. A new type of "progressive" caudillo—Porfirio Díaz in Mexico, Rafael Núñez in Colombia, Antonio Guzmán Blanco in Venezuela—symbolized the politics of acquisition. The cycle of dictatorship and revolution continued in many lands, but the revolutions became less frequent and less devastating.

These major trends in the political and economic history of Latin America in the period extending from about 1820 to 1900 were accompanied by other changes in the Latin American way of life and culture, notably the development of a powerful literature that often sought not only to mirror Latin American society but to change it. In Part Two, we present short histories of Mexico, Argentina, Chile, Brazil, Peru, Cuba, the United Provinces of Central America, and Gran Colombia in the nineteenth century. All these histories contain themes and problems common to Latin America in that period, but each displays variations that reflect the specific backgrounds of the different states.

# 9    Dictators and Revolutions

I
NDEPENDENCE DID NOT bring Latin America the ordered freedom and prosperity the liberators had hoped for. In most of the new states, decades of civil strife followed the passing of Spanish and Portuguese rule. Bolívar reflected the disillusionment of many patriot leaders when he wrote in 1829: "There is no good faith in America, nor among the nations of America. Treaties are scraps of paper; constitutions, printed matter; elections, battles; freedom, anarchy; and life, a torment." The contrast between Latin American stagnation and disorder and the meteoric advance of the former English colonies—the United States—intensified the pessimism and self-doubt of some Latin American leaders and intellectuals.

## The Fruits of Independence

Frustration of the great hopes with which the struggle for liberation began was inevitable, for independence was not accompanied by economic and social changes that could shatter the colonial mold. Aside from the passing of the Spanish and Portuguese trade monopolies, the colonial economic and social structures remained intact. The hacienda, fazenda, or estancia, employing archaic techniques and a labor force of peons or slaves, continued to dominate agriculture; no significant class of small farmers arose to challenge the economic and political might of the great landowners. Indeed, the revolutions strengthened the power of the landed aristocracy by removing the agencies of Spanish rule—viceroys, audiencias, intendants—and by weakening among the landowners the ingrained habits of obedience to a central authority. In contrast, all other colonial elites—the merchant class, weakened by the expulsion or emigration of many loyalist merchants; the mine owners, ruined by wartime destruction or confiscation of their properties; and the church hierarchy, often in disgrace for having sided with Spain—emerged from the conflict with diminished weight.

To their other sources of influence, members of the landed aristocracy added the prestige of a military elite crowned with the laurels of victory, for many revolutionary officers had arisen from its ranks. The militarization of the new states as a result of years of destructive warfare and postwar instability assured a large political role for this officer group. Standing armies that often consumed more than half of the national budgets arose. Not content with the role of guardians of order and national security, military officers became the arbiter of political disputes, as a rule intervening in favor of the conservative landowning interests and the urban elites with whom the great landowners were closely linked.

## ECONOMIC STAGNATION

Revolutionary leaders had expected that a vast expansion of foreign trade would follow the passing of Spanish commercial monopoly and aid economic recovery. In fact, some countries, favored by their natural resources or geographic position, soon recovered from the revolutionary crisis and scored modest to large economic advances; these included Brazil (coffee and sugar), Argentina (hides), and Chile (metals and hides). But others, such as Mexico, Bolivia, and Peru, whose mining economies had suffered shattering blows, failed to recover colonial levels of production.

Several factors accounted for the economic stagnation that plagued many of the new states in the first half of the nineteenth century. Independence was not accompanied by a redistribution of land and income that might have stimulated a growth of internal markets and productive forces. The anticipated large-scale influx of foreign capital did not materialize, either, partly because political disorder discouraged foreign investment, partly because Europe and the United States, then financing their own industrial revolutions, had as yet little capital to export. Exports of Latin American staples remained below expectations, for Europe still viewed Latin America primarily as an outlet for manufactured goods, especially English textiles. The resulting flood of cheap, factory-made European products damaged local craft industries and drained the new states of their stocks of gold and silver, creating a chronic balance-of-trade problem. The British conquest of the Latin American markets further weakened the local merchant class, which was unable to compete with its English rivals. By mid-century the wealthiest and most prestigious merchant houses, from Mexico City to Buenos Aires and Valparaíso, bore English names. Iberian merchants, however, continued to dominate the urban and provincial retail trade in many areas.

Taken together, these developments retarded the development of native capitalism and capitalist relations and reinforced the dominant role of the hacienda in the economic and political life of the new states. The deepening stagnation of the interior of these nations, aggravated by the lack of roads and by natural obstacles to communication (such as jungles and mountains), intensified tendencies toward regionalism and the domination of regions by caudillos great and small, who were usually local large landowners.[1] The sluggish tempo of economic activity encouraged these caudillos to employ their private followings of peons and retainers as pawns in the game of politics and revolution on a national scale. Indeed, politics and revolution became in some countries a form of economic activity that compensated for the lack of other opportunities, because the victors, having gained control of the all-important customhouse (which collected duties on imports and exports) and other official sources of revenue, could reward themselves and their followers with government jobs, contracts, grants of public land, and other favors. This reliance by members of the elite on political and military activity as a career and on the customhouse as a source of government revenue had two negative results. One was the rise of bloated military and bureaucratic establishments that diverted resources from economic development; the other was a stress on foreign trade that intensified the trend toward dependency.

## POLITICS: THE CONSERVATIVE AND LIBERAL PROGRAMS

The political systems of the new states made large formal concessions to the liberal ideology of the nineteenth century. With the exception of Brazil,

---

[1] The term *caudillo* is commonly applied to politico-military leaders who held power on the national and regional level in Latin America before more or less stable parliamentary government became the norm in the area beginning about 1870. Military ability and charisma are qualities often associated with caudillos, who came in many guises, but not all possessed the same qualities. Because the semifeudal conditions that gave rise to the caudillo still survive in parts of Latin America, it can be said that caudillos and *caudillismo* still exist.

all the new states adopted the republican form of government (Mexico had two brief intervals of imperial rule) and paid their respects to the formulas of parliamentary and representative government. Their constitutions provided for presidents, congresses, and courts; often they contained elaborate safeguards of individual rights.

These façades of modernity, however, poorly concealed the dictatorial or oligarchical reality behind them. Typically, the chief executive was a caudillo whose power rested on force, no matter what the constitutional form; usually, he ruled with the support of a coalition of lesser caudillos, each more or less supreme in his own domain. The supposed independence of the judicial and legislative branches was a fiction. As a rule, elections were exercises in futility. Because the party in power generally counted the votes, the opposition had no alternative but revolt.

Literacy and property qualifications disfranchised most natives and mixed-bloods; where they had the right to vote, the *patrón* (master) often herded them to the polls to vote for him or his candidates. The lack of the secret ballot (voting was usually open, with colored ballots) made coercion of voters easy. Whether liberal or conservative, all sections of the ruling class agreed on keeping the peasantry, gauchos, and other "lower orders" on the margins of political life, on preventing their emergence as groups with collective philosophies and goals. The very privileges that the new creole constitutions and law codes granted indigenous peoples—equality before the law, the "right" to divide and dispose of their communal lands— weakened their solidarity and their ability to resist the creole world's competitive individualism. But especially gifted, ambitious, and fortunate members of these marginal groups were sometimes co-opted into the creole elite and provided some of its most distinguished leaders; two examples are the Zapotec Benito Juárez in Mexico and the mestizo president Andrés Santa Cruz in Bolivia.

At first glance, the political history of Latin America in the first half-century after independence, with its dreary alternation of dictatorship and revolt, seems pointless and trivial. But the political struggles of this period were more than

disputes over spoils between sections of a small upper class. Genuine social and ideological cleavages helped produce those struggles and the bitterness with which they were fought. Such labels as "conservative" and "liberal," "unitarian" and "federalist," assigned by the various parties to themselves or each other, were more than masks in a pageant, although opportunism contributed to the ease with which some leaders assumed and discarded these labels.

Generally speaking, conservatism reflected the interests of the traditional holders of power and privilege, men who had a stake in maintaining the existing order. Hence, the great landowners, the upper clergy, the higher ranks of the military and the civil bureaucracy, and monopolistic merchant groups tended to be conservatives. Liberalism, in contrast, appealed to those groups that in colonial times had had little or no access to the main structures of economic and political power and were naturally eager to alter the existing order. Thus, liberalism drew much support from provincial landowners, lawyers and other professionals (the groups most receptive to new ideas), shopkeepers, and artisans; it also appealed to ambitious, aspiring indígenas and mixed-bloods. But regional conflicts and clan or family loyalties often cut across the lines of social and occupational cleavage, complicating the political picture.

Liberals wanted to break up the hierarchical social structure inherited from the colonial period. They had a vision of their countries remade into dynamic middle-class states on the model of the United States or England. Inspired by the success of the United States, they usually favored a federal form of government, guarantees of individual rights, lay control of education, and an end to a special legal status for the clergy and military. In their modernizing zeal, liberals sometimes called for the abolition of entails (which restricted the right to inherit property to a particular descendant or descendants of the owner), dissolution of convents, confiscation of church wealth, and abolition of slavery. The federalism of the liberals had a special appeal for secondary regions of the new states, eager to develop their resources and free themselves from domination by capitals and wealthy primary regions.

Conservatives typically upheld a strong centralized government, the religious and educational monopoly of the Roman Catholic church, and the special privileges of the clergy and military. They distrusted such radical novelties as freedom of speech and the press and religious toleration. Conservatives, in short, sought to salvage as much of the colonial social order as was compatible with the new republican system. Indeed, some conservative leaders ultimately despaired of that system and dreamed of implanting monarchy in their countries.

Neither conservatives nor liberals displayed much interest in the problems of the indigenous, black, and mixed-blood masses that formed the majority of the population in most Latin American countries. Liberals, impatient with the supposed backwardness of indigenous peoples, regarded their communalism as an impediment to the development of a capitalist spirit of enterprise and initiated legislation providing for the division of communal lands—a policy that favored land grabbing at the expense of indigenous villages. Despite their theoretical preference for small landholdings and a rural middle class, liberals recoiled from any program of radical land reform. Conservatives correctly regarded the great estate as the very foundation of their power. As traditionalists, however, the conservatives sometimes claimed to continue the Spanish paternalist policy toward indigenous communities and often enjoyed their support.

This summary of the conservative and liberal programs for Latin America in the first half-century after independence inevitably overlooks variations from the theoretical liberal and conservative norms, variations that reflected the specific conditions and problems of the different states. A brief examination of the history of Mexico, Argentina, Chile, Brazil, Peru, Cuba, the United Provinces of Central America, and Gran Colombia reveals not only certain common themes but also a rich diversity of political experience.

## Mexico

The struggle for Mexican independence, begun by the radical priests Hidalgo and Morelos, was completed by Agustín de Iturbide, who headed a coalition of creole and peninsular conservatives terrified at the prospect of being governed by the liberal Spanish constitution of 1812, which was reestablished in 1820. Independence, achieved under such conservative auspices, meant that Mexico's economic and social patterns underwent little change. To be sure, recent scholarship has shown that the popular insurgency begun by Hidalgo had at least a short-term impact on the social, economic, and political patterns of Mexican development. John Tutino, for example, has shown that in the Bajío the insurgency destroyed commercial hacienda production, which generated profit by storing maize until prices peaked with scarcity, and forced a shift to tenant ranchero production, which maximized maize production, bringing "real and enduring benefits to both rural producers and urban consumers of maize across the Bajío during the first half-century of national life." Similarly, Florencia Mallon and Peter Guardino stress the revolutionary participation of popular urban and rural groups in Mexican nineteenth-century political struggles, revealing their long-term impact on Mexican state formation and peasant consciousness. Nonetheless, the great hacienda continued to dominate the countryside in many areas. Although indigenous villages managed to retain substantial community lands until after mid-century and even improved their economic and political position somewhat with the passing of Spanish centralized authority, the trend toward usurpation of indigenous lands grew stronger as a result of the lapse of Spanish protective legislation. Peons and tenants on the haciendas often suffered from debt servitude, miserable wages, oppressive rents, and excessive religious fees. At the constitutional convention of 1856–1857, the liberal Ponciano Arriaga declared:

> With some honorable exceptions, the rich landowners of Mexico . . . resemble the feudal lords of the Middle Ages. On his seigneurial lands, with more or less formalities, the landowner makes and executes laws, administers justice and exercises civil power, imposes taxes and fines, has his own jails and irons, metes out punishments and tortures,

**Latin America in 1830**

monopolizes commerce, and forbids the conduct without his permission of any business but that of the estate.

The church continued to wield diminished but still considerable economic and spiritual power. An anonymous contemporary writer reflected the disillusion of the lower classes with the fruits of independence: "Independence is only a name. Previously they ruled us from Spain, now from here. It is always the same priest on a different mule. But as for work, food, and clothing, there is no difference."

### THE MEXICAN ECONOMY

The ravages of war had left mineshafts flooded, haciendas deserted, the economy stagnant. The end of the Spanish commercial monopoly, however, brought a large increase in the volume of foreign trade; the number of ships entering Mexican ports jumped from 148 in 1823 to 639 in 1826. But exports did not keep pace with imports, leaving a trade deficit that had to be covered by exporting precious metals. The drain of gold and silver aggravated the problems of the new government, which had inherited a bankrupt treasury and had to support a swollen bureaucracy and an officer class ready to revolt against any government that suggested a cut in their numbers or pay. The exodus of Spanish merchants and their capital added to the economic problems of the new state. Complicating those problems was the disorder that was a legacy of the war; bands of robbers made travel on the roads so unsafe that "whether coming or going from Puebla or Veracruz, the Mexico City traveler expected to be robbed."

Foreign loans appeared to be the only way out of the crisis. In 1824–1825, English bankers made loans to Mexico amounting to 32 million pesos, guaranteed by Mexican customs revenues. Of this amount the Mexicans received only a little more than 11 million pesos, as the bankers went bankrupt before all the money due to Mexico from the loan proceeds was paid. By 1843 unpaid interest and principal had raised the nation's foreign debt to more than 54 million pesos. This mounting foreign debt not only created crushing interest burdens, but it also threatened Mexico's independence and territorial integrity, for behind foreign capitalists stood governments that might threaten intervention in case of default.

Foreign investments, however, mainly from Britain, made possible a partial recovery of the decisive mining sector. Old mines, abandoned and flooded during the wars, were reopened, but the available capital proved inadequate, the technical problems of reconstruction were greater than anticipated, and production remained on a relatively low level.

An ambitious effort to revive and modernize Mexican industry also got under way, spurred by the founding in 1830 of the *Banco de Avío*, which provided governmental assistance to industry. Manufacturing, paced by textiles, made some limited progress in the three decades after independence. Leading industrial centers included Mexico City, Puebla, Guadalajara, Durango, and Veracruz. But shortages of capital, lack of a consistent policy of protection for domestic industry, and a socioeconomic structure that sharply limited the internal market hampered the growth of Mexican factory capitalism. By 1843 the Banco de Avío had to close its doors for lack of funds. The Mexican economy, therefore, continued to be based on mining and agriculture. Mexico's principal exports were precious metals, especially silver, and such agricultural products as tobacco, coffee, vanilla, cochineal, and henequen (a plant fiber used in rope and twine). Imports consisted primarily of manufactured goods that Mexican industry could not supply.

### POLITICS: LIBERALS VERSUS CONSERVATIVES

A liberal-conservative cleavage dominated Mexican political life in the half-century after independence. That conflict was latent from the moment that the "liberator" Iturbide, the former scourge of insurgents, rode into Mexico City on September 27, 1821, flanked on either side by two insurgent generals, Vicente Guerrero and Guadalupe Victoria, firm republicans and liberals. The fall of Iturbide in 1823 cleared the way for the establishment of a republic. But it soon became apparent that the republicans were divided into liberals and conservatives, federalists and centralists.

The constitution of 1824 represented a compromise between liberal and conservative interests. It appeased regional economic interests, which were fearful of a too-powerful central government, by creating nineteen states that possessed taxing power; their legislatures, each casting one vote, chose the president and vice president for four-year terms. The national legislature was made bicameral, with an upper house (Senate) and a lower house (Chamber of Deputies). By assuring the creation of local civil bureaucracies, the federalist structure also satisfied the demand of the provincial middle classes for greater access to political activity and office. But the constitution had a conservative tinge as well: although the church lost its monopoly on education, Catholicism was proclaimed the official religion, and the fueros of the church and the army were specifically confirmed.

A hero of the war of independence, the liberal general Guadalupe Victoria, was elected first president under the new constitution. Anxious to preserve unity, Victoria brought the conservative Lucas Alamán into his cabinet. But this era of good feeling was very short-lived; by 1825, Alamán was forced out of the government. The liberal-conservative cleavage now assumed the form of a rivalry that reflected the Anglo-American competition for economic and political influence in Mexico. Founded by the American minister Joel Roberts Poinsett, the York Rite Masonic lodge favored liberals and federalists, who regarded the United States as a model for their own reform program. Its rival, the Scottish Rite lodge, sponsored by the British chargé d'affaires Henry Ward, appealed to the Conservative Party, which represented the old landed and mining aristocracy, the clerical and military hierarchy, monopolistic merchants, and some manufacturers. Its intellectual spokesman and organizer was Lucas Alamán, statesman, champion of industry, and author of a brilliant history of Mexico from the conservative point of view.

The Liberal Party represented a creole and mestizo middle class—provincial landowners, professional men, artisans, the lower ranks of the clergy and military—determined to end special privileges and the concentration of political and economic power in the upper class. A priest-economist, José María Luis Mora, presented the liberal position with great force and lucidity. But the Liberal Party was divided: its right wing, the *moderados*, wanted to proceed slowly and sometimes joined the conservatives; its left wing, the *puros*, advocated sweeping antifeudal, anticlerical reforms.

During the first decade after independence, none of these factions could consolidate its control over the nation, but the year 1833 was a high-water mark of liberal achievement. Aided by Mora, his minister of education, the puro President Valentín Gómez Farías pushed through Congress a series of radical reforms: abolition of the special privileges and immunities of the army and church (meaning that officers and priests would now be subject to the jurisdiction of civil courts), abolition of tithes, secularization of the clerical University of Mexico, creation of a department of public instruction, reduction of the army, and creation of a civilian militia. These measures were accompanied by a program of internal improvements designed to increase the prosperity of the interior by linking it to the capital and the coasts. In their use of the central government to promote education and national economic development, the liberals showed that they were not doctrinaire adherents of laissez faire.

This liberal program inevitably provoked clerical and conservative resistance. Army officers began to organize revolts; priests proclaimed from their pulpits that the great cholera epidemic of 1833 was a sign of divine displeasure with the works of the impious liberals. Meanwhile, General Antonio López de Santa Anna, a classic caudillo who earlier had supported liberal movements, now placed himself at the head of the conservative rebellion, occupied the capital, and sent Gómez Farías and Mora into exile. Assuming the presidency, he summoned a hand-picked reactionary congress that repealed the reform laws of 1833 and suspended the constitution of 1824. Under the new conservative constitution of 1836, the states were reduced to departments completely dominated by the central government, upper-class control of politics was assured through high property and income qualifications for holding office, and the fueros of the church and army were restored.

Santa Anna and the conservatives ruled Mexico for the greater part of two decades, 1834 to 1854. Politically and economically, the conservative rule subordinated the interests of the regions and the country as a whole to a wealthy, densely populated central core linking Mexico City, Puebla, and Veracruz. Its centralist trend was reflected in the Tariff Act of 1837, which restored the alcabala, or sales tax system, inland customhouses, and the government tobacco monopoly, ensuring the continuous flow of revenues to Mexico City.

Thereafter, conservative neglect and abuse of outlying or border areas like northern Mexico and Yucatán contributed to the loss of Texas in 1836 and almost led to the loss of Yucatán. Santa Anna's destruction of provincial autonomy enabled American colonists in Texas, led by Sam Houston, to pose as patriotic federalists in revolt against Santa Anna's tyranny. In Yucatán, the Caste or Social War of 1839 combined elements of a regional war against conservative centralism and an indigenous war against feudal landlords. For almost a decade, Yucatán remained outside Mexico.

After the United States annexed Texas in 1845, the North American Invasion or Mexican War (1846–1848) marked another conservative disaster. Its immediate cause was a dispute between Mexico and the United States over the boundary of Texas, but the decisive factor was the determination of the Polk administration to acquire not only Texas but California and New Mexico as well. The war ended in catastrophic Mexican defeat, basically due to U.S. superiority in resources, military training, and leadership, but the irresponsible, selfish attitudes of the Mexican aristocracy and church contributed to the debacle. Most particularly, conservatives, dreading the mobilization of peasant armies in a prolonged guerrilla war against the U.S. invasion, concluded a hasty surrender.

Naturally, puro leaders, including Benito Juárez, Melchor Ocampo, and Ponciano Arriaga, urged continued resistance. "Give the people arms," said Ocampo, "and they will defend themselves." In some regions of the country, peasant revolts broke out that combined demands for division of large haciendas among the peasantry and other reforms with calls for a continued resistance to the invaders. But the aristocratic creoles—some of whom favored a total takeover of Mexico by the United States—and their clerical allies feared the consequences of partisan warfare to their wealth and privileges and hastened to make peace. "The Mexican government," says Mexican historian Leticia Reina, "preferred coming to terms with the United States rather than endanger the interests of the ruling class." By the treaty of Guadalupe Hidalgo (1848), Mexico gave up half the country, ceding Texas, California, and New Mexico to the United States; in return, Mexico received $15 million and the cancellation of certain claims against it.

Even after the signing of the treaty, a vocal opposition in and outside the Mexican congress argued against ratification and urged continuing the war. In his "Observations on the Treaty of Guadalupe Hidalgo," the liberal Manuel Rejón predicted that the treaty would mean the inevitable economic conquest of Mexico by the United States. He foresaw that the new boundary, bringing American commerce closer to the Mexican heartland, would lead to the americanization of Mexico; he argued that "we will never be able to compete in our own markets with the American imports. . . . The treaty is our sentence of death." Finally, in view of the intense American racism, he questioned whether Mexican citizens in the ceded territories would be protected in their civil and property rights as promised by the treaty.

Rejón's fears concerning the treatment of Mexican citizens in the newly annexed territories were soon justified. The gold rush in California caused a wave of attacks by Anglo-American miners against native Californians. In his reminiscences, Antonio Coronel, from Los Angeles, described "stabbings, extortions, and lynchings as commonplace American reactions to native Californios, whom they regarded as interlopers." Even worse was the fate of indigenous Californians, who were considered full Mexican citizens under the constitution of 1824. Denied the protection specified in the treaty of Guadalupe Hidalgo, they "became the victims of murder, slavery, land theft, and starvation." In two decades the indigenous population of the state declined by more than one hundred thousand. "Genocide," writes Richard Griswold del Castillo, "is not too strong a word to use in describing what happened to the California Indians during that period." In New Mexico, which became a territory rather than a state, Hispanic inhabitants did not gain citizenship status until New Mexico achieved statehood in 1912, and its native peoples were denied the vote until 1953.

Violation of their land rights, the protection of which was promised by the treaty of Guadalupe Hidalgo, was and remains a major grievance of many Mexican Americans. Claiming that the great majority of Mexican land grants in the ceded territory were "imperfect," American courts ruled that the U.S. government had inherited the right to complete the process of land confirmation. In California and New Mexico, this process, creating for Mexican American landowners an immense expense of litigation and legal fees, aggravated by usurious interest rates and falling cattle prices, resulted in the loss of their land by most rancheros. Even the few who survived the confirmation process came under great pressure from squatters, mostly wealthy and influential Anglo-Americans, to surrender their land. In New Mexico, a fraternity of predatory lawyers and politicians, the so-called Santa Fe Ring, "used the long legal battles over land grants to acquire empires extending over millions of acres." Here, the struggle of Mexican Americans to regain the lost lands of their ancestors, based on the claim that the United States violated the articles of the treaty of Guadalupe Hidalgo that guaranteed the citizenship and property rights of Mexicans, continues to this day.

## LA REFORMA, CIVIL WAR, AND THE FRENCH INTERVENTION

The disasters suffered by Mexico under conservative rule had created widespread revulsion against conservative policies and stimulated a revival of puro liberalism. In 1846, during the war, liberal administrations came to power in the states of Oaxaca and Michoacán. In Michoacán the new governor was Melchor Ocampo, a scholar and scientist profoundly influenced by Rousseau and French utopian socialist thought. In Oaxaca a Zapotec lawyer, Benito Juárez, became governor and earned a reputation for honesty, efficiency, and democratic simplicity.

Ocampo and Juárez were two leaders of a renovated liberalism that ushered in the movement called *La Reforma*. Like the older liberalism of the 1830s, the Reforma sought to destroy feudal vestiges and implant capitalism in Mexico. Its ideology, however, was more spirited than the aristocratic, intellectual liberalism of Mora; and its puro left wing included a small number of figures, such as Ponciano Arriaga and Ignacio Ramírez, who transcended liberal ideology with their attacks on the latifundio, defense of labor and women's rights, and other advanced ideas.

This revived liberal ferment inspired alarm among the reactionary forces led by Alamán and Santa Ana, who in 1853 had proclaimed himself perpetual dictator, with the title of His Most Supreme Highness.

Santa Anna's return to power, accompanied by a terrorist campaign against all dissenters, spurred a gathering of opposition forces, including many disgruntled moderados and conservatives. In early 1854 the old liberal caudillo from the state of Guerrero, Juan Alvarez, and the moderado general Ignacio Comonfort issued a call for revolt, the Plan of Ayutla, demanding the end of the dictatorship and the election of a convention to draft a new constitution. Within a year, Santa Anna's regime began to disintegrate, and in August 1855, seeing the handwriting on the wall, he went into exile for the last time. Some days later, a puro-dominated provisional government took office in Mexico City. The seventy-five-year-old Juan Alvarez was named provisional president; to his cabinet he named Benito Juárez as minister of justice and Miguel Lerdo de Tejada as treasury minister.

One of Juárez's first official acts was to issue a decree, the *Ley Juárez*, proclaiming the right of the state to limit the clerical and military fueros to matters of internal discipline. The *Ley Lerdo* (Lerdo Law) of 1856, drafted by Miguel Lerdo de Tejada, also struck a heavy blow at the material base of the church's power, its landed wealth. The law barred

Mexico's famous muralist, José Clemente Orozco, celebrated Mexican national resistance to French colonialism and the heroic leadership of Benito Juárez in this painting entitled *The Triumph of Juárez*. It depicts ordinary Mexican citizens rising to assist outgunned and overmatched Mexican regular army soldiers in a great victory over the French Legion at the Battle of Puebla on May 5, 1862. [Archivo Iconografico, S.A./Corbis]

the church from holding land not used for religious purposes and compelled the sale of all such property to tenants, with the rent considered to be 6 percent of the sale value of the property. Real estate not being rented was to be auctioned to the highest bidder, with payment of a large sales tax to the government.

The law's intent was to create a rural middle class, but because it made no provision for division of the church estates, the bulk of the land passed into the hands of great landowners, merchants, and capitalists, both Mexican and foreign. Worse, the law barred indigenous villages

from owning land and ordered that such land be sold in the same manner as church property, excepting only land and buildings designed exclusively for the "public use" of the inhabitants and for communal pastures (*ejidos*). As a result, land-grabbers descended on the native villages, "denounced" their land to the local courts, and proceeded to buy it at auction for paltry sums. The law provided that the native owners should have the first opportunity to buy, but few could pay the minimum purchase price. When they responded with protests and revolts, Lerdo explained in a circular that the intent of his law was that their community lands should be divided among the natives, not sold to others. But he insisted that "the continued existence of the Indian communities ought not to be tolerated . . . , and this is exactly one of the goals of the law." He was also adamant on the right of those who rented indigenous lands to buy them if they chose to do so. So, during the summer and fall of 1856 many pueblos lost crop and pasturelands from which they had derived revenues vitally needed to defray the cost of their religious ceremonies and other communal expenses. Indigenous resistance and the liberals' need to attract popular support during their struggle with the conservative counterrevolution and French interventionists in the decade 1857–1867 seem to have slowed enforcement of the Lerdo Law as it applied to native villages, but the long-range tendency of liberal agrarian policy was to compel division of communal lands, facilitating their acquisition by hacendados and even small and middle-sized farmers. The result was a simultaneous strengthening of the latifundio and some increase in the size of the rural middle class.

While the provisional government was causing consternation among conservatives with the Ley Juárez and the Ley Lerdo, a constitutional convention dominated by moderate liberals had been completing its work. The constitution of 1857 proclaimed freedom of speech, press, and assembly; limited fueros; forbade ecclesiastical and civil corporations to own land; and proclaimed the sanctity of private property. It restored the federalist structure of 1824, with the same division of Mexico into states, but replaced the bicameral national legislature with a single house and eliminated the office of vice president.

A few voices were raised against the land monopoly, peonage, and immense inequalities of wealth. "We proclaim ideas and forget realities," complained the radical delegate Ponciano Arriaga. "How can a hungry, naked, miserable people practice popular government? How can we condemn slavery in words, while the lot of most of our fellow citizens is more grievous than that of the black slaves of Cuba or the United States?" Despite his caustic attack on the land monopoly, Arriaga

offered a relatively moderate solution: the state should seize and auction off large uncultivated estates. The conservative opposition promptly branded Arriaga's project "communist"; the moderate majority in the convention passed over it in silence.

Because the new constitution incorporated the Lerdo Law and the Juárez Law, the church now openly entered the political struggle by excommunicating all public officials who took the required oath of loyalty. Counterrevolution had been gathering its forces for months, and the Three Years' War soon erupted in 1857. In regional terms, the war pitted the rich central area, dominated by the conservatives, against the liberal south, north, and Veracruz. Controlling extensive regions and enjoying the support of a clear majority of the population, the liberals, relying on largely undisciplined guerrilla forces, nevertheless suffered serious defeats in the first stage of the war.

As the struggle progressed, both sides found themselves in serious financial difficulties. The conservatives, however, had the advantage of generous support from the church. In July 1859, Juárez struck back at the clergy with reform laws that nationalized without compensation all ecclesiastical property except church buildings; the laws also suppressed all monasteries, established freedom of religion, and separated church and state. The reform laws were designed to encourage peasant proprietorship by dividing church estates into small farms, but this goal proved illusory; thanks to the Ley Lerdo, wealthy purchasers had already acquired much of the church land.

By the middle of 1860, although conservative bands in the provinces continued to make devastating raids, the tide of war had turned in favor of the liberals and Juárez reentered the capital in 1861. The war was effectively over, but diehard reactionaries now looked for help abroad. The conservative governments of England, France, and Spain had no love for the Mexican liberals and Juárez. Moreover, there were ample pretexts for intervention, for both sides had seized or destroyed foreign property without compensation, and foreign bondholders were clamoring for payments from an empty Mexican treasury. The three European powers demanded compensation for damages to their nationals and payment of just debts. Noting the dubious nature of some of the claims, Juárez vainly pleaded poverty, but the three powers nonetheless invaded and occupied Veracruz in 1862. England and Spain, having received assurances of future satisfaction of their claims, soon withdrew, but the French government rejected all Mexican offers, and its troops remained.

But Napoleon III wanted more than payment of debts. A group of Mexican conservative exiles had convinced the ambitious emperor that the Mexican people would welcome a French army of liberation and the establishment of a monarchy. Napoleon had visions of a French-protected Mexican Empire that would yield him great political and economic advantages. It remained only to find a suitable unemployed prince, and one was found in the person of Archduke Ferdinand Maximilian of Hapsburg, brother of Austrian emperor Franz Josef.

To prepare the ground for the arrival of the new ruler of Mexico, the French army advanced from Veracruz into the interior toward Puebla. At Puebla, instead of being received as liberators, the interventionists met determined resistance from a poorly armed Mexican garrison and were thrown back with heavy losses. The date—Cinco de Mayo de 1862—is still celebrated as a Mexican national holiday. On June 10, however, French reinforcements finally entered the city to the rejoicing of the clergy; by the end of the year the interventionists had occupied Querétaro, Monterrey, San Luis Potosí, and Saltillo. But the invaders had secure control only of the cities; republican guerrilla detachments controlled most of the national territory.

Meanwhile, a delegation of conservative exiles called on Maximilian to offer him a Mexican crown, which he and his wife Carlota gratefully accepted in 1864. The conservative conspirators had counted on Maximilian to help them recover their lost wealth and privileges, but the emperor, mindful of realities, would not consent to their demands; the purchase of church lands by native and foreign landlords and capitalists had created new interests that Maximilian refused to antagonize. Confident of conservative support, Maximilian even wooed moderate liberals and won the support of notable intellectuals like historians José Fernando Ramírez and Manuel Orozco y Berra, who were impressed by Maximilian's goodwill and cherished the illusion of a stable, prosperous Mexico ruled by an enlightened monarch.

But the hopes of both conservatives and misguided liberals were built on quicksand. The victories of Maximilian's generals could not destroy the fluid and elusive liberal resistance, firmly grounded in popular hatred for the invaders and aided by Mexico's rugged terrain. A turning point in the war came in the spring of 1865, with the Union triumph over the Confederacy in the U.S. Civil War. U.S. demands that the French evacuate Mexico, a region regarded by Secretary of State William Seward as a U.S. zone of economic and political influence, grew more insistent, and U.S. troops were massed along the Rio Grande. Facing serious domestic and diplomatic problems at home, Napoleon decided to cut his losses and liquidate the Mexican adventure.

Captured on May 14, 1867 and tried by court-martial, Maximilian and his leading generals, Miguel Miramón and Tomás Mejía, were found guilty of treason, sentenced to death, and executed by a *Juarista* firing squad.

## POSTWAR ATTEMPTS AT RECONSTRUCTION AND THE DEATH OF *LA REFORMA*

Juárez, symbol of Mexican resistance to a foreign usurper, assumed the presidency in August 1867. His government inherited a devastated country. Agriculture and industry were in ruins; as late as 1873, the value of Mexican exports was below the level of 1810. To reduce the state's financial burdens and end the danger of military control, Juárez dismissed two-thirds of the army, an act that produced discontent and uprisings that his generals managed to suppress. He also devoted the state's limited resources to the development of a public school system, especially on the elementary level; by 1874 there were about eight thousand schools with some three hundred and fifty thousand pupils.

However, his agrarian policy continued the liberal program that aimed to implant capitalism in the countryside, at the expense not of the haciendas but of indigenous communities. Indeed, the period of the "Restored Republic" (1868–1876) saw an intensified effort by the federal government to implement the Lerdo Law by compelling dissolution and partition of indigenous communal lands, opening the way for a new wave of fraud and seizures by neighboring hacendados and other land-grabbers. The result was a series of nationwide peasant revolts, the most serious occurring in the state of Hidalgo (1869–1870). Proclaiming the rebels to be "communists," the hacendados, aided by state and federal authorities, restored order by the traditional violent methods. A few liberals raised their voices in protest, but they were ignored; one was Ignacio Ramírez, who condemned the usurpations and fraud practiced by the hacendados with the complicity of corrupt judges and officials and called for suspension of the law.

Reelected president in 1871, Juárez put down a revolt by a hero of the wars of the Reforma, General Porfirio Díaz, who charged Juárez with attempting to become a dictator. But Juárez died the next year of a heart attack and was succeeded as acting president by the chief justice of the Supreme Court, Sebastían Lerdo de Tejada, who governed until 1876 when Díaz, aided by a group of Texas capitalists with strong links to New York banks, successfully overthrew him.

Díaz had seized power in the name of the ideals of the Reforma. In fact, however, the year 1876 marked the death of the Reforma and the libertarian creed to which Juárez subscribed, no matter how often he deviated from it. Thereafter, a new, profoundly anti-revolutionary ideology of positivism, which ranked order and progress above freedom, dominated Mexico.

The Reforma had paved the way for this change by transforming the Mexican bourgeoisie from a revolutionary class into a ruling class that was more predatory and acquisitive than the old creole aristocracy. The remnants of that aristocracy speedily adapted to the ways of the new ruling class and merged with it. The interests of the old and the new rich required political stability, a docile labor force, internal improvements, and a political and economic climate favorable to foreign investments. The mission of the "honorable tyranny" of Porfirio Díaz was to achieve those ends.

# Argentina

In 1816 delegates to the congress of Tucumán proclaimed the independence of the United Provinces of the Río de la Plata. "Disunited," however, would have better described the political condition of the La Plata area, for the creole seizure of power in Buenos Aires in 1810 brought in its train a dissolution of the vast viceroyalty of the Río de la Plata.

### The Liberation of Paraguay, Uruguay, and Upper Peru

Paraguay was first to repel the Buenos Aires junta's efforts to "liberate" it, and, under the dictatorial rule of the creole lawyer José Gaspar Rodríguez de Francia, it declared its own independence. Thereafter, Francia effectively sealed it off from its neighbors to avoid submission and payment of tribute to Buenos Aires, which controlled Paraguay's river outlets to the sea. Francia did permit a limited licensed trade with the outside world by way of Brazil, chiefly to satisfy military needs.

Francia's state-controlled economy brought certain benefits: the planned diversification of agriculture, which reduced production of such export crops as yerba maté, tobacco, and sugar, ensured a plentiful supply of foodstuffs and the well-being of the indigenous and mestizo masses. An interesting feature of Francia's system was the establishment of state farms or ranches—called *estancias de la patria*—that successfully specialized in the raising of livestock and ended Paraguay's dependence on livestock imports from the Argentine province of Entre Ríos. Those who suffered most under Francia's dictatorship were Spaniards, many of whom he expelled or penalized in various ways, and creole aristocrats, who were kept under perpetual surveillance and subjected to severe repression.

The gaucho chieftain José Artigas also resisted the efforts of the Buenos Aires junta to dominate the area and led Uruguay, then known as the Banda Oriental, toward independence. In 1815 the junta abandoned these efforts, evacuated Montevideo, and turned it over to Artigas. No ordinary caudillo, Artigas not only defended Uruguayan nationality but sought to achieve social reform. In 1815 he issued a plan for distributing royalist lands to the landless, with preference shown to blacks, indigenous peoples, zambos, and poor whites. But he was not given the opportunity to implement this radical program. In 1817 a powerful Brazilian army invaded Uruguay and soon had a secure grip on the Banda Oriental. Artigas had to flee across the Paraná River into Paraguay. He received asylum from Francia but was never allowed to leave again; he died in Paraguay thirty years later.

Meanwhile, Uruguay was occupied by foreign armies until 1828, when Great Britain, unwilling to see it fall under the control of either Brazil or Argentina, intervened to negotiate its independence.

Upper Peru, the mountainous northern corner of the old viceroyalty of La Plata, also escaped the grasp of Buenos Aires after 1810. Three expeditions were sent into the high country, won initial victories, then were rolled back by Spanish counteroffensives. Logistical problems, the apathy of the native population, and the hostility of the creole aristocracy, which remained loyal to Spain until it became clear that the royalist cause was doomed, contributed to the patriot defeats. Not until 1825 did General Antonio José de Sucre, Bolívar's lieutenant, finally liberate Peru. Renamed Bolivia in honor of the liberator, it began its independent life the next year under a complicated, totally impractical constitution drafted by Bolívar himself.

## THE STRUGGLE FOR PROGRESS AND NATIONAL UNITY

Even among the provinces that had joined at Tucumán to form the United Provinces of La Plata, discord grew and threatened the dissolution of the new state. The efforts of the wealthy port and province of Buenos Aires to impose its hegemony over the interior met with tenacious resistance. The end of the Spanish trade monopoly brought large gains to Buenos Aires and lesser gains to the littoral provinces of Santa Fe, Entre Ríos, and Corrientes; their exports of meat and hides increased, and the value of their lands rose. But the wine and textile industries of the interior, which had been protected by the colonial monopoly, suffered from the competition of cheaper and superior European wares imported through the port of Buenos Aires.

The interests of the interior provinces required a measure of autonomy or even independence to protect their primitive industries, but Buenos Aires preferred a single free-trade zone under a government dominated by the port city. This was one cause of the conflict between Argentine *federales* (federalists) and *unitarios* (unitarians). By 1820 the federalist solution had triumphed: the United Provinces had in effect dissolved into a number of independent republics, with the interior provinces ruled by caudillos, each representing the local ruling class and having a gaucho army behind him.

A new start toward unity came in 1821 when Bernardino Rivadavia, an ardent liberal strongly influenced by the English philosopher Jeremy Bentham, launched an ambitious program of educational, social, and economic reform. He promoted primary education, founded the University of Buenos Aires, abolished the ecclesiastical fuero and the tithe, and suppressed some monasteries. Rivadavia envisioned a balanced development of industry and agriculture, with a large role assigned to British investment and colonization. But the obstacles in the way of industrialization proved too great, and little came of efforts in this direction. The greatest progress was made in cattle raising, which expanded rapidly southward into territory formerly claimed by native peoples. To control the large floating population of gauchos, Rivadavia enacted vagrancy laws requiring them to have passports for travel and to have written permission from the *estanciero* to leave his ranch.

In 1822, hoping to raise revenue and increase production, Rivadavia introduced the system of emphyteusis, a program that distributed public lands to leaseholders at fixed rentals. Some writers have seen in this system an effort at agrarian reform, but there were no limits on the size of

## GÉNERAL ROSAS.

Although he cultivated the populist image of a *gaucho*, Juan Manuel Rosas was a wealthy *estanciero* and military *caudillo*, whose policies inevitably defended the interests of Argentina's landed aristocracy. [Culver Pictures, Inc.]

grants, and the measure actually contributed to the growth of latifundia. The lure of large profits in livestock raising induced many native and foreign merchants, politicians, and members of the military to join the rush for land. The net result was the creation not of a small-farmer class but of a new and more powerful estanciero class that was the enemy of Rivadavia's progressive ideals.

Rivadavia's planning went beyond the province of Buenos Aires; he had a vision of a unified Argentina under a strong central government that would promote the rounded economic development of the whole national territory. In 1825 a constituent congress met in Buenos Aires at Rivadavia's call to draft a constitution for the United Provinces of the Río de la Plata. Rivadavia, who was elected president of the new state, made a dramatic proposal to federalize the city and port of Buenos Aires. The former capital of the province would henceforth belong to the whole nation, with the revenues of its customhouse used to advance the general welfare.

Rivadavia's proposal reflected his nationalism and the need to mobilize national resources for a war with Brazil (1825–1828) over Uruguay. Congress approved Rivadavia's project, but the federalist caudillos of the interior, fearing that the rise of a strong national government would mean the end of their power, refused to ratify the constitution and even withdrew their delegates from the congress. In Buenos Aires a similar stand was taken by the powerful estancieros, who had no intention of surrendering the privileges of their province and regarded Rivadavia's program of social and economic reform as a costly folly. Defeated on the issue of the constitution, Rivadavia resigned the presidency in 1827 and went into exile. The liberal program for achieving national unity had failed.

After an interval of factional struggles, the federalism espoused by the landed oligarchy of Buenos Aires triumphed in the person of Juan Manuel Rosas, who became governor of the province in 1829. He forged (in 1831) a federal pact under which Buenos Aires assumed representation for the other provinces in foreign affairs but left them free to run their own affairs in all other respects. Federalism, as defined by Rosas, meant that Buenos Aires retained the revenues of its customhouse for its exclusive use and controlled trade on the Río de la Plata system for the benefit of its merchants. A network of personal alliances between Rosas and provincial caudillos, backed by use of force against recalcitrant leaders, ensured for him a large measure of control over the interior.

Rosas's long reign saw a reversal of Rivadavia's policies. For Rosas and the ruling class of estancieros, virtually the only economic concern was the export of hides and salted meat and the import of foreign goods. The dictator also showed some favor to wheat farming and artisan industry, which he protected by the Tariff Act of 1835, but the competition for land and later from livestock raising and the primitive character of artisan industry prevented both from taking much advantage of the act. Rosas himself was a great estanciero and owner of a *saladero* (salting plant) for the curing of meat and hides. He vigorously pressed the conquest of indigenous territory, bringing much new land under the control of the province of Buenos Aires; this land was sold for low prices to estancieros, and Rivadavia's policy of retaining ownership of land by the state was abandoned.

Although he professed to favor the gauchos, Rosas enforced the vagrancy laws against them even more rigorously, seeking to convert so-called idlers into ranch hands or soldiers for his army. The notion propagated by some historians that Rosas represented the rural masses against the urban aristocracy is contradicted by his own words. Fearing the masses, he cultivated gauchos and urban blacks to control them. "As you know," he wrote in a letter, "the dispossessed are always inclined to rise against the rich and the powerful. So . . . I thought it very important to gain a decisive influence over this class in order to control and direct it." But Rosas's "populism," his cultivation of gaucho manners and dress, did nothing to improve their condition. Under Rosas discipline on the estancias was enforced by punishments inherited from the colonial past that included torture, the lash, the stocks, and staking delinquent peons out "like hides in the sun." His government, observes John Lynch, was a seigneurial regime based on an informal alliance of estancieros and militia commanders, often the same people.

By degrees the press and all other potential dissidents were cowed or destroyed. To enforce the dictator's will there arose a secret organization known as the *Mazorca* (ear of corn—a reference to the close unity of its members). In collaboration with the police, this terrorist organization beat up or even murdered Rosas's opponents. The masthead of the official journal and all official papers carried the slogan "Death to the savage, filthy unitarians!" Even horses had to display the red ribbon that was the federalist symbol. Those opponents who did not knuckle under to escape death fled by the thousands to Montevideo, Chile, Brazil, or other places of refuge.

Under Rosas, the merchants of the city and the estancieros of the province of Buenos Aires enjoyed a measure of prosperity. But this prosperity bore no proportion to the possibilities of economic growth; technical backwardness marked all

aspects of livestock raising and agriculture, and port facilities were totally inadequate.

Meanwhile, the littoral provinces, which had experienced some advance of livestock raising and agriculture, became increasingly aware that Rosas's brand of federalism was harmful to their interests and that free navigation of the river system of La Plata was necessary to assure their prosperity. In 1852 the anti-Rosas forces formed a coalition that united liberal émigrés with the caudillo Justo José de Urquiza of Entre Ríos, who together defeated Rosas's army and sent him fleeing to an English exile.

Victory over Rosas did not end the dispute between Buenos Aires and the other provinces, between federalism and unitarianism. Only the slower process of economic change would forge the desired unity. A rift soon arose between the liberal exiles who assumed leadership in Buenos Aires and the caudillo Urquiza of Entre Ríos, who still sported the red ribbon of federalism. A sincere convert to the gospel of modernity and progress, he had proposed a loose union of the provinces, with all of them sharing the revenues of the Buenos Aires customhouse. But the leaders of Buenos Aires feared the loss of their economic and political predominance to Urquiza, whom they wrongly considered a caudillo of the Rosas type.

After Urquiza had attempted unsuccessfully to make Buenos Aires accept unification by armed force, the two sides agreed to a peaceful separation. As a result, delegates from Buenos Aires were absent from the constitutional convention that met at Santa Fe in Entre Ríos in 1852.

The constitution of 1853 reflected the influence of the ideas of the journalist Juan Bautista Alberdi on the delegates. His forcefully written pamphlet, *Bases and Points of Departure for the Political Organization of the Argentine Republic*, offered the United States as a model for Argentina. The new constitution strongly resembled that of the United States in certain respects. The former United Provinces became a federal republic, presided over by a president with significant power who served a six-year term without the possibility of immediate reelection. Legislative functions were vested in a bicameral legislature, a senate and a house of representatives. The Catholic religion was proclaimed the official religion of the nation, but freedom of worship for non-Catholics was assured. The states were empowered to elect governors and legislatures and frame their own constitutions, but the federal government had the right of intervention—including armed intervention—to ensure respect for the provisions of the constitution. General Urquiza was elected the first president of the Argentine Republic.

The liberal leaders of Buenos Aires, joined by the conservative estancieros who had been Rosas's firmest supporters, refused to accept the constitution of 1853, for they feared the creation of a state they did not control. As a result, two Argentinas arose: the Argentine Confederation, headed by Urquiza, and the province of Buenos Aires. For five years, the two states maintained their separate existences. In Paraná, capital of the confederation, Urquiza struggled to repress gaucho revolts, stimulate economic development, and foster education and immigration. Modest advances were made, but the tempo of growth lagged far behind that of the wealthy city and province of Buenos Aires, which prospered on the base of a steadily increasing trade with Europe in hides, tallow, salted beef, and wool.

Hoping to increase the confederation's scanty revenues, Urquiza began a tariff war with Buenos Aires, levying surcharges on goods landed at the Paraná River port of Rosario if duties had been paid on them at Buenos Aires. Buenos Aires responded with sanctions against ships sailing to Rosario and threatened to close commerce on the Paraná altogether. In 1859 war between the two Argentine states broke out and the forces of Bartolomé Mitre, governor of Buenos Aires, emerged victorious.

The military and economic superiority of Buenos Aires, the need of the other provinces to use its port, and an awareness on all sides of the urgent need to achieve national unity dictated a compromise. At an 1862 congress representing all the provinces, it finally was agreed that the city should be the provisional capital of both the Argentine Republic and the province and that the Buenos Aires customhouse should be nationalized, with the proviso that for a period of five years the revenues of the province would not fall below the

1859 level. Bartolomé Mitre—distinguished historian, poet, soldier, and statesman—was elected the first president of a united Argentina.

Mitre promoted economic progress and consolidated national unity. The customhouse was nationalized, as had been promised, and plans were made for the federalization of the capital. The construction of railways and telegraph lines that would forge closer links between Buenos Aires and the interior had begun, and European immigrants arrived in growing numbers. Some advances were made in the establishment of a public school system. But great problems remained, the most difficult of which was the long, exhausting Paraguayan War (1865–1870).

### THE PARAGUAYAN WAR

On the death of the dictator Francia in 1840, power in Paraguay was assumed by a triumvirate in which Carlos Antonio López soon emerged as the dominant figure. In essence, López continued Francia's dictatorial system but gave it a thin disguise of constitutional, representative government. Since he had inherited a stable, prosperous state, López could afford to rule in a less repressive fashion than his predecessor. More flexible than Francia, too, with a better understanding of the outside world, López made a successful effort to end Paraguay's diplomatic and commercial isolation. After the fall of Rosas, a stubborn enemy of Paraguayan independence, López obtained Argentine recognition of his country's independence, and the Paraná was at last opened to Paraguayan trade. López also established diplomatic relations with a series of countries, including England, France, and the United States.

The end of the policy of isolation was accompanied by a major expansion of the Paraguayan economy. Although agriculture (especially the production of such export crops as tobacco and yerba maté) continued to be the principal economic activity, López assigned great importance to the development of industry. One of his proudest achievements in this field was the construction of an iron foundry, the most modern enterprise of its type in Latin America. Transportation was improved with the building of roads and canals, the creation of a fleet of merchant ships, and the construction of a short railroad line.

Continuing Francia's policy, López enlarged the role of the state sector in the national economy. In 1848 he transferred to state ownership forest lands producing yerba maté and other commercial wood products and much arable land. The lucrative export trade in yerba maté and some other products became a government monopoly, and the number of state-owned ranches rose to sixty-four. López promoted education as well as economic growth; by the time of his death, Paraguay had 435 elementary schools, with some 25,000 pupils, and a larger proportion of literate inhabitants than any other Latin American country.

At the same time, López took advantage of his position to concentrate ownership of land and various commercial enterprises in his own hands and those of his children, relatives, and associates; thus, there arose a bourgeoisie that profited by its close connection with the state apparatus, which enabled it to promote its own interests. The number of large private estates, however, was small; the private agricultural sector was dominated by small or medium-sized farms cultivated by owners or tenants, sometimes aided by a few hired laborers. In contrast with the situation in other Latin American countries, peonage and debt servitude were rare and slavery was gradually abolished by an 1842 manumission law. The relative absence of peonage and other feudal survivals contributed to a rapid growth of Paraguayan capitalism and the well-being of its predominantly indigenous and mestizo population. When López died in 1862, Paraguay was one of the most progressive and prosperous states in South America.

His son, Francisco Solano, succeeded him as dictator. The younger López inherited a tradition of border disputes with Brazil that erupted into open war when Brazil sent an army into Uruguay in 1864 to ensure the victory of a pro-Brazilian faction in that country's civil strife. López could not be indifferent to this action, which threatened the delicate balance of power in the basin of La Plata. López also feared that Brazilian control of Uruguay would end unrestricted Paraguayan access to the port of Montevideo, which would make Paraguayan trade dependent entirely on the good will of Buenos Aires.

When the Brazilian government disregarded his protests, López declared war and Brazil quickly concluded a Triple Alliance with Argentina and Uruguay; a separate secret treaty between Brazil and Argentina provided for the partition of more than half of Paraguay's territory between them. Paraguay thus faced a coalition that included the two largest states in South America, with an immense superiority in manpower and other resources.

Yet the war dragged on for five years, for at its outset Paraguay possessed an army of some 70,000 well-armed and disciplined soldiers that outnumbered the combined forces of its foes. By 1870, however, the Triple Alliance had depleted Paraguay's economic strength and defeated its military forces. Perhaps as much as 20 percent of Paraguay's prewar population of some 300,000 perished as a result of military action, famine, disease, and a devastating Brazilian occupation. The peace treaty assigned much Paraguayan territory to the victors and burdened Paraguay with extremely heavy reparations. Brazil, the occupying power, installed a puppet regime that radically reconstructed the Paraguayan economy and state.

The essence of the new policy was to liquidate the progressive changes made under the Francia and López regimes. Most of the state-owned lands were sold to land speculators and foreign businessmen at bargain prices, with no restriction on the size of holdings. Tenants who could not present the necessary documents were ejected even though they and their forebears had cultivated the land for decades. By the early 1890s, the state-owned lands were almost gone. Foreign penetration of the economy through loans, concessions, and land purchases soon deprived Paraguay of its economic as well as its political independence.

## PROGRESS AND DEVELOPMENT UNDER SARMIENTO

The Paraguayan War also changed Argentina, which obtained its share of Paraguayan reparations and territorial concessions (Formosa, Chaco, and Misiones). Politically, it ushered in a transfer of power to Domingo Faustino Sarmiento (1868–1874), a gifted essayist, sociologist, and statesman, who worked for Argentine unity and economic and social progress.

Even more importantly, however, a flood of technological change began to sweep over Argentina. Railways penetrated the interior, extending the stock-raising and farming area. The gradual introduction of barbed-wire fencing and alfalfa ranges made possible a dramatic improvement in the quality of livestock. In 1876 the arrival of an experimental shipload of chilled carcasses from France prepared the way for the triumph of frozen over salted meat, which led to a vast expansion of European demand for Argentine beef. Labor was needed to exploit the rapidly expanding pasturelands and farmlands, so Sarmiento's administration promoted immigration; some three hundred thousand immigrants poured into the country. Sarmiento, believing it necessary to educate the citizens of a democratic republic, expanded the public school system and introduced to Argentina teacher-training institutions of the kind his friend Horace Mann had founded in the United States. But there also was a darker side to Sarmiento's policies. Regarding native peoples and gauchos as obstacles to the advance of "civilization," he waged a war of extermination against the indígenas and used vagrancy laws, press gangs, and other repressive measures to control the gauchos.

When Sarmiento left office, Argentina presented the appearance of a rapidly developing, prosperous state. But there were clouds in the generally bright Argentine sky. The growth of exports and the rise in land values did not benefit the forlorn gauchos, aliens in a land over which they had once freely roamed, or the majority of European immigrants. Little was done to provide newcomers with homesteads. Immigrants who wished to farm usually found the price of land out of reach; as a result, many preferred to remain in Buenos Aires or other cities of the littoral, where they began to form an urban middle class largely devoted to trade. Meanwhile, foreign economic influence grew as a result of increasing dependence on foreign—chiefly British—capital to finance the construction of railways, telegraph lines, gasworks, and other needed facilities. The growing concentration of landownership reinforced a colonial land tenure pattern; the tightening British control of markets and the country's economic infrastructure reinforced a colonial pattern—dependence on a foreign metropolis, with London replacing Seville as commercial center. But Mitre, Sarmiento, and other builders of the new Argentina were dazzled by their successes in nation-building and by a climate of prosperity they believed permanent. These men did not suspect the extent of the problems in the making, nor did they anticipate the nature of the problems future generations of Argentines would face.

## Chile

The victories of José de San Martín's Army of the Andes over royalist forces at Chacabuco and Maipú in 1817 and 1818 gave Chile its definitive independence. From 1818 until 1823, Bernardo O'Higgins, a hero of the struggle for Chilean liberation and a true son of the Enlightenment, ruled the country with the title of supreme director. O'Higgins energetically pushed a program of reform designed to weaken the landed aristocracy and the church and promote rapid development of the Chilean economy along capitalist lines. His abolition of titles of nobility and entails angered the great landowners of the fertile Central Valley between the Andes and the Pacific; his expulsion of the royalist bishop of Santiago and his restrictions on the number of religious processions and the veneration of images infuriated the church. Dissident liberals who resented his sometimes heavy-handed rule joined the opposition to O'Higgins. In 1823, O'Higgins resigned and went into exile in Lima. There followed seven turbulent years, with presidents and constitutions rising and falling.

### PORTALES AND ECONOMIC GROWTH

In Chile, as in other Latin American countries, the political and armed struggle gradually assumed the form of a conflict between conservatives, who usually were also centralists, and liberals, who were generally federalists. The conservative-centralists were the party of the great landowners of the Central Valley and the wealthy merchants of Santiago; the liberal-federalists spoke for the landowners, merchants, and artisans of the northern and southern provinces, who were resentful of political and economic domination by the wealthy central area. By 1830 the conservatives emerged victorious under the leadership of Joaquín Prieto and his cabinet minister Diego Portales.

Until 1837, Portales, who never held an elective office, indelibly stamped his ideas on Chilean politics and society. A businessman of aristocratic origins, owner of a successful import house, he faithfully served the interests of an oligarchy of great landlords and merchants that dominated the Chilean scene for decades. Although Portales expressed atheist views in private, he supported the authority of the church as an instrument for keeping the lower classes in order. He understood the importance of trade, industry, and mining and promoted their interests by removing remaining obstacles to internal trade. He introduced income and property taxes to increase the state's revenues and trimmed government spending by dismissing unnecessary employees. Agriculture was protected by high tariffs on agricultural imports. Port facilities were improved, measures were taken to strengthen the Chilean merchant marine, and in 1835 a steamship line began to connect Chilean ports. Under the fostering care of the conservative regime and in response to a growing European demand for Chilean silver, copper, and hides, the national economy made steady progress in the 1830s.

Measures designed to stimulate economic growth were accompanied by others that fortified the social and political power of the oligarchy. Portales restored the privileges the church had lost under liberal rule and normalized the troubled relations between Chile and the papacy.

In 1833 a conservative-dominated assembly adopted a constitution that further consolidated the power of the oligarchy. Elections were made indirect, with the suffrage limited to men of twenty-five years or over who could satisfy literacy and property qualifications. Still higher property qualifications were required of members of the lower and upper houses. The constitution restored entails, ensuring perpetuation of the latifundio. Catholicism was declared the state religion, and the church was given control over marriage. The president enjoyed an absolute veto over congressional legislation, appointed all high officials, and could proclaim a state of siege. The process of amending the constitution was made so difficult as to be virtually impossible. Since the president controlled the electoral machinery, the outcome of elections was a foregone conclusion.

## ECONOMIC EXPANSION UNDER BULNES

In 1841, General Manuel Bulnes succeeded Prieto to the presidency; he was reelected to a second five-year term in 1846. Victorious at home and abroad, the conservative leadership decided it could relax the strict discipline of the Portales period. Chile's economic life began a renewed advance. Commerce, mining, and agriculture prospered as never before. The Crimean War and the gold rushes to California and Australia of the 1850s created large new markets for Chilean wheat, stimulating a considerable expansion of the cultivated area. In 1840 a North American, William Wheelright, established a steamship line to operate on the Chilean coast, using coal from newly developed hard coal mines. Wheelright also founded a company that in 1852 completed Chile's first railroad line, providing an outlet to the sea for the production of the mining district of Copiapó. The major Santiago-Valparaíso line, begun in 1852, was not completed until 1863. Foreign—especially British—capital began to penetrate the Chilean economy; Britain dominated foreign trade and had a large interest in mining and railroads, but Chilean capitalists constituted an important, vigorous group and displayed much initiative in the formation of joint stock companies and banks.

The great landowners were the principal beneficiaries of this economic upsurge; their lands appreciated in value without any effort on their part. Some great landowners invested their money in railroads, mining, and trade. But the essential conservatism of the landed aristocracy and the urge to preserve a semifeudal control over its peons discouraged the transformation of the great landowners into capitalist farmers. A pattern of small landholdings arose in southern Chile, to which German as well as Chilean colonists came in increasing numbers in the 1840s and 1850s. The rich Central Valley, still dominated by the latifundio, reflected inefficient techniques and reliance on the labor of *inquilinos*—tenants who also had to work the master's fields. Thus, alongside an emerging capitalist sector based on mining, trade, banking, intensive agriculture, and some industry, there existed a semifeudal sector based on the latifundio, peonage, and an aristocracy that hindered the development of Chilean capitalism.

Although Chile appeared more progressive than most other Latin American states, militants like José Victorino Lastarria—historian, sociologist, and a deputy of the Liberal Party—were dissatisfied with the new conservatives' modest concessions to modernity. They wanted to accelerate the rate of change and demanded both a radical revision of the constitution of 1833 and an end to oligarchical rule.

To the left of Lastarria stood the firebrand Francisco Bilbao, author of a scorching attack on the church and Hispanic heritage, "The Nature of Chilean Society" (1844). Later, he spent several years in France and was profoundly influenced by utopian socialist and radical republican thought. He returned to Chile in 1850 to found, with Santiago Arcos, the Society of Equality, uniting radical intellectuals and artisans, which advocated these advanced ideas. The society carried on an intensive antigovernmental campaign and within a few months had a membership of four thousand.

## MONTT'S MODERATE REFORMS

The Society of Equality was founded on the eve of the election of 1850, for which President Bulnes had designated Manuel Montt his heir. Despite Montt's progressive educational policies and patronship of the arts and letters, liberals identified him with the repressive system of Portales and the constitution of 1833. Liberals like Lastarria and radical democrats like Bilbao proclaimed the impending election a fraud and demanded constitutional reforms. The government responded by proclaiming a state of siege and suppressing the Society of Equality. Regarding these acts as a prelude to an attempt to liquidate the opposition, groups of liberals in Santiago and La Serena rose in revolts that were quickly crushed. Lastarria was exiled; Bilbao and Arcos fled to Argentina. Montt became president and immediately crushed another liberal revolt, but thereafter took steps to resolve future crises by granting amnesty to the insurgents and abolishing both entails and the tithe.

The abolition of entails, which was designed to encourage the breakup of landed estates among the children of the great landowners, affected a dwindling number of great aristocratic clans. Its effects were less drastic than the anguished cries of the affected parties suggested, for the divided estates were almost invariably acquired by other latifundists, and the condition of the *inquilinos* who worked the land remained the same. The elimination of the tithe, and Montt's refusal to allow the return of the Jesuits, greatly angered the reactionary clergy. Responding to their attacks, Montt promulgated a new civil code in 1857 that placed education under state control, gave the state jurisdiction over the clergy, and granted non-Catholics the right of civil marriage.

The abolition of entails and the tithe represented a compromise between liberals and conservatives, between the new bourgeoisie and the great landowners. In the process, the bourgeoisie gained little, and the landowners lost almost nothing; the chief loser was the church. Although Montt's reforms alienated the most reactionary elements of the Conservative Party, they gained him the support of moderate liberals who joined with moderate conservatives to form a new coalition, the National Party. Its motto was the typically positivist slogan "Freedom in Order."

In the last years of his second term, President Montt faced severe economic and political problems. The 1857 depression caused a sharp fall in the price of copper and reduced Australian and Californian demand for Chilean wheat. The economic decline fed the fires of political discontent, and another large-scale revolt erupted in January 1859. The rebels included radical intellectuals, northern mining capitalists and their workers, artisans, and small farmers, all groups with grievances against the dominant Central Valley alliance of great merchants and landowners. Their demands included a democratic republic, state support for mining and industry, the splitting up of the great estates, and abolition of the semifeudal *inquilinaje* system of peonage as incompatible with democratic principles. Before the revolt was crushed, it had taken five thousand lives. Some of the bourgeois leaders of the revolt were imprisoned, others were deported, and others fled into exile, but a large number of miners, artisans, and peasants were executed. Maurice Zeitlin regards it as a crucial turning point in Chilean history: "Defeat of the revolutionary bourgeoisie amounted to virtual suppression of an alternative and independent path of capitalist development for Chile—a realm of objective historical possibilities unfulfilled because of the failure of the bourgeois revolution."

By 1861 the depression had lifted and another boom began, creating new fortunes and bringing large shifts of regional influence. A growing stream of settlers, including many Germans, flowed into southern Chile, founding cities and transforming woodlands into farms.

But Chile's true center of economic gravity became the desert north, rich in copper, nitrates, and guano; the last two, in particular, were objects of Europe's insatiable demand for fertilizers. The major nitrate deposits, however, lay in the Bolivian province of Antofagasta and the Peruvian province of Tarapacá. Chilean capital, supplemented by English and German capital, began to pour into these regions and soon dominated the Peruvian and Bolivian nitrate industries. In the north there arose an aggressive mining capitalist class that demanded a place in the sun for itself and its region. A rich mine owner, Pedro León Gallo, abandoned the liberals to form a new middle-class party, called Radical, that fought more militantly than the liberals for limited constitutional changes, religious toleration, and an end to repressive policies.

**LIBERAL CONTROL**

The transition of Chile's political life to liberal control, begun under Montt, was completed in 1871 with the election of the first liberal president, Federico Errázuriz Zañartú. Between 1873 and 1875 a coalition of liberals and radicals pushed through the congress a series of constitutional reforms: reduction of senatorial terms from nine to six years; direct election of senators; and freedom of speech, press, and assembly. These victories for enlightenment also represented a victory of new capitalist groups over the old merchant-landowner oligarchy that traced its beginnings back to colonial times. By 1880, of the fifty-nine Chilean personal fortunes of over 1 million pesos, only twenty-four were of colonial origin and only twenty had made their fortunes in agriculture; the rest belonged to coal, nitrate, copper, and silver interests or to merchants whose wealth had been formed only in the nineteenth century. Arnold Bauer has observed that the more interesting point is "not that only twenty made their fortune in agriculture, but that the remaining thirty-nine—designated as miners, bankers, and capitalists— subsequently invested their earnings in rural estates. This would be comparable to Andrew Carnegie sinking his steel income into Scarlett O'Hara's plantation." Bauer's comment points to the "powerful social model" that the Chilean agrarian oligarchy continued to exert. For the rest, the victories of the new bourgeoisie brought no relief to the Chilean masses, the migrant laborers and tenant farmers on the haciendas, and the young working class in Chile's mines and factories.

# Brazil

Brazil took its first major step toward independence in 1808, when the Portuguese crown and court, fleeing before a French invasion of Portugal, arrived in Rio de Janeiro to make it the new capital of the Portuguese Empire. Formal national independence came in 1822 when Dom Pedro, who ruled Brazil as regent for his father, João VI, rejected a demand that he return to Portugal and issued the famous Cry of Ipiranga: "Independence or Death!"

## DOM PEDRO, EMPEROR

Dom Pedro acted with the advice and support of the Brazilian aristocracy, which was determined to preserve the autonomy Brazil had enjoyed since 1808. It was equally determined to make a transition to independence without the violence that marked the Spanish-American movement of liberation elsewhere. The Brazilian aristocracy had its wish; Brazil made a transition to independence with comparatively little disruption and bloodshed. But separation from Portugal with a minimum of internal dislocation meant that independent Brazil retained not only monarchy and slavery but also the large landed estate and monoculture; a wasteful, inefficient agricultural system; a highly stratified society; and a free population that was 90 percent illiterate and prejudiced against manual labor.

Dom Pedro had promised to give his subjects a constitution, but the constituent assembly he summoned in 1823 drafted a document that seemed to the emperor to place excessive limits on his power. He responded by dissolving the assembly and assigning to a hand-picked commission the task of making a new constitution, which he approved and promulgated by imperial proclamation. This constitution, under which Brazil was governed until the fall of the monarchy in 1889, concentrated great power in the hands of the monarch. In addition to a Council of State, it provided for a two-chamber parliament—a lifetime Senate, the members of which were chosen by the emperor, and a Chamber of Deputies elected by voters who met property and income requirements. The emperor had the right to appoint and dismiss ministers and summon or dissolve parliament at will. He also appointed the provincial governors or presidents.

Resentment over Dom Pedro's highhanded dissolution of the constituent assembly and the highly centralist character of the constitution of 1824 was particularly strong in Pernambuco, a center of republican and federalist ferment. Here in 1824 a group of rebels, led by the merchant Manoel de Carvalho, proclaimed the creation of a Confederation of the Equator that would unite the six northern provinces under a republican government. A few leaders voiced antislavery sentiments, but nothing was done to abolish slavery, which deprived the movement of the potential support of a large slave population. Within a year imperial troops had smashed the revolt and executed fifteen of its leaders.

Dom Pedro had won a victory, but resentment of his autocratic tendencies continued to smolder, and his popularity steadily waned. The emperor's foreign policies contributed to this growing discontent. In 1826, in return for recognition of Brazilian independence and a trade agreement, Dom Pedro signed a treaty with Great Britain that obligated Brazil to end the slave traffic by 1830. Despite this ban and the efforts of British warships to intercept and seize the slaveships, the trade continued with the full knowledge and approval of the Brazilian government. But British policing practices caused the price of slaves to rise sharply. The prospering coffee growers of Rio de Janeiro, São Paulo, and Minas Gerais could afford to pay high prices for slaves, but the cotton and sugar growers of the depressed north could not compete with them for workers and blamed Dom Pedro for their difficulties.

News of the July Revolution of 1830 in France, a revolution that toppled an unpopular, autocratic king, produced rejoicing and violent demonstrations in Brazilian cities. *Exaltados* (radical liberals) placed themselves at the head of the movement of revolt and called for the abolition of the monarchy and the establishment of a federal republic. In the face of the growing crisis, Dom Pedro abdicated in favor of his five-year-old son Pedro, and two weeks later he sailed for Portugal, never to return. These developments, eliminating the dominant influence of Portuguese merchants and Portuguese-born courtiers under Emperor Pedro I, completed the transition to full Brazilian independence.

## REGENCY, REVOLT, AND A BOY EMPEROR

The revolution had been the work of radical liberals, who viewed Dom Pedro's downfall as the first step toward the establishment of a federal republic, but its fruits were garnered by the moderates. In effect, the radicals had played the game of the monarchist liberals, who had guided the movement of secession from Portugal and later lost influence at court as a result of Dom Pedro's shift to the right. Dom Pedro's departure was a victory for these moderates, who hastened to restore their ascendancy over the central government and prevent the revolution from getting out of hand.

As a first step, parliament appointed a three-man regency composed of moderate liberals to govern for the child emperor until he reached the age of eighteen. Another measure created a national guard, recruited from the propertied classes, to repress urban mobs and slave revolts. Simultaneously, the new government began work on a project of constitutional reform designed to appease the strong federalist sentiment. After a three-year debate, parliament approved the Additional Act of 1834, which gave the provinces elective legislative assemblies with broad powers, including control over local budgets and taxes. This provision assured the great landowners a large measure of control over their regions. The Council of State, identified with Dom Pedro's reactionary rule, was abolished. But centralism was not abandoned, for the national government continued to appoint provincial governors with a partial veto over the acts of the provincial assemblies.

Almost immediately, the regency government struggled against a rash of revolts, most numerous in the northern provinces, where the economy suffered from a loss of markets for their staple crops, sugar and cotton. None occurred in the central southern zone (the provinces of Rio de Janeiro, São Paulo, and Minas Gerais), whose coffee economy prospered and whose planter aristocracy had secure control of the central government. These revolts had a variety of local causes. Some were elemental, popular revolts; such was the so-called *cabanagem* (from the word *cabana*, "cabin") of Pará, which originated in the grievances of small tradesmen, farmers, and lower-class elements against the rich Portuguese merchants who monopolized local trade. Others, like the republican and separatist revolt in Bahia (1837–1838), reflected the frustrations of the planter aristocracy of this once-prosperous area over its loss of economic and political power.

Most serious of all was the revolt that broke out in 1835 in the province of Rio Grande do Sul. Although it was dubbed the *Revolução Farroupilha* (Revolution of the Ragamuffins) in contemptuous reference to its supposed lower-class origins, the movement was led by cattle barons who maintained a more or less patriarchal sway over the gauchos who formed the rank-and-file of the rebel armies. An intense regionalism, resentment over taxes and unpopular governors imposed by the central government, and the strength of republican sentiment all induced the revolt that established the independent republic of Rio Grande in 1836. The presence of considerable numbers of Italian exiles such as Giuseppe Garibaldi, ardent republicans opposed to slavery, gave a special radical tinge to the revolt. For almost a decade, two states—one a republic, the other an empire—existed on Brazilian territory.

The secession of Rio Grande and the inability of imperial troops to quell the revolt further weakened the regency government. Soon the political struggle began to assume an organized form, with the emergence of a Liberal Party composed chiefly of moderate liberals who favored concessions to federalism, and a Conservative Party, which preferred to strengthen the central government. However, on such essential issues as the monarchy, slavery, and the maintenance of the status quo in general, liberals and conservatives saw eye to eye.

They also agreed on the need to suppress the Rio Grande rebellion and other regional revolts in the north. The Rio Grande experiment in republican government and its offer of freedom to all slaves who joined the republic's armed forces posed an especially serious threat to monarchy and slavery. To strengthen the central government in its war against these subversive and separatist movements, liberals and conservatives decided to call the young Pedro to rule before his legal majority. In 1840 the two legislative chambers orchestrated a parliamentary coup d'état and proclaimed the fourteen-year-old Dom Pedro emperor. He empowered a conservative government that dismantled the federalist reforms in the Additional Act of 1834, sharply curtailed the powers of provincial assemblies, and stripped locally elected judges of their judicial and police powers.

The liberals of São Paulo and Minas Gerais responded with a revolt (1842) that had little popular support, for it was dictated solely by the desire for the spoils of office. Conservative troops swiftly crushed the uprising, but the emperor treated the vanquished rebels leniently and, a short time later, he called on the liberals to form a new ministry. Once returned to power, the liberals made no effort to repeal the conservative revisions of the constitution and made use of the broad police powers vested in the central government for their own ends.

With the unity of the ruling class restored, the government undertook to settle scores with the rebels of Rio Grande. As a result of internal squabbles and the cessation of aid from friendly Uruguay after Argentina invaded it in February 1843, the situation of the republic became extremely difficult. Facing the prospect of military defeat, the republican leaders accepted an offer from Rio de Janeiro to negotiate a peace, which was signed in February 1845. The peace treaty extended amnesty to all rebels but annulled all laws of the republican regime. The cattle barons won certain concessions, including the right to nominate their candidate for provincial governor and retain their military titles.

The last large-scale revolt in the series that shook Brazil in the 1830s and 1840s was the uprising of 1848 in Pernambuco. Centered in the city of Recife, its causes included hostility toward the Portuguese merchants who monopolized local trade, the appointment of an unpopular governor by the conservative government, and hatred for the greatest landowners of the region, the powerful Cavalcanti family. The rebel program called for the removal from Recife of all Portuguese merchants, expansion of provincial autonomy, work for the unemployed, and division of the Cavalcanti lands. Even this radical program, however, contained no reference to the abolition of slavery. The movement collapsed after the capture of Recife by imperial troops in 1849. Many captured leaders were condemned to prison for life, but all were amnestied in 1852.

Underlying these rebellions and armed conflicts of the 1830s and 1840s was economic stagnation caused by the weakness of foreign markets for Brazil's traditional exports. The expansion in the center-south of coffee, already important in the 1830s but flourishing after 1850, strengthened the hand of the central government with increased revenues and laid the basis for a new era of cooperation between regional elites and the national government. The new coffee prosperity, confirming the apparent viability and rationality of the neocolonial emphasis on export agriculture, also discouraged any thought of taking the more durable but difficult path of Brazilian autonomous development.

## THE GAME OF POLITICS AND THE CRISIS OF SLAVERY

By 1850, Brazil was at peace. The emperor presided over a pseudoparliamentary regime, exercising his power in the interests of a tiny ruling class. He paid his respects to parliamentary forms by alternately appointing conservative and liberal prime ministers at will; if the new ministry did not command a majority in parliament, one was obtained by holding rigged elections. Because the ruling class was united on essential issues, the only thing at stake in party struggles was patronage, the spoils of office. An admirer of Dom Pedro, Joaquim Nabuco, described the operation of the system in his book *O abolicionismo*:

> The representative system, then, is a graft of parliamentary forms on a patriarchal government, and senators and deputies only take their roles seriously in this parody of democracy because of the personal advantage they derive therefrom. Suppress the subsidies, force them to stop using their positions for personal and family ends, and no one who had anything else to do would waste his time in such shadow-boxing.

The surface stability of Brazilian political life in the decades after 1850 rested on the prosperity of the coffee-growing zone of Rio de Janeiro, São Paulo, and Minas Gerais, itself the product of growing demand and good prices for Brazilian coffee. But the sugar-growing northeast and its plantation society continued to decline because of exhausted soil, archaic techniques, and competition from foreign sugars.

The crisis of the northeast grew more acute as a result of English pressure on Brazil to enforce the Anglo-Brazilian treaty banning the importation of slaves into Brazil after November 7, 1831. Before 1850 this treaty was never effectively enforced; more than fifty thousand slaves a year were brought to Brazil during the 1840s. In 1849 and 1850, however, the British government pressured Brazil to pass the Queiroz anti–slave-trade law and instructed its warships to enter Brazilian territorial waters if necessary to destroy Brazilian slave ships. By the middle 1850s, the importation of slaves had virtually ended.

Abolition of the slave trade had major consequences. Because of the high mortality among slaves due to poor food, harsh working conditions, and other negative factors, the slave population could not be maintained by natural reproduction, and the eventual doom of the slave system was assured. The end of the slave trade created a serious labor shortage, with a large flow of slaves from the north to the south because of the coffee planters' greater capacity to compete for slave labor. This movement aggravated the imbalance between the declining north and the prosperous south-central zone, where Brazil's first telegraph lines were established in 1852 and the first railroad line was begun in 1854. In these years, a pioneer of Brazilian capitalism, Irineu Evangelista de Sousa, later the Baron Mauá, laid the foundations of a veritable industrial and banking empire.

By the 1860s, a growing number of Brazilians had become convinced that slavery brought serious discredit to Brazil and must be ended. The abolition of slavery in the United States as a result of the Civil War, which left Brazil and the Spanish colonies of Cuba and Puerto Rico the only slaveholding areas in the Western Hemisphere, sharpened sensitivity to the problem. The Paraguayan War also promoted the cause of emancipation. In an effort to fill the gaps caused by heavy losses at the front, a decree was issued granting freedom to government-owned slaves who agreed to join the army, and some private slave owners followed the official example. Criticism of slavery was increasingly joined with criticism of the emperor, censured for his cautious posture on slavery.

Alongside the antislavery movement there arose a nascent republican movement. In 1869 the Reform Club, a group of militant Liberals, issued a manifesto demanding restrictions on the powers of the emperor and the grant of freedom to the newborn children of slaves. The crisis of slavery was fast becoming a crisis of the Brazilian Empire.

## Peru

The liberation of Peru from Spanish rule had come from without, for the creole aristocracy, whose wealth was derived from the forced labor of indigenous peoples and enslaved Africans in mines, workshops, and haciendas, rightly feared that revolution might set fire to this combustible social material. The liberators, General José de San Martín and Simón Bolívar, had attempted to reform the social and economic institutions of the newly created Peruvian state. Before he left to meet Bolívar in Guayaquil, San Martín had decreed a ban on slave importation, the automatic emancipation of all children born of slaves in Peru, and the abolition of native tribute as well as the mita and all other kinds of indigenous forced labor; he also proclaimed that all inhabitants of Peru, whether native or creole, were Peruvians.

Because these reforms did not conform to the interests of the creole elite, however, they were never implemented after San Martín left Lima to meet Bolívar in Guayaquil. When Bolívar assumed power in Peru in 1823, he enacted reforms reflecting the same liberal ideology. Wishing to create a class of independent small-holders, he decreed the dissolution of indigenous communities and ordered the division of communal lands into individual parcels; each family was to hold its plot as private property, with the surplus to become part of the public domain. While attacking communal property, Bolívar left alone feudal property, the great haciendas serviced by *yanaconas* or *colonos* (native sharecroppers or serfs) who had to pay their landlords a rent that amounted to as much as 50 to 90 percent of the value of their crops, in addition to *pongueaje* (free personal service).

The well-intentioned Bolivarian land reform played into the hands of hacendados, public officials, and merchants, who used it to build up vast estates at the expense of indigenous communal lands; the process began slowly but gathered momentum as the century advanced. Bolívar's efforts to abolish native tribute had no greater success. After he left Peru in 1826, Peru's creole government reinstituted the tribute for *serranos* under the name *contribución de indígenas,* and for good measure it also reintroduced the *contribución de castas* for the mestizo population of the coast.

The new government's heavy dependence on such tribute as a source of revenue reflected the stagnant condition of the Peruvian economy. The revolution completed the ruin of the mining industry and coastal plantation agriculture, both of which had been declining since the close of the eighteenth century, and the scanty volume of exports could not pay for the much greater volume of imports of manufactured goods from Britain. As a result, the new state, already burdened with large wartime debts to English capitalists, developed a massive trade deficit with Great Britain, its largest trading partner. There was some growth of wool exports after 1836, and in 1840 a new economic era opened on the coast with the exploitation of guano, but in its first stage the guano cycle failed to provide the capital accumulation needed to revive coastal agriculture.

# Cuba

Because of its distinctive colonial past, Cuba's nineteenth-century development differed markedly from that of most other Latin American countries. For three centuries after Christopher Columbus landed in 1492, the island served primarily as a strategic stopover for the Spanish treasure fleet. Largely isolated from expanding transatlantic markets and without precious metals or a large indigenous population to exploit, Cuba remained a neglected, sparsely populated outpost of the empire. The island's inhabitants engaged, for the most part, in small-scale farming for domestic consumption. Unlike the sugar-producing islands of the Caribbean, at the end of the seventeenth century Cuba had few slaves (its population of African descendents numbered 40,000, only one-tenth that of Haiti), many of whom worked in nonagricultural occupations, often as skilled craftsmen.

## ECONOMIC AND SOCIAL CHANGE: THE BITTER HARVEST OF KING SUGAR

The second half of the eighteenth century, however, had brought profound economic and social change as Cuba was transformed into a classic case of monoculture—an area dependent on the production and export of a single crop for its economic livelihood. Spurred by the short-lived British occupation of Havana in 1762 and further stimulated by the growing U.S. market produced by independence in 1783, the island experienced a commercial awakening. Most important, Cuba developed into a major sugar producer and slave importer in the aftermath of the Haitian Revolution of the 1790s, which ruined that island as a sugar producer (until then, it had been the world's leader). During the next half-century, sugar production in Cuba skyrocketed, and nearly 600,000 enslaved Africans arrived on its shores. From 1774 to 1861, the island's population leaped from 171,620 to 1,396,530, 30 percent of whom were of African descent. Havana and Santiago de Cuba became large, busy urban centers and ports, and no fewer than eight other cities attained populations exceeding 10,000.

Initially, the transfer to sugar did not stimulate the creation of the latifundio—first, because much of the land converted to sugar was the underused acreage of large cattle haciendas, and second, because many farmers did not change over to sugar, preferring instead to produce coffee and tobacco, which then enjoyed high prices resulting from the abolition of the royal monopoly on these commodities. Furthermore, the sugar mills themselves stimulated demand for livestock (to turn the mills) and food crops for the slaves. During the first decades of the nineteenth century, the number of farm proprietors increased markedly, and from their ranks came the leaders of Cuban society for the next century.

The boom that followed the destruction of Haitian sugar production ended by the turn of the century because other Caribbean islands expanded and initiated production in response to the same stimuli, thereby creating an enormous glut on the market. Just as the industry recovered from this setback, diplomatic maneuvering during the Napoleonic wars closed U.S. ports. Shortly thereafter, two new challenges to the Cuban economy arose: the introduction of beet sugar in Europe and the British campaign to end the slave trade. (England forced Spain to end the trade in 1821.) Further impediments resulted from the restrictions imposed by Spanish hegemony: high tariffs, scarce and expensive credit, and the disruptions brought on by the Spanish-American wars of independence.

By 1820 the first of a series of technological innovations began to transform the character of the sugar industry in Cuba. Mill owners had to invest heavily in steam-operated machinery to compete with beet sugar. Modern machinery allowed the mills to expand in size, but they could do so only gradually because of limited transportation facilities. Because railroads were enormously expensive, and in any case there was not sufficient capital on the island or in Spain for large projects of this type, they did not become important until much later.[2] The mills also carried a huge overhead because they were largely unused during the off-season. Slaves and livestock had to be fed and sheltered even when the harvest was completed. The problem of fuel for the mills also slowed their expansion. The forests close to the mills were quickly consumed, and transport of wood to the mills proved prohibitively costly. As a result, sugar production was expanded in the first half of the century through an increase in the number of mills. In 1827 there were 1,000 mills, by 1846 there were 1,442, and by 1860 there were 2,000.

The expansion of trade and the introduction of large-scale sugar production created a fantastic economic boom and delayed the development of the spirit of rebellion against Spanish rule that swept the rest of Spanish America. Cuba stayed loyal to Spain during the Spanish-American wars of independence, for its creole leaders saw no reason to tamper with their newfound prosperity.

[2] The first railroad in Cuba was built in 1836.

Discontent grew among slaves and free blacks, however, as a result of the rise of an increasingly harsh plantation system; in addition to everyday acts of resistance, such as work slowdowns, feigned illness, equipment sabotage, and abortion, African men and women periodically punctuated their protests against enslavement with major slave rebellions, led by free blacks, in 1810, 1812, and 1844.

But during the last half of the nineteenth century, wealthy creoles became increasingly resentful of the arbitrary ways of corrupt Spanish officialdom, which was determined to enforce continued obedience from Spain's last and richest colony in the New World. The colony grew increasingly dissatisfied with repressive Spanish rule and less dependent economically on the mother country. As Cuba turned increasingly toward the United States as a market for its products and a source of needed imports, schemes for the annexation of Cuba to the United States emerged both on the island and in some North American circles. In Cuba, conservative creole planters saw in annexation an insurance policy against the abolition of slavery; in the United States, some pro-slavery groups regarded annexation as a means of gaining a vast new area for the expansion of plantation slavery. Some of these groups even dreamed of carving Cuba up into three or five states that would give the South increased power in the national government. The U.S. Civil War put an end to these projects.

Meanwhile, large plantations developed in Cuba in response to the necessity of building bigger and bigger mills (centrales). Sugar technology was continually improving, and Cuban mills had to expend huge sums to remain competitive. The larger the mill, the more sugar it could process, the more fuel it consumed, and the more employees it needed. Smaller and less efficient mills were at a severe competitive disadvantage.

Sugar production traditionally had been set up in one of two ways: the land was cultivated by resident or temporary labor, or the land was parceled out to farmers, known as colonos, who worked the land for a salary or a share of the crop. The landowners, in either situation, might or might not also be the millowners. As the number of mills grew smaller, the colonos became the main suppliers of sugar to the mills. They planted and harvested the cane and brought it to the mill to be processed. They paid for the processing in sugar. By the 1860s production was specialized into these components, colonos and centrales. The number of large plantations did not increase; instead, the number of colonos gradually rose.

During the 1860s creole discontent grew and was heightened by a developing national and class consciousness. The creole elite rejected various reform proposals offered by a weak Spanish government that was battered by internal dissension and economic difficulties. It became increasingly clear to the creoles that Spanish economic and political policies were severely restricting Cuban development— a feeling sharpened by a serious economic downturn. On October 10, 1868, in the small town of Yara in Oriente Province, a group of landowners proclaimed Cuban independence and initiated a struggle that was to continue for ten years.

## THE TEN YEARS' WAR

The Ten Years' War, a long, bitter, devastating guerrilla struggle, ended in 1878 when the Cubans accepted a peace that granted them some concessions but withheld independence. The Pact of Zanjón ended hostilities, but some rebel leaders, like the black revolutionary Antonio Maceo, the "Bronze Titan," rejected the settlement because it did not achieve the main goals of the revolution— independence and the abolition of slavery. Ironically, the Spanish government, hoping to win the loyalty of the black population, abolished slavery in 1880, with provision for an eight-year patronato, or period of apprenticeship, for the liberated slaves. The abolition of slavery removed the last major factor tending to keep creole planters loyal to Spain. Thereafter, the prospect of independence, offering free, unlimited trade with the United States, became increasingly attractive.

The Ten Years' War had a far-reaching impact on the development of Cuban society. It decimated the creole landowning class, hindering the formation of a traditional Latin American landed elite

on the island. Moreover, the shakeout of mills during the war, the financial crisis of 1885–1890, and the expansion of the island's railroad network combined to stimulate the spread of the latifundio. As they grew, the mills required more cane, which came from a wider geographic area than previously. At the same time, the introduction of cheap rails spurred railroad construction in Cuba (and all over the world). In their quest for more cane, owners of centrales began to lay their own track, and competition among centrales for cane, a condition previously unknown because of transportation limitations, resulted.

The owners of centrales confronted the necessity of guaranteeing enough cane at the lowest possible prices for the zafra (harvest). They could do this either by reducing the independence of the colonos or by acquiring their own cane land. The first method transformed the once-free farmers into satellites of the giant mills. The second led to the creation of latifundia. Small- and medium-sized growers fell by the wayside, to be replaced by tenants or day labor. The colonos managed to hold their own until independence, after which time the massive influx of foreign capital into the sugar mills overwhelmed them. With their lesser financial resources, they were doomed.

Entrepreneurs from the United States filled the vacuum created by the ruin of the creole aristocracy and the bankruptcy of Spanish interests by the war. Thousands of North Americans accompanied their investment dollars to the island to run the sugar mills and merchant houses. The McKinley Tariff Act of 1890, which abolished import duties on raw sugar and molasses, greatly increased American trade with and economic influence in Cuba; by 1896, U.S. interests had invested $50 million in Cuba and controlled the sugar industry. The United States purchased 87 percent of Cuba's exports. The growth of U.S. investment in Cuba also brought about an increasing concentration of sugar production, a trend signaled by the entry of the "Sugar Trust" (the American Sugar Refining Company of Henry O. Havemeyer) into the island in 1888.

Although the Ten Years' War had transformed Cuba into a haven for North Americans, it had done nothing to eliminate racial segregation and discrimination, even after emancipation. Elite Spanish and creole white supremacists dominated late nineteenth-century Cuba and routinely blamed Afro-Cubans for all manner of Cuban social ills, denied them access to education and adequate health care, engaged in employment discrimination, and created obstacles to full citizenship. Interracial marriage, prohibited by law until 1881, remained socially stigmatized thereafter.

This racial apartheid created two Cubas—one steeped in Spanish cultural traditions and ritual practices like Catholicism and Freemasonry, and the other centered in African *santería*, a syncretic popular religion, and *ñáñigos*, secret mutual aid societies. According to historian Aline Helg, Afro-Cubans, frustrated by limits imposed on their ability to rise in Spanish society, increasingly relied on their African heritage to protect themselves and to organize social protest movements that demanded their "rightful share."

# United Provinces of Central America

On the eve of independence, the five republics—Guatemala, El Salvador, Honduras, Nicaragua, and Costa Rica[3]—were provinces of the captaincy general of Guatemala, with its capital at Guatemala City. Under the captain general and his audiencia, a small group of wealthy creole merchants, organized in a powerful consulado, had dominated the economic, social, and political life of the colony. But Spain's hold over its American colonies had weakened after 1800 as a result of its involvement in European wars, the resulting disruption of trade, and growing political turmoil at home. Central America drifted toward independence. When Mexico proclaimed its independence in 1821, Central America followed suit. City after city declared its independence, not only from Spain, but from Guatemala and rival cities and towns. The captaincy general dissolved into a mul-

titude of autonomous *cabildo* (municipal) governments. The transition to independence was complicated by the efforts of Agustín de Iturbide to incorporate Central America into his Mexican empire, efforts supported by Central American conservatives and opposed by many liberals. In 1822 a majority of cabildos voted in favor of union with Mexico, but Iturbide's overthrow the next year permanently ended the Mexican connection.

## INDEPENDENCE AND THE FAILURE OF UNION, 1810–1865

Despite provincial rivalries and resentment against Guatemalan domination, a tradition of Central American unity remained and attempts were made to strengthen that unity. In 1823 a constituent assembly met and created the federal republic of Central America out of the five former provinces: Guatemala, Honduras, Nicaragua, Costa Rica, and El Salvador. The constitution provided for a federal government with free and independent state governments and had a strong liberal tinge: it abolished slavery and the special privileges of the clergy and established the principles of laissez faire, free trade, and free contract of labor. The next year a Salvadoran liberal, Manuel José Arce, was elected as the first president of the republic. Meanwhile, the states were forming their own governments. On the state as on the federal level, conservatives and liberals struggled for power: conservatism—the ideology of the old monopolistic merchant clique, many great landowners, and the church—had its base in Guatemala; liberalism was the dominant doctrine among many large and small landowners of the other states and the small middle class of artisans, professionals, and intellectuals. Behind the façade of elections and universal male suffrage, power throughout the area was held by great landowning and mercantile families, who often mobilized their private armies of retainers and tenants in a struggle for control of regions and states.

The superficial unity of Central America soon dissolved as it became clear that the states were neither willing nor able to finance both their own governments and the federal government in Guatemala

---

[3]Although, for descriptive convenience, Belize and Panama are usually included in Central America, the former was a British colony and the latter a province of Colombia. Neither, therefore, was linked historically to the region.

City. Efforts by Arce's federal government to assert its prerogatives by the establishment of a strong army and the collection of taxes led him to abandon liberalism, which ignited a destructive civil war between 1826 and 1829. The struggle ended with the defeat of the national government and its conservative leadership by liberal forces headed by Francisco Morazán and the reorganization of the union on a basis of liberal hegemony.

Morazán, elected president of the federal republic and commander of its armed forces, both based in San Salvador, defended it against conservative plots and attacks. At the same time, a former conservative turned liberal, Mariano Gálvez, governor of Guatemala, launched a program for the economic and social reconstruction of his state. The program included the establishment of civil marriage and divorce and secular schools on all levels, anticlerical measures that allowed nuns to leave their orders and reduced the number of church holidays, large land concessions to British companies that were to colonize the land with foreign immigrants and provide it with an infrastructure, and even an agrarian reform that allowed squatters to buy land for half its value and permitted natives to settle on vacant land. Gálvez also sought to reform Guatemala's judicial system by basing it on the Livingston Code,[4] which provided for trial by jury and *habeas corpus* and vested power to appoint all judges in the governor of the state. This last feature alienated powerful landed interests who often served as *jefes políticos*, local officials who combined judicial and administrative functions and were permitted to keep a share of tax collections.

The loss of the support of local landed interests combined with the ravages of a cholera epidemic that spread over Central America in 1837 to bring down the Gálvez regime and its ambitious reform program. Stirred up by local clergy who proclaimed the epidemic to be divine retribution for the heresies of civil marriage and divorce, the native and mixed-blood masses rose in revolt against Gálvez's radical innovations in law and taxation, attacks on their landholdings by creole landowners, and sanitary

measures instituted to prevent the spread of disease. The principal revolt in February 1838 was led by the mestizo Rafael Carrera, whose army of indígenas and castas cried, "Long live religion and death to all foreigners!"

Carrera took Guatemala City, defeated Morazán in 1842, and ended the federal republic. He then established a conservative regime in Guatemala, which he controlled until his death in 1865. In 1854, dispensing with the formality of elections, he had Congress name him president for life and implemented a reactionary program that revived the authority of the church, returned church and indigenous communal properties to their original owners, brought back native forced labor, and even changed the title of local officials from jefe político to the old colonial title of corregidor. But what had begun as a lower-class protest against radical innovations and the spoliation of communal lands was soon taken over by the conservative merchant oligarchy, who provided the taxes Carrera needed to pay his army and foreign loans. Conservative ministers drawn from the elite surrounded the dictator. Alongside the traditional labor arrangements, there existed free labor and a money economy, with landless natives and mestizos working, sometimes under debt peonage, on the plantations.

Similar trends prevailed throughout Central America in the age of Carrera, although labor was freer in most of the area than it was in Guatemala. By the 1850s, a rising world demand for coffee stimulated expansion of the crop, which had been grown on a large scale in Costa Rica since the 1830s, and spurred attacks on indigenous communal lands. Coffee in Costa Rica and indigo and coffee in El Salvador made for relative political stability in those countries. In the more backward republics of Nicaragua and Honduras, where cattle barons warred with each other, little centralized authority existed.

The discovery of gold in California gave a new importance to Central America as a transoceanic transit route and sharpened the rivalry of the United States and Great Britain in the area. The threat to the sovereignty and territorial integrity of the Central American republics grew acute as a

---

[4]An influential code of legal and penal reform completed by U.S. lawyer and statesman Edward Livingston in 1824.

result of the folly of Nicaraguan liberals, who in 1855 invited William Walker, an adventurer from the United States, to help them overthrow a conservative regime. Having brought the liberals to power, Walker, supported by a band of some three hundred countrymen, staged a coup, proclaimed himself president, legalized slavery, and made English the official language. By mid-1856, in a rare display of unity, Nicaraguan liberals and conservatives, joined by all the other Central American republics, had combined in the National War against the Yankee intruders, but the Central American army opposing Walker was essentially a conservative army. Defeated in 1857, Walker returned to the United States. He nevertheless made two other attempts to conquer Central America, the last ending in his death before a Honduran firing squad in 1860.

The National War revived the moribund movement for Central American unity. The liberal Salvadoran president Gerardo Barrios was a leading advocate of federation. His efforts to realize Morazán's dream provoked Carrera, who was determined to maintain conservative domination over Central America, to send troops into El Salvador and its ally Honduras. The war ended with Barrios's defeat and exile; there were now conservative regimes in every Central American republic. In 1865 Barrios attempted to make a comeback, but he was captured and executed by his enemies. Carrera died in the same year. With his death the violence-filled formative period of Central American history came to an end.

## Gran Colombia

The early history of Venezuela and Colombia is inseparably linked to the name of the liberator Simón Bolívar. Venezuela was his homeland; Colombia (then called New Granada) and Venezuela, the theaters of his first decisive victories in the war for Latin American independence. Bolívar sought to unite Venezuela and New Granada into a single large and powerful state and looked toward the creation of a vast federation of all the Spanish-American republics, extending from Mexico to Cape Horn. In 1819 the Congress of Angostura (in Venezuela) approved the formation of the state of Colombia (later called Gran Colombia, or Greater Colombia) that would combine Venezuela, New Granada, and Ecuador (then still in Spanish hands). In 1821, at Cúcuta on the Venezuelan-Colombian border, the union was formalized with the adoption of a centralized constitution drafted according to Bolívar's wishes, and he was elected provisional president of the new state. But he soon went off to launch a campaign for the liberation of Peru and Bolivia and entrusted the administration of the new state, with its capital at Bogotá, to his vice president, Francisco de Paula Santander, a veteran revolutionary leader whose policies in general conformed to Bolívar's.

Santander presided over the implementation of a liberal reform program that included the gradual abolition of slavery, the abolition of native tribute, the division of indigenous communal lands into private parcels (a "reform" that opened the door to land-grabbing), the suppression of smaller male convents and the seizure of their property for the support of public secondary education, and a general expansion of education.

The major threat to Gran Colombia's survival came from its geographic, economic, and social realities. Immense distances separated its component parts, and a mountainous terrain made communication very difficult; it took about a month for a letter to reach Bogotá from Caracas. These conditions also hindered the development of economic ties between Venezuela and New Granada, and also Ecuador; Caracas and other Venezuelan coastal cities communicated more easily with Europe than overland via the Andes with Bogotá. Finally, the Venezuelan elite of cacao planters and merchants, joined by a new elite of military leaders or caudillos, had little sympathy for Bolívar's idea of fusing several independent Spanish-American republics into one and even less for his vision of a confederation that would unite all the Spanish-American states.

The latent conflict broke out into the open in 1826, when José Antonio Páez, the principal Venezuelan military commander, refused to appear before Congress in Bogotá to answer charges that he had violated the rights of citizens by sending soldiers to round them up for militia service. Supported by his army of llaneros and other caudillos, Páez proclaimed a revolt against the Bogotá government. Bolívar finally returned to deal with Páez's rebellion and the growing unrest. But Bolívar's efforts to keep the union alive were in vain. In 1829 in Venezuela, "popular assemblies," carefully organized by the caudillos, voted overwhelmingly in favor of independence, for Páez against Bolívar. In mid-1830, Ecuador followed the example of Venezuela and seceded from the union. Gran Colombia was dead. Months before, Bolívar, filled with despair and terminally ill with tuberculosis, had resigned from office. Attended by a retinue of faithful officers and soldiers, he left Bogotá and made his way to the coast, planning to go into self-imposed exile in Europe. But he died near Santa Marta in 1830.

## PÁEZ, THE CONSERVATIVE-LIBERAL SPLIT, AND THE FEDERAL WAR IN VENEZUELA, 1830–1863

On May 6, 1830, a congress assembled in Valencia to provide the independent state of Venezuela with a constitution, the third in the country's short history. The document limited suffrage to males who were twenty-one, literate, and had a high income. These requirements excluded most of the population, numbering under 900,000, from participation in political life. Of that number some 60 percent were descended from Africans. Another 15 percent were natives and a quarter identified themselves as white. A tiny minority of these, about ten thousand, composed the ruling class of wealthy merchants, great landowners, and high officeholders and military officers, who usually were also landowners. The members of this class, often linked through family networks, dominated politics.

Military hero, longtime champion of Venezuelan independence, and former ranch hand José Antonio Páez was elected president, a post he combined with that of supreme army commander. His rise illustrates the renewal of the old colonial ruling class through the admission of a new elite of military caudillos, frequently of very humble origins. The Venezuelan society and economy over which

Páez presided essentially resembled the colonial social and economic order. The latifundio continued as the basic unit of economic activity; concentration of landownership increased after independence because of the rapid acquisition of royalist estates and public lands by a small group of military caudillos. A decree of October 15, 1830, compelling the sale of so-called uncultivated indigenous lands, gave the latifundists more opportunities to expand their landholdings. Labor relations in the countryside continued to be based on slavery, peonage, and various forms of tenancy, including sharecropping and obligatory personal service. Slavery in Venezuela, as in other parts of Latin America, had long been in decline. Enslaved Africans' defiant opposition to enslavement, either through passive forms of resistance, rebellions, or escape to *cumbes* (runaway slave settlements), had made slavery socially destabilizing and less economically efficient. So the Constituent Congress of 1830 adopted a manumission law freeing the children of slaves but requiring them to work for their masters until the age of twenty-one. Continuing a tendency that began in the late colonial period, however, many slave owners found it more profitable to free their slaves voluntarily, because they generally remained on their former masters' land as tenants or peons bound by debts and other obligations. By 1841, 14,000 had been freed in this manner and only 150 because they had reached the age of manumission.

The long revolutionary war had caused immense material damage and loss of life—the population had been reduced by 262,000—and destroyed the fragile economic links between the country's different regions. By the time Páez became president, however, a partial recovery had taken place, leading to a boom based on the switch from cacao to coffee as Venezuela's principal export and the country's integration into the capitalist world market, which henceforth absorbed about 80 percent of Venezuela's exports of coffee, cacao, indigo, tobacco, and hides.

The high coffee prices that accompanied the 1830s boom made planters hungry for credit to expand production by obtaining new land. Foreign merchant capitalists, the Venezuelan export-import merchants who were their agents, and native moneylenders obliged, using coffee crops and the planters' estates as security, but colonial legislation that regulated interest rates and punished usury posed an obstacle. The Venezuelan congress removed this impediment by passing a credit law in 1834 that abolished all traditional Spanish controls on contracts; the state then enforced legally executed contracts, no matter how exorbitant the interest rates. By the late 1830s, with the world price of coffee in decline, the Venezuelan economy was in serious trouble. Creditors refused to refinance their debtors, and by the 1840s Venezuela was in a severe depression.

The economic crisis caused a rift in the elite, with the emergence of factions that turned into political parties in the 1840s. One called itself Conservative, but opponents dubbed its members *godos* (Goths), to identify them with the unpopular Spanish colonial rule. Páez was its acknowledged leader, and it represented the views and interests of the export-import merchants and their foreign partners, the moneylenders, the high civil and military bureaucracy, and some great landowners. The Liberal Party was led by Antonio Leocadio Guzmán and was a loose coalition of debt-ridden planters, the urban middle class, artisans, intellectuals seeking reform, and disaffected caudillos resentful of Páez's long reign.

Guzmán's rhetorical press attacks on Conservative economic policies and on the elections of 1842 and 1846 as fraudulent contributed to the growing social tension. A series of popular uprisings, which Páez described as open warfare against private property, terrified the Conservatives, who raised the specter of a general social race war, waged by pardos and slaves, which they blamed on Guzmán's inflammatory propaganda. In fact, Guzmán and most Liberals feared social revolution as much as their opponents and had no links to the popular revolts of 1846–1847. But the government determined to crush these revolts at their supposed source, brought Guzmán to trial, found him guilty of instigating the revolutionary movements, and sentenced him to death.

In 1848 war hero General José Tadeo Monagas, an eastern caudillo, became the Conservative president through the customary controlled election. If Páez had expected to find a pliant executor of Conservative policies, he was disappointed. Monagas, determined to free himself from Páez's control and establish his own dynasty, favored moderate Liberals for posts in his cabinet and other government positions. His commutation of Guzmán's death sentence to exile was a virtual declaration of independence from Páez and the Conservatives. But those Liberals who expected substantial social and political reforms from Monagas were also disillusioned. He paid his political debt to his planter allies by supporting congressional passage of several laws designed to give relief to distressed planters. Under his brother José Gregorio, slavery was abolished in Venezuela (March 23, 1854), with compensation to the slave owners. Slavery had been increasingly unprofitable as a result of falling coffee prices; even as Congress was discussing emancipation, some planters were voluntarily freeing their slaves to avoid paying their support.

Emancipation brought little change in the lives of most freedmen. In the absence of a modern factory system to provide alternative employment or any program for distributing land to them, most were doomed to remain on their former owners' estates as tenants burdened with heavy obligations or peons whose scanty wages were paid in *vales* (tokens) redeemable only for goods purchased in the estate store (*tienda de raya*) at inflated monopoly prices.

Hard times continued in the late 1850s: depressed coffee prices; the unwillingness of foreign capitalists to invest in Venezuela because of the debt-relief legislation, which increased the risk of investment; elite fears of a social explosion; and general resentment of the greed and nepotism of the Monagas dynasty persuaded Conservatives and Liberals to join forces in March 1858 in a revolution that overthrew the hated regime. The coalition soon fell apart, however, when a group of extreme Conservatives seized power and installed a government even more repressive than the Monagas regime, imprisoning or deporting many Liberals, who responded with an uprising that began the Federal War (1858–1863).

The term "federal" here had different meanings for the Liberal elite and its rank-and-file followers, most of whom were pardos or blacks who rallied to the federalist battle cry: "Death to the whites." But whereas Conservatives denounced the Liberal elite for fomenting a "race war," the "colored population" saw it as a war of the poor majority against the wealthy, propertied elite. After their victory, Liberal leaders gave the country a new constitution (1864) with many reforms, including universal male suffrage and increased autonomy for the twenty states. But without substantive social reform, these rights were virtually meaningless. "Federalism" under these conditions simply meant the continued supremacy of the local caudillo, who often was a great landowner as well, and whose arbitrary rule was tolerated by the Caracas government as long as he remained its loyal proconsul.

For the peasants and artisans who rose in spontaneous revolt against the reactionary Conservative regime and rallied to the Liberal leadership's slogan of federalism, the term had a different meaning. Their vague hopes were expressed in a manifesto by Ezequiel Zamora, the veteran guerrilla fighter who had been freed by the revolution of 1858 and then exiled by the Conservative regime, and who returned to Venezuela in February 1859 to open another front of a rapidly expanding peasant war. The advance of Zamora's troops was accompanied by the occupation of large estates by their former peons and tenants, the creation of federal states, and the election of local governments by the citizenry. Zamora's death by an assassin's bullet in 1860 cut short the life of a leader who represented a genuinely democratic, social revolutionary tendency in the Federal War.

Conservatives rejoiced, moderate Liberals heaved sighs of relief, and both, fearing the growing power of peasant revolutionists, agreed to a negotiated peace. The 1863 Treaty of Coche, negotiated by Antonio Guzmán Blanco, son of the famous Liberal caudillo, ended the war. It had cost some fifty thousand lives and inflicted immense damage on the economy. Many haciendas had been destroyed, and the cattle herds of the llanos had virtually disappeared as a result of wartime depredations and neglect. Like the War of Independence, the Federal War produced limited social changes. The old Conservative oligarchy disintegrated and victorious Liberal military officers, some of plebeian background, occupied their estates. But for the revolutionary rank-and-file, the war's end forced them to surrender the parcels of land they had occupied and return as peons to the great estates.

### SANTANDER AND THE BIRTH OF A TWO-PARTY SYSTEM IN COLOMBIA, 1830–1850

Following the secession of Venezuela and Ecuador from Gran Colombia in 1830, the remaining territory went its separate way under the name of the Republic of New Granada (present-day Colombia plus Panama). Struggles for control of the governmental apparatus in Bogotá between followers of Bolívar and those of Santander ended in the latter's victory. He became the first president of an independent New Granada under a constitution that provided for a president elected for four years, a bicameral Congress, and provincial legislatures. The constitution granted suffrage to all free males who were married or aged twenty-one and were not domestic servants or day laborers. In practice, political life was dominated by a small aristocratic ruling class.

The geographic, economic, and social conditions of the new state posed even greater obstacles to the creation of a true national society than those facing Venezuela. The country's difficult geography, dominated by the towering Andean cordillera, whose ranges, valleys, and plateaus were the home of the overwhelming majority of a population numbering less than one and a half million, offered formidable barriers to communication and transport; as late as the end of the nineteenth century, it was cheaper to transport goods from Liverpool to Medellín than from Medellín to Bogotá. This geography contributed to the formation of an economic structure called an "economic archipelago," consisting of a number of isolated regions having little contact with each other. The economy of some of these regions was characterized by traditional haciendas mainly dedicated to growing wheat, barley, potatoes, and raising cattle.

Their labor force usually consisted of mestizo peons or tenants who paid rent in labor or in kind for the privilege of cultivating their own small parcels of land; their freedom of movement could be restricted by debts, and sometimes they owed personal service to their patrón.

Alongside these haciendas and on marginal lands and mountain slopes lived other peasants whose precarious independence came from subsistence farming and supplying food to nearby towns. The northwest region of Antioquia, with its rugged terrain and low population, had few haciendas and numerous small- and medium-size landholdings; a more independent peasantry had also arisen in neighboring Santander. The Spanish had enslaved thousands of Africans and their descendants to labor on plantations and in gold-mining districts in the western states and on the Caribbean coast, but the institution, greatly weakened by the revolutionary wars, slave resistance, and legislation providing for the freedom of the children of slaves, was in decline. In fact, by the nineteenth century, many Africans had escaped enslavement and established *palenques*, free villages that had negotiated with the crown for rights to communal lands and political autonomy. Although the 1821 Congress of Cúcuta had ordered the division of *resguardos* (native communal lands) to conform with the prevailing liberal ideology, indigenous peoples had resisted. The dissolution of the resguardos was implemented in 1839. A large part of remaining indigenous lands was acquired for low prices by white landowners and merchants. Some of the former owners became peons or tenants on haciendas; others became *minifundio* farmers, peasant proprietors of small plots.

New Granadan industry in 1830, like agriculture, displayed many precapitalist features. Most industrial activity (weaving and spinning, pottery making, shoeware) was done in the home, chiefly by women. The 1830s saw numerous state-sponsored efforts to establish factories making soap, glassware, textiles, and iron in Bogotá, but most ended in failure. By the 1840s sizable artisan groups had arisen in larger towns like Bogotá, Medellín, and Cali, but despite moderate tariff protections for local industries, they had difficulty competing with imported foreign goods. The backwardness of economic life was most apparent in transportation; in parts of the country porters and pack mules were used for transport well into the twentieth century. Even after steamboat navigation became regular on the Magdalena River in the 1840s, it took between four and six weeks to make the voyage from Atlantic ports to Bogotá. The limited development of productive forces and the sluggish tempo of economic activity were reflected in the modest wealth of even the upper classes. In the first half of the nineteenth century, the income of Bogotá's upper class came to about $5,000 per capita and the number of persons whose capital exceeded $100,000 could be counted on one hand.

The lack of a dynamic export base to stimulate the economy and provide resources for a strong nation-state was a major factor in Colombia's economic and political difficulties in its first half-century. Efforts to replace gold production—which had been in decline even before independence—with tobacco, cotton, cinchona bark, and other products as export staples produced a series of short booms that quickly collapsed because of declining markets and prices, competition from foreign producers whose prices or quality Colombia could not match, or exhaustion of resources. The absence of an export base and a nationally dominant elite helps explain the "economic archipelago" or regional isolation and self-sufficiency that developed. A corollary of this economic autarchy was political autarchy, an almost permanent instability punctuated by frequent civil wars or threats of war and even secession by hacendado-generals, who could mobilize private armies of peons to settle scores with rival caudillos or the weak central government.

Under Santander's successor, José Ignacio de Márquez (1837–1841), whose policies continued Santander's brand of moderate liberalism, the political climate turned stormy. Responding to a measure of Congress that closed some small convents in the fervently Catholic province of Pasto in the far South, the population rose up in arms. By 1841 the revolt had been defeated, but it had one lasting effect: its contribution to the formation of the classic Colombian two-party system—Liberals versus Conservatives. Until the late 1840s the difference between the ideologies and programs of the two groups was far from absolute. Actually both had more in common with the moderate liberalism of Santander than with Bolívar's late conservatism. Both represented upper-class interests but accepted the formal democracy of representative, republican government; both had faith in social and technological progress, believed in the freedoms of speech and of the press as well as other civil liberties, and in economic policy accepted laissez-faire and liberal economics. Neither party cared about the agrarian problem or other problems of the rural and urban masses. The only genuine issue separating them was the relation between church and state and the church's role in education. The emergent Liberal party was distinctly anticlerical, regarding the church as hostile to progress; they did, however, favor freedom of worship and separation of church and state. The nascent Conservative party endorsed religious toleration but favored cooperation between church and state, believing that religion promoted morality and social peace.

In 1849 the ideological gap between Liberals and Conservatives widened and three new political factions emerged: *Gólgotas*, urban artisans, and *Draconianos*, military from the lower officer ranks, who would later align themselves with the artisans. Shaped by the rapid expansion of tobacco cultivation, the beginnings of the coffee cycle, internal improvements of the Conservative administrations, and a resulting growth of foreign and domestic trade, the Gólgotas were the sons of a merchant class whose population increased to 2,000,000 in 1850. Well educated and influenced by French romanticism, utopian socialism, and the Revolution of 1848 in France, they developed a peculiar sentimental brand of liberalism based on a romantic interpretation of Christianity in which Christ, described as the "Martyr of Golgotha," appeared as a forerunner of nineteenth-century secular reformism. This ideology's practical essence was its demand for the abolition of slavery, the ecclesiastical and military fuero, compulsory tithing, and all restraints on free enterprise.

The third element in the Liberal coalition was the urban artisan group, whose numbers also had increased in the preceding decade. Competition with foreign imported manufactures had caused serious unemployment among these artisans, who attributed their distress to lower tariffs; perhaps an equally important cause was the then-recent establishment of permanent steam navigation on the Magdalena River, which ended the protective isolation of their markets from the outside world. These artisans created a network of "Democratic Societies," beginning with the Democratic Society of Bogotá (1847), which had almost four thousand members. These clubs were mutual-aid societies and carried on educational and philanthropic activities, but they also served as important political vehicles for the Liberal leadership that triumphed in 1849, enabling the new merchant elite, with large support from regional landed oligarchies, to seek the triumph of laissez faire and modernity. This noisy revolution, although full of drama, produced little change in the basic structures of Colombian economy and society.

# The Triumph of Neocolonialism

B EGINNING ABOUT 1870, the quickening tempo of the Industrial Revolution in Europe stimulated a more rapid pace of change in the Latin American economy and politics. Responding to a mounting demand for raw materials and foodstuffs, Latin American producers increased their output of those commodities. The growing trade with Europe helped stabilize political conditions in Latin America, for the new economic system demanded peace and continuity in government.

Encouraged by the increased stability, European capital flowed into Latin America, creating railroads, docks, processing plants, and other facilities needed to expand and modernize production and trade. Latin America became integrated into an international economic system in which it exchanged raw materials and foodstuffs for the factory-made goods of Europe and North America. Gradual adoption of free-trade policies by many Latin American countries, which marked the abandonment of efforts to create a native factory capitalism, hastened the area's integration into this international division of labor.

## The New Colonialism

The new economic system fastened a new dependency on Latin America, with Great Britain and later the United States replacing Spain and

Portugal in the dominant role; it may, therefore, be called "neocolonial." Despite its built-in flaws and local breakdowns, the neocolonial order displayed a certain stability until 1914. By disrupting the markets for Latin America's exports and making it difficult to import the manufactured goods that Latin America required, World War I marked the beginning of a general crisis the area has not yet overcome.

Although the period from 1870 to 1914 saw rapid overall growth of the Latin American economy, the pace and degree of progress were uneven, with some countries (like Bolivia and Paraguay) joining the advance much later than others. A marked feature of the neocolonial order was its one-sidedness (monoculture). One or a few primary products became the basis of prosperity for each country, making it highly vulnerable to fluctuations in the world demand and price of these products. Argentina and Uruguay depended on wheat and meat; Brazil on coffee, sugar, and briefly rubber; Chile on copper and nitrates; Honduras on bananas; Cuba on sugar.

In each country, the modern export sector became an enclave largely isolated from the rest of the economy; this enclave actually accentuated the backwardness of other sectors by draining off their labor and capital. The export-oriented nature of the modern sector was reflected in the pattern of the national railway systems, which as a rule were not designed to integrate each country's regions but to satisfy the traffic needs of the export industries. In addition, the modern export sector often rested on extremely precarious foundations. Rapid, feverish growth, punctuated by slumps that sometimes ended in a total collapse, formed part of the neocolonial pattern; such meteoric rise and fall is the story of Peruvian guano, Chilean nitrates, and Brazilian rubber.

The triumph of neocolonialism in Latin America in the late nineteenth century was not inevitable or predetermined by Europe's economic "head start" or the area's past history of dependency. The leap from a feudal or semifeudal economy and society to an autonomous capitalist system, although difficult, is not impossible, as the case of Japan makes clear. Following independence, the new states had to choose between the alternatives of autonomy or dependency, or in the words of historian Florencia Mallon, "between focusing on internal production and capital formation, on the one hand, and relying increasingly on export production, foreign markets, and ultimately foreign capital, on the other." Given Latin America's history, however, the formation of the dynamic entrepreneurial class and the large internal market required by autonomous capitalism could not be achieved without such sweeping reforms as the breakup of great estates, the abolition of peonage and other coercive labor systems, and the adoption of a consistent policy of supporting native industry, reforms that most sections of the elite found too costly and threatening. Most Latin American elites, therefore, chose the easier road of continued dependency, with first Great Britain and later the United States replacing Spain as the metropolis.

Latin America in the nineteenth century, however, produced some serious efforts to break with the pattern of dependence. We have already described two such efforts. A remarkable and temporarily successful project for autonomous development was launched in Paraguay under the rule of Dr. Francia and the Lópezes, father and son. Their state-directed program of agrarian reform and industrial diversification transformed Paraguay from a backward country into a relatively prosperous and advanced state, but the disastrous Paraguayan War interrupted this progress and returned Paraguay to backwardness and dependency. In Chile, in the 1850s, an alliance of mining capitalists, small farmers, and artisans attempted to overthrow the landed and mercantile oligarchy and implement a radical program of political and social reform; their "frustrated bourgeois revolution" was drowned in blood. In the present chapter we describe a second Chilean effort to achieve autonomous development under the slogan "Chile for the Chileans"; it too ended in defeat and in the death of the president who led it.

## EXPANSION OF THE HACIENDA SYSTEM

The neocolonial order evolved within the framework of the traditional system of land tenure and labor relations. Indeed, it led to an expansion of the hacienda system on a scale far greater than the colonial period had known. As the growing European demand for Latin American products and the growth of national markets raised the value of land, the great landowners in country after country launched assaults on the surviving indigenous community lands. In part at least, this drive reflected an effort to eliminate indigenous competition in the emerging market economy. In Mexico the Reforma laid the legal basis for this attack in the 1850s and 1860s; it reached its climax in the era of Porfirio Díaz. In the Andean region similar legislation turned all communal property into individual holdings, leading to a cycle of indigenous revolt and bloody governmental repressions. Not all native peoples opposed the nineteenth-century drive to dissolve the ancient communal landholding system, however. In both Mexico and the Andean regions, where market relations had induced significant socioeconomic differentiation within villages, indigenous leaders often willingly accepted privatization of communal lands, viewing it as a road to personal enrichment.

Seizure of church lands by liberal governments also contributed to the growth of the latifundio. Mexico again offered a model, with its Lerdo Law and the Juárez anticlerical decrees.

Following the Mexican example, Colombian liberal governments confiscated church lands in the 1860s, the liberal dictator Antonio Guzmán Blanco seized many church estates in Venezuela in the 1870s, and Ecuadoran liberals expropriated church lands in 1895.

Expansion of the public domain through railway construction and wars also contributed to the growth of great landed estates. Lands taken from the church or wrested from indigenous communities were usually sold to buyers in vast tracts at nominal prices. Concentration of land, reducing the cultivable area available to native and mestizo small landowners, was accompanied by a parallel growth of the *minifundio*, an uneconomical small plot worked with primitive techniques.

The seizure of indigenous community lands, to use immediately or to hold for a speculative rise in value, provided great landowners with another advantage by giving them control of the local labor force at a time of increasing demand for labor. Expropriated natives rarely became true wage earners paid wholly in cash, for such workers were too expensive and independent in spirit. A more widespread labor system was debt peonage, in which workers were paid wholly or in part with vouchers redeemable at the *tienda de raya* (company store), whose inflated prices and often devious bookkeeping created a debt that was passed on from one generation to the next. The courts enforced the obligation of peons to remain on the estate until they had liquidated their debts. Peons who protested low wages or the more intensive style of work demanded by the new order were brought to their senses by landowners' armed retainers or by local police or military authorities.

In some countries, the period saw a revival of the colonial repartimiento system of draft labor for indigenous peoples. In Guatemala, this system required able-bodied natives to work for a specified number of days on haciendas. It was the liberal president Justo Rufino Barrios who issued instructions to local magistrates to see to it "that any Indian who seeks to evade his duty is punished to the full extent of the law, that the farmers are fully protected and that each Indian is forced to do a full day's work while in service."

Slavery survived in some places well beyond mid-century—for example, in Peru until 1855, in Cuba until 1886, in Brazil until 1888. Closely akin to slavery was the system of bondage, under which some ninety thousand Chinese coolies were imported into Peru between 1849 and 1875 to work on the guano islands and in railway construction. The term *slavery* also applies to the system under which political deportees and captured native rebels were sent by Mexican authorities to labor in unspeakable conditions on the coffee, tobacco, and henequen plantations of southern Mexico.

More modern systems of agricultural labor and farm tenantry arose only in such regions as southern Brazil and Argentina, whose critical labor shortage required the offer of greater incentives to the millions of European immigrants who poured into those countries between 1870 and 1910.

Labor conditions were little better in the mining industry and in the factories that arose in some countries after 1890. Typical conditions were a workday of twelve to fourteen hours, miserable wages frequently paid in vouchers redeemable only at the company store, and arbitrary, abusive treatment by employers and foremen. Latin American law codes usually prohibited strikes and other organized efforts to improve working conditions, and police and the armed forces were commonly employed to break strikes, sometimes with heavy loss of life.

## FOREIGN CONTROL OF RESOURCES

The rise of the neocolonial order was accompanied by a steady growth of foreign corporate control over the natural and human-made resources of the continent. The process went through stages. In 1870 foreign investment was still largely concentrated in trade, shipping, railways, public utilities, and government loans; at that date, British capital enjoyed an undisputed hegemony in the Latin American investment field. By 1914 foreign corporate ownership had expanded to include most of the mining industry and had deeply penetrated real estate, ranching, plantation agriculture, and manufacturing; by that date, Great Britain's rivals had effectively challenged its domination in Latin America. Of these rivals, the most spectacular advance was made by the United States, whose Latin American investments had risen from a negligible amount in 1870 to over $1.6 billion by the end of 1914 (still well below the nearly $5 billion investment of Great Britain).

Foreign economic penetration went hand in hand with a growth of political influence and even armed intervention. The youthful U.S. imperialism proved to be the most aggressive of all. In the years after 1898, a combination of "dollar diplomacy" and armed intervention transformed the Caribbean into an "American lake" and reduced Cuba, the Dominican Republic, and several Central American states to the status of dependencies and protectorates of the United States.

### THE POLITICS OF ACQUISITION

The new economy demanded new politics. Conser-vatives and liberals, fascinated by the atmosphere of prosperity created by the export boom, the rise in land values, the flood of foreign loans, and the growth of government revenues, put aside their ideological differences and joined in the pursuit of wealth. The positivist slogan "Order and Progress" now became the watchword of Latin America's ruling classes. The social Darwinist idea of the struggle for survival of the fittest and Herbert Spencer's doctrine of "inferior races," frequently used to support claims of the inherent inferiority of the native, mestizo, and mulatto masses, also entered the upper-class ideological arsenal.

The growing domination of national economies by the export sectors and the development of a consensus between the old landed aristocracy and more capitalist-oriented groups caused political issues like the federalist-centralist conflict and the liberal-conservative cleavage to lose much of their meaning; in some countries, the old party lines dissolved or became extremely tenuous. A new type of "progressive" caudillo—Porfirio Díaz in Mexico, Rafael Núñez in Colombia, Justo Rufino Barrios in Guatemala, Antonio Guzmán Blanco in Venezuela—symbolized the politics of acquisition.

As the century drew to a close, dissatisfied urban middle-class, immigrant, and entrepreneurial groups in some countries combined to form parties, called Radical or Democratic, that challenged the traditional domination of politics by the creole landed aristocracy. They demanded political, social, and educational reforms that would give more weight to the new middle sectors. But these middle sectors—manufacturers, shopkeepers, professionals, and the like—were in large part a creation of the neocolonial order and depended on it for their livelihood; therefore, as a rule they did not question its viability. The small socialist, anarchist, and syndicalist groups that arose in various Latin American countries in the 1890s challenged both capitalism and neocolonialism, but the full significance of these movements lay in the future.

The trends just described lend a certain unity to the history of Mexico, Argentina, Chile, Brazil, Central America, Venezuela, and Colombia in the period from 1870 to 1914. Each presents significant variations on the common theme, however—variations that reflect distinctive historical backgrounds and conditions.

## Mexican Politics and Economy

### DICTATORSHIP UNDER DÍAZ

General Porfirio Díaz seized power in 1876 with the support of disgruntled regional caudillos and military personnel, liberals angered by the old regime's patronage politics, and indigenous and mestizo small landholders who believed that Díaz would protect them. He also owed his success to the open support of American capitalists, army commanders, and great Texas landowners who, regarding his predecessor as "anti-American," supplied Díaz with arms and cash. Having installed himself as president, Díaz paid his respects to the principle of no reelection by allowing a trusted crony, General Manuel González, to succeed him in 1880. However, he returned to the presidential palace in 1884 and continued to occupy it through successive reelections until his resignation and flight from Mexico in 1911. Thus, Díaz, who had seized power in the name of republican

Beginning in the 1920s, with considerable support from the state, there arose in Mexico a school of socially conscious artists who sought to enlighten the masses about their bitter past and the promise of the revolutionary present. One of the greatest of these artists was David Alfaro Siqueiros, whose painting depicts with satire the former President Porfirio Díaz, who tramples on the constitution of 1857 as he diverts his wealthy followers with dancing girls. [Artes e Historia México]

legality, erected the *Porfiriato*, one of the longest personal dictatorships in Latin American history.

But the construction of the dictatorship was a gradual process. During his first presidential term, Congress and the judiciary enjoyed a certain independence, and the press, including a vocal radical labor press, was free. The outlines of Díaz's economic and social policies, however, soon became clear. Confronted with an empty treasury, facing pressures from above and below, Díaz decided in favor of the great landowners, moneylenders, and foreign capitalists, whose assistance could ensure his political survival. In return, he assured these groups of protection for their property and other interests. Díaz, who had once proclaimed that in the age-old struggle between the people and the haciendas he was on the side of the people, now sent troops to suppress peasant resistance to land seizures. And although before taking power, he had denounced generous concessions to British capitalists, by 1880 Díaz had granted even more lavish subsidies for railway construction to North American companies. Economic development had become for Díaz the great object, the key to the solution of his own problems and those of the nation.

Economic development required political stability; accordingly, Díaz promoted a policy of conciliation, described by the formula *pan o palo* (bread or the club). This consisted of offering an olive branch and a share of spoils to all influential opponents, no matter what their political past or persuasion. A dog with a bone in its mouth, Díaz cynically observed, neither kills nor steals. In effect, Díaz invited all sections of the upper class and some members of the middle class, including prominent intellectuals and journalists, to join the great Mexican barbecue, from which only the poor and humble were barred. Opponents who refused Díaz's bribes—political offices, monopolies, and the like—suffered swift reprisal. Dissidents were beaten up, murdered, or arrested and sent to the damp underground dungeons of San Juan de Ulúa or the grim Belén prison, a sort of Mexican Bastille. An important instrument of this policy was a force of mounted police, the *rurales*, originally composed of former bandits and vagrants who later were gradually replaced by artisan and peasant recruits dislocated by the large social changes that took place during the *Porfiriato*. Aside from chasing unrepentant bandits, the major function of the rurales was to suppress peasant unrest and break strikes.

By such means, Díaz virtually eliminated all effective opposition at the end of his second term (1884–1888). The constitution of 1857 and the liberties it guaranteed existed only on paper. Elections to Congress, in theory the highest organ of government, were a farce; Díaz simply circulated a list of his candidates to local officials, who certified their election. The dictator contemptuously called Congress his *caballada*, his stable of horses. The state governors were appointed by Díaz, usually from the ranks of local great landlords or his generals. In return for their loyalty, he gave them a free hand to enrich themselves and terrorize the local population. Under them were district heads called *jefes políticos*, petty tyrants appointed by the governors with the approval of Díaz; below them were municipal presidents who ran the local administrative units. One feature of the Díaz era was a mushrooming of the administrative and coercive apparatus; government costs during this period soared by 900 percent.

The army, as indispensable to Díaz as it had been to Santa Anna, naturally enjoyed special favor. Higher officers were well paid and enjoyed many opportunities for enrichment at the expense of the regions in which they were quartered. But the Díaz army was pathetically inadequate for pur-

poses of national defense. Generals and other high officers were appointed not for their ability but for their loyalty to the dictator. Discipline, morale, and training were extremely poor. A considerable part of the rank-and-file were recruited from the dregs of society; the remainder were young native conscripts. These soldiers, often used for brutal repression of strikes and agrarian unrest, were themselves harshly treated and miserably paid: the wage of ranks below sergeant was fifty cents a month.

The church became another pillar of the dictatorship. Early in his second term, Díaz reached an accommodation with the hierarchy. The church agreed to support Díaz; in return he allowed the anticlerical Reforma laws to fall into disuse. In disregard of those laws, monasteries and nunneries were restored, church schools were established, and wealth again began to accumulate in the hands of the church. Faithful to its bargain, the church turned a deaf ear to the complaints of the lower classes and taught complete submission to the authorities. As in colonial times, many priests were utterly venal and corrupt. Only in the closing years of the dictatorship did the church, sensing the coming storm, begin to advocate modest social reforms.

The Díaz policy of conciliation was directed at prominent intellectuals as well as more wealthy and powerful figures. A group of such intellectuals, professional men, and businessmen made up a closely knit clique of Díaz's advisers. Known as *Científicos*, they got their name from their insistence on "scientific" administration of the state and were especially influential after 1892. About fifteen men made up the controlling nucleus of the group. Their leader was Díaz's all-powerful father-in-law, Manuel Romero Rubio, and after his death in 1895, the new minister of finance, José Yves Limantour.

For the Científicos, the economic movement was everything. Most Científicos accepted the thesis of the inherent inferiority of the native and mestizo population and the consequent necessity for relying on the native white elite and on foreigners and their capital to lead Mexico out of its backwardness. In the words of the journalist Francisco

.G. Cosmes, "the Indian has only the passive force of inferior races, is incapable of actively pursuing the goal of civilization."

Thanks to the devoted efforts of educators like Justo Sierra, Díaz secured modest advances in public education, such as a federal law making primary education obligatory. Despite the law, however, on average only one out of three children between the ages of six and twelve were enrolled, the vast majority of whom probably completed only the first year and remained functionally illiterate. The principal beneficiaries of educational progress under Díaz were the sons of the rich: for every student enrolled in the primary schools in 1910, the state spent about seven pesos; for every student in the college preparatory schools, it spent nearly a hundred pesos.

In the last analysis, however, supporters of the dictatorship rested their case on the "economic miracle" that Díaz had allegedly worked in Mexico. A survey of the Mexican economy in 1910 reveals how modest that miracle was.

## CONCENTRATION OF LANDOWNERSHIP

At the opening of the twentieth century, Mexico was still predominantly an agrarian country; 77 percent of its population of 15,000,000 still lived on the land. The laws of the Reforma had already promoted the concentration of landownership, and under Díaz this trend was greatly accelerated. There is some evidence of a link between the rapid advance of railway construction, which increased the possibilities of production for export and therefore stimulated a rise in land values, and the growth of land-grabbing in the Díaz period.

A major piece of land legislation was a law of 1883 that provided for the survey of so-called vacant public lands, *tierras baldías*. The law authorized real estate companies to survey such lands and retain one-third of the surveyed area; the remainder was sold for low fixed prices in vast tracts, usually to Díaz's favorites and their foreign associates. The 1883 law opened the way for vast territorial acquisitions. One individual alone obtained nearly 12,000,000 acres in Baja California and other northern states. But the land

companies were not satisfied with the acquisition of true vacant lands. Another law, in 1894, declared that a parcel of land to which a legal title could not be produced could be declared vacant land, opening the door to expropriation of land from indigenous villages and other small landholders whose forebears had tilled their lands from times immemorial but who could not produce the required titles. If the victims offered armed resistance, troops were sent against them, and the vanquished rebels were sold like slaves to labor on henequen plantations in Yucatán or sugar plantations in Cuba. This was the fate of the Yaquis of the northwest, defeated after a long, valiant struggle.

Another instrument of land seizure was an 1890 law designed to give effect to older Reforma laws requiring the distribution of indigenous village lands among the villagers. The law created enormous confusion. In many cases, land speculators and hacendados cajoled the illiterate villagers into selling their titles for paltry sums. Hacendados also used other means, such as cutting off a village's water supply or simply brute force, to achieve their predatory ends. By 1910 the process of land expropriation was largely complete. More than 90 percent of the indigenous villages of the central plateau, the most densely populated region of the country, had lost their communal lands. Only the most tenacious resistance enabled villages that still held their lands to survive the assault of the great landowners. Landless peons and their families made up 9,500,000 of a rural population of 12,000,000.

As a rule, the new owners did not use the land seized from indigenous villages or small landholders more efficiently. Hacendados let much of the usurped land lie idle. They waited for a speculative rise in value or for an American buyer. By keeping land out of production, they helped keep the price of maize and other staples artificially high. The technical level of hacienda agriculture was generally extremely low, with little use of irrigation, machinery, and commercial fertilizer, although some new landowning groups—northern cattle raisers and cotton growers, the coffee and rubber growers of Chiapas, and the henequen producers of Yucatán—employed more modern equipment and techniques.

The production of foodstuffs stagnated, barely keeping pace during most of the period with the growth of population, and per capita production of such basic staples as maize and beans actually declined toward the end of the century. This decline culminated in three years of bad harvests, 1907 to 1910, due principally to drought. As a result, the importation of maize and other foodstuffs from the United States steadily increased in the last years of the Díaz regime. Despite the growth of pastoral industry, per capita consumption of milk and cheese barely kept pace with the growth of population, for a considerable proportion of the cattle sold was destined for the export market.

The only food products for which the increase exceeded the growth of population were alcoholic beverages. Some idea of the increase in their consumption is given by the fact that the number of bars in Mexico City rose from 51 in 1864 to 1,400 in 1900. At the end of the century, the Mexican death rate from alcoholism—a common response to intolerable conditions of life and labor—was estimated to be six times that of France. Meanwhile, inflation, rampant during the last part of the Díaz regime, greatly raised the cost of the staples on which the mass of the population depended. Without a corresponding increase in wages, the situation of agricultural and industrial laborers deteriorated sharply.

## The Economic Advance

Whereas food production for the domestic market declined, production of food and industrial raw materials for the foreign market experienced a vigorous growth. By 1910, Mexico had become the largest producer of henequen, a source of fiber in great demand in the world market. Mexican export production became increasingly geared to the needs of the United States, which was the principal market for sugar, bananas, rubber, and tobacco produced on plantations that were largely foreign owned. U.S. companies dominated the mining industry, whose output of copper, gold, lead, and zinc rose sharply after 1890. The oil industry, controlled by U.S. and British interests, developed spec-

tacularly, and by 1911, Mexico was third among the world's oil producers. French and Spanish capitalists virtually monopolized the textile and other consumer-goods industries, which had a relatively rapid growth after 1890.

Foreign control of key sectors of the economy and the fawning attitude of the Díaz regime toward foreigners gave rise to a popular saying: "Mexico, mother of foreigners and stepmother of Mexicans." The ruling clique of Científicos justified this favoritism by citing the need for a rapid development of Mexico's natural resources and the creation of a strong country capable of defending its political independence and territorial integrity. Thanks to an influx of foreign capital, some quickening and modernization of economic life did take place under Díaz. The volume of foreign trade greatly increased, a modern banking system arose, and the country acquired a relatively dense network of railways. But these successes were achieved at a very heavy price: a brutal dictatorship, the pauperization of the mass of the population, the stagnation of food agriculture, the strengthening of the inefficient latifundio, and the survival of many feudal or semifeudal vestiges in Mexican economic and social life.

## Labor, Agrarian, and Middle-Class Unrest

The survival of feudal vestiges was especially glaring in the area of labor relations. There was some variation in labor conditions from region to region. In 1910 forced labor and outright slavery, as well as older forms of debt peonage, were characteristic of the southern states of Yucatán, Tabasco, Chiapas, and parts of Oaxaca and Veracruz. The rubber, coffee, tobacco, henequen, and sugar plantations of this region depended heavily on the forced labor of political deportees, captured indigenous rebels, and contract workers kidnapped or lured to work in the tropics by a variety of devices.

In central Mexico, where a massive expropriation of village lands had created a large landless native proletariat, tenantry, sharecropping, and the use of migratory labor had increased and living standards had declined. The large labor surplus of this area diminished the need for hacendados to

Striking workers at the Rio Blanco textile works in Mexico in 1909; the business was controlled by French capital. Troops broke up the strike and much blood was shed.
[Brown Brothers]

tie their workers to their estates with debt peonage. In the north the proximity of the United States, with its higher wage scales, and the competition of hacendados with mine owners for labor made wages and sharecropping arrangements somewhat more favorable and weakened debt peonage. In all parts of the country, however, the life of agricultural workers was filled with hardships and abuses of every kind.

Labor conditions in mines and factories were little better than in the countryside. Workers in textile mills labored twelve to fifteen hours daily for a wage ranging from eleven cents for unskilled women and children to seventy-five cents for highly skilled workers. Employers found ways of reducing even these meager wages. Wages were discounted for alleged "carelessness" in the use of tools or machines or for "defective goods"; workers were usually paid wholly or in part with vouchers good only in company stores, the prices of which were higher than in other stores. Federal and state laws banned trade unions and strikes. Scores of workers, both men and women, were shot down by troops who broke the great textile strike in the Orizaba (Veracruz) area in 1909, and scores were killed or wounded in putting down the strike at the U.S.-owned Consolidated Copper Company mine at Cananea (Sonora) in 1906. Despite such repressions, the trade union movement continued to grow in the last years of the Díaz era, and socialist, anarchist, and syndicalist ideas began to influence the still-small urban working class.

The growing wave of strikes and agrarian unrest in the last, decadent phase of the Díaz era indicated an increasingly rebellious mood among even broader sections of the Mexican people. Alienation spread among teachers, lawyers, journalists, and other professionals, whose opportunities for advancement were sharply limited by the monolithic control of economic, political, and social life by the Científicos, their foreign allies, and regional oligarchies. In the United States in 1905 a group of middle-class intellectuals, headed by the Flores Magón brothers, organized the Liberal Party, which called for the overthrow of Díaz and advanced a platform whose economic and social provisions anticipated many articles of the constitution of 1917.

Even members of the ruling class began to join the chorus of criticism. These upper-class dissidents included liberal reformers, like the wealthy hacendado and businessman Francisco Madero, and national capitalists who resented the competitive advantages enjoyed by foreign companies in Mexico. They also feared that the static, reactionary Díaz policies could provoke the masses to overthrow the capitalist system itself. Fearing revolution, these upper-class critics urged Díaz to end his personal rule, shake up the regime, and institute modest reforms needed to placate popular protest and preserve the existing economic and social order. When their appeals fell on deaf ears, some of these bourgeois reformers reluctantly prepared to take the road of revolution.

The simultaneous advent of an economic recession and a food crisis sharpened this growing discontent. The depression of 1906–1907, which spread from the United States to Mexico, caused a wave of bankruptcies, layoffs, and wage cuts. At the same time the crop failures of 1907–1910 provoked a dramatic rise in the price of staples like maize and beans. By 1910, Mexico's internal conflicts had reached an explosive stage. The workers' strikes, the agrarian unrest, the agitation of middle-class reformers, and the disaffection of some great landowners and capitalists all reflected the disintegration of the dictatorship's social base. Despite its superficial stability and posh splendor, the house of Díaz was rotten from top to bottom. Only a slight push was needed to send it toppling to the ground.

# Argentine Politics and Economy

Although the principal source of conflict in Argentina remained rivalry between provincial caudillos and Buenos Aires, Nicolás Avellaneda, a lawyer from Tucumán and his protégé, a fellow Tucumano, Julio Roca, dominated late nineteenth-century Argentine politics and shared Sarmiento's interest in unifying the nation. Avellaneda promoted education, immigration, and domestic tranquility. In 1876 he inaugurated railroad service between Buenos Aires and his native city of Tucumán. The new line forged stronger economic and political links between the port city and the remote northwest, contributing to the end of the long quarrel between Buenos Aires and the interior.

## CONSOLIDATION OF THE STATE

Julio Roca, Avellaneda's presidential successor, institutionalized this new unification by carrying out a long-standing pledge to federalize the city of Buenos Aires, which now became the capital of the nation, while La Plata became the new capital of Buenos Aires province. The interior seemed to have triumphed over Buenos Aires, but that apparent victory was an illusion; the provincial lawyers and politicians who carried the day in 1880 had absorbed the commercial and cultural values of the great city and wished not to diminish but to share in its power. Far from losing influence, Buenos Aires steadily gained in wealth and power until it achieved an overwhelming ascendancy over the rest of the country.

The federalization of Buenos Aires completed the consolidation of the Argentine state, the new leaders of which were closely identified with and often recruited from the ruling class of great landowners and wealthy merchants. The "generation of 1880," or the oligarchy, as it was called, shared a faith in economic development and the value of the North American and European models, but it was also deeply tinged with cynicism, egotism, and a profound distrust for the popular classes. These autocratic liberals prized order and progress above freedom. They regarded the gauchos, indigenous peoples, and the mass of illiterate

European immigrants flooding Argentina as unfit to exercise civic functions. Asked to define universal suffrage, a leading oligarch, Eduardo Wilde, replied, "It is the triumph of universal ignorance."

The new rulers identified the national interest with the interest of the great landowners, wealthy merchants, and foreign capitalists. Regarding the apparatus of state as their personal property or as the property of their class, they used their official connections to enrich themselves. Although they maintained the forms of parliamentary government, they were determined not to let power slip from their hands and organized what came to be called the *unicato* (one-party rule), exercised by the National Autonomist Party, which they formed. Extreme concentration of power in the executive branch and systematic use of fraud, violence, and bribery were basic features of the system.

## ECONOMIC BOOM AND INFLATION

The ominous new trends of the oligarchy emerged in the administration of President Julio Roca (1880–1886) and flowered exuberantly under his political heir and brother-in-law, Miguel Juárez Celman (1886–1890). Roca presided over the beginnings of a great boom that appeared to justify all the optimism of the oligarchy. As secretary of war under Avellaneda, Roca had led a military expedition—the so-called Conquest of the Desert—southward against native peoples of the pampa in 1879–1880. This conquest added vast new areas to the province of Buenos Aires and to the national public domain. The campaign created a last opportunity for implementing a democratic land policy directed toward the creation of an Argentine small-farmer class. Instead, the Roca administration sold off the area in huge tracts for nominal prices to army officers, politicians, and foreign capitalists. The aging Sarmiento, who had seen the defeat of his own effort to acquire and distribute to settlers public land suitable for farming, lamented: "Soon there will not remain a palm of land for distribution to our immigrants."

Coming at a time of steadily mounting European demand for Argentine meat and wheat, the Conquest of the Desert triggered an orgy of land speculation that drove land prices ever higher and caused a prodigious expansion of cattle raising and agriculture. This expansion took place under the sign of the latifundio. Few of the millions of Italian and Spanish immigrants who entered Argentina in this period realized the common dream of becoming independent small landowners. Although some immigrant agricultural colonies were founded in the provinces of Santa Fe and Entre Ríos in the 1870s and 1880s, by the mid-1890s, with wheat prices now declining, there was a shift from small-scale farming to extensive tenant farming. The traditional unwillingness of the estancieros to sell land forced the majority of would-be independent farmers to become ranch hands or tenant farmers, whose hold on the land was very precarious; because leases were usually limited to a few years, these immigrants broke the virgin soil, replaced the tough pampa grass with the alfalfa pasturage needed to fatten cattle, and produced the first wheat harvests but then had to move on, leaving the landowner in possession of all improvements.

As a result, the great majority of new arrivals settled in Buenos Aires, where the rise of meat-salting and meat-packing plants, railroads, public utilities, and many small factories created a growing demand for labor. True, the immigrant workers received very low wages, worked long hours, and crowded with their families into one-room apartments in wretched slums. But in the city barrio they lived among their own people, free from the loneliness of the pampa and the arbitrary rule of great landowners, and had some opportunity of rising in the economic and social scale. As a result, the population of Buenos Aires shot up from 500,000 in 1889 to 1,244,000 in 1909. The great city, which held the greater portion of the nation's wealth, population, and culture, grew at the expense of the interior—particularly the northwest—which was impoverished, stagnant, and thinly peopled. Argentina, to use a familiar metaphor, became a giant head set on a dwarf body.

Foreign capital and management played a decisive role in the expansion of the Argentine economy in this period. The creole elite obtained vast profits from the rise in the price of their land

and the increasing volume of exports but showed little interest in plowing those gains into industry or the construction of the infrastructure required by the export economy, preferring a lavish and leisurely lifestyle over entrepreneurial activity. Just as they left to English and Irish managers the task of tending their estates, so they left to English capital the financing of meat-packing plants, railroads, public utilities, and docks and other facilities. As a result, most of these resources remained in British hands. Typical of the oligarchy's policy of surrender to foreign interests was the decision of Congress in 1889 to sell the state-owned Ferrocarril Oeste, the most profitable and best-run railroad in Argentina, to a British company. Service on a growing foreign debt claimed an ever larger portion of the government's receipts.

Meanwhile, imports of iron, coal, machinery, and consumer goods grew much faster than exports. Combined with the unfavorable price ratio of raw materials to finished goods, the result was an unfavorable balance of trade and a steady drain of gold. New loans with burdensome terms brought temporary relief but aggravated the long-range problem. Under President Miguel Juárez Celman, the disappearance of gold and the government's determination to keep the boom going at all costs led to the issue of great quantities of unbacked paper currency and a massive inflation.

The great landowners did not mind, for they were paid for their exports in French francs and English pounds, which they could convert into cheap Argentine pesos for the payment of local costs; besides, inflation caused the price of their lands to rise. The sacrificial victims of the inflation were the urban middle class and the workers, whose income declined in real value.

## THE FORMATION OF THE RADICAL PARTY

In 1889–1890, just as the boom was turning into a depression, the accumulated resentment of the urban middle class and some alienated sectors of the elite over the catastrophic inflation, one-party rule, and official corruption produced a protest movement that took the name Unión Cívica (Civic

Union). Although the new organization had a middle-class base, its leadership united such disparate elements as disgruntled urban politicians like Leandro Além, its first president; new landowners and descendants of old aristocratic families denied access to patronage; and Catholics outraged by the government's anticlerical legislation. Aside from the demand for effective suffrage, the only thing uniting these heterogeneous elements was a common determination to overthrow the government.

The birth of the new party in 1890 coincided with a financial storm: the stock market collapsed, bankruptcies multiplied, and in April the cabinet resigned. Encouraged by this last development, and counting on support from the army, the leaders of the Unión Cívica planned a revolt against Juárez Celman that ended in defeat for the rebels.

The oligarchy now showed its ability to maneuver and divide its enemies. Carlos Pellegrini (1890–1892) replaced Juárez Celman, appeased disgruntled elements of the elite by revising the system of state patronage, and took steps to improve economic conditions by a policy of retrenchment that reduced inflation, stabilized the peso, and revived Argentine credit abroad. Thanks to these measures and a gradual recovery from the depression, popular discontent began to subside.

These reforms isolated Leandro Além and other dissidents, who now formed a new party committed to a "radical" democracy—the Unión Cívica Radical. The party named Bernardo de Yrigoyen as its presidential candidate in 1892 but, knowing that rigged elections made his victory impossible, they also prepared for another revolt—a move that Pellegrini effectively squelched by deporting Além and other Radical leaders until after the election of Luis Sáenz Peña (1892–1895).

On his return from exile, Além organized a new revolt in July 1893. The rebels briefly seized Santa Fe and some other towns, but after two and a half months of fighting, the revolt collapsed for lack of significant popular support. Depressed by his failures and the intrigues of his nephew, Hipólito Yrigoyen, to seize control of the Radical Party, Além committed suicide in 1896. Until 1910, the Radical Party, now led by Yrigoyen, proved unable to achieve political reform by peaceful or revolutionary means, as the reunited oligarchy consolidated its power.

In Yrigoyen, however, the Radicals possessed a charismatic personality and a masterful organizer who refused to admit defeat. Yrigoyen, a one-time police superintendent in Buenos Aires, was formerly a minor politician who used his official party connections to acquire considerable wealth, which he invested in land and cattle. As a Radical caudillo, Yrigoyen was the architect of a program whose vagueness was dictated by the party's need to appeal to very diverse elements and by its wholehearted acceptance of the economic status quo. "Abstention," refusal to participate in rigged elections, and "revolutionary intransigence," the determination to resort to revolution until free elections were achieved, were the party's basic slogans.

The Radical Party represented the bourgeoisie, but it was a dependent bourgeoisie that did not champion industrialization, economic diversification, or nationalization of foreign-owned industries. Far from attacking the neocolonial order, the Radical Party proposed to strengthen it by promoting cooperation between the landed aristocracy and the urban sectors, which were challenging the creole elite's monopoly of political power. In all respects, it was much more conservative than the contemporaneous reformist movement of José Batlle y Ordóñez in Uruguay.[1]

---

[1] Under the leadership of José Batlle y Ordóñez (1856–1929), president of Uruguay from 1903 to 1907 and again from 1911 to 1915, Uruguay adopted an advanced program of social reform that made it "the chief laboratory for social experimentation in the Americas and a focal point of world interest." The program included the establishment of the eight-hour day, old-age pensions, minimum wages, and accident insurance; abolition of capital punishment; separation of church and state; education for women; recognition of divorce; and a system of state capitalism that gradually brought under public ownership banks, railroads, electric systems, telephone and telegraph companies, street railways, and meat-packing plants. Batlle supported labor in its strikes against foreign-owned enterprises. But he did not challenge the land monopoly of the great estancieros and refused to apply his social legislation to their peons.

The Radical Party went into eclipse after the debacles of 1890 and 1893 but gradually revived after 1900, due in part to Yrigoyen's charismatic personality and organizing talent. The most important factor, however, was the steady growth of an urban and rural middle class largely composed of sons of immigrants. The domination of the export sector, which limited the growth of industry and opportunities for entrepreneurial activity, focused middle-class ambitions more and more on government employment and the professions, two fields dominated by the creole elite. Signs of growing unrest and frustration in the middle class included a series of student strikes in the universities, caused by efforts of creole governing boards to restrict enrollment of students of immigrant descent.

## ELECTORAL REFORM AND THE GROWTH OF THE LABOR MOVEMENT

Meanwhile, a section of the oligarchy, headed by Carlos Pellegrini, had begun to advocate electoral reform. These aristocratic reformers argued that the existing situation created a permanent state of tension and instability; they feared that sooner or later the Radical efforts at revolution would succeed. It would be much better, they believed, to make the concessions demanded by the Radicals, open up the political system, and thereby gain for the ruling party—now generally called Conservative—the popular support and legitimacy it needed to remain in power. Moreover, the conservative reformers were aware of a new threat from the left—from the labor movement and especially its vanguard, the socialists, anarchists, and syndicalists—and hoped to make an alliance with the bourgeoisie against the revolutionary working class. They therefore supported a series of measures known collectively as the Sáenz Peña Law (1912). The new law established universal and secret male suffrage for citizens when they reached the age of eighteen. This law, which historian David Rock calls "an act of calculated retreat by the ruling class," opened the way for a dependent bourgeoisie to share power and the spoils of office with the landed aristocracy.

The principal political vehicle for working-class aspirations was the Socialist Party, founded in 1894 as a split-off from the Unión Cívica Radical by the Buenos Aires physician and intellectual Juan B. Justo, who led the party until his death in 1928. Despite its professed Marxism, the party's socialism was of the parliamentary reformist kind, appealing chiefly to highly skilled, native-born workers and the lower-middle class. The majority of workers, foreign-born noncitizens who still dreamed of returning someday to their homelands, remained aloof from electoral politics but readily joined trade unions that valiantly resisted deteriorating wages and working conditions; a series of great strikes was broken by the government with brutal repression and the deportation of so-called foreign agitators. Despite these defeats, the labor movement continued to grow and struggle, winning such initial victories as the ten-hour workday and the establishment of Sunday as a compulsory day of rest.

## Chilean Politics and Economy

### Nitrates and War

In 1876 the Liberal president Aníbal Pinto inherited a severe economic crisis (1874–1879). Wheat and copper prices dropped, exports declined, and unemployment grew. The principal offset to these unfavorable developments was the continued growth of nitrate exports from the Atacama Desert as a result of a doubling of nitrate production between 1865 and 1875. But nitrates, the foundation of Chilean material progress, also became the cause of a major war with dramatic consequences for Chile and its two foes, Bolivia and Peru.

The nitrate deposits exploited by the Anglo-Chilean companies lay in territories belonging to Bolivia (the province of Antofagasta) and Peru (the province of Tarapacá). In 1866 a treaty between Chile and Bolivia defined their boundary in the Atacama Desert as the twenty-fourth parallel, gave Chilean and Bolivian interests equal rights to exploit the territory between the twenty-third and twenty-fifth parallels, and guaranteed each government half of the tax revenues obtained from the export of minerals from the whole area. Anglo-Chilean capital soon poured into the region, developing a highly efficient mining-industrial complex. By a second treaty of 1874, Chile's northern border with Bolivia was left at the twenty-fourth parallel. Chile relinquished its rights to a share of the taxes from exports north of that boundary but received in return a twenty-five-year guarantee against increase of taxes on Chilean enterprises operating in the Bolivian province of Antofagasta.

Chile had no boundary dispute with Peru, but aggressive Chilean mining interests, aided by British capital, soon extended their operations from Antofagasta into the Peruvian province of Tarapacá. By 1875, Chilean enterprises in Peruvian nitrate fields employed more than ten thousand workers, engineers, and supervisory personnel. At this point, the Peruvian government, on the brink of bankruptcy as a result of a very expensive program of public works, huge European loans, and the depletion of the guano deposits on which it had counted to service those loans, decided to expropriate the foreign companies in Tarapacá and establish a state monopoly over the production and sale of nitrates. Meanwhile, Peru and Bolivia had negotiated a secret treaty in 1874 providing for a military alliance in the event either power went to war with Chile.

Ejected from Tarapacá, the Anglo-Chilean capitalists intensified their exploitation of the nitrate deposits in Antofagasta. In 1878, Bolivia, counting on its military alliance with Peru, challenged Chile by imposing higher taxes on nitrate exports from Antofagasta, in violation of the treaty of 1874. When the Chilean companies operating in Antofagasta refused to pay the new taxes, the Bolivian government threatened them with confiscation. The agreement of 1874 provided for arbitration of disputes, but the Bolivians twice rejected Chilean offers to submit the dispute to arbitration.

In February 1879, despite Chilean warnings that expropriation of Chilean enterprises would void the treaty of 1874, the Bolivian government ordered the confiscation carried out. On February 14, the day set for the seizure and sale of the

Chilean properties, Chilean troops occupied the port of Antofagasta, encountering no resistance, and proceeded to extend Chilean control over the whole province. Totally unprepared for war, Peru made a vain effort to mediate between Chile and Bolivia. Chile, however, having learned of the secret Peruvian-Bolivian alliance, charged Peru with intolerable duplicity and declared war on both Peru and Bolivia on April 5, 1879.

In this war, called the War of the Pacific, Chile faced enemies whose combined population was more than twice its own; one of these powers, Peru, also possessed a respectable naval force. But Chile enjoyed major advantages. By contrast with its neighbors, it possessed a stable central government, a people with a strong sense of national identity, and a disciplined, well-trained army and navy. Chile also enjoyed the advantage of being closer to the theater of operations, because Bolivian troops had to come over the Andes and the Peruvian army had to cross the Atacama Desert.

All three powers had serious economic problems, but Chile's situation was not as catastrophic as that of its foes. Equally important, Chile had the support of powerful English capitalist interests, who knew that the future of the massive English investment in Chile depended in large part on the outcome of the war. The prospect of Chilean acquisition of the valuable nitrate areas of Antofagasta and Tarapacá naturally pleased the British capitalists. British capital was also invested in Bolivia and Peru, but whereas the Chilean government had maintained service on its debt, Bolivia and Peru had suspended payment on their English loans. Besides, the Peruvian nationalization of the nitrate industry in Tarapacá had seriously injured British interests.

With British assistance, Chile won the war in 1883 and imposed its terms. By the Treaty of Ancón (October 20, 1883), Peru ceded the province of Tarapacá to Chile in perpetuity. The provinces of Tacna and Arica would be Chilean for ten years, after which a plebiscite would decide their ultimate fate. But the plebiscite was never held, and Chile continued to administer the two territories until 1929, when Peru recovered Tacna

and Arica went to Chile. An armistice signed in April 1884 by Bolivia and Chile assigned the former Bolivian province of Antofagasta to Chile, but for many years no Bolivian government would sign a formal treaty acknowledging that loss. Finally, in 1904, Bolivia signed a treaty in which Chile agreed to pay an indemnity and to build a railroad connecting the Bolivian capital of La Paz with the port of Arica. That railroad was completed in 1913.

## AFTERMATH OF THE WAR OF THE PACIFIC

Chile took advantage of the continued mobilization of its armed forces during the negotiations with Peru to settle scores with the Araucanians, whose struggle in defense of their land against encroaching whites had continued since colonial times. After two years of resistance against very unequal odds, the Araucanians were forced to admit defeat and sign a treaty (1883) that resettled them on reservations but retained their tribal government and laws. The Araucanian campaign of 1880–1882, which extended the Chilean southern frontier into a region of mountain and forest, sparked a brisk movement of land speculation and colonization in that area.

From the War of the Pacific, which shattered Peru economically and psychologically and left Bolivia more isolated than before from the outside world, Chile emerged the strongest nation on the west coast, in control of vast deposits of nitrates and copper, the mainstays of its economy. But the greater part of these riches would soon pass into foreign hands. In 1881 the Chilean government made an important decision: it decided to return the nitrate properties of Tarapacá to private ownership; that is, to the holders of the certificates issued by the Peruvian government as compensation for the nationalized properties.

During the war, uncertainty as to how Chile would dispose of those properties had caused the Peruvian certificates to depreciate until they fell to a fraction of their face value. Speculators, mostly British, had bought up large quantities of these depreciated certificates. In 1878 British capital controlled some 13 percent of the nitrate industry of Tarapacá; by 1890 its share had risen to at least

70 percent. British penetration of the nitrate areas proceeded not only through formation of companies for direct exploitation of nitrate deposits, but also through the establishment of banks that financed entrepreneurial activity in the nitrate area and the creation of railways and other companies more or less closely linked to the central nitrate industry. An English railway company with a monopoly of transport in Tarapacá, the Nitrate Railways Company, controlled by John Thomas North, paid dividends of up to 20 and 25 percent, compared with earnings of from 7 to 14 percent for other railway companies in South America.

The Chilean national bourgeoisie, which had pioneered the establishment of the mining-industrial-railway complex in the Atacama, offered little resistance to the foreign takeover. Lack of strong support from the state, the relative financial weakness of the Chilean bourgeoisie, and the cozy and profitable relationships maintained throughout the nineteenth century between the Chilean elite and British interests facilitated the rapid transfer of Chilean nitrate and railway properties into British hands and the transformation of Chilean mine owners into a dependent bourgeoisie content with a share of the profits of British companies.

But elsewhere in Chile, the war had energized the national economy and mobilized local manufacturers and workers, who pressed for electoral reform; in 1884 the property qualification for voting was replaced with a literacy test. Because the great majority of Chilean males were illiterate *rotos* (seasonal farm workers) and inquilinos, this change did not materially add to the number of voters; as late as 1915, out of a population of about 3.5 million, only 150,000 persons voted. But it did secure the 1886 victory of liberal president José Manuel Balmaceda, who took office with a well-defined program of state-directed economic modernization. By the 1880s factory capitalism had taken root in Chile. In addition to consumer goods industries—flour mills, breweries, leather factories, furniture factories, and the like—there existed foundries and metalworking enterprises that served the mining industry, railways, and agriculture. Balmaceda proposed to consolidate and expand this native industrial capitalism.

## BALMACEDA'S NATIONALISTIC POLICIES

Balmaceda came to office when government revenues were at an all-time high (they had risen from about 15 million pesos a year before the War of the Pacific to about 45 million pesos in 1887). The chief source of this government income was the export duty on nitrates. Knowing that the proceeds from this source would taper off as the nitrate deposits diminished, Balmaceda wisely planned to employ those funds for the development of an economic infrastructure that would remain when the nitrate was gone. Hence, public works figured prominently in his program. In 1887 he created a new ministry of industry and public works, which expended large sums on extending and improving the telegraphic and railway systems and on the construction of bridges, roads, and docks. Balmaceda also generously endowed public education, needed to provide skilled workers for Chilean industry. During his presidency the total enrollment in Chilean schools rose in four years from some 79,000 in 1886 to over 150,000 in 1890. He also favored raising the wages of workers but was inconsistent in his labor policy; yielding to strong pressure from foreign and domestic employers, he sent troops to crush a number of strikes.

Central to Balmaceda's program was his determination to "Chileanize" the nitrate industry. In his inaugural address to Congress, he declared that his government would consider what measures it should take "to nationalize industries which are, at present, chiefly of benefit to foreigners," a clear reference to the nitrate industry. Later, Balmaceda's strategy shifted; he encouraged the entrance of Chilean private capital into nitrate production and exportation to prevent the formation of a foreign-dominated nitrate cartel whose interest in restricting output clashed with the government's interest in maintaining a high level of production to collect more export taxes. In November 1888 he scolded the Chilean elite for their lack of entrepreneurial spirit:

> Why does the credit and the capital which are brought into play in all kinds of speculations in our great cities hold back and leave the foreigner to establish banks at Iquique and aban-

don to strangers the exploiting of the nitrate works of Tarapacá? . . . The foreigner exploits these riches and takes the profit of native wealth to give to other lands and unknown people the treasures of our soil, our own property and the riches we require.

Balmaceda waged a determined struggle to end the monopoly of the British-owned Nitrate Railways Company, whose prohibitive freight charges reduced production and export of nitrates. His nationalistic policies inevitably provoked the hostility of English nitrate "kings" like North, who had close links with the Chilean elite and employed prominent liberal politicians as their legal advisers.

But Balmaceda had many domestic as well as foreign foes. The clericals opposed his plans to further curb the powers of the church. The landed aristocracy resented his public works program because it drew labor from agriculture and pushed up rural wages. The banks, which had profited from an uncontrolled emission of notes that fed inflation and benefited mortgaged landlords and exporters, were angered by his proposal to establish a national bank with a monopoly of note issue. The entire oligarchy, liberals as well as conservatives, opposed his use of the central government as an instrument of progressive economic and social change.

Meanwhile, the government's economic problems multiplied, adding to Balmaceda's political difficulties by narrowing his popular base. By 1890 foreign demand for copper and nitrates had weakened. Prices in an overstocked world market fell, and English nitrate interests responded to the crisis by forming a cartel to reduce production. Reduced production and export of nitrates and copper sharply diminished the flow of export duties into the treasury and caused growing unemployment and wage cuts even as inflation cut into the value of wages. The result was a series of great strikes in Valparaíso and the nitrate zone in 1890. Despite his sympathy with the workers' demands and unwillingness to use force against them, Balmaceda, under pressure from domestic and foreign employers, sent troops to crush the strikes. These repressive measures ensured much working-class apathy

or even hostility toward the president in the eventual confrontation with his foes.

Indeed, Balmaceda had few firm allies at his side when that crisis came. The industrial capitalist group whose growth he had ardently promoted was still weak. The mining interests, increasingly integrated with or dominated by English capital, joined the bankers, the clericals, and the landed aristocracy in opposition to his nationalist program of economic development and independence. The opposition mobilized its forces in parliament, where Balmaceda lacked a reliable congressional majority, forcing him to abolish the system of parliamentary government and return to the traditional system of presidential rule established by the constitution of 1833. His rash act, made without any serious effort to mobilize popular forces, played into the hands of his enemies, who were already preparing for civil war.

On January 7, 1891, congressional leaders proclaimed a revolt against the president in the name of legality and the constitution. The navy, then as now led by officers of aristocratic descent, promptly supported the rebels, who seized the ports and customhouses in the north and established their capital at Iquique, the chief port of Tarapacá.

English-owned enterprises also actively aided the rebels. Indeed, by the admission of the British minister at Santiago, "our naval officers and the British community of Valparaíso and all along the coast rendered material assistance to the opposition and committed many breaches of neutrality." Many nitrate workers, alienated by Balmaceda's repression of their strike, remained neutral or even joined the rebel army, organized by a German army officer, General Emil Korner. Politically isolated and militarily defeated, Balmaceda sought refuge in the Argentine embassy and, on September 19, 1891, the day on which his legal term of office came to an end, Balmaceda put a bullet through his head.

The death of Chile's first anti-imperialist president restored the reign of the oligarchy, a coalition of landowners, bankers, merchants, and mining interests closely linked to English capital. A new era began, the era of the so-called Parliamentary

Republic. Taught by experience, the oligarchy now preferred to rule through a congress divided into various factions rather than through a strong executive. Such decentralization of government favored the interests of the rural aristocracy and its allies. A new law of 1892, vesting local governments with the right to supervise elections both for local and national offices, reinforced the power of the landowners, priests, and political bosses who had fought Balmaceda's progressive policies.

### The Parliamentary Republic, Foreign Economic Domination, and the Growth of the Working Class

The era of the Parliamentary Republic was accompanied by a growing subordination of the Chilean economy to foreign capital, which was reflected in a steady increase in the foreign debt and foreign ownership of the nation's resources. English investments in Chile amounted to 24 million pounds in 1890; they rose to 64 million pounds in 1913. Of this total, 34.6 million pounds formed part of the Chilean public debt. In the same period, North American and German capital began to challenge the British hegemony in Chile. England continued to be Chile's principal trade partner, but U.S. and German trade with Chile grew at a faster rate. German instructors also acquired a strong influence in the Chilean army, and the flow of German immigrants into southern Chile continued, resulting in the formation of compact colonies dominated by a Pan-German ideology. The revival of the Chilean economy from the depression of the early 1890s brought an increase of nitrate, copper, and agricultural exports and further enriched the ruling classes, but it left inquilinos, miners, and factory workers as desperately poor as before. Meanwhile, the working class grew from 120,000 to 250,000 between 1890 and 1900, and the doctrines of trade unionism, socialism, and anarchism achieved growing popularity in its ranks.

Luis Emilio Recabarren (1876–1924), the father of Chilean socialism and communism, played a decisive role in the social and political awakening of the Chilean proletariat. In 1906 Recabarren was elected to Congress from a mining area but was not allowed to take his seat because he refused to take his oath of office on the Bible. In 1909, he organized the Workers Federation of Chile, the first national trade union movement. Three years later, he founded the Socialist Party, a revolutionary Marxist movement, and became its first secretary.

The growing self-consciousness and militancy of the Chilean working class found expression in a mounting wave of strikes. Between 1911 and 1920, almost three hundred strikes, involving more than 300,000 workers, took place. Many were crushed with traditional brutal methods that left thousands of workers dead.

## Brazilian Politics and Economy

### The Antislavery Movement

From the close of the Paraguayan War (1870), the slavery question surged forward, becoming the dominant issue in Brazilian political life. Dom Pedro, personally opposed to slavery, was caught in a crossfire between a growing number of liberal leaders, intellectuals, and urban middle-class groups who demanded emancipation and slave owners determined to postpone the inevitable as long as possible. In 1870 Spain freed all the newborn and aged slaves of Cuba and Puerto Rico, leaving Brazil the only nation in the Americas to retain slavery in its original colonial form. Yielding to pressure, a conservative ministry pushed the Rio Branco Law through parliament in 1871. This measure freed all newborn children of slaves but obligated the masters to care for them until they reached the age of eight. At that time, owners could either release the children to the government in return for an indemnity or retain them as laborers until they reached the age of twenty-one. The law also freed all slaves belonging to the state or crown and created a fund to be used for the manumission of slaves.

The Rio Branco Law was a tactical retreat designed to put off a final solution of the slavery problem. As late as 1884, when Brazil still had over 1 million slaves, only 113 had been freed by this means.

Slaves drying coffee on a plantation in Terreiros, in the state of Rio de Janeiro, about 1882. [Courtesy of Hack Hoffenburg]

Abolitionist leaders denounced the law as a sham and illusion and advanced ever more vigorously the demand for total and immediate emancipation. From 1880 on, the antislavery movement developed great momentum. Concentrated in the cities, it drew strength from the process of economic, social, and intellectual modernization under way there. To the new urban groups, slavery was an anachronism, glaringly incompatible with modernization.

Among the slave owners themselves, divisions of opinion appeared. In the north, where slavery had become economically inefficient, a growing number of planters shifted to wage labor, drawing on the pool of freedmen made available by the Rio Branco Law and the *sertanejos* (inhabitants of the interior), poor whites and mixed-bloods who lived on the fringes of the plantation economy. Another factor in the decline of the slave population in the northeast was the great drought of 1877–1879, which caused many of the region's wealthier folk to sell their slaves or abandon the area, taking their slaves with them. States like Amazonas and Ceará, where black slaves were few and most of the work was done by natives and mixed-bloods, abolished slavery within their borders in 1884. By contrast, the coffee planters of Rio de Janeiro, São Paulo, and Minas Gerais, joined by northern planters who trafficked in slaves, selling them to the coffee zone, offered the most tenacious resistance to the advance of abolition.

The abolitionist movement produced leaders of remarkable intellectual and moral stature. One was Joaquim Nabuco, son of a distinguished liberal statesman of the empire, whose eloquent dissection and indictment of slavery, *O abolicionismo*, had a profound impact on its readers. Another was a mulatto journalist, José de Patrocinio, a master propagandist noted for his fiery, biting style. Another mulatto, André Rebouças, an engineer and teacher whose intellectual gifts won him the respect and friendship of the emperor, was a leading organizer of the movement. For Nabuco and his comrades-in-arms, the antislavery struggle was the major front in a larger struggle for the transformation of Brazilian society. Abolition, they hoped, would pave the way for the attainment of other goals: land reform, public education, and political democracy.

Yielding to mounting pressure, parliament adopted another measure on September 28, 1885, that liberated all slaves when they reached the age of sixty but required them to continue to serve their masters for three years and forbade them to leave their place of residence for five years. These conditions, added to the fact that few slaves lived beyond the age of sixty-five, implied little change in the status of the vast majority of slaves. The imperial government also promised to purchase the freedom of the remaining slaves in fourteen years—a promise that few took seriously, in the light of experience with the Rio Branco Law. Convinced that the new law was another tactical maneuver, the abolitionists spurned all compromise solutions and demanded immediate, unconditional emancipation. By the middle 1880s, the antislavery movement had assumed massive proportions and a more militant character. Large numbers of slaves began to vote for freedom with their feet; they were aided by abolitionists who organized an underground railway that ran from São Paulo to Ceará, where slavery had ended. Efforts to secure the return of fugitive slaves encountered growing resistance. Army officers, organized in a *Club Militar*, protested against the use of the army for the pursuit of fugitive slaves.

In February 1887, São Paulo liberated all slaves in the city with funds raised by popular subscription. Many slave owners, seeing the handwriting on the wall, liberated their slaves on condition that they remain at work for some time longer. By the end of 1887 even the die-hard coffee planters of São Paulo were ready to adjust to new conditions by offering to pay wages to their slaves and improve their working and living conditions; they also increased efforts to induce European immigrants to come to São Paulo. These efforts were highly successful; the flow of immigrants into São Paulo rose from 6,600 in 1885 to over 32,000 in 1887 and to 90,000 in 1888. As a result, coffee production reached record levels. With its labor problem solved, São Paulo was ready to abandon its resistance to abolition and even join the abolitionist crusade.

On May 13, 1888, Brazil finally abolished slavery, but contrary to a traditional interpretation, this decision was not the climax of a gradual process of slavery's decline and slave owners' peaceful acceptance of the inevitable. The total slave population dropped sharply only after 1885, as a result of abolitionist agitation, mass flights of slaves, armed clashes, and other upheavals that appeared to threaten anarchy. In effect, abolition had come not through reform but by revolution.

The aftermath of abolition refuted the dire predictions of its foes. Freed from the burdens of slavery and aided by the continuance of very high world coffee prices (until about 1896), Brazil made more economic progress in a few years than it had during the almost seven decades of imperial rule. For the former slaves, however, little had changed. The abolitionist demand for the grant of land to the freedmen was forgotten. Relationships between former masters and slaves in many places remained largely unchanged; racist traditions and the economic and political power of the fazendeiros gave them almost absolute control over their former slaves. Denied land and education, freedmen were now compelled by the "whip of hunger" to labor at the hardest, most poorly paid jobs. Fazendeiros replaced freedmen with immigrants on the coffee plantations; in the cities, black artisans lost their jobs to immigrants.

## THE FALL OF THE MONARCHY

But abolition did sabotage slavery's sister institution, the monarchy, which had long rested on the support of the planter class, especially the northern planters, who saw in it a guarantee of slavery's

*Allegory of the Departure of Dom Pedro II for Europe After the Declaration of the Republic.* This romantic painting suggests the respect and affection many Brazilians, including supporters of the republic, felt for the ousted emperor. [Anonymous, 1890, oil on canvas. Fundaçao Maria Luisa e Oscar Americano, São Paolo]

survival. Before 1888 the Republican Party had its principal base among the coffee interests, who resented the favor shown by the imperial government to the sugar planters and wished to achieve political power that corresponded to their economic power. Now, angered by abolition and embittered by the failure of the crown to indemnify them for their lost slaves, those planters who had opposed abolition now joined the Republican movement. The monarchy that had served the interest of regional elites for the previous sixty-seven years had lost its reason for existence.

Republicanism and a closely allied ideology, positivism, also made many converts in the officer class, disgruntled by the imperial government's neglect and mistreatment. Many of the younger officers came from the new urban middle class or, if of aristocratic descent, were discontented with the ways of their fathers. Positivism, it has been said, became "the gospel of the military academy," where it was brilliantly expounded by a popular young professor of mathematics, Benjamin Constant Botelho de Magalhães, a devoted disciple of Auguste Comte, the doctrine's founder. The positivist doctrine, with its stress on science, its ideal of a dictatorial republic, and its distrust of the masses, fit the needs of urban middle-class groups, progressive officers, and businessmen-fazendeiros who wanted modernization but without drastic changes in land tenure and class relations. On

November 15, 1889, a military revolt led by Benjamin Constant and Marshal Floriano Peixoto overthrew the government, proclaimed a republic with Marshal Deodoro da Fonseca as provisional chief of state, and sent Pedro II into exile in France.

Like the revolution that gave Brazil its independence, the republican revolution came from above; the coup d'état encountered little resistance but also inspired little popular enthusiasm. Power was firmly held by representatives of the business, landed, and military elites.

The new rulers promptly promulgated a series of reforms, including a decree that ended corporal punishment in the army, a literacy test that replaced property qualifications for voting (because property and literacy usually went together, this measure did not significantly enlarge the electorate), and successive decrees that established a secular state and civil marriage.

## The New Republic

Two years after the revolt, a constituent assembly met in Rio de Janeiro to draft a constitution for the new republic. It provided for a federal, presidential form of government with the customary three branches—legislative, executive, and judicial. The principal debate was between the partisans of greater autonomy for the states and those who feared the divisive results of an extreme federalism. The coffee interests, which dominated the wealthy south-central region, sought to strengthen their position at the expense of the central power. The urban business groups, represented in the convention chiefly by lawyers, favored a strong central government that could promote industry, aid the creation of a national market, and offer protection from British competition.

The result was a compromise tilted in favor of federalism. The twenty provinces in effect became self-governing states with popularly elected governors, the exclusive right to tax exports (a profitable privilege for wealthy states like São Paulo and Minas Gerais), and the right to maintain militias. The national government was given control over the tariffs and the income from import duties, whereas the president obtained very large powers:

he designated his cabinet ministers and other high officers, he could declare a state of siege, and he could intervene in the states with the federal armed forces in the event of a threat to their political institutions. The constitution proclaimed the sanctity of private property and guaranteed freedom of the press, speech, and assembly.

If these freedoms had some relevance in the cities and hinterlands touched by the movement of modernization, they lacked meaning over the greater part of the national territory. The fazendeiros, former slave owners, virtually monopolized the nation's chief wealth, its land. The land monopoly gave them absolute control over the rural population. Feudal and semifeudal forms of land tenure, accompanied by the obligation of personal and military service on the part of tenants, survived in the backlands, especially in the northeast. Powerful *coronéis* maintained armies of *jagunços* (full-time private soldiers) and waged war against each other.[2]

In this medieval atmosphere of constant insecurity and social disintegration, there arose messianic movements that reflected the aspirations of the oppressed sertanejos for peace and justice. One of the most important of such movements arose in the interior of Bahia, where the principal activity was cattle raising. Here, Antônio Conselheiro (Anthony the Counselor) established a settlement at the abandoned cattle ranch of Canudos. Rejecting private property, Antônio required all who joined his sacred company to give up their goods, but he promised a future of prosperity in his messianic kingdom through the sharing of the treasure of the "lost Sebastian" (the Portuguese king who had disappeared in Africa in 1478 but would return as a redeemer) or through division of the property of hostile landowners.

Despite its religious coloration, the existence of such a focus of social and political unrest was intolerable to the fazendeiros and the state authorities. When the sertanejos easily defeated state forces

---

[2]The title *coronel* (Portuguese for "colonel"; *coronéis* is the plural) was often honorary and did not necessarily indicate a military command or landownership; especially after 1870, a coronel might be simply a political boss, a merchant, or even an influential lawyer or priest.

sent against them in 1896, the governor called on the federal government for aid. Four campaigns were required to break the epic resistance of the men, women, and children of Canudos, nearly all of whom were killed in the final assault by the national army. A Brazilian literary masterpiece, *Os sertões (Rebellion in the Backlands)* by Euclides da Cunha (1856–1909), immortalized the heroism of the defenders and the crimes of the victors. It also revealed to the urban elite another and unfamiliar side of Brazilian reality.

## THE ECONOMIC REVOLUTION

An enormous historical gulf separated the bleak sertão—in which the tragedy of Canudos was played out—from the cities, the scene of a mushrooming growth of banks, stock exchanges, and corporations. In Rio de Janeiro, writes Pedro Calmon, there was "a multitude of millionaires of recent vintage—commercial agents, bustling lawyers, promoters of all kinds, politicians of the new generation, the men of the day." Even the physical appearance of some of Brazil's great urban centers changed. These changes were most marked in the federal capital of Rio de Janeiro, which was made into a beautiful and healthful city between 1902 and 1906 when Prefect Pereira Passos mercilessly demolished narrow old streets to permit the construction of broad, modern avenues, and the distinguished scientist Oswaldo Cruz waged a victorious struggle to conquer mosquito-borne disease by filling in swamps and installing adequate water and sewage systems.

The economic policies of the new republican regime reflected pressures from different quarters: the planter class, urban capitalists, the military. Many planters, left in a difficult position by the abolition of slavery, demanded subsidies and credits to enable them to convert to the new wage system. The emerging industrial bourgeoisie, convinced that Brazil must develop an industrial base to emerge from backwardness, asked for protective tariffs, the construction of an economic infrastructure, and policies favorable to capital formation. Within the provisional government, these aspirations had a fervent supporter in the minister

of finance, Ruy Barbosa, who believed that the factory was the crucible in which an "intelligent and independent democracy" would be forged in Brazil. Finally, the army, whose decisive role in the establishment of the republic had given it great prestige and influence, called for increased appropriations for the armed services. These various demands far exceeded the revenue available to the federal and state governments.

The federal government solved this problem by resorting to the printing press and allowing private banks to issue notes backed by little more than faith in the future of Brazil. In two years, the volume of paper money in circulation doubled, and the foreign-exchange value of the Brazilian monetary unit, the *milréis*, plummeted disastrously. Because objective economic conditions (the small internal market and the lack of an adequate technological base, among other factors) limited the real potential for Brazilian growth, much of the new capital was used for highly speculative purposes, including the creation of fictitious companies.

The resulting economic collapse brought ruin to many investors, unemployment and lower wages to workers, and a military coup that replaced President da Fonseca with his vice president, Marshal Floriano Peixoto.

The urban middle-class sector briefly gained greater influence in the Peixoto government, and inflation continued unchecked. The rise in the cost of many imported items to almost prohibitive levels stimulated the growth of Brazilian manufactures: the number of such enterprises almost doubled between 1890 and 1895.

But the suppression of a new revolt with strong aristocratic and monarchical overtones increased Peixoto's reliance on the financial and military support of the state of São Paulo, whose coffee oligarchy resolved to use its clout to end the ascendancy of the urban middle classes. The oligarchy distrusted their policies of rapid industrialization and blamed them for the financial instability that had plagued the first years of the republic. In 1893 the old planter oligarchies, whose divisions had temporarily enabled the middle classes to gain the upper hand in coalition with the military, reunited to form the Federal Republican Party, with a program of support for federalism and fiscal responsibility. Because they controlled the electoral machinery, they easily elected Prudente de Morais president in 1894, and his administration again institutionalized the domination of the coffee interests, relegating urban capitalist groups to a secondary role in political life.

Morais's successor, Manuel Ferraz de Campos Sales (1898–1902), continued and expanded his program of giving primacy to agriculture. Campos Sales fully endorsed the system of the international economic division of labor as it applied to Brazil. "It is time," he proclaimed, "that we take the correct road; to that end we must strive to export all that we can produce better than other countries, and import all that other countries can produce better than we." This formula confirmed the continuity of neocolonialism from the empire through the early republic. Determined to halt inflation, Campos Sales drastically reduced expenditures on public works, increased taxes, and made every effort to redeem the paper money to improve Brazil's international credit and secure new loans to cover shortfalls in government revenues.

Coffee was king. Whereas Brazil produced 56 percent of the world's coffee output from 1880 to 1889, it accounted for 76 percent from 1900 to 1904. Its closest competitor, rubber, supplied only 28 percent of Brazil's exports in 1901. Sugar, once the ruler of the Brazilian economy, now accounted for barely 5 percent of the nation's exports. Minas Gerais and especially São Paulo became the primary coffee regions, and Rio de Janeiro declined in importance. Enjoying immense advantages—the famous rich, porous *terra roxa* (red soil), an abundance of immigrant labor, and closeness to the major port of Santos—the *Paulistas* harvested 60 percent of the national coffee production.

The coffee boom from the late 1880s through the mid-1890s soon led to overproduction, falling prices, and the accumulation of unsold stocks after 1896. Because coffee trees came into production only four years after planting, the effects of expansion into the western frontier of São Paulo continued to be felt even after prices fell; between 1896 and 1900 the number of producing trees in São Paulo alone went from 150 million to 570 million. Large international coffee-trading firms controlled the world market, and they added to planters' difficulties by paying depressed prices during the height of each season and selling off their reserves in periods of relative shortage when prices edged up.

Responding to the planters' clamor for help, the São Paulo government took the first step for the "defense" of coffee in 1902, forbidding new coffee plantings for five years. Other steps soon proved necessary. Faced with a bumper crop in 1906, São Paulo launched a coffee price-support scheme to protect the state's economic lifeblood. With financing from British, French, German, and U.S. banks and the eventual collaboration of the federal government, São Paulo purchased several million bags of coffee and held them off the market in an effort to maintain profitable price levels. Purchases continued into 1907; from that date until World War I, the stocks were gradually sold off with little market disruption. The operation's principal gainers were the foreign merchants and bankers who, because they controlled the Coffee Commission formed to liquidate the purchased stocks, gradually disposed of them with a large margin of profit. The problem, temporarily exorcised, was presently to return in an even more acute form.

The valorization scheme, which favored the coffee-raising states at the expense of the rest, reflected the coffee planters' political domination. Under President Campos Sales, this ascendancy was institutionalized by the so-called *política dos governadores* (politics of the governors). Its essence was a formula that gave the two richest and most populous states (São Paulo and Minas Gerais) a virtual monopoly of federal politics and the choice of presidents. Thus, the first three civilian presidents from 1894 to 1906 came from São Paulo; the next two, from 1906 to 1910, came from Minas Gerais and Rio de Janeiro, respectively.

In return, the oligarchies of the other states were given almost total freedom of action within their jurisdictions, the central government intervening as a rule only when it suited the local oligarchy's interest. Informal discussions among the state governors determined the choice of president, whose election was a foregone conclusion since less than two percent of the population was eligible to vote. No official candidate for president lost an election before 1930. Similar reciprocal arrangements existed on the state level between the governors and the coronéis, urban or rural bosses who rounded up the local vote to elect the governors and were rewarded with a free hand in their respective domains.

Despite the official bias in favor of agriculture, industry continued to grow in the period from 1904 to 1914. By 1908, Brazil could boast of more than three thousand industrial enterprises. Foreign firms dominated the fields of banking, public works, utilities, transportation, and the export and import trade. Manufacturing, on the other hand, was carried on almost exclusively by native Brazilians and permanent immigrants. This national industry was concentrated in the four states of São Paulo, Minas Gervais, Rio de Janeiro, and Rio Grande do Sul. Heavy industry did not exist; over half of the enterprises were textile mills and food-processing plants. Many of these "enterprises" were small workshops employing a few artisans or operated with archaic technology, and Brazilians in the market economy continued to import most quality products. The quantitative and qualitative development of industry was hampered by the semifeudal conditions prevailing in the countryside; by the extreme poverty of the masses, which sharply limited the internal market; by the lack of a skilled, literate labor force; and by the hostility of most fazendeiros and foreign interests to industry.

Together with industry there arose a working class destined to play a significant role in the life of the country. The Brazilian proletariat was partly recruited from sharecroppers and minifundio peasants fleeing to the cities to escape dismal poverty and the tyranny of coronéis, but above all it was composed of the flood of European immigrants, who arrived at a rate of 100,000 to 150,000 each year. Working and living conditions of the working class were often intolerable. Child labor was common, for children could be legally employed from the age of twelve. The workday ranged from nine hours for some skilled workers to more than sixteen hours for various categories of unskilled workers. Wages were pitifully low and often paid in vouchers redeemable at the company store. There was a total absence of legislation to protect workers against the hazards of unemployment, old age, or industrial accidents.

Among the European immigrants were many militants with socialist, syndicalist, or social-democratic backgrounds who helped organize the Brazilian labor movement and gave it a radical political orientation. National and religious divisions among workers, widespread illiteracy, and quarrels between socialists and anarcho-syndicalists hampered the rise of a trade union movement and a labor party.

But trade unions grew rapidly after 1900, and the first national labor congress, representing the majority of the country's trade unions, met in 1906 to struggle for the eight-hour workday. One result of the congress was the formation of the first national trade union organization, the Brazilian Labor Confederation, which organized a number of strikes that authorities and employers tried to suppress by arresting labor leaders, deporting immigrants, and sending dissidents to forced labor on a railroad under construction in distant Mato Grosso. The phrase "the social question is a question for the police" was often used to sum up the labor policy of the Brazilian state.

## Peruvian Politics and Economy

Peru's backward, stagnant economy, the profound cleavage between the sierra and the coast, and the absence of a governing class (such as arose in Chile) capable of giving firm and intelligent leadership to the state produced chronic political turbulence and civil wars.

Under these conditions, military caudillos, sometimes men of plebeian origin who had risen in the ranks during the wars of independence, came to play a decisive role in the political life of the new state. Some were more than selfish careerists or instruments of aristocratic creole cliques. The ablest and most enlightened of the military caudillos was the mestizo general Ramón Castilla, who served as president of Peru from 1845 to 1851 and again from 1855 to 1862. Castilla presided over an advance of the Peruvian economy based on the rapid growth of guano exports. This export trade was dominated by British capitalists, who obtained the right to sell guano to specified regions of the world in return for loans to the Peruvian government (secured by guano shipments). Exorbitant interest and commission rates swelled their profits. Although Castilla gave some thought to direct government exploitation of some guano deposits, to setting controls over the amount and price of guano to be sold, and to plowing guano revenues into development projects, he did nothing to implement these ideas. The guano boom, however, stimulated some growth of native Peruvian commerce and banking and created the nucleus of a national capitalist class. Guano prosperity also financed the beginnings of a modern infrastructure; thus, in 1851 the first railway line began to operate between Lima and its port of Callao.

The rise of guano revenues enabled Castilla to carry out a series of social reforms that also contributed to the process of modernization. In 1854 he abolished slavery and indigenous tribute, relieving natives of a heavy fiscal burden and freeing enslaved Africans, who numbered some twenty thousand. Abolition had an initial disruptive effect on coastal agriculture, but in the long run it was very advantageous to the planter aristocracy, who received compensation of up to 40 percent of their slaves' value. With these indemnities, planters could buy seeds, plants, and Chinese coolies brought to Peru on a contract basis that made them virtual slaves. Meanwhile, the freed blacks often became sharecroppers who lived on the margins of the hacienda and supplied a convenient unpaid labor force and a source of rent. Stimulated by these developments, cotton, sugar cane, and grain production expanded on the coast. Highland economic life also quickened, though on a smaller scale, with the rise of extensive cattle breeding for the export of wool and leather through Arequipa and Lima.

The general upward movement of the Peruvian economy after 1850 was aided by such favorable factors as the temporary dislocation of the cotton industry of the southern United States

and large inflows of foreign capital. As a result, exports of cotton and sugar increased sharply. The coastal latifundia continued to expand at the expense of indigenous communities, sharecroppers, and tenants, all of whom were expelled from their lands. This process was accompanied by the modernization of coastal agriculture through the introduction of cotton gins, boilers, refinery equipment for sugar, and steam-driven tractors.

Although profits from the agricultural sector enabled the commercial and landed aristocracy of Lima to live in luxury, the Peruvian state sank even deeper into debt. The guano deposits, Peru's collateral for its foreign borrowings, were being depleted at an ever-accelerating rate, and the bulk of the proceeds from these loans went to pay interest on old and new debts. In 1868, during the administration of the military caudillo José Balta, his minister of the treasury, Nicolás de Piérola, devised a plan for extricating Peru from its difficulties and providing funds for development. The project eliminated the numerous consignees to whom guano had been sold and awarded a monopoly of guano sales in Europe to the French firm of Dreyfus and Company. In return, the Dreyfus firm agreed to service its foreign debt and to make Peru a loan that would tide it over immediate difficulties. The contract initiated a new flow of loans that helped create a boundless euphoria, an invincible optimism, about the country's future.

U.S. adventurer and entrepreneur Henry Meiggs, who had made a reputation as a railway builder in Chile, easily convinced Balta and Piérola that they should support the construction of a railway system to tap the mineral wealth of the sierra. As a result, much of the money obtained under the Dreyfus contract, and a large part of the proceeds of the dwindling guano reserves, were poured into railway projects that could not show a profit in the foreseeable future.

## PARDO AND THE CIVILIANIST PARTY

The good fortune of Dreyfus and Company displeased the native commercial and banking bourgeoisie that had arisen in Lima. A group of these men—including former guano consignees who had been eliminated by the Dreyfus contracts—headed by the millionaire businessman Manuel Pardo, challenged the legality of the contract before the Supreme Court, arguing that assignment of guano sales to a corporation of native consignees that they proposed to form would be more beneficial to Peru's economic development. The native bourgeoisie suffered defeat, but in 1871 they organized the *Civilista*, or Civilianist Party (in reference to their opposition to military caudillos), which ran Pardo as its candidate for president. An amalgam of "an old aristocracy and a newly emerging capitalist class," the Civilianist Party opposed clerical and military influence in politics and advocated a large directing role for the state in economic development. Pardo won handily over two rivals and took office in 1872.

Pardo presided over a continuing agricultural boom, with exports reaching a peak in 1876. Foreign capital poured into the country. In those years, an Irish immigrant, W. R. Grace, began to establish an industrial empire that included textile mills, a shipping line, vast sugar estates, and Peru's first large-scale sugar-refining plants. Whereas private industry prospered, the government sank ever deeper into a quagmire of debts and deficits. The guano cycle was nearing its end, with revenues steadily declining as a result of falling prices, depletion of guano beds, and competition from an important new source of fertilizer: nitrates exploited by Anglo-Chilean capitalists in the southern Peruvian province of Tarapacá. In 1875, wishing to control the nitrate industry and make it a dependable source of government income, Pardo expropriated the foreign companies in Tarapacá and established a state monopoly over the production and sale of nitrates. This measure angered the Anglo-Chilean entrepreneurs, whose holdings had been nationalized and who were indemnified with bonds of dubious value. Meanwhile, due to unsatisfactory market conditions in Europe, the nationalization measure failed to yield the anticipated economic benefits.

In 1876, Peru felt the full force of a worldwide economic storm. In a few months, all the banks of Lima had to close; by the following year, the government had to suspend payments on its foreign debt and issue unbacked paper money. The economic collapse was followed by a military disaster: the War of the Pacific. Despite heroic resistance, Peru suffered a crushing defeat at the hands of a Chilean state that enjoyed more advanced economic organization, political stability, and the support of British capitalists. The war completed the work of economic ruin begun by the depression. The Chileans occupied and ravaged the economically advanced coastal area: they levied taxes on the hacendados; dismantled equipment from the haciendas and sent it to Chile; and sent troops into the sierra to exact payment from hacendados, towns, and villages. Their extortions infuriated the native peasantry. Led by General Andrés Cáceres, they began to wage an effective guerrilla war of attrition against the Chilean occupiers. The war was finally ended by the 1883 Treaty of Ancón.

# Central American Politics and Economy

In the last third of the nineteenth century, the three Central American countries selected for special study—Guatemala, Nicaragua, and El Salvador—underwent major economic changes in response to growing world demand for two products the area was ideally fitted to produce: coffee and bananas. The changes included a "liberal" reform that sought to modernize economic and social structures but left intact existing class and property relations; the rise of a new dependency based on the export of one or two products and foreign control of key natural resources and infrastructure; and acceptance of U.S. political hegemony. Everywhere, these changes were accompanied by concentration of landownership, intensified exploitation of labor, and a growing gulf between the rich and the poor.

## GUATEMALA, 1865–1898

Rafael Carrera's death in 1865 was followed by six years of continuous liberal political and military challenge to conservative rule in Guatemala. The liberals responded to changes in the world economy, in particular to the mounting foreign demand for coffee and the adjustments this required in Guatemala's economic and social structures. In 1871 they seized power, and two years later the energetic Justo Rufino Barrios became president. Although a hard, dictatorial man, Barrios had a genuine passion for reform and was an apostle of Central American unity; he died in battle in 1885 trying to unify Central America by force. His successors grew increasingly cynical, corrupt, and repressive in their efforts to consolidate state power, subjugate relatively autonomous indigenous communities, and create a unified national market for land, labor, and commodities.

The liberal reform program included major economic, social, and ideological changes. The ideological reform introduced doctrines of white supremacy then current in Europe and the United States to justify racist immigration policies designed to "whiten" the population. It also rejected clerical and metaphysical doctrine in favor of a firm faith in science and material progress. This called for the secularization and expansion of education. The shortage of public funds, however, greatly limited public education; as late as 1921 the Guatemalan illiteracy rate was over 86 percent. Seeking to reduce the power and authority of the church, the liberal governments nationalized its lands, ended its special privileges, and established freedom of religion and civil marriage.

The economic transformation encompassed three major areas: land tenure, labor, and infrastructure. A change in land tenure was necessary for the creation of the new economic order. The old staples of Guatemalan agriculture, indigo and cochineal, had been grown by thousands of small- and medium-sized producers; coffee, however, required large expanses of land concentrated in relatively few hands. Under Barrios, there began an "agrarian reform" designed to make such land available to the coffee growers. Church and monastery lands, confiscated by Barrios, were the first target. Next came uncultivated state holdings, which were divided and sold cheaply or granted to private interests, and indigenous communal lands. Legislation requiring titles to private property provided the legal basis for this expropriation. The principal native beneficiaries of this process were

small- and medium-sized coffee growers who could purchase or otherwise obtain land from the government. But foreign immigrants, warmly welcomed by the liberal regimes, also benefited from the new legislation. By 1914 foreign-owned (chiefly German) lands produced almost half of Guatemala's coffee. By 1926 concentration of landownership had reached a point where only 7.3 percent of the population owned land.

The land reform helped achieve another objective of the liberal program—the supply of a mass of cheap labor to the new group of native and foreign coffee growers. Many highland natives who had lost their land migrated to the emerging coffee-growing areas near the coast. The most common labor system was debt peonage—legal under Guatemalan law—in which indígenas were tied to the *fincas* (plantations) by hereditary debts. This was supplemented by the recruitment of native peoples who came down from the mountains to work as seasonal laborers on haciendas and plantations to add to their meager income from their own tiny landholdings. Barrios also revived the colonial system of mandamientos, under which indígenas were required to accept offers of work from planters. The registers of native peoples maintained by local officials for this purpose were also used to conscript them for military service and public works. Those who could not pay the two-peso head tax—the great majority—were required to work (two weeks a year) on road construction.

Constituting 70 percent of the nation's 1,000,000 people in the late nineteenth century, indigenous peoples naturally resisted this liberal onslaught, occasionally through overt acts of localized rebellion. But in the face of a ruthless military state prepared to obliterate them, they more commonly survived by deploying "weapons of the weak," modes of resistance designed to limit the risk of annihilation. In rural Guatemala, these indigenous communities relied on *guachibales*, independent religious brotherhoods rooted in colonial Catholic traditions, to maintain their cultural identities, defend their autonomy, and preserve communal customs, ancestral languages, and religious rituals against the homogenizing power of liberalism's unfettered market forces.

## NICARAGUA, 1870–1909

The history of Nicaragua for two decades after the collapse of the Central American federation in 1838 also was dominated by a struggle between liberals and conservatives. Their responsibility for inviting William Walker to assist them, followed by Walker's attempt to establish his personal empire in Central America, so discredited the liberals that the conservatives were able to rule Nicaragua with very little opposition for more than three decades (1857–1893).

Although coffee was grown commercially as early as 1848, the principal economic activities in Nicaragua until about 1870 were cattle ranching and subsistence agriculture. Indigenous communities still owned much land, there existed a class of independent small farmers who lived on public land, and peonage was rare. On the Atlantic coast, however, the autonomous Kingdom of Mosquitia, controlled by the British since 1678, was inhabited by traditional Miskitos, Sumus, and Afro-creoles, who labored at low wages on thriving British- and U.S.-owned banana plantations, timber lands, gold mines, and commercial port facilities. But the sudden growth of the world market for coffee created a nationalist demand by some members of the Nicaraguan elite for land suitable for coffee growing and for a supply of cheap labor.

Beginning in 1877 a series of laws required these villages to sell their communal lands and effectively drove the indigenous and mestizo peasants off their land, gradually transforming them into a class of dependent peons or sharecroppers. The passage of vagrancy laws and laws permitting the conscription of native peoples for agricultural and public labor also ensured the supply of cheap labor needed by the coffee growers. These laws provoked a major indigenous revolt, the War of the Comuneros (1881), which ended in defeat for the indígenas and was followed by a ferocious repression that took five thousand lives.

The new class, made up of coffee planters, was impatient with the traditional ways of the conservative cattle raisers who had held power in Nicaragua since 1857. In 1893 the planters staged a revolt that brought the liberal José Santos

Zelaya to the presidency. A modernizer, Zelaya ruled for the next seventeen years as dictator-president. He undertook to provide the infrastructure needed by the new economic order through the construction of roads, railroads, port facilities, and telegraphic communications. He reorganized the military, separated church and state, and promoted public education. Like other Latin American liberal leaders of his time, he believed that foreign investment was necessary for rapid economic progress and granted large concessions to foreign capitalists, especially U.S. firms. By 1909, North Americans controlled much of the production of coffee, gold, lumber, and bananas—the principal sources of Nicaragua's wealth.

## EL SALVADOR, 1876–1911

By the mid-nineteenth century, El Salvador had already passed through two economic cycles. The first was dominated by cacao, the prosperity of which collapsed in the seventeenth century; the second by indigo, which entered a sharp decline in the latter half of the nineteenth century, first as a result of competition from other producing areas and then as a result of the development of synthetic dyes. The search for a new export crop led to the enthronement of coffee. Coffee cultivation began at about the time of independence, but it did not expand rapidly until the 1860s. As elsewhere in Central America, the rise of coffee was marked by expropriation and usurpation of native lands—carried out in the name of private property and material progress—because most of the land best suited to coffee cultivation was held by indigenous communities.

Unlike indigo, which was planted and harvested every year, coffee trees did not produce for three years. Producers, therefore, had to have capital or credit, and the people with capital or access to credit were the hacendados who had prospered from the growing of indigo. To help these hacendados in their search for land and labor, a government decree of 1856 declared that if two-thirds of a pueblo's communal lands were not planted in coffee, ownership would pass into the hands of the state. Later, the liberal president and military strongman, Rafael Zaldívar, directly attacked native landholdings with passage of an 1881 law that ordered all communal lands to be divided among the co-owners (which opened the way for their acquisition by legal or illegal means by the expanding coffee growers); thirteen months later he decreed the abolition of all communal land tenure. The new legislation harmed not only these communities but *ladino* (mestizo) small farmers as well. These farmers often relied on municipal *tierras comunes* (the free pasture and woodlot where they could graze their stock) for an important part of their subsistence. In 1879, 60 percent of the people depended upon communal properties, which composed 40 percent of arable lands.

The result of this new legislation was a rapid concentration of landownership in the hands of a landed oligarchy often referred to as "the fourteen families." The number, though not an exact figure, expresses symbolically the reality of the tiny elite that dominated the Salvadoran economy and state. Throughout most of the nineteenth century, the great landowners used their own private armies to deal with the problem of recalcitrant peasants. Governmental decrees of 1884 and 1889 made these private armed forces the basis of the public Rural Police, later renamed the National Police. In 1912 the *Guardia Nacional* (National Guard), modeled after the Spanish National Guard, was established. Like the National Police, the National Guard patrolled the countryside and offered police protection to haciendas. The national army, created in the 1850s, did not become an instrument of repression until the late twentieth century.

For the rural poor, the social consequences of the coffee boom were disastrous. A few of the dispossessed peasants were permitted to remain on the fincas, or new estates, as colonos—peons who were given a place to live and a milpa, or garden plot, where they could raise subsistence crops. Unlike the old indigo or sugar latifundia, however, which required a large permanent labor force, the need for labor on the coffee plantations was seasonal, so for the most part planters relied on hired hands. This circumstance determined the pattern of life of most Salvadoran campesinos. They might farm a small plot as squatters or as colonos on a

plantation, but their tiny plots did not as a rule provide subsistence for their families. They would therefore tend to follow the harvests, working on coffee fincas during the harvest season, moving on to cut sugar cane or harvest cotton during August and September, and finally returning to their milpas, hopeful that the maize had ripened. This unstable migratory pattern created many social problems.

## Venezuelan Politics and Economy

Turmoil in the aftermath of the Federal War ended in 1870 when Antonio Guzmán Blanco, the ablest of Venezuela's nineteenth-century rulers, seized power. Like his father, Guzmán Blanco was a master of demagogic rhetoric. He was a self-proclaimed liberal and foe of the oligarchy, an anticlerical and devout believer in the positivist creed of science and progress whose ambition was to create a "practical republic" of "civilized people." To secure this vision, he forged pacts with the conservative merchant class of Caracas, which viewed him with suspicion when he came to power; with the regional caudillos, traditionally identified with the principle of local autonomy; and with foreign economic interests, whose support he needed for his ambitious program to construct roads, railroads, and telegraph systems. In the end Guzmán Blanco's dream of a developed capitalist Venezuela proved to be a mirage; after two decades of his rule, Venezuela remained rural, monocultural, and dependent, a country in which caudillos again ran rampant as they struggled for power.

His system has been called "a national alliance of caudillos," but over this alliance "the illustrious American," as he came to be called by his sycophantic Congress and press, presided as the supreme caudillo. The constitution of 1864 was periodically replaced by new constitutions that reinforced the centralization of power. Although Guzmán's dictatorship was mild by comparison with some others in Venezuelan history, he did not hesitate to use repressive measures against his foes.

By his pact with the caudillos, Guzmán secured a relatively stable peace (though there were several large-scale revolts against him between 1870 and 1888 and local uprisings were common throughout the period). Soon after coming to power he established a *compañía de crédito* with a powerful group of Caracas merchants. This gave him the resources needed to initiate a program of public works designed to improve transportation and communication. Between 1870 and 1874 fifty-one road-building projects were begun. But local funding did not suffice; Guzmán needed the cooperation of foreign capital, hesitant to invest in a country whose recent history had been marked by recurrent episodes of civil war. In 1879 he secured his first foreign contract, with a group of British investors for the construction of a railroad connecting Caracas with its major port, La Guaira. By the time he left office, Venezuela had eleven railroad lines completed or under construction, all designed to serve the export-import trade by connecting Caracas and the major agricultural and mining areas with the ports. Given Venezuela's unfavorable terms of trade—the long-term tendency for the prices of its exports to decline and those of its manufactured imports to rise—the net result was to reinforce Venezuela's economic dependency, promote decapitalization, and leave the country a legacy of large unpaid foreign debt that in time posed a threat of foreign intervention and loss of sovereignty.

Guzmán Blanco's anticlerical policies led to a further weakening of the church. Tithing had already been abolished as "an excessive tax burden" on the citizenry. Under Guzmán Blanco the priestly fuero was ended, civil marriage and civil registration of birth and deaths established, and convents and seminaries closed. The church was also forbidden to inherit real estate, and many church estates were seized by the government. Guzmán Blanco also tried to prohibit black and Asian immigration, even as he enticed Europeans with generous subsidies. Ultimately this failed, and Venezuela remained a society in which a small, self-proclaimed "white" wealthy minority ruled a "black" majority.

For the rest, Guzmán Blanco's development programs caused little change in the country's economic and social structures. In 1894 the population, numbering some 2,500,000, was overwhelmingly rural; only three cities had a population of more than 10,000. Most of the working population was employed in agriculture; what little modern industry existed was limited to light industry such as food processing and textiles. Artisan shops, employing some 50,000 workers, were economically much more important.

In 1888 "the illustrious American," whose interest in modernizing Venezuela appeared to flag, departed for Europe, leaving a hand-picked successor in charge. After a chaotic decade during which governments rose and fell, in 1899 Cipriano Castro, an energetic young caudillo from the Andean state of Táchira, seized power with his *compadre* (buddy) Juan Vicente Gómez, a prosperous cattle raiser and coffee grower. Castro's seizure of power reflected the growing economic importance of the Andean coffee-growing region. Announcing a program of "new men, new ideals, new methods," Castro formed a provisional government of national unity that included all political factions. In 1901 a constituent assembly elected him president and framed a constitution that extended the executive's term of office to six years.

Castro continued Guzmán Blanco's policy of centralization, appointing or confirming local officials and state governors, and sought to establish a strong national armed force that would replace the old-time personal armies and state militias. His program of military reform was handicapped by declining coffee prices that reduced state revenues, a series of caudillo revolts repressed at heavy cost, and a major conflict with foreign powers whose blockade of Venezuelan ports deprived the government of a vital source of income, custom duties.

Castro presided over a country in ruin due to devastating civil wars and a prolonged depression. Hard-pressed for funds, in December 1900 he demanded that Manuel Antonio Matos, Guzmán Blanco's brother-in-law and the country's wealthiest man, and his fellow financiers loan the government money. When they refused, he paraded them through the streets of Caracas on the way to jail. The loan was made, but Matos took his revenge, organizing a large-scale revolt that brought together Caracas financiers, foreign investors, and regional caudillos. This *Revolución Libertadora* received considerable aid from foreign firms. Despite this assistance and Matos's own resources, Castro, leading the government forces in person, inflicted a decisive defeat on the rebels at La Victoria in November 1902.

The German and British governments chose this time to demand immediate settlement of their nationals' claims for unpaid debts and damages suffered in various civil wars. The government, having thrown all its resources into the struggle against the Matos revolt, could not pay these claims. In December 1902, despite Castro's offer to negotiate, the two powers sent an Anglo-German squadron of twelve warships into Venezuelan waters with orders to seize or destroy Venezuela's tiny fleet and blockade its ports. The powerful guns of the Anglo-German squadron soon silenced the answering fire of Venezuelan coastal batteries, and the aggressors occupied several Venezuelan ports. The unequal nature of the struggle, the catastrophic economic impact of the Anglo-German blockade, and the continuing Matos revolt in some areas of the country made a settlement necessary. Accordingly, Castro asked the U.S. ambassador to serve as mediator in negotiating a settlement. The terms required Venezuela to allocate 30 percent of its customs duties to the payment of claims and provided for an end to the blockade and reestablishment of diplomatic relations between the parties but denied Venezuela the right to demand compensation for its losses.

Castro's last years in power were troubled by new clashes with foreign states—France, Holland, the United States—usually caused by his insistence that foreign nationals were subject to Venezuelan courts and laws. As Castro's health declined, Juan Vicente Gómez conspired to take power. The regime divided into two bands—one supporting Castro, the other Gómez. Gómez also had the support of foreign powers, notably the United States, which was eager to get rid of Castro. On November 24, 1908, on the advice of his physicians, Castro left for Europe to seek medical aid. Gómez, assuming the duties of president, staged a coup d'état. Castro attempted to return but was blocked by U.S. warships off the Venezuelan coast and by French

authorities on Martinique, who put him on board a ship sailing for Europe. He spent the rest of his life in exile, dying in Puerto Rico in 1924.

## Colombian Politics and Economy

Dominating the presidency and Congress, the Liberals in Colombia began to establish a reign of liberty and reason in New Granada. The new constitution of 1853 provided for universal male suffrage, a provision that troubled some Liberals, who knew that illiterate proclerical peasants were most likely to vote Conservative. As a matter of fact, because in most areas voters continued to vote the wishes of the local *gamonales*, or bosses, the new electoral law did not significantly change anything.

In economics the Liberals sought a decisive break with the colonial tradition of restriction and monopoly. The abolition of the state tobacco monopoly finally took effect in 1850. An 1850 law ceded to the provinces revenues from tithes (hitherto collected by the state but used for support of the church), the *quinto* tax on gold and other precious metals, and other traditional sources of state revenue. The provinces were also empowered to abolish these taxes. To compensate for the resulting loss of state revenues, Congress adopted a tax on individuals.

Slavery was completely abolished in 1851, and slave owners were compensated. The measure, freeing about twenty-five thousand individuals, had its most severe impact on gold-mining areas, which generally relied heavily on slave labor. Some of the freedmen became peons on haciendas; others turned to subsistence farming.

But the Liberals always equated emancipation with *mestizaje*, a belief in "one God, one race, one tongue" that required the sacrifice of African and indigenous ethnic identities and the invention of a unified national Hispanic culture. This naturally led to the sacrifice of indigenous and African communal lands and their autonomous political traditions. Thereafter, the Liberals intensified the attack on resguardos, and land "liberated" by forced division often passed into the hands of neighboring hacendados by legal or illegal means. Natives made landless by such means often became peons serving the hacendados. Vagrancy laws similarly coerced the labor of "free" blacks.

Having achieved their ends with artisan support, the Liberal elite now ignored their allies' demands for tariff protection. This triggered a new political crisis in 1854 when a coup, supported by artisans who formed workers' battalions to defend the revolution, briefly installed General José María Melo. But Liberal and Conservative generals, putting aside their differences, raised private armies and defeated Melo in a short campaign. His artisan allies were imprisoned and three hundred were deported to Panama. The economic, political, and military rout of the artisans was complete.

In 1860, Liberals carried their religious and political reforms to their extreme and logical conclusions. Compulsory tithes and ecclesiastical fueros were abolished. All religious orders were suppressed, all convents and monasteries were closed, and all church wealth was seized by the government and sold. The transfer of massive amounts of church land into private hands produced little or no change in the land tenure system; clerical latifundia simply became lay latifundia, contributing to a further concentration of landownership. The principal buyers were Liberal merchants, landowners, and politicians, but Conservatives also participated in the plunder of church land.

In 1863, Liberal political reform reached its climax when a new constitution carried the principle of federalism to great lengths. The nine sovereign states became, in effect, independent nations, each with its own armed forces, possessing all the legislative powers not explicitly granted to the central government, which was made as weak as possible. The Liberals remained in power until 1885 in a political climate that approximated institutionalized anarchy, as the central government was powerless to intervene against the local revolutions that toppled and set up state governments.

The economic movement and its quest for the export base that could firmly integrate Colombia into the capitalist world economy continued. By the 1870s tobacco exports were down sharply, but this decline was made up by exporting coffee, qui-

nine, and other products. Coffee was emerging as the country's major export product, but its development lagged behind that of Brazil, which relied increasingly on European immigrant free labor. In Colombia coffee production in its principal centers of Santander and Cundinamarca was based on traditional haciendas worked by peons and tenants who lived and labored under oppressive conditions. A more satisfactory situation existed in Antioquia and Caldas, characterized by a mix of haciendas with more enlightened forms of sharecropping and small holdings, operations marked by high productivity. It was in these states that the twentieth-century takeoff of the Colombian coffee industry occurred.

The development of coffee as the major export, the growing ties between foreign and domestic merchants and coffee planters, and the stimulus given to trade and speculation by the expropriation of church lands created economic interests that required a new political model—a strong state capable of imposing order and creating the railroads and the financial infrastructure needed for the expansion of the coffee industry. The Liberal reform had removed many obstacles to capitalist development but had created others by its federalist excesses. By the early 1880s not only Conservatives but many moderate Liberals were convinced that political and social stability required making peace with the church and restoring its traditional role. The unlikely instrument for the creation of this new conservative, unitary order was the poet and intellectual Rafael Núñez, whom his party elected president in 1879.

### RAFAEL NÚÑEZ, THE "REGENERATION," AND THE WAR OF A THOUSAND DAYS, 1880–1903

Núñez began political life as a radical Liberal and had spent thirteen years in the consular service in Europe. He returned home in 1875 and was elected president in 1879, governing with a coalition of right-leaning elements from both the Liberal and Conservative Parties. Elected again in 1884 he swiftly crushed a radical Liberal revolt and announced that the 1863 constitution had "ceased to exist." In 1886 he presented the country with a new constitution that replaced the sovereign states with departments headed by governors appointed by the president, extended the presidential term to six years, established literacy and property qualifications for voting for representatives, and provided for indirect election of senators. Under that constitution, personally or through surrogates, Núñez ruled Colombia until his death in 1894.

Like another religious skeptic, Bolívar, Núñez believed the authority of religion and the church was the foundation of the social order and must be fully supported by the state. The 1886 constitution made Catholicism the official religion and entrusted education to the clergy. The other foundations of Núñez's authoritarian republic were a strong standing army and a national police force. The Liberal regimes had virtually dismantled the regular army; the revolts and civil wars of the federal period had been fought by private armies formed by the great landowners with their tenants and peons. The existence of these regional private armies and militias was incompatible with Núñez's unitary project. The 1886 constitution created a permanent army and reserved to the central government the right to possess arms and ammunition. The national police, organized in 1891, kept under vigilance political suspects and disrupted most plots against the government.

Núñez is credited with two major economic innovations. Claiming that the Liberal policy of free trade or low tariffs was the cause of economic decadence and poverty, which had caused the civil war, he proposed to use tariff protection to stimulate the growth of certain industries. He believed this would create a new middle class that would form a buffer between the governing social class and the unlettered multitude. But his implementation of this program was timid and inconsistent. The new policy succeeded, however, in providing a modest level of protection for domestic industry.

Núñez's other innovation was the creation in 1881 of a national bank designed to relieve the financial distress of a government always on the verge of bankruptcy. The bank had the exclusive right to issue money; this monopoly enabled the state to provide for its needs and was managed prudently until 1890. Then its uncontrolled emissions of paper money caused a galloping inflation. An expensive civil war in 1899 provoked the emission of paper money on such a scale that the printers could not keep up with the demand, and the country was flooded with millions of pesos of depreciated currency.

The "Regeneration," as the Núñez era is known, represented an effort to achieve national unification from above under reactionary auspices; it has been compared with Bismarck's project for German national unification, a compound of feudal and capitalist elements. Under Núñez the conditions for the rise of a modern, capitalist state began. An important step in this direction was his creation of a permanent army and the assumption of a monopoly of the use of force by the state. His removal of internal barriers to trade and his policy of tariff protection, however modest, contributed to the formation of an internal market; his national bank, despite its later scandalous mismanagement, represented an initial effort to create a national system of credit; and he gave impulse to the construction of internal improvements, especially railroads. Finally, he sought to give private enterprise access to frontier lands by formally denying the existence of ethnic Afro-Colombian and indigenous communities, voiding their proprietary claims. These policies, combined with the coffee boom, created national markets in land, labor, and commodities and contributed to a growth of capitalism in Colombia.

When he died, Núñez's leadership was assumed by Conservative politicians who lacked his intelligence and iron will. Their corruption, flagrant rigging of elections, and division over freedom of the press and electoral reform collided with Liberal anger at their long exclusion from power and an economic slump caused by a sharp decline of coffee prices. The result was a political crisis followed by a resort to arms. Confident of victory over a thoroughly unpopular government, the Liberals launched a revolt in 1899 that ushered in the disastrous War of a Thousand Days. It raged for three years, caused an estimated loss of 100,000 lives, and created immense material damage. It ended in a government victory.

# Society and Culture in the Nineteenth Century

INDEPENDENCE LEFT MUCH of the colonial social structure intact. This fact was very apparent to liberal leaders of the postindependence era. "The war against Spain," declared the Colombian liberal Ramón Mercado in 1853, "was not a revolution. . . . Independence only scratched the surface of the social problem, without changing its essential nature." A modern historian, Charles C. Griffin, comes to much the same conclusion. "Only the beginnings of a basic transformation took place," he writes, "and there were many ways in which colonial attitudes and institutions carried over into the life of republican Spanish America."

## How New Was the New Society?

We should not minimize, however, the extent and importance of the changes that did take place. Independence produced, if not a major social upheaval, at least a minor one. It opened wide fissures within the elite, dividing aristocratic supporters of the old social order from modernizers who wanted a more democratic, bourgeois order. Their struggle is an integral aspect of the first half-century after the end of Spanish and Portuguese rule. Independence also enabled such formerly submerged groups as artisans and gauchos to enter the political arena, although in subordinate roles, and even allowed a few to climb into the ranks of the elite. The opening of Latin American ports to foreign goods also established a relatively free market in ideas, at least in the capitals and other cities. With almost no time lag, such new European doctrines as utopian socialism, romanticism, and positivism entered Latin America and were applied to the solution of the continent's problems. These new winds of doctrine, blowing through what had lately been dusty colonial corridors, contributed to the area's intellectual renovation and promoted further social change.

## The Passing of the Society of Castes

Verbally, at least, the new republican constitutions established the equality of all before the law, destroying the legal foundations of colonial caste society. Because little change in property relations took place, however, the ethnic and social lines of division remained essentially the same. Wealth, power, and prestige continued to be concentrated in the hands of a ruling class that reproduced colonial racial structures and identified itself with whiteness, although in some countries, such as Venezuela, it became more or less heavily tinged with individuals of darker skin who had managed to climb the social ladder through their prowess in war or politics.

## INDIGENOUS PEOPLES

Of all the groups composing the old society of castes, the status of indígenas changed least of all. Mexican historian Carlos María Bustamante was one of the few creole leaders who recognized that independence had not freed them from their yoke. "They still drag the same chains," he wrote, "although they are flattered with the name of freemen." Even native tribute and forced labor, abolished during or after the wars of independence, soon reappeared in many countries under other names. What was worse, indigenous communal landholding, social organization, and culture, which Spanish law and policy had to some extent protected in colonial times, came under increasing attack, especially from liberals who believed that these communal traditions constituted as much of an obstacle to progress as the Spanish system of castes and special privileges did.

Until about 1870, however, large, compact indigenous populations continued to live under the traditional communal landholding system in Mexico, Central America, and the Andean region. Then, the rapid growth of the export economy, the coming of the railroads, and the resulting rise in land values and demand for labor caused "white" and mestizo landowners and landowner-dominated governments to launch a massive assault on native lands. The expropriation of these lands was accompanied, as noted in Chapter 10, by a growth of peonage and tenantry. Employers used a variety of devices, ranging from debt servitude to outright coercion, to attach laborers to their estates. In some areas, there arose a type of indigenous serfdom that closely resembled the classic European model. In the Andean region, for example, Aymara tenants, in addition to working their masters' land, had to render personal service in their households, sometimes at the hacienda, sometimes in the city. During their term of domestic service, these serfs could be given or sold to their masters' friends. This and other forms of serfdom survived well into the twentieth century.

The master class, aided by the clergy and local magistrates, sought to reinforce the economic subjection of indigenous peoples with psychological domination. There evolved a pattern of relations and role-playing that assigned to the *patrones* the role of benevolent figures who assured their peons or tenants of a livelihood and protected them in all emergencies in return for their absolute obedience. In countries with large indigenous populations, the relations between masters and peons often included an elaborate ritual that required natives to request permission to speak to *patrones*, to appear before them with head uncovered and bowed, and to seek their approval for all major personal decisions, including marriage.

But these relationships and attitudes of submission and servility, more characteristic of resident peons, were not accepted by all indigenous peoples. In the Andean area, Mexico, and elsewhere during the second half of the nineteenth century, the surviving native landowning communities fought stubbornly to prevent the absorption of their lands by advancing haciendas and to halt the process by which they became landless laborers. They fought with all the means at their disposal, including armed revolts as a last resort. Such revolts occurred in Mexico in the 1860s and 1870s and were called "communist" by the landowners and government officials, who crushed them with superior military force.

The greater freedom of movement that came with independence, the progressive disappearance of indigenous communities, and the growth of the hacienda, in which natives mingled with mestizos, strengthened a trend toward acculturation that had begun in the late colonial period. This acculturation was reflected in a growth of bilingualism: indigenous peoples increasingly used Spanish in dealing with whites, reserving their native languages for use among themselves. To the limited extent that public schools entered their regions, they contributed to the adoption of Spanish as a second language or sometimes led to total abandonment of their native tongues. Mexican historian Eduardo Ruiz recalled that as a child he spoke only Tarascan but had forgotten it during his twelve years of study at the colegio. "I did not want to remember, I must confess, because I was ashamed of being thought to be an Indian." Some acculturation also occurred in dress, with frequent abandonment of regional fashions in favor of a quasi-European style, sometimes enforced by legislation and fines. Over much of Mexico, for example, the white trousers and shirt of coarse cotton cloth and the broad-brimmed hat became almost a native "uniform."

Yet pressures toward indigenous acculturation or assimilation failed to achieve integration into "white" society that well-meaning liberals had hoped to secure through education and employment in the modern world of industry and trade. At the end of the nineteenth century, the processes of acculturation had not significantly reduced the size of the indigenous sector in the five countries with the largest native populations: Mexico, Guatemala, Ecuador, Peru, and Bolivia. There were various reasons for this. The economic stagnation and political troubles of the first postrevolutionary decades tended to reinforce the isolation and cultural separateness of their communities. When the Latin American economies revived as a result of the expansion of the export sector, this revival was achieved largely at the expense of indigenous peoples and served mainly to accentuate their poverty and backwardness. Their economic marginality; their almost total exclusion from the political process; the intense exploitation to which they were subjected by white and mestizo landowners, priests, and officials; and the barriers of distrust and hatred that separated them from the white world prevented any thoroughgoing acculturation, much less integration.

Indigenous communities made such concessions to the pressures for assimilation as were necessary but preserved their traditional housing, diet, social organization, and religion, which combined pagan and Christian features. In some regions, the pre-Conquest cults and rituals, including occasional human sacrifice, survived. The existence in a number of countries of large native populations, intensely exploited and branded as inferior by the ruling social Darwinist ideology, constituted a major obstacle to the formation of a national consciousness in those lands. With good reason, pioneer Mexican anthropologist Manuel Gamio wrote in 1916 that Mexico did not constitute a nation in the European sense but was composed of numerous small nations, differing in speech, economy, social organization, and psychology.

## A QUESTION OF COLOR

The wars for independence, by throwing "careers open to talent," enabled a few natives and a larger number of mestizos of humble origins to rise high on the military, political, and social scale. The liberal caudillos Vicente Guerrero and Juan Alvarez in Mexico and such talented leaders as Juan José Flores of Ecuador, Andrés Santa Cruz of Bolivia, and Ramón Castilla of Peru illustrate the ascent of mixed-race people.

The rise of these mestizo or mulatto leaders inspired fears in some members of the creole elite, beginning with Bolívar, who gloomily predicted a race war that would also be a struggle between haves and have-nots. Bolívar revealed his obsessive race prejudice in his description of the valiant and generous Mexican patriot Vicente Guerrero as the "vile abortion of a savage Indian and a fierce African." These fears proved groundless; although some mixed-race leaders, like Guerrero and Alvarez, remained to one degree or another loyal to the humble masses from which they had sprung, the majority were soon co-opted by the creole aristocracy and firmly defended its interests.

On the other hand, creole politicians of the postrevolutionary era had to take account of the new political weight of the mixed-race middle and lower classes, especially the artisan groups. They were exploited politically by white elites who promised to satisfy the aspirations of the masses, promises they failed to fulfill. This happened in Bogotá, where Colombian liberals courted the artisans in their struggle against conservatives, and in Buenos Aires, where Rosas demagogically identified himself with the mixed-race gauchos and urban artisans against the aristocratic liberal *unitarios*.

After mid-century, the growing influence of European racist ideologies, especially Spencerian biological determinism, led to a heightened sensitivity to color. From Mexico to Chile, members of the so-called white elite and even the middle class claimed to be superior to natives and mestizos. Dark skin increasingly became an obstacle to social advancement. Typical of the rampant pseudoscientific racism by the turn of the century was the remark of the Argentine Carlos Bunge, son of a German immigrant, that mestizos and mulattos were "impure, atavistically anti-Christian; they are like the two heads of a fabulous hydra that surrounds, constricts, and strangles with its giant spiral a beautiful, pale virgin, Spanish America."

As a rule, neither liberals nor conservatives were free from the pervasive racism of the time. Carried away by his enthusiasm for "civilization," which he identified with the European bourgeois order and white supremacy, the Argentine liberal Sarmiento proclaimed: "It may appear unjust to exterminate savages, destroy nascent civilizations, conquer peoples who occupy land that is rightly theirs, but thanks to this injustice America, instead of being abandoned to savages who are incapable of progress, is today occupied by the Caucasian race, the most perfect, intelligent, beautiful, and progressive of all the races that inhabit the earth." A handful of Latin American intellectuals dissented from such a view. One was the Chilean Bilbao, who condemned "the great hypocrisy of covering up every crime and outrage with the word *civilization*" and pointedly referred to Sarmiento's war against native peoples and gauchos. Another was the Cuban José Martí, who denounced "the pretext that 'civilization,' the name commonly given to the present state of Europe, has the natural right to seize the land of 'barbarians,' the name given by those who hunger for other people's land to everyone who is not European or of European descent."

Even before the revolutions, black slavery had declined in various parts of Latin America. This occurred in part because of economic developments that made slavery unprofitable and favored manumission or commutation of slavery to tenantry. An even more significant reason, perhaps, was the frequent flight of slaves to remote jungles and mountains, where they formed self-governing communities. In Venezuela, in about 1800, it was estimated that alongside some eighty-seven thousand slaves there were twenty-four thousand fugitive slaves.

The wars of independence gave a major stimulus to emancipation. Patriot commanders like Bolívar and San Martín and royalist officers often offered slaves freedom in return for military service, and black slaves sometimes formed a majority of the fighting forces on both sides. About a third of San Martín's army in the campaign of the Andes was black. Moreover, the confusion and disorder produced by the fighting often led to a collapse of plantation discipline, easing the flight of slaves and making their recovery difficult if not impossible.

After independence, slavery further declined, partly because of its patent incompatibility with the libertarian ideals proclaimed by the new states but even more as a result of the hostile attitude of Great Britain, which had abolished the slave trade in all its possessions in 1807 and henceforth brought pressure for similar action by all countries still trading in slaves: we have seen that British pressure on Brazil contributed to the crisis of Brazilian slavery and its ultimate demise.

Emancipation came most easily and quickly in countries where slaves were a negligible element in the labor force; thus, Chile, Mexico, and the Federation of Central America (1823–1839) abolished slavery between 1823 and 1829. In other countries, the slave owners fought a tenacious rear-guard action. In Venezuela a very gradual manumission law was adopted in 1821, but not until 1854 was slavery finally abolished. Slavery was abolished in Peru in 1855 by Ramón Castilla. The Spanish Cortes decreed the end of slavery in Puerto Rico in 1873 and in Cuba in 1880, but in Cuba the institution continued in a disguised form (the *patronato*) until 1886, when it was finally abolished.

The record of Latin American slavery in the nineteenth century, it should be noted, does not support the thesis of some historians that cultural and religious factors made Hispanic slavery inherently milder than the North American variety. In its two main centers of Cuba and Brazil, under conditions of mounting demand for Brazilian coffee and Cuban sugar and a critical labor shortage, there is ample evidence of systematic brutality with use of the lash to make slaves work longer and harder. The slaves responded with a resistance that varied from slowdowns to flight to open rebellion—a resistance that contributed to the final demise of the institution.

## The Process of Modernization

### THE LANDOWNERS

Patriarchal family organization, highly ceremonial conduct, and leisurely lifestyle continued to characterize the landed aristocracy and Latin American elites after independence. The kinship network of the large extended family ruled by a patriarch was further extended by the institution of *compadrazgo*, which established a relationship of patronage and protection on the part of an upper-class godparent toward a lower-status godchild and his or her parents. The lower-class family members in turn were expected to form part of the godparent's following and to be devoted to the godparent's interests.

As in colonial times, great landowners generally resided most of the time in the cities, leaving their estates in the charge of administrators (but it must not be assumed that they neglected to scrutinize account books or were indifferent to considerations of profit and loss). From the same upper class came a small minority of would-be entrepreneurs who challenged the traditional agrarian bias of their society and, in the words of Richard Graham, were "caught up by the idea of capitalism, by the belief in industrialization, and by a faith in work and practicality." Typical of this group was the Brazilian Viscount Mauá, who created a banking and industrial empire between 1850 and 1875 against the opposition of traditionalists. Mauá's empire collapsed, however, partly because the objective conditions for capitalist development in Brazil had not fully matured, partly because of official apathy and even disfavor. The day of the entrepreneur had not yet come; the economic history of Latin America in the nineteenth century is strewn with the wrecks of abortive industrial projects. These fiascos also represented defeats for the capitalist mentality and values.

After mid-century, with the gradual rise of a neocolonial order based on the integration of the Latin American economy into the international capitalist system, the ruling class, although retaining certain precapitalist traits, became more receptive to bourgeois values and ideals. An Argentine writer of the 1880s noted that "the latifundist no longer has that semibarbarous, semifeudal air; he has become a scientific administrator, who alternates between his home on the estate, his Buenos Aires mansion, and his house in Paris." In fact, few estancieros or hacendados became "scientific administrators." They preferred to leave the task of managing their estates to others, but the writer accurately pointed to a process of modernization or Europeanization of elites under way throughout the continent.

The process began right after independence but greatly accelerated after mid-century. Within a decade after independence, marked changes in manners and consumption patterns had occurred. "Fashions alter," wrote Fanny Calderón de la Barca, Scottish-born wife of the Spanish minister to Mexico, who described Mexican upper-class society in the age of Santa Anna in a series of sprightly letters. "The graceful mantilla gradually gives place to the ungraceful bonnet. The old painted coach, moving slowly like a caravan, with Guido's Aurora painted on its gaudy panels, is dismissed for the London-built carriage."

The old yielded much more slowly and grudgingly to the new in drowsy colonial cities like Quito, capital of Ecuador, but yield it did, at least in externals. The U.S. minister to Ecuador in the 1860s, Friedrich Hassaurek, who was harshly critical of Quitonian society and manners, noted that "in spite of the difficulty of transportation, there are about one hundred and twenty pianos in Quito, very indifferently tuned." Another U.S. visitor to Quito in this period, Professor James Orton, observed that "the upper class follow *la mode de*

These fine sketches of Colombian mestizo farmers and upper-class figures effectively make the point that in nineteenth-century Latin America, clothes still made the man. [Carmelo Fernandez, *Mestizo Farmers of Anis, Ocana Province, Colombia*, 1850–59, watercolor, Biblioteca Nacional de Colombia, Bogotá]

*Paris*, gentlemen adding the classic cloak of Old Spain." He added sourly that "this modern toga fits an Ecuadoran admirably, preventing the arms from doing anything, and covers a multitude of sins, especially pride and poverty."

Under the republic, as in colonial times, dress was an important index of social status. According to Orton, "no gentleman will be seen walking in the streets of Quito under a poncho. Hence citizens are divided into men with ponchos and gentlemen with cloaks." Dress even served to distinguish followers of different political factions or parties. In Buenos Aires under Rosas, the artisans who formed part of

the dictator's mass base were called *gente de chaqueta* (wearers of jackets), as opposed to the aristocratic unitarian liberals, who wore dress coats. In the army of Urquiza, Rosas's conqueror, a gaucho army like that of Rosas, the only Argentine officer dressed as a European was Sarmiento, a strange sight in his frock coat and kepi (a French military cap) among the gauchos with their lances and ponchos. For Sarmiento, writes John Lynch, "it was a matter of principle, a protest against barbarism, against Rosas and the caudillos. . . . 'As long as we do not change the dress of the Argentine soldier,' said Sarmiento, 'we are bound to have caudillos.'"

By the close of the century, European styles of dress had triumphed in such great cities as Mexico City and Buenos Aires and among all except native peoples. Attitudes toward clothes continued to reflect aristocratic values, especially scorn for manual labor; dress still made the man. In Buenos Aires, for example, at the turn of the century, a worker's blouse would bar the entrance of its wearer to a bank or the halls of Congress. As a result, according to James Scobie, "everyone sought to hide the link with manual labor," and even workingmen preferred to wear the traditional coat and tie.

## THE IMMIGRANTS

After 1880 there was a massive influx of European immigrants into Argentina, Uruguay, and Brazil and of lesser numbers into such countries as Chile and Mexico. Combined with growing urbanization and continued expansion of the export sector, this helped accelerate the rate of social change. These developments helped create a small, modern industrial working class and swelled the ranks of blue-collar and middle-class white-collar workers.

But aside from that minority of the working class that adopted socialist, anarchist, or syndicalist doctrines, the immigrants posed no threat to the existing social structure or the prevailing aristocratic ideology; instead, many were conquered by that ideology. The foreigners who entered the upper class as a rule already belonged to the educated or managerial class. Movement from the middle class of immigrant origin to the upper class was extremely difficult and rare; for the lower-class immigrant it was almost impossible. A few immigrants made their fortunes by commerce or speculation. Their children or grandchildren took care to camouflage the origins of their wealth and to make it respectable by investing it in land. These nouveaux riches regarded natives and workers with the same contempt as their aristocratic associates.

## WOMEN

Independence did not better the status of women. Indeed, their civil status probably worsened as a result of new bourgeois-style law codes that strengthened husbands' control over their wives' property. More than ever, women were relegated to the four walls of their houses and household duties. Church and parents taught women to be submissive, sweetly clinging, to have no wills of their own. Typical of the patriarchal attitudes that prevailed with regard to relations between the sexes was the advice that the Colombian Mariano Ospina Rodríguez gave in an 1864 letter to his daughter Maria on the eve of her marriage to José Mariano Roma y Batres. "Your happiness depends . . . on the sincere and constant practice of these modest virtues: humility, patience, resignation, abnegation, and . . . the proper conduct of the domestic relations that depend on those same Christian virtues." Mariano Ospina went on to caution his daughter: "One of your first cares must be to study your husband's inclinations, habits, and tastes, so that you never contradict them. Never seek to impose your will or make him give up his habits or tastes, no matter how insignificant they may seem; on the contrary, act in such a manner that he may continue them without disturbance. . . . Frequently you will find that you have different tastes and habits; never hesitate for a moment to sacrifice your own tastes and habits in favor of his." The double standard of sexual conduct prevailed; women were taught to deny their sexuality and believe that procreation was the sole end of sexual intercourse. But women's actual conduct did not necessarily conform to the law and ideology. Silvia Arróm has shown, for example, that the restrictions did not deter women in early nineteenth-century Mexico from engaging in extramarital affairs.

Few Latin American women of the elite class, however, strayed so far beyond the bounds of propriety as did Flora Tristán (1803–1844), pioneer feminist and socialist. Daughter of an aristocratic Peruvian landowner and a French mother, she spent most of her life in France, but Peruvian feminists and socialists regard her as one of their own. A woman of striking beauty, she separated early from her husband and became active in French feminist and socialist circles. In 1835 she published a novel, *Méphis*, which proposed the transformation of society on socialist and feminist principles, and in 1840 *Promenades in London*, a description of the monstrous contrasts between wealth and poverty in the English metropolis. In her last book, *The Workers' Union* (1844), she called on "the working men and women of the world" to unite, anticipating by four years Marx's appeal in *The Communist Manifesto*. Tristán clearly identified the gendered layers of exploitation. " The most oppressed male can oppress another human being who is his own wife," she wrote. "Woman is the proletariat of the proletariat." She also presaged theoretical formulations of twentieth-century feminists by arguing that "the liberation of women is the necessary condition for the liberation of men."

The democratic, liberal movements of the first half-century after independence stimulated some developments in favor of women. In Argentina, Sarmiento wrote that "the level of civilization of a people can be judged by the social position of its women"; his educational program envisaged a major role for women as primary-school teachers. In Mexico, the triumph of the Reforma was followed by promulgation of a new school law that called for the establishment of secondary schools for girls and normal schools for the training of women primary-school teachers. In both countries after 1870 there arose small feminist movements, largely composed of schoolteachers, that formed societies, edited journals, and worked for the cultural, economic, and social improvement of women.

Even in a backward slave society like Brazil, there arose a women's rights press, pioneered by Joana Paula Manso de Noronha, who stated in the introductory editorial to *O Jornal das Senhoras* (1852) her intention to work for "social betterment and the moral emancipation of women." In the last decades of the century, with the development of industry, women in increasing numbers entered factories and sweatshops, where they often were paid half of what male workers earned, becoming a source of superprofits for capitalist employers. By 1887, according to the census of Buenos Aires, 39 percent of the paid work force of that city was composed of women.

## THE CHURCH

The church, which in some countries had suffered discredit because of the royalist posture of many clergy during the wars of independence, experienced a further decline in influence as a result of increasing contacts with the outside world and a new and relatively tolerant climate of opinion. In country after country, liberals pressed with varying success for restrictions on the church's monopoly over education, marriage, burials, and the like. Because the church invariably aligned itself with the conservative opposition, liberal victories brought reprisals in the form of heavy attacks on its accumulated wealth and privileges.

The colonial principle of monolithic religious unity was early shattered by the need to allow freedom of worship to the prestigious and powerful British merchants. It was, in fact, the reactionary Rosas, who disliked foreigners and brought the Jesuits back to Argentina, who donated the land on which the first Anglican church in Buenos Aires was built. Despite the efforts of some fanatical clergy to incite the populace against foreign heretics, there gradually evolved a system of peaceful coexistence between Catholics and dissenters, based on reciprocal goodwill and tact.

The Inquisition, whose excesses had made it odious even to the faithful, disappeared during the wars of independence. In many countries, however, the civil authorities assumed its right to censor or ban subversive or heretical writings. Occasionally, governments exercised this right. In the 1820s clerical and conservative opposition forced the liberal vice president of Gran Colombia, Francisco de Paula Santander, to authorize the dropping of a textbook by the materialist Jeremy Bentham from law school courses. In Buenos Aires, under Rosas, subversive books and other materials were publicly burned. According to Tulio Halperin-Donghi, however, a reading of the press advertisements of Buenos Aires booksellers suggests that this repression was singularly ineffective. In Santiago in the 1840s, Francisco Bilbao's fiery polemic against Spain and Catholicism was burned by the public hangman. According to Sarmiento, however, it was not the content of

Bilbao's book but its violent, strident tone that caused this reaction; Bilbao, he added, had been justly punished for his clumsiness.

After mid-century, with the enthronement of positivism, which glorified science and rejected theology as an approach to truth, efforts to suppress heretical or anticlerical writings diminished or ended completely in many countries. In general, during the last half of the nineteenth century, there existed in Latin America a relatively free market in ideas—free, that is, as long as these ideas were couched in theoretical terms or referred primarily to other parts of the world and were not directed against an incumbent regime. Governments were often quick to suppress and confiscate newspapers and pamphlets whose contents they considered dangerous to their security, but they remained indifferent to the circulation of books containing the most audacious social theories. By way of example, the Díaz dictatorship in Mexico struck at opposition journalists and newspapers but permitted the free sale and distribution of the writings of Marx and anarchist theoretician Peter Kropotkin.

As a result of the ascendancy of positivism, the church suffered a further decline in influence and power. Conservative victories over liberalism sometimes produced a strong pro-clerical reaction, typified by Gabriel García Moreno, who ruled Ecuador from 1860 to 1875 and carried his fanaticism to the point of dedicating the republic to the Sacred Heart of Jesus. Rafael Núñez, dictator of Colombia from 1880 to 1894, drafted a concordat with the Vatican that restored to the church most of the rights it had enjoyed in colonial times. But such victories failed to arrest the general decline of the church's social and intellectual influence among the literate classes. Anticlericalism became an integral part of the ideology of most Latin American intellectuals and a large proportion of other upper-class and middle-class males, including many who were faithful churchgoers and observed the outward forms and rituals of the church. But church influence continued to be strong among women of all classes, indigenous peoples, and the submerged groups generally.

# The Romantic Revolt

The achievement of political independence did not end Latin American cultural dependence on Spain and Portugal. The effort of Latin American writers to find their own means of self-expression, to create national literatures, fused with the larger effort to liquidate the Hispanic colonial heritage in politics, economics, and social life. Thus, Latin American literature was from the first a literature of struggle; the concept of art for art's sake had little meaning for the writers of the first half-century after independence. Many writers were also statesmen and even warriors, alternately using pen and sword in the struggle against tyranny and backwardness. This unity of art and politics is expressed by the famous comment of Ecuadoran essayist and polemicist Juan Montalvo when he learned that the dictator García Moreno had been assassinated; "*Mi pluma lo mató*" ("My pen killed him"). That unity found its most perfect embodiment in the Cuban José Martí, who devoted himself almost from childhood to the struggle against Spanish rule in Cuba and died in 1895 in action against Spanish troops. He also blazed new trails in Latin American poetry and prose.

Latin American writers took the first step toward literary independence by breaking with Hispanic classic traditions and adopting as their models the great French and English poets and novelists of the romantic school. Romanticism, which Sarmiento once defined as "a true literary insurrection, like the political uprising that preceded it," seemed peculiarly appropriate for the achievement of the tasks the revolutionary young writers of Latin America had set themselves.

Victory over classicism, however, did not come without a struggle. In 1842 a famous debate took place in Chile between the Venezuelan Andrés Bello, conservative arbiter of literary taste, and the Argentine Domingo Sarmiento, who upheld a democratic freedom of expression and the superiority of contemporary French literature over all others. Their opposition was by no means absolute, for Bello was not a true reactionary in politics or literature. A distinguished poet, scholar, and educator, he had made major contributions to the development of Hispanic culture. His Spanish grammar, published in 1857, ended the domination of Latin grammatical rules and forms over the language and won acceptance by the Spanish Academy. His poem "The Agriculture of the Torrid Zone," despite its classic form, stimulated the rise of literary Americanism.

But Bello had a conservative's love for order and decorum and regarded himself as a guardian of the purity of the Castilian language. He was shocked when Sarmiento, in a review of a recently published grammar, wrote that "teachers of grammar are useless, for people learn by practical example and general discussion . . . the people are the real creators of a language, while grammarians are only the maintainers of tradition and compilers of dictionaries." Writing in a conservative journal, Bello retorted with praise of linguistic purity and academic standards; it would make as little sense, he wrote, to allow the people to make their own laws as to permit them to dictate the forms of their language. Sarmiento countered with an ardent defense of democracy in language and style. Bello, who disliked polemics, soon withdrew from the fray, but his disciples continued the debate.

Before the controversy ended, Sarmiento had silenced his opponents and converted Bello's chief disciple, José Victorino Lastarria, to his own beliefs. Romanticism soon triumphed everywhere, but Latin American romanticism was not a simple carbon copy of the European original; it bore its own vigorous stamp, displayed its own distinctive character.

## Romanticism in Argentine Writing

By no coincidence, Esteban Echeverría, the founder of Argentine romanticism, gave the name *Dogma socialista (Socialist Teaching)* to his first important writing, in which *socialism* stood for a nebulous concept of the primacy of the general interest of society over individual interests. "Association, progress, liberty, equality, fraternity: these sum up the great social and humanitarian synthesis; these are the divine symbols of the happy future of nations and of humanity." By the time *Dogma socialista* was published in 1839,

Echeverría had been forced by the Rosas terror to flee from Buenos Aires to Montevideo, where a group of young exiles combined literary activity with plots to overthrow the Rosas regime.

In his short prose masterpiece *The Slaughterhouse* (published posthumously but probably written about 1840), Echeverría rejects one element of European romanticism: its idealized view of the common people. With unsparing realism, he describes the repellent sights and smells of a slaughterhouse that is also a gathering place of the Mazorca, the band of thugs who terrorize Rosas's enemies. The story is also a political allegory: the slaughterhouse, with its butchers in gaucho dress and the black and mulatto women who carry away entrails, empty stomachs and bladders, and wade in blood, is a symbol of Rosas's Argentina, in which barbarous lower-class elements are given a free hand to torture and kill. The climax of the story comes when the butchers intercept a passing unitarian, a young man who wears stylish European dress and has his beard cut in the shape of a U. They tie him up, taunt him, and prepare to beat him. He scornfully replies to their taunts, breaks loose with a supreme effort, and dies from a hemorrhage before their very eyes. In the words of Arturo Torres-Rioseco, "the whole story is a sombre and terrible vignette, against a background of howling curs, bedraggled Negresses, circling vultures— a slaughterhouse that represents the real *matadero* [slaughterhouse] tyranny of Rosas."

A few years after Echeverría's death in 1851, another Argentine émigré, José Marmol, began to publish in serial form in Montevideo the first Argentine novel, *Amalia*. Again, as in *The Slaughterhouse*, literature and political attack fuse. The young unitarian Eduardo Belgrano tries to escape from his federalist pursuers; he takes refuge in the house of the widowed Amalia, and the two fall deeply in love. But the dictator's secret police discover Eduardo's hiding place and kill the lovers. Despite a stilted style and the artificiality of some of the characters, its intensity of feeling and the vivid descriptions of various social types and life in Buenos Aires lend portions of the book a genuine power.

Another exile from Rosas's Argentina, Domingo Sarmiento, illustrated his artistic theories in his formless masterpiece, *Life of Juan Facundo Quiroga: Civilization and Barbarism* (1845). Sarmiento offers a geographical and sociological interpretation of Argentine history, showing how the pampa had molded the character and lifestyle of the gauchos, the mass base of the Rosas dictatorship and the petty caudillos who ruled under him. From this tough, self-reliant breed of men springs the "hero" of Sarmiento's book, the provincial caudillo Facundo. Facundo was master of the Argentine western provinces and Rosas's lieutenant until the greater tyrant, who brooked no rival, had him ambushed and killed.

The ambiguity of Sarmiento's posture toward the gaucho—condemnation tempered by recognition of his admirable qualities—gave way to total defense and vindication of the gaucho and his values in the climactic work of gaucho literature, the epic poem *The Gaucho Martín Fierro* (1872) of José Hernández. Written some thirty years after Sarmiento's *Facundo*, its poignant, nostalgic mood reflects the uprooting of the old patriarchal estancia, the unfenced pampa, and the freedom of the gaucho's life by triumphant bourgeois "civilization" championed by Sarmiento. Hernández, a federalist who opposed Mitre and Sarmiento, supported the revolt of the last untamed gaucho chieftain, General López Jordán, and believed the city, the seat of the central government, was exploiting and strangling the countryside. He portrayed the gaucho as a victim of the forces of "civilization"— judges, recruiting officers, corrupt police. The poem is strongly influenced by the folk songs of the gaucho *payador* (minstrel) and makes restrained but effective use of gaucho dialect.

## MEXICAN NATIONAL LITERATURE

The beginnings of a Mexican national literature are linked to the founding in 1836 of the Academy of Letrán, an informal literary circle whose members met to talk of literature or listen to readings of poetry and prose. Here, according to Mexican literary historian González Peña, "was incubated the generation which later filled half a century of the history of Mexican literature." One of its founders, Guillermo Prieto, wrote that "the great and transcendent significance of the Academy was its decided tendency to 'Mexicanize' our literature, emancipating it from all other literatures and giving it a specific character." Prieto also noted that the academy "democratized literary studies, recognizing merit without regard to social position, wealth, or any other considerations." The effort to create a Mexican literature was closely linked to the struggle for political and social reform. Most major Mexican literary figures of the first half-century after independence—such men as Guillermo Prieto, Ignacio Altamirano, and Ignacio Ramírez—took an active part in that struggle.

The most serious effort to create a national Mexican literature was made by Ignacio Altamirano, like his comrade-in-arms Benito Juárez, born of indigenous parents. Believing that Mexican poetry and literature should be as completely original as "are our soil, our mountains, our generation," Altamirano rejected the imitation of foreign models. He attempted to offer an example of such originality in his novel *Clemencia* (1869), set in the period of the French intervention. More successful, because of its fresh, unpretentious descriptions of life in a small Mexican village, was his *Christmas in the Mountains* (1870).

From the Academy of Letrán also issued a school of romantic poetry whose most remarkable creation was the "Prophecy of Cuauhtemoc" (1839) by Ignacio Rodríguez Galván. The poem sounds some major themes of Mexican romanticism: nationalism, anti-Spanish sentiment, and the glorification of pre-Cortesian Mexico. The magnificent coloring of the poem, its authentic romantic agony, the restless alternation in the poet's mind between thoughts of his personal sorrow and the woes of his people, make it, in the words of Menéndez y Pelayo, "the masterpiece of Mexican romanticism."

## CHILEAN WRITERS

Chile lagged behind some of the other republics in the development of a national literature, perhaps— as Sarmiento suggested in his duel with Bello—

The Chilean writer Francisco Bilbao was an activist intellectual and radical democrat whose literary works denounced equally slavery, the Catholic church, U.S. expansionism, and racist assaults on indigenous peoples. [Frontispiece for *Obras Completas*, 1897]

own way promoted the ideal of Chilean cultural emancipation.

Francisco Bilbao threw a bombshell into staid Santiago society with his essay "The Nature of Chilean Society" (1844), in which he declared: "Slavery, degradation: that is the past. . . . Our past is Spain. Spain is the Middle Ages. The Middle Ages are composed, body and soul, of Catholicism and feudalism." Later (1856), in *America in Danger*, Bilbao issued a powerful cry of warning to Latin America to unite under a regime of freedom and democracy. He sounded a special alarm against the expansionist designs of the United States in Latin America. In *The American Gospel* (1864), he offered much the same message: Latin America must throw off its Hispanic heritage of repression and obscurantism, and it must adopt rationalism rather than Catholicism as its guide if the Disunited States of Latin America were to achieve the place the United States had gained among the nations of the earth.

Lastarria, more moderate and scholarly than Bilbao, caused a lesser stir with his address, "Investigations of the Social Influence of the Conquest and the Colonial System of the Spaniards in Chile" (1844). Despite an occasional factual error, it remains an effective summary of the liberal case against the Spanish colonial regime. Andrés Bello undertook to review it. Conceding the general correctness of Lastarria's criticism of Spanish policy and work in Latin America, he offered a partial defense that stressed the mildness of Spanish rule and its civilizing mission in the New World. Whereas Bilbao was profoundly influenced by French left-wing republican and utopian socialist ideas, Lastarria's thought reflected the more conservative positivist teachings of the French philosopher Auguste Comte. Like Bilbao, however, Lastarria waged a consistent struggle against the backwardness he identified with Spanish civilization, which he felt was "the principal cause of our political and social disasters. . . . We cannot remedy these disasters except by reacting frankly, openly, and energetically against that civilization, in order to free our minds and adapt our country to the new form, democracy."

because the absolute sway of Bello's classicist doctrines had created inertia, or perhaps because the relative stability of Chilean politics and the upward movement of the Chilean economy deprived its writers of the spur that the more dramatic contrasts of Argentine and Mexican life gave to creative literary activity. But if Chile lacked a Sarmiento or an Echeverría, it produced, in José Victorino Lastarria and Francisco Bilbao, two major writers on sociological topics who in their

## BRAZILIAN ROMANTIC LITERATURE

A strong nationalism characterized the Brazilian romantic literature of the first decades after independence. In contrast with the Argentine writers of the same period, Brazilian writers expressed their nationalism in glorification of the indigenous past. This reflected differences in the historical experience of the two countries: Brazilian natives had long ceased to pose a serious threat to white society, and mixed-race peoples were common in Brazilian society. The celebration of its indigenous past, moreover, represented an effort to find roots for Brazilian nationalism, roots that could not be found in Portugal or Europe generally.

The greatest romantic poet of the first generation was Antônio Gonçalves Dias, whose ancestry included Portugal, Africa, and indigenous Brazil. Basing himself on a careful study of native languages and culture, Gonçalves Dias conjured up the image of indigenous defeat with extraordinary emotive power in his *American Poems* (1846) and in the narrative poem "The Timbiras" (1857). He also celebrated the beauty of the Brazilian landscape in poems like the nostalgic "Song of Exile" (1846), which opens with the line: "My land has palm trees where the sabiá sings."

This identification with native traditions also found expression in the novels of José de Alencar, whose two most popular novels, *Iracema* (1865) and *The Guarani* (1856), deal with the theme of love between native and Portuguese. Despite the improbable plots and the sentimentality and artificiality of the dialogue and characters, Alencar's limpid, poetic style successfully evokes, somewhat in the manner of James Fenimore Cooper, the drama of the clash of indigenous and European cultures and the grandeur of the Brazilian wilderness, with its majestic rivers, dense forests, and great waterfalls.

After the optimistic nationalism of the first generation of Brazilian romantic poets came the introspection, pessimism, and escapism of the second generation, which perhaps were a reaction to the defeat of the republican revolts of the 1830s and 1840s. In sharp contrast to these second-generation poets, who appeared to be sensitive to their own sufferings and misfortunes only, Antônio de Castro Alves devoted his poetic talent above all to the struggle against slavery. Because of his lofty, impassioned style, he is known as the founder of the *condoreira*, or condor school of poetry. Castro Alves's verses, read at countless abolitionist meetings and frequently published in the abolitionist press, gave a major stimulus to the growth of the abolitionist and republican movements in Brazil.

In 1867, Latin American romanticism, already in decline, produced its finest prose flower, the delicate love story *María* by the Colombian Jorge Isaacs. The story is set in a patriarchal country estate in the Cauca River Valley. Told in a simple, elegiac style, pervaded by a mood of gentle nostalgia, it relates the unfolding of an idyllic romance between a landowner's son and his cousin María. The story ends tragically when María dies during her lover's absence in London.

## THE HISTORICAL NOVEL

The romantic movement yielded an abundant harvest of historical novels, most of which dealt with episodes from the Spanish Conquest and the colonial era. Often their authors seemed chiefly concerned with exposing Spanish cruelty and the horrors of the Inquisition. Whether or not faithful to the historical facts, they generally lacked originality, talent, and psychological realism.

In 1872, however, Ricardo Palma began to publish his ironic and sparkling evocations of colonial Lima, *The Peruvian Traditions* (1872–1906). With these "traditions," Palma created a new genre: "a short sketch that was not history, anecdote, or satire, but a distillation of all three." Drawing on his immense knowledge of the colonial period (he was director of the National Library of Peru during the latter part of his life), Palma applied his own formula for the traditions: "a little bit, and quite a little bit of lying, a dose of the truth be it ever so infinitesimal, and a great deal of nicety and gloss in the style." From these elements Palma spun a long succession of cheerfully malicious tales that played on the follies and frailties of viceroys, priests, and highborn ladies as well as lesser folk. Palma's "traditions" evoked the past far more successfully than the typical historical novel of this period.

# Literature and Social Change, 1880–1910

By 1880 the romantic movement in Latin American literature had almost completed its tasks and exhausted its creative possibilities. As a result of the economic and political changes that we have surveyed, a new social reality had arisen. The growth of industry, immigration, and urbanization gave a new face to Latin American society. The ruling classes were increasingly acquisitive, arrogant, and philistine; the condition of the masses had not improved and may even have deteriorated. Latin America had become more European; in the process, it had failed to solve some old problems and had acquired some new ones.

In conformity with the specific conditions of their countries and their own backgrounds, writers responded to the new environment in a variety of ways. Generally speaking, romanticism survived as a vital force only in those countries where the old problems had not been solved. (Examples are Ecuador, the scene of a bitter struggle between liberals and conservatives, and Cuba, whose struggle for independence did not reach its climax until the 1890s.)

## POETRY AND MODERNISM

In poetry, the most important new phenomenon was the movement called modernism. Because the movement comprises an immense variety of stylistic and ideological tendencies, it is difficult to define. The common feature of modernist poets, however, was their search for new expressive means, for new stylistic forms, in reaction against the outworn language and forms of romanticism. The artistic creed of many modernist poets included rejection of literature as an instrument of social and political struggle. Turning their backs on "a world they never made," the world of shoddy and unstable prosperity ruled, in Rubén Darío's

words, by *el rey burgués* (the bourgeois king), these escapists sought refuge in the ivory tower of art.

Most escapist of all was the prodigiously gifted Nicaraguan Rubén Darío (1867–1916), who defined modernism as the rejection of any explicit message in art; stress on beauty as the highest value (in Darío's poems, the swan is the recurrent symbol of beauty as an end in itself); and the determination to free verse from the tyranny of traditional forms. Not unexpectedly, in view of their conception of the artist as an outcast from bourgeois society, bohemianism, alcohol, and drugs were elements in the lifestyle of many escapist poets, and not a few came to tragically early ends.

In their effort to achieve a renovation of poetry (and prose as well), the modernists drew on a variety of foreign sources (French Parnassianism, impressionism, symbolism; Whitman and Poe; Spain's medieval ballads). But they did not imitate; they appropriated these foreign methods for the creation of poetry and prose that were "entirely new, new in form and vocabulary and subject matter and feeling."

Escapism was a major current of modernism but not the only one. Indeed, before the movement had run its course, some of the leading escapist poets had risen to a new awareness of the continent's social and political problems and the writer's responsibility to the people. Darío himself exemplifies this evolution. If in the first, escapist phase of his poetic career he peopled his verses with satyrs, nymphs, centaurs, peacocks, and swans, in its second phase he gave voice to a powerful public poetry that reflected his new Americanism and concern with political and social themes. Darío's Americanism led him to a search for symbols in both the Spanish and the indigenous past, regarded as the sources of a Latin American culture threatened by the aggressive expansionism of the United States.

Literary critics dispute whether the Cuban José Martí was a precursor of modernism or one of its major figures and creators. Certainly, his spirit was alien to the escapist tendency of many modernist poets. Far from seeking refuge in an ivory tower, he dedicated his life to the struggle for

Cuban independence; Cubans of all political faiths still call him "the Apostle." Martí's faith in humanity and progress reflected his links to Enlightenment thought, to romanticism, and to the optimistic evolutionism of the late nineteenth century. "I have faith," he wrote in the preface to his first book of verse (1882), "in the improvement of man, in the life of the future, in the utility of virtue." In a time of rampant racism, he denounced race prejudice of every kind.

From 1881 to 1895, Martí lived in exile in New York. As a correspondent for various Latin American newspapers, he wrote a vast number of articles in which he subjected political, economic, and cultural developments in the United States to searching analysis. Martí fervently admired Lincoln, Emerson, Mark Twain, and the abolitionist Wendell Phillips but expressed growing concern over the rise of monopolistic and imperialist tendencies. He especially feared and disliked the Republican leader James G. Blaine, whom he regarded as the chief exponent of North American imperialist designs on Latin America. In 1895 he left the United States to launch the Cuban Revolution. On the day before his death on May 19, 1895, while fighting Spanish troops, he set down his fears concerning U.S. policy toward Cuba: "I know the monster because I have lived in its lair, and my sling is that of David."

Martí's artistic ideas reflected his belief in the organic links between art and society, in the social responsibility of the artist. Art should reflect the joys and sorrows of the masses; in that sense it is a collective product. "Poetry is durable when it is the work of all. Those who understand it are as much its authors as those who make it." Simplicity and directness characterize his poems, but he was capable of using vivid, concrete imagery of great symbolic power. The very simplicity of his verse makes it difficult to render into English. In prose he achieved a genuine stylistic revolution. "The style he achieved," writes Pedro Henríquez-Ureña, "was entirely new to the language. He follows no single rhythmical pattern, but constantly varies it . . . he combines words—and meanings—in many unfamiliar ways. The effect is a constantly varied inter-play of light and color. In style, as well as in what lies beyond style and becomes expression, his power of invention was inexhaustible." Darío said of Martí: "He writes more brilliantly than anyone in Spain or America."

## The Romantic Revolt Continued: Ecuador and Peru

The fires of romantic revolt continued to burn in two Andean republics where small groups of intellectuals battled the rule of reactionary landowners, generals, and the church. In Ecuador, the writer Juan Montalvo, exiled by the fanatical dictator Gabriel García Moreno, leveled polemical attacks against him and claimed credit for García Moreno's assassination. Unhappy with the new rulers of Ecuador, Montalvo spent much of his life in exile from his native country. His *Seven Essays* (1882), reflecting a somewhat old-fashioned liberalism, propose the regeneration of Latin America through the formation of a model elite. His curious *Chapters That Cervantes Forgot*, a continuation of *Don Quijote*, published posthumously, displays Montalvo's virtuosity in the use of sixteenth-century Castilian and expresses his ideas on a wide variety of topics.

The Peruvian writer Manuel González Prada advanced more radical ideas. A member of that generation of Peruvian youth that witnessed with feelings of profound humiliation the swift defeat of their country in the War of the Pacific, he initiated a new era of social unrest and intellectual ferment in Peru. He launched his "prose thunderbolts" against all that was sacrosanct in Peruvian society: the army, the church, the state, the creole aristocracy. In 1886 he founded a *círculo literario* (literary circle) with the declared aim of creating a nationalistic literature of "propaganda and attack." He proclaimed that "the people must be shown the horror of their degradation and misery; a good autopsy was never made without dissecting the body, and no society can be thoroughly known until its skeleton is laid bare."

González Prada made good his promise of dissecting the Peruvian organism by the ferocity of his attacks. Peru, he wrote, was a great boil: "press down anywhere and the pus comes out." He described the Peruvian Congress as a sewer where all the filth of the country had come together. He called for the creation of a vigorous new literature that would deal with national problems; this required writers to reject tradition and forge a new language: "Archaism implies backwardness: show me an archaic writer and I show you a reactionary thinker."

A woman writer who formed part of González Prada's literary circle and shared many of his progressive ideas, Clorinda Matto de Turner (1854–1909), wrote the first protest novel, *Birds Without a Nest* (1889). Set in an indigenous village of the sierra, the novel denounces the abuses committed against natives by the exploitive trinity of judge, priest, and governor. However, its lesson is that the well-being of Peru's indigenous peoples must depend upon the charity and benevolence of well-disposed upper-class whites. With all its weaknesses, however, *Birds Without a Nest* was the forerunner of a genre.

# PART THREE

# Latin America Since 1900

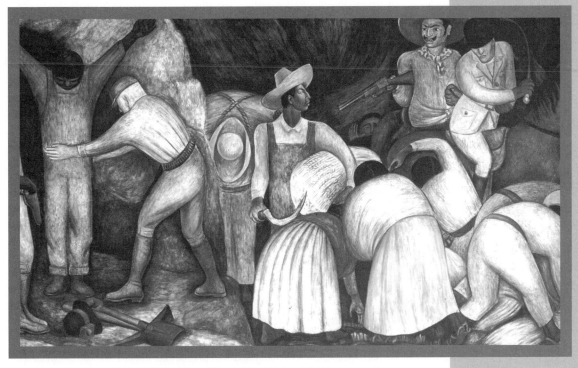

*Los explotatores*, 1926–1927, by Diego Rivera. Mural Universidad Autonoma de Chapingo Chapel, Mexico. Schalkwijk/Art Resource, NY.

UNDERSTANDING THE COMPLEXITY of Latin America's evolution in the twentieth century requires particular attention to the social, political, economic, and cultural histories of each nation and its integration into the international economic order. Throughout this text, we consistently have emphasized both internal and external factors that have shaped and constrained Latin American development. These have included domestic class conflicts; gender, racial, and ethnic struggles; strategic rivalries among the United States and certain European powers; and the shifting demands of international markets.

Internally, the struggle of Latin America's peoples to eliminate neocolonialism and *latifundismo*, the chief obstacles to the achievement of a more just economic and social order, gives meaning and direction to the turbulent flow of modern Latin American history. Viewed in the large, that history, with all its contradictory aspects, its gains and setbacks, appears to form a sequence of stages, each representing a higher level of effort to achieve complete economic and political emancipation. Such an overview inevitably ignores the great differences between the Latin American countries, but it helps make clear the general unity of problems and the common direction of movement of all the Latin American states.

The single most significant external factor in Latin America's twentieth-century development was the emergence of the United States as first a hemispheric and then a global hegemonic power. Its recurrent military, economic, and diplomatic interventions in the region established the international context within which local events unfolded. Changes in the global economy also impacted greatly on Latin America, giving rise to three distinct periods.

## 1900–1930

From 1900 to 1930, a fierce competition among industrially developed capitalist countries for overseas markets led to recurrent imperialist interventions, chiefly by the United States. U.S. and European statesmen and corporate businessmen continued their competition for privileged access to Latin American markets for strategic raw materials, cheap labor, and direct investment. This typically required alliances with traditional latifundistas and the oligarchical or dictatorial governments that protected their interests. It also reinforced late nineteenth-century trends toward urbanization, the decline of independent peasantries and relatively autonomous indigenous communities, and the parallel growth of new national bourgeoisies and a wage-earning working class in which women would play an increasingly decisive role. Throughout the region, market forces steadily eroded traditional barriers between public and private life and doubly exploited women—as menial, poorly paid wage earners and as unpaid labor in the patriarchal household. Simultaneously, these same market forces assaulted the rural, relatively isolated, provincial hinterland and drove a steady stream of migrant workers first to urban slums in search of industrial employment and then as immigrants to new lands.

Not surprisingly, these new social actors sought out political alliances and often joined social protest movements that challenged the power of traditional oligarchs like Porfirio Díaz in Mexico, Cipriano Castro and Juan Vicente Gómez in Venezuela, and Gerardo Machado in Cuba. By the end of this period, these opposition groups, which formed the core constituency of an emerging regional "populism," had taken advantage of the political space created by intra-elite conflicts and international rivalries to demand the creation of a more modern nation-state that would regulate private sector relations in a way that would promote greater economic independence, social justice, and political stability.

The Mexican Revolution of 1910 and the start of World War I offer two points of departure for this period. The revolution swiftly developed into the first major effort in Latin American history to uproot the system of great estates and peonage and curb foreign control of the area's natural resources. The famous constitution of 1917 spelled out this social content of the revolution. In the leadership struggle between agrarian and bourgeois revolutionaries, the latter emerged victorious and adopted a program that subordinated the interests of peasants and workers to the goals of rapid capitalist development. Nonetheless, the determined struggles of Mexico's lower classes made lasting contributions to the construction of a new, modern state that incorporated popular demands for reform and political participation. Moreover, despite discrepancies between its professed social ideals and its practical political-economic achievements, the revolution also unleashed creative energies in art, literature, and the social sciences that gave Mexico a leading role in the cultural life of Latin America.

World War I seriously disrupted the markets for Latin America's goods and placed difficulties in the way of importing needed manufactured products. As a result, some local capital and labor were diverted from agriculture to manufacturing in an effort to supply these goods. Although the postwar period saw some revival of the export economy, declines in the price levels of Latin America's exports encouraged a further growth of manufacturing. But at the end of this period, industrialization was still almost completely limited to light consumer goods industries.

The United States, which emerged from World War I as the world's principal industrial and financial power, soon replaced Great Britain as the major source of foreign investments in Latin America. Continuing the "big stick" and "dollar diplomacy" policies of their predecessors, Democratic and Republican administrations used armed intervention and economic pressure to expand U.S. control over the Caribbean area. By the end of the period, deep Latin American resentment of these strong-arm tactics had forced Republican policy makers to consider a change in dealing with Latin America.

# 1930–1970

In rapid succession, the devastation of the Great Depression and World War II brought substantial changes to the nations of Latin America, the world economic order, and the international balance of power. With the emergence of the United States as a global hegemonic power and the absorption of Japanese and European capitalists in the herculean postwar task of national reconstruction, international competition for access to and control over foreign markets in Latin America diminished, at least temporarily. This left traditional latifundista oligarchies vulnerable to the political challenges of popular movements from below and often required military dictatorships to preserve their interests. As an alternative to these dictatorships, newly emerging national industrial bourgeoisies were forced to join with, or even help mobilize, alienated peasants, militant workers, indigenous peoples, racial minorities, and women's groups to create a new national corporative state committed to an ambiguous notion of collective social justice, the specific elements of which each constituent faction defined differently.

Ultimately, in virtually every Latin American country, these struggles produced a populist state dominated by a new national bourgeoisie. This new state, in turn, typically subsumed a plethora of local class, ethnic, racial, and clientelist identities to fashion a single new national identity, the foundation of which was national private sector industrial and agricultural development that would benefit, however unequally, all domestic social sectors. To secure this objective, these populists typically pursued programs that included limited agrarian reform, greater social welfare expenditures, nationalistic and state-centered economic policies like import substitution and export-led industrialization, and an expansion of citizenship rights among workers, women, and racial minorities.

Naturally, from country to country, the scope and intensity of these populist reforms varied proportionately with the level of internal popular political mobilization and its success in shaping the ideology and practice of the new bourgeoisies that occupied the corridors of power. Nonetheless, without substantial foreign competition, these new rulers could afford to raise wages, pay higher taxes, and submit to otherwise expensive state regulations by passing these higher costs on to consumers through a protected price system. Despite the obvious tensions and contradictions that divided the social constituents of Latin American populism, these developmental strategies often produced dynamic economies that expanded the local working class, simultaneously fortified the power of a sometimes fiercely nationalistic bourgeoisie, and consolidated populist political alliances—even as they reinforced the region's capitalist social structures and long-term dependency on external markets.

The Great Depression dramatically exposed the vulnerability of a neocolonial, monocultural economy: the area's foreign markets collapsed, and the prices of its raw materials and foodstuffs fell much more sharply than those of the manufactured goods it had to import. Latin America's unfavorable balance of trade made necessary exchange controls and other trade restrictions that encouraged the growth of industries to produce goods formerly supplied through importation. World War II, which caused a virtual suspension of imports of manufactured goods, gave further stimulus to the movement for Latin American industrialization.

The nationalist temper of the times also found expression in the formation of state enterprises in such fields as oil exploitation and in efforts to nationalize some foreign-owned utilities and natural resources. The most dramatic example of this trend was the seizure of foreign oil properties in Mexico by President Lázaro Cárdenas in 1938. The new nationalist regimes also made concessions to labor in the form of social legislation but maintained tight control over working-class organizations.

By 1945 the movement for Latin American industrialization could point to some successes. Consumer-goods industries had arisen in all the Latin American republics, and some countries had laid the foundations of heavy industry. Industrial development, however, was everywhere hampered by shortages of capital, lack of advanced technology, and the extremely low purchasing power of the masses. Latin American economists often related these deficiencies to such background conditions as latifundismo and its corollary of wretchedly small farms (minifundismo), widespread disease and illiteracy, and absorption of a large part of the area's economic surplus by foreign investors in the form of dividends, interest, and the like. Meanwhile, aside from the massive assault of Lázaro Cárdenas on the Mexican latifundio, little or nothing was done in the way of agrarian reform.

In the same period, the United States, reacting to the diplomatic and economic losses caused by the old-style imperialism and a wave of "anti-Yanqui" feeling throughout the continent, adopted the Good Neighbor Policy, which proclaimed the principle of nonintervention by one American state in the affairs of another. But the policy represented more of a change in form than in content. Washington's friendly, cooperative relations with such tyrannies as those of Anastasio Somoza in Nicaragua, Rafael Trujillo in the Dominican Republic, and Fulgencio Batista in Cuba ensured a continuance of North American hegemony in the Caribbean. For the rest, the immense economic power of the United States in Latin America, exercised through investments and its role as the area's main trading partner, usually sufficed to obtain approval of its policies in most parts of the continent.

In the new postwar era, the Latin American drive to industrialize continued, but after 1950, with the gradual restoration of competition among the industrially developed capitalist countries, the pace of Latin America's advance slowed and the industrialization process underwent a certain deformation. Perceiving the changes taking place in the Latin American society and economy as a result of industrialization and the growth of urban markets, foreign firms began to shift the bulk of their new investments from agricultural and mining activities to manufacturing. This shift allowed them to leap over tariff walls and penetrate the Latin American market. The immensely superior resources of foreign firms and their advanced technology gave them a great advantage over national companies. The result was that many small and middle-sized national companies failed or were swallowed up by subsidiaries of foreign firms.

A favorite device of foreign economic penetration was the mixed company, dominated by foreign capital, with native capitalists reduced to the role of junior partners or directors. The huge sums exported annually by foreign companies in profits, dividends, and other types of income led to a process of "decapitalization" that slowed down the rate of Latin American capital accumulation and industrial growth.

The failure to reform archaic agrarian structures and improve income distribution also held back industrialization. Indeed, the experience of those countries that had the largest growth of capitalism, such as Brazil and Argentina, suggested that the new industrial and financial oligarchies were as fearful of social change, as prone to come to terms with foreign economic interests, as the old landed aristocracy had been. During the 1950s and 1960s ruling elites in various Central and South American countries increasingly abandoned the populistic, more or less democratic, state-centered, nationalistic strategies of industrialization that earlier had achieved considerable success in modernizing the region.

A similar rightward swing took place in Mexico, where the conservative successors of President Lázaro Cárdenas pursued policies favorable to big business and large landowners but neglected the peasantry. As a result, a new corporate hacienda arose and soon dominated Mexican agriculture. By the end of the 1960s, the once-fashionable hope that a dynamic entrepreneurial class could lead Latin America out of dependence and underdevelopment had largely faded.

Meanwhile, the discontent of the masses, sharpened by the "revolution of rising expectations," continued to erupt in revolts: in 1944, a revolution in Guatemala had established a standard of democracy and social justice against which later popular movements there and throughout Latin America would measure themselves; a spontaneous rising of Bolivian peasants and miners in 1952 similarly demanded political and economic democracy; a 1964 democratic upheaval in Brazil forced a moderate president, João Goulart, to radicalize his policies with a call for nationalization of oil and wholesale land reform; popular mobilizations in Peru led to a reformist military coup in 1968; in the same year, the Latin American Bishops' Conference, announcing its intent to exercise "a preferential option for the poor," introduced the idea of Liberation Theology and, in Mexico, a general protest against authoritarian politics led to the massacre of university students and workers in Tlatelolco Square; urban uprisings, led by Montoneros and Tupamaros, spread throughout the industrial cities of Argentina and Uruguay; and in 1970 a popular coalition of Chilean industrial workers, peasants, women, and students freely elected the first avowedly Marxist president in the hemisphere. But the single most important popular mobilization in the region was the armed struggle begun by Fidel Castro and his comrades against the Cuban dictator Batista in July 1953. Their long guerrilla war ended with the victorious entry of the rebel army into Havana on January 1, 1959.

The victory of the Cuban Revolution, soon transformed into a socialist revolution, marked a turning point in Latin American history. The swift, thoroughgoing Cuban agrarian reform and nationalization of foreign enterprises and the revolution's successes in raising living standards offered Latin America a radical alternative to development along capitalist lines.

Washington responded to the Cuban threat to the old order in Latin America with a variety of tactics. In 1961, President John F. Kennedy proclaimed the establishment of the Alliance for Progress, designed to show that Latin America's social revolution, with U.S. help, could be achieved peacefully within the framework of capitalism. But within a few years, the failure of the corruption-ridden program to achieve structural change was apparent.

Simultaneously, the U.S. government sought to undermine and destroy the Castro regime, first by economic blockade and political isolation and then by a CIA-sponsored effort by Cuban exiles to invade Cuba (1961), an effort that met with a swift and humiliating defeat. The Soviet Union stepped up its flow of arms to Cuba, which led to the Cuban missile crisis (1962). For ten days, a jittery world lived under the threat of nuclear war between the United States and the Soviet Union. The crisis ended with a pledge on the part of the United States not to invade Cuba in return for the withdrawal of Soviet missiles from the island.

Forced to retreat in Cuba, the United States, supported by the old and new Latin American elites fearful of radical social change, redoubled its efforts to prevent a spread of the Cuban "contagion" to other parts of the hemisphere. In 1964 a coalition of reactionary Brazilian military, great landowners, and large capitalists overthrew the mildly progressive government of President João Goulart, whose heresies included a modest program of agrarian and electoral reform. It was succeeded by a heavy-handed military dictatorship that offered large incentives to foreign investors and proclaimed its unswerving loyalty to the United States, which responded with generous financial assistance.

But the movement for structural social change and economic independence proved irrepressible. Nationalist military officers sometimes played a leading role in these upheavals, disproving the common assumption that the Latin American officer class is one reactionary group. Thus, the military takeover in Peru 1968 was quickly followed by nationalization of key foreign-owned industries and land reform that transferred many large estates to peasants and workers, organized into cooperatives. The Peruvian Revolution—a revolution from above, without significant participation by the masses—soon faltered, however, primarily because of its failure to break with the traditional strategy of development based on foreign loans and export expansion.

The struggle against neocolonialism scored a temporary major victory with the triumph of the Marxist presidential candidate Salvador Allende and his Popular Unity coalition in Chile in 1970. In three years, it carried out the nationalization of copper mines and banks and a massive agrarian reform and made significant advances in housing, health, and education. But the Allende government also made serious errors. Most serious was its failure to take preventive action against a coup by reactionary military. In September 1973, military plotters overthrew the Allende government. Published evidence has since confirmed the complicity of the United States in a "destabilization" of his government that prepared the way for the coup.

## 1970–2003

By the 1970s the global marketplace once again had shifted dramatically. The system of international capitalism would no longer tolerate the relatively modest nationalist constraints imposed on foreign corporations in Latin America by populist governments, much less those of democratically elected socialists like Allende. Japanese and European capitalists, with the assistance of the United States and, ironically, a host of local statist protections, had fully reconstructed their war-ravaged economies and once again looked to overseas markets to acquire strategically valuable raw materials, sell surplus products, invest surplus capital, and exploit cheap labor. Meanwhile, the United States itself had experienced a serious economic decline and international competitive crisis, largely the product of its expensive investment in a military establishment designed to police the postwar new world order.

Peaceful resolution of these resurgent international capitalist rivalries seemed to require that the core capitalist countries have freer access to the world's resources; transnational corporate capitalist elites, through their control of national governments and private organizations like the Trilateral Commission, thereafter sought to promote a neoliberal strategy of economic development that emphasized free trade, an open door for foreign investment, state deregulation of business, privatization, free convertibility of local currencies, tax and spending cuts beneficial to investors and disastrous to workers, balanced federal budgets, currency devaluation, and liquidation of public sector debt. These new "reforms" attacked the material foundation of the old populist political alliances that had supported the region's state-led industrialization during the previous forty years.

Latin America's established industrial, commercial, agricultural, and financial elites, all of whom had profited handsomely from the nationalistic policies promoted by populists, now found themselves squeezed between resurgent, aggressive foreign interests and growing domestic popular mobilizations that continued to demand expansion of social programs that redistributed power and wealth. Always suspicious of the goals and methods of these popular social movements, these elites also were increasingly attracted to the relatively low-cost loans and lucrative business partnerships that transnational corporations and core capitalist governments promised.

Populist redistributive policies, whose success had always depended on a dynamic economic expansion, increasingly came to rely on foreign loans. However, under President Ronald Reagan, the Federal Reserve Board raised the prime rate from 9 percent in 1979 to 21.5 percent in January 1981, "the highest interest rate since the birth of Jesus Christ," according to West German chancellor Helmut Schmidt. Trapped by these high floating interest rates, in just three years (1981–1983) Latin America had to pay out $94.8 billion in interest payments, twice the outlay on interest for the whole of the 1970s. Despite the negative impact of the skyrocketing external debt on redistributive policies and state-sponsored economic growth, Latin American elites quickly became enthusiastic champions of foreign-inspired neoliberal strategies. These appeared first in Brazil in 1964, when General Humberto de Alencar Castelo Branco overthrew the democratically elected government of João Goulart. But they reached their fullest expression in the policies of General Augusto Pinochet, who ousted Allende in 1973. His new, openly terrorist military junta, in league with the most reactionary elements of Chile's ruling class and its foreign allies, not only reversed the progressive policies of the Allende regime but transformed Chile into a concentration camp, torturing and killing thousands of opponents. Its economic policies reduced the living standards of the masses to near-starvation levels.

The destruction of Chilean democracy was part of a general counteroffensive by Latin American cities and their foreign allies to halt and roll back the movement for structural economic and social change. By mid-1976 a block of authoritarian states—Brazil, Chile, Bolivia, Uruguay, and Paraguay—had taken shape. Following the overthrow of the government of President Isabel Perón by a right-wing military in early 1976, they were soon joined by Argentina.

But these regimes, whose policies included the systematic use of torture and assassination against political opponents and the abandonment of the effort to achieve economic independence, offered no solutions for the deep-seated problems of their countries. Their most shining success, the "Brazilian miracle" of steady economic growth since 1964, was made possible by reducing wages to the subsistence level, an annual inflation rate of about 20 percent, and massive foreign investments that hastened the foreign conquest of Brazilian industry. By the mid-1970s the Brazilian miracle was running down; by 1980 Brazil was in a deep recession, with factories closing, unemployment rising, and a balance of payments problem growing steadily worse.

Other military regimes, such as Argentina and Chile, faced similarly grave economic problems. But the crisis was not one of dictatorships alone; it confronted all the countries of the region, whatever their political systems, that pursued a strategy of dependent development based on foreign loans and investments.

At the heart of the continuing debt problem lay the unequal exchange between advanced capitalist countries, such as the United States, and Latin America. A major factor in Latin America's balance of payments deficit is the imbalance between the low prices of Latin American export commodities and the high prices of the manufactured goods and oil that most of the countries in the area must buy. In recent decades falling commodity prices, themselves the product of growing global competition, have greatly aggravated the problem. These unfavorable terms of trade help to explain Latin America's mountainous debt.

Certain changes in the Latin American industrialization programs contributed to the growing gap between its exports and imports. Since about 1955, countries like Brazil and Mexico increasingly stressed production of consumer durables and capital goods that required the importation of expensive machinery, equipment, and technical licenses from countries like the United States. The result was a growing surplus of imports over exports. The transnational companies' takeover of much of the Latin American manufacturing sector contributed to the same result. In the 1970s, for every dollar invested in Latin America, transnationals repatriated approximately $2.20 to their home countries. To cover the deficits in their balance of payments, Latin American countries had to borrow from Western bankers at interest rates that reached double digit figures by 1980.

By 1982, with their national treasuries almost empty of foreign exchange, a number of major Latin American countries faced the prospect of immediate default. This posed immense dangers to the international banking system, for defaults by Mexico and Brazil alone could have wiped out 95 percent of the capital of the nine largest U.S. banks. Defaults were averted by emergency aid packages provided by Western governments and bankers in return for agreements by the recipient governments to carry out "austerity" programs that further reduced the living standards of their workers and peasants. Nevertheless, the problem had been postponed, not resolved. There was no prospect that even a portion of the huge Latin American debt could be repaid without large write-offs and long delays in payment. Meanwhile the flow of new loans by commercial banks sharply declined.

In the later 1980s, despite populist rhetoric about resisting the tyranny of the International Monetary Fund and the World Bank, which monitored debtor countries' compliance with the "structural adjustment programs"—privatization of state companies, an end to subsidies, opening their economies to foreign investment—imposed as a condition for new loans, Latin American governments did little more than demand reschedulings and lower interest payments. Efforts by Latin American governments to reduce their debt burdens under the Brady Plan proposed by the United States included debt-bond swaps, in which foreign debt was exchanged at a discount for new government bonds, and debt-equity swaps, in which foreign debt was exchanged for equity, that is, shares in local companies. None of this made a serious dent in the region's foreign debt, which grew between 1990 and 2000 from $439 billion to $774 billion, an increase of 76 percent. In the same period exports grew from $147 billion to $359 billion. The debt problem was complicated by the fact that Latin America's imports grew more rapidly than its exports, with the area's balance of payments deficit rising from $6.171 billion in 1990 to $45.5 billion in 2001. By 1996, despite paying back $648 billion, the area's foreign debt had risen to $611 billion. Four years later, despite devoting 38.7 percent of its export earnings to service the external debt, Latin America's foreign debt rose to $774 billion. Without an expansion of exports, a new debt crisis was likely to arise. Meanwhile, major Western banks reduced their Latin American exposure by selling parts of the debt at a discount, by setting aside huge reserves to cover possible losses on loans to developing countries, and by the debt-bond swaps and debt-equity swaps mentioned above.

The United States, under successive Presidents Reagan, Bush, and Clinton, used debt as a weapon of coercion and played a leading role in imposing the neoliberal or "structural adjustment" system. The logical next step was the incorporation of Latin America into a U.S.-dominated Western Hemisphere common market that would aid the United States in its competition with Japan and the European Community. A major move toward that goal was approval of the North American Free Trade Agreement with Mexico (1993). By eliminating remaining tariff restrictions and restrictions on investment, the pact ensured that Mexico would become a cheap-labor preserve for U.S industry, with a loss of better-paying jobs in the United States. The opening of Mexico to U.S. low-cost agricultural products, especially corn, had a devastating effect on less efficient and less productive Mexican small farmers. Similar pacts were planned with other Latin American countries, beginning with Chile.

Now, after more than a decade of experience with neoliberal policies that promised to produce economic growth, reduce poverty, and promote development in Latin America, the people of the region appear to have become increasingly disillusioned with it. According to polling by Latinobarómetro, by the end of the 1990s almost half the population described the current economic situation as either bad or very bad; 60 percent said that their parents lived better, more than 20 percent described unemployment as the most important problem in their country, and 40 percent described their economic situation as unstable. Even more important, almost 80 percent complained that income distribution was either unfair or very unfair. Even José Manuel Salazar-Xirinachs, a neoliberal trade adviser to the Organization of American States, reluctantly acknowledged that "liberalization was not the miracle or the magic formula that many expected."

The chapters that follow document in detail the staggering economic and social costs of the neoliberal or structural adjustment program for Latin America. Here we offer a few social indicators of Latin American "underdevelopment": between 1980 and 1990 the number of poor people in the region increased by 66 million and a decade later, despite a slight decline in that rate, a record 211 million people remained mired in poverty. Morever, of these, some 89 million lived in extreme poverty, meaning they did not have the means to acquire a basic family food basket.

To emerge from underdevelopment, Latin American countries will have to learn from the historical successes and failures of reforms undertaken from the 1930s to the 1970s when the region, largely left alone to pursue developmental strategies consistent with its internal social, political, and cultural needs, experienced substantial growth and a significant reduction of social inequality. This will require the reinvigoration of "positive government" and its collaboration with nongovernmental organizations to formulate more autonomous, inward-directed strategies of development based on more rational exploitation of human and natural resources. But such strategies cannot be implemented without profound changes in the relations between Latin America and the developed countries and in Latin America's economic and social structures, particularly in land tenure and use, ownership of industry, and income distribution. Nor can such strategies be implemented without powerful, well-organized social movements that can spearhead a democratic revitalization of Latin American political life that would allow popular interests and wishes to influence the direction of economic and social policy.

In the early 1980s, in fact, it appeared that a democratic revival had begun as the reactionary tide of the 1970s began to recede and in country after country—Argentina, Brazil, Bolivia, Uruguay—discredited military regimes gave way to popularly elected governments. By 1990 the last military or personal dictatorships, in Chile and Paraguay, had fallen. In part because of the long repression of left-wing parties and trade union movements, the emerging democratic movements of the 1980s and 1990s as a rule had a centrist or conservative complexion. Often they cultivated accommodation with the former military rulers, granting pardons or amnesties for their crimes, and thus perpetuated a climate of impunity for human rights abuses. Sometimes, too, the new democratic regimes displayed a broad authoritarian streak, resorting to free use of rule by decree to bypass Congress and other arbitrary measures. Peruvian President Alberto Fujimori's seizure of power by a "self-coup" (*autogolpe*) (1992), the overthrow of populist President Jean-Bertrand Aristide by Haiti's military leaders (1991), the collapse of the Argentine economy and the elected government of Fernando de la Rua, and the aborted coup against Venezuela's populist President Hugo Chávez all revealed the fragility of the recent democratic revival.

None of the new democracies made a clean break with the failed economic policies of the past. This was reflected in their usual acquiescence in payment of the immense foreign debt and their acceptance of the harsh neoliberal remedies prescribed by the International Monetary Fund and the World Bank. In particular, the acceptance by Latin America's old and new democracies of privatization and tariff-reduction policies represented a virtual abandonment of half a century of struggle to achieve independent capitalist development. To date, in countries like Mexico, Brazil, Argentina, Peru, and Bolivia, these policies have resulted in increases in unemployment and declines in living standards, relieved in Peru and Bolivia by a thriving informal or underground economy based on the production of coca and cocaine. The reliance by Peru, Colombia, and Bolivia on the demand for cocaine in the United States and Europe represents a grotesque new kind of Latin American "dependency" on the advanced countries.

But as the new millennium opened, neoliberalism, which demolished Latin America's statist institutions and the old populist, corporative consensus that underwrote them, was unable to fashion a cohesive new social order. In this age of neoliberalism, the fruits of an unregulated marketplace proved incompatible with basic human needs; everywhere the signs of discontent proliferated as the insistent political-economic demands of foreign bankers and Latin America's "new billionaires" conflicted with popular democratic political aspirations. In the Mexican state of Chiapas, the dramatic 1994 revolt led by the self-styled Zapatista Army of National Liberation was called an "armed critique" of Mexico's neoliberal policies.

Electoral opposition to neoliberalism also continued to grow. Brazil's Lula (Luis Inaçio da Silva) of the Socialist Workers' Party won the 2002 presidential elections with the support of women, blacks, and diverse social movements like the Landless People's Movement (MST). In Ecuador, Paraguay, and Bolivia, indigenous people, trade union activists, women's organizations, and student groups mobilized to resist neoliberal austerity programs.

Environmentalists, indigenous groups, and trade union organizations in Venezuela similarly organized to support the election of President Hugo Chávez, running on a populist platform opposed to neoliberalism. He inaugurated new policies that reinforced state control of the Venezuelan oil industry to promote the public interest.

In Argentina, the neoliberalism of Carlos Menem, another politician who betrayed his electoral promises, produced high rates of unemployment and provoked massive street demonstrations. More recently, Argentina's problems spiraled out of control, forcing the nation to close its banks and default on its foreign debt payments. Spreading poverty, popular political protest, and food riots quickly swept Fernando de la Rua, Menem's elected successor, from the presidency in 2001. Everywhere angry Argentines blamed the wealthy bankers and industrialists who had benefited from a decade of neoliberal policies. "We're somewhat less popular than serial killers," one banker candidly confessed to *The Economist.*

In 1997 hundreds of thousands of Haitians participated in a series of national strikes to protest the economic hardships imposed by the IMF, the World Bank, and the U.S. government, which had successfully engineered both a restoration of formal democratic rule and the power of a Haitian elite committed to the principles of neoliberalism. By 2000, however, the impoverished majority managed to mobilize its resources in support of the Family Lavalas Party, which won control of the Haitian Senate, and a year later it reelected former president Jean Bertrand Aristide, a populist priest whose radical ambition was to promote economic growth and an equitable distribution of its fruits in a nation that throughout the twentieth century had suffered from dictatorship, crushing poverty, and brutal political violence.

In Central America, the popular struggle against market deregulation and the sale of state companies to private corporations occurred in the midst of a transition from armed insurrection to peacetime political struggle. A formidable guerrilla offensive in El Salvador forced the right-wing government to the bargaining table, and by 1992 the two sides had reached a U.N.-sponsored agreement that provided for a sweeping reduction and cleansing of the armed forces and full integration of the insurgents into the country's political life. But twelve long years of revolution and counterrevolution had rendered the government utterly dependent on the United States, devastated the nation's economy, and left it vulnerable to foreign pressure to adopt neoliberal policies. The leftist coalition that had championed the armed struggle now had to monitor implementation of the peace accords and simultaneously resist the privatization of the national patrimony. Proclaiming its commitment to a "social market economy" that promised to expand public accessibility to potable water, subsidize the poor, and "make public services accessible to the people," the FMLN triumphed in the March 2000 legislative elections, took control of the National Assembly, and won 77 mayoral races, retaining its control of San Salvador. According to former Guatemalan guerrilla leader Jorge Monsanto, the FMLN's victory portended dramatic changes for the rest of the region because it was "an answer to the neoliberal-style policies applied by [other Central American] governments, which only drag the people down into deeper poverty than they already suffered."

Meanwhile, Guatemala's insurgent forces tried a slightly different tactic. In exchange for an agreement to end the thirty-six-year-old civil war and demobilize guerrilla armies, they negotiated peace accords in 1996 that required popular input into government plans to reconstruct civil society in a way that, in the words of long-time revolutionary activist Alfonso Bauer Paiz, offered "some resistance to current trends of economic globalization and neoliberalism." This agreement, for example, identified poverty as a problem that government policies must address, and it further required a tax system that was "fair, equitable, and on the whole, progressive, in keeping with the constitutional principle of ability to pay"; the agreement also provided a legal basis for indigenous people, who constituted 60 percent of the nation's population, to make claims against the state. Of course, the extent to which these accords were actually enforced would determine the success or failure of this strategy; but this, as elsewhere in Latin America, would depend on popular political mobilization and struggle.

By 2002 the neoliberal model, for over a decade the dominant policy prescription for Latin American development, ceased to offer credible solutions to the region's many social, economic, and political problems. Its patent failure to promote genuine development, raise living standards, and reduce the gigantic Latin American foreign debt gave new life to broad regional and national social and political movements, uniting trade unions, activist women, peasant cooperatives, church groups, and community organizations intent on securing social justice and democratic models of development. Even stalwart neoliberals like Joseph Stiglitz, the World Bank's chief economist, appeared to have lost faith in the developmental potential of the "free movement of capital." As the new millennium opened, Latin America appeared to be perched on the precipice of a new era in its historic struggle for development and social justice.

# 12

# The Mexican Revolution— and After

O N THE EVE of the presidential election of 1910, signs of unrest multiplied in Mexico. Peasant risings and workers' strikes became more frequent, and the Mexican Liberal Party (PLM), founded and led by the exiled revolutionary journalist Ricardo Flores Magón, intensified its conspiratorial activities. Drawn by the PLM's programmatic commitment to "equality between the sexes" and repelled by miserably low wages, abusive working conditions, and legal discrimination, women like Juana Gutiérrez de Mendoza and Dolores Jiménez became influential activists, organizers, and propagandists in this growing opposition to Porfirio Díaz's dictatorial regime. Divisions soon appeared within the oligarchy. Bernardo Reyes, a foe of the Científicos and the powerful governor of Nuevo León whose rule combined iron-fisted repression with reformist rhetoric, announced his candidacy for the post of vice president. Reyes saw this office as a stepping-stone to the presidency when Díaz, who was eighty years old in 1910, died or retired.

In an unusual atmosphere of political ferment and debate, there appeared a tract for the times, *The Great National Problems* (1909) by the lawyer Andrés Molina Enríquez. Financed by Reyes, the book combined the customary eulogies of Díaz with incisive criticism of his political system and especially of his agrarian policy. Its denunciation of the latifundio and appeal for land reform anticipated the radical slogans of the coming revolution.

Díaz had contributed to this ferment by announcing in 1908 that Mexico was now ready for democracy and that he would welcome the emergence of an opposition party. Francisco Madero, a Coahuila hacendado whose extensive family interests included cattle ranches, wheat farms, vineyards, textile factories, and mines, took Díaz at his word. A member of the elite, Madero was no revolutionary, but he feared that continuance of the existing political order would inevitably breed social revolution. Madero made clear, however, that by democracy he meant control by an elite. "The ignorant public," he wrote, "should take no direct part in determining who should be the candidate for public office."

Madero criticized Díaz's social policies—his genocidal Indian wars and violent repression of strikes—as counterproductive; in place of those brutal tactics, he proposed a policy of modest concessions to peasants and workers that would reduce mounting tensions and check the growth of radical ideas. Madero regarded democracy as an instrument of social control that would promote the acceptance of capitalism through the grant of limited political and social reforms, with a large stress on education.

In December 1909, Madero began to tour the country, making speeches in which he explained his reform program. In April 1910 an opposition anti-reelectionist party was formed and announced Madero as its candidate for president.

Díaz at first refused to take Madero seriously but soon became alarmed by his growing popularity. In early June he had Madero arrested and charged with preparing an armed insurrection; arrests of many of his supporters followed. On June 21 the election was held, and it was announced that Díaz and his hand-picked vice-presidential candidate, Ramón Corral, had been elected by an almost unanimous vote.

After the election, Díaz no longer considered Madero dangerous and allowed him to be released on bail. Convinced that the dictator could not be removed by peaceful means, Madero also feared the demands of radical women, peasants, and workers; in September 1910, for example, Dolores Jiménez, a working-class leader of the feminist Daughters of Cuauhtémoc, advocated women's empowerment in their "economic, physical, intellectual, and moral struggles." Caught between the Scylla of reaction and the Charybdis of lower-class revolution, Madero opted for armed struggle. On October 7 he fled across the border to Texas and from there announced the Plan of San Luis Potosí. Declaring the recent elections null and void, Madero assumed the title of provisional president of Mexico but promised to hold free elections as soon as conditions permitted. The plan made a vague reference to the return of usurped peasant lands, but most of its articles dealt with political reforms. That Madero was allowed to organize the revolution on U.S. soil with little interference by the authorities suggests the U.S. government's displeasure with Díaz. Fearing that North American domination of investments in Mexico threatened Mexican economic and political independence, the dictator had recently favored British over North American capitalists in the grant of concessions and had given other indications of an anti-U.S. attitude. The administration of President Taft evidently hoped that Madero would display a more positive attitude toward U.S. interests.

## The Great Revolution, 1910–1920

The revolution got off to a shaky start when Madero, having crossed back into Mexico, found only twenty-five supporters waiting for him and hurriedly returned to Texas. But it soon gathered momentum as two major movements of peasant revolt responded to his call. In the huge northern border state of Chihuahua, where peons and small farmers suffered under the iron rule of the Terrazas-Creel clan, masters of a vast landed empire, the rising began under the leadership of Pascual Orozco, a mule driver, and Pancho Villa, a bandit with a reputation for taking from the rich to give to the poor. By the end of 1910, guerrilla armies had seized control of most of the state from federal troops.

Another seat of rebellion was the mountainous southern state of Morelos, where Indian communities had long waged a losing struggle against encroaching sugar haciendas. Here the mestizo insurgent leader Emiliano Zapata, attracted by the promise of land reform in the Plan of San Luis Potosí, proclaimed his loyalty to Madero.

Meanwhile, in March 1911, former PLM leaders Camilo Arriaga and Dolores Jiménez, now *maderistas*, organized Mexico City's Complot de Tacubaya, an urban revolt against Díaz that advocated a revolutionary social agenda including protection of indigenous rights, agrarian reform, an eight-hour workday, equal pay for equal work, and equal access to education. In the political context of a countryside in arms, the Tacubaya uprising, though prematurely betrayed and suppressed, nonetheless successfully undermined Díaz's confidence in his ability to rule and led directly to a decision to seek compromise with Madero a month later.

In May 1911, moreover, the Zapatistas won two decisive victories. Rather than face an invasion of the poorly defended capital by Zapata's dreaded agrarian rebels, Díaz and his advisers decided to reach an agreement with Madero. Disregarding urgent warnings by the left wing of the revolutionary movement against compromises with the Díaz regime, Madero signed the Treaty of Ciudad Juárez on May 21, which provided for the removal of Díaz but left intact all existing institutions. It was completely silent on the subject of social change. On May 25 the aged dictator resigned the presidency; a few days later he left for Europe. Francisco León de la Barra, the Mexican ambassador to the United States, assumed the interim presidency.

The *soldaderas*, women who joined their lovers or husbands and often fought at their side, made their own contribution to the victory of the Mexican Revolution. [Library of Congress]

On June 7, 1911, Madero entered Mexico City in triumph, but the rejoicing of the crowds who thronged into the streets to greet the "apostle of democracy" was premature. The provisional president was closely tied to the old regime and had no sympathy with the revolution. The *Porfirista* aristocracy and its allies had not given up hope of regaining power; they regarded the compromise that made León de la Barra provisional president a tactical retreat, a means of gaining time to allow the revolutionary wave to subside so they could prepare a counterblow. Under the interim president, the huge Díaz bureaucracy remained largely intact. The reactionary officer corps remained in command of the federal army and burned for revenge over the revolutionary peasant armies that had defeated it.

Social conditions throughout the country remained largely unchanged, and the provisional government sought a total restoration of the status quo. Efforts were made to disband the revolutionary troops, and León de la Barra sent federal forces into Morelos to initiate hostilities against the Zapatistas, who had begun to confiscate large estates and distribute land to the villages. Madero's ineffective efforts to halt the fighting and mediate between Zapata and León de la Barra only deepened the reactionaries' hatred for the visionary meddler who had unleashed anarchy in Mexico. But the revolutionary wave was still running strong, and reaction had to bide its time. In October 1911, Madero and his running mate, José María Pino Suárez, were elected president and vice president by overwhelming majorities. Despite numerous public protests and petitions, led by leaders like Juana Gutiérrez de Mendoza and her *Amigas del Pueblo* (AP), feminists failed to secure voting rights, but their political agitation in support of the "apostle of democracy" was undiminished.

## MADERO'S PRESIDENCY: INADEQUACY AND REVOLT

It soon became evident that the "apostle" had no fundamental solutions for Mexico's grave social and economic problems. Even on the political plane, Madero's thought was far from advanced. His conception of democracy was a formal democracy that would give the masses the illusion of power and participation in political life but would vest all decision making in the hands of an elite.

In regard to economic and social democracy, his vision was even more limited. Madero allowed workers to organize trade unions and to strike and permitted a national workers' center, the *Casa del Obrero Mundial*, to be formed in Mexico City. But his answer to the agrarian problem was a totally inadequate program of purchase of land from large landowners and recovery of national land for distribution among landless peasants. In fact, Madero, who believed that only large landholdings would permit Mexican agriculture to modernize, was totally opposed to land reform at the expense of the haciendas. Madero's retreat on the land issue led to a break with his most faithful ally, Emiliano Zapata. Zapata urged Madero to carry out the agrarian provisions of the Plan of San Luis Potosí. Madero refused, arguing that the treaties that set up the interim government of León de la Barra obliged him to accept the legality of the legal and administrative decisions of the Díaz regime. Madero also demanded the total surrender and disarmament of Zapata's peasant troops.

Convinced that Madero did not intend to carry out his pledges to restore land to the villages, Zapata announced his own program on November 28, 1911. The Plan of Ayala proclaimed that "the lands, woods, and waters usurped by the hacendados, Científicos, or caciques through tyranny and venal justice" would be returned to their owners, and Zapata began to put the plan into effect. The Zapatista movement soon spread to other states in central and southern Mexico. Historian John Womack paints a vivid portrait of these peasant armies,

one of which, composed of "the widows, wives, daughters, and sisters of rebels," was commanded by a woman warrior known as "La China." Clad "in rags, some in plundered finery, wearing silk stockings and dresses, sandals, straw hats, and gun belts," these women so terrorized federales and hacendados in the region that even veteran Zapatista commanders "treated La China with respect." Madero sent a series of generals against Zapata and his allies but failed to crush the revolt.

Madero's failure to carry out a genuine agrarian reform lost him the trust and support of the revolutionary peasantry without mollifying the reactionaries, who resented his modest concessions to labor and his efforts to transform Mexico into a bourgeois democracy with freedom of speech and press and the rule of law. They also feared that under pressure from the peasantry and under the influence of urban middle-class reformers like Luis Cabrera, a strong advocate of land reform, Madero might move farther to the left.

The aristocracy, its possessions and influence almost intact, dreamed of restoring the lost paradise of Don Porfirio, when peasants, workers, and natives knew their place. Almost from the day that Madero took office in November 1911, therefore, counterrevolutionary revolts sprouted in various parts of Mexico. Most serious was a revolt in the north led by Pascual Orozco, who was encouraged and bribed by conservative elements in Chihuahua, especially the Terrazas-Creel clan. Federal troops under General Victoriano Huerta crushed the Orozco revolt in a series of battles, but Huerta's victory, joined with the alienation of Zapata and other of Madero's old revolutionary allies, increased Madero's dependence on an officer corps whose loyalty to his cause was highly dubious.

Abortive revolts followed one after another throughout the rest of 1912. The danger to Madero increased as it became clear that he had lost the support of the United States. Although Madero had made it clear that he favored foreign investments and guaranteed their security, he refused to show special favors to U.S. capitalists and warned foreign investors that the crony system that had operated under Díaz was dead. This

**Modern Mexico**

independent spirit, plus Madero's legalization of trade unions and strikes and his inability to cope with the peasant revolution and establish stability, alienated the United States, whose foreign policy, originally favorable to Madero, turned against him.

U.S. Ambassador Henry Lane Wilson became increasingly hostile to Madero. In February 1912 a hundred thousand U.S. troops were stationed along the border, and throughout the year Wilson made vehement threats of intervention if the Madero government failed to protect U.S. lives and property.

Meanwhile, preparations for a coup d'état were under way in the capital. Implicated in the conspiracy were General Huerta, the recent conqueror of Orozco; General Miguel Mondragón, former chief of artillery under Díaz; Bernardo and Rodolfo Reyes, father and son; and Félix Díaz, nephew of the old dictator.

The blow fell on February 9, 1913, when the military garrison at Tacubaya "pronounced" against Madero and marched on the National Palace. Meanwhile, the U.S. ambassador, in complete sympathy with the counterrevolutionary revolt, was secretly negotiating with Huerta and Díaz. On February 12, Wilson sent Madero a sharp protest against the conduct of military operations in Mexico City because they threatened U.S. life and property. At his urging, the British, German, and Spanish representatives sent similar demands. As the crisis moved toward a climax, Wilson became feverishly active. On February 14 he demanded that the Mexican government begin negotiations with the other warring parties; otherwise, U.S. marines would be landed in Mexican ports. The same day, Wilson invited other foreign diplomats to a conference at which it was agreed to force Madero to resign. A message to that effect was sent to Madero from the diplomatic corps. Madero firmly rejected the demand. He would rather die, he said, than allow foreign intervention.

## HUERTA'S DICTATORSHIP

Ambassador Wilson's activities were clearly coordinated with those of the conspirators and encouraged Huerta to arrest the president and other members of his government. A dispute between Huerta and Díaz over who should head the new regime was settled through Wilson's mediation. At a meeting at the U.S. embassy, agreement was reached that Huerta should head a provisional government, with Díaz to succeed him as soon as an election could be held. Wilson then called a meeting of foreign diplomats to whom he introduced Huerta as the "savior of Mexico."

To give some semblance of legality to his usurpation, Huerta obtained the "voluntary" resignations of Madero and Pino Suárez in return for the promise that they would then be free to leave Mexico. An intimidated Congress accepted the resignations and recognized Huerta as provisional president, almost without dissent. There remained the question of what should be done with Madero. Asked by Huerta for his advice, the U.S. ambassador replied that he should do "what was best for the country." Despite urgent requests by other members of the diplomatic corps and Madero's wife that he intercede to save Madero's life, Wilson refused. On the evening of February 22, Madero and Pino Suárez were murdered as they were being transferred from the National Palace to the penitentiary; the official explanation was that they had been killed during an attempt by armed men to release them. The two assassins, officers of the rurales, were quickly advanced in rank, one being made a general.

Huerta's seizure of power, which was greeted with rejoicing by the landed aristocracy, the big capitalists, and the church, was an effort to set the Mexican clock back, to restore the Díaz system of personal dictatorship. The promise to Félix Díaz that he would succeed Huerta as president was soon broken, and Díaz was shunted aside by sending him off on a diplomatic mission to Japan.

Hoping to broaden the social base of his dictatorship and conceal its reactionary character as long as possible, Huerta for a time continued Madero's labor policies, but as the terrorist nature of the regime became more apparent and labor more and more allied itself with the anti-Huerta movement, he proceeded to arrest its leaders and eventually closed down the Casa del Obrero Mundial.

## THE OPPOSITION: ZAPATA, VILLA, CARRANZA, AND OBREGÓN

Huerta had counted on a quick victory over the peasant revolutionaries of the south and favorable reception of his coup d'état by conservative economic and political interests in the north. However, the revolutionary wave, still running strong, rose even higher in reaction to Madero's brutal murder and the imposition of Huerta's terrorist regime. Zapata intensified his struggle against local great landowners, Huerta's allies, and federal troops. In the northern border states of Sonora, Chihuahua, and Coahuila, meanwhile, an anti-Huerta coalition of disparate social groups—liberal hacendados, middle classes, miners, industrial workers, vaqueros, and peasants—began to take form.

By forcing Huerta to commit a considerable part of his troops to the campaign in the south, Zapata assured the success of the revolutionary movement that sprang up anew in the north. Pancho Villa assumed leadership of the Constitutionalists, as Huerta's northern opponents called themselves. Enjoying an immense popularity among the state's vaqueros, he soon recruited an army of three thousand men who soon controlled almost all Chihuahua, including Ciudad Juárez and Chihuahua City.

Master of Chihuahua, Villa imposed a revolutionary new order on the state. He employed his soldiers as a civil militia and administrative staff to restore normal life. Villa ordered a reduction of meat prices and distributed money, clothing, and other goods to the poor. Education was a passion with the almost illiterate Villa; according to the U.S. correspondent John Reed, who accompanied him, Villa established some fifty new schools in Chihuahua City.

Clearly, Villa's social policies were more radical than those implemented by the Constitutionalist leaders in the neighboring states of Sonora and Coahuila. In December 1913 he announced the expropriation without compensation of the holdings of the pro-Huerta oligarchy in Chihuahua. His agrarian program, however, differed in significant ways from that of Zapata. Whereas in the area ruled by Zapata confiscated estates were promptly distributed among the peasants, Villa's decree provided that they should remain under state control until the victory of the revolution. The revenues from these estates would be used to finance the revolutionary struggle and support the widows and orphans of the revolutionary soldiers. Once victory had been achieved, they were to be used to pay pensions to such widows and orphans, to compensate veterans of the revolution, to restore village lands that had been usurped by the hacendados, and to pay taxes left unpaid by the hacendados.

Meanwhile Villa turned control of some confiscated haciendas over to his lieutenants; the rest were administered by the state. Cattle were sold in the United States to secure arms and ammunition for Villa's army, and meat was distributed on a large scale to the urban unemployed, to public institutions like orphanages and children's homes, and for sale in the markets. The differences between the agrarian programs of Villa and Zapata may be explained in part by the fact that the economy of the north was based not on agriculture but on cattle raising, which required large economic units. These units had to be administered by the state or on a cooperative basis. In addition, the percentage of peasants in the population was much smaller in the north, and the problem of land hunger much less acute.

In the neighboring state of Coahuila, meanwhile, the elderly Venustiano Carranza, a great landowner who had once served Díaz but joined Madero in 1911 and was appointed by him governor of the state, raised the standard of revolt against Huerta. On March 26, 1913, he announced his Plan of Guadalupe, which called for the overthrow of the dictator and the restoration of constitutional government but did not mention social reforms. Carranza assumed the title of first chief of the Constitutionalist Army. By April he commanded some forty thousand men. He was soon joined by Villa, who placed himself under Carranza's command but retained much autonomy in Chihuahua; Villa's troops were renamed the Northern Division. Carranza gained another important recruit in the young ranchero Álvaro Obregón, who led the anti-Huerta forces in the state of Sonora. Named commander of the Army of the Northwest, he soon proved his large military gifts by driving the federal troops out of almost all Sonora; in April the state legislature recognized Carranza as first chief of the revolution.

Meanwhile, within Mexico City, Huerta also faced clandestine opposition, led by prominent intellectuals like José Vasconcelos and Martín Luís Guzmán. Just as troublesome, however, was the public resistance of the feminist Loyalty Club, headed by María Árias Bernal, which protested the regime's brutality and organized a public demonstration at the site of Madero's tomb.

## INTERVENTION BY THE UNITED STATES

By the beginning of 1914, the Constitutionalist revolt had assumed significant proportions and Huerta's fall appeared inevitable. Meanwhile, in March 1913, Woodrow Wilson had succeeded Taft as president of the United States. Alone among the great powers, Wilson's government refused to recognize the Huerta regime, although it continued to embargo revolutionary arms purchases while permitting U.S. arms sales to Huerta to consolidate his rule. Wilson justified his nonrecognition policy with moralistic rhetoric, refusing to recognize a government that had come to power illegally. More important, he was convinced that Huerta could not provide the stable political climate U.S. interests required in Mexico. Noting Huerta's strong support among European governments, Wilson also suspected that Huerta had cut a deal to grant British and German investors privileged access to Mexican markets at the expense of U.S. business. In the first six months of his regime, Huerta clearly favored British interests, thereby solidifying his support in London and further alienating Washington.

Wilson's concern with a suitable political climate for U.S. investments emerged from a note sent to British officials in November 1913, in which he assured those officials that his U.S. government "intends not merely to force Huerta from power, but also to exert every influence it can exert to secure Mexico a better government under which all contracts and business concessions will be safer than they have been."

Shortly thereafter, growing tensions between England and Germany, ultimately leading to World War I, dramatically affected the Huerta regime's security and international backing. Both nations now openly courted the United States and began to distance themselves from Huerta. By yielding to a British request for uniform rates on all goods shipped through the nearly completed Panama Canal, Wilson obtained an end of British support for Huerta in early 1914. As a result, Huerta's financial position became increasingly difficult. Seeking to avert a catastrophe, he suspended payment on the interest on the national debt for six months, but that extraordinary measure only increased Huerta's difficulties. Foreign creditors began to demand the seizure of Mexican customhouses, and some even clamored for immediate intervention. By February 1914, Wilson decided force must be used. After receiving assurances from Carranza's agent in Washington that the Constitutionalists would respect foreign property rights, including "just and equitable concessions," Wilson lifted the existing embargo on arms shipments to the Carranza forces.

Wilson found a pretext for intervention when a party of U.S. sailors from the cruiser *Dolphin* landed in a restricted area of Tampico and were arrested. They were almost immediately released with an apology, but the commander of the *Dolphin*, under orders from Washington, demanded a formal disavowal of the action, severe punishment for the responsible Mexican officer, and a twenty-one-gun salute to the U.S. flag. For Huerta to grant these demands might have meant political suicide, and he refused.

President Wilson now sent a fleet into the Gulf of Mexico, and on April 21, 1914, learning that a German merchant ship was bound for Veracruz with munitions, he ordered the seizure of the city. When Mexican batteries at the fortress of San Juan de Ulua attempted to prevent a landing, they were silenced by answering fire from the U.S. ships. Huerta's forces evacuated Veracruz the same day, but the local population and cadets of the naval academy continued a courageous resistance until April 27, when U.S. troops occupied Veracruz, setting off a wave of anti-Yankee sentiment in Mexico and a number of Latin American countries. Meanwhile Carranza, whom Wilson had hoped to control, bitterly denounced the U.S. action and demanded the immediate evacuation of Veracruz.

The rising storm of Mexican anger and Carranza's defiant stand placed Wilson in a quandary. He sought a way out of his difficult situation by obtaining an offer from Argentina, Brazil, and Chile to mediate the dispute between the United States and Mexico. A conference was convened at Niagara Falls, Canada, in May 1914. Wilson hoped to do more than reduce tensions; he intended to use the mediation as a means of eliminating Huerta and establishing a new provisional Mexican government that he could control. The U.S. candidate to head this provisional government was the moderate Carranza, because the revolutionary peasant leaders Zapata and Villa were obviously unacceptable. But Carranza would not rise to Wilson's bait. The conservative but fiercely nationalist first chief sent representatives to the Niagara Falls conference but did not give them official status and refused the conference's mediation. Mexico, his representatives informed the U.S. delegates, would settle its own problems without interference from foreign sources.

By this time the fall of the Huerta regime was imminent. With the northern tier of states securely in Constitutionalist hands, Pancho Villa's Northern Division drove south to Zacatecas. Meanwhile, Obregón's Army of the Northwest seized the important railroad and industrial center of Guadalajara. Recognizing that his situation had become hopeless, Huerta took flight for Europe on July 15. On August 15, Obregón's troops entered Mexico City.

Huerta's fall deprived the United States of any pretext for continuing its armed intervention, but Wilson delayed the evacuation of Veracruz as long as possible in the hope of securing commitments from Carranza that would have effectively prevented any basic changes in Mexico's social and economic structure. Despite hints that "fatal consequences" might follow, Carranza resolutely rejected these demands and continued to insist on the end of the military intervention. U.S. troops finally evacuated Veracruz on November 23, 1914.

## FIGHTING AMONG THE VICTORS

As the day of complete victory drew near, differences emerged within the Constitutionalist camp, especially between Carranza and Villa. There were personal factors, such as Carranza's jealousy of Villa as a potential rival, but more important was Carranza's failure to define his position on such fundamental issues as the agrarian question, the role of the church, and the new political order. Villa proposed to incorporate in an agreement a clause drawn up by one of his intellectuals that defined "the present conflict as a struggle of the poor against the abuses of the powerful" and committed the Constitutionalists "to implant a democratic regime . . . to secure the well-being of the workers; to emancipate the peasants economically, making an equitable distribution of lands or whatever else is needed to solve the agrarian problem." Under pressure from his generals, who recognized the potential dangers of an open break with Villa, Carranza permitted his representatives to sign the agreement containing this radical clause, which he personally found unacceptable. Villa, however, continued to distrust Carranza, and his distrust was confirmed by various of Carranza's actions, notably his unilateral occupation of the capital.

Relations also deteriorated between Carranza and Zapata, who had waged war against Huerta independently and refused to recognize Carranza's leadership; a Zapatista manifesto proclaimed that the Plan of Ayala must prevail and all adherents of the old regime must be removed.

In October 1914 a convention of revolutionary leaders and their delegates met at Aguascalientes to settle the conflict between Carranza and Villa. At the insistence of the *Villistas*, Zapata was invited to attend, and presently a delegation from "the Liberating Army of the South" arrived. The convention endorsed the Plan of Ayala, assumed supreme authority, called for the resignation of Carranza as first chief, and appointed General Eulalio Gutiérrez provisional president of the nation. Gutiérrez was a compromise candidate pushed by delegates equally opposed to Carranza and Villa. Because Aguascalientes swarmed with Villa's troops, Gutiérrez had no choice but to name

In early December 1914, Pancho Villa (*on throne*) met with Emiliano Zapata (*center right, with sombrero*) in Mexico City, where both attended the installation of a new president. Earlier, Villa and Zapata had reached agreement on a course of action for the revolution, but the arrangement soon fell apart. [Culver Pictures, Inc.]

Villa commander in chief of the Conventionist Army, as the Northern Division now came to be called.

But Carranza refused to accept the decisions of the Aguascalientes convention, claiming it had no authority to depose him. When he failed to meet the deadline for his resignation, November 10, the armies of Zapata and Villa advanced on the capital and occupied it. Carranza retreated with his depleted forces to Veracruz, which had been evacuated by the Americans shortly before. According to historian John Hart, although the United States remained suspicious of Carranza's nationalism, its decision to withdraw from Veracruz in favor of the Constitutionalists reflected U.S. fears of the revolutionary convention's radical threat to U.S. economic interests, especially investments in Mexican oil production. Veracruz became a safehouse for *Carrancista* forces led by Obregón, who had remained loyal to Carranza and rebuilt his army with the aid of arms and munitions stockpiled in Veracruz during the U.S. occupation.

On December 4, Villa and Zapata held their first meeting and came to full agreement. But although the peasant revolutionaries controlled the capital and much of the country, they could not consolidate their successes. Unskilled in politics, they entrusted state power to the unreliable provisional president, Gutiérrez, a former general in Carranza's army, who sabotaged the Conventionist war effort and opened secret negotiations with Obregón. Meanwhile a conservative wing in the convention strongly opposed land reform, expropriation of foreign properties, and other radical social changes. Villa's sympathies on land reform were with the radicals, but he avoided taking sides in the dispute, probably because he believed that unity was necessary to gain both a rapid military victory and recognition by the United States, which he also regarded as essential to his final triumph. For these and other reasons the convention proved unable to forge a clear national program of socioeconomic reforms that could unite the interests of the peasantry, industrial workers, and the middle class. His later attempts to broaden his program to attract labor, the middle class, and even national capitalists were too little and too late.

The Constitutionalists did not make the same mistake. At the insistence of Obregón and intellectuals like Luis Cabrera, who were aware of the need for broadening the social base of the Constitutionalist movement, the conservative Carranza adopted a program of social reforms designed to win the support of peasants and workers. In December 1914, during the darkest days of the Constitutionalist cause, Carranza issued his "Adiciones" to the Plan of Guadalupe, promising agrarian reform and improved conditions for industrial workers. Other decrees followed: on January 6, 1915, he restored lands usurped from the villages and expropriated additional needed land from haciendas. (Simultaneously, Carranza secretly promised the hacendados that he would return the haciendas that had been confiscated by revolutionary authorities—promises that in the end he would keep.) Carranza's agrarian decrees gained him a certain base among the peasantry. Carranza courted labor support by the promise of a minimum-wage law applying to all branches of industry and by affirming the right of workers to form trade unions and to strike. He also appealed for women's support, and thousands flocked to his ranks from diverse social classes. According to historian Shirlene Soto, working-class radicals like Artemisa Sénz Royo, a labor organizer who later served in the "red battalions," joined with middle-class feminists such as Hermila Galindo de Topete, Carranza's private secretary, to demand "women's complete equality, including sexual equality."

After Obregón's troops reoccupied Mexico City in January 1915, an alliance was formed between the Carranza government and the Casa del Obrero Mundial, which was restored after the fall of Huerta. Members of the Casa agreed to join "the struggle against reaction," meaning above all the revolutionary peasantry. Six "red battalions" of workers were formed and made an important contribution to the offensive launched by Obregón against Villa and Zapata in January 1915. Inadequate understanding on the part of the peasant and working-class leaders of their common interests and the skillful opportunism of the middle-class politicians in Carranza's camp contributed to this disastrous division between labor and the peasantry.

With growing support from a diverse, cross-class political constituency and emboldened by financial and arms transfusions from the United States, the Constitutionalists benefited from a dramatic shift in the balance of forces in Mexico. Under pressure from Carranza's troops, Villa was forced on January 19 to evacuate Mexico City, which Obregón soon occupied. In April 1915, Obregón advanced toward the important railroad center of Celaya, occupied it, and awaited Villa's attack. Obregón had studied accounts of the great war in progress in Europe and had learned that trenches and barbed wire could stop mass attacks. His army received Villa's furious infantry and cavalry assault with a withering fire from machine-gun emplacements and entrenched infantry. For the first time in his military career, Villa suffered a disastrous defeat, with thousands of men killed or taken prisoner. By the end of 1915, the Constitutionalists had destroyed Villa, whom they regarded as the primary danger.

There remained the Zapatistas, who threatened the capital and who had temporarily occupied it in July. But Zapata's battered forces could not check the advance of General Pablo González's army. In August the Constitutionalists returned to Mexico City to stay, while González, one of Carranza's ablest generals, pursued the Zapatistas into Morelos in a campaign of devastation and plunder.

In October 1915, after unsuccessful efforts to play off the revolutionary chiefs against each other or to achieve a coalition under U.S. leadership, President Wilson acknowledged Carranza's ascendancy and extended de facto recognition of his regime; equally important, he placed an arms embargo on Carranza's opponents. But the United States had not abandoned its efforts to influence the course of the Mexican Revolution. A memorandum to Carranza dictated the conditions he must meet before he could obtain *de jure* recognition. They amounted to a claim to determine Mexican policy not only in the area of foreign economic rights but in such internal matters as the role of the church, elections, and the like. These demands were as unacceptable to Carranza in October 1915 as they had been a year before.

In early 1916 relations between the United States and Mexico deteriorated sharply. In part, this resulted from initial efforts by Mexican federal and state authorities to regulate the operations of foreign oil companies. A crisis arose in March when Villa, angered by the arms embargo and wrongly convinced that Carranza had bought U.S. recognition by agreeing to a plan to convert Mexico into a U.S. protectorate, raided Columbus, New Mexico, in an apparent effort to force Carranza to show his hand. The Wilson administration responded by ordering General John Pershing to pursue Villa into Mexico. The United States counted on the enmity between Villa and Carranza to secure the latter's neutrality. But Carranza denounced the invasion, demanded the immediate withdrawal of U.S. forces, and began to prepare for war. In a note to other Latin American nations, the Mexican government declared its belief that the basic reason for U.S. intervention was its opposition to the Mexican policy of eliminating privileged treatment of foreign capital and affirmed that the "foreign invasion" must be repelled and Mexican sovereignty respected.

The United States had anticipated an easy victory, but Pershing's hot pursuit of the elusive Villa proved a fiasco, and Wilson accepted Carranza's offer to negotiate a settlement. Wilson was unsuccessful in his efforts to link the evacuation of U.S. forces with acceptance of the U.S. formula for Mexican domestic policy. In January 1917, influenced by the troubled international scene and his conviction that a war with Mexico would involve at least half a million men, Wilson decided to liquidate the Mexican venture. Mexican nationalism had won a major victory over yet another effort by the United States to impose its hegemony.

## THE CONSTITUTION OF 1917

In the fall of 1916, Carranza issued a call for the election of deputies to a convention that was to frame a new constitution and prepare the way for his election as president. The convention opened in Querétaro on December 1, 1916. Because the call effectively excluded women and those who had not sworn loyalty to his 1913 Plan of Guadalupe, it seemed likely that the constitution would be what Carranza wanted. The draft did not contemplate a radical agrarian reform; for labor, it limited itself to proclaiming the "right to work" and the right of workers to form organizations for "lawful purposes" and to hold "peaceful" assemblies.

These abstract proposals were unsatisfactory to a majority of the deputies, who formed the radical wing of the convention. The principal spokesman for this left wing was Francisco J. Múgica, a young general who helped make the first land distribution of the revolution. The radicals obtained majority approval to create a commission to revise Carranza's project. Múgica himself was largely responsible for Article 3, which struck a heavy blow at church control of education by specifically forbidding "religious corporations" and "ministers of any cult" to establish or conduct schools.

Hermila Galindo and other women revolutionaries were very interested in Articles 34 and 35, which dealt with citizenship and voting rights. Addressing the convention, Galindo appealed to the delegates' "sense of justice as popular representatives" and argued that women should have an equal right to vote and hold office precisely because working women paid taxes, obeyed the same laws as men, and participated fully in the revolutionary struggle for social justice. But others, especially the more radical delegates like Luís Monzón and Inés Malváez, early supporters of the PLM and principled proponents of gender equality, opposed women's suffrage for practical political reasons: they feared that the vast majority of women, sheltered from the harsh realities of the working world (less than 20 percent worked for wages in 1917) and seduced by a conservative Catholic church, would use the franchise to restrain the revolution's radical anticapitalist, anticlerical tendencies. Fear triumphed over principle and women were denied citizenship and political rights.

But wage-earning women did win important protections in Article 123, dealing with the rights of labor. Carranza had asked only that the federal government be empowered to enact labor legislation. The convention went much further. The finished article, a true labor code, provided for the eight-hour day; secured childbirth benefits for women, including paid prenatal and postnatal maternity leaves; required companies employing more than fifty women to provide on-site childcare; abolished the tienda de raya, or company store, and debt servitude; guaranteed the right of workers to organize, bargain collectively, and strike; and granted many other rights and privileges, making it the most advanced labor code in the contemporary world.

Article 27, dealing with property rights, had an equally advanced character. It proclaimed the nation the original owner of all lands, waters, and the subsoil; the state could expropriate them, with compensation to the owners. National ownership of water and the subsoil was inalienable, but individuals and companies could obtain concessions for their exploitation. Foreigners to whom that privilege was granted must agree that they would not invoke the protection of their governments in regard to such concessions. Of prime importance were the same article's agrarian provisions. It declared that all measures passed since 1856 alienating ejidos (communal lands) were null and void; if the pueblos needed more land, they could acquire it by expropriation from neighboring haciendas.

These and other provisions of the constitution of 1917 made it the most progressive law code of its time. It laid legal foundations for a massive assault on the latifundio, for weakening the power of the church, and for regulating the operations of foreign capital in Mexico. But the constitution was not anticapitalist. It sanctioned and protected private property; it sought to control rather than eliminate foreign enterprises, creating more favorable conditions for the development of national capitalism.

Nonetheless, Carranza expressed reservations about the new constitution but promised to uphold it. Shortly after its promulgation on February 5, 1917, Carranza became the first legally elected president since Madero. On inauguration day, Obregón, his secretary of war, resigned and retired to private life. Obregón, who had been moving to the left, distrusted many of the men around Carranza as reactionaries of Porfirista stamp.

## CARRANZA'S PRESIDENCY

The three remaining years of the Carranza regime were marked by a sharp swing to the right. Carranza soon made it clear that he did not intend to implement the reform articles of the constitution. Only a trifling amount of land was distributed to the villages. Carranza returned many confiscated haciendas to their former owners; others he turned over to his favorite generals. Official corruption existed on a massive scale. The working class suffered severe repression. Carranza shut down the Casa del Obrero Mundial. The constitution's promise of free education was ignored. Only in Carranza's foreign policy, marked by a genuine revolutionary nationalism, did the spirit of the constitution live. Carranza staunchly resisted U.S. pressure to give guarantees that Article 27 of the constitution would not be implemented against foreign interests. He kept Mexico neutral in World War I and insisted on an independent Mexican diplomatic position in the hemisphere, postures that the United States regarded as unfriendly.

Carranza also appealed to upper- and middle-class women with decrees that legalized civil divorce, established alimony rights, and authorized women to own and manage property. On April 9, 1917, he signed the Law of Family Relations, which guaranteed women equal rights to exercise guardianship and child custody, file lawsuits, and sign contracts. But cultural taboos against divorce and other legal inequities institutionalized what historian Shirlene Soto calls a "sexual double standard" in Mexico.

Meanwhile, Carranza continued to battle the tenacious Zapatista movement in the south and Villa in the north. Against the Zapatistas, Carranza's favorite general, Pablo González, launched campaign after campaign. Zapata's forces diminished and the territory under his control shrank to the vanishing point, but he remained unconquerable, supported by the affection and loyalty of the peasantry. His fall came through treachery. Invited to confer with a Carrancista officer who claimed to have gone over to his side, Zapata was ambushed and slain on April 10, 1919. But his people continued their struggle for *tierra y libertad* (land and liberty).

Carranza's legal term was due to end in 1920, but the president had no intention of relinquishing power. Barred from running again by the constitutional rule of no reelection, he nonetheless tried to extend his power by imposing a weak puppet president. But Obregón, supported by a Labor Party formed to further his interests, rejected both Carranza and his surrogate. In May 1920, Carranza fled from the capital toward Veracruz, taking with him 5 million pesos in gold and silver from the national treasury. He was slain on May 21.

On May 24, Adolfo de la Huerta, a loyal Obregón ally, became interim president and sought to reconcile with Zapatistas by implementing agrarian reform. Villa, who also aided the anti-Carranza movement, was rewarded with a hacienda, and other lands were given to his men. Villa did not long enjoy his newfound peace and prosperity; he was assassinated in the summer of 1923 under obscure circumstances.

In November 1920, Obregón assumed the presidency. Peace had come to Mexico, and the work of reconstruction could begin. It would not be an easy task. The great wind that swept through Mexico had left a devastated land, with hundreds of thousands dead or missing; the Mexican population had actually declined by 1 million since 1910. The constitution of 1917 offered a blueprint for a new and better social order, but major obsta-

cles to change remained. Not the least were the hundreds of generals thrown up by the great upheaval, men of humble origins who once had nothing and now had an incurable itch for wealth and power. With his characteristic wry humor, Obregón summed up the problem when he said that the days of revolutionary banditry had ended because he had brought all the bandits with him to the capital to keep them out of trouble.

# Reconstructing the State: Rule of the Millionaire Socialists

## Obregón and Reform

With Obregón there came to power a group of northern generals and politicians who began the work of economic and social reconstruction that Madero, Huerta, and Carranza were unable or unwilling to achieve. Obregón and his successor, Calles, were of middle-class or even lower-class origins—Obregón had been a mechanic and farmer, Calles, a schoolteacher. They both were products of a border region where U.S. cultural influence was strong and where capitalism and capitalist relations were more highly developed than in any other part of Mexico. Obregón and Calles thus possessed a pragmatic business mentality as far removed from the revolutionary agrarian ideology of Zapata as it was from the aristocratic reformism of Carranza. These men deliberately set out to lay the economic, political, and ideological foundations of a Mexican national capitalism.

Aware that the revolution had radicalized the masses, aware of the appeal of socialism and anti-imperialism to the workers on whose support they counted, Obregón and Calles employed a revolutionary rhetoric designed to mobilize popular support and conceal how modest were the social changes that actually took place. In practice, Obregón's program was revolutionary only by contrast with the reactionary trend that characterized the last years of Carranza's rule. Far from promoting socialism, Obregón sought accommodation with all elements of Mexican society except the most reactionary clergy and landlords. He allowed exiles of the most varied political tendency to return to Mexico, and radical intellectuals rubbed shoulders with former Científicos in his government. Power was held by a ruling class of wealthy generals, capitalists, and landlords. Labor and the peasantry were the government's obedient clienteles.

Regarding agrarian reform as a useful safety valve for peasant discontent, Obregón distributed some land to the pueblos. But the process proceeded slowly, haltingly, against the intense opposition of the hacendados and the church, which condemned the agrarian reform because it did not take account of the "just rights of the landlords." Litigation by landlords, their use of armed force to resist occupation of expropriated land, and the opposition of the clergy slowed down the pace of the land reform.

Even after a village had received land, its prospect for success was poor, for the government failed to provide the peasants with seeds, implements, and adequate credit facilities or modern agricultural training. Such credit assistance as they received usually came from government rural banks, which exercised close control over land use, intensifying the client status of the peasantry, or from rural loan sharks. The Obregón land reform was neither swift nor thoroughgoing; by the end of his presidency, only some 3 million acres had been distributed among 624 villages, whereas 320 million acres remained in private hands.

Obregón also encouraged labor to organize, for he regarded trade unions as useful for stabilizing labor-capitalist relations and as an important bulwark of his regime. The principal trade union organization was the *Confederación Regional Obrera Mexicana* (CROM), formed in 1918. Despite the rhetoric of its leaders about "class struggle" and freedom from the "tyranny of capitalism," CROM was about as radical as the American Federation of Labor, with which it maintained close ties. Its perpetual boss was Luis Morones, known for his flashy dress, diamonds, and limousines. As the only labor organization sponsored and protected by the government, CROM had virtually official status. Despite this official protection, Morones's method of personal negotiation with employers yielded scanty benefits to labor; wages barely kept pace with the rising cost of living.

Perhaps the most solid achievements of the Obregón regime were in the areas of education and culture. The creation of a native Mexican capitalism demanded the development of a national consciousness, which meant the integration of indigenous peoples—still made up of so many small nations—into the national market and the new society. From this point of view, they were the key problem of Mexican reconstruction. Because incorporating them into the modern world required a thorough understanding of their past and present conditions of life, the revolutionary regimes encouraged scientific study of the indigenous peoples.

An integral part of *indigenismo* was a reassessment of indigenous cultural heritage. To insist on the greatness of the old native arts was one way of asserting the value of one's own, of revolting against the tyranny of the pallid, lifeless French and Spanish academicism over Mexican art during the last decades of the Díaz era.

From Europe returned two future giants of the Mexican artistic renaissance, Diego Rivera and David Alfaro Siqueiros, to join another gifted artist, José Clemente Orozco, in creating a militant new art that drew much of its inspiration from the indigenous peoples and their ancient art. Believing that "a heroic art could fortify the will to reconstruction," Obregón's brilliant young secretary of education, José Vasconcelos, offered the walls of public buildings for the painting of murals that glorified the natives, past and present.

The "Indianist" cult had great political significance. The foes of the revolution, unregenerate Porfiristas, clericals, and reactionaries of all stripes, looked back to Spain as the sole source of enduring values in Mexican life and regarded Cortés as the creator of Mexican nationality; partisans of the revolution tended to idealize Aztec Mexico (sometimes beyond recognition) and elevated the last Aztec warrior-king, Cuauhtémoc, to the status of a demigod.

Convinced that the school was the most important instrument for unifying the nation, that "to educate was to redeem," Vasconcelos, with ample budgetary support from Obregón, launched an imaginative program of cultural missions designed to bring literacy and health to indigenous villages. Professor Elena Torres, a founding member of the Mexican National Council of Women and a fiery socialist feminist, supervised the training of more than 4,000 rural teachers, the majority of whom were women, commissioned to bring the gospel of sanitation and literacy to remote pueblos. Torres acquired practical experience in this field during her collaboration with Yucatán state governor Felipe Carrillo Puerto, whose progressive reform agenda included "socialist education," state-supported birth control, women's suffrage, and civil equality.

Vasconcelos also founded teacher-training colleges, agricultural schools, and other specialized schools. An achievement in which he took special pride was the publication of hundreds of classic works in cheap editions for free distribution in the schools. Although these state education programs aimed to promote capitalist land and labor relations by building a patriarchal solidarity with peasants otherwise hostile to this goal, the result was much more ambiguous; according to historian Mary Kay Vaughan, the rural literacy crusades "injected new notions of women's work and personhood" into traditional rural images of women, thereby empowering *campesinas* and their local communities in ways unanticipated by national leaders. These villagers soon took advantage of the growing institutional rivalry between church and state to expand their autonomy.

The new secular, nationalist school provoked clerical anger, for it threatened to supplant the priest with the teacher as the guiding force of the rural community and to replace the religious world outlook taught by the Catholic church with a scientific world outlook. The church fought back with all the means at its disposal. Some priests denounced secular education from their pulpits and threatened parents who sent their children to state schools with excommunication. As a result of this campaign, many teachers were attacked and some killed by fanatical villagers. Despite this campaign, Obregón made no effort to implement Article 3 of the constitution, which banned reli-

gious primary schools, for he believed that in the absence of enough resources on the part of the state it was better that Mexican children receive instruction from priests than remain illiterate.

The Catholic issue joined with other issues to cause Obregón difficulties in his relations with the United States. For three years, the U.S. government withheld diplomatic recognition from Obregón in an effort to force him to recognize that Article 27 of the constitution should not apply to mineral concessions obtained by foreigners before 1917. Like Carranza, Obregón was willing to respect the principle of nonretroactivity but refused to formalize it in a treaty as a condition of U.S. diplomatic recognition, which he considered humiliating and politically destabilizing.

Obregón's practical policies, however, confirmed his interest in securing the rights of private property essential to foreign investment and capitalist growth. He signed agreements that renewed Mexico's foreign debt service payments, returned the National Railways to private ownership, and resolved various indemnity claims; he also secured Supreme Court rulings that declared unconstitutional any attempt to apply Article 27 retroactively. Faced with Obregón's uncompromising demand for unconditional U.S. recognition and a growing counterrevolutionary insurgency that threatened once again to destabilize Mexico, thereby undermining these agreements, the United States formally recognized the Mexican government in August 1923. When the expected revolt broke out in December, the United States allowed Obregón to procure large quantities of war materiel. Together with the help of the organized labor and peasant movements, this aid enabled Obregón to crush the uprising, which was supported by reactionary landowners, clergy, and military. On November 30, 1924, Obregón's hand-picked successor, Plutarco Elías Calles assumed the presidency of Mexico.

## CALLES'S REGIME

In and out of office, as legal president or de facto dictator, Calles dominated the next decade of Mexican politics. Building on the foundations Obregón had laid, he continued his work with much the same methods. His radical phraseology tended to conceal the pragmatic essence of his policy, which was to promote the rapid growth of Mexican national capitalism, whose infrastructure he helped to establish. To strengthen the fiscal and monetary system, he created the Bank of Mexico, the only bank permitted to issue money. A national road commission was organized, and a national electricity code was enacted to aid the electric power industry. These measures stimulated the growth of construction and consumer goods industries, in which members of Calles's official family—or the "revolutionary family," as the ruling elite came to be called—were heavily involved. Protective tariffs, subsidies, and other forms of aid were generously extended to industry, both foreign and domestic. In 1925 an assembly plant of the Ford Motor Company began operations in Mexico after Calles and the company negotiated an agreement providing for numerous concessions.

Calles showed more enthusiasm for land reform than Obregón, and the tempo of land distribution increased sharply during his presidency. Like Obregón, Calles regarded land reform as a safety valve for peasant unrest. During the four years of his term, Calles distributed about twice as much land as Obregón had.

But less than one-fourth of that amount consisted of arable land, for Calles did not require the hacendados to surrender productive land, and most of the land given up came from pasture or forest lands, or even land that was completely barren. Nor did Calles make a serious effort to provide the peasantry with irrigation, fertilizer, implements, or seed. He established a government bank that was supposed to lend money to the ejidos, promote modern farming techniques, and act as agents for the sale of their produce. But four-fifths of the bank's resources were loaned not to ejidos but to hacendados with much superior credit ratings, and many of the bank's agents took advantage of their position to enrich themselves at the expense of the peasants.

Under these conditions, it is no wonder that the land reform soon appeared to be a failure. By 1930 grain production had fallen below the levels of 1910, and Calles, concluding that peasant proprietorship was economically undesirable, announced the abandonment of land distribution. Meanwhile, on his own large estates Calles introduced machinery and other modern agricultural techniques and advised other large landowners to do the same.

Like Obregón, Calles regarded labor unions as desirable because they helped stabilize labor-capitalist relations and avert radical social change. But by the end of the *Callista* decade, Mexican labor, disillusioned with a corrupt leadership that kept wages at or below the subsistence level, had begun to break away from CROM and form independent unions.

Although Calles had announced his rhetorical support for women's rights, he did little to advance them, prompting women to organize themselves to secure their political, social, and economic liberation. Socialist Elvia Carrillo Puerto, sister of the Yucatecan *caudillo*, and communist María "Cuca" García organized women government employees; Elena Torres joined García to establish the Mexican Feminist Council, and the Mexican Feminist League appeared a few years later. At successive national and international conferences, however, these women inevitably clashed over issues of class. For example, when a middle-class delegate argued for prohibitions on begging, García objected: "How can one prevent begging when there is no work, when salaries are so meager, and you have the poor in complete helplessness?" Carrillo Puerto concluded the ensuing debate, scorning "the people of class" as "parasites that suck the lifeblood from the country."

Calles continued the Carranza and Obregón policies of asserting Mexico's right to regulate the conditions under which foreign capital could exploit its natural resources, but he was far from hostile to foreign capital. Indeed, he gave assurances that "the government will do everything in its power to safeguard the interests of foreign capitalists who invest money in Mexico."

But a serious dispute with the United States arose in 1925 when the Mexican Congress passed laws to implement Article 27. The most important of these measures required owners of oil leases to exchange their titles for fifty-year concessions dating from the time of acquisition, to be followed, if necessary, by a thirty-year renewal, with the possibility of yet another extension if needed. No Mexican oil well had ever lasted more than eighty years. Far from injuring the foreign oil companies, the law eliminated the vagueness of their status under Article 27, gave them firm titles emanating from the government, and served to quiet more radical demands for outright nationalization. However, a number of U.S. oil companies denounced the law as confiscatory and threatened to continue drilling operations without confirmatory concessions.

The U.S. State Department vigorously protested the restrictive legislation, and the U.S. ambassador, James R. Sheffield, pursued a hardline, uncompromising policy. By late 1926 the United States appeared to be moving toward war with Mexico.

Fortunately, the interventionist policy came under severe attack from progressive Republican senators, the press, church groups, and the academic world. President Calvin Coolidge and Secretary of State Kellogg, realizing that war with Mexico would have little national support, sought a way out of the impasse and were aided by U.S. international bankers, who had a firmer grasp of Mexican policies and intentions. The appointment of Dwight Morrow, a partner in the financial firm of J. P. Morgan, as ambassador to Mexico in September 1927 marked a turning point in the crisis. Morrow managed to persuade Calles that portions of the oil law had the potential for injuring foreign property rights, with the result that the Mexican Supreme Court found unconstitutional that portion of the law setting a time period on concessions. But as rewritten the law still provided for confirmatory concessions and reaffirmed national ownership of the subsoil.

In addition, a serious domestic dispute arose as a result of the government's alienation of peasant communities disadvantaged by its market reforms and the growing opposition of the church to the whole modernizing thrust of the revolution. Under Calles this opposition assumed the proportions of a civil war. In January 1926 the church hierarchy signed a letter declaring that the constitution of 1917 "wounds the most sacred rights of the Catholic Church" and disavowed the document. Calles responded by enforcing the anticlerical clauses of the constitution, which had lain dormant. The Calles Law, as it was called, ordered the registration of priests with the civil authorities and the closing of religious primary schools. The church struck back by suspending church services throughout Mexico, a powerful weapon in a country so overwhelmingly Catholic.

But neither this strike nor the boycott organized by the church, which urged the faithful to buy no goods or services except absolute necessities, brought the government to its knees. By the end of 1926, militant Catholics, in frequent alliance with local hacendados, had taken up arms. Guerrilla groups were formed, with the mountainous backcountry of Jalisco the main focus of their activity. Government schools and young teachers sent into remote areas were frequent objects of clerical fury; many teachers were tortured and killed. The total number of Catholic guerrillas, known as *Cristeros* from their slogan, *Viva Cristo Rey* (Long Live Christ the King), was small, but federal commanders helped keep the insurrection alive by the brutality of their repressions. By the summer of 1927, however, the revolt had largely burned itself out.

In 1928, fearing the divisiveness historically associated with Mexico's democratic electoral transitions, Obregón and Calles sought a constitutional amendment to extend the presidential term to six years and allow former presidents to seek reelection after one term out of office. Although this was designed to rotate the presidency between Obregón and Calles, Obregón's assassination by a fanatical *Cristero* in July spawned a new political crisis.

With the passing of the formidable Obregón, Calles became the *jefe máximo*, the maximum chief of the revolution. The presidents who successively held office during what was to have been Obregón's six-year term—Emilio Portes Gil, Pascual Ortiz Rubio, and Abelardo Rodríguez—were Calles's stooges and obediently resigned when they incurred his displeasure. In 1929, after crushing a rebellion that proved to be almost the last hurrah of the regional military caudillos, Calles organized the National Revolutionary Party

(PNR) as an instrument for pacifying the country and institutionalizing the rule of the "revolutionary family," the military leaders and politicians who had ruled the country since 1920. Under different names and with leaderships of differing composition, the party formed by Calles remained the ruling party of Mexico for six decades. The official party's candidates for president did not lose an election until 2000.

As the "revolutionary family" consolidated its power and its wealth increased, its members became even more corrupt and predatory than the old Porfirista aristocracy. As large landowners, they were naturally hostile to agrarian reform; as owners of construction firms and factories, they were hostile to strikes and unions.

Calles and his cronies had never been committed to a radical reconstruction of Mexican society, but after 1928, they retreated from their own modest reform program. To camouflage this shift of emphasis and validate their revolutionary credentials they indulged freely in anticlerical demagoguery and excesses. Their acts blew new life into the dying Cristero movement, causing a brief but bitter new conflict that took many lives.

This change in the Callista regime coincided with the beginning in 1929 of the Great Depression, which exposed the bankruptcy of capitalist economics and added to the misery of Mexican peasants and workers. Their growing unrest created fears of a new revolutionary explosion. Rumblings of protest were heard even within the ruling party. A new generation of young, middle-class reformers demanded vigorous implementation of the constitution of 1917. Some were intellectuals influenced by Marxism and the success of the Soviet example, especially by its concept of economic planning, but their basic message was the need to resume the struggle against the latifundio, peonage, and economic and cultural backwardness; that is, to resume the advance of the bourgeois revolution, stalled by the corruption and cynicism of the Callistas.

This message was loudly trumpeted at successive meetings of the National Congress of Women Workers and Peasants in the early 1930s. Here, "Cuca" García, for example, accused the Callistas of murdering campesinos and denounced their neglect of poor peasant women: "the agrarian legislation," she thundered, "condemns them always to live in their father's, husband's, or brother's poverty," denying them the "economic independence [that] is the foundation of women's political independence." García was promptly arrested but was later released when thousands of women rallied to her defense at the jail. Despite rancorous debate, these meetings typically pressed for more progressive state action to expand indigenous rights, protect women workers, raise the minimum wage, increase land reform, and promote women's suffrage.

By 1933 the influence of the progressive wing within the PNR had grown. Its acknowledged leader was General Lázaro Cárdenas, governor of Michoacán, who had established an enviable record for honesty, compassion, and concern for commoners. He had spent almost 50 percent of his budget on education, doubling the number of schools in the state. Despite his progressive ideas, he was close to the inner circle of the "revolutionary family," and the jefe máximo supported Cárdenas for president in 1933. Although there was no doubt that he would be elected, Cárdenas campaigned vigorously, visiting the most remote areas of the country, patiently explaining to workers and peasants his Six-Year Plan to strengthen the ejidos, build modern schools, and develop workers' cooperatives. Although Calles remained confident that the loyal Cárdenas would carry out his orders as the puppet presidents who preceded him had done, Cárdenas had established his political independence.

## Cárdenas and the Populist Interlude

Under Cárdenas, the Mexican Revolution resumed its advance. Land distribution to the villages on a massive scale was accompanied by a many-sided effort to raise agricultural productivity and improve the quality of rural life. Labor was encouraged to replace the old, corrupt leadership with militant leaders and to struggle for improved conditions. A spirit of service began to pervade at least a part of the governmental bureaucracy. Cárdenas set an example to subordinates by the democratic simplicity of his manners, by cutting his own salary in half, and by making himself available to the delegations of peasants and workers who thronged the waiting rooms of the National Palace.

These and other policies of the new president—such as the closing down of illegal gambling houses, most of which were owned by wealthy Callistas—angered the jefe máximo. In 1935, Calles denounced the labor movement and its alleged radicalism and threatened to depose Cárdenas, who responded by forming a new cabinet dominated by the left wing but representing a broad coalition of anti-Callista elements. By the end of 1935, Cárdenas was the undisputed master of Mexico, and he ordered Calles's immediate deportation to the United States in 1936.

## LAND REFORM

Having consolidated his political control, Cárdenas proceeded to implement his reform program. He regarded land distribution as of prime importance. Land was distributed to the peasantry in a variety of ways, according to the climatic and soil conditions of the different regions. The principal form was the ejido, the communal landholding system under which land could not be mortgaged or alienated (except under very special conditions), with each *ejidatario* entitled to use a parcel of community land. The ejido was the focal point of the agrarian reform. But Cárdenas also distributed land in the form of the *rancho*, the individual small holding widely prevalent in the northern Mexican states. Finally, in regions where natural conditions favored large-scale cultivation of such commercial crops as sugar, cotton, coffee, rice, and henequen, large cooperative farms (collective ejidos) were organized on a profit-sharing basis. The government generously endowed these enterprises with seeds, machinery, and credit from the *Banco de Crédito Ejidal*.

During the Cárdenas years, some 45 million acres of land were distributed to almost twelve thousand villages. The Cárdenas distribution program struck a heavy blow at the traditional, semi-feudal hacienda and peonage, satisfied the land hunger of the Mexican peasantry for the time being, and promoted a general modernization of Mexican life and society. By 1940, thanks to the land reform and supplemented by the provision of villages with schools, medical care, roads, and other facilities, the standard of living of the peasantry had risen, if only modestly. These progressive changes in turn contributed to the growth of the internal market and therefore of Mexican industry. The land reform also justified itself in terms of productivity; average agricultural production during the three-year period from 1939 to 1941 was higher than it had been at any time since the beginning of the revolution.

Granted these benefits and Cárdenas's excellent intentions, the fact remains that the land reform suffered from the first from certain structural defects. To begin with, it was basically conceived as a means of satisfying land hunger by the grant or restitution of land to the villages, and it overlooked the need to establish agricultural units that would be viable from an economic point of view. In many cases, the *ejidal* parcel, especially in areas of very dense population, was so small as to form a minifundio. Much of the distributed land was of poor quality (the agrarian law always allowed the landowner to retain a portion of his estate, and naturally landowners kept the best portions for themselves), and aid in the form of seeds, technical assistance, and credit was frequently inadequate.

In addition, peasants received their land from the government, which controlled their activities through the operations of the *Departamento Agrario*, the Banco de Crédito Ejidal, and officially organized peasant leagues; thus, they were increasingly dependent on public authorities. Under Cárdenas, officials of these agencies often worked in a spirit of disinterested service and sought to develop peasant collective initiative and democracy; under his successors in the presidency, they tended to become corrupt and self-seeking, to enmesh the peasantry and its organizations in a bureaucratic network that manipulated them to satisfy its own interests. After 1940, Mexican governments increasingly favored large private property and neglected the ejido. In concert with the structural defects of the land reform, this produced a gradual decline of the ejido system and a parallel growth of large landed property, leading to the emergence of a new latifundio.

## LABOR REFORM

Under Cárdenas the labor movement was revitalized. Aware of the sympathetic attitude of the new regime, workers struck in unprecedented numbers for higher wages and better working conditions; in 1935 there were 642 strikes, more than twice the number in the preceding six years. In 1936 the young radical intellectual Vicente Lombardo Toledano organized a new labor federation, the *Confederación de Trabajadores Mexicanos* (CTM), to replace the dying and discredited CROM. Labor supported and in turn was supported by Cárdenas.

Labor, the peasantry, and the army became the three main pillars of the official party, reorganized in 1938 and renamed the Party of the Mexican Revolution (PRM). The power of the generals was weakened by a policy of raising wages and improving the morale of the rank-and-file and by the distribution of weapons to the peasantry, formed into a militia.

Like the land reform, the labor reform had structural flaws that created serious problems for the future. In return for concessions from a paternal government, labor, like the peasantry, was invited to incorporate itself into the official apparatus and to give automatic and obligatory support to a government that in the last analysis represented the interests of the national bourgeoisie. In the domestic and international situation of the 1930s, which was dominated by a struggle between profascist and antifascist forces, the interests of that bourgeoisie and Mexican labor largely coincided, but in the changed conditions after 1940, labor's loss of independence and the meshing of its organizations with the official apparatus led to a revival of corruption and reactionary control of the trade unions.

## ECONOMIC REFORM

Although Cárdenas was sympathetic to labor's demands for better conditions, he was no foe of private enterprise, despite efforts by his foes to link him to socialism and communism. In fact, industrial capitalism made significant strides under Cárdenas. If Cárdenas supported labor's efforts to raise wages where the financial condition of an enterprise warranted it, he also favored Mexican industry with government loans and protective tariffs that insured the creation of a captive market for high-priced consumer goods. In 1934 his government established the *Nacional Financiera*, a government bank and investment corporation that used funds supplied by the federal government and domestic investors to make industrial loans, finance public welfare projects, and issue its own securities. The coming of World War II, which sharply reduced the availability of imports, greatly stimulated the movement toward industrialization and import substitution.

Mexico's struggle for economic sovereignty reached a high point under Cárdenas. In 1937 a dispute between North American and British oil companies and the unions erupted into a strike, followed by legal battles between the contending parties. When the oil companies refused to accept a much-scaled-down arbitration-tribunal wage finding in favor of the workers, Cárdenas intervened. On March 18, 1938—a date celebrated by Mexicans as marking their declaration of economic independence—the president announced in a radio speech that the properties of the oil companies had been expropriated in the public interest. With support from virtually all strata of the population, Cárdenas was able to ride out the storm caused by economic sanctions against Mexico on the part of the United States, England, and the oil companies. The oil nationalization was a major victory for Mexican nationalism. It provided cheap, plentiful fuel for Mexican industry, and the needs of the nationalized oil industries further stimulated industrialization. But the oil nationalization did not set a precedent; some 90 percent of Mexico's mining industry remained in foreign hands.

## WOMEN'S RIGHTS

Pressured by a well-organized, increasingly cohesive women's movement, Cárdenas supported constitutional reform "to grant equal rights" and pledged to create a women's section of the PNR to guarantee that "working women have the right to participate in electoral struggles." Meanwhile, women consolidated their organizational efforts in the United Front for Women's Rights, under the leadership of veteran feminist "Cuca" García and other socialist and communist women. The Front, incorporating some eight hundred women's groups with more than fifty thousand members, demanded women's right to vote and hold office, civil equality, protective legislation for women workers, social integration of indigenous women, and women's centers for cultural education and vocational training.

In 1937, even though the law forbade women to hold elective office and the PNR refused to slate her, the Front supported García's successful primary race for a seat in the Chamber of Deputies. It also secured congressional and state legislative approval of a constitutional amendment permitting woman suffrage beginning in 1939, but thereafter the PNR-dominated Congress, split by fractious party infighting and fearful of a resurgent Catholic conservatism that might have benefited politically from women's enfranchisement, neglected to pass the necessary enabling legislation. Woman suffrage would have to wait until 1953, when a more conservative ruling party had reached a *modus vivendi* with the Catholic church.

### CÁRDENAS'S GROWING MODERATION AND THE ELECTION OF 1940

Education, especially the rural school system, made considerable progress under Cárdenas. Of Tarascan origin, Cárdenas displayed much concern for indigenous welfare. He created a *Departamento de Asuntos Indígenas* to serve and protect their interests and encouraged the study of their culture, past and present, by founding the *Instituto Nacional de Antropología de México*.

But in the last years of his presidency, in apparent deference to clerical and conservative opposition, Cárdenas abandoned many reforms and soft-pedaled the so-called socialist character of Mexican education. He also slowed down the

pace of land distribution and displayed a conciliatory attitude toward the entrepreneurial class, assuring its members that he regarded them as part of the *fuerzas vivas* (vital forces) of the country and that they need not fear for the safety of their investments.

On the eve of the presidential election of 1940, Cárdenas and the official party, an amalgam of social forces including increasingly conservative and influential industrialists, nominated General Manuel Ávila Camacho, a Cárdenas loyalist, a devout Catholic, and a man of generally conservative views. Ávila Camacho was elected with almost 99 percent of the vote and soon began to reassure foreign and domestic capital. He dissociated himself from the radical leadership of the unions, expressed a flexible attitude toward the question of whether the ejido or small private property was the best form of agrarian organization, and assured the Catholics that he was a *creyente* (believer).

## The Big Bourgeoisie in Power, 1940–1976: Erosion of Reform

The Cárdenas era was the high-water mark of the struggle to achieve the social goals of the revolution. Under his successors, there began an erosion of the social conquests of the Cárdenas years. During those years the material and cultural condition of the masses had improved, if only modestly; peasants and workers managed to secure a somewhat larger share of the total national income. After 1940 these trends were reversed. The new rulers of Mexico favored a development strategy that sharply restricted trade union activity, slowed the tempo of agrarian reform, and reduced the relative share of total income of the bottom two-thirds of the Mexican population.

Ávila Camacho presided over the first phase (1940–1946) of this policy reversal. Regarding unlimited private profit as the driving force of economic progress, he proposed to create a favorable climate for private enterprise. In practice, this meant the freezing of wages, the repression of strikes, and the use of a new weapon against dissidents, a vaguely worded law dealing with the "crime of social dissolution."

Meanwhile, World War II stimulated both the export of Mexican raw materials and import substitution through industrialization. Significant advances were made in food processing, textiles, and other consumer goods industries, and the capital goods industry, centered in the north, was considerably expanded. Steel production increased, with Monterrey Steel and other companies producing structural and rolled steel for buildings, hotels, highways, and steel hardware. The Nacional Financiera played a leading role in this process of growth through loans to industry for plant construction and expansion. In view of this spontaneous economic growth, the concept of planning was forgotten; the second Six-Year Plan remained on paper. No effort was made to produce a balanced development of the Mexican regions; most of the development took place in the Federal District and the surrounding area. Meanwhile, land distribution was sharply reduced.

In 1946 the official party changed its name to the PRI (*Partido Revolucionario Institucional*), and Ávila Camacho was succeeded as president by the lawyer Miguel Alemán (1946–1952), who continued the policies of his predecessor. Alemán made every effort to encourage private investment through tariff protection, import licensing, subsidies, and government loans. This favorable economic climate attracted domestic and foreign investors looking for outlets for their surplus capital after World War II. A characteristic of the new foreign capital investment was that it flowed primarily into manufacturing rather than the traditional extractive industries.

Under Alemán and his successor, Adolfo Ruiz Cortines (1952–1958), land distribution and efforts to increase the productivity of the ejidos were neglected in favor of the large private landholding. To provide an incentive to capitalist entrepreneurs, Alemán had Article 27 of the constitution amended. This "reform" consisted in the grant of certificates of "inaffectibility" to landowners, which exempted them from further expropriation for holdings up to 100 hectares of irrigated land or 200 hectares of land with seasonal rainfall. For the production of certain specified crops, the size of inaffectible holdings was made even larger.

A massive program of irrigation contributed to the explosion of capitalist agriculture that began in this period. The irrigation projects were concentrated in northern and northwestern Mexico, where much of the land was owned directly or indirectly by prominent Mexican politicians, their friends, and relatives. Alemán presided over a great boom in public works construction, accompanied by an orgy of plunder of the public treasury by entrepreneurs and officials; his was probably the most corrupt administration in modern Mexican history.

There arose a new hacienda, technically efficient and often arrayed in modern corporate guise, that soon accounted for the bulk of Mexico's commercial agricultural production and shared its profits with processing plants that were usually subsidiaries of foreign firms. By 1961, fifty years after the revolution began, less than 1 percent of all farms possessed 50 percent of all agricultural land. Increasing numbers of small landholders meanwhile, starved for credit and lacking machinery, had to abandon their parcels of land and become peons on the new haciendas or emigrate to the cities in search of work in the new factories.

Industry continued to grow but was increasingly penetrated and dominated by foreign capital. A favorite device for foreign penetration of Mexican industry was the mixed, or joint, company, which had a number of advantages. It satisfied the requirement of Mexican law that Mexican nationals hold 51 percent of most companies operating in Mexico; it camouflaged actual domination of such enterprises by the foreign partners through control of patents, licensing agreements, and other sources of technological and financial dependence; and it formed strong ties between foreign capitalists and the native industrial and financial bourgeoisie.

The economic and social policies of Presidents Adolfo López Mateos (1958–1964) and Gustavo Díaz Ordaz (1964–1970), did not differ significantly from those of their predecessors. Under Díaz Ordaz discontent among workers mounted as their real income shrank as a result of chronic inflation, a virtual freeze on wages, and official control of trade union organizations, known as *charrismo*. Demetrio Vallejo of the independent railway workers epitomized this growing instability and led a series of strikes that quickly spread to other workers. The teachers' strike was especially disturbing to the PRI's authoritarian state and its proponents, such as the newspaper *Excelsior*, which promptly lamented the lack of respect for "authority" that this inculcated among students who consequently were not taught about "the inviolable and absolute respect for private property."

The 1957 death of Pedro Infante also gave voice to this growing social alienation. Arguably Mexico's premier entertainer, Infante, born to poverty, became famous for his good looks, quick wit, anarchic lifestyle, enormously popular films, and *ranchera* songs that proclaimed "it's better to die while dreaming than to live in reality." According to cultural historian Anne Rubenstein, his funeral and the riots that it occasioned among his mostly working-class fans represented this same social turmoil and growing popular resistance to Mexico's authoritarian state. Angered at his untimely death in an airplane crash, Infante's working-class fans empathized with their hero, whom they saw as a victim of the same forces of modernization that daily assaulted their lives, and lashed out at Mexico City's police, the most visible and proximate representatives of an authoritarian state that had relentlessly promoted modernization in the postwar world.

Popular resistance to modernization also was reflected in the experience of Mexican workers at the General Motors plant in Mexico City, which further illustrated the impact of global market changes in the 1960s. For many years, General Motors had been the symbol par excellence of postwar modernity, the populist state's import-substitution industrialization strategy, and paternalistic transnational corporate managerial relations with workers. The company, according to historian Steven Bachelor, traditionally had prided itself on creating a family environment with which Mexican workers would readily identify. This included relatively high wages; paid vacations; educational scholarships for workers' children; and company-sponsored baseball, soc-

cer, and bowling leagues. These collaborative relationships began to deteriorate, however, as international markets for automobile production became increasingly competitive and domestic demand grew in response to the 1962 Integration Decree, which required domestic production of all cars sold in Mexico. Thereafter, GM's corporate management forcibly retired older workers, hired younger replacements at half the wages, restricted their bathroom breaks, and dramatically increased the speed of assembly line operations to maximize productivity and profits. One worker, unable to endure the relentless pressure of the accelerated assembly line, broke down in tears. Others naturally resisted these pressures through open acts of defiance: one, whose boss refused to authorize a bathroom break, simply urinated on the spot; others, like Clemente Zaldívar, sabotaged the assembly line. By 1965 these tensions exploded into a month-long strike against General Motors that won some considerable wage benefits but failed to achieve the workers' goal of greater control over production decisions.

Student unrest also grew. Historian Eric Zolov argues that this was, at least in part, the consequence of the invasion of British and U.S. rock and roll music in the late 1950s and 1960s. Initially embraced by the López Mateos's government as a symbol of Mexico's newly achieved modernity, Mexico's cultural industries celebrated rock and roll, along with other musical imports like *cha-cha-chá* and *mambo* from Cuba and *cumbia* from Colombia. Epitomized by the lyrics, facial expressions, and body movements of Elvis Presley, however, upper- and middle-class Mexican youth seemed more interested in rock's sneering contempt for traditional values, associated in Mexico with *buenas costumbres* or "good behavior." Because this threatened the stability of the nation's patriarchal, authoritarian power, it was quickly denounced in the press as *"rebeldismo sin causa"* (rebellion without a cause), and an effort to discredit foreign rock shortly ensued. For example, rumors soon circulated that Presley had said he would "rather kiss three black girls than a Mexican," and an advertising campaign entitled "Die Elvis Presley" was soon initiated.

But this did not dampen the enthusiasm of Mexican middle-class youth for rock-and-roll music. On the contrary, it became more popular than ever; Mexican bands like Los Loud Jets, Los Rebeldes del Rock, and Los Teen Tops became national icons, at least in part as a result of nationalistic laws that placed high tariffs on foreign imports and required radio stations to feature play lists, 25 percent of the artists of which were Mexican. Ironically, the popularity of these Mexican bands was a reflection of their skill at producing accurate English-language covers (*refritos*) of British and U.S. rock songs by bands like The Doors, The Beatles, The Rolling Stones, Jimi Hendrix, and Janis Joplin, whose music increasingly celebrated freedom, rebellion, and disrespect of tradition. By the end of the 1960s, the rock music that flourished in Mexico City's *cafes cantantes* (musical coffeehouses) unleashed *La Onda* (The Wave), which became Mexico's counterculture, championing alike the cultural contributions of Che Guevara, Allen Ginsberg, and Mick Jagger. Denouncing these coffeehouses as "centers of perversion" influenced by decadent foreigners, the authorities organized a campaign to close them down in 1965 and instructed border officials to deny visas to "dirty, long-haired North American youth."

This was the cultural background against which the student protest movement of 1968 unfolded. Many of those who rallied in support of student demands for an end to state repression were initially attracted to the movement by its association with the rock-and-roll subculture that had developed over the previous decade. Zolov interviewed one student who confessed that in his early teens he had known little about the movement except that it was composed of students from the national university who "listened to rock." Others recalled that the student movement recruited supporters for its opposition to an authoritarian patriarchal social order by invoking state and parental repression of rock music: "Isn't it true they don't let you listen to rock?"

This student movement denounced police brutality against student protesters and violations of the constitutional autonomy of the national university. The student protest broadened into a nationwide movement demanding democratiza-

tion of Mexican economic and political life. The government responded with a savage assault by army troops on a peaceful assembly of students and others in the Plaza of Three Cultures in Mexico City (October 2, 1968), leaving a toll of dead and wounded running into the hundreds.

This massacre of students at Tlatelolco Square ignited a fierce repression of popular resistance that forced political opposition underground and channeled it into cultural forms. The student movement fractured into two groups: political radicals and *jipitecas*, who joined foreign "hippies" in their common search for psychedelic mushrooms and an escape from the modern world into the "pristine poverty" of indigenous Mexico. During the next decade, Mexico's angry young urban working class laid its claim to the rebellious rock-and-roll culture that middle- and upper-class youth increasingly abandoned after 1968. Nurtured in the *hoyos fonquis* or "funky holes," bands like Los Dug-Dugs, with their "dirty and disheveled look" and "insolent gestures that offend," used these urban "raves" to reflect and represent their youthful working-class protest. This protest found its ultimate outlet at the Avándaro music festival in 1971. Here, Mexican rock bands attracted an audience of 200,000 that included *fresas* (wealthy, privileged elites), middle-class *onderos*, and a large number of *nacos*, lower-class youth from the "proletarian neighborhoods of the Federal District." Critics on the left and right alike denounced the cultural anarchy unleashed at Avándaro, but the participants themselves more closely identified with one of the featured bands, who insisted that "Rock isn't about peace and love; rock is about revolution." Although the rock subculture was self-consciously—even aggressively—antipolitical, it gave voice to anti-authoritarian popular protest and provided a potentially powerful instrument of political organization that seemingly transcended class barriers. "Avándaro," according to Zolov, "had revealed the political dangers of rock." Not surprisingly, the PRI thereafter tried to close it down.

The economic strategy of the Díaz Ordaz administration centered on providing the greatest possible incentives to private investment, foreign

Rock-and-roll music offered alienated Mexican youth a forum for their collective protest against cultural conformity, social inequality, and political repression. Organized in the aftermath of the Mexican government's slaughter of rebellious students at Tlatelolco Square, the 1971 Avándaro Music Festival provided some 250,000 young people an opportunity to express their enthusiasm for a music that defied Mexico's established traditions. [Alberto Cruz Molina]

and domestic. The foreign debt grew alarmingly, with the volume of foreign loans reaching a figure four times that of the Ruiz Cortines era. This heavy influx of loans increased the dependent character of the Mexican economy.

The official presidential candidate, Luis Echeverría, took office in 1970 amid deepening political, social, and economic storm clouds. Echeverría signaled a tactical shift when he released a large number of students and intellectuals imprisoned after the 1968 student disturbances, promised to struggle against colonialism and corruption, and condemned the unjust distribution of land and income in Mexico. However, recent publication of archival materials, memoirs, and other testimony removed any doubt about Echeverría's leading role in the Tlatelolco mas-

sacre and the *guerra sucia* (dirty war) thereafter waged by PRI regimes against leftist opposition.

But conservative Mexican capitalists, closely linked with foreign capital, struck back by withholding investment funds from the market, setting off a serious recession. Under intense pressure from the right, Echeverría retreated. During his last three years in office he reverted to traditional policies and methods, poorly concealed by a populist rhetoric. He publicly denounced colonialism and multinational corporations, but his government did its utmost to attract foreign investments, especially from the United States. With the investments came growing foreign penetration and domination of Mexican industry, especially of its most strategic sectors. By the mid-seventies, 70 percent of earnings from the capital goods industry went to foreign capital, leaving 20 percent for public firms and 10 percent for national private companies.

As the investments increased, so did Mexico's indebtedness and the drain of its capital in the form of dividends, interest, and other returns on foreign investment. By June 1976, Mexico's foreign debt had reached $25 billion. Mexico and Brazil shared the distinction of having the highest foreign debts among Third World countries. By September of that year the growing trade deficit had forced the government to order a 60 percent devaluation of the peso, causing a sharp rise in inflation and greater hardship for the masses. The problem of landlessness or inadequate land and rural unemployment and underemployment remained as stubborn as ever. Some 6 million peasants were landless.

Prospects for the solution of Mexico's urgent problems through the electoral process appeared dim because the PRI, dominated by the industrial and financial oligarchy, had an unshakable grip on power. That power rested in the last analysis on a system of institutionalized coercion and fraud. But other methods included the co-optation of dissidents into the state apparatus; the provision of greater access to medical services, schools, low-cost housing, and other benefits to such strategic groups as state employees, professionals, and organized workers; the paternalistic distribution of goods and services to the urban poor; and a populist rhetoric that identified the ruling party with the great ideals of the Revolution. These policies slightly reduced mass poverty and income inequalities in Mexican society, but they reinforced a precarious popular base and legitimacy for the PRI's monopoly of political power. By the 1970s, however, both were threatened by rampant inflation and a stagnant economy.

## Deconstructing the State: Neoliberalism and the Second Conquest of Mexico, 1977–2003

José López Portillo assumed the presidency on December 1, 1976, and continued the long-established policy of favoring the country's elites, making it clear that he was opposed to further large-scale land distribution and would not touch efficiently run large estates even if their size exceeded legal limits. In the words of one Mexican weekly, "the constitution is to protect peasants wearing collars and ties, and not those wearing rope sandals." Amid growing optimism over Mexico's economic prospects, López Portillo announced the discovery of vast new oil and gas deposits on Mexico's east coast. Figures for the country's estimated and proven oil reserves steadily rose; by 1980 they were put at 200 billion barrels, and Mexico ranked among the world's major oil producers. With oil prices increasing steeply due to the Arab oil embargo, government planners counted on the oil and gas bonanza to alleviate Mexico's balance-of-payments problem and to finance the purchase of the goods needed for further development and the creation of new jobs. The resulting expansion of production, however, was largely concentrated in capital-intensive industries—petrochemical factories, steel mills, and the like—that generated relatively few jobs and required expensive imports of capital equipment. In agriculture, too, the main growth was in capital-intensive, export-oriented agribusiness operations that created little employment and diverted labor and acreage from staple food production, which actually declined during the 1970s; by 1980 one-third of the maize consumed in Mexico came from the United States.

The cost of imported equipment and technology required to expand oil production came very high and had to be covered by new loans. Despite increasing revenues from oil and gas exports, Mexico's trade deficit steadily rose from $1.4 billion in 1977 to $3 billion in 1979. Inflation again moved upward; Mexican workers lost 20 percent of their purchasing power between 1977 and 1979. Despite these troubling signs, the international bankers appeared eager to lend more, advancing Mexico $10 billion in 1980. Who could question the credit of a country that seemed to float on a sea of oil?

The oil boom and the massive infusions of foreign loans gave a new dimension to the familiar problem of corruption in Mexican political life.[1] One of its signs was a wave of monumental private construction. But "the dance of the billions" was drawing to a close. In the first months of 1981, responding to weakening demand and a developing world oil glut, oil prices fell sharply. Mexico's projected earnings in 1982 from oil and gas exports, the source of 75 percent of Mexico's foreign exchange, fell from $27 billion to under $14 billion. Many wealthy Mexicans, losing confidence in their currency, hurried to buy dollars and deposit them in U.S. banks. In February 1982, with the government's foreign-exchange reserves dwindling at an alarming rate, López Portillo allowed the peso to fall by 60 percent. Fear of further devaluations provoked another flight of dollars. The growing shortage of dollars, vitally needed fuel for Mexican industry, caused a widening recession and unemployment.

## Debt Crisis, the IMF, and NAFTA

Bankruptcies and closings multiplied as more and more businesses lacked the dollars needed to obtain imported parts and raw materials or to pay debts contracted in dollars. With the Banco de México almost drained of reserves, López Portillo announced the nationalization of all private (but not foreign) banks and the establishment of stringent exchange controls. The bank nationalization, the most radical measure taken by a Mexican president since the "Mexicanization" of the oil industry by Cárdenas in 1938, was greeted with cries of protest from the private banking sector and great demonstrations of support by the PRI and its client organizations, the trade unions, and the parties of the left.

In Washington, usually so allergic to all measures smacking of collectivism or socialism, the bank nationalization did not arouse the hostility that might have been expected, probably because even conservative U.S. officials regarded it as a necessary step, given the circumstances. The prime

concern of the Reagan administration was to save Mexico, the third largest trading partner of the United States, from a default that could wreck the international banking system and bring down the great U.S. banks to which Mexico owed $25.8 billion, almost a third of its foreign debt. Consequently, Mexican and U.S. officials negotiated a rescue operation that provided for U.S. aid of $2.9 billion for Mexico's current-accounts problem; a seven-month freeze on the repayment of principal due to foreign bankers; and an eventual IMF (International Monetary Fund) loan of $3.9 billion, which could initiate a new cycle of commercial bank loans to Mexico. The IMF loan was, of course, subject to the usual conditions: Mexico must accept certain austerity measures—reduction of subsidies, restraints on wage increases, and other economies that were bound to hit Mexico's poor the hardest.

Even before he took office, the PRI's designated successor, Harvard-trained economist Miguel De la Madrid had indicated his approval of the strong financial medicine prescribed by the IMF. These politically unpalatable steps included price increases of 100 percent and 50 percent on gasoline and natural gas, respectively, and the lifting of price controls and subsidies for consumer items ranging from shoes to television sets. Another measure was a new devaluation of the peso that was expected to stimulate exports. It would, however, also make imports more costly, increase the burden of foreign debt service, and reduce real wages.

The solution for the Mexican crisis consisted, in essence, of adding new debts to old ones, without the slightest prospect that the huge foreign debt of some $85 billion could ever be paid or even significantly reduced without a large write-off, and of imposing heavy new burdens on already impoverished groups of the Mexican population. Four years after the rescue operation, the debt problem was more intractable than ever. By the fall of 1986, Mexico's foreign debt had risen to more than $100 billion.

The economic crisis was intertwined with a growing crisis in U.S.-Mexican relations. The Reagan administration, fanatically devoted to a "free market" economy and committed to the

---

[1]One Mexican news magazine, *Proceso*, estimated that officials of López Portillo's administration had misused or stolen $3 billion of public funds.

overthrow of the Sandinist government in Nicaragua, sought to use negotiations with Mexico over its foreign debt as a means of reshaping Mexico's economic structures and even its foreign policy. The U.S. economic demands included the opening up of Mexican industry to foreign investments, selling off state-owned enterprises, liberalizing foreign trade, and abandoning regulation of direct foreign investment. Despite the many concessions made by the De la Madrid government in economic policy, the Reagan administration demanded more.

Thus Mexico faced a profound, many-sided crisis. In essence, it was a crisis of the import-substitution model of development institutionalized by Cárdenas and continued by his successors. That model was based on state ownership of key industries, protection and subsidies for private industry, and such redistributive policies as the provision of social services, subsidized food prices, and land reform. It also called for the alternate use of co-optation and repression by the one-party state to keep restive labor, peasants, and intellectuals in line. By the early 1980s, however, that model, encumbered by a suffocating foreign debt, had exhausted its possibilities for growth.

Confronted with this crisis, a dominant section of the Mexican elite opted for a new, neoliberal model of development that abandoned the internal market in favor of exports of manufactured goods and integration with the world economy, especially with the United States. The economic program of President De la Madrid marked the formal transition to the new economic order. Two important steps in that direction were Mexico's signing in 1986 of the General Agreement on Tariffs and Trade, designed to lower tariffs and eliminate quotas and other restrictions on trade, and the liberalization under U.S. and Japanese pressure of foreign investment laws. The full implementation of the neoliberal project, however, had to await the outcome of the historic election of 1988, which pitted the PRI candidate, another Harvard-trained economist, Carlos Salinas de Gortari, against Cuauhtémoc Cárdenas, son of former president and national hero Lázaro Cárdenas. Cárdenas's program called for an end to political corruption

and electoral fraud, suspension of foreign debt payments and renegotiation of the debt with creditor banks and governments, a mixed economy, and state assistance to the ejido farming sector. His candidacy inspired a wave of popular enthusiasm and mobilization unknown since the election of 1934 that had brought his own father to power.

Most political observers believe that Cárdenas actually won the general election, but because the PRI counted the votes, Salinas was declared the winner with 50.1 percent of the 19 million ballots cast. Despite mass protests, including a march of thousands on Mexico City, Salinas assumed office and immediately slated for privatization almost all of Mexico's remaining 770 state-owned enterprises, presiding over a fire sale of some of Mexico's choicest properties, including mines, sugar mills, a five-star hotel chain, and the national insurance company. Two government airlines, state-owned steel companies, 70 percent of the petrochemical industry, and the Teléfonos de México were sold, many well below their market value, and only some were operating inefficiently at a loss. The process was accompanied by widespread layoffs and wage cuts and growing foreign conquest of Mexican industry, aided by repeal of the law that restricted foreign control to 49 percent ownership of Mexican businesses. Observers noted that the state companies were being sold to the same small group of people and their foreign partners who already controlled most of Mexico's economy, with no effort to promote "popular capitalism" through stock offerings in the open market. "Crony capitalism," ran one comment, "seems to be the current government's style."

The denationalization of Mexican industry through privatization was accompanied by the demise of many small and medium-sized domestic businesses as a result of the removal of most tariff barriers. These developments reflected a general tendency on the part of Mexico's recent rulers to abandon the struggle for economic independence that had been a major goal of the Mexican Revolution, of Lázaro Cárdenas, and even of the conservative but nationalistic presidents who followed him. The foreign conquest of the Mexican consumer goods market since 1986 was very evident: "Everything from Italian pasta and Diet Coke to European cookies and Italian loafers is now available. . . . In many cases local manufacturers have closed down because imports are cheaper and better made."

The decision to abandon the struggle for economic independence was reflected in the Mexican government's encouragement of the program that permitted U.S. companies to establish plants (called *maquiladoras* or *maquilas*) for production of parts and their assembly on the Mexican side of the border. The program allowed duty-free entry of parts and machinery into Mexico and total U.S. ownership of the plants. U.S. customs regulations permitted the finished products to enter the United States with duty paid only on the value of the labor, not on that of the goods themselves. The lure of low wages (averaging between $3.75 and $4.50 per day) caused an explosive growth of maquiladora plants, whose number grew from some 455 with 130,000 workers in 1982 to over 2,000 with more than 600,000 workers, two-thirds of them women, in 1998. In these plants workers assembled television sets, radios, computer hardware, and the like for the American market.

Many of these plants were unorganized; in others the workers were represented by government-controlled unions that usually offered employers "protection contracts" that kept wages low and did not meet the labor standards mandated by the Mexican Federal Labor Law. For example, the predominantly male supervisors in these U.S. companies routinely subjected a mostly poor, uneducated female labor force to sexual violence, harassment, and discrimination. To avoid the expense of complying with Mexican laws that mandated paid pre- and post-partum maternity leaves, these companies, according to a 1998 U.S. Labor Department report, often screened out pregnant job applicants, forced women employees to take birth control pills, checked their monthly menstruation flows, required them to submit to regular urine tests, and arbitrarily fired pregnant women or reassigned them to physically challenging tasks designed to induce voluntary resignations or miscarriages. Moreover, according to University of Chicago sociologist Leslie Salzinger,

this "sexualization of factory life," symbolized by annual industrywide "Señorita Maquiladora" beauty contests, discouraged worker solidarity and contributed directly to skyrocketing rates of violent crime against women.

Nonetheless, Mexican officials defended the program by arguing that it relieved high Mexican unemployment. But because many of the plants were true sweatshops, with health and safety problems widespread among the workers, it tended to institutionalize poverty on both sides of the border, for the program inevitably tended to depress wages in the U.S. border zone. In the United States, unions were concerned about the loss of thousands of jobs and the prospect of more to come. Environmentalists and health workers were alarmed by the shockingly poor environmental and health record of the maquiladoras, which freely released various toxins into the air and water and routinely neglected to treat hazardous wastes. The American Medical Association declared that the maquiladora program had created "a virtual cesspool" on the border.

The neoliberal assault on state regulation especially affected women. Privatization eliminated relatively high-paying jobs for men and thereby placed additional burdens on women to supplement family income by working outside the home, often as salaried employees but more commonly as self-employed street vendors in the "informal sector." The maquiladoras especially sought out women workers, largely because management viewed them as more docile and likely to accept lower wages. Consequently, between 1970 and 1993, women's waged employment almost doubled from 17.6 to 33 percent of the total work force. But, according to a recent study, 40 percent of women workers were paid less than the minimum wage and 60 percent received no additional benefits; moreover, 44 percent worked part time (less than thirty-five hours per week), and more than 54 percent were self-employed, working in microenterprises or on the streets.

All these economic, social, and environmental problems were exacerbated by the North American Free Trade Agreement, which was approved in November 1993 by the U.S. Congress after a bitter debate. In Mexico the treaty was denounced by independent labor, peasant unions, and Cuauhtémoc Cárdenas, all of whom called for a new trade agreement, providing workers in the three countries (Mexico, Canada, and the United States) with the same workplace conditions, collective bargaining rights, and occupational safety and health standards. But Mexico's PRI-dominated Senate swiftly brushed aside all objections and ratified the treaty on November 22.

NAFTA eliminated tariffs between Canada, the United States, and Mexico over fifteen years and permitted the free flow of investment capital across borders. To meet the concerns of labor unions and conservationists, negotiators from Canada, the United States, and Mexico worked out side agreements dealing with labor and the environment. But the commissions created by the accords were simply "watchdog" bodies, with no enforcement powers or minimum standards to enforce. Moreover, the Mexican government routinely manipulated or juggled workplace information.

U.S. labor unions had good reason to fear that free trade with Mexico, where wages were only one-tenth of those in the U.S.,[2] would result in the loss of many thousands of jobs. Estimates of the probable job losses in the United States as a result of the implementation of NAFTA ranged from 150,000 by President George H. W. Bush's Secretary of Labor Lynn Martin to the forecast of 550,000 jobs lost over ten years by Jeff Faux, president of the Economic Policy Institute. Aside from the actual job loss, NAFTA pressured U.S. labor to make wage and other concessions to employers. President Clinton and his Secretary of Labor Robert Reich argued that the United States would lose low-paid, unskilled jobs to Mexico but retain high-tech, high-paid jobs. In fact, three-quarters of the new manufacturing jobs created by U.S. com-

panies in Mexico were precisely in the high-tech, capital-intensive fields of automobiles and electronics, and the productivity of Mexican labor was rising rapidly. The claim that job creation through increased exports to Mexico would more than compensate for any job losses in the United States was equally dubious. The primary targets of NAFTA were the United States and Canada, not the impoverished Mexican market. Over 50 percent of the Mexican population lived below poverty levels set by the United Nations. Only one-third of the population had sufficient income to constitute an effective market for more than basic necessities.

Meanwhile the De la Madrid and Salinas policies created an unprecedented crisis for the ejido sector of Mexican agriculture. Even before the passage of NAFTA, Mexican small farmers faced increasing competition from foreign agricultural imports as a result of Mexico's entry into the General Agreement on Tariffs and Trade (GATT) and steadily reduced import restrictions. NAFTA, allowing the free entrance of U.S. corn into Mexico, dealt a death blow to Mexican maize producers, since maize costs about two or three times as much to produce per ton in Mexico as in the United States. Moreover, U.S. farmers still benefited from various government subsidies that enabled them to undersell their Mexican competitors. According to one estimate, as a result of NAFTA the number of maize farmers in Mexico would decline from about 2.8 million to 420,000 in a few years.

The very existence of the ejido system was threatened by a February 1992 reform of Article 27 of the constitution. This constitutional reform allowed the division of the ejidos into individual lots and their rental, sale, or joint cultivation with domestic or foreign partners. The provision for rental of ejido land legalized a previously existing practice, but it was predicted that the lure of cash would induce many impoverished ejidatarios to sell their land. Others lost their land through foreclosure by banks. Increasingly, companies with easier access to credit and capital bought the most productive areas of the Mexican countryside.

Where did the hundreds of thousands of farmers who abandoned the land as a result of NAFTA

---

[2]In October 1993 the Economic Research Institute of Vienna issued a report showing just how low average wages were in Mexico: about $2.35 per hour, compared with $17.02 in the United States, $16.16 in Japan, and $25.94 in Germany. They were even lower than those of the "Asian Tigers": $3.89 in Hong Kong, $4.93 in South Korea, and $5.19 in Taiwan.

and the agrarian reform go? Many left for the over-crowded cities, swelling the numbers of unemployed or underemployed Mexicans; others found low-wage jobs in the border maquiladoras or on farms producing fruit or vegetables for the U.S. market. Many headed for the United States to join the pool of Mexican undocumented workers, numbering in the millions and growing between 200,000 and 300,000 a year, who worked in agriculture, domestic service, small industry, and food service. The existence of this pool of low-paid, vulnerable workers—vulnerable precisely because they were undocumented, subject to deportation—represented a source of superprofits to employers and contributed to the weakness of organized labor. In general, U.S. unions did little to incorporate the migrants into their ranks or protest their abuse by police and border guards. A wave of anti-Mexican, anti-immigrant sentiment, with strong racist overtones, swept through the United States and heightened tension on both sides of the border. This sentiment was reflected in California's 1994 passage of Proposition 187, which denied social services to illegal immigrants.

## NEOLIBERAL CRISIS AND POPULAR RESISTANCE

Despite widespread poverty, repression, and discontent, there appeared to be little effective opposition in 1993 to the PRI's monolithic control of Mexican politics and its neoliberal economic program. In late November the PRI held the traditional *destape* or "unveiling" of the party's presidential candidate, Luis Donaldo Colosio, who had managed the fraud-riddled 1988 election.

Then a succession of dramatic events shattered Mexico's surface calm and raised serious doubts about the ruling party's secure grip on power and its internal unity. On New Year's Day 1994, a revolt led by a self-styled "Zapatista Army of National Liberation" (EZLN), believed to number several thousand members, broke out in the southern state of Chiapas, one of the poorest regions of Mexico, with a largely Mayan population. The rebels proclaimed NAFTA and its free trade program "a death certificate" for the native peoples of Mexico and demanded sweeping politi-

cal and economic reforms, including self-rule for Mexico's indigenous communities, repeal of the reforms to Article 27, and fraud-free elections. The rebels seized and briefly held the highland city of San Cristóbal de las Casas and three other towns before melting back into the Lacandon rain forest after a savage counteroffensive by fourteen thousand Mexican army troops, accompanied by bombing of villages, summary executions, torture of suspects, and other repressive measures.

With some specific features that reflected its tragic history, Chiapas's problems epitomized those of rural Mexico. The Mexican Revolution of 1910 never really reached Chiapas, with the result that no agrarian reform took place there. The great landowners still owned about 40 percent of the land, while 63 percent of the campesinos owned plots of less than 2.5 acres. Emboldened by the crisis and the standoff with the government, land-hungry campesinos, not waiting for the government to act, occupied nearly 100,000 acres of farmland, resulting in armed clashes with paramilitary groups organized by the great landowners.

The problems of the campesinos were aggravated by severely eroded soils, cutbacks in credits and subsidies by the Salinas administration since 1988, and the collapse of world coffee prices. According to economist José Luis Calva, the "time bomb" that exploded in Chiapas resulted from the government's structural adjustment plan and the official free trade policy, which resulted in a greatly increased importation of cheap corn from the United States. In his view, the reforms to Article 27 of the constitution, threatening what remained of the communal ejido system, "detonated" the crisis.

The Chiapas crisis deeply wounded the PRI and the Salinas regime, exposing sharp disagreements that widened appreciably with the shocking assassination of Colosio. Although Salinas quickly named another U.S.-trained economist, Ernesto Zedillo Ponce de León, as the PRI's new presidential candidate, a large majority of the Mexican public did not expect honest elections. So widespread skepticism greeted the government's announcement that Zedillo's margin of victory topped 50.08 percent, the "magic number" needed to retain control of the Congress and ensure a presidential mandate. Charging "colossal fraud," Cárdenas's opposition party discovered more than six thousand polling places in which more votes were cast than the number of voters on the voting list. An unknown number of persons was erased from the voting rolls; the independent observer group Civic Alliance (AC) found that 65 percent of the nation's polling stations featured shaved registries.

In the midst of the regime's crisis of delegitimacy, the Zapatistas of Chiapas convened a National Democratic Convention in the Lacandon forest to which it invited all sectors of "civil society," including all political parties except PRI, "the common enemy to us all." The convention, modeled on the 1914 revolutionary convention summoned by Zapata and Villa, reflected the Zapatista decision to broaden the scope of their movement—to develop electoral activity as an adjunct to armed struggle, leading to the drafting of a new constitution.

Consequently Zedillo faced a sea of troubles. In Chiapas the military standoff continued, but there was widespread and growing disorder. Meanwhile, indigenous and mestizo farmers established four autonomous zones in different regions of Chiapas. They blocked roads, refused to pay taxes and electricity bills to federal and state authorities, and ejected local PRI officials. The Zapatista leadership proclaimed these areas "zones of rebellion." A wave of land takeovers continued, producing the unfamiliar spectacle of over one hundred wealthy landowners staging a hunger strike in Mexico City to call attention to their plight. Zedillo was forced to choose between coming to terms with the rebels or crushing them with armed force. From the PRI's point of view, both options could have had dangerous consequences.

Mexican public opinion, as expressed in polls and demonstrations, favored a peaceful solution that took into account the just grievances of the Chiapas peasants. But PRI hardliners, the right-wing PAN, and foreign investors demanded a military solution of the problem. A January 1995 memorandum written by Chase Manhattan Bank advisor Riordan Roett and leaked to an investigative newsletter warned that "the government will need to eliminate the Zapatistas to demonstrate [to the investment community] their effective control of the national territory and of security policy." In addition to calling for the Zapatistas' liquidation, the memo warned the Zedillo administration "to consider carefully whether or not to allow opposition victories if fairly won at the ballot box," because "a failure to retain PRI controls runs the risk of splitting the government party."

Facing these rival pressures, Zedillo initially sought compromise. But on February 9, 1995, on the pretext that Zapatista arms caches had been found in Mexico City and Veracruz, Zedillo sent thousands of troops, backed by tanks and heavy artillery, into the rebel-held territory, with orders to arrest the Zapatista leadership. The rebels, along with thousands of their supporters, fled into the jungle area near the Guatemalan border. The government's action provoked angry protests, including a march of almost a hundred thousand people in Mexico City, that forced Zedillo to halt the military operation.

A more immediate threat to the regime was the prospect of an economic collapse. NAFTA, which was supposed to bring prosperity to Mexico, instead had deepened the recessive tendencies of the Mexican economy. The removal of trade barriers had ruined many small farmers who found themselves unable to compete with the influx of cheaper U.S. grain, milk, and other agricultural products. Mexican national industries like the shoe and textile industries were threatened with destruction by competition from more technologically advanced U.S. and Canadian producers. An overvalued peso—deliberately overvalued to promote confidence in the Mexican economy, ensure the passage of NAFTA, and attract foreign investment—contributed to the flood of imports. This in turn caused a chain of events: a growing trade deficit, a decline in the value of the peso against the dollar, and the flight of domestic and foreign capital out of the country.

Mexico had long financed its account deficits with foreign loans; its total foreign debt was about $174 billion, which cost more than $25 billion in interest and principal in 1997. Of the $80 billion borrowed in recent years, only some $15 billion

Thousands of supporters crowded into Mexico City's main square in March 2001 to greet a caravan of Zapatista commanders who had traveled from the southern state of Chiapas to press their claims for indigenous rights, popular democracy, and an end to neoliberal policies. [Gamma]

was invested in plant and equipment, and the rest was used to service previous loans and restore Mexico's exhausted currency reserves. In December 1994, with $20 billion in short-term loans coming due in a few months, the peso free-falling, and capital flight accelerating, Mexico faced a replay of the 1982 debacle of inflation and looming default. Mexican stocks fell sharply, sending shock waves through the hemisphere's money markets.

Once again foreign governments, led by the United States, and international lending agencies came to Mexico's rescue with a bailout package of loans and loan guarantees amounting to some $50 billion to pay or renegotiate the huge loans coming due and to stem the peso's collapse. But the price of the February 1995 bailout was high. In return for $20 billion from the United States in loan guarantees, Mexico had to put up $7 billion a year in oil-export revenues as collateral, to be deposited at the New York Federal Reserve. Another $27.5 billion came from the IMF and the Bank for International Settlements, with the usual conditions: Mexico must cut social spending, restrain wage increases, and expand the privatization program to include PEMEX, the nation's prized petrochemical industry. Many Mexicans viewed the deal not as a bailout but as a sellout. "The gringos have us by the throat again," commented one Mexico City taxi driver.

The cost for ordinary Mexicans was more austerity and more hardships. With the peso down 55 percent since 1994 and inflation expected to top 15 percent in 1998, the real minimum wage, according to an economics writer for the national daily *La Jornada*, dropped from $4.00 a day to $2.82. These sacrifices did not restore the Mexican economy's health. The bailout, filling the pockets of bankers and multinationals, did nothing to promote economic development. "The immediate consequence of the $47.5 billion package," concluded a report in *The Nation*, "is to allow resumption of the speculative merry-go-round, with investment banks swiftly resuming their lucrative practice of underwriting and trading Mexican securities."

But, by the decade's end, recurrent economic troubles, combined with the regime's growing vacillation, had produced a crisis of state legitimacy, fractured elite consensus, and fueled widespread popular discontent. In 1996, the government signed the San Andrés Accords, halting troop movements in Chiapas and recognizing indigenous rights to create "autonomous municipalities." A grassroots coalition of human rights groups in neighboring oil-rich Tabasco state promptly mobilized 10,000 Chontal natives, declared local petroleum reserves "an autonomous region," and blocked access to sixty wells; meanwhile, the powerful oil workers' union successfully lobbied the PRI leadership to condemn Zedillo's plans to privatize PEMEX. The Chiapas revolt continued to seethe, even as its rebellious message spread.

Still another guerrilla group, the Popular Revolutionary Army (EPR), emerged in Guerrero and coordinated an armed campaign in six southern states that included seizure of radio stations, raids on police stations, and assaults on army posts. Although government leaders scoffed at the EPR's popularity and dismissed its threat to regime stability, Father Máximo Gómez, a local parish priest, concluded that "90 percent of the people here support the guerrillas in their hearts."

Popular opposition to the PRI and its neoliberal program, although clearly centered in the impoverished south, also continued to grow in central Mexico. *El Barzón*, a debtors' group initially composed of middle-class farmers and ejidatarios damaged by free trade and high interest rates, filed some 350,000 lawsuits to block mortgage foreclosures; organized mass protests to obstruct the nation's commercial highways; and staged sit-ins in government buildings, banks, courtrooms, and factories to demand debt relief. Under the leadership of leftist Juan José Quirino, the *barzonistas* expanded and became more politically partisan.

With an estimated membership of half a million to a million, the Barzón demanded that the banks return to ejidos over a million acres of land illegally foreclosed during the debt crisis and announced an alliance with the Zapatistas to establish a democratic front to resist neoliberalism.

But the most convincing evidence of massive popular resistance to the PRI and its neoliberal agenda were successive electoral repudiations in 1997 and 2000. This first secured a majority for opposition parties in the Chamber of Deputies that denied the PRI its traditional veto-proof Senate, thereby undermining the presidency's nearly unlimited de facto power, and gave Cuauhtémoc Cárdenas control of metropolitan Mexico City, home to a quarter of the nation's people. The second shattered the PRI's historic monopoly of presidential power, which dated to its founding in 1929, and elected Vicente Fox Quesada, the candidate of the National Action Party (PAN), to the presidency. Fox, a wealthy former Coca-Cola business executive, had campaigned on populist themes and was a founding member of "Latin American Alternatives," a group that denounced neoliberalism for its failure "to generate growth and development, and particularly to meet the challenge of achieving a more equitable distribution of income and wealth." He promised to support indigenous rights and negotiate a peaceful resolution of the Chiapas crisis; dismantle the structure of political authoritarianism; promote economic growth; protect the state-owned oil company, PEMEX, from privatization; reduce poverty and inequality throughout Mexico; and double state funding of education.

Once in office, however, Fox seemed to abandon his populist promises and surrounded himself with neoliberal advisors from the Mexican and transnational corporate business community: the World Bank, Union Carbide, DuPont-Mexico, Procter and Gamble, and Avantel, a subsidiary of WorldCom. His Minister of the Interior, Santiago Creel, was heir to an agricultural, mining, and timber fortune whose origins lay in the nineteenth-century world of Porfirio Díaz. Given their social backgrounds, it was no surprise that these men supported policies that favored investors, not social justice. During its first year in office, the Fox administration sought to cut subsidies to small farmers, open Mexico's energy and telecommunications industry to privatization, eliminate legal protections for workers, facilitate debt collection, and secure passage of a regressive 15 percent, value-added tax on food and medicine, which, opponents insisted, would fall disproportionately on 40 million poor people, 17 million of whom were desperately poor. Largely because he lacked a congressional majority, however, Fox failed to win legislative support for these proposals. His own party helped defeat a presidential initiative that would have protected indigenous rights, while other legislative coalitions blocked the president's remaining agenda. Fox himself even failed to win congressional authorization to leave the country to meet with Microsoft CEO Bill Gates! By December 2001 polls showed that his popularity had declined to 50 percent from an historical high of 75; moreover, according to another poll published by the Mexico City newspaper *El Universal*, only 37 percent said they would vote for Fox again.

Meanwhile, the economy, which grew at an annual average rate of 5.5 percent between 1997 and 2000, nonetheless produced slightly higher rates of poverty. After two decades of neoliberal policies and steady economic growth (averaging 2.8 percent), punctuated by major declines in 1982 and 1994, the share of poor Mexicans, according to conservative estimates of the InterAmerican Development Bank, had grown from 32 percent in 1977 to 36 percent in 1994 and to 38 percent in 1998. Using different standards and methods, Julio Bolvitnik, an economics professor at the Colegio de México and an advisor to the Fox government, reported in March 2001 that some 70 million Mexicans were poor, 27 million of whom earned less than was necessary to purchase their basic nutritional requirements. Moreover, the World Bank, a champion of neoliberalism, reported that in 1998, after two decades of neoliberal policies, income inequality in Mexico was greater than ever: the poorest 10 percent of the population earned 1.3 percent of national income, while the wealthiest 10 percent received 41.7 percent. This growing inequality was largely a function of unregulated

markets that empowered investors rather than workers. But fewer than 2 percent of Mexican households relied upon investment income, while 72 percent depended upon waged labor. Since 1993 about a million manufacturing jobs were created, but half of these were created in the *maquila* industry and the other half in the informal sector, both of which were renowned for low wages and part-time, insecure employment. In 1990, 40 percent of the Mexican work force was self-employed in these "microenterprises," but this rose to more than 50 percent in 2001. Between 1994 and 2000 average wages declined 21 percent.

By 2002, Mexico was utterly dependent on foreign export and investment-capital markets. Since 1990 its external debt rose steadily from $104 billion to $152 billion, it relied on the United States for 80 percent of its export sales, and it paid foreign bankers $1 of every $3 that it earned. Ominously, however, Mexico's economic boomlet recently began to wither, as the U.S. market contracted: export prices fell, export income dropped, economic output declined, and unemployment grew. Yet another economic crisis loomed, based on whether the U.S. economy rebounded strongly in 2003 and whether new foreign capital investment followed these declining economic indicators. Because the previous five years of growth had failed to reduce income inequality and poverty, even a normal cyclical economic downturn, compounded by an ineffective government response, threatened to produce a social catastrophe.

Whatever the outcome, at the heart of Mexico's continuing economic, political, and social crisis was the debt problem and the system of dependent capitalism that produced it. North American scholar Peter Evans had presciently written in 1979:

> Like Brazil, Mexico has found that dependent development requires a mass of imported outputs even larger than the exports it generates, and that even when the multinationals cooperate in the promotion of local accumulation they still ship more capital back to the center than they bring in. . . . Dependent development does not correct the imbalances in semiperipheral relations with the center; it replaces old imbalances with new ones.

# 13

# Argentina: The Failure of Democracy

AFTER THIRTY YEARS of explosive economic growth and sustained political stability, Argentina seemed ready to take a place among the developed nations by the first decade of the twentieth century. Argentines could proudly point out that their nation was the world's greatest exporter of grain and one of the most important exporters of meat; they could boast of a railroad network unsurpassed outside western Europe and the United States and of a capital, Buenos Aires, that ranked among the world's most beautiful and cultured cities. Argentines were seemingly prosperous, relatively well educated, and increasingly urban. The burgeoning population (nearly 8 million in 1910) and transportation system promised to create an internal market that would stimulate the rise of native manufacturing and elevate Argentina to the position of one of the world's modern industrialized countries.

The full flowering of democracy, too, seemed close at hand. The landed oligarchy, known as *estancieros*, historically had monopolized Argentine politics by relying on military force and restricting the vote to propertied males, most of whom traditionally resided on rural estates. By the early twentieth century, however, Argentina had become a much more urban society and a propertied middle class consisting of shopkeepers, artisans, manufacturers, and government bureaucrats emerged. New political organizations like the Radical Party soon developed and began to compete effectively for this new constituency. Moreover, with the gradual professionalization of the army, the social composition of the officer corps also changed. Middle-class men, mostly the sons of immigrants, replaced the old officer groups and the oligarchy gradually lost its predominance. These developments and a series of unsuccessful Radical coups apparently convinced the estancieros that the time had come for electoral reform. Consequently, in the hope of attracting a significant share of newly enfranchised voters, they embraced the Saenz Peña Law, which provided for universal male suffrage and a secret ballot.

The appearance of prosperity and emerging democracy, however, proved illusory. Stagnation, interspersed with periods of depression and runaway inflation, marked the Argentine economy during succeeding decades. Military coups, disorder, and brutal repression afflicted the nation's politics. At the base of these problems lay Argentina's structural dependence on foreign markets and capital, a dependence that placed the country's economy at the mercy of foreign events and decisions made abroad. This helped perpetuate a deformed social and political system.

# The Export Economy

Argentina's dynamic economic development during the last quarter of the nineteenth century and the early twentieth century was due to three factors: the appearance of a large market in Europe for its products—wool, mutton, beef, and wheat; the inflow of millions of immigrants, who provided cheap labor for the expanding agricultural sector; and the influx of large quantities of foreign investment capital, which went to construct railroads, put more land under cultivation, and establish food (mainly meat) processing plants. The nation's prosperity depended on its ability to export huge amounts of agricultural commodities, to import the manufactured goods it required, and to attract a steady stream of large-scale foreign investment.

Consequently, Argentina was critically vulnerable to fluctuations in international market and finance conditions. Any reduction in overseas trade reverberated disastrously throughout the economy. Because Argentines usually imported more than they exported—a tendency made worse by the fact that the market price for raw materials remained steady or declined while the prices of manufactured goods rose—the country suffered from chronic trade deficits that habitually depleted the national economy of circulating coin and restricted local market development. To attract new sources of wealth, successive Argentine governments had opened Argentina to foreign capital.

Foreign investment reached enormous proportions in the first decades of the twentieth century. During the years 1900 to 1929, foreigners came to control between 30 and 40 percent of the nation's fixed investments. Argentina absorbed nearly 10 percent of all foreign investment carried out by capital-exporting nations, one-third of all the foreign investment in Latin America, and more than 40 percent of the total foreign investment of Great Britain, the world's leading capitalist power. Investment was concentrated in railroads and government bonds, the proceeds from which subsidized the construction of railroads and public works.

Although foreign investment unquestionably helped fuel economic growth, it simultaneously created immense economic difficulties. Huge interest payments on foreign debts and the profit remittances of foreign-owned companies, often representing between 30 and 50 percent of the value of Argentina's exports, produced serious balance-of-payments problems. Because government bodies owed much of the foreign debt, a substantial portion of government revenue went to service payments. Rigid interest rates and repayment schedules meant that the burden remained the same, even when state revenues declined because of adverse economic conditions, and that revenues earmarked for debt service could not be diverted to other areas.

Every sector of the Argentine economy depended on exports. Agriculture and livestock raising employed 35 percent of the work force. The nation's greatest agricultural area, the pampas, exported 70 percent of its production. Argentine industry centered on food processing, mainly meat packing. As late as 1935 food-stuff processing accounted for 47 percent of all industrial production, and textiles for another 20 percent. The transportation industry—railroads and coastal shipping—handled mostly export commodities.

Rich and poor alike relied on the export economy for their livelihood. The ruling elite was composed of large landowners, who produced almost entirely for the export trade. Their income and their political power rested squarely on the export economy. In addition to large numbers of farm laborers, many urban and industrial workers depended on exports for their jobs. The major trade and industrial unions in Argentina arose in those industries—coastal shipping, railroads, dock work, and packinghouses—whose workers owed their well-being to overseas trade. Because the government relied on revenues derived from import taxes, significant numbers of white-collar workers and professionals employed by the government also were intimately tied to the export economy.

Foreign control and influence permeated the economy. Most of the large merchant houses, which carried on the all-important export-import trade, were either owned by or closely affiliated with foreign houses. The major shipping lines (both intercoastal and interoceanic), the railroads, and the *frigoríficos* (meat-packing plants) were owned and operated by British or U.S. companies.

The export economy brought indisputable benefits to Argentina, but those benefits were unequally distributed. There were, for example, sharp differences in economic development among regions. Whereas the pampas and Buenos Aires boomed, most of the interior provinces stagnated. Mendoza and Tucumán with their wine and sugar made some headway, but all the other central and northwestern provinces—Jujuy, La Rioja, Santiago del Estero, and Salta—experienced social and economic decline.

The inequalities of property and income between the various classes were equally glaring. The rich were very rich and growing richer; the poor grew poorer. In the countryside, the estancieros, masters of thousands of acres of rich land, built palaces, while the majority of foreign-born immigrant sharecroppers eked out a miserable living. In Buenos Aires, wealthy landowners, merchants, and lawyers gathered at the sumptuous Jockey Club, while laborers struggled to make ends meet as inflation eroded their already insufficient paychecks.

The expansion of market forces also dissolved traditional barriers between private and public spheres, forcing women into low-paid, menial positions in urban factories and sweatshops without releasing them from their unpaid responsibilities in the home. According to a late nineteenth-century Buenos Aires census, women composed 39 percent of the paid work force, and a 1904 report by Dr. Juan Bialet Masse confirmed that, in an industrial environment generally characterized by intolerable working conditions and low wages, Argentine women "suffered the most intense discrimination and exploitation." Apparently male employers preferred women workers because they were cheaper, more reliable, more efficient, and more docile than men. A 1913 report for the National Labor Department revealed that, on average, children employed in industry received half the wages of women, whose income, in turn, was half that of men.

Argentina's greatest treasure was its land, but only a few Argentines owned sizable portions of it.

In 1914 farm units larger than 2,500 acres accounted for only 8.2 percent of the total number of farms but held 80 percent of the nation's farm area. Over 40 percent of farms were worked by tenants, most on terms that were less than favorable. In 1937 a mere 1 percent of the active rural population controlled over 70 percent of Argentina's farmland, much of which they left idle. Yet the land was fertile and suitable for intensive agriculture. Thousands of immigrants came to Argentina in search of land only to discover that virtually all had long since been monopolized by the estanciero oligarchy.

Income distribution followed the same pattern. Less than 5 percent of the active population garnered 70 percent of the gross income derived from agriculture. Not only did workers and rural laborers receive little benefit from the export system, but the operation of the system's finances and taxation eroded what little return they did receive for their labor. Faced with chronic deficits in the balance of payments and unwilling or unable to tax the land or income of the landed elite, the government had no alternative but to resort to the printing press to finance its costs. The result was inflation. Exporters also demanded a fluctuating currency-exchange rate, which had an adverse effect on wage earners. Finally, the tax structure burdened the mass of consumers with high sales taxes that discouraged internal market expansion.

## Argentine Society

Argentine society divided roughly into three classes—upper, middle, and lower. The upper class acquired its wealth and prestige through its virtual monopoly of landownership. These large landholders used the late nineteenth-century export boom to solidify and enhance their power. Cattle fatteners, who supplied beef for both the domestic and foreign markets, constituted the most powerful faction within this elite. This inner circle was composed of approximately four hundred families who were closely allied through social clubs and business associations. Geographically, most of the wealth was located in the cattle and cereal regions of the pampas near Buenos Aires. From 1880 to

**Modern South America**

1912 this landed oligarchy also controlled national politics. It used its control over the government to promote meat and grain exports, guarantee easy credit for members, and provide more favorable taxation and currency policies. The other great institutions of Argentine society, the military and the church, also reflected the views of the elite.

Late nineteenth-century economic growth stimulated urbanization, which transformed the nation's class structure. An urban middle class arose. This middle class, heavily concentrated in the bureaucracy and professions, depended on the export economy and attached itself to the Radical Party.

The lower class divided into two groups: urban marginals and workers. Urban marginals were a racially and ethnically diverse group, composed largely of immigrant foreigners, including Eastern European Jews, against whom regular employers routinely discriminated. Not surprisingly, according to historian Donna Guy, women constituted a large share of this underclass, a considerable number of whom became involved in prostitution, which the Argentine government had legalized in 1875. For elites, legalized prostitution—which required prostitutes to undergo regular medical examinations and restricted their activities to particular urban zones—aimed to stabilize the patriarchal family by providing a safe, secure outlet for the release of men's sexual frustrations; it also enabled elites to collect revenues from, and establish control over, a population considered "dangerous." But for the prostitutes and pimps, these licensed bordellos became a means of survival and, ironically, gave birth to a cultural form—the tango—that eventually defined Argentina's national identity.

The tango, first as dance and later as song, had emerged in the early nineteenth century among the nation's lower classes, especially its black population, which composed 25 percent of Buenos Aires. According to historian John Charles Chasteen, the dance originally was performed by enslaved Africans to celebrate their individual black kings and distinguish their African national identities. Later, it evolved into *candombe*, a dance style typical of the Argentine black community, and by the middle of the nineteenth century, it was

adopted by Argentine elites to mock Afro-Argentine culture. By the early twentieth century, however, the tango or *milonga* had become, according to the *Dictionary of Argentine Expressions*, "a dance found only among people of the lower orders." It was featured routinely in the brothels, nightclubs, and *academios* (dancehalls) of Buenos Aires, where poor women mixed with men of all social classes. Its songs typically addressed themes about life in the tenements (*conventillos*), criminals, slum dwellers, and the relentless intrusion of poverty on the dreams of young girls.

By contrast, most members of the working class labored in small factories, where Argentina's industrial expansion was concentrated until 1914. (The primary exception to the predominance of small industries were the frigoríficos.) A considerable number of workers were employed by the shipping industry, railroads, and urban tramways in the Port of Buenos Aires, where organizations like *La Fraternidad*, the railroad workers' union, and the Maritime Workers' Federation were especially strong. Numerous strikes occurred after the turn of the century and throughout the first Radical regime (1916–1922). The labor movement, however, was weakened by diverse viewpoints on political activity and by internecine rivalries among Socialists, anarchists, and syndicalists.

# The Radical Era, 1916–1930

## THE RISE OF THE RADICAL PARTY

Naturally, increasing social inequality produced growing unrest among the urban middle class, university students, women, workers, ethnic minorities, and small groups of junior military officers. The Radicals drew upon this discontent in their efforts to overthrow the oligarchy by force in 1905. Despite their failure, the Radicals attracted growing popular support in the decade that followed.

Radical Party strength rested on twin pillars: its local urban organization, which acted to meet the needs of the middle class, and its leader, Hipólito Yrigoyen, who played a dual role as the titular head of the Radical Party. First, he was the great mediator who managed to reconcile the

Carolina Muzzilli and Alicia Moreau were militant Argentine feminists who agitated for civil and political equality, social justice, and international solidarity in the early twentieth century. [From the cover of *Nuestra Causa,* a feminist newspaper published in Argentina. Biblioteca Juan B. Justo, Buenos Aires. Photograph courtesy of Asunción Lavrín]

often conflicting interests of the middle class and large landowners who made up his political coalition. Second, although inarticulate and a recluse, Yrigoyen managed to project an austere democratic image that made him the party's charismatic leader. This clever deal maker and manipulator symbolized for the middle class the Radical dedication to democracy. Despite a checkered past that included shady business deals, he furnished the party with much of its moral appeal.

The Radical propaganda effectively presented an image of a national party, transcending the narrow regional and class interests that had previously governed Argentine politics. The Radical program was purposely vague. It straddled the line between its two major constituencies, the middle class and the landed elite. The Radicals therefore never challenged the basic premises of the export economy and its dependence on foreign capital. The party advocated neither land reform nor industrialization.

During the Radical era, Argentine women, who historically had been treated like children or, worse, the legal property of men (*patria potestad*), continued to organize and agitate for equality both within and outside the formal structure of political parties. Cecelia Grierson, Argentina's first female doctor, formed the National Women's Council to lobby for women's greater access to education and professional employment. These women's groups, like others in Latin America, typically sought to protect and conserve the primary power of women within the family. Although some viewed this as an implicitly "conservative" role, in the context of a traditional society battered by unfettered market forces, the communal maternal values of family life quickly translated into civic actions, which Francesca Miller calls "social motherhood."

This meant that, irrespective of class, ethnic, racial, or regional identity, women activists came to expect the state to intervene to monitor, regulate, protect, and harmonize the interests of all members of the Argentine national family, especially when these were threatened by outsiders. "The aristocratic women and the proletarian women are equally victims," thundered Carolina Muzzilli, a prominent feminist. "It is time that the Argentine woman recognizes that she is not inferior to men and, even if she has a different mission, her civil and natural rights must be restored."

In practice, however, class interests often distinguished the activities of various women's organizations. For example, feminist leaders like Alicia Moreau de Justo, founder of the Socialist Feminist Center in 1900, pressured her husband, Juan Bautista Justo, the nation's premier Socialist, and his male colleagues to sponsor Law 5291, which attempted to regulate working conditions for women and children, providing them special legal protections against the ravages of unfettered market forces.

By 1910 these and other women's organizations had coalesced to sponsor Argentina's first International Feminist Congress, which attracted women's groups throughout Latin America to its agenda for civil equality, better working conditions for women, equal pay for equal work, school reform, and revision of divorce laws to allow divorced mothers custody of themselves, their children, and their property. Not content merely with equality of opportunity, delegates from the Socialist Women's Center argued that this would only reinforce the existing inequality of social condition between men and women; they consequently called on male leaders in government, business, and education to institute affirmative action in support of women's issues. They demanded special treatment that would consider women's historical responsibilities in both public and private realms; for example, they wanted a special commercial school for women and legal provisions that would give wage-earning women thirty-four days of paid leave before and after giving birth.

European ethnic immigrant groups also protested against the elite's discriminatory laws designed to "ghettoize," stigmatize, and limit the civil rights of the non-native-born, who also—not coincidentally—happened to be either prosperous small farmers, urban petty proprietors, or "organized proletarians." Ironically, the late nineteenth-century white supremacist oligarchy had encouraged their arrival in Argentina in order to "whiten" the nation's population and provide relatively cheap labor on the great estates and in export-oriented urban industry. But continuous harassment greeted those immigrants who either resisted acculturation, demanded worker rights, or successfully competed against the creole estancieros. Swiss and German immigrant farmers, for example, organized a revolt in the province of Santa Fe to denounce the oligarchy's discriminatory policies. Similarly, Jewish schools, especially in the province of Entre Ríos, had been the target of racist violence in 1910, which prompted Jewish organizations to protest. Finally, a coalition of immigrant groups including Italians, Germans, and Russian Jews, many of whom were sympathetic to socialist, anarchist, and trade unionist ideas, challenged the Social Defense Law of 1910, which authorized the expulsion of foreign "agitators" and defined some immigrant groups as "undesirable elements."

## THE FIRST RADICAL GOVERNMENT: YRIGOYEN, 1916–1922

With a finely tuned grassroots political organization, a well-known presidential candidate, and a vague program promoting "class harmony," the Radicals won the 1916 presidential elections. But they were limited by their tenuous bond with the conservative landowner elite. The elite controlled the military and the major agricultural lobbying groups and had close contacts with powerful foreign business interests. Yrigoyen continually walked an unsteady tightrope between the middle class, which wanted a piece of the governmental pie, and the oligarchy, which was still wary of the party that had rebelled three times in three decades and that had won an election campaigning against the selfish interests of that oligarchy. He could not push too hard too fast or the oligarchy would surely overthrow him.

The Radical government's program combined a conservative fiscal policy and moderate social reforms designed to secure political stability, in return for which the oligarchy was to allow the middle class wider access to the governmental bureaucracy and the professions. There were inherent contradictions in this strategy. First, expansion of access to government employment meant that government expenditures necessarily had to increase. But this violated the tenet of fiscal conservatism, unless the economy continued to expand at a rapid rate. Second, Yrigoyen had to maintain the fragile alliance of landowners and members of the middle class within his own party. In sum, the key to the Radicals' staying in power was Yrigoyen's ability to distribute the fruits of Argentine economic development to the middle class without antagonizing the oligarchy.

There was growing discontent on the part of the middle class, too, because the decline in government revenues from imports meant fewer government jobs for its members. Yrigoyen's balancing act became even more difficult with the emergence of labor agitation for improved wages and working conditions. Wartime demand for Argentine exports had brought on inflation, and as a result, the purchasing power of wages was seriously eroded. Yrigoyen had to move cautiously in attempting to alleviate labor's plight, for the oligarchy might look upon such moves as interference in their economic domain. The problem was complicated by the fact that much of the labor agitation was directed against foreign-owned companies with close ties to the elite. Facing bitter opposition from the ruling elite, Yrigoyen abandoned his modest efforts to incorporate labor into his coalition.

Consequently, from 1916 to 1919, Yrigoyen's policy toward workers' struggles was clearly determined by expediency and, in the last analysis, by the degree of pressure exerted by the landed elite. Major strikes occurred against foreign-owned companies engaged in export-related enterprises. Because Argentine governments often sent in the police and armed forces to break strikes, the attitude of the Yrigoyen regime was decisive. The Maritime Workers' Federation struck twice, in 1916 and 1917, for higher wages. The first strike was timed to coincide with harvest shipments. In both instances the union gained access to Yrigoyen, the government kept out of the dispute, and the union won. But in late 1917, the government abandoned the unions when a general strike began to jeopardize export interests. With the strike threatening the entire harvest, the British government and the elite brought joint pressure on Yrigoyen to intervene, and troops were used. The strike collapsed. The frigorífico strike of 1917–1918 met the same fate when the government sent in marines to subdue the strikers.

The climactic episode came in January 1919 and is known in Argentine history as the *Semana Trágica* (Tragic Week), in reference to the heavy loss of life that followed when Yrigoyen, apparently fearing intervention by the army to topple his government, abandoned his original conciliatory position and sent police and armed forces to break a general strike that had grown out of a strike in a metal works. This violence was accompanied by a wave of brutal pogroms against Russian Jewish immigrants by members of the elite and the middle class, organized in an Argentine Patriotic League. Instead of denouncing the anti-"communist" witch hunt, the Radical government added its voice to the right-wing cry that the strike was a revolutionary conspiracy and even encouraged party members to join the vigilante bands. Thereafter, Yrigoyen concentrated on catering to his middle-class constituency through the use of patronage and on strengthening his popular electoral base.

The Radicals also faced growing opposition among women, who, according to the 1914 national census, composed 22 percent of the total work force. These women activists continued to press the government for greater access to the professions and government jobs, equal pay, the right to vote and hold office, and a variety of regulations designed to protect women from the brutality of unfettered market forces. In 1919, Elvira Rawson de Dellepiane, a veteran feminist leader, organized the Women's Rights Association (ADF) to rally women, regardless of political affiliation, around this progressive platform. Within a relatively short time, the ADF claimed some eleven thousand members and worked closely with other feminist organizations like the Women's Union and Labor Group to pressure the Yrigoyen administration. The last three years of Yrigoyen's term were a struggle merely to survive.

The Argentine university reform of 1918, which had continental reverberations, reflected Yrigoyen's desire to cater to his middle-class constituency. The series of events leading to this famous reform began with a student strike at the University of Córdoba; the students demanded, among other changes, simplification of the entrance requirements and secularization of the curriculum. When the strike deteriorated into violence, Yrigoyen intervened and acceded to the student demands. But he went further, establishing a series of new universities that increased middle-class access to the professions and the government jobs for which so many middle-class aspirants hungered. This especially benefited Argentine women.

The Radicals also sought to strengthen their electoral position by expanding the patronage system and removing provincial governors on the pretext that they had violated the federal constitution.

By 1921 the boom unleashed by World War I had ended, and depression followed. The union movement disintegrated. Layoffs eroded union membership, and internal bickering rendered the unions ineffective. The Radicals actually experienced some success in recruiting among workers during the Depression, because their local committees were able to provide charitable services.

## THE SECOND RADICAL GOVERNMENT: ALVEAR, 1922–1928

Despite adverse economic conditions, Marcelo de Alvear, Yrigoyen's hand-picked successor, became president. Immediately, however, the party began to come apart. Although couched in personal terms—Alvear against Yrigoyen—the division more accurately reflected the growing split between the middle-class and elite sectors of the party.

Alvear cut the payroll to trim expenses and hiked tariff rates to increase revenue. The tariff increase was also aimed at reducing imports and alleviating the balance-of-payments problem, thereby satisfying the middle class. A balanced budget, however, appealed to estancieros but directly contradicted middle-class demands for even more government employment opportunities. In 1924 the Radicals split into two factions, with the Anti-Personalist wing under Alvear's leadership.

Meanwhile, although largely excluded from these debates, subordinate social sectors nonetheless sought to organize popular movements to take advantage of the political discord within the Radical Party and between propertied elites and the middle class. Although workers, women's rights organizations, and ethnic minorities were themselves often internally divided, the devastating impact of external market forces on their daily lives helped to mobilize a common agenda that occasionally managed to intrude on the national political discourse. In 1924, for example, a coalition of trade unions and women's groups, including the Socialist Feminist Center and the Women's Rights Association, successfully secured the passage of Law 11.317, which established an eight-hour workday for women, limited a woman's workweek to forty-eight hours, and prohibited night work.

The law also required large, typically foreign-owned, companies to obey special rules for pregnant workers, including a stipulation that factories hiring at least fifty women should provide facilities for nursing mothers. Two years later, women's groups pressured Argentina's patriarchal political parties to pass another law, this time empowering adult married women to sign contractual agreements and pursue personal, educational, and career goals without their husbands' permission. Naturally, none of this legislation protected women employed in agriculture or domestic service, nor did it address the gender wage gap. But these victories, no matter how seemingly modest, laid the foundation for future state intervention on behalf of women and other historically oppressed people disadvantaged by an unregulated market.

The decade also pioneered the expansion of radio, a new technology that assisted the Radicals in their efforts to fashion a unified national culture. Although "decent" women historically had been precluded from participation in Argentina's rich cultural night life, the radio brought the tango from the dancehalls and brothels into middle-class homes, where women thrilled to its raunchy disrespect for an established social order that confined them to their kitchens and bedrooms. Moreover, the tango had been widely acclaimed in Paris, which lent it still greater credibility as a national cultural expression acceptable to Francophile elites and the middle-class folk who simultaneously envied and mimicked their lifestyle. From this moment onward, the tango became the new symbol of Argentine modernity and national identity.

### Yrigoyen's Second Term, 1928–1930

Yrigoyen made a smashing comeback in 1928, winning his second presidential term with an overwhelming 57 percent of the vote. But in October 1929 the Great Depression hit Argentina. The Radicals, whose strength had been increasing, suffered a mortal blow. Exports dropped 40 percent; foreign investment stopped. Unemployment was widespread. Government efforts to spark a recovery served only to induce inflation. The decline in imports severely undermined the government's fiscal position, since it relied on import duties for most of its revenue.

The government incurred a huge deficit, which it tried to cover by borrowing. As a result, it found itself in the position of competing for increasingly scarce credit resources with the landed elite, which desperately needed money to ride out the decline in the export market. Yrigoyen's policy threatened the interests of the landed elite, and he became expendable. Further, his meddling with the military had seriously undercut his standing with that powerful institution. Finally, the Depression destroyed his personal popularity among the middle class, his main base.

Yrigoyen became the scapegoat. His enemies pictured him as senile and corrupt, incapable of ruling the nation in a time of crisis. The Depression ruined the party apparatus, for there was no patronage to dispense. The political situation continued to disintegrate, and violence increased. Yrigoyen was overthrown by the military on September 6, 1930.

## The "Infamous Decade," 1930–1943: The Conservative Restoration

The coup marked the end of Argentina's short experiment with democracy and the entry of the military into the nation's politics; it ushered in a period of harsh repression and corruption, which came to be known as the "Infamous Decade." Lieutenant General José F. Uriburu, who had led the group of conspirators that overthrew Yrigoyen, became the head of a coalition of widely diverse elements, including traditional conservatives, right-wing nationalist-fascists, and such center and left parties as the Progressive Democrats, Independent Socialists, and Socialists. These strange bedfellows had agreed on the elimination of Yrigoyen, but little else. Consequently, the loosely built alliance soon fell apart.

Following the coup, Uriburu conducted a campaign of brutal repression against opponents of his provisional government. He especially targeted prostitutes, whose defiance of established law had spread venereal disease and undermined the patriarchal family. Their scandalous behavior threatened public authority and led the military to abolish prostitution in 1934. Fearful that the abrupt abolition of the sex industry would create a new wave of unemployed in the midst of a global depression, however, the military government passed the Law of Social Prophylaxis, which offered former prostitutes state-sponsored medical care and employment opportunities in the public and private sector. The military also strictly controlled radio, decreeing the Dry Law, which censored electronic broadcasts that featured tango music, soap operas, and other lewd activities that corrupted public morality.

With its political and social opposition dispersed and defenseless, the military sought to reorganize Argentina's civilian political institutions and created a new coalition, the *Concordancia*, which united conservative aristocrats, dissident Radicals, the Catholic church, and the military. With the help of fraud, the intimidation tactics of goon squads and gangsters, and the general apathy of an embittered and cynical electorate, the Concordancia won control of the national government.

The Great Depression, the first modern crisis of the international capitalist system, powerfully proclaimed the fragility of the nation's economically dependent, externally oriented national development policies and ushered in a new era of internal sociopolitical struggle that dramatically transformed Argentine society. The global economic collapse bankrupted Argentina's largest companies and inundated the nation with a tidal wave of unemployment, which, not surprisingly, disproportionately afflicted women, who lost jobs at a much higher rate than men.

It also precipitated a pronounced demographic shift in the social origins of the national labor force: before 1930, urban industrial and rural agricultural employers alike had relied upon more than 6 million European immigrants, half of whom had arrived after 1880; in the ensuing decades, expansion of Argentine industry and agriculture would have to depend on internal migration from rural to urban areas.

Naturally, women constituted an increasingly important segment of this population; during the Depression and World War II, twice as many women as men migrated to Buenos Aires and other cities. This reflected both the destructive impact of market forces on rural life and the patriarchal nature of Argentine families. Unable to make a living in rural areas, men who lost their jobs or small agricultural plots often abandoned their families as well; under the circumstances, single female heads of households could not sustain their families' subsistence in the low-paying jobs traditionally available to women in agriculture, where wages were one-fourth those of urban industry. Not surprisingly, women's employment nationwide increased 27.4 percent from 1935 to 1939. In the textile, tobacco, and clothing industries, women composed a majority of the labor force by the end of the decade.

Although the military's intrusion into Argentine politics during the 1930s effectively reduced opportunities for democratic popular participation, trade union leaders still organized and agitated in defense of male workers' rights and for state regulation of the market. Here, they were joined by women's groups, which, reflecting their increased visibility in the public sector, also demanded an activist national government that would recognize their political rights and protect their socioeconomic interests. That is why the Argentine Association for Women's Suffrage, founded by Carmela Horne de Burmeister in 1932 and claiming a membership of eighty thousand, campaigned vigorously both for women's right to vote and for state-subsidized subsistence, maternity leave and health care benefits, and child care for working mothers. Argentina's conservative Concordancia faced one inescapable conclusion: an enduring social stability could not be imposed militarily; it would require an expanding economic pie, which the unfettered international market forces of a dependent capitalism could no longer guarantee.

Abandoning the free-trade, laissez-faire economic doctrines on which the prewar export economy was based, Conservative economic policy of the 1930s established state intervention as a decisive factor in the economy. The basic aim of their policy was to protect the nation from the effects of the cyclical nature of the world capitalist economy. To accomplish this, they sought to protect their main foreign market, Great Britain, limit production of farm commodities, and restrict imports through indirect methods, such as the establishment of a currency-exchange system that discriminated against non-British imports. They also sought to establish new import-substitution industries primarily through foreign investment.

In this period, finding that they could not export manufactured goods to Argentina on a competitive basis because of high tariffs and the discriminatory exchange system, U.S. manufacturers established plants in Argentina. As a result, foreign capital played an increasingly important role in the economy during the 1930s, accounting for 50 percent of the total capital invested in

Argentine industry. Foreign companies virtually monopolized the meat-packing, electric power, cement, automobile, rubber, petroleum, pharmaceutical, and several other industries.

The British market for beef and grain was critical for the Argentine export economy. During the late 1920s and early 1930s, the British government was under constant pressure to reduce Argentine imports, to protect producers within the empire. The result of Argentine efforts to secure the British market was the controversial Roca-Runciman Treaty of 1933. By this treaty, Britain guaranteed Argentina a fixed, though somewhat reduced, share of the chilled beef market. It also promised to eliminate tariffs on cereals. Argentina, in return, lowered or eliminated tariffs on British manufactures. It also agreed to spend its earnings from the British market on British goods to be imported into Argentina.

The economy improved after 1934, and by 1936 the crisis had passed. Cereal prices rose gradually on the world market until 1937, when they again dropped. Meat prices rose until 1936 and then remained steady. Industrial investment reached pre-Depression levels. Although real wages declined, unemployment fell sharply as a result of public works and industrial investment. In general, Argentines were relatively well off during the 1930s. Consumption of consumer goods and food rose considerably.

The process of industrialization was accompanied by a growth of the native industrialist class and a parallel increase in the size of the working class and its organizations. In 1930 the General Confederation of Labor (CGT) arose from the merger of two large unions. By 1943 the membership of the trade union movement was estimated to be between three hundred and three hundred and fifty thousand.

The growth of the Argentine industrial bourgeoisie, a class profoundly dissatisfied with the economic policies of the landed oligarchy, and of the working class, still relatively small and unorganized but gaining in self-consciousness and developing new social and political aspirations, heightened the tensions within Argentine society. These ultimately exploded in 1943 when a coup

d'état, organized by a secret officers' lodge known as the Group of United Officers (GOU), overthrew the Concordancia government and established a ruling military junta headed successively by Generals Arturo Rawson, Pedro P. Ramírez, and Edelmiro Farrell, who ruled from 1944 until the elections of 1946.

## The Perón Era, 1943–1955

### PERÓN'S RISE TO POWER

The 1943 military coup had deep and tangled roots. The fraud and corruption that tainted both conservative and Radical politics in the "Infamous Decade" no doubt offended military sensibilities. During the 1930s, the officer corps of the Argentine armed forces, predominantly middle class in its social origins, had developed an ardent nationalism that saw the solution for Argentina's problems in industrialization and all-around technical modernization. The interest of the military in industrialization also was closely linked to its desire to create a powerful war machine capable of creating a Greater Argentina that could exercise hegemony in a new South American bloc. To industrialize it was necessary to end Argentina's neocolonial status, to free it from dependence on foreign markets. The pro-German attitude of many officers stemmed in part from the German military instruction that they had received and from their admiration for the supposed successes of the Nazi New Order, but even more, perhaps, from the conviction that England and the United States had conspired to keep Argentina a rural economic colony. Their pro-German attitude was not translated into a desire to enter the war on Germany's side but rather into the wish to keep Argentina neutral in the great conflict.

World War II had a lasting impact on the ideology and practical political-economic needs of Argentina's military leaders. First, absorbed with waging global war, neither the United States, Great Britain, France, Germany, nor Japan could intervene effectively in Argentina's internal affairs. Second, with the war's disruption of international commercial trade and the conversion of the great powers' industrial production to military needs, an externally dependent Argentina lacked the essential inputs—capital equipment, technology, replacement parts, and private sector investment—necessary to sustain economic expansion and social stability. In the absence of any organized and effective foreign opposition and pressed by domestic popular movements for a social justice based on economic growth, these military leaders had no alternative except to expand the state-centered, import-substitution industrialization policies inaugurated during the 1930s.

Consequently, the military proposed a massive government investment in industrialization and technical modernization, even though it feared the social changes and forces that such transformations might unleash. In particular, it feared the revolutionary potential of the working class. In effect, the military proposed to build Argentine industrial capitalism with a thoroughly cowed, docile working class.

As a result, one of the first acts of the military regime was to launch an offensive against organized labor. The government took over the unions, suppressed newspapers, and jailed opposition leaders. It also sought to silence women's public voice and force them to return to their gendered lives as mothers, wives, and daughters—to be the familial anchor of a revitalized Catholic morality within their private households. Here, gender discrimination aimed to undermine class solidarity by blaming male workers' economic difficulties on women's highly visible presence in the workplace. This policy of direct confrontation and collision with labor and women had disastrous results and threatened to wreck the industrialization program. The military was saved from itself by an astute young colonel, Juan Domingo Perón, who took over the Department of Labor in October 1943, promptly raised it to the status of the Ministry of Labor and Welfare, and opened a new bureau, the Women's Division of Labor and Assistance. As he noted in his inaugural speech, Perón wanted officially to recognize that "more than 900,000 Argentine women are part of the paid work force."

Born in 1895, the son of immigrant and creole parents of somewhat marginal economic status (his father was a farmer), Perón entered the military college at sixteen and very slowly rose in rank to captain in 1930. During the next decade, he spent several years in Europe, where he was much impressed by the German and Italian dictatorships. In 1941, Perón joined the Group of United Officers; although only a junior colonel, he quickly rose to its leadership ranks.

His genius lay in his recognition of the potential of women, ethnic minorities, and the working class and the need to broaden the social base of the nationalist revolution. He became the patron of the urban proletariat and, under considerable pressure from a well-organized and vocal women's rights movement, immediately courted its support by endorsing woman suffrage. Within a year, such legislation was submitted to the Congress and approved in 1947. Perón secured the enactment of protective legislation designed to increase women's access to education and improve their wages and working conditions. Not surprisingly, from 1941 to 1950, the number of women admitted to universities more than doubled.

As Minister of Labor in 1944, Perón established a minimum wage for piecework produced in the home, largely by women; naturally, this raised the issue of a broader minimum wage, and workers in the food industry, mostly women, received this protection the following year. By 1949 women constituted 45 percent of the industrial workers in Buenos Aires. In this year, again pressed by women's groups and apparently recognizing the potential divisiveness of a gendered wage gap between men and women workers, Perón supported legislation to require equal pay for equal work in Argentina's flourishing textile industry. As a result, by 1959 the differential wage between men and women ranged between 7 and 15 percent, which historian Nancy Caro Hollander characterizes as "one of the lowest in the non-Socialist world."

Perón also cultivated a political constituency among Argentina's male work force. Workers were not only encouraged to organize but favored in bargaining negotiations, in which his department participated. As a result, workers' wages not only rose in absolute terms, but their share of the national income also grew. This, of course, increased mass purchasing power and thereby promoted the process of industrialization. Perón also created a state system of pensions and health benefits, with the result that employers' contributions for pensions, insurance, and other benefits rose steadily until the year of Perón's fall (1955). In return for these real gains, however, the unions lost their independence and became part of a state-controlled apparatus in Perón's hands.

Naturally, Perón's progressive social policies created considerable opposition both within certain factions of the military and among the landed oligarchy. In October 1945 these groups staged a coup that led to Perón's imprisonment. But the organizers of the coup were divided and unclear about their objectives, and Perón's followers mobilized rapidly. Loyal labor leaders organized the Buenos Aires working class for massive street demonstrations to protest Perón's jailing. The workers virtually took over the city, without opposition from the armed forces. The bewildered conspirators released Perón from prison. Thereupon, he resigned from his various government posts, retired from the army, and began his campaign for the presidency in the 1946 elections.

In preparation for those elections, Perón, taking due account of the defeat of fascism in Europe, cast himself in the role of a democrat. He created a Labor Party to mobilize the working class, the principal component in a class alliance whose other major elements were the national industrial bourgeoisie and the army. Perón's chief opponent was a heterogeneous coalition of conservative landed elite, middle-class Radicals, and even the Socialists and Communists. Perón, who was greatly assisted by the blundering foreign policy of the United States, won easily.

Once in office, Perón turned to confront a new cultural threat. Since the Great Depression and the advent of movie theaters had bankrupted many small cabarets frequented by middle- and working-class men, Argentina's national obsession with the tango had been displaced by *fútbol* (soccer). Whereas the tango had celebrated unbridled heterosexual passion, soccer had emerged as an all-male sport in its appeal to participants and spectators alike. According to historian Donna

Guy, the Peronistas increasingly feared what appeared to be an increase in homosexual relationships and their open representation in national artistic and cultural expression; they therefore determined to use state power to revive the tango and legal prostitution in the hope that this would stimulate more interest in heterosexuality. According to historian Donald Castro, Perón understood the tango's popular appeal and fostered its reemergence for his own political ends. During his administration, the state-owned movie company produced *La historia del tango* and three films that celebrated the life of Argentina's most famous tango artist, Carlos Gardel.

## POSTWAR ECONOMICS

After the war, the United States bestrode the emerging new world order like a colossus, but its extraordinary economic output found ample demand in wartorn Europe, Asia, and Africa, where domestic policies focused on internal socioeconomic reconstruction. Consequently, Argentine industrialists and landed oligarches alike faced relatively little postwar competition as they sought to develop internal markets and expand agricultural raw materials exports. International prices remained high, profits were secure, and domestic tariff protection meant that local companies could afford to pay higher wages and benefits to workers without jeopardizing their control over production.

The postwar boom enabled Perón to keep his coalition together. The export sector produced large surpluses in the balance of payments, making available funds for industrialization, mainly in labor-intensive manufactures. Perón also nationalized railroads and public utilities and created powerful state-owned companies that dominated local shipping, steel, and banking industries. Between 1945 and 1948 real wages for industrial workers rose 20 percent. Personal consumption also rose. Because there was only a slight decline in the share of the national income that went to profits, the redistribution of income to the working class did not come at the expense of any other segment of the alliance. Industrialists kept profits up and benefited from increased domestic consumption,

Juan and Evita Perón, 1952. [Bettmann/Corbis]

which provided a growing market for their products. The only sector of the economy that was slighted was agriculture.

Perón managed to win over a considerable sector of the dependent middle class through his use of government patronage, just as Yrigoyen had done before. He kept the military happy by his commitment to industrialization, which was an important aspect of the military's desire for national self-sufficiency, and by providing it with generous salaries and the latest equipment for modern warfare.

One of Perón's greatest allies was his beautiful and stylish wife Eva Duarte de Perón, known affectionately by Argentines as "Evita" (little Eva), who relished her role as his liaison to the working class.

"The people can be sure," she triumphantly announced to admiring throngs at Perón's presidential inaugural, "that between them and their government, there could never be a separation, because in this case, in order to divorce himself from his people, the President would have to first divorce his wife!" Shortly after the enfranchisement of women in 1947, Evita joined with other feminists to create the Peronist Feminist Party, an organization to mobilize women in support of the Peronist political platform. She also formed the Eva Perón Foundation, a charitable institution that distributed large sums of money to neighborhood groups; financed various women's centers to link impoverished women to vital social, medical, and legal services; and built a large patronage army for Peronism.

Although her role as a feminist in Argentina's history is controversial, one thing is indisputable: Eva Perón's activism showed women and her working-class supporters, the adoring *descamisados* (shirtless ones), that they should not rely on the beneficence of any politician to defend their rights. "Just as only workers could wage their own struggle for liberation," she insisted, "so too could only women be the salvation of women." In the presidential election of 1951, this was a lesson that was not lost on women or the working class; 90 percent of registered women, eligible to vote for the first time, went to the polls and some 65 percent cast their votes for Perón, but they also elected seven women senators and twenty-four women deputies, the largest female delegation of government representatives in the Americas. Evita's vision of a government and people linked by her marriage to Perón seemed prophetic, but a year later death, not divorce, intervened; Evita's tragic demise in 1952 at the age of thirty-two dramatically weakened the populist caudillo's attachment to Argentine workers and women.

Perhaps more significant, the global economy had begun to shift, as did Perón's policies. Except for a short-lived recovery during the Korean war, Argentina entered a period of severe recession, which included several drought-induced bad harvests. The late 1940s brought the first signs that Argentina would face serious long-term economic difficulties. Its export commodities began to confront increased competition from the United States and from revitalized Western European agriculture. Later, the advent of the Common Market worsened Argentina's position. Balance-of-payments deficits replaced the large surpluses that had financed the nation's import-substitution industrialization. Industrial production fell, as did per capita income. Real wages dropped 20 percent from the 1949 level in 1952–1953. It was in this decline that Perón's political failure was rooted.

## PERÓN'S DOWNFALL

After his reelection in 1952 and in response to the economic crisis of the early 1950s, Perón formulated a new plan (the Second Five-Year Plan, 1953–1957) that to a great extent reversed his previous strategy. He tried to expand agricultural production by paying higher prices to farmers for their produce and by buying capital equipment for this sector (tractors and reapers). He sought to increase the agricultural production available for export by means of a wage freeze, which he hoped would restrict domestic consumption. Although real wages declined, workers did not suffer proportionately more than other groups. But the industrial bourgeoisie was unhappy, for labor productivity declined while the regime's prolabor policies propped up wages. The industrialists, supported by a considerable portion of the army, wanted deregulation of the economy so they could push down wages. But the major problem of the industrial sector was lack of capital, since the agricultural sector no longer generated a large surplus.

To solve the capital shortage, Perón abandoned his previously ultranationalistic stand and actively solicited foreign investment. In 1953 the government reached an agreement with a North American company, the Standard Oil Company of California, for exploration, drilling, refining, and distribution rights in Argentina. Perón hoped thereby to reduce the adverse effect of oil purchases abroad on the balance of payments. Foreign capital, however, used the most modern technology and machines, which required fewer workers and tended to create unemployment in the affected industrial sectors.

To maintain government expenditures and a bloated bureaucracy in the face of declining revenues, Perón printed more money. The amount in circulation increased from 6 to 45 billion pesos during his two terms. By 1954 he had had some success in stabilizing the economy; he achieved a balance-of-payments surplus, and capital accumulation showed an upward curve. But his new economic strategy had alienated key elements of his coalition of workers, industrialists, and the armed forces. Perón then sought to divert attention from economic issues—with disastrous results.

Perón adopted two new strategies. First, he attempted to enhance his moral and ideological appeal. Second, he began to employ greater coercion to suppress a growing opposition. The vehicle for his ideological and moral appeal was *justicialismo*, Perón's ideal of justice for all—a third route to development that was neither communist nor capitalist.

Perón's strategy included attacking the church. Starting in 1951 the regime grew more repressive. The government suppressed and took over Argentina's most famous newspaper, *La Prensa* (1951). Further, Perón used his National Liberating Alliance, a private army of thugs, and the thirty-five-thousand-man federal police force to intimidate the political opposition. Torture, imprisonment, censorship, purges, and exile became the order of the day. After 1954 even the General Confederation of Labor became a coercive force, whose prime function seemed to be to suppress opposition within the labor movement.

Perón's reluctance to go along with the industrialists' desire to push down wages and increase productivity alienated that group; the industrial bourgeoisie then joined forces with the agrarian interests, which had long and bitterly opposed Perón. This desertion ended Perón's once highly successful coalition. Inevitably, Perón's hold on the working class loosened as the wage freeze and inflation reduced the value of their wages.

Despite economic adversity, Perón could not have been overthrown had not the military abandoned him. For the better part of a decade, he had masterfully balanced, divided, and bribed the military. Most of the senior officers owed him both their rank and their prosperity. The army was heavily involved in industrial production, and this provided an excellent means to become rich. In addition, to win its allegiance, Perón had showered the military with expensive military hardware and excellent wages. However, his relations with the armed forces began to disintegrate when he altered his economic policy to lessen emphasis on industrialization and self-sufficiency. On this score, his concession to Standard Oil in 1953 was the last straw for the nationalist military.

Thus, in struggling to extricate the nation from an economic quagmire, Perón undermined the multiclass coalition that had brought him to power and sustained him there. When the final successful revolt took place in 1955, enough of the working class was alienated to assure the military's success. Perón briefly threatened to arm the descamisados but instead fled into exile.

Although there is considerable scholarly debate about Perón and his populist policies, the fact remains that he solved none of the country's major economic problems. The main roadblocks remained. Transportation continued to be inadequate and obsolete, and a scarcity of electric power stood in the way of industrial modernization. Argentina did not produce enough fuel to meet domestic needs, and this created an enormous drain on the balance of payments. The nation's industry remained limited for the most part to import-substitution light industry. Despite his anti-imperialist rhetoric, Perón did not nationalize such key foreign-owned industries as meat packing and sugar refining. Most serious of all, Perón did nothing to break the hold of the latifundio on the land. As a result, agriculture was marked by inefficient land use, which impeded long-range development.

## The Shadow of Perón, 1955–1973

### ECONOMIC STAGNATION

The gradual restoration of global economic competition among the leading capitalist countries led to chronic, sometimes violent, economic fluctuations during this period. At the base of these difficulties lay continuous balance-of-payments deficits, which were caused by the decline in agricultural prices. The nation could not earn enough from its exports to pay for the large expenditures necessary to fuel domestic industry. Periods of rapid economic growth were invariably followed by acute depressions, which wiped out all previous gains. Runaway inflation accompanied these cyclical conditions.

The governments of this period, whether military or civilian, tended to promote the inflow of foreign investment as a development strategy. Arturo Frondizi (1958–1962), for example, was elected on a political platform of "Peronismo Without Perón," that is, nationalism and state regulation of market forces. Nonetheless, he quickly bowed to pressure from the U.S. State Department and the International Monetary Fund (IMF), a multilateral institution created after World War II to manage the postwar global economy. These agencies promised low-interest loans to ease the economic pain produced by mounting trade deficits, but in return they insisted that Frondizi break his political promises to the Argentine people and slash social welfare spending, deregulate private sector business, and expand investment opportunities for foreign capital.

But this development strategy had severe drawbacks. Foreign companies tended to monopolize credit opportunities, certain key industries became concentrated in foreign hands, and profits earned by foreign subsidiaries and remitted to the home company added to the balance-of-payments deficits. Moreover, since the IMF's principal concern was inflation, its stabilization programs invariably increased the cost of credit, deepened economic recessions, and contributed to growing business failures. Finally, foreign investment was usually technologically intensive and therefore created unemployment. It was during the post-Perón era of development spurred by foreign capital that Argentina saw the emergence of large numbers of underemployed and unemployed urban workers.

This economic insecurity was politically untenable for working men and women who recurrently joined with students, small businesspersons, and other disadvantaged groups in publicly protesting these intolerable policies that disproportionately benefited wealthy foreigners and Argentine elites. The resulting political disorder inevitably led to a cycle of political violence and periodic military coups d'état against Frondizi in 1962 and his civilian successor, Arturo Illia, in 1966.

## THE MILITARY IN POLITICS

In the past, military interventions had been brief, largely designed to destroy popular political opposition, intimidate the lower classes, and reconstruct civil society so that civilian governments favorable to the ruling elites could be elected. However, General Juan Carlos Onganía, who replaced Illia, was determined to govern longer.

Consequently, he suspended the constitution; dismissed all civilian government entities, including the Congress, the Supreme Court, and provincial governors; abolished all political parties; and purged the universities of moderates and leftists, reserving a special hatred for Jewish intellectuals.

As minister of the economy, Onganía sought foreign investment by removing all restrictions on profit remittances; he also stimulated the process of industrial denationalization by devaluating the peso by 40 percent. This meant that many local companies could no longer afford expensive capital imports and royalty payments to owners of foreign technology. These local companies disappeared, leaving their share of the market to foreign firms. In this way, Coca-Cola and Pepsi gained control of 75 percent of the soft-drink market. Between 1963 and 1971, foreign interests bought out fifty-three Argentine companies representing almost every industrial sector, particularly the automotive, chemical, petrochemical, metallurgical, and tobacco industries. Meanwhile, wages were frozen although prices continued their steady rise.

Growing outrage on the part of workers and students over the government's economic program, especially its policy of industrial denationalization and the wage freeze, erupted into violence in the interior in the spring of 1969. Major riots took place in Rosario, Corrientes, and Córdoba, the most industrialized city of Argentina. There, workers and students rose in the famous Cordobaza revolt, occupying major sectors of the city until they were ousted by troops. At the same time, there was an upsurge of urban guerrilla activity by groups like the Montoneros, who represented the left wing of the Peronist movement. Their tactics included raids on police stations, assassinations, and robberies.

Onganía's failure to cope with the mounting wave of guerrilla activity precipitated the 1970 military coup, which installed General Roberto M. Levingston as president. An expert in military intelligence and counterinsurgency, Levingston decreed the death penalty for terrorist acts and kidnappings, but his repressive decrees failed to establish a permanent social peace that would restore investors' confidence and reverse Argentina's 1970–1971 economic decline.

### THE RETURN OF PERÓN

Displeased with a resurgence of labor unrest, the military ousted Levingston in March 1971. His replacement, General Alejandro Lanusse, carried out a dual policy combining brutal repression of leftist guerrillas with a general liberalization of the political climate. In effect admitting the military's failure to renovate Argentine politics, Lanusse undertook negotiations that led to the restoration of political activity and the return of the Peronists to full electoral participation for the first time since 1955.

The military briefly held out hope that the moderate political parties would unite to stand against the Peronists, but the latter's superior organization and their leader's unchallenged popularity assured their victory. At the heart of the Peronist program were formal agreements with labor (*Pacto Social*) and industry (*Acto Compromiso del Campo*) that pledged compliance with a wage and price freeze. This cooperation lasted for about a year, while the Argentine economy, buoyed by high world-market prices for beef and grain, boomed. The agreements disintegrated in mid-1974 with the onset of renewed inflation brought on by a huge increase in international oil prices.

Even before these economic arrangements ended, the Peronist movement had begun to disintegrate, divided between left and right wings. By the time Perón died in July 1974, the level of violence had increased. In 1975 left- and right-wing thugs reportedly killed eleven hundred people. In the face of this escalating violence and economic chaos, the military stepped in again and installed General Jorge Rafael Videla as president.

# Military Dictatorship, 1974–1983

In the ensuing years, the military unleashed a reign of terror unprecedented in the nation's history and imposed an equally harsh neoliberal economic policy that decimated Argentine society. By the summer of 1982, the annual rate of inflation shot up to a catastrophic 500 percent, the highest in the world. Economic growth fluctuated wildly.

Worst of all, the free market policies of finance minister José Alfredo Martínez de Hoz led to record numbers of bankruptcies and bank failures. By eliminating tariffs on imported industrial goods and reducing government involvement in the economy, Martínez de Hoz presided over the destruction of many of Argentina's largest corporations. The real wages of Argentine workers plummeted 40 percent between 1976 and 1979, before recovering in 1980 and falling again in the severe crisis of 1982.

Between 1975 and 1990, Argentina experienced a prolonged period of economic stagnation: low or erratic growth coupled with high inflation, declining manufacturing production, and sharply rising unemployment that contributed to falling real wages, increasing income inequality, and the dramatic growth of an "informal sector" comprised mostly of impoverished urban female street vendors. Misery spread as the share of households earning income below the poverty line steadily expanded from 2.6 percent in 1974 to 7.5 percent in 1980 to an all-time high of 38.3 percent in 1989.

Naturally, this economic devastation contributed to political discontent and social turmoil. To defend its power, Videla's military junta banned all normal political activity and embarked on a "dirty war" against the left. Under military rule, perhaps as many as thirty thousand Argentines disappeared, many victims of illegal rightist death squads. Argentines came to fear the knock on the door at midnight, after which unknown kidnappers would take family and friends who were never to be heard from again.

Opposition to the military's barbaric cruelty grew steadily, if clandestinely. Direct political action was replaced by popular movements among human rights advocates, labor, youth, community groups, and women. Human rights organizations, with a longer history of social activism, were most influential and included veteran groups like the Communist party–affiliated Argentine League for Human Rights, established in 1937, and the Permanent Assembly for Human Rights, co-founded in 1977 by Raul Alfonsín, who parlayed his prestige into a convincing presidential electoral victory in 1983.

Labor, on the other hand, long the most powerful organized social group in Argentina, suffered dramatic declines because it was a special target of the military's political and economic violence. Determined to eradicate all vestiges of working-class resistance and heroic struggle, military officials attacked the gender identities of union leaders by subjecting them to what Jean Franco calls the "feminization" of torture: systematic assaults on the reproductive organs of men and women. Economically, union membership fell as privatization, government budget cuts, and foreign competition combined to increase unemployment. Under these conditions, important sectors of the labor movement, especially the leadership of the General Labor Confederation (CGT), collaborated with the military government. Some even testified years later that they "did not remember" the massive disappearance of workers and shop stewards during the dictatorship.

Young people also resisted the military's invasion of their schools, disruption of home life, and wholesale assault on youth culture. With traditional vehicles for expressing youth activism closed, their outrage found new channels of discontent, the most influential of which was "national rock." Outdoor concerts during the dictatorship regularly drew as many as sixty thousand youth who routinely defied the authorities with collective chants of *"Se va a acabar"* ("the dictatorship will soon end") and thrilled to the subversive lyrics of Argentine rock stars like Fito Paez, León Gieco, and Charley García. For example, García's *"Los dinosaurios"* ("The Dinosaurs"), lampoons the military as witless prehistoric beasts destined to extinction, and Paez's *"Tiempos difíciles"* ("Hard Times") envisions the fires of hell emerging from the nation's cemeteries to avenge the youthful disappeared.

Community organizations offered a similar outlet to adults threatened by the military's economic and political war against citizens. With the moral, logistical, and financial support of local parish priests, squatters—impoverished, homeless, and unemployed families—organized to reclaim vacant lands in urban centers. The first such group, the Neighbor's Commission, organized

some twenty thousand people for a land invasion in San Francisco Solano, a working-class neighborhood in Buenos Aires. Thereafter, these neighborhood groups spread rapidly, protesting higher taxes, skyrocketing food prices, decreased social services, the lack of affordable housing, and inadequate schools and health clinics.

Drawing on a rich historical legacy of "social motherhood," Argentine women, in the words of Jean Franco, "subverted the boundaries between public and private and challenged the assumption that mothering belonged only to the private sphere." The best-known of these women's groups, the Mothers and Grandmothers of the Plaza de Mayo, became the country's moral conscience; they refused to be intimidated by the military's daily death threats and routinely marched in the Plaza de Mayo, the nation's "symbolic center," demanding the return of their "disappeared" children and calling for the end of a dictatorship whose political and economic policies destroyed family life.

Women also campaigned for the abolition of compulsory military service, joint child custody, reproductive rights, sex education, and legal rights for children born to unmarried mothers. An organization known as Housewives of the Country denounced the high cost of living, sponsored shopping boycotts, and coordinated voluntary blackouts to protest the regime's neoliberal economic policies. Collectively, these popular protest movements weakened the military dictatorship and laid the organizational foundation for a return to democratic civilian government in 1983.

## THE MALVINAS WAR

Facing growing domestic opposition and international pressure, the military sought to divert the nation from the government's program of economic and political violence by manipulating traditional *peronista* populist themes of nationalism and anti-imperialism. Suddenly, Argentine soldiers, who earlier had been ordered to root out domestic opposition to the dictatorship's sale of the national patrimony, were now sent to defend Argentina's national dignity against British colonialism by capturing the Malvinas Islands (also known as the Falklands) in the south Atlantic, three hundred miles off the coast.

The invasion was the culmination of a series of colossal miscalculations by the Argentine military. First, it had not expected Britain to fight to retain the islands. The British, however, sensitive to their position as a declining world power, chose to fight as a matter of national honor. The Argentines also misjudged the position of the United States. They believed that the United States, which had recently made a number of friendly overtures, would remain neutral in the conflict. Instead, after an initial period during which it tried to mediate a peaceful agreement, the United States actively supported the British.

The war was a disaster for Argentina. Thoroughly humiliated and discredited, the military faced an unprecedented political and economic crisis. Inevitably, the generals had to yield power to a civilian government.

## Return to Democracy and the Death of Peronismo

Argentina ended nine years of nightmarish military rule in the fall of 1983 with the landslide victory of Raul Alfonsín, whose visibility in the human rights movement had earned him popular support. Alfonsín thus became the first democratically elected majority president since Perón in 1946.

Alfonsín first attacked inflation, which soared to 1,200 percent in 1985, by instituting the "austral plan." This established wage and price controls, replaced the peso with a new currency, the *austral*, and reduced government spending. Almost overnight currency stabilized. Inflation fell to 25 percent. Though the immediate crisis ended, the nation's economic problems remained manifold and profound. Argentina's industrial base was technologically backward, its foreign debt exceeded $50 billion by the late 1980s, and it was still dependent on primary export markets plagued by low prices. Unemployment in 1985 was the highest it had been in twenty years.

Alfonsín faced the difficult problem of the trials of the military accused of atrocities during the

so-called dirty war of the 1970s and failures during the war with Great Britain. When the military refused to try officers in its own courts, the president transferred the cases to civilian jurisdiction and appointed a commission to investigate military terrorism. The commission found the armed forces responsible for 8,971 disappearances; it documented torture, kidnapping, and other crimes, and labeled the acts as "the greatest and most savage tragedy in our history." In the trials that followed, several generals were convicted and given long prison sentences. But in 1987, against overwhelming public opposition, Alfonsín ended prosecutions of lower-rank military for human rights abuses on the grounds that they had simply carried out orders.

Alfonsín also faced an economic crisis of unprecedented proportions in 1989 when Argentina's per capita gross product fell more than 15 percent. To cope with the crisis he resorted to neoliberal remedies, seeking to push exports and enacting the austerity measures—cuts in government services and wage restraints—demanded by the IMF as a condition for new foreign loans to keep the Argentine economy afloat. By spring 1989 the foreign debt stood at about $60 billion. Payment on the debt took some $6 billion a year, but the country's earnings in 1988 were below $3 billion. The deficit had to be made up by new loans, which only increased the country's dependency. The policy of austerity and faithful service of the foreign debt meant that little capital was available for development. The economic program contributed to a deterioration of the infrastructure, with long daily blackouts and energy rationing.

The situation sparked a week of food riots that spread across the country, with desperate thousands of people taking over supermarkets, cleaning out the shelves but usually leaving the cash in the registers. The government responded by declaring a nationwide state of emergency and banning all demonstrations and strikes.

Against this background of economic collapse, Alfonsín lost to the Peronist candidate Carlos Saúl Menem, governor of La Rioja province, who had campaigned against the Radical Party's liquidation of the national patrimony. Menem's follow-

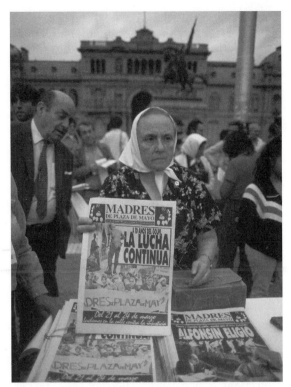

Mothers of the Plaza de Mayo wear white kerchiefs in silent protest against the disappearance of their loved ones and distribute newspapers that report the trials of those held responsible for the "dirty war." [Owen Franklin/Corbis]

ers, including the powerful Peronist-controlled unions, naturally expected him to repudiate the policies that had led to an unprecedented economic and social crisis. What followed was a stunning surprise. Convinced that an even more powerful dose of those policies offered the only solution for the crisis, Menem, who professed his admiration for Ronald Reagan, Margaret Thatcher, and Augusto Pinochet, abandoned his party's traditional economic and political positions in favor of a thoroughgoing neoliberal program.

Contrary to all expectations, therefore, Menem included in his cabinet many conservatives, including representatives of big business like the great firm of Bunge and Born, representing one of the most powerful multinational groups,

with links to the agricultural oligarchy that Peronists had traditionally distrusted, and announced a program of privatization of state-owned companies, the dismissal of thousands of state employees, and cuts of billions in government spending over the next year. The program represented a deepening of the policies attempted without much success by the brutal military governments between 1976 and 1983 and by the Alfonsín regime, with equal lack of success.

The process of privatization was carried out with frenzied haste and clearly favored large economic groups. Typical of the process was the "fire-sale" aspect of the privatization of two profitable state firms, Entel (the telephone company) and Aerolineas Argentinas (the national airline). The *Wall Street Journal* commented that these two privatizations "more resemble corporate raids than stockholders' sales. Both Aerolineas Argentinas and Entel are being sold for a fraction of their net worth." In July 1993 bidding began for the jewel of the state properties, the state oil company, Yacimientos Petrolíferos Fiscales, a profitable company with assets calculated at $7.4 billion and projected revenues of $5 billion. Among Latin America's oil producers, Argentina alone sold off its oil state monopoly, usually regarded as a "strategic" asset.

Menem's "shock therapy" on his way to the goal of a free market economy provoked resistance. The Peronist trade union movement, once his ardent supporter, split into pro- and anti-Menem wings, followed by a series of strikes to which Menem responded by firing strike leaders and seeking to curtail the right to strike by law or decree. The generally ineffective resistance of the once powerful labor movement to Menem's policies reflected a number of factors: the decline in size of the blue-collar labor force; the increase in the number of unemployed and underemployed, creating a substantial reserve labor force that weakened militancy; labor's traditional loyalty to the Peronist party; and the opportunism and greed of Peronist labor bosses, who were accustomed to live off state money and collaborate with the party, whatever its policies. To these factors one should add the weakness of the Argentine left, divided and decimated by state terrorism during the years of military rule.

To combat inflation, Menem's finance minister, Domingo Cavallo, unveiled the "ultimate anti-inflation shock," a plan making the Argentine currency convertible in relation to the dollar and forbidding the Central Bank to print money that was not backed by gold or foreign currency. To ensure wage and price stabilization Cavallo pledged government budget cuts of $6 billion, largely at the expense of public sector jobs. The policy entailed extensive budget cuts in health, education, welfare, and pensions. From the government's point of view, the Cavallo plan was a great success. Prices plummeted, the stock market exploded, and the Buenos Aires financial district hailed the start of the "Argentine miracle." The United States and the IMF rewarded Menem's fiscal orthodoxy by approving a Brady Plan that refinanced $21 billion of Argentina's foreign debt over thirty-five years.

This latest round of neoliberal orthodoxy deepened national income inequality, especially damaging women workers. During the next few years, unemployment soared from 13.1 percent in 1993 to 17.4 percent in 1995; the share of households that fell below the poverty line similarly increased from 13 percent in 1993 to 20 percent in 1996. During Menem's administration, women were forced to compensate for the decline in family income caused by higher male unemployment and falling real wages by entering the job market at much lower wage levels than men. In 1992, 45.9 percent of women were employed in waged work, but only three years later almost 52 percent worked for wages. Even as more women were forced to enter the job market, however, unemployment among women grew, from 6.3 percent in 1992 to more than 20 percent in 1995.

These neoliberal policies had a significant impact on family relations. The number of families with a primary male breadwinner declined steadily from 73 percent in 1980 to 65 percent in 1994, with these trends intensifying between 1992 and 1994, when the number of families with primary female breadwinners increased by 62 percent. The resulting double burden on

women both within the household and in the public sector undermined the traditional family; divorce rates rose markedly and, since 1980, the number of single-mother households increased by 93 percent while the number of nontraditional families tripled between 1992 and 1994. What's more, under the relentless pressure of global market forces, the working conditions of wage-earning women deteriorated: sociologist Rosa Geldstein concludes that, under the neoliberal regime, women suffered greater gender discrimination in the workplace and were required to work faster, with shorter and less frequent breaks, longer and less flexible hours, for lower wages.

Another legacy of Menem's neoliberalism was the appearance of a class of "new poor," including many members of Argentina's once substantial middle class. It was estimated that nearly 30 percent of Argentina's population over age sixty fell into this category. An agricultural crisis, itself the result of low international prices, declining local markets, and the high cost of credit contributed to this state of affairs. Moreover, the removal of tariff protections, which caused a flood of cheap textiles and other imports, forced many small businesses to close. Lastly, there were savage budget cuts for education and other social welfare programs, all of which prompted the Argentine social scientist Atilio Borón to disparage "democracy that demonstrates by its deeds that it has no obligation to the poor and weak and has no concern for their fate, a democracy that manipulates injustice to protect the powerful and its favorites while it imposes the law of the jungle on the shantytowns." More to the point, he wondered, "Can a democracy of this kind consolidate itself through successive endorsements at the polls?"

With the utter collapse of the economy in 1999, however, growing popular discontent removed all doubt about this possibility. If poverty and social inequality grew ominously even during Argentina's "miraculous" growth in the early 1990s, they skyrocketed thereafter when Menem's economic house of cards, battered by low export prices, high debt, and the flight of foreign investment, came crashing down. Between 1999 and 2002 the economy shrank 3 percent per year, unemployment increased from 15 to 25 percent, and Argentina's capital account fell from a surplus of $16.8 billion to a deficit of $4.1 billion. Poverty, which rose during Argentina's prosperous years from 7 percent in 1987 to 19 percent in 1996, swelled to half the population in 2002. It was not uncommon to see families scouring garbage piles, competing with flies and maggots in their search for scraps of food to eat. One such man, cooking a small pot of fetid potatoes retrieved from a local dumpster, reflected simultaneously the anger and resiliency of a proud people victimized by foreign bankers and Argentina's elite: "Tell Mr. Bush we still want to pay back the debt, but give us more time," he laughed derisively.

Indeed, as the new millennium opened, Argentina found itself mired in a virtually unpayable foreign debt that, since 1990, had grown steadily to $155 billion. To service this debt between 1990 and 1996, Argentina had paid foreign bankers $3 of every $10 that it earned in export sales, but thereafter this rose precipitously to an average of $6. Nonetheless, to be eligible for low-interest loans that might have prevented national bankruptcy, the IMF insisted that the national government ignore the urgent cry of its own citizens and implement a domestic austerity program that balanced its budget on the backs of the Argentine people, whom it expected to pay the costs of these economic hard times. Not surprisingly, "capitalism in Argentina," according to an investment banker at Salomon Smith Barney, "has become a dirty word; profit has become a dirty word." Another banker put the issue much more starkly: "We're somewhat less popular than serial killers."

It did not take long for this simmering contempt for the inequities produced by unregulated markets to boil over in open revolt, as unemployed *piqueteros* (picketers) blockaded roads and middle-class youth burned cars, smashed windows, and looted stores; in the process, this popular wrath ignited a political tempest that led to the resignations of President Fernando de la Rua, only recently elected in 1999 on a populist platform, and Alejandro Rodríguez Saa, his interim successor. To combat the economic mess bequeathed by

Menem and generate the revenues necessary to appease the foreign bankers, de la Rua had deserted his own constituents and slashed pension benefits, cut state workers' wages 13 percent, reduced public expenditures 20 percent, and raised taxes. This apparent surrender to wealthy foreign interests again reinforced a growing popular disdain for politicians and the political process. In the last elections, 40 percent of voters registered their protest by casting blank or defaced ballots. More recently, at weekly demonstrations throughout the nation, protesters ritualistically abused politicians, sometimes physically, chanting "*Que se vayan todos!*" ("Throw the bums out!").

By early 2002, Eduardo Duhalde, a Peronist and frequent critic of Argentina's decade-long neoliberal experiment, assumed the presidency with a popular mandate to defy the foreign bankers and rescue the nation from this devastating crisis. He immediately defaulted on the external debt; abandoned the dollar as Argentina's monetary standard; and devalued the peso to make Argentine exports more affordable, raise the cost of imports, and create more jobs. He regulated the largely foreign-owned utilities industries to lower electricity, gas, and telephone rates; imposed new energy taxes that mostly affected foreign companies; developed contingency plans for price controls; continued to limit the amounts that bank depositors could withdraw; regulated currency convertibility; expanded an emergency relief program that paid $42 per month to over a million families; and allowed Argentines to use devalued pesos to repay credit card debt at par. Although foreign bankers expressed skepticism about these reforms, workers, farmers, and small business owners clearly approved. In 2003 they elected as president Néstor Kirchner, Duhalde's populist political ally, who pledged not to be "a prisoner of the big corporations." After a decade of neoliberal addiction unregulated foreign markets and privatization, however, it remained unclear whether or not this modest methadone prescription would be sufficient to ease the nation's cold turkey convulsions of withdrawal, much less induce an independent recovery.

# 14    The Chilean Way

F OR A CENTURY and a half, Chile set a relatively high standard of political
behavior on a continent notorious for
its turmoil and dictatorships. Compared to its
neighbors, Peru, Bolivia, and Argentina, Chile was
a model of domestic tranquility. Chilean democracy appeared so firmly rooted that it permitted the
election and installation of a Marxist head of state,
President Salvador Allende Gossens, in 1970. Only
three years later, however, amid growing economic
and political chaos, military rebels overthrew
Chile's legitimate government and established a
right-wing dictatorship whose rule was characterized by brutal oppression.

How could Chile maintain its parliamentary
democracy so long when the rest of Latin America
could not? Why, after almost a hundred and fifty
years of respect for parliamentary democracy, did
it crumble so swiftly? In retrospect, the bounds of
Chilean democracy were narrowly drawn; the elite
never allowed political freedom and the practice of
politics to endanger its basic interests. Instead of
seeking to solve the nation's desperate economic
and social problems, successive governments
merely evaded them. When, finally, a coalition
government headed by Chile's working-class parties came to power in 1970 and inaugurated structural reforms that threatened oligarchical
privilege, the elite responded by calling in the army,
abolishing parliamentary democracy, and establishing a reactionary dictatorship.

## Foreign Dependency and the Parliamentary Republic, 1891–1920

The defeat and suicide of President José Manuel
Balmaceda during the civil war of 1891 ushered in
an era of unrestrained foreign investment and
export-dependent trade, presided over by the so-
called Parliamentary Republic, dominated by the
Liberal and Conservative political parties, which represented the great landowners of the Central Valley.

A third major party, the Radicals, founded in
1861 by dissident Liberals, enjoyed the support of
low-level professionals, bureaucrats, teachers,
artisans, and other middle-class groups, as well as
that of large landowners on the southern frontier
around Concepción, northern mine owners from
the Copiapó region, and businessmen from
Santiago, the capital. A fourth party, the
Democrats, had some base in the lower-middle
class and among workers.

The only issue separating the major parties
was the role of the church in education. The chief
concerns of the parties appeared to be the preservation of the status quo and the distribution of the
spoils of office. Corruption and inefficiency pervaded the political life of the era.

### ECONOMIC GROWTH AND THE EXPORT SECTOR

While politics stagnated in an atmosphere of fraud
and apathy, Chilean society underwent a profound

transformation. The export sector played a crucial and basically detrimental role in this transformation. Raw material exports generated enormous profits, but relatively few benefits flowed to the nation as a whole. Like the "banana republics" of Central America and the sugar islands of the Caribbean, Chile relied for its revenues on one export commodity, first nitrate and then copper, making it extremely vulnerable to cyclical world market demands for its products. Moreover, the copper industry, which produced the nation's major export in the twentieth century, was operated as an enclave, almost totally isolated from the rest of the economy. Finally, and most important, the presence of an export sector that produced sufficient revenue to operate the government and provide employment for a growing middle class enabled the Chilean oligarchy to retain political power and maintain an obsolete system of land tenure and use; these conditions severely hampered the growth of democracy and economic development.

Nonetheless, the nation grew increasingly urbanized and industrialized, and new classes emerged from these processes. An industrial working class rose in the mining regions of the north, first in the nitrate fields and then in the copper mines. Although their wages were higher than elsewhere in the country, the miners suffered from low pay, inadequate housing, the tyranny of company stores, and unsafe working conditions. In the cities, where wages were even lower, workers lived in wretched slums and were periodically battered by epidemic disease.

After the turn of the century, workers struggled against these dismal conditions. The first major strike broke out in Iquique in the northern mining region in 1901 and lasted for two months. In 1907 the nitrate workers of Iquique again struck against inhuman living and working conditions; the government responded by sending in troops who slaughtered two thousand workers. The wave of strikes continued, with a notable upsurge during World War I. After the war, a cheaper synthetic product displaced Chilean nitrates in world markets and the industry collapsed, leaving thousands of miners unemployed and plunging the entire country into a severe

depression. In 1919, faced with growing unrest, the government declared a state of siege (suspending civil liberties) in the mining areas.

Copper soon became Chile's leading export. Initially small-scale, low-technology operations had mined most of Chile's copper, but shortly after 1900 a downturn in copper prices had forced many of these producers to close. At the same time, the introduction of improved methods for the extraction of low-grade ore and the lower transportation costs promised by the opening of the Panama Canal attracted large North American companies, which dominated the industry after World War I. The Guggenheim interests and Anaconda Copper Co. now accounted for more than 80 percent of the nation's copper production. Foreigners also controlled Chile's other mineral exports: Bethlehem Steel monopolized iron ore and Guggenheim's *Compañía de Salitres de Chile* (COSACH) held 70 percent of the nitrate industry.

Labor had meantime begun to organize in the effort to achieve better conditions. Luis Emilio Recabarren played a leading part in establishing the Workers' Federation of Chile (*Federación de Obreros de Chile*, or *FOCH*) in 1909. Three years later he founded the first workers' party, the Socialist, or Socialist Labor, Party. In 1922 it became the Communist Party and joined the Third (Communist) International. By contrast with the Argentine Socialist Party, with its large middle-class base, Chile's first working-class party grew directly out of the labor movement.

In the same period, the middle class became larger and more diverse. The growth of industry and commerce and the expansion of the state created many new white-collar jobs. This growing middle class displayed few of the entrepreneurial traits commonly associated with the North American and European middle classes. The domination of decisive sectors of the economy by large-scale enterprise effectively barred small- and medium-size entrepreneurs from playing an important role in economic life. Aristocratic control of choice government jobs through clientele and kinship ties also restricted the sphere of middle-class activity. As the twentieth century opened, the middle class began to agitate for a place in the sun.

Meanwhile, the composition of the oligarchy was also changing, for it began to incorporate new elements from among industrialists and businessmen. More completely than elsewhere in Latin America, the Chilean landed elite fused with the new urban upper and upper-middle classes. They intermarried, and the urban rich acquired land, adopting the values of the traditional elite. This was a serious impediment to reform. Missing in Chile, too, were the large number of immigrants that in some measure had challenged the values and hegemony of the elite in Argentina.

### WOMEN AND THE WORKPLACE

The lack of immigrants also meant there was only a limited supply of native-born Chilean workers to satisfy growing industrial and agricultural needs. But market demand for cheap labor quickly broke down the gendered walls of work and family; in addition to their unpaid labor in the household, women played an increasingly important role as wage-earning workers in the Chilean economy. By 1913, 21 percent of the labor force was women, almost all of whom were native-born and employed in blue-collar occupations; three years later, this figure rose rapidly to 26 percent. Most women worked in "*trabajo a domicilio*," sweatshops in which they performed household chores like sewing and weaving for piece-rate wages. In a report on working conditions in the industry, Elena Caffarena showed that these workshops were "neither hygienic nor safe" and paid miserably low wages. This also inevitably damaged women's reproductive capacity; not surprisingly, child mortality rose from an average of 273 infant deaths per thousand in 1871 to 325 in 1908. To remedy this, Caffarena and other feminists advocated "strong government regulation" to abolish the sweatshop system and "female exploitation."

Ironically, they drew on traditional gendered ideals of womanhood and the family to lay the foundation for Chile's modern feminist movement. Needleworker and feminist leader Esther Valdés de Díaz, for example, denounced the "wolves" who waited to seduce women, made vulnerable by long hours of work and constant verbal abuse on the shop floor, and she argued the need for a paternalistic state to protect them. Like many working-class feminists, she stressed the class oppression of capitalism rather than the gendered tyranny of patriarchy. "Women who work in factories, pushed by the need to earn their daily bread, not only are not in their place, but, without knowing it, are competing with men and, in so doing, becoming victims of capitalism." Women, she believed, unconsciously and unavoidably contributed to the "devaluation of men's work."

But for these feminists, this lamentable state of affairs could be remedied only by an aggressive, activist state that defended women and workers against the predatory interests of capitalists. So they mobilized to pressure Chile's political leadership to regulate sweatshops; enforce minimum-wage protections for women and children; establish the legal right to equal pay for equal work; restrict women's workweek to six eight-hour days; prohibit work by children under fourteen years of age; abolish night work for women; require companies to provide partially paid pre- and post-partum leaves for pregnant women; compel industries employing more than twenty women to provide on-site child-care facilities; and allow nursing mothers periodic breaks to feed their children.

# Alessandri and the Rise of Populism, 1920–1970

By 1920 even sections of the oligarchy were aware that they could no longer ignore the needs of the rest of Chilean society. Foreign interests like the Braden Copper Company actively contributed to this expanded social consciousness. According to Braden, a sturdy nuclear family could stabilize labor turnover; decrease such antisocial behavior as gambling, drinking, and fighting; deter absenteeism and the celebration of "*San Lunes*" (Saint Monday), the unofficial international workers' holiday; and discourage militant trade unionism that frequently led to strikes, industrial sabotage, and worker slowdowns—all of which reduced labor productivity. Braden therefore had developed a comprehensive private social welfare program to encourage family life, but workers typically opposed these paternalistic policies, which were transparently designed to control their labor; for example, they scorned the company's *Departamento de Bienestar* (Welfare Department) as the *Departamento de Bienfregar* (Molest Well Department).

However, state welfare programs enjoyed a social legitimacy that a company's private plan did not. Moreover, public welfare was an effective means of socializing private costs and thus increasing the competitive advantage of large companies over smaller businesses that routinely ignored workers' welfare. Finally, these state-sponsored programs also appealed to middle-class progressives who sought to "moralize" working-class culture and to radicals who sought to cultivate a "proletarian morality" that discouraged workers' fractious individualism and encouraged a politically disciplined, class-based solidarity. The stage was set for a populist reform program that would appeal to diverse political constituencies, and Arturo Allessandri, nicknamed the "Lion of Tarapacá," became its agent.

A former corporation lawyer turned populist politician, Alessandri appealed to the lower and middle classes with promises to reform the constitution and relieve the bleakness of working-class life. He promised a social security system, a labor code, cheap housing, educational reform, women's rights, and state control of banks and insurance companies. With considerable support from sections of the oligarchy, which hoped that he could placate the restless masses with a minimum of effective social change, Alessandri became president in 1920.

During the first four years of Alessandri's term, he proved unable to make good his campaign pledges. Congress, representing entrenched oligarchical interests, stood squarely in the way of any meaningful social and political reforms. Accordingly, Alessandri urged the passage of laws that would restore the balance of power between Congress and the executive branch, a balance destroyed after the civil war of 1891. He also sought such social reforms as a shorter workday,

labor laws to protect women and children, the right of workers to strike, and health insurance. These modest proposals certainly did not threaten the status quo, but they would require money. In view of the catastrophic decline of the nitrate industry, this money could be raised only by taxing the oligarchy's land and income, a solution the elite found unthinkable. As a result of the parliamentary deadlock, the Chilean government could not cope with the mounting economic and social crisis.

The Chilean military, predominantly of middle-class origins, had observed the unfolding crisis with growing impatience and resentment. Many junior and middle-grade officers favored the enactment of Alessandri's social and political reform program; they also felt that Congress had neglected the needs of the armed forces. A succession of military coups, the last of which was led by reformist officers Carlos Ibáñez del Campo and Marmaduke Grove, ultimately enabled Alessandri to accomplish the political reforms for which he had campaigned. The result was the constitution of 1925, which ended the Parliamentary Republic and restored the balance of power between Congress and the president. It provided that the president would be elected by direct vote, serve a six-year term, be ineligible for immediate reelection, and have control over his cabinet and government finance. The constitution proclaimed the inviolable right of private property but stated that this right could be limited in the interest of social needs. Other measures included a new and extensive labor code, the grant of the vote to literate males over twenty-one, the establishment of an electoral registry to reduce electoral fraud, a nominal income tax on income over ten thousand pesos a year, and the establishment of a central bank.

## IBÁÑEZ AND THE GREAT DEPRESSION

But Ibáñez and the military remained powerful, and they initially sought an alliance with the working and middle classes for the achievement of structural reforms, but this ended in the military dictatorship of 1927 to 1931.

To implement his program and secure the position of state employees, which was necessary to maintain political stability, Ibáñez needed substantial amounts of money; his populist program of welfare, public works, and modernization was based above all on huge loans from foreign bankers. The armed forces were a special beneficiary of government largesse, obtaining generous promotions and salary increases. Most of the protective legislation for which women had lobbied during the previous decade was enacted. Meanwhile, all opposition was suppressed, political foes were jailed or deported, and efforts were made to split the Communist-led labor movement by the sponsorship of government-backed unions.

Aided by a temporary revival of copper and nitrate sales and massive foreign loans, the Chilean economy prospered for the first two years of Ibáñez's rule. But the Wall Street crash of 1929 unmasked Chile's dependency on external markets. It cut off the all-important flow of capital and loans, and by the following year the nitrate and copper markets had both collapsed. Because the government relied heavily on copper taxes for revenue, the Depression forced it to curtail daily operations severely and default on its large foreign debt. In 1932 the United States, Chile's main market for copper, adopted a high tariff on copper imports, which caused mine closings and severe unemployment. The Depression also accentuated gender-based wage inequities and unleashed a backlash against women in the work force. Conservatives called for women's return to the home to stabilize the family and reduce job competition among men, thereby increasing male wages and employment. Although the political left advocated elimination of gendered wage inequalities so that all workers could unite against capitalists on the basis of their shared class interest, they nonetheless agreed to identify certain industries, like copper and teaching, as exclusively male and female. In a vain effort to find a solution for the economic crisis, the government tried to limit nitrate sales to push up prices. Ibáñez trimmed social services and his public works program and hiked taxes, but the financial situation grew increasingly desperate.

In July 1931, confronted by a general strike that involved not only workers but professionals, white-collar employees, women, and students and faced with growing doubts about the army's loyalty to him, Ibáñez resigned and went into exile in Argentina. The next seventeen months brought a succession of military coups. One such coup, led by Marmaduke Grove, commander of the air force, led to the proclamation of a Socialist Republic of Chile, which lasted barely twelve days before it was overthrown by a new military revolt. Ironically, the program of the socialist republic was not socialist; it proposed, rather, to create jobs through public works financed by the issue of paper money.

Finally, in September 1932 a new coup installed a caretaker regime that presided over new elections, which returned Arturo Alessandri to the presidency.

### THE RETURN OF ALESSANDRI

Alessandri began his second term in the depths of the Depression, with one hundred and sixty thousand people unemployed in Santiago alone, while a typhoid epidemic ravaged the country. Income from nitrates was one-twentieth the 1927 figure; public employees, including soldiers and policemen, had not been paid for months. In the succeeding five years, 1932 to 1937, the president and his finance minister, Gustavo Ross, presided over an economic recovery that reflected a partial revival and stabilization of the world market. Copper prices recovered in 1935, and by 1937 copper production exceeded pre-Depression levels. As the economy revived, government revenues generated from copper taxes enabled the government to avoid taxing large landholdings. Without the spur of equitable taxes, latifundists continued to leave vast tracts of fertile land uncultivated or underutilized. Although it had the potential to feed its own people, Chile had to import foodstuffs—a policy that drained the nation of foreign exchange that would have been better used to purchase capital goods for industrialization or to build roads and harbors.

With its coffers swelled by revenue from the export sector, the Chilean government expanded its role in the economy. A large bureaucracy developed, staffed by an emerging middle class. As the government became the major employer of the middle class and the nation's most important

In the 1930s, Chile's Women's Liberation Movement (MEMCH) mobilized thousands of women and influenced populist policies with a demand that the state guarantee women's right to equality in the home, in the workplace, and in politics. [Photograph courtesy of Asunción Lavrín]

venture capitalist, Chile grew ever more dependent for its economic development on factors beyond its control.

But Alessandri had no greater success in solving Chile's structural problems in the 1930s than he had in the 1920s. Foreign capital controlled the lucrative mining sector of the economy, and the inefficient latifundio continued to dominate Chilean agriculture. Workers' strikes for better wages and living conditions were often brutally suppressed.

Middle-class critics of the regime fared little better. Following the example of Ibáñez, Alessandri closed down hostile newspapers, exiled political critics, and dealt highhandedly with

Congress. These conditions produced a major new effort to mobilize workers, peasants, and the urban middle sector to defend democracy and promote social progress. This effort was called the Chilean Popular Front.

### WOMEN AND THE RISE OF THE POPULAR FRONT

The Chilean left had its roots in the Communist Party during the 1920s. The Communists won considerable support among organized labor, particularly the railroad workers' union and the Confederation of Chilean Workers (FOCH), which claimed two hundred thousand members. Although they had had a part in framing the constitution of 1925, Communist leaders were imprisoned and exiled during the Ibáñez regime. After the fall of Ibáñez in 1931, however, the party revived under the leadership of Carlos Contreras Labarca and gained considerable popularity among workers and intellectuals.

Chile in the 1930s was fertile ground for the growth of left-wing parties and ideologies, many of which coalesced to form the Chilean Popular Front. Composed of Socialists, Communists, and Radicals, the Front's candidate, Radical Pedro Aguirre Cerda, won the presidency in 1938. The Popular Front's electoral platform called for the restoration of constitutional rule and civil liberties and basic social reforms, summed up in the slogan *pan, techo, y abrigo* (bread, clothing, and a roof ).

The short, stormy life of the Popular Front yielded some achievements. In 1938 the State Development Agency, CORFO, was formed to foster industrialization. Aided by relatively high wartime copper prices, a virtual cessation of imports as a result of World War II, and by governmental subsidies, low taxes, and protective tariffs on imported consumer goods, native manufacturing made steady progress between 1940 and 1945.

The policy of state-supported industrialization also promoted the growth of the Chilean industrial working class; between 1940 and 1952, the number of workers employed in manufacturing rose from 15 percent of the work force to 19 percent. The industrialization process was accompanied, at least until 1945, by improvement in workers' real purchasing power—up 20 percent between 1940 and 1945—while that of white-collar workers increased 25 percent. After 1945, as Radical administrations moved to the right and the basis of the Popular Front strategy disintegrated, the working class's relative share of the national income declined.

Women also were active both as workers and mothers, but increasingly they insisted that they would need more than the "aura of dignity and respect, but should also receive the aid of the state when economic conditions demand it." For many women in the 1930s, this meant state protections against exploitation, prenatal health care, and subsidies for child care. But feminists like Clara de la Luz also wanted support for family planning. She defended "scientific procreation"—that is, birth control—and called on women to organize a "strike of the wombs" to liberate themselves from unwanted family responsibilities that increased the supply of new workers for industry and agriculture, lowered workers' wages, and reduced their freedom to resist capitalist exploitation. Others criticized the moral and legal double standard that gave "men impunity and women responsibility" in reproductive matters.

Although Chile's Catholic traditions made abortion illegal, it was widely practiced by midwives and amateurs. In 1936 five hospitals identified 10,514 cases of botched abortions that required medical attention; the following year, the Ministry of Health reported that 24 percent (13,351) of women in public maternity hospitals were there to be treated for complications from bungled abortions. Growing numbers of women, especially poor working-class women, viewed abortion, contraception, and family planning as one way to escape what the leftist Women's Liberation Movement (MEMCH) called "compulsory motherhood" and the "slavery of unwanted children."

Women also won basic political and civil rights. Conservatives, influenced by upper-class women's groups like the Club de Señoras, historically had supported enfranchisement of literate women because they believed that, as guardians of home, church, and family life, they were a natural conservative constituency necessary to counter the political advantages accruing to Socialist, Communist, and Radical Parties from the enfranchisement of illiterate men. Meanwhile, MEMCH insisted on the "integral emancipation of women, especially the economic, juridical, biological, and political emancipation." All pressed for civil equality and the right to vote, a campaign that achieved partial success in 1934 with the granting of municipal voting rights to literate women.

Local leftist parties failed to offer women candidates for municipal posts, preferring to emphasize class struggle while ignoring gender difference. This created an electoral void that conservatives filled by offering women candidates like Elena Doll de Díaz, whose populist campaign defended the moral center of family life and called for an aggressive program of state intervention to protect it against the injustice of market forces: workers' welfare, equal wages, sanitation, "popular restaurants" to feed the hungry, and electric trolleys to provide workers with cheap transportation. Not surprisingly, by 1941 two-thirds of the women registered to vote identified themselves as Conservatives; thereafter, the Popular Front coalition fractured and party leaders abandoned interest in woman suffrage.

World War II decisively reinforced the politics of the Popular Front and reignited the campaign for women's right to vote in national elections. Wartime alliances with the Soviet Union, a growing democratic discourse, and the decline of anti-imperialist rhetoric within the Chilean left contributed to the emergence of a cross-class, gender-based movement in support of women's suffrage. The Chilean Federation of Feminine Institutions (FECHIF), for example, which represented 213 women's organizations, mobilized massive street demonstrations that attracted thousands of women to its militant calls for "social democracy."

Although freed from traditional external constraints during the war, the Popular Front era produced no structural changes in the Chilean economy or society because the members of the governing coalition had irreconcilable differences over domestic and foreign policy. In the 1946 election, the Socialists, reflecting historic factional disputes within the party, abandoned the Popular Front, but Radical Gabriel González Videla (1946–1952) won with the support of the Communist Party. Soon, responding to the pressures of the cold war, González Videla moved to the right, ousted the Communist members of his cabinet, broke a strike of Communist-led coal miners, and passed the *Ley Maldita* (the Accursed Law), which outlawed the Communist Party and eliminated Communists from Congress. González Videla also established a concentration camp for Communist Party members and other left-wing militants in an abandoned mining camp in the northern desert.

With the repression and disenfranchisement of Communists like Elena Caffarena, who had written the women's suffrage legislation and organized on behalf of women's rights for decades, González Videla finally signed into law a 1949 bill to give literate women the vote in national elections. Thereafter, he tried to consolidate his political support among working-class women by organizing Women's Centers to provide education, training, and career services.

But massive discontent with skyrocketing inflation, the freezing of workers' wages, and González Videla's repressive policies paved the way for a comeback by the old ex-dictator Carlos Ibáñez del Campo in 1952. Ibáñez promised repeal of the Ley Maldita, a minimum salary, a family allowance for workers, and a sympathetic hearing for just wage demands. But the decline in Chilean copper revenues following the end of the Korean war made it impossible for Ibáñez to make good on his populist promises. To stabilize the economy he sought loans from North American banks and the International Monetary Fund; meanwhile, he sought to force the working class to absorb inflation through cuts in real wages. Threatened with labor unrest, Ibáñez embarked on a course of harsh repression. By the end of his term, he had alienated all sectors of the Chilean people.

## New Alignments: The Emergence of Christian Democracy

Between 1953 and the presidential election year of 1958, the parties of the left restored their unity by forming the *Frente de Acción Popular* (Popular Action Front, or FRAP), which included the Socialist Party and the Communists. Simultaneously, a new Christian Democratic Party emerged, led by Eduardo Frei; it appealed to Catholic workers, especially white-collar sectors, with a vague ideology that claimed to be neither capitalist nor socialist. In its first try for office in 1958, this party demonstrated its electoral force.

Four major candidates contested the presidency in 1958. They were the Conservative Jorge Alessandri, a son of the former president and a leading industrialist; Eduardo Frei, a Christian Democrat; Salvador Allende, of FRAP; and Luis Bossay, a Radical. Surprisingly, Alessandri beat Allende by a threadbare margin of only 33,500 votes. Allende would probably have won if an obscure minor-party candidate had not drawn away some slum and rural poor votes.

Despite booming copper prices, however, Alessandri had no more success than his predecessors in coping with Chile's problems of inflation and economic stagnation. His formula for recovery was to restore the free market, reduce state intervention in the economy, and employ foreign loans and investment as the basis for economic development.

Although depression and war had slowed the inflow, foreign capital now surged into Chile in the postwar period, not only into the extractive sector but into manufacturing and commerce as well. From 1954 to 1970, foreigners invested $1.67 billion in Chile. U.S. companies continued to dominate copper, nitrate, and iodine production. Foreign companies conducted approximately half the nation's wholesale trade, monopolized the telephone and telegraph industries, and had important stakes in electric utilities and banking. Even the major advertising agencies were foreign subsidiaries or affiliates.

In 1960 the three great mines of the Gran Minería, all owned by the foreign giants Anaconda and Kennecott, accounted for 11 percent of the country's gross national product, 50 percent of its exports, and 20 percent of government revenues. But the millions of dollars in sales, profits, and tax revenues generated by copper mining provided little stimulus for Chilean commerce and industry. Their huge profits, which they remitted to their parent corporations in the United States, added to the outflow of capital from the country.

Chile depended not only on direct investment from abroad but on loans as well. Payment of interest and amortization on the national debt consumed an increasing share of its revenue from the export sector. Because most foreign investment, like the copper enclave, was capital-intensive, it provided little employment and few linkages to the rest of the economy. Employment in the mines declined steadily in the post–World War II era, and the surplus of miners made it possible for the companies to pay the largely unskilled labor force relatively low wages. Until the 1950s, machinery, equipment, and technical skills were imported entirely from abroad. The benefits to Chile's long-range economic development were minimal. Without a doubt, Chile was not the master of its own economic fate.

Politics in Chile during the early 1960s was profoundly affected by changes in United States policy in response to the Cuban Revolution (1959). The United States sought to bolster reform movements throughout Latin America as an alternative to social revolution. As part of this policy, it covertly financed the Christian Democrats. Combined with the backing of the conservative parties, which were badly scared by Allende's near-election six years earlier, U.S. support enabled Frei to win the 1964 election with 56 percent of the vote.

Eduardo Frei came to the presidency with promises of a "revolution in freedom" that would correct the extreme inequities of Chilean society without a violent class struggle. He especially appealed to women to preserve the sanctity of the Catholic family against Allende's "godless communist revolution" and opened 6,000 Women's Centers. The problems he faced were familiar ones: inflation and stagnation, a domestic market too narrow to support an efficient mass industry, an extractive industry dominated by foreign ownership, and an agriculture incapable of supplying the basic needs of the population. To create the market needed for a modern mass industry, Frei proposed agrarian reform, tax reform, and other measures to redistribute income to the lower classes.

When Frei took office, there was an extreme concentration of landownership, the condition of rural laborers was wretched, and the inefficient great landed estates were clearly incapable of providing enough food to feed Chile's growing urban centers. By contrast with the situation in most underdeveloped nations, Chile's agricultural sector played only a small role in the economy. The inability of agriculture to provide employment, on the one hand, and sufficient food, on the other, resulted in an overurbanized, underemployed, and undernourished population.

The statistics of landholding indicate that there was little change in these patterns between 1930 and 1970. In 1930 holdings of over 2,500 acres composed only 2 percent of the total number of farms but constituted 78 percent of the cultivable land. Eighty-two percent of all farms were under 125 acres but held only 4 percent of the land. By the 1960s, 11,000 units, accounting for 4.2 percent of the farms, composed 79 percent of the land. Farms under 100 acres—77 percent of all farms—held 10.6 percent of the land. Over 700,000 people, the majority of the rural labor force, had no land at all. The living and working conditions of agricultural laborers were appalling—and getting worse. Agricultural wages had consistently declined since the 1940s, falling 23 percent from 1953 to 1964.

Government credit and tax policies before 1964 assured that the maldistribution of land and agricultural income would continue. Small landholders, having no access to bank or government loans, had to rely on moneylenders or store owners, who charged outrageous interest. Smallholders and agricultural laborers also bore a disproportionate burden of taxes. Taxes on land, capital, income, and inheritance, on the other hand, were light. The large estates, especially those that were not farmed, went virtually untaxed.

Frei's program of agrarian reform had mixed results. He began by attempting to improve conditions in rural areas by increasing wages, establishing peasant unions, and instituting a more equitable system of taxation; he also redistributed some land to the peasants, but inflation eroded wage gains and land redistribution fell far short of what was promised. As a gradualist, Frei shied away from precipitous or widespread expropriations. Peasants who received land faced a difficult time, for the government did not provide them with credit needed to start off as independent farmers.

Frei's plan for the Chileanization of the copper industry was designed both to appease widespread nationalist sentiment and to obtain new government revenue through increased copper production. The plan required the government to buy 51 percent of the shares in the foreign-owned mines. In return for a promise to increase production and refine more ore in Chile, the foreign companies retained control of management and obtained new concessions with respect to taxation and repatriation of profits. But the plan failed to expand production significantly or to increase government revenues.

Other sectors of the Chilean economy also were concentrated. A few powerful clans controlled a wide variety of industrial and financial enterprises and thus exerted a decisive influence on the national economy as a whole. In 1967, 12 companies out of 2,600 transacted nearly half the total wholesale business in the country. One bank, Banco de Chile, furnished 32 percent of the nation's private bank credit; the five largest banks furnished 57.4 percent.

These facts, however, tell only part of the story, for control of the economy was even more concentrated. Fifteen large economic groups controlled the Chilean economy. The most powerful of the clans, the Edwards family, controlled one commercial bank, seven financial and investment corporations, five insurance companies, thirteen industries, and two publishing houses and was closely associated with North American companies active in the country. The family's newspaper chain accounted for over half the circulation of daily newspapers in Chile; together with another publishing house, it virtually controlled the entire market for periodicals. As early as 1965, the president had decided to abandon his campaign promise to redistribute income and instead he implemented an economic policy that would attract foreign and domestic investors. During 1966 the government froze wages and reacted

harshly to strikes in the copper mines, at one point sending in troops. Increased worker militancy made Socialist and Communist union leadership more influential.

The need to appease his political constituency and the economic decline after 1966 defeated Frei's efforts at reform. Upper-class Catholic intellectuals had founded and provided the leadership of the Christian Democratic party. Its membership was overwhelmingly middle class, including urban professionals, white-collar workers—especially from the public sector—skilled workers, and managers, all groups that had emerged during the preceding two decades as the Chilean economy diversified. The party did well in the larger towns, among urban slum dwellers, and among women. In 1964 Frei got considerable support from industrialists and bankers who feared the election of Allende. These were hardly the elements of a revolutionary party. Frei's program of reform depended entirely on a healthy, expanding economy that would enable the government to distribute benefits to the lower class without injuring the middle class or altering the basic economic and social structures.

When Frei came to office in 1964, the economy was expanding rapidly, for the Vietnam War kept copper prices high. Frei's moderate reform goals insured good relations with the United States and a resulting flow of loans and private investment. Even Chile's chronic inflation slowed. Two good years, however, were followed by four bad ones. After 1967 the economy stagnated while inflation surged again. Income inequalities increased, and living standards declined sharply. Frei's rhetoric brought hope to Chileans, but he fulfilled few of his promises. During his term, the working class grew increasingly restive. Groups like *pobladores* (urban slum dwellers) and rural workers organized for the first time. As the Christian Democrats proved less and less capable of dealing with Chile's economic woes, these newly organized groups and the trade unions moved further to the left.

This transformation of Chilean politics was both reflected in and shaped by powerful cultural changes, the most significant of which was the birth of *Nueva Canción*, the New Song movement. First developed in Peronist Argentina, the New Song movement utilized indigenous musical instruments and typically explored folkloric lyrical themes. But in Chile and elsewhere throughout Latin America in the 1960s, it quickly became associated with revolution and the democratic struggle against poverty, social injustice, and tyranny. Violeta Parra, the daughter of a schoolteacher and seamstress in Chile's rural south, had pioneered the study of the nation's folkloric art and music in the 1950s. Her ballads, like her paintings and colorful *arpilleras* (tapestries), typically commemorated the struggles of poor folk and condemned the wealthy *pitucos* who profited from their exploitation.

Parra's work made an indelible impression on a young Víctor Jara, arguably Chile's most famous New Song musician. Born to a poor peasant family, Jara, whose songs celebrated the lives of ordinary Chileans, often combined traditional Catholic rituals with lyrics that reflected his leftist social conscience. Perhaps the most famous of these was his *"La plegaria del labrador"* ("Farmworkers' Prayer"), modeled on the Lord's Prayer. But Jara, giving voice to Chile's impoverished peasants, did not ask to be saved from some abstract evil; on the contrary, accompanied by his searing *charango*, an indigenous guitar made from an armadillo shell, he raised his powerful voice to demand: "Deliver us from the master who keeps us in misery, thy kingdom of justice and equality come."

In 1969, after Frei's police savagely attacked a group of peasants who illegally had occupied vacant lands in Puerto Montt, Jara wrote a stirring new song that became the battle cry of a generation. *"Preguntas por Puerto Montt"* ("Questions about Puerto Montt") denounced the barbaric murderers and declared that "All the rains in the south (of Chile) will not be enough to wash your hands clean." But Jara was not only interested in politics. He believed that the role of artists was to be cultural rebels. "An artist must be an authentic creator," he once said, "and in essence a revolutionary . . . a man as dangerous as a guerrilla because of his great power of communication." Artists became revolutionaries by celebrating a popular culture that all too often was ignored or scorned by a mass media monopolized by the wealthy. "We should ascend to the people, not feel

that we are lowering ourselves to them," Jara once wrote. "Our job is to give them what belongs to them— their cultural roots." Jara and others later collaborated on a popular new musical, *"La Cantata de Santa María,"* which commemorated the 1907 slaughter of 3,000 striking nitrate miners, a massacre that sparked the development of Chile's modern trade union movement.

This leftward move also was reflected within the Christian Democratic Party itself. In 1969 disillusioned progressives split off to form the Movement for United Popular Action (MAPU), which later joined the Popular Unity Coalition. This break left Frei the leader of the right wing of the party and Radomiro Tomic the head of what remained of the left wing. Because Frei was ineligible to run again under the constitution and the party could not risk further erosion of its social base by running a hard-liner, it advanced Tomic as its presidential candidate in 1970. He ran on a platform almost indistinguishable from that of Allende, the candidate of the left coalition, Popular Unity (UP), whose main elements were the Socialist, Communist, and Radical Parties.

The right backed ex-President Jorge Alessandri of the National Party. The right, already alienated by Frei's agrarian reform, found Tomic totally unacceptable and refused to join forces with the Christian Democrats as it had in 1964. Allende won the election with 36 percent of the vote, whereas Alessandri got 35 percent and Tomic 28 percent. Preferring to stress class solidarity, Allende had not targeted the women's vote, but his share of it grew by 13 percent from 1958 and doubtlessly provided his razor-thin margin of victory. Because Allende failed to receive a majority, the election went to Congress which, after much-publicized maneuvering, approved Allende as president.

## The Chilean Road to Socialism, 1970–1973

### THE OPPOSITION

When Allende took office in 1970, domestic political conditions appeared favorable to his program for the achievement of socialism in Chile within a

Salvador Allende, president of Chile, died during the military coup of September 1973. [Bruno Barbey/Magnum Photos]

framework of legality and nonviolence. The assassination in October 1970 of General René Schneider, the commander in chief of the army, who had kept the army neutral during the period after the election just before Allende assumed the presidency, had discredited the right. Prospects were excellent that the Popular Unity would receive the cooperation of the left wing of the Christian Democratic Party in Congress. For the time being, the UP coalition remained united behind a program that called for expropriation of all landholdings over 80 hectares, and the progressive takeover of large foreign companies and monopolies.

Nonetheless, the forces against the UP were formidable. It did not have a majority in Congress. Both the judiciary and the *Controlaría General* (the

government's fiscal arm) opposed Allende's policies. The entire domestic economic establishment, foreign interests, much of the officer corps of the military and national police, and the Catholic church were also aligned against the UP. The anti-UP political coalition, the *Confederación Democrática* (Democratic Confederation) controlled virtually all of the nation's media—two of the three television stations, 95 percent of the radio stations, 90 percent of the newspaper circulation, and all of the weekly magazines.

Even more significantly, however, substantial shifts were occurring in global markets. The European and Japanese economies had fully recovered from their wartime collapse and had emerged as vigorous competitors with the United States, whose economic and technological strength had been sapped by the Vietnam War and a host of other Third World military interventions. By the early 1970s, the leading capitalist countries were on the verge of an international trade war, looking to industrially developing, "semiperipheral" countries like Chile to earn profits otherwise unavailable to them in their own markets.

But this meant that foreign interests would no longer tolerate nationalistic, statist restrictions on their activities, no matter how popular these might be with local democratic electoral constituencies. Consequently, when the democratically elected UP coalition of Socialists and Communists sought to implement their campaign promises, U.S. government leaders like Henry Kissinger, President Richard Nixon's National Security Council adviser, imperiously intervened. "I don't see why we have to let a country go Marxist," Kissinger arrogantly insisted, "just because its people are irresponsible." Nixon immediately ordered the Central Intelligence Agency (CIA) to orchestrate a coup to overthrow Allende before the Congress could validate his election, but, even after this failed, he advised U.S. operatives to "make the economy scream." The ensuing economic chaos, according to Nixon, would undermine Allende's legitimacy and force his government to reopen Chile to foreign control.

But a lack of internal cohesion also hindered the UP. The old problem of how to satisfy the claims of both the working-class—even more militant than during the Popular Front days—and the middle-class sectors—who worried that their interests were being threatened by the structural reforms undertaken by the UP—was never fully resolved.

This competition between middle- and working-class constituents also had been reflected in cultural conflict among the nation's youth. During the tumultuous 1960s, the folk music of Parra and Jara, with its social conscience, political protest, and identification with Chile's popular classes, had starkly contrasted with a Chilean rock music that self-consciously emulated British and U.S. (counter)culture. Jara himself had campaigned for the UP, and he wrote *"Venceremos"* ("We Shall Overcome"), which quickly became the campaign's theme song.

On the other hand, rock musicians like *Los Macs* identified more with foreign cultures they defined as modern; they especially appealed to alienated upper- and middle-class youth who, like the later supporters of Pinochet's bloody dictatorship, rebelled against Chilean popular traditions they associated with backwardness. Chilean rockers typically sang their songs, even original compositions, in English and were greatly influenced by Elvis Presley, The Beatles, The Kinks, and The Byrds. So disgusted were these bands with Chilean popular cultural traditions and the nation's stormy politics that some rock musicians, like Juan Mateo O'Brien of *Los Vidrios Quebrados* (Broken Glass), "thought only about leaving Chile" and declined invitations to return to play for a Chilean audience. Others, like Willy Morales of *Los Macs*, specifically cited Allende's democratic socialist revolution, "the social and political events between 1970 and 1973," for his disinterest in returning to Chile.

Ironically, countercultural *gringos* who visited Chile to help build a peaceful, democratic socialist alternative to western capitalism often discovered to their amazement that the young Chilean rockers, who dressed like them, wore long hair, smoked marihuana, and listened to Jimi Hendrix, increasingly were politically more sympathetic to Richard Nixon. Middle- and upper-class countercultural Chilean rockers defined the dominant culture against which they rebelled as primitive, uneducated, undeveloped, and working class; in 1970, Salvador Allende had become its political symbol. But the countercultural *gringos* and folk enthusiasts like Víctor Jara defined the dominant culture against which they rebelled as modern, capitalistic, socially unjust, and foreign dominated; its political symbols were Richard Nixon and Jorge Alessandri, upon whom the Nixon administration had lavished covert financial support in the 1970 presidential elections.

## THE FIRST YEAR, 1971

The UP's immediate goal was to improve the living standard of the working class and get the economy moving. The government accomplished this by increasing purchasing power, which in turn stimulated demand, industrial production, and employment. During the first year of Allende's term, worker income rose a startling 50 percent. The government instituted a massive program of public spending, especially for labor-intensive projects such as housing, education, sanitation, and health. At the same time, the government expanded its appeal to women. It developed a Ministry of the Family, created community daycare centers, organized low-income milk distribution programs, financed *Almacenes del Pueblo* (People's Grocery Cooperatives), and established price controls, which were monitored by local, housewife-operated price and supply committees. The rate of inflation fell to 22.1 percent in 1971 from 34.9 percent in 1970, and as a result, real income rose 30 percent. The Organization of American States independently confirmed that Allende's program had produced "high growth levels" during its first year.

For the first year, middle-class businessmen, industrialists, and peasants fared very well and cooperated with the Allende regime. There were scattered cases of larger owners sabotaging their own property but, for the most part, business was not hostile. The government also employed coercion to gain cooperation from industry, threatening companies with intervention if they did not agree to increase production. Coercion and increased demand combined to bring about an expansion of industrial production and employment.

The short-term policies of the UP government increased popular support for the minority regime, a success reflected in the municipal elections of April 1971, in which the Popular Unity won over 50 percent of the vote. In the long run, however, the depletion of stocks, the outflow of foreign exchange to pay for the import of consumer goods, and the fall of profits in what was still basically a market economy proved very damaging to the government's economic program.

Allende's first problems arose when the United States in effect declared economic war on Chile's fragile democratic socialist experiment. The United States covertly embargoed Chilean loans, imports, and exports, especially copper, whose price declined sharply, leading to an imbalance in terms

of trade and the depletion of foreign-exchange reserves. In addition, the expropriation of the Gran Minería in July 1971 virtually halted the flow of private investment capital from the United States. The resulting economic difficulties led Allende to stop servicing the national debt, but he eventually managed to reach satisfactory agreements with all of Chile's creditors except the United States.

## THE LEFT'S OLD DILEMMA: CAUGHT IN THE MIDDLE, 1972–1973

The first year's gains gave way to economic stagnation and a resurgence of inflation. Although Allende's popularity remained high in 1971, he struggled unsuccessfully to reach a delicate balance between the needed structural reform demanded by the working class and the special interests of the middle class. The government's policy of expropriating large enterprises alienated owners of small- and medium-size businesses, who employed 80 percent of the working population. Workers began occupying and operating factories. State enterprises were badly mismanaged.

The socialist government was also unable to solve the agricultural crisis. Chile's inefficiently managed agricultural production was perhaps the biggest economic roadblock, for it neither raised enough to feed the country's inhabitants nor provided employment for the large pool of rural labor. A hostile Congress forced Allende to operate with reform laws inherited from the Frei administration; nonetheless, by the end of 1972, Allende had effectively liquidated the latifundio system. Expropriation and redistribution proceeded, but with considerable cost to production. The amount of land under cultivation decreased by 20 percent, and the harvest of 1972–1973 was poor.

The Allende administration faced a full-fledged economic and political crisis by the fall of 1972. The inevitable disruptions that accompany revolutionary conditions were aggravated by mistakes and shortcomings of the UP government and conflicts within the coalition. Moreover, the Chilean oligarchy and its North American allies were formidable, unrelenting opponents. The United States was deeply involved in Chilean politics. According to its director, William Colby, the CIA spent $11 million between 1962 and 1970 to help prevent Allende from being elected president. Thereafter the CIA, with authorization from President Richard Nixon and Secretary of State Henry Kissinger, spent $8 million between 1970 and 1973 to "destabilize" the Chilean economy. Nixon told the U.S. ambassador to Chile that he would "smash that son-of-a-bitch Allende."

The Chilean upper class, although it had lost much of its economic base due to the nationalization of large industries and expropriation of large landholdings, retained control over much of the mass media, the judiciary, a majority in Congress, and the armed forces.

The struggle hinged, finally, on the middle sectors. Soaring inflation eroded their economic position. All of Allende's efforts to reassure and win over the middle class failed to overcome its traditional hostility toward socialism and its association with the bourgeoisie. This middle class provided the mass base for the coup that overthrew the Popular Unity.

Allende's opponents took advantage of the growing economic crisis to embark on a program of sabotage and direct action that included the mobilization of middle-class women in "empty pots" protest marches and a strike of truck drivers (subsidized by the CIA), which developed into a full-scale lockout by a majority of Chilean capitalists. The strike ended when Allende made major concessions to his opponents, guaranteeing the security of small- and medium-size industries. He also agreed to the inclusion of generals in his cabinet to ensure law and order and to supervise the congressional election scheduled for March 1973.

Relying on long established electoral trends, which saw the party in power lose congressional seats, the opposition expected to gain a sweeping victory in the election; it hoped to have the two-thirds majority needed to impeach Allende and legally oust his government. Instead, the UP vote rose from 36 percent (in 1970) to 44 percent, proof that its socialist policies had substantially increased its support among the working class and peasantry. Once again women now known as "hacedoras de presidentes" (makers of presidents)

provided Allende his margin of victory. The UP coalition received 41 percent of the women's vote, a 14 percent increase since the last congressional elections in 1969 and an 11 percent improvement over the 1970 presidential election totals. Allende also benefited from 1971 electoral reforms that enfranchised younger voters and eliminated literacy restrictions, all of which boosted women's participation from 47 percent of the electorate in 1970 to 56 percent in 1973.

But the opposition still commanded a majority in Congress and it redoubled efforts to create economic and political chaos by disruptive strikes, the organization of terrorist bands, and calls on the armed forces to intervene. The Chilean military, itself internally divided over the Allende government, was greatly influenced by the United States. Many Chilean officers had had counterinsurgency training either in the United States or in the Panama Canal Zone. Throughout the Allende presidency, even after the United States economically embargoed Chile, U.S. military aid continued. The United States even doubled its usual contribution in 1973.

By the spring of 1973, the balance of forces within the military had shifted in favor of conservatives. On June 29 a premature coup was put down by loyal troops under the direction of General Carlos Prats. Following the defeat of the coup, workers called for occupation of the factories and distribution of arms among them. Instead, Allende renewed his efforts to achieve a compromise with the Christian Democrats, foolishly relying on the armed forces, who raided factories in search of illegal weapons while making no effort to disarm rightist paramilitary groups. Control of many localities effectively passed from the UP administration to the armed forces. On September 10, 1973, a military coup led by General Augusto Pinochet toppled Allende and inaugurated a brutal dictatorship.

## Neoliberalism and Democratic Constraints, 1973–2003

### PINOCHET, STATE TERRORISM, AND FREE MARKETS

After the coup, Chileans endured a brutal and large-scale repression. The four-man military

During the 1980s, as the popular mobilization against the Pinochet dictatorship grew in numbers and audacity, the walls once used to divide and control neighborhoods became a national canvas upon which cultural resistance to oppression was graphically inscribed. This mural in Santiago celebrates the art of Violeta Parra and Víctor Jara (see page 352), two martyred champions of social justice and popular democracy. [Art by Alberto Díaz Parra, in Santiago, Chile, August 1989. Published in *Muralismo: Art in the Popular Chilean Culture*, © 1990 Committee of Defense of the Chilean Culture]

junta headed by General Pinochet set about to "regenerate" Chilean society. To this end they abolished all political parties, suppressed civil liberties, dissolved the Congress, banned union activities, prohibited strikes and collective bargaining, and erased the Allende administration's agrarian and economic reforms. The junta jailed, tortured, and put to death thousands of Chileans, including Víctor Jara, who had reportedly defied military authorities by singing "Venceremos." The dreaded secret police, DINA (*Dirección de Inteligencia Nacional*)—with guidance from Colonel Walter Rauff, a former Nazi who had supervised the extermination of Jews at Auschwitz—spread its network of terror throughout Chile and carried out assassinations abroad. The junta also set up at least six concentration camps. It is estimated that one of every one hundred Chileans was arrested at least once under the military regime.

Meanwhile, Pinochet worked to legitimize his brutal regime and, under cover of The Feminine Power (EPF), an organization of aristocratic and middle-class women who had opposed Allende, he sought to cultivate a female constituency committed to "traditional family values," self-sacrifice, and loyalty to the motherland. He established a National Ministry of Women and his wife, Lucía Hiriart, rejuvenated the Mothers' Centers, eventually organizing 10,000 groups that claimed 230,000 members. But the family was an early victim of the regime's political terror, and its economic policies also alienated working-class women.

Pinochet, influenced by a group of economists known as the Chicago Boys because many had studied at the University of Chicago under Milton

Friedman, implemented his neoliberal, free-market doctrines. Public spending was cut drastically, almost all state companies privatized, the peso devalued, and import duties sharply reduced. The social consequences of the "shock treatment" soon became apparent. Gross domestic product fell 16.6 percent in 1975. Manufacturing suffered particular injury, with some industries, like the textile industry, devastated by foreign imports. Wages had fallen by 1975 to 47.9 percent of their 1970 level. Unemployment stood at 20 percent, or 28 percent if the people working in government emergency programs were included.

A recovery partly based on export products—minerals, timber, and fish—but above all on a speculative spree of immense proportions began in 1977 and turned into a boom that lasted until 1980, with annual growth rates averaging 8 percent. The Chilean "economic miracle," however, was superficial and short-lived. Hoping to attract heavy foreign investment that would turn Chile into a South Korea or Taiwan, the Chicago Boys deliberately kept interest rates high. Foreign capital poured in, but almost all of it came in the form of loans to Chilean banks, which profited enormously by borrowing abroad at 12 percent and lending at 35 to 40 percent. The borrowing companies, subsidiaries of a few huge conglomerates, did not invest in production, which the high interest rates made unprofitable, but used the loans for speculation in real estate or to buy up at fire-sale prices the state companies sold under the privatization program. The bubble burst in 1980. By the end of 1981 the government, in violation of its own free-market principles, was forced to take over the nation's largest banks in order to forestall economic calamity. Bankruptcies multiplied. Production declined sharply. Between 1982 and 1986 unemployment rose to more than 30 percent and real wages fell by as much as 20 percent. An earthquake in 1985 added to the country's economic woes. By the late 1980s the economy was heavily dependent on foreign loans. With a population of 12.5 million, Chile's foreign debt in 1991 stood at $17 billion, in per capita terms one of the heaviest debt burdens in the world. In its last years the Pinochet regime pursued a policy of

swapping debt for ownership of Chilean industries and natural resources, with a resulting growth of foreign control of the economy.

Great landowners who controlled the production, commercialization, and export of agricultural products profited handsomely. Exports of fruit and agricultural products sharply increased in these years. But the modernization and expansion of Chilean agriculture did not benefit the mass of the rural population, who lost most of the land and other gains made during the Allende years, suffered police repression, and endured chronic unemployment. Farm workers, prevented from forming labor unions and denied welfare benefits, worked no more than three or four months at a time and often lived in intolerable conditions.

The situation was even worse in urban areas, whose high levels of unemployment and underemployment forced workers to live with their families in squalid, overcrowded shantytowns. Even the middle class suffered a sharp decline in its standard of living. Between 1978 and 1988 the wealthiest 20 percent of the population increased their share of the national income from 51 to 60 percent. The next 60 percent, which includes Chile's large middle class, suffered a substantial drop in income, their share falling from 44 to 35 percent. And the poorest 20 percent continued to receive a meager 4 percent.

## WOMEN AND RESISTANCE TO DICTATORSHIP

During the dictatorship's first decade, the opposition to Pinochet was fragmented. Nonetheless, Pinochet's harsh repression and unsuccessful economic policies soon gave rise to mass opposition. Although the Catholic church had initially supported the *Pinochetazo*, the Vicariate of Solidarity organized community support networks to provide legal aid, health care, and employment in craft workshops to working-class communities devastated by the dictatorship's political terror and economic war against the poor. Within a few months after the coup, the Vicariate served 700,000 people, many of whom were women who became involved in what political anthropologist James Scott calls "infrapolitics," a dissident political cul-

Mass opposition to the economic policies and repressive tactics of President Augusto Pinochet erupted in 1983 and 1984. Here thousands of Chilean youths march through Santiago calling for democracy and jobs for unemployed copper workers. [Carlos Carrión/Sygma]

ture largely hidden from the powerful but actively engaged in everyday forms of resistance. For example, these women hid people fleeing Pinochet's terror, baked and distributed bread containing secret messages about clandestine opposition activities, circulated information about the "disappeared," and created *arpilleras*, a folk art that used burlap and other common materials to fashion powerful political indictments of the dictatorship. These *arpilleristas* later participated in hunger strikes and *encadenamientos* (chain-ins), chaining themselves to the Supreme Court building, Pinochet's house, and various other government buildings to protest against the dictatorship.

The dictatorship especially damaged women's social position in Chilean society. It restored the *potestad marital*, authorizing a husband's legal control over his wife and her property, eliminated women's protective labor legislation, restricted women's access to unemployment compensation, disqualified women for legislative positions, and reduced women's median income to 36 percent of men's—a decline from a pre-coup high of 68 percent. These reverses in women's wage rates, coupled with skyrocketing male unemployment, created greater market demand for women's labor and the female work force grew 4.5 percent by 1985 even as the proportion of female heads of households increased 4 percent.

Women therefore played an active role in the political opposition; for example, to commemorate International Women's Day on March 8, 1978, the Women's Department (DF), a women's trade union group, organized the first public demonstration against Pinochet. But women's antidictatorial struggles also became increasingly antipatriarchal as well, and a decade later, at the Days of Protest demonstrations, women's groups like the Feminist Movement (MF) called for "Democracy in the Nation and in the Home," that is, a comprehensive democratic agenda to end the dictatorship, reform the constitution, eliminate misogynistic civil, criminal, and labor legislation, create a ministerial office for women's issues, revise educational curricula, and establish a government affirmative action goal of 30 percent female employment.

Under growing pressure from this swelling democratic movement, Pinochet made limited concessions to the demands for liberalization and amnesty for political prisoners and exiles, even as the repression sometimes intensified. Maneuvering to remain in power, Pinochet called a plebiscite for October 1988, in which Chileans voted by a resounding 54.6 percent to 43 percent to deny Pinochet a new term as president. But the old dictator had fallback positions. By the terms of an undemocratic constitution imposed on the country in 1980, even if defeated, Pinochet was to remain in power for one more year until new elections determined his successor. But Pinochet would still preside over a military council with broad powers, be able to appoint one-third of the new Senate, and himself become a senator for life. The civilian opposition's fatal decision to cut a deal with Pinochet, to accept his imposed constitution instead of obeying the thousands of Chileans whose jubilant street celebrations after the plebiscite demanded the general's resignation from the army, meant the continuing reign of Pinochet's economic model, his power to veto any significant political or social change, and an abiding impunity for the military killers and torturers protected by the dictatorship's self-serving amnesty law.

Nonetheless, pro-democratic forces, despite their differences, coalesced around Patricio Aylwin, who won the 1989 elections.

## Popular Struggle for Democracy and Social Justice, 1990–2003

The new president assumed office on March 11, 1990, with a cabinet dominated by Christian Democrats and Socialists. The first democratically elected government since 1970 faced enormous problems. First, Pinochet's power remained solidly entrenched in the state apparatus, especially the judiciary and security forces.

His 1980 constitution, which made it a crime even to think Marxist thoughts, also severely limited the new government's democratic options. Nonetheless, popular movements pressed for the release of all political prisoners, dissolution of the security forces, abolition of torture and other human rights abuses, and punishment of officials who had committed such abuses. Here a major obstacle was the amnesty decreed by Pinochet for acts committed during the so-called internal war between 1973 and 1978, but that amnesty did not cover the many brutal murders committed after that date. The discovery early in 1990 of secret cemeteries, generally located near armed forces bases, containing the remains of numerous victims who had frequently been tortured before being murdered, brought home to all Chileans the full horror of the regime under which they had suffered for seventeen years. One year later, a "Commission of Truth and Reconciliation," documented the horrific record of human rights violations committed under the Pinochet dictatorship; it identified 2,279 known deaths and disappearances, assigned direct responsibility for these crimes to the armed forces, and charged the courts with negligence for failing to respond properly to such violations of human rights.

But the process of settling accounts with the military murderers and torturers proceeded with excruciating slowness, due in part to the grim resistance offered by Pinochet and the army and in part to the government's anxiety to achieve compromise and "reconciliation" with the military. This led the president to support a "gentle accommodation" with them and to abandon efforts to make Pinochet step down as commander in chief, which angered organizations of relatives of the "disappeared" and many other Chileans who claimed that Aylwin's policies tended to institutionalize impunity.

Another major problem facing the new democratic government was the need to define its attitude toward the economic and social policies of the old regime, which benefited foreign transnationals and their domestic allies at the expense of long-range national interests and the welfare of Chilean workers. Aylwin had promised to make no major changes in the old regime's free-market policies but also committed himself to improve the living and working conditions of the Chilean masses. In fact, under Aylwin the government considerably increased spending for health care, education, and social services. This resulted in a significant reduction in poverty. Overall poverty fell from 40 percent of the population in 1990 to 28 percent in late 1994, and absolute poverty (defined as insufficient income to buy a basic food basket) fell from 14 percent to 9 percent.

But the decline in Chile's poverty rate did not reverse historic patterns of income inequality. After almost a decade of democratic reforms, the wealthiest 10 percent of the Chilean population still received almost 50 percent of national income while the poorest 40 percent, who had received only 10.5 percent in 1989, watched their share fall steadily during the 1990s.

This growing inequality was largely the product of the government's neoliberal economic model, which privileged employers' rights at the expense of labor. "Over the past twenty years," writes Orlando Caputo, a prominent Chilean economist, "$60 billion has been transferred from salaries to profits." Like its predecessor, the Aylwin government prohibited farm workers' strikes during harvest season, which effectively undermined their collective bargaining power. It also disguised unemployment rates by "privatizing" unemployment, that is, by forcing the unemployed into the "informal sector" of low-income, self-employed peddlers who composed 50 percent of the work force. Real wage and salary income, which was still 18 percent lower than it was during the Allende period, declined 10 percent since 1986. By the late 1990s, a third of the nation earned less than $30 a week.

Aylwin continued to stress such export products as seafood, lumber, fruit, and agricultural products, with production and commercialization dominated by agribusiness companies, many of them foreign-owned. Typical is the case of wood exports. There was a veritable explosion of Chilean lumbering, which increased by 57 percent and grew 6.4 percent per year in the 1990s. In south-central Chile the new tree farms replaced such traditional crops as wheat, corn, and rice. Environmentalists charged that the new forests were damaging the soil, drying up water sources, and causing a rapid decrease of many species of plants and animals. Chile's export-based economic strategy also had serious health costs. A study carried out in the large fruit-growing region around the city of Rancagua, south of the capital of Santiago, revealed an alarming increase in children born with physical deformities to parents whose work exposed them to dangerous pesticides.

The explosive growth of raw-material exports was accompanied by the collapse of large-scale industry in such areas as textiles and construction. This was reflected in the decline in the number of unionized workers, who by 1996 composed only 12 percent of the total labor force, compared with 41 percent in 1972. Meanwhile the number of Chileans who worked alone or owned firms with fewer than four employees (the so-called *microempresas*) greatly increased; these "microenterprises" employed more than 45 percent of the labor force in 1992. Typically, they contracted out to or serviced in a variety of ways the large conglomerates called AFPs (*Asociaciones de Fondos Provisionales*) or Mutual Funds, controlled by the ten richest families in Chile. "Workers in *microempresas*," writes Cathy Schneider, "are paid salaries barely above subsistence, without fringe benefits or job security. Irregular hours, unstable employment, and low caloric intake have increased levels of physical and mental exhaustion."

The AFPs also managed Chile's privatized pension system, to which all workers (but no employers) had to make contributions. This system empowered employers to withhold employees' contributions from their paychecks, but there were no mechanisms to ensure that the employers promptly deposited those sums into AFPs, leading to frequent complaints about delays of months or even years in so doing. Moreover, because so many Chileans were marginally employed in the "informal sector," almost half the enrolees did not keep their contributions up to date and consequently accumulated less than a $1,000 balance, clearly insufficient to support retirement. Finally, because the return on pensions depended on the value of the stocks in which contributions were invested, a prolonged decline in the Chilean stock market could have had a catastrophic effect on the system's health.

In December 1993 Chilean voters elected Eduardo Frei of the ruling center-left coalition, son of the reformist president of the same name. Frei's populist program pledged to eradicate extreme poverty by the year 2000, reform the labor laws and the public health system, and regain civilian control of the military, but he also declared his support for free markets. This meant that Chile's prosperity and democratic institutions, already severely compromised by civil society's Faustian bargain with the military, would depend on increasing exports, attracting new foreign investment, and expanding domestic consumer credit, all of which could easily collapse as the world market fluctuated. The 1997 Asian economic crisis, which briefly panicked the Chilean stock market, alerted many Chileans to the fragility of their government's developmental model.

As a result, there were significant indicators of growing popular resistance. First, labor unions became more defiant. The Teachers' Guild (*Colegio de Profesores*), led by Jorge Pávez, a long-time Communist party militant, organized a successful strike in 1996 and continued to coalesce with youth groups, environmentalists, women, and indigenous organizations like those of the Mapuches and Aymaras, all of whom had been damaged by the expansion of unregulated market forces.

Second, disenchanted with the political options available to them, none of which seemed to challenge the neoliberal orthodoxy, Chileans increasingly abandoned the political process altogether. In the December 1997 congressional election, 41 percent of eligible voters either failed to register, abstained from voting, or defaced the ballot. Young people especially lost interest in politics and increasingly associated all political parties with corruption; during the last decade, the percentage of 18- and 19-year-olds registered to vote declined from 5 percent of the electorate to less than 1 percent. Even more startlingly, the share of voters between 20 and 24 plummeted from 15.6 to 4.8 percent.

Third, there emerged greater public support for bringing to justice those accused of brutal crimes during the fifteen-year Pinochet dictatorship. A particularly courageous judge, Juan Guzmán Tapia, successively indicted Pinochet himself on murder and kidnapping charges, authorized a criminal investigation into the murders of two U.S. citizens, Charles Horman and Frank Teruggi, who had supported Allende's Socialist government thirty years ago, and declared former U.S. Consul General Fred Purdy *inculpado* (a suspect) in the crime. Intimating that he formally would seek their extradition to Chile if voluntary arrangements could not be made, Guzmán also respectfully asked the United States to make available to his investigation some sixteen other former U.S. government officials, including then U.S. Ambassador Nathaniel Davis and National Security Adviser Henry Kissinger. A recently declassified U.S. State Department document seemed to confirm the wisdom of Guzmán's inquiry into the activities of these U.S. government officials: "There is some circumstantial evidence," it reported, "to suggest U.S. intelligence may have played an unfortunate part in Horman's death."

Finally, Chileans elected Ricardo Lagos, presidential candidate of the ruling *Concertación* coalition and a lifelong member of the Socialist Party. Although Lagos's political platform was not remotely similar to that of Salvador Allende, the Socialist president who had died defending democracy against a vicious military coup, the martyred president was clearly on the minds of the massive crowd that wildly celebrated Lagos's election with electrifying cries of *"¡Se siente! ¡Se siente! ¡Allende está presente!"* ("I feel it! I feel it! Allende is here among us!"). However, Lagos found himself in an awkward political position.

He had campaigned on social themes, promising to sustain Chile's economic expansion, reduce unemployment, eliminate extreme poverty, promote equality for women and indigenous peoples, and guarantee workers' rights. But, thanks to undemocratic constitutional provisions imposed by the Pinochet dictatorship, his political opponents still controlled the Senate and blocked most of his legislative agenda, including a national heath care initiative, a dramatic increase in the minimum wage, and greater spending on education. Meanwhile, as global markets began to contract, unemployment continued to grow from 5.3 percent in 1997 to almost 10 percent in 2002; before the Asian economic crisis flattened Chile, its gross domestic product had peaked at 6.6 percent, but it averaged a meager 2.9 percent during the first two years of the Lagos presidency. Equally disheartening was the steady growth of Chile's external debt and the steady rise in the share of export revenues diverted to repay it.

Nonetheless, Lagos could point to some modest successes. He reformed the nation's labor laws to defend workers' rights, make workplace discrimination illegal, and strengthen trade unions. This legislation extended state protection to some 400,000 women, annually hired as temporary workers by *enganchadores* to harvest fruit in Chile's booming export industry. His government cut the military budget by severing its historical connection to copper exports and reallocated the resulting savings to social programs. During the Pinochet dictatorship, the military had been allocated $225 million or 10 percent of all export revenues earned by the state-owned copper company, CODELCO, whichever was higher. Even though world copper prices generally rose during the 1990s, successive Christian Democratic presidents, still fearful of the military's power, had continued this practice, paying as much as $341 million to the military account in 1995.

Finally, he worked to reduce Chilean poverty, which had rocketed to 40 percent by the end of the Pinochet dictatorship, the "glory days" of the "free market." Steady economic growth and increasing state social programs since 1990 had produced a gradual decline in poverty rates to 20 percent in 1996, but Lagos sought to reduce these numbers still further and to eliminate extreme poverty by the end of his presidential term in 2006. Declaring that "the poor cannot wait and these poor families will no longer have to wait," Lagos pledged to pay a monthly "protection bonus" of $16 to indigent families earning a dollar per day or less.

No matter how well-intentioned the current government was, however, it remained clear that history would judge Chile by its performance. But this judgment ultimately depended upon two factors: popular struggle to overcome the considerable institutional constraints imposed by almost two decades of dictatorship and a growing global economy upon which thirty years of neoliberal policies had rendered the nation utterly dependent. As the new millennium opened, progress on the former seemed assured even as the latter appeared increasingly uncertain; the fate of Chile's peculiar democracy thus continued to be clouded by its troubled past.

# 15

# Republican Brazil

**O**N THE EVE of World War I, Brazil's economic, political, and social structures showed growing strain and instability. Between 1910 and 1914 the Amazonian rubber boom began to fade as a result of competition from the new and more efficient plantations of the Far East. The approaching end of the rubber cycle revealed the vulnerability of Brazil's monocultural economy to external factors beyond its control and heightened its dependence on coffee. The coffee industry was itself plagued by recurrent crises of overproduction that required periodic resort to valorization—governmental intervention to maintain coffee prices by withholding stocks from the market or restricting plantings.

Violence was endemic over large areas of the country. In the backcountry, feudal coronéis with private armies recruited from dependents and *jagunços* (hired gunmen) maintained a patriarchal but frequently tyrannical rule over the peasantry. Over large areas of the country, peasants lived in feudal bondage, obligated to give one or more days per week of free labor as homage to the landowners. Lacking written contracts, they could be evicted at any moment and could find work elsewhere only on the same conditions. The interior was also the scene of mystical or messianic movements that sometimes assumed the character of peasant revolts. Banditry, especially widespread in the northeast, was another response to the tyranny of rural coronéis and the impotence of

officials. A few *cangaceiros* (outlaws) took the part of the peasantry against their oppressors; most, however, served as mercenaries in the coronéis's private wars.

Violence was not confined to the countryside. Even in the growing cities, proud of their European culture and appearance, popular anger at the arbitrary rule of local oligarchies, or divisions within those oligarchies, sometimes flared up into civil war. Intervention by the federal government in these armed struggles on the side of its local allies greatly enlarged the scale of violence.

## Decline and Fall of the Old Republic, 1914–1930

### ECONOMIC IMPACT OF WORLD WAR I

The outbreak of World War I in August 1914 had a negative initial impact on Brazil. Exports of coffee, a nonessential product, declined, and in 1917 the government came to the rescue of the planters with a new valorization (price maintenance) program. However, the growing demand of the Allies for sugar, beans, and other staples had by 1915 sparked a revival that turned into a boom.

The war accelerated some changes under way in Brazilian economic life. It weakened British capitalism and therefore strengthened the North American challenge to British financial and commercial preeminence in Brazil. The virtual cessation of imports of manufactured goods also gave a strong stimulus to Brazilian industrialization. Profits derived from coffee, an industry protected by the state, provided a large part of the resources needed for industrialization. Favored by its wealth, large immigrant population, and rich natural resources, the state of São Paulo led the movement, replacing Rio de Janeiro as the foremost industrial region. Brazil doubled its industrial production during the war, and the number of enterprises (which stood at about 3,000 in 1908) grew by 5,940 between 1915 and 1918. But these increases were concentrated in light industry, especially food processing and textiles, and most of the new enterprises were small shops.

The advance of industry and urbanization enlarged and strengthened both the industrial bourgeoisie and the working class, which became racially, sexually, and ethnically more diverse. After emancipation, Brazil's late nineteenth-century white supremacist policies, drawing on foreign ideologies and elite fears of Afro-Brazilian power, had discriminated against blacks and encouraged European immigration to "whiten" the country's labor force and undermine the black majority's ability to negotiate favorable wages and working conditions. Thus immigrant women, especially from Italy, played a central role in the early development of Brazil's industrial working class and dominated employment in the rapidly expanding textile industry. Of the nine thousand workers hired in thirty-one representative textile mills in São Paulo in 1912, almost seven thousand were women.

In response to wartime inflation that eroded the value of workers' wages, the trade union movement grew, and strikes became more frequent. In 1917 a general strike—the first in Brazilian history—gripped the city and state of São Paulo. The strike was organized and initiated by women weavers whose paid and unpaid work responsibilities in the factory and in the home made them especially aware of the negative impact of wartime inflation on workers' wages. They therefore demanded a 20 percent wage increase, "more respect" from male supervisors, improvement of working conditions, and a promise that "in every-

thing there should be reason and justice." These women's grievances rapidly spread to other factories, mobilized thousands of strikers who won significant concessions from the city's industrialists, and energized the national labor movement. Although the strike wave of 1917 to 1920 forced many employers to grant higher wages, the living conditions of most workers did not permanently improve. The labor movement, composed largely of foreign-born workers, remained small and weak, without ties with the peasantry, who formed the overwhelming majority of the Brazilian people.

The economic expansion associated with the war also had a dramatic impact on the development of Brazilian culture. Displaced from their homelands and lured by new economic opportunities in Brazil, new immigrants from Japan and the Ottoman Empire joined with migrants of African descent from the nation's hinterland, especially the drought-ridden Northeast, in search of high-paying jobs that never seemed to materialize. Together they gathered in the urban centers of Rio de Janeiro and São Paulo in the sprawling slums known as *favelas* or *morros* and gave birth to the *samba*, a song and dance that drew heavily on Angolan and Congolese cultural traditions. The samba was closely associated with the ritualistic celebration of *carnival*, a popular street festival that preceded the Lenten season of self-sacrifice and created a safe public space for the lower classes to challenge established social hierarchies, to mock the customs, attitudes, dress, and beliefs of their social rivals; in fact, in its early days, the Brazilian aristocracy, which greatly feared the unruliness of its exploited work force, was scandalized by the wanton sexuality and the wild, irrepressible, and defiant behavior associated with carnival.

Samba lyrics similarly raised serious social and political issues, often using clever word play, double entendre, and the juxtaposition of contrasting images to scorn the arrogant power of the upper classes. In 1917, for example, one of Brazil's greatest samba artists, Ernesto dos Santos, better known as Dongo, recorded the first samba, "*Pelo Telefone*," which simultaneously celebrated the new technology and lamented its use by police officials to harass a poor man. During the postwar period, the radio broadened the popular appeal of the samba, repeatedly broadcasting the songs produced by competing *escolas da samba* ("samba schools"), the neighborhood clubs that organized community participation in carnival. Suddenly, the precise meaning of what it meant to be Brazilian had ceased to be as clear as the traditional light-skinned, Eurocentric plantation elites had imagined it. Change was in the air.

## POSTWAR INDUSTRY AND LABOR

Industrialization and urbanization further weakened the foundations of the neocolonial order, which was based on the primacy of agriculture and dependence on foreign markets and loans, but it emerged from the war essentially intact, although its stabilization proved temporary and precarious. A chronically adverse balance of trade and a declining rate of exchange against foreign currencies gave Brazilian industry a competitive advantage in goods of popular consumption. It continued to grow, but it had little support from a central government dominated by the coffee interests. Bitter debates between the friends and foes of tariff protection for industry marked the political life of the 1920s.

As that decade opened, Brazil remained an overwhelmingly rural country. A few export products—coffee, sugar, cotton—dominated Brazilian agriculture; food production was so neglected that the country had to import four-fifths of its grain. There was an extreme concentration of landownership: 461 great landowners held more than 27 million hectares of land, while 464,000 small- and medium-sized farms occupied only 15.7 million hectares. Archaic techniques prevailed in agriculture: the hoe was still the principal farming instrument and the wasteful slash-and-burn method the favored way of clearing the land. Even relatively progressive coffee planters gave little attention to care of the soil, selection of varieties, and other improvements. As a result, the productivity of plantations rapidly declined, even in regions of superior soil.

In the cities, most workers toiled and lived under conditions that recalled those of the early Industrial Revolution in Europe. In 1920 the average industrial worker in São Paulo earned about four milréis (sixty cents) a day; for this wage he or she worked ten to twelve hours, six days a week. Women earned only 60 percent of men's wages and suffered from abusive patriarchal power in the workplace. Historian Joel Wolfe documents the case of one such woman, Ambrosina Pioli, who was beaten savagely when she complained about her foreman's threats to fire her to make room for his lover.

Malnutrition, parasitic diseases, and lack of medical facilities limited Brazilians' average life span in 1920 to twenty-eight years. In the same year, more than 64 percent of the population over the age of fifteen was illiterate. Since literacy was a requirement for voting, the general lack of schools kept the people not only ignorant but politically powerless. As expanding market forces dissolved traditional rural patron-client social relations, the impoverished peasantry often sought refuge in a culture of resistance that focused on daily survival strategies. Although periodically engaged in overt acts of sedition like the Contestado Rebellion of 1912–1916, peasants typically did not organize to transform Brazilian society.

## CULTURAL CRISIS AND POLITICAL UNREST

The task of transforming society fell to the rapidly growing urban bourgeois groups, and especially to the middle class, which began to voice ever more strongly its discontent with the rule of corrupt rural oligarchies. In the early 1920s, there arose a many-faceted movement for the renovation of Brazilian society and culture. Intellectuals, artists, junior military officers, professional men, and a small minority of radical workers participated in this movement. But they had no common program and did not comprehend the convergence of their aims and work.

Three seemingly unrelated events of 1922 illustrate the diverse forms that the ferment of the times assumed. First, in February São Paulo intellectuals organized a Modern Art Week to commemorate the centenary of Brazilian independence. Influenced by rebellious European artists, these young poets, painters, and composers

One of the original organizers of Brazil's famous "Modern Art Week" in 1922 and a pioneer of Brazilian modernism was Emiliano di Cavalcanti. His *Samba* (1925) broke with artistic traditions that stressed the nation's European origins and instead celebrated Brazil's African and indigenous cultural roots. [Collection of Genevieve and Jean Boghici]

rejected the staid traditions of naturalism that had dominated the late nineteenth century Brazilian art world, declared their independence from old forms and content, and insisted upon the need to develop indigenous Brazilian culture. Among the young intellectuals gathered there were Heitor Villa-Lobos, who became the nation's premier samba artist, and Oswaldo de Andrade, who later shocked Brazilian audiences by proclaiming the need to become "cultural cannibals"; that is, to consume foreign artistic ideas, mix them with Brazil's digestive enzymes, and thereby produce an authentically Brazilian national cultural identity that was neither xenophobic nor nativist.

Then in March 1922, after the appearance of Marxist groups in a number of cities, the Brazilian Communist Party was founded at a congress in Rio de Janeiro and began a struggle against the anarcho-syndicalist doctrines that still dominated much of the small labor movement.

Last, in July *tenentes* (junior officers) at the Copacabana garrison in Rio de Janeiro rose to prevent the seating of Artur da Silva Bernardes, who had been elected president according to the agreement between the two dominant states of São Paulo and Minas Gerais. The rebel program denounced the rule of the coffee oligarchy, political corruption, and electoral fraud. Government forces easily crushed the revolt, but it left a legend when a handful of insurgents refused to surrender and fought to the death against overwhelming odds.

The officers' revolt signaled the beginning of a struggle by the Brazilian bourgeoisie to seize power from the rural oligarchy. Given the closed political system, it inevitably assumed the character of an armed struggle; that is why its spearhead was the nationalist young officer group, mostly of middle-class origins, which called for democratic elections, equal justice, and similar political reforms.

President Bernardes (1922–1926) took office amid growing economic and political turmoil. As a result of a massive increase in coffee plantings between 1918 and 1924, the industry again suffered from overproduction and falling prices. In 1924 another military revolt, organized by junior officers, broke out in São Paulo. The city's large working class was sympathetic to the revolt, but its conservative leaders rejected the workers' request for arms.

Meanwhile, the revolt had spread to other states. Another group of rebels in Rio Grande do Sul, led by Captain Luís Carlos Prestes, moved north to join the insurgents from São Paulo, and their combined forces, known in history as the Prestes column, began a prodigious fourteen-thousand-mile march through the interior. The tenentes hoped to enlist the peasantry in their struggle against Bernardes. But they knew little of the peasants' problems and offered no program of agrarian reform. The peasants, for their part, had no interest in fighting the "tyrant" Bernardes in distant Rio de Janeiro.

The long march had much educational value for the officers who took part in it. For the first time in their lives, many of these young men came face to face with the reality of rural Brazil and began to reflect on its problems. As a result, the tenente reform program acquired an economic and social content. It began to speak of the need for economic development and social legislation, including agrarian reform as well as minimum wages and maximum working hours.

Naturally, these conflicts provided additional political space for lower-class mobilization in the 1920s. Black Brazilians in Salvador da Bahia and elsewhere joined Marcus Garvey's black power movement, prompting the government to solicit the covert assistance of the FBI in the United States to monitor and disrupt their activities. Meanwhile, others flocked to the practice of *candomble,* a popular religion that evoked consciousness of the African past and created a spiritual community of resistance to white supremacist policies.

Brazilian women likewise mobilized in the militant tradition of nineteenth-century feminist Motta Diniz, who had declared that "in all the world, barbarous or civilized, woman is a slave." In 1922 women's rights activist Berta Lutz organized the Brazilian Federation for the Advancement of Women (FBPF). Largely composed of middle-class professionals, it nonetheless advocated state intervention against market forces and called on the Bernardes government to protect "female labor, which has been subject to inhuman exploitation, reducing women to an inferior position in the competition for industrial and agricultural salaries."

Although Bernardes survived this political opposition, he continued to be plagued by economic problems, with the coffee problem paramount. Bernardes applied the now orthodox remedy of valorization, but gave it a decentralized form. The central government turned over the supervision of the scheme to the individual coffee-producing states. The state of São Paulo established an agency, the Coffee Institute, which undertook to control the export trade in coffee by regulating market offerings to maintain a balance between supply and demand. This was done by withdrawing unlimited stocks of coffee, storing them in warehouses, and releasing them according to the needs of the export trade. The plan required financing the producers whose coffee was withheld from the market. The program appeared to work, for prices rose and remained stable until

1929. But the burdens of valorization steadily grew, for high prices stimulated production, requiring new withdrawals and new loans to finance the unsold output. To make matters worse, Brazil's competitors—especially Colombia—were attracted by the high coffee prices and expanded their own output.

## ECONOMIC CRISIS

In 1926 Bernardes turned over the presidency to the Paulista Washington Luís de Sousa Pereira (1926–1930). During his administration, a series of new loans was made to support the valorization program. This especially alienated the nation's industrial bourgeoisie, whose interests and power had continued to expand. The coffee oligarchs and their foreign bankers siphoned off financial and labor resources needed by industry. High, state-sponsored coffee prices created greater demand for labor, which led to high turnover rates and increased costs in urban industry. By 1930 foreign loans had produced an external debt of $1,181 million, and Brazil was required to pay $200 million annually—one-third of the national budget—to service the debt. Squeezed between the conflicting demands of coffee planters and militant workers, these industrialists relied on local repression and privately funded social welfare programs to co-opt and control their labor force, even as they increasingly pressured the state to regulate economic activity in their interests.

By 1930, U.S. investment in Brazil had reached $400 million, considerably larger than the British total, and the United States had supplanted England as Brazil's chief trading partner. But Brazil's heavy dependence on foreign markets and loans made it extremely vulnerable to the crisis that shook the capitalist world after the New York stock market collapsed in October 1929. Coffee prices fell from 22.5 to 8 cents a pound between 1929 and 1931, and immense stocks of coffee piled up in the warehouses. By the end of 1930, Brazil's gold reserves had disappeared and the exchange rate plummeted to a new low. As foreign credit dried up, it became impossible to con-

tinue to finance the valorization program, which collapsed, leaving behind a mountain of debt.

The presidential campaign and election of 1930 took place against a background of economic crisis the principal burdens of which—unemployment, wage cuts, and inflation—fell chiefly on the working classes. But the crisis sharpened all class and regional antagonisms, especially the conflict between the coffee oligarchy and the urban bourgeois groups, who regarded the Depression as proof of the bankruptcy of the old order. A rift even appeared within the coffee oligarchy, and the traditional alliance of São Paulo and Minas Gerais fell apart. This emboldened a new coalition, the Liberal Alliance, that linked urban groups, great landowners—like the ranchers of Rio Grande do Sul—who resented São Paulo's dominant position, and disaffected politicians from Minas Gerais and other states. It named Getúlio Vargas, a wealthy rancher and politician from Rio Grande do Sul, as its candidate.

The working class was not a participant in the Liberal Alliance, but many workers sympathized with its program and openly pressured Vargas to improve working conditions, establish a minimum wage and mandatory vacations, organize consumer cooperatives, and regulate labor relations. Women's groups, in search of freedom from the tyranny of market forces, also lobbied the anti-oligarchical movement. Berta Lutz and the FBPF announced their "Thirteen Principles," which advocated women's suffrage, civil equality, equal pay for equal work, paid maternity leave for working women, affirmative action in government employment, a minimum wage, the eight-hour day, paid vacations, and medical, disability, and retirement insurance. All these provisions would eventually be incorporated into the 1934 constitution.

The most ardent supporters of Vargas were the veterans of the 1924 Tenentes revolt, but their former leader, Luís Carlos Prestes, an exile in Buenos Aires, would not endorse Vargas or his program. Instead Prestes, now a Marxist, proclaimed that the chief task before the Brazilian people was to struggle against the latifundio and Anglo-American imperialism. A few years later, he would join the Communist Party and become its leader.

During the 1930 campaign, Vargas, although careful not to give offense to his latifundist supporters, spoke of the need to develop industry, including heavy industry, advocated high tariffs to protect Brazilian industry using local raw materials, and called on Brazilians to "perfect our manufactures to the point where it will become unpatriotic to feed or clothe ourselves with imported goods." Reflecting the influence of the tenentes, he advanced a program of social welfare legislation and political, judicial, and educational reform. He even made a cautious pledge of "action with a view to the progressive extinction of the latifundio, without violence, and support for the organization of small landed property through the transfer of small parcels of land to agricultural laborers."

When the coffee oligarchs sought to deny Vargas the presidency, he overthrew the Washington Luís government. The successful revolt meant that the Old Republic, born in 1889 and dominated since 1894 by the coffee oligarchy, was dead. A new era had begun that may with fair accuracy be called the era of the bourgeois revolution. The political career of its chieftain, Getúlio Vargas, faithfully mirrored its advances, retreats, and ultimate defeat.

# Vargas and the Bourgeois Revolution, 1930–1954

The liberal revolution of 1930 represented a victory for the urban bourgeois groups who favored industrialization and the modernization of Brazil's economic, political, and social structures. But the bourgeoisie had gained that victory with the aid of allies whose interests had to be taken into account. Getúlio Vargas presided over a heterogeneous coalition that included conservative fazendeiros—who had joined the revolution from jealousy of the overweening Paulista power but feared radical social change—and intellectuals and tenentes who called for agrarian reform, the formation of cooperatives, and the nationalization of mines. Women's groups and others disadvantaged by oligarchical rule and market forces pressured Vargas to endorse their campaign for liberation. The

Brazilian Black Front (FNB), established in 1931, organized massive protests against racial discrimination, advocated laws to require racial integration of all public places, educated Afro-Brazilians about Pan-Africanist political movements, and sought black representation in the national Congress. Of course, the working class, vital to the development of Brazilian capitalism, remained a potential threat to its very existence. Finally, Vargas had to take account of foreign capital interests, temporarily weakened but capable of applying great pressure on the Brazilian economy when the capitalist world emerged from the depths of the Great Depression. Vargas's strategy of attempting to balance and reconcile these conflicting interests helps to explain the contradictions and abrupt shifts of course that marked his career.

## VARGAS'S ECONOMIC AND POLITICAL MEASURES

The most pressing problem facing the new government was to find some way out of the economic crisis. Vargas did not abandon the coffee industry, the base of his political enemies, to its fate; he attempted to revive it by such classic valorization measures as the restriction of plantings, the purchase of surplus stocks, and the more drastic expedient of burning excess coffee. But the level of coffee exports and prices remained low throughout the 1930s. The government had more success with efforts to diversify agriculture. Production of cotton, in particular, grew with the aid of capital and labor released by the depressed coffee industry, and cotton exports rose steadily until 1940, when the outbreak of war interrupted their advance. But diversification of agriculture could not compensate for the steep decline in Brazil's import capacity. The key to recovery was found in import substitution through industrialization.

The Great Depression did not create Brazilian industrialization, but it created the conditions for a new advance. Beginning as a spontaneous response to the loss of import capacity that resulted from the catastrophic decline of exports and a falling rate of exchange, industrialization received a fresh impetus from Vargas, who encouraged industry through exchange controls, import quotas, tax

During a long and complex political career, Getúlio Vargas struggled to create an autonomous Brazilian capitalist state. Here the populist president is surrounded by military officers after the 1930 revolution briefly united a broad coalition of disparate political interests and swept him to power. [Bettmann/Corbis]

incentives, lowered duties on imported machinery and raw materials, and long-term loans at low interest rates. Thanks to the combination of favorable background conditions and the Vargas policy of state intervention, Brazilian industrialization, based entirely on production for the home market, made notable strides in a few years: industrial production doubled between 1931 and 1936. As early as 1933, when the United States was still deep in the Depression, Brazil's national income had begun to increase, which indicated that for the moment, at least, the economy no longer depended on external factors but on internal ones.

Meanwhile, Vargas sought to centralize political power by making strategic concessions to his coalition allies. He appeased the political elite of São Paulo with conservative ministerial appointments. He also tried to conciliate São Paulo's workers, who, again sparked by the women weavers in the textile industry, openly rebelled against industrialists in May 1932, demanding an eight-hour day, 20 percent wage increases, night-work bonuses, equal pay for equal work, prohibition of forced overtime, and recognition of their local bargaining units called "factory commissions." Tens of thousands joined the general strike, and Vargas was forced to intervene, co-opting the workers' movement by agreeing to most of their demands but requiring that future disagreements over working conditions be negotiated peacefully by tripartite "conciliation commissions" composed of workers, employers, and government appointees.

In February 1932 Vargas had promulgated an electoral code that established the secret ballot, lowered the voting age from twenty-one to eighteen, and extended the vote to working women, but the code still denied the vote to illiterates. Although these electoral reforms still left 95 percent of Brazilians ineligible to vote, they expanded suffrage sufficiently to allow women to get elected in eighteen of twenty state legislatures. Moreover, reflecting women's new political muscle, the state government of Rio de Janeiro appointed women to the cabinet portfolios of Labor and Education. The constituent assembly elected under this code also drafted a new constitution, which was promulgated on July 16, 1934. This document retained the federal system but considerably strengthened the powers of the executive. The assembly, constituting itself the first Chamber of Deputies, elected Vargas president for a term extending to January 1938.

The section of the constitution on "economic and social order" stressed the government's responsibility for economic development. Article 119 declared that "the law will regulate the progressive nationalization of mines, mineral deposits, and waterfalls or other sources of energy, as well as of the industries considered as basic or essential to the economic and military defense of the country."

The section on the rights and duties of labor revealed the importance Vargas attached to the imposition of a tutelage over the working class, a class to be courted through concessions but denied independence of action. The constitution of 1934 established a labor tribunal system, gave the government power to fix minimum wages, and guaranteed the right to strike. Subsequent decrees set the working day at eight hours in commerce and industry, fixed minimum wages throughout the country, and created an elaborate social security system that provided for pensions, paid vacations, safety and health standards, and employment security.

In exchange for these gains, the working class lost its freedom of action. The trade unions, formerly subject to harsh repression, but militant and jealous of their autonomy, became official agencies controlled by the Ministry of Labor. The workers had no voice in the drafting of labor legislation.

Police and security agencies brutally repressed strikes not approved by the government.

The labor and social legislation, moreover, was unevenly enforced, and employers frequently evaded the law. The legislation did not apply to the great majority of agricultural workers, who comprised 85 percent of the labor force. Determined to maintain his alliance with the fazendeiro wing of his coalition, Vargas left intact the system of patrimonial servitude that governed labor relations in the countryside, just as he left intact the latifundio. The promises of agrarian reform made during the campaign of 1930 were forgotten.

Vargas's rightward shift grew more pronounced in 1934 and alienated liberal tenentes, intellectuals, radical workers, and the Communist Party, founded in 1922 by Luís Carlos Prestes. As honorary president of the *Aliança Nacional Libertadora* (National Liberation Alliance, or ANL), a popular front movement that attracted middle-class as well as working-class support, Prestes advocated the liquidation of the latifundio, nationalization of large foreign companies, and cancellation of imperialist debts.

Meanwhile, Vargas harassed the leftist opposition as "subversive." In 1935 after Prestes attacked Vargas's failure to implement the tenente ideals and called for the creation of a truly "revolutionary and anti-imperialist government," Vargas responded by banning the ANL and ordering the arrest of many leftist leaders.

With the legal avenues of opposition for the left disappearing, the ANL and one wing of the Communist Party began an armed uprising in November. Despite some initial successes, it was quickly crushed by government forces and followed by a savage repression. There were fifteen thousand arrests, and prisoners were tortured, some to death. Prestes and other leaders of the revolt were captured, tried, and sentenced to many years in prison. The Communist Party was banned and went underground for a decade.

## VARGAS AS DICTATOR

The repression of the left paved the way for the establishment of Vargas's personal dictatorship.

On November 10 he canceled the 1938 presidential elections, dissolved Congress as an "inadequate and costly apparatus," and assumed dictatorial power under a new constitution patterned on European fascist models. On December 2, all political parties were abolished.

The new regime, baptized the *Estado Novo* (New State), copied not only the constitutional forms of the fascist regimes but also their repressive tactics. Strict press censorship was established, and prisons filled with workers, teachers, military officers, and others suspected of subversion. The apparatus of repression included a special police force for hunting down and torturing dissidents. The Estado Novo also dealt women workers a decided setback in their struggle for freedom and equality by actively soliciting their return to the private patriarchal province of home and family. The tax code penalized single women and childless families, while other laws provided special protections to mothers and children and actively discouraged women from working outside the home or joining trade unions. Yet there was little organized resistance to the regime. Labor, its most likely opponent, was neutralized by a paternalist social legislation and doped by populist rhetoric, and it remained passive or even supportive of Vargas.

By decade's end, Brazil's growing trade and increasingly friendly relations with Germany and Italy led to fears that the country was moving into the fascist orbit. Between 1933 and 1938, Germany became the chief market for Brazilian cotton and the second largest buyer of its coffee and cacao. German penetration of the Brazilian economy also increased, and the German Bank for South America established three hundred branches in Brazil.

But Brazil's economic rapprochement with Germany and Italy did not reflect sympathy with the expansionist goals of the fascist bloc; Vargas, the great realist, sought only to open up new markets for Brazil and to strengthen his hand in bargaining with the United States. Despite its authoritarian, repressive aspects, the Estado Novo continued the struggle against neocolonialism in its effort to achieve economic independence and modernization.

Indeed, under the new regime the state intervened more actively than before to encourage the growth of industry and provide it with the necessary economic infrastructure. Rejecting laissez faire, the Estado Novo pursued a policy of planning and direct investment for the creation of important industrial complexes in the basic sectors of mining, oil, steel, electric power, and chemicals. In 1940 the government announced a Five-Year Plan whose goals included the expansion of heavy industry, the creation of new sources of hydroelectric power, and the expansion of the railway network. In 1942 the government established the *Companhia Vale do Rio Doce* to exploit the rich iron-ore deposits of Itabira; in 1944 it created a company for the production of materials needed by the chemical industry; and in 1946 the National Motor Company began the production of trucks. In the same year, Vargas saw the realization of one of his cherished dreams: the National Steel Company began production at the Volta Redonda plant between Rio de Janeiro and São Paulo. Aware of the need of modern industry for abundant sources of power, Vargas created the National Petroleum Company in 1938 to press the search for oil.

By 1941, Brazil had 44,100 plants employing 944,000 workers; the comparable figure for 1920 was 13,336 plants with about 300,000 workers. Aside from some export of textiles, the manufacturing industries served the domestic market almost exclusively. State and mixed public-private companies dominated the heavy and infrastructural industries and private Brazilian capital predominated in manufacturing, but the 1930s also saw a significant growth of direct foreign investment as foreign corporations sought to enlarge their share of the internal market and overcome tariff barriers and exchange problems by establishing branch plants in Brazil. By 1940 foreign capital represented 44 percent of the total investment in Brazilian stock companies. Vargas made no effort to check the influx of foreign capital, perhaps because he believed that the growth of Brazilian state and private capitalism would keep the foreign sector in a subordinate status.

The Estado Novo banned strikes and lockouts but retained and even expanded the body of protective social and labor legislation. In 1942 the labor laws were consolidated into a labor code, regarded as one of the most advanced in the world. But it was unevenly enforced and brought no benefits to the great mass of agricultural workers. Moreover, spiraling inflation created a growing gap between wages and prices; prices rose 86 percent between 1940 and 1944, whereas between 1929 and 1939 they had risen only 31 percent. In effect, inflation, by transferring income from wages to capitalists, provided much of the financing for the rapid economic growth of the 1940s.

World War II accelerated that growth through the new stimulus it gave to industrialization. Brazil exported vast quantities of foodstuffs and raw materials, but the industrialized countries, whose economies were geared to war, could not pay for their purchases with machinery or consumer goods. As a result, Brazil built up large foreign-exchange reserves, $707 million in 1945. Most of the economic advance of the war years was due to expansion and more intensive exploitation of existing plants or the technical contributions of Brazilian engineers and scientists.

However, Vargas adroitly exploited Great Power rivalries to secure financial and technical assistance from the United States for the construction of the huge state-owned integrated iron and steel plant at Volta Redonda. U.S. companies and government agencies were notably cool to requests for aid for establishing heavy industry in Latin America. But Vargas's hints that he might have to turn for help to Germany removed all obstacles. Volta Redonda was a great victory for the Vargas policies of economic nationalism and state intervention in economic life. In return for its assistance, Vargas allowed the United States to lease air bases in northern Brazil even before it entered the war against the Axis.

The paradox of Brazil's participation in an antifascist war under an authoritarian regime was not lost on Brazilians; the demands for an end to the Estado Novo grew stronger as the defeat of the Axis drew near. Although the dictatorship and war had limited the political agenda of women's rights groups, their organizational strength continued to grow under the auspices of the Women's Division

of the League for National Defense, whose members staffed neighborhood committees to monitor food prices and demand social justice. This led to the creation of the Woman's Committee for Amnesty, which by war's end had built a broad coalition to restore civil liberties and secure political liberalization. During the war the struggle for Afro-Brazilian rights also took refuge in cultural organizations like the Black Experimental Theater (TEN), which rooted "antiracist civil and human rights demands" in the cultivation of African consciousness among blacks.

Likewise, a simmering worker discontent, blunted by repression and wartime co-optation of union leadership, could express itself only in popular protest sambas, clandestine factory commissions, spreading absenteeism, and personal appeals to Vargas for justice. But in February 1945 this dissatisfaction boiled over in a riot involving hundreds of protestors. In the summer, women textile workers in São Paulo again led a strike movement that mobilized thousands, destabilized Brazilian industrial society, and threatened Vargas's regime. Ever sensitive to changes in the political climate and the balance of forces, Vargas announced an amnesty for political prisoners, promulgated a law allowing political parties to function openly, and set December 2 as the date for presidential and congressional elections.

## A MILITARY COUP

Vargas announced that he would not run for president but set the stage for a well-organized campaign by his supporters, called *queremistas* (from the Portuguese verb *querer*, "to want"), who wanted Vargas to declare himself a candidate in the forthcoming election. Soon after issuing the decrees restoring political freedom, Vargas, proclaiming himself the "father of the poor," authorized the expropriation of any organization whose practices were harmful to the national interest.

The authorization decree, which was aimed at keeping down the cost of living, inspired alarm in conservative foreign and domestic circles. Senior military officers regarded Vargas's leftward move with growing uneasiness. The wartime alliance with the United States had accentuated their inherent conservatism and made them ready to accept the gospel of free enterprise and U.S. leadership in the cold war against the Soviet Union and world communism.

On October 29, 1945, Generals Goes Monteiro and Eurico Dutra staged a coup, forced Vargas to resign, promptly repealed Vargas's authorization decree, and suppressed the Communist Party. They refused to expand the vote to illiterates and organized elections that guaranteed the victory of President Eurico Dutra (1946–1951), under whom neocolonial interests regained much of the influence they had lost under Vargas. In his foreign and domestic policies, Dutra displayed a blind loyalty to the anticommunist creed propounded by Washington.

In the 1945 elections, the Communist Party (PCB) had polled over half a million votes, and two years later the Brazilian Women's Federation, the country's leading feminist organization, joined the Communist-sponsored Women's International Democratic Federation. Alarmed by the growing influence of the Communist Party, Dutra outlawed it, and Congress followed by expelling the party's elected representatives. Dutra exploited the resulting witch-hunt to smash the independent, left-led labor movement; the Workers' Federation, organized in 1946, was declared illegal; and the government intervened in a large number of unions to eliminate "extremist elements." The imposition of a wage freeze and the failure to raise the officially decreed minimum wage caused the real income of workers to drop sharply.

With respect to economic development, Dutra pursued a laissez-faire policy that meant the virtual abandonment of the Vargas strategy of a state-directed movement toward economic independence. Dutra removed all import and exchange controls and allowed the large foreign exchange reserves accumulated during the war—reserves that Vargas had proposed to use for re-equipping Brazilian industry—to be dissipated on imported consumer goods, luxury goods in large part.

Attracted by the new economic climate, foreign capital flowed into Brazil. Meanwhile, seeking to curb inflation according to the prescription of U.S. advisers, the government pursued a restrictive credit policy harmful to Brazilian entrepreneurs and industrial growth.

Despite these setbacks, popular movements continued to organize and agitate for progressive reform. Afro-Brazilians, for example, created the National Black Convention and the Black Women's National Congress to expose the hypocrisy of the government's claim that Brazil was a "racial democracy." After years of public pressure—culminating in 1950 with a well-publicized incident in which a São Paulo hotel refused to accommodate the famous African American choreographer Katherine Dunham but reserved a room for her white secretary—the Dutra regime finally adopted a relatively timid, but nonetheless significant, antidiscrimination law, the Afonso Arinos Act.

## VARGAS'S RETURN TO POWER

In 1950, having assured himself of the neutrality of the armed forces, Vargas drew upon *this* popular dissatisfaction and ran for president with the support of a broad coalition of workers, industrialists, and members of the urban middle class. His campaign concentrated on the need to accelerate industrialization and expand and strengthen social welfare legislation. Riding a wave of discontent with the economic and social policies of the Dutra regime, Vargas easily defeated his two opponents.

Vargas inherited a difficult economic situation. After a brief boom in coffee exports and prices in 1949–1951, the balance of trade again turned unfavorable and the inflation rate increased. In the absence of other major sources of financing for his developmental program, Vargas had to rely largely on a massive increase in the money supply, with all its inevitable social consequences. Meanwhile, his national program of state-directed industrialization, using state corporations as its major instrument, encountered increasing hostility from neocolonial interests at home and abroad. In the United States, the Eisenhower administration decided that the Vargas government had not created the proper climate for private investment and terminated the Joint United States–Brazilian Economic Commission. Within Brazil, Vargas's program faced sabotage at the hands of the rural forces that continued to dominate the majority of state governments and Congress. This hardening of attitudes signified that Vargas's options and his capacity for maneuvering between different social groups were greatly reduced.

Nonetheless, Vargas pursued his populist program. He created a mixed public-private petroleum corporation, called *Petrobrás,* which would give the state a monopoly on the drilling of oil and new refineries. Petrobrás illustrated Vargas's belief that the state must own the commanding heights of the economy and represented an attempt to reduce the balance-of-payments deficit by substituting domestic sources of oil for imported oil. Vargas sought to appease domestic and foreign opponents by leaving the distribution of oil in private hands and allowing existing refineries to remain privately owned. Vargas also proposed to create a similar agency for electric power, to be called *Electrobras.*

Vargas's labor policy became another political battleground. Under Vargas, labor regained much of the freedom of action it had lost during the Dutra years. In December 1951, under pressure from militant workers, the government decreed a new minimum wage that compensated for the most recent price rises. In 1953 three hundred thousand workers went on strike for higher wages and other benefits. In June of that year, Vargas appointed a young protégé, João Goulart, minister of labor. Goulart, a populist in the Vargas tradition, was sympathetic with labor's demands. In January 1954, Goulart recommended a doubling of the minimum wage.

The battle lines between Vargas and his foes were being drawn ever more sharply. In speeches to Congress, Vargas attacked foreign investors for aggravating Brazil's balance-of-payments problem by their massive remittances of profits and claimed that invoicing frauds had cost Brazil at least $250 million over an eighteen-month period. Meanwhile, attacks on him by conservatives grew even more bitter. On August 24, the military ordered him to resign or be deposed. Isolated and betrayed, the seventy-two-year-old Vargas found the way out of his dilemma by suicide. But he left a message that was also his political testament. It ended with the words:

I fought against the looting of Brazil. I fought against the looting of the people. I have fought bare-breasted. Hatred, infamy, and calumny did not beat down my spirit. I gave you my life. Now I offer my death. Nothing remains. Serenely I take the first step on the road to eternity and I leave life to enter history.

As in life, so also in death, Vargas remained a controversial figure. But a woman textile worker, Odette Pasquini, offered perhaps the most astute epitaph for Vargas and his populist programs. "Vargas," she opined, "oh he was the 'father of the poor,' as they used to say on the radio, but of course he was truly the mother of the rich!"

## Reform and Reaction, 1954–1964

The death of Vargas foreshadowed the demise of the nationalist, populist model of independent capitalist development over which he had presided for the better part of a quarter century. That model, based on a strategy of maneuver and compromise, of reconciling the clashing interests of the national bourgeoisie, fazendeiros, foreign capitalists, and the working class, of avoiding such structural changes as agrarian reform, had about exhausted its possibilities.

Two options remained. One was for Vargas's political heirs to mobilize the working class and the peasantry for the realization of a program of structural changes, including agrarian reform, that could impart a new dynamic to Brazilian national capitalism. The alternative was for Vargas's political enemies to impose a streamlined neocolonial model based on the denationalization and modernization of Brazilian industry, on its transformation into an extension of the industrial park of the great capitalist powers, accompanied by a shift in emphasis from the export of raw materials to the export of manufactured goods. Because such a course entailed immense sacrifices for the Brazilian people, it also required the imposition of a dictatorship of the most repressive kind. The balance of forces in 1954 already favored the second option. For a decade, however, Brazil would sway uncertainly between the two alternatives.

## THE KUBITSCHEK ERA

The presidential election of 1955 took place under the watchful gaze of the military. Juscelino Kubitschek, governor of Minas Gerais, with João Goulart as his running mate, stressed the defense of democracy and the acceleration of economic growth. Kubitschek was not an economic nationalist in the Vargas mold, but the nationalist and reformist groups, knowing the limits of military tolerance, gave him their support. As the campaign progressed, there grew a clamor on the right for a coup to prevent the victory of Kubitschek and Goulart. However, they won the election in October, with the popular Goulart polling more votes than the president-elect.

Kubitschek took office in January 1956 with a promise of "fifty years of progress in five." But this progress was to be achieved with the aid of massive foreign investments, to which Kubitschek offered most generous incentives. Foreign capital flowed into Brazil; the total inflow between 1955 and 1961 amounted to $2.3 billion. The bulk came from the United States, whose investments in Brazil reached $1.5 billion in 1960.

This influx of capital, which benefited from advantages denied to Brazilian enterprises, promoted a rapid foreign conquest of Brazilian national industry. In the process, the native entrepreneurs were frequently transformed into directors or partners of the foreign-controlled firms. The takeover concentrated on the most modern and fastest-growing industries (chemical, metallurgy, electrical, communications, and automotive). In 1960 foreign investment accounted for 70 percent of the capital invested in the 34 largest companies and more than 30 percent in the 650 corporations with capital of a million dollars or more.

The Kubitschek era was a heady time of unprecedented economic growth that averaged 7 percent per year between 1957 and 1961. By 1960, Brazil had been transformed from an agrarian country into an agrarian-industrial country with a base of heavy industry, for it could boast that it produced half its heavy-industry needs. Construction of a series of great dams provided much of the power needed by Brazil's growing industry. Kubitschek's decision to build a new capital, Brasilia, in the frontier state of Goias reflected his exuberant optimism about Brazil's future. Completed in three years, the new capital was inaugurated on April 21, 1960. A network of "highways of national unity" was constructed to link Brasilia with the rest of the country but failed to solve the many difficulties—housing and resettlement problems, cultural isolation, and the like—that faced its inhabitants.

These triumphs of development had to be paid for, and their cost was high. A major source of financing was foreign loans, which swelled Brazil's already large foreign debt from $1.6 billion in 1954 to $2.7 billion in 1961. Service of the foreign debt took an ever-increasing share of the national budget, rising from $180 million to $515 million (more than half the value of Brazil's exports) in the same period. This source of financing had its limits; by 1959 the International Monetary Fund (IMF) threatened to withhold loans if Brazil did not adopt a stabilization program and live within its means. Kubitschek responded by breaking off negotiations with the IMF and increasing the money supply. The result was an unprecedented inflation rate and a catastrophic decline in the value of the cruzeiro. This in turn greatly diminished the value of Brazil's exports. Inflation, like foreign loans, appeared to have reached its limits as a source of financing Brazilian development.

This economic growth, the resulting expansion of Brazil's middle class, and the ideology of modernity that accompanied both also affected Brazilian culture. *Bossa nova* (literally, the new beat), which emerged from fashionable cabarets in middle- and upper-class communities, sought to rescue Brazilian national music from the wild, seemingly uncontrollable, undulating rhythms of the samba, traditionally associated with mixed-race popular classes; instead it redefined Brazil's cultural identity in a way that emphasized modernity, personal freedom, and the pursuit of individual pleasure. Like the country's modernization during the 1950s, bossa nova relied heavily on imports from the United States, in this case syncopated jazz rhythms that artists like Antonio Carlos

(Tom) Jobim, João Gilberto, and Nara Leão fused with a samba drumbeat. Lyrically, bossa nova music like the internationally renowned "Girl from Ipanema," written by Brazilian beat poet extraordinaire Vinicius de Moraes, celebrated the bohemian lifestyles of young middle-class men who were more interested in the beach, beautiful girls, and drinking whiskey than the daily struggles of Brazil's popular classes, which samba songs traditionally memorialized.

### THE QUADROS REGIME

The election of 1960 took place amid growing social unrest and intense debate over domestic and foreign policy. Women actively participated in this national dialogue, demanding civil equality and organizing a massive protest demonstration to commemorate the tenth anniversary of the Brazilian Women's Federation, which Kubitschek had outlawed in 1956. Workers also agitated for an end to inflation, corruption, and foreign control of the economy. Brazilian popular culture reflected and reinforced this social turmoil. According to cultural historian Eduardo Carrasco Pirard, bossa nova songs, which earlier had eschewed controversial subjects like exploitation, inequality, and oppression now increasingly discussed "social themes which presented a rather idealized and paternalistic vision of the black *favela*-dweller and the worker from the fringe areas of the big cities." Songs like "The Farmworker's Funeral," by Chico Buarque de Holanda, sarcastically lamented the misfortunes of a peasant who finally won in death that which in vain he had sought in life: a plot of latifundio land ("large enough for a grave, not too big, not too deep!").

The campaign oratory and programs of all the principal candidates reflected the ascendancy that the nationalist, populist ideology had gained over public opinion. Even conservatives supported the presidential candidacy of the flamboyant Jânio da Silva Quadros, former governor of São Paulo, whose populist campaign denounced "foreign exploiters" and promised to "sweep out of the government the corrupt elements, the thieves and exploiters of the people."

Without breaking with the traditional dependence on the capitalist countries for markets and loans, Quadros sought to reduce that dependence by developing new trade and diplomatic relations with the socialist countries and the Third World. Accordingly, he initiated negotiations for the resumption of diplomatic relations with the Soviet Union, sent a trade mission to the People's Republic of China, and denounced the CIA-backed Bay of Pigs invasion of Cuba in April 1961. Although he stressed the need for foreign investments and guaranteed their security, Quadros opposed foreign investment in Brazilian oil and proposed to modify the "laws and regulations which place the Brazilian company in an inferior position." He also restricted the remittance of profits abroad.

However moderate, Quadros's policies aroused the hostility of military and civilian conservatives. Quadros's problems were compounded by an increasingly recalcitrant Congress dominated by conservative fazendeiros. Determined to break the legislative deadlock by some dramatic act, Quadros submitted his resignation on August 25, 1961, after only seven months of rule. His resignation message claimed that hostile foreign forces had obstructed his program of Brazil for the Brazilians. Convinced that the military would not permit the prolabor vice president Goulart to succeed him, Quadros evidently believed that public clamor for his return would bring him back to office with the powers he needed to govern.

But he had miscalculated. Led by war minister Odílio Denys, military officers took control of the government and declared that, for reasons of "national security," Goulart, whom they distrusted as a dangerous radical, should not return from his trade mission to China. Naturally, this ignited a national popular uprising that caused a split within the military; in Goulart's home state of Rio Grande do Sul, the commander of the Third Army announced his support for Goulart, and the governor of the state rallied the population to defend the constitution and ensure Goulart's elevation to the presidency. The threat of civil war loomed, but the military ministers, facing divisions within the armed forces and feeling the pressure of public opinion, agreed to a compromise. Goulart took office, but a constitutional amendment restrained the power of democracy and required the president to share power with a parliamentary council drawn from the conservative legislature.

## GOULART'S PRESIDENCY

Taking office in September 1961, Goulart steered a cautious course designed to allay conservative suspicions at home and abroad. In April 1962 he paid a visit to Washington. Addressing a joint session of Congress, he promised reasonable treatment of foreign-owned utilities in Brazil. The United States provided $131 million in aid for Brazil's depressed northeast, but the IMF, whose approval was a condition for the cooperation of private bankers, remained skeptical of Goulart's intentions.

The first year and a half of Goulart's rule under the parliamentary system saw few major legislative achievements. One was the passage of a Brazilian civil code that, under pressure from women's rights groups, prohibited gender discrimination in employment and gave married women legal control over their earnings and shared ownership of commonly acquired property. Another law established Electrobras, the national agency proposed by Vargas for the control of the production and distribution of electric power. Still another required foreign capital to be registered with the Brazilian government and barred profit remittances abroad in excess of 10 percent of invested capital, certainly not a radical measure. Yet it produced a sharp drop in foreign investments, from $91 million in 1961 to $18 million in 1962. Lacking other sources for financing development, Goulart had to resort to the Kubitschek formula of a massive increase of the money supply. The new inflationary spiral brought the collapse of the cruzeiro and a wave of strikes and food riots, as well as a growing radicalization of labor and sections of the peasantry. But the economic slowdown apparent since 1961 continued. Import substitution as a stimulus to industrialization appeared to have reached its limits, and further advance was blocked by the small domestic market, the inequities of Brazilian income distribution, and the

drain of capital through debt repayment and profit remittances (amounting to $564 million, or 45 percent of the value of Brazil's exports, in 1962).

With the advice of the brilliant young economist Celso Furtado, who had directed an ambitious effort to develop Brazil's backward, poverty-ridden northeast, Goulart drafted a program of structural reforms that aimed to expand Brazil's democracy and impart a new dynamism to its faltering economy. Reform of the archaic land tenure system would expand the domestic market and increase agricultural production. Tax reform would reduce the inequities of income distribution and provide funds needed for public education and other social welfare purposes. The grant of votes to illiterates would, it was hoped, drastically reduce the power of the rural oligarchy in the national and state legislatures.

To implement these changes, however, the legislative deadlock in Congress had to be broken, so in mid-1962 Goulart launched a campaign for a plebiscite to let the people choose between presidential and parliamentary government. Under great public pressure, Congress agreed to the plebiscite, and on January 1, 1963, more than 12 million voters decided by a three to one majority to restore to Goulart his full presidential powers under the constitution of 1946.

But Goulart's victory only deepened a growing polarization of opinion in the country, with the bourgeoisie and the middle class joining the landed oligarchy in opposition to Goulart's domestic program. Goulart's moderate reform proposals in reality favored the industrial bourgeoisie and should have enjoyed its support. But the dynamic industrialist class that had arisen and thrived under Getúlio Vargas was now much weaker. The progressive foreign conquest of Brazilian industry had greatly reduced that class's influence as more and more national entrepreneurs gave up an unequal struggle and solved their personal problems by becoming directors or associates of foreign-owned firms. This dependent bourgeoisie shared the fears of social change of its foreign and rural allies. But even the more militant nationalists within the ranks of the progressive industrial bourgeoisie—industrialists long affiliated with organizations like the Industrial Social Service (SESI) and the National Service for Industrial Training (SENAI), which had collaborated with *getulista* populism— feared a growing radicalism of Brazil's peasant and urban industrial working class. As historian Barbara Weinstein argues, by the late 1950s and early 1960s, workers had become a more significant political force: they had expanded their autonomy from state controls, they increasingly relied on strikes and uncompromising demands for wage hikes to secure their interests, and they tended to elect leftist union leaders less inclined to collaborate with industrialists or the state.

The industrialists' apprehension increased as a result of the spread of radicalism to the countryside. Under the leadership of the lawyer Francisco Julião, peasants in the bleak northeast, afflicted by drought, famine, and oppressive land tenure and labor systems, joined Peasant Leagues and invaded fazendas. Their activities endangered the latifundio, which was also threatened by Goulart's proposal to give the vote to illiterates and enact agrarian reform.

By the end of 1963, the forces on the right— the fazendeiros, the big bourgeoisie, the military, and their foreign allies—had begun to mobilize against the threat from the left. Industrialists had long cultivated support among army officers, inviting generals like Humberto Castelo Branco, the future dictator, to speak at their Forum Roberto Simonsen, a regular meeting sponsored by the São Paulo Federation of Industrialists. But in early 1962 they began plotting in earnest and by March of 1964, according to Weinstein, the industrialists "had collected more than 1.5 billion cruzeiros equal to more than a million dollars, to aid the armed forces in the seizure of power."

Meanwhile, under strong pressure from impatient radicals, Goulart moved to the left. Appearing at a mass rally in Rio de Janeiro in March 1964, he signed two decrees. One nationalized all private oil refineries. The other made liable to expropriation all large and "underutilized" estates close to federal highways or railways and lands of over seventy acres near federal dams, irrigation works, or drainage projects. At the same meeting, Goulart announced that he would shortly issue a decree on

rent control. He asked Congress to pass reforms that included tax reform, the vote for illiterates and enlisted men, an amendment to the constitution providing for land expropriation without immediate compensation, and legalization of the Communist Party.

By the middle of March, the military-civilian conspiracy for Goulart's overthrow was well advanced. The governors of a number of important states met with a view to transferring the Congress to São Paulo, where a "legalist government" would be installed. An emissary returned from the United States with assurances from the State Department that the United States would immediately recognize the new government. Then, if it became necessary, the legalist government would solicit aid from the United States, and the dispatch of U.S. troops would not constitute intervention but a response to a legitimate government's request for aid to suppress communism and subversion.

On March 31 army units in Minas Gerais and São Paulo began to march on Rio de Janeiro. The U.S. ambassador to Brazil, Lincoln Gordon, was well informed of the conspiracy; five days before the coup he cabled Secretary of State Dean Rusk naming General Humberto de Alencar Castelo Branco as the probable head of the new military junta. Published documents also show that the United States was prepared to give military aid, if needed, to the rebels. But Operation Uncle Sam (its code name) proved unnecessary; the Goulart regime fell almost without a struggle on April 1, and the president fled into exile in Uruguay.

As the new military regime consolidated its power, it became clear that the generals had come to install the alternative to the nationalist economic model, a neocolonial model based on the thorough integration of a dependent Brazilian economy into the international capitalist economy and the rapid modernization of Brazilian industry and agriculture without regard to its social consequences. Because of the regime's combination of brutally repressive policies with primary economic and political dependence on the United States, the Brazilian scholar Hélio Jaguaribe has aptly called it "colonial fascism."

# Brazil's "Colonial Fascism"

The first acts of the military leaders of the self-proclaimed "democratic revolution" on April 1964 revealed their long-range intentions. On April 9 the Supreme Revolutionary Command issued the First Institutional Act, permitting the president to rule by decree, declare a state of siege, and deprive any citizen of civil rights for a period of ten years. A docile Congress approved the military's choice for president, General Humberto de Alencar Castelo Branco. Like many of his colleagues, Castelo Branco was a product of the *Escola Superior de Guerra* (School of Higher Military Studies), dominated in recent years by advocates of a *linha dura* (hard line), whose main tenets were fanatical anti-communism, favorable treatment of foreign capital, and acceptance of the leadership of the United States in foreign affairs.

## ENCOURAGEMENT OF FOREIGN CAPITAL AND REPRESSION OF LABOR

It was in the area of economic policy that the new government most clearly defined its character and long-range aims. Roberto Campos, minister of planning, worked out a program for stimulating the entry of foreign capital by incentives that included the free export of profits, reduced taxes on the income of foreign firms, and a special type of exchange for the payment of external financing in case of devaluation. At the same time, internal credit was severely reduced in compliance with the anti-inflationary prescriptions of the IMF, while the level of consumption of the domestic market fell as a result of a wage freeze and the decline in the real value of wages. These policies, placing Brazilian-owned companies in an unfavorable position, caused many to go under; 440 went bankrupt in 1966, 550 in 1967.

The new government's economic policies accelerated the foreign takeover of Brazilian industry. By 1968 foreign capital controlled 40 percent of the capital market of Brazil, 62 percent of its foreign trade, 82 percent of its maritime transport, 77 percent of its overseas air transport, 100 percent of its motor vehicle production, 100 percent of its tire production, more than 80 percent of its pharmaceutical industry, and 90 percent of its cement industry. The United States led, with about half of the total foreign investment, followed by Germany, Britain, France, and Switzerland.

To ensure foreign and domestic capital of an abundant supply of cheap labor, the government froze wages and banned strikes, with the result that workers' living standards fell sharply. In 1968 the minister of labor estimated that the real value of wages had fallen between 15 and 30 percent in the preceding four years. Labor was further shackled by the appointment of military intervenors to oversee more than two thousand of the country's leading industrial unions.

Further, the government suppressed dissent in all areas of Brazilian life and suspended the political rights of thousands of so-called extremists. Thousands of federal employees were fired, and hundreds of nationalist military officers were arbitrarily retired or dismissed. The government shut down the Brazilian Institute of Higher Studies, a major center of nationalist economic theory, suppressed the National Student Union, and outlawed the Peasant Leagues.

In 1965, Castelo Branco issued the Second Institutional Act, which dissolved all political parties and instituted indirect elections of the president and vice president. The Third Institutional Act (February 1966) ended the popular election of governors of states and mayors of state capitals. Yet Brazil's military rulers chose to maintain a façade of democracy and representative government. They established an official party and a legal opposition party, whose ranks were carefully screened to exclude "subversives." Its elected representatives had little or no impact on policy and legislation.

With electoral politics closed to serious democratic debate, opposition to the military dictatorship was increasingly reflected in popular youth culture, where lyrical metaphors and a driving musical beat initially avoided dictatorial censorship and substituted for political manifestos. Born in urban musical theaters that sponsored socially conscious plays like *"Roda Viva"* ("Commotion"), this new Brazilian popular music (MPB) soon provided a catalyst for youthful protest against the dictatorship. It quickly reached a mass audience because television, radio, and record companies, to attract a younger generation of consumers, sponsored competitions among musicians who were eager to play at music festivals originally held in large theaters and later in outdoor stadiums. Six months before each festival and following the carnival tradition, songs were played repeatedly on the radio and the most popular artists were invited to perform at the festival. Among them were the musicians like Geraldo Vandré and Chico Buarque who used love songs and traditional ballads to thinly disguise lyrics that railed against social injustice and oppression. Vandré's *"Disparada"* ("Stampede"), for example, tells the story of a cowboy from Brazil's arid and poverty-stricken Northeast who, tired of having the fazendeiro treat him worse than the cattle, violently rebels.

But perhaps the most popular song was *"Caminhando"* ("Walking"), which became a national anthem of youthful social protest, even after the dictatorship, citing its "subversive lyrics, its offensiveness to the armed forces, and its use as a slogan for student demonstrations," banned its publication and dissemination. It called upon workers, peasants, students, and intellectuals to unite and mobilize against dictatorship in defense of song, a metaphor for freedom and democracy: "Walking and singing and following the song/ We're all equal, arms linked or not/ In the schools, in the streets, fields, and construction sites/ Walking and singing and following the song." More ominously still for Brazil's military leaders, "Caminhando" insisted that "Those who know, take action now and don't wait for it to happen."

## COSTA E SILVA AND A NEW CONSTITUTION

In March 1967, Castelo Branco turned over the presidency to his hand-picked successor Marshal Artur da Costa e Silva. His first act was to give Brazil a new constitution, the sixth in its history, which incorporated the successive institutional acts. In general, Costa e Silva continued the policies of his predecessor but allowed a certain thaw in the climate of repression; this encouraged a

revival of opposition activity and demands for changes in policy. Nationalists inside and outside the armed forces called for a return to the nationalist model of economic development, workers for an end to the wage freeze, intellectuals and students for an end to censorship and a return to academic freedom. A portion of the clergy, headed by the courageous archbishop of Recife and Olinda, Helder Câmara, added their voices to the general cry for social, political, and economic reforms.

During this period, a new musical force appeared that made a dramatic impact on Brazilian popular culture and the struggle against dictatorship. Known as *tropicália*, this new genre criticized the bossa nova and another musical style, *a jovem guarda* (new guard), as hopelessly romantic, fundamentally "bourgeois," and insufficiently willing to confront the brutality of the repressive military dictatorship; it called not only for the ouster of the military regime, but also for a revolution of Brazilian culture and national identity.

Ironically, tropicália music alienated both the military regime and traditional left-wing political opponents, because it self-consciously fused Brazilian and foreign instruments and musical styles to create a "universal sound." This contradicted the interests of the dictatorship, which sought to maintain social control by celebrating Brazil's national cultural traditions, but it also undermined the left's critique of foreign domination and cultural imperialism. Led by artists like Caetano Veloso and Gilberto Gil, the *tropicalistas* were greatly influenced by The Beatles' *"Sergeant Pepper's Lonely Hearts Club Band"* and drew heavily on Oswaldo de Andrade's concept of "cultural cannibalism" to shock their audiences with raucous, electric guitars and lyrics that juxtaposed contradictory images of modernity and repression. At the International Music Festival, Veloso and his band, *Os Mutantes* (The Mutants), dressed like futuristic automatons, initially were booed off the stage when they performed "To Prohibit Is Prohibited." Veloso, in an angry rage, chastised his audience for seeking "to police Brazilian music" in the same way that the dictatorship sought to police Brazil; by contrast, he and his tropicália comrades aimed "to abolish the imbecility that rules Brazil." Indeed,

Gilberto Gil, Caetano Veloso, Tom Ze, and Os Mutantes shocked Brazilians with their new sound, which combined traditional Brazilian rhythms with the electrified guitar sounds of Jimi Hendrix. Before their arrest and exile in 1968, their psychedelic music scorned middle-class Brazilian consumerism and the military dictatorship that protected it. [© Universal Music Group. Photo from University of North Carolina Press]

Veloso, Gil, and their comrades equally savaged the dictatorship and its agenda of capitalist modernization. According to cultural historian Christopher Dunn, in the title song of his first album in 1968, "Tropicália," Veloso contrasted the bossa nova, cultural symbol of Brazilian modernity in the late 1950s with *palhoça*, "the ubiquitous mud huts of the Brazilian backlands." Although this seemed harmless enough, the song concluded with still more disturbing images, ultimately describing a modern metaphorical Brasilia inhabited by a "smiling, ugly dead child" begging for coins.

The tropicalistas' sophisticated allegories confused the military censors and even secured their approval for a time. In fact, the military dictators were unsure how to classify the political meaning of the tropicalía movement, especially because it was also the target of their left-wing opponents. By late 1968, however, the dictatorship, according to

Veloso, was convinced that their music "represented anarchy, violence, and a threat to families, relations between generations, respect, and religion." According to Gilberto Gil, the military viewed tropicalía as "a threat, something new, something that can't quite be understood, something that doesn't fit into any of the well-defined compartments of existing cultural practices." The military government consequently incarcerated them and later exiled them to Europe because they were "sort of illegible, and that won't do, that is dangerous."

Heartened by this show of popular resistance to the dictatorship, Congress and the Supreme Court reasserted their independence. The Supreme Court defied the military by granting a writ of habeas corpus for three student leaders who had been imprisoned for three months. Congress protected the immunity of a deputy who had bitterly criticized the military for its brutal treatment of political prisoners and student dissenters.

These acts of defiance precipitated a governmental crisis that exposed a struggle within the regime between adherents of the hard line and a group of military officers who proposed to reduce foreign economic influence, pursue a more independent foreign policy, and make some concessions to the clamor for social and political reform. The hard-liners won out; under their pressure, Costa e Silva issued a Fifth Institutional Act in 1968 that dissolved Congress, imposed censorship, suspended the constitution, and granted the president dictatorial powers.

This "coup within a coup" escalated the use of terrorist tactics by a variety of police forces, local and national. The official security forces were joined by vigilante groups, operating with the covert approval of the government. The systematic use of torture by special units of the military police and the "death squads" reached a level without precedent in Brazilian history. The victims included intellectuals, students, workers, and even priests and nuns, as well as common criminals. Increasingly, Brazilians could express their opposition only in the allegorical style by now made famous by Brazilian popular music and the tropicalistas. On December 14, 1968, *Jornal do Brasil* published such a weather report that forecast "black weather, suffocating temperature, unbreathable air, and a country beset by strong winds." It could not have been more accurate.

The intensified campaign of repression convinced some elements of the Brazilian left that there was no alternative to armed struggle against the dictatorship. There arose some half-dozen guerrilla groups, but they never achieved a mass character. The slaying in 1969 by members of a death squad of the most prominent guerrilla leader, Carlos Marighella, dealt a heavy blow to the movement, which soon ceased to pose a serious problem for the regime. Brazil remained a police state.

### THE ECONOMY AND DENATIONALIZATION

This vicious assault on Brazilian democracy and civil liberties aimed to preserve the military's power and to protect its neoliberal economic policies, which favored foreign investment and export production but attacked the living standards of Brazil's impoverished majority. By 1970 the denationalization of key sectors of Brazilian industry was almost complete. One or a few giant multinational firms dominated each major industry. The automotive industry, which was dominated by three firms—Volkswagen, General Motors, and Ford—typified the concentration of industrial ownership and production. The military champions of free enterprise did not dismantle the state sector, however, as one might expect. Instead they assigned to it the function of providing cheap steel, power, and raw materials to the profitable foreign-owned enterprises.

A counterpart of the concentration of production was the concentration of income. Brazil's gross national product grew at an average annual rate of 8 percent, one of the highest in the world, but there was no parallel growth of mass capacity to consume.

The contradiction between a highly productive, technologically advanced industrial plant and an extremely small domestic market had to be resolved somehow. The regime's economic planners found the answer by programming a vast increase in Brazil's exports. Primary products continued to dominate the export trade, but exports of

manufactured goods increased at a rate of about 12 percent between 1968 and 1972. Most Brazilians lacked shoes and were poorly clad, but Brazil became a major exporter of shoes and textiles. Increasingly, however, primacy was placed on the export of durable consumer and capital goods, such as cars, electrical products, and machine tools.

Government planners hoped that exports would help solve the problem of the balance of payments, a problem that grew ever more acute. But even as the volume of exports increased, so did the annual trade deficit. Meanwhile, the foreign debt, which stood at $12.5 billion in 1973, climbed to $17.6 billion in 1974 and stood at about $30 billion by the end of 1976. Service on this foreign debt, an important component of which was the increased cost of imported oil, amounted to nearly the total value of Brazil's exports in 1977. The problem was compounded by the heavy drain of interest and dividends in amounts considerably greater than the foreign investments that generated them. The deficits in the balance of payments contributed to a steep fall in the exchange value of the cruzeiro and an inflationary spiral that reached a rate of about 46 percent in 1976.

The recession that spread throughout the capitalist world in 1973–1974, combined with much higher oil prices, added to Brazil's economic difficulties. The passage of "antidumping" laws[1] in various countries, including the United States, cut into Brazil's exports of manufactured goods, creating overproduction and unemployment in various industries. By the mid-1970s, the bloom was off Brazil's "economic miracle."

The government's own figures documented the devastating effect of the "economic miracle" on the general welfare. By 1974 the minimum wage was only half the minimum income required to buy food for subsistence. When the costs of rent, clothing, and transportation were added, a worker needed four times the minimum wage. Official data revealed an intolerable situation with respect to public health. Nearly half the population over the

---

[1]These laws imposed duties designed to prevent the sale of goods in international trade at below-market prices.

age of twenty suffered from tuberculosis and about 150,000 people died every year from the disease; about 42 million suffered from parasitic diseases that caused general debility and reduced working capacity. The great majority of Brazilian houses lacked running water and sanitary facilities, a condition that contributed to the prevalence of parasitic disease. According to the president of the National Institute of Nutrition, 12 million preschool children—70 percent of all children in that category—suffered from malnutrition in 1973.

The government's agrarian reform was primarily directed at prodding and assisting semifeudal great landowners to transform their estates into agribusinesses at the expense of their tenants. It threatened to expropriate latifundia that had not been exploited for four years. But the stress on "voluntary" adherence gave landowners time for delay and circumvention of the law by dividing the land among relatives or forming it into commercial enterprises exempt from the law's provisions. Thus, its principal result was to stimulate the development of capitalist large-scale agriculture, accelerating a process that had been under way since the 1930s. Sociologists warned that the "agrarian reform" was spurring a new wave of rural emigration, throwing a new mass of cheap labor on an overstocked urban labor market.

## THE OPPOSITION AND THE STRUGGLE FOR RIGHTS

Ruled by a brutal military dictatorship, the Brazilian people expressed their dissent and discontent through the few available channels. Brazilian music quickly reemerged as an effective means through which popular discontent with the military dictatorship, especially among the nation's youth, was expressed. Strongly influenced by a decade of rigid internal military censorship of Brazilian artists and the regime's free-market exposure to the innovative electric sounds of foreign music (especially jazz), a new generation of Brazilian youth grew up less interested in a song's words, but very much aware of the liberating power of its sound. Milton Nascimento, perhaps the best known of these young artists, reflected this awareness in his *"Milagre dos Peixes"* ("Miracle

of the Fishes"), a popular song sung without lyrics to protest military censorship. To overcome the limitations imposed by television and radio censors, these musicians increasingly relied upon massive outdoor music festivals to communicate their ideas to the public; these became important sites for the organization of popular opposition to dictatorship.

Urban theater was another form of popular culture through which opposition to the military was expressed. Professional theater battled the dictatorship, using metaphor and historical narrative to escape the censors' disapproval. Chico Buarque's *"Calabar: O Elogio da Traição"* ("Calabar: In Praise of Treason"), for example, used a famous story of betrayal in the seventeenth-century Portuguese-Dutch colonial wars to celebrate Brazilian independence from Portuguese tyranny, an all too obvious metaphor that, after three months, ultimately failed to survive the regime's censorship. Largely because of the military's omnipresent censors, there was a dramatic expansion of local, decentralized amateur theater. These dramas likewise challenged the power of the military and sought to avoid individual recriminations by collectivizing all production decisions. They used narratives of well-known historical events to communicate themes of popular rebellion and resistance to oppression that resonated with contemporary antidictatorial struggles. *Teatro da rua* (street theater) also flourished during this dark period. It used the techniques of mime and clowning to scorn dictatorship and helped galvanize popular resistance in the nation's favelas, whose residents could not afford the price of a theater ticket. By the mid-1970s there was a thriving national subculture of popular protest and rebellion that belied the surface calm imposed by the military regime's brutal repression.

Influenced by liberation theology and its "preferential option for the poor," Christian Base Communities also emerged to play a key role in this struggle. Under church protection, women organized community and neighborhood groups that initially limited themselves to "feminine" demands for clean water, better housing, and lower food prices but increasingly became more overtly "political," agitating for the release of political prisoners, a restoration of democracy, and the "reconquest of lost equality." By decade's end, this had spawned a feminist movement, whose media voice, *Brasil Mulher*, claiming a circulation of ten thousand readers, concluded that "capitalism is the origin of numerous forms of the oppression of women."

Afro-Brazilians also created cultural organizations like the Center for Black Culture and Art, which advocated the abolition of racial discrimination and cultivated racial pride associated with a Pan-African consciousness. By 1978, however, these organizations had begun to coalesce in the Unified Black Movement (MNU), which organized *centros de luta* (struggle centers) to protest against racism, "the inevitable consequence of capitalist development." Likewise, a substantial minority of the Catholic church hierarchy, led by Archbishop Helder Câmara, openly began to oppose capitalism and neocolonialism.

Meanwhile, workers, whose average wages under the military regime's neoliberal economic program had fallen to two-thirds of their 1964 levels and one-half of their 1957 high, had become more vocal. A "new unionism" emerged to challenge the military government's policies and led directly to the formation of the Workers' Party (PT), which participated in the social struggle demanding an end to dictatorship, respect for human rights, and economic justice.

Finally, congressional elections in 1978 reflected Brazilians' immense discontent with the economic and social results of dictatorial rule and the growing strength of an opposition that united ever wider sections of the population.

## THE DICTATORSHIP IN CRISIS, 1978–1983

There were three major developments on the Brazilian scene between 1978 and 1983. First, a weak recovery from the recession of 1974–1975 soon gave way to an even more severe recession, culminating in a balance-of-payments crisis that brought Brazil to the verge of national bankruptcy. Second, the living standards of the masses continued to decline as a result of mounting unemployment, skyrocketing inflation, and the government's

austerity measures, causing increased discontent and resistance on the part of the working class and the peasantry. At the same time, opposition to the military regime grew among the middle class and sections of the capitalist class. Third, in an effort to defuse the growing opposition, the regime applied the policy of *abertura*, or "opening toward democracy." This policy of limited political concessions aimed to preserve the military's power.

The economic crisis resulted from the interplay of domestic and external factors. An important cause was the inability of the domestic market to absorb the growing output of Brazilian industry. For almost two decades, the dictatorship had pursued a policy of promoting the growth of profits and capital by keeping wage increases below the cost of living; this policy sharply limited the purchasing power of the people. The economic downturn of the 1970s and the 1980s, however, also reduced the purchasing power of the middle classes, who provided a major part of the market for cars, television sets, and other durable consumer goods.

The most direct cause of the crisis was an unmanageable balance of payments and debt service problem. By 1980, Brazil had a foreign debt of $55 billion, largest in the Third World, and service of the debt absorbed 40 percent of the nation's export earnings. Even Brazil's president complained that because of the drain of interest, Brazil had "nothing left over for development." The high interest rates caused by the monetarist tight money policies of the Reagan administration added to Brazil's debt service burden. The export of a considerable part of the profits made by multinational companies in Brazil also increased Brazil's payments deficit. By 1980 these companies controlled 40 percent of the major industrial and mining enterprises of the country and were sending home 55 percent of their profits.

By 1982 the balance-of-payments problem had reached a critical point. Brazil had almost run out of the foreign exchange it needed to meet its financial obligations. The foreign debt stood at about $89 billion, and many of the approximately 1,400 banks that had lent money to Brazil, grown suddenly nervous, were refusing to renew outstanding loans to Brazilian entities. A Brazilian default, however, would have sent shock waves through the world financial system. Once more, as in the similar Mexican emergency, the self-interest of the Western financial community dictated a rescue operation. The plan, organized by the IMF with strong support from the U.S. government, provided for rollover loans that allowed Brazil to continue paying the interest on its debt, thus maintaining the profits of the international banks. At the same time, austerity measures imposed by the agreement meant that the mass of impoverished Brazilians, already hard-pressed, suffered further. The new loans gave Brazil a breathing space, but the balance-of-payments problem remained as intractable as ever, and the financial juggling act of 1982 could not be indefinitely repeated.

The austerity program imposed by the IMF was a new blow at popular living standards, which had sharply declined since the establishment of the military dictatorship in 1964. In mid-1978 one study concluded that at least 70 percent of the population lived below the officially calculated economic survival level. In 1982 the minimum monthly wage was 23,000 cruzeiros, about $95. According to Brazilian sociologists, however, a family of five needed three times that amount to survive. The superexploitation of Brazilian workers took its heaviest toll on the weakest group of the population—its children. A partial census taken in 1982 indicated that half of all Brazilian children over ten worked.

These abysmal social conditions led to rural conflict that was intensified by an explosion of land concentration and land-grabbing. In part this process of land concentration reflected the expansion of capitalist, mechanized agriculture, producing such crops as soya beans or sugar cane,[2] primarily into marginal and frontier land that had not been cultivated previously. In part it was due to the pattern of occupation of the new lands opened up for settlement in the Amazon by the construction of the Trans-Amazonian Highway and other roads. Instead of settling thousands of landless peasant families on the new agricultural frontier, the Amazon Development Agency gave big companies large sums of money to set up vast cattle ranches. As a result, some 95 percent of the new landholdings in the Amazon were of 10,000 hectares or more. Unlike coffee plantations, the large new soya bean and sugar-cane farms and cattle estates employed little labor. Many of the dispossessed or discharged tenants and rural laborers migrated to the cities, swelling the ranks of the unemployed and underemployed and aggravating all the urban social problems.

Thousands of others drifted to the Amazon frontier, becoming *posseiros* (squatters) who raised subsistence crops of rice, cassava, and maize on their small plots. They enjoyed considerable rights under Brazilian law, but these rights had little value on the violent frontier. The posseiros were (and are) frequently threatened with eviction by powerful land-grabbers, who arrived with their gunmen and sometimes enjoyed the open or covert support of the local military or other officials. The posseiros responded by organizing rural unions and defending their land by all the means at their disposal; they found allies in courageous Catholic clergy who on occasion were arrested, tortured, and even murdered for their humanitarian activities.

Discredited and isolated on account of its failed economic policies and corruption, the military regime sought a way out of its impasse by a strategy of détente with the opposition. This policy of abertura included the lifting of most censorship; an amnesty that permitted the return of political exiles and the restoration of their political rights; and an overhaul of the political system that allowed the formation of new parties in addition to the official government and opposition parties.

These concessions were certainly not without significance, but their limited, calculated character must be understood. They were hedged about by constitutional amendments designed to ensure the continuation of military rule. Although the opposition made large gains in the 1982 elections under the constitution imposed by the military, the all-powerful president controlled both the federal budget and the operating funds of the states. It still

[2] A major factor in the expansion of sugar-cane cultivation was the success of Brazil's program for developing alcohol as a fuel.

seemed certain that a military man or a nominee of the military would be the next president of Brazil.

## The Transition to Democracy, 1983–2003: "The New Republic"

The march of events upset the calculations of the military rulers. The dictatorship had counted on an easy win over opposition candidate Tancredo Neves, but popular mobilization against the military swept Neves to victory. On the eve of his inauguration, however, Neves died, leaving his vice president, José Sarney, to carry out Neves's program of structural reforms, which included land reform and the grant of a larger voice in government to workers and unions. But Sarney took office without Neves's mandate and with little popular support.

### THE MILITARY AND EXTERNAL CONSTRAINTS ON DEMOCRACY

The transition to democracy and civilian rule, made under the watchful eyes of the military, was a gradual process. Behind the scenes, the military continued to influence the decision-making process on all major issues. Consequently, the Sarney administration made little progress in solving Brazil's great social and economic problems, the chief of which was land reform. This was not simply a question of redistributive justice; it was a prerequisite for the creation of a modern national capitalism based on a large domestic market. In 1985, for example, Sarney signed into law an agrarian reform bill that provided for the distribution of 88 million acres of land to 1.4 million families through 1989. But a 1986 decree limited the land available for distribution and expropriation to state-owned lands and to private holdings whose production was below the land-use standards set by government agronomists.

So sluggish was the program's implementation that Minister of Agrarian Reform and Development Nelson Ribeiro resigned in protest. The major obstacle to land reform was the fierce resistance of the landowners. Organized under the Rural Democratic Union (UDR) and the Brazilian Society for the Defense of Tradition, Family, and Property, the landowners hired thousands of former military personnel to staff private militias, paying, it was reported, salaries three times higher than those of the army.

If land reform was the most acute, violence-ridden issue of the "New Republic," Brazil's greatest external problem remained the immense foreign debt, which in 1990 stood at about $120 billion. The continuous drain of foreign exchange had a profoundly negative impact on Brazil's efforts to achieve social reform and economic growth. To many Brazilians, it appeared that the nation must choose between paying the interest and supporting social and economic development.

Sarney defined his position on the debt in a 1985 speech to the United Nations General Assembly: "Brazil will not pay its foreign debt with recession nor with unemployment, nor with hunger . . . a debt paid for with poverty is an account paid with democracy." These were brave words, in sharp contrast to the docility with which military governments had accepted the debt status quo. But this revolt by a timid president did not last long. Under pressure from foreign bankers and right-wing domestic groups, Sarney lifted the debt moratorium and in 1988 began negotiations with the banks for a conventional rescheduling.

On taking office the Sarney administration found the economy in recession, racked by galloping inflation and high unemployment. To combat this economic crisis, he announced a stabilization program, *Plan Cruzado*, which established a freeze on wages, prices, and rents, and replaced Brazil's monetary unit, the cruzeiro, with a new and strong monetary unit, the *cruzado*. He also announced a series of devaluations designed to maintain export effectiveness; the immediate closing or merger of fifteen state companies and of thirty-two more in the coming months; and, most painful of all, large increases in postal rates, the cost of utilities, fuel, and sugar, and 100 percent increases in taxes on cigarettes and alcoholic beverages.

An explosion of popular wrath followed these announcements. Brazilian wage earners' purchasing power, already slashed 30 percent since 1986, faced another decline of 29 percent. Consequently, the two labor federations, the leftist *Central Unica dos Trabalhadores* (CUT) and its rival, the more conservative *Central Geral dos Trabalhadores* (CGT), joined in a general strike designed to bring about the total repeal of the austerity program; organizers claimed that the strike brought 70 percent of the nation to a standstill. By mid-1987 Sarney's popularity had declined to the vanishing point. The U.S. banker David Rockefeller astutely noted the source of this decline: "In all my visits to Brazil, I have never before come across such desperate poverty."

In 1988 the national Congress, acting as a constituent assembly and influenced by this massive popular mobilization, gave the country a new democratic constitution that represented a sweeping rejection of all the late military regime had stood for. It provided for popular election of the president and mandated that Brazilians should vote in 1993 to choose between the presidential and parliamentary systems. Presidential rule by decree, so often used by the military regime, was abolished. The basic civil rights of freedom of assembly, speech, and the press were guaranteed, workers were given the right to strike and engage in collective bargaining, and the workweek was reduced from forty-eight to forty-four hours. Another provision nationalized oil- and mineral-mining rights.

The constitution promised protection of indigenous rights but contained no concrete measures to prevent the destruction of their culture and habitat, the Amazon rain forest. With the approval and financial support of the military regimes and their civilian successors, big ranchers and mine companies, both Brazilian and foreign, cut down or burned vast stretches of forest to graze cattle or strip-mine, threatening the livelihoods and very survival of the indigenous peoples and *seringueiros* (rubber tappers), who depended on the forests for their existence. Those who protested the exploitive practices of the ranchers and mine owners were often murdered by hired gunmen protected by corrupt and racist government officials.

Sarney's administration received a stunning rebuff from Brazilian voters in the November 1988

municipal elections. In a sharp swing to the left, labor and socialist parties captured control of the major Brazilian cities and a majority of state capitals, and there was a rapid growth of left-wing parties, especially the Workers' Party, led by the militant trade union leader Luís Inaçio da Silva (Lula), whose membership grew into millions.

### NEOLIBERAL WINE IN POPULIST BOTTLES

The election results and a general strike in March 1989, which mobilized 20 million workers, sounded an alarm bell to Brazil's elites and their political managers, preparing for the first popular presidential election in nearly thirty years, to be held in 1989. The new democratic environment required the right to present a populist, charismatic presidential candidate who could convince the Brazilian people to swallow the ill-tasting free-market prescription of austerity and privatization, something Sarney had been unable to do.

Such a candidate was found in the person of Fernando Collor de Mello, a dapper sportsman and athlete from a wealthy family. Sharply critical of official state corruption and inefficiency, his campaign focused on promises to reduce the bloated bureaucracy, attract foreign capital, and institute a free-market economy.

Although he combined populist initiatives with policies that reflected his hard-line free-market principles, the basic thrust of Collor's program conformed to the most traditional IMF recipes for economic solvency. Reduction of government spending and services, a halt to wage indexation (adjustment of wages to changing price levels), an end to collective bargaining except on the firm level, and wholesale privatization of state enterprises became the order of the day. A freeze of savings and banking deposits, designed to check inflation, helped produce the desired effect but had major recessive results; by 1990 industrial production had plummeted 25 percent and layoffs nationwide were well over 300,000. Caught between the scissors of declining sales and interest rates of 6 percent a month, many companies filed for bankruptcy; almost a million workers were unemployed in Rio de Janeiro, São Paulo, and four

Chico Mendes with his family, shortly before his death in 1988. The murder of Mendes, a leader of the crusade to save the Brazilian rain forest, shocked environmentalists around the world. [Denise Zmekhol]

other state capitals (this figure did not include workers in the so-called informal sector). Meanwhile, talks with foreign commercial banks that held much of Brazil's $121 billion foreign debt had bogged down, the banks rejecting Brazil's proposal to tie debt service payments to its future "capacity to pay."

Meanwhile, Brazil's land problem remained without solution. Amazonia continued to be the scene of violent clashes between great landowners who frequently acquired their land illegally and small farmers whose tiny plots would not support their families. Peasants who resisted usurpation and exploitation faced threats, harassment, and murder. Rent-a-killer agencies (*agências de pistolagem*) operated in many areas; they offered a sliding scale ranging from $600 for a peasant to $4,000 for an elected official. In southern Pará

state 172 rural activists were killed. A judge in Rio Maria (Pará state) expressed surprise about the excitement caused by such killings; "they were only peasants," he said. The Collor government did little to protect peasant leaders or punish their assassins. Arrests were rare and prosecutions rarer still. The conviction in December 1990 of a cattle rancher and his son for the murder of the celebrated Chico Mendes, an organizer of the rubber tappers and defender of the rain forest, was largely driven by international attention and pressure.

Responding to the devastating effects of the Collor program on wages, employment, and living standards, many unions went on strike and in some cases wrung concessions from employers and government. Collor's declining popularity was reflected in growing congressional and judicial resistance to his decrees. Left-of-center parties now held 246 votes in the new Congress, forming a strong opposition to President Collor.

Then, in a series of dramatic events in 1992, President Collor's administration collapsed amid accusations of personal corruption on a large scale. Congressional investigations established that Collor and his associates had accumulated at least $32 million in public funds and payoffs, but that amount was considered only a fraction of the total involved. After months of investigations, revelations, and legal maneuvering, Collor, who had campaigned on an anticorruption platform, resigned just before Congress would have voted to subject him to an impeachment trial.

## ELECTORAL *ENGANOS* AND POPULAR PROTEST

Following Collor's resignation, his vice president, Itamar Franco, was named acting president. Franco, who was known for his nationalistic stands, had opposed Collor's neoliberal market reforms, including the privatization of state companies. On assuming the presidency, however, the unpredictable Franco announced that he would continue Collor's privatization program and honor Brazil's debt commitments but would assign priority to a campaign against hunger and poverty; he claimed the income of Brazil's poorest citizens had fallen 30 percent as a result of Collor's "false modernization program." Governing elites now understood clearly that the unadulterated neoliberal reforms so enthusiastically championed by the IMF, foreign investors, and Brazil's bourgeoisie were widely unpopular with the lower classes and therefore impossible to realize within the context of democracy, however carefully circumscribed.

This realization shaped a new debate between two groups within Franco's coalition cabinet: advocates of social reform who argued that growth to relieve hunger and poverty should take first place in a country where millions were destitute, where a "social time bomb" was ticking; and advocates of neoliberal economic reform who put first the need to achieve fiscal stability (the monthly inflation rate in late 1993 was over 30 percent) through reduced government spending, the sale of state companies, and improved tax collection. The conflict between

the cabinet's "social sector" and its "economic sector" and Franco's own unpredictability sometimes made it difficult to know in which direction the government was moving, but in general the neoliberal tendency had the better of it. To head his economic reform team Franco appointed as finance minister his former foreign minister, the major political figure and prominent sociologist Fernando Henrique Cardoso. Cardoso's program centered on deficit reduction through budget cuts and on securing the constitutional and fiscal changes needed to achieve tax reform, privatize state companies in such sensitive areas as oil, mining, and telecommunications, and promote foreign investment. But the program encountered strong resistance from left-wing parties who opposed the austerity and privatization plans, from state governments dismayed by demands that they pay their large debts to the federal government, and from members of congress who had their eyes fixed on the 1994 general election and feared the impact of unpopular measures like tax increases on their own fortunes.

That election would be the most sweeping in Brazilian history, with the president, two-thirds of the Senate, the Chamber of Deputies, the governors of all twenty-seven states, and deputies in the state assemblies all coming up for election. It also promised to be the most important election in Brazil's history, with voters likely to be offered a choice between the neoliberal profit-driven model of economic growth, based on exports and foreign investment, and a more statist, autonomous model of development, oriented toward the internal market and the solution of the country's great social problems. Workers' Party leader Lula, himself an automobile worker and trade unionist who had opposed the military dictatorship, championed the latter and campaigned tirelessly throughout the country, repeating his pledge to implement agrarian reform, fight unemployment, increase agricultural production, and improve health and education.

But Lula's chief rival was Cardoso, a distinguished academic who even described himself as representing the "viable left" (in contrast to Lula's "utopian left"). This reflected the increasingly leftward leanings of the Brazilian electorate. Cardoso's trump card was a new economic stabilization plan, the "Real Plan" (*Plan Real*), named after the new currency that was introduced on July 1. Under this tight-money plan, the monthly inflation rate fell from 50 percent in June to 6.1 percent in July 1994. Cardoso counted on the support of workers, whose salaries had been readjusted every two months but quickly lost their value as a result of uncontrollable price increases. Cardoso's plan, combined with promises of sweeping social reform and the right's fear of a leftist victory, led moderates and conservatives to unify behind Cardoso, who won decisively.

Cardoso faced staggering problems when he took office in 1995. True, the Brazilian economy grew strongly, with exports for the first five months of the year reaching $15.5 billion, an all-time record. But these exports consisted mainly of raw materials like soya products, coffee beans, iron ore, and some manufactured goods like footwear and auto parts that were extremely vulnerable to fluctuations in market demand. Moreover, the growth of these exports, produced mostly by highly mechanized agribusinesses and plants, had little or no multiplier effect. This was reflected in continuing high unemployment figures and the rapid growth of the informal sector of the economically active population, believed to range between 30 and 60 percent of the total. Cardoso's program of a balanced budget and the Real Plan tamed the monster of inflation, but other economic and social problems still loomed large.

Revealing once again Brazil's extraordinary vulnerability to global economic changes, the Asian financial crisis in the fall of 1997 panicked the Brazilian stock market and unleashed a speculative assault on its currency, the real. To defend the real against devaluation and still attract the foreign capital on which it depended to finance the nation's fiscal deficit (then 6 percent of gross domestic product, or GDP), Cardoso doubled interest rates to 40 percent and announced an austerity package of spending cuts and tax increases designed to save $17.7 billion, or 2.5 percent of GDP. Although Cardoso, facing reelection in the fall of 1998, sought to immunize social spending

from these draconian budget cuts, they plunged Brazil into a severe recession. Industrial production and unemployment rates continued to climb; in São Paulo, the country's industrial heartland, even official estimates of unemployment rose to 17 percent in 1997.

Another major social problem was the grossly inequitable distribution of land. Less than 3 percent of the population owned almost 60 percent of Brazil's arable land, 62 percent of which lay uncultivated and unoccupied. Meanwhile, 5 million rural families were landless and lacked the means to earn an income with which to purchase their survival. Although Cardoso acknowledged that "we need agrarian reform," his government was slow to enforce a 1993 law permitting the government to expropriate (with adequate compensation) lands that were 75 percent idle. Consequently, under the auspices of the Catholic Church, some 42,000 landless families joined together to form the Landless People's Movement (MST), which organized a campaign of direct action to invade uncultivated lands and establish "squatter" communities that gave more than 140,000 families access to land and pressured the Cardoso government to promise land to an additional 280,000 families.

But these popular victories often came with a heavy price. Jorge Neri, an indigenous leader and MST activist whose own family lost their communal lands during the construction of the Trans-Amazonian Highway, participated in more than sixty-seven land invasions, many of which ended in violence, but none so graphic as the wholesale slaughter of nineteen squatters by policemen and hired thugs in full view of television cameras. Despite international protests, however, no one was ever arrested, much less tried and convicted. For his part, although he deplored the violence, President Cardoso also chastised the MST as a "threat to democracy," thereby revealing the extraordinary shadow that historical memories of military dictatorship still cast over Brazil's "free institutions." Lest Cardoso's subtle allusion be lost, the local president of a landowners' organization was characteristically more blunt: if the government failed to curb the MST's activities, he boldly announced, "we could have a repeat of the coup d'état."

The Landless People's Movement (MST) demanded a more equitable distribution of land, occupied uncultivated lands, and galvanized a popular resistance that effectively forced President Cardoso to moderate his government's neoliberal policies. [Wide World Photos]

Widespread poverty was yet another problem that successive neoliberal policies only seemed to aggravate. According to government figures, the number of people living in poverty increased steadily from 50.9 million in 1979 to 61.03 million in 1987 to 64.7 million in 1989 and jumped 10 percent in 1990 to 69.8 million, almost half the entire population. Moreover, 32 million people, 21 percent of all Brazilians, lived in extreme poverty. Sixty percent of this indigent population lived in the Northeast, racked by recurrent droughts that wiped out crops and jobs and produced a water shortage that threatened the area with a large-scale spread of cholera. Anthropologist Nancy Scheper-Hughes, with many years of work and residence in the region, noted that throughout the 1980s diseases like typhoid, tuberculosis, leprosy, and bubonic plague, once thought to be under control, resurfaced in Brazil, especially in the Northeast. Calling them diseases of "disorderly development," she traced their roots to the "social relations that produce rural to urban migration, unemployment, *favelas* [shantytowns], illiteracy, and malnutrition." She described an area that was still "in a transitional stage of state formation that contained many traditional and semifeudal structures, including its legacy of local political bosses (coronéis) spawned by an agrarian *latifundista* class of powerful plantation estate masters and their many dependents." And she quoted the words of a woman factory worker, disillusioned with civilian and military governments: "We need a government that will take care of the people, but I have begun to think that this doesn't exist; that it is another *engano* [deceit]."

The Northeast and the Amazon may provide the most extreme illustrations of the "disorderly development" that characterized contemporary Brazil, but the crisis pervaded every part of the country and most dramatically affected urban women, who were forced to shoulder increasing burdens in the workplace, working for low wages, even as their unpaid familial responsibilities in the home grew proportionately with the decline of public services in health care, education, and day-care. This crisis actually sharpened under the civilian, democratically elected regimes in power since 1985, regimes that embraced even more ardently than the discredited military rulers their neoliberal economic policies and their model of dependent capitalist development. Official figures told the story. According to the World Bank, in the 1980s the percentage of Brazilians surviving on less than $2 a day rose from 34 percent to 41 percent. At the same time the income gap between the rich and poor widened. According to Brazil's 1991 census, the poorest 10 percent of the population had less than 1 percent of the nation's wealth. The richest 10 percent, on the other hand, held 49 percent of the nation's wealth.

But this "disorderly development" could have created still more problems were it not for the determined opposition of diverse nationalist groups, including trade unions like the Central Federation of Workers, environmental clubs, social protest organizations like the Landless People's

Movement, various political parties, and certain loyal coroneis—all of whom defended popular interests against the worst excesses of neoliberalism. Senator Benedita da Silva, the nation's first elected *favelada* (slum dweller) and most prominent Afro-Brazilian woman activist, proudly claimed that "Brazil is perhaps the country in Latin America that has most resisted the neoliberal model, and our unions are on the forefront of this resistance."

Although politically divided, this social opposition nonetheless influenced the contours of Brazilian political debate. Even Cardoso, defending his leftist, nationalist credentials, sought to identify his policies with these popular interests, insisting that his privatization of government services never sought to eliminate the role of the state in Brazil's national development but merely to transform its function from a "producer state" to a "regulatory state." State social programs, he conceded, "are necessary because we cannot expect the market to solve the problem of poverty." This blend of neoliberal, market-centered policies and state-supported social services made Cardoso an elusive target for his political enemies, enabling him to win reelection in fall 1998 with slightly more than 50 percent of the votes.

For almost a decade, Cardoso worked to integrate the nation's economy into the global marketplace, adopting neoliberal reforms endorsed by the IMF and relying on a steady expansion of exports, foreign investment, privatization, and overseas loans to finance modest social programs and produce economic growth that averaged 2 percent since 1997. As a result, debt service as a share of export income rose steadily from 26 percent in 1993 to an improbable 122 percent in 1999. More distressingly, however, income inequality remained the highest in Latin America and poverty likewise stayed stubbornly high, falling only slightly from

46 to 45 percent between 1990 and 2001. This record ordinarily would not be expected to win considerable public support, but Cardoso's populist rhetoric and a divided political opposition ensured repeated electoral success.

Cardoso was unable to pass his good fortune to his successor, however. By 2002 the collapse of neighboring Argentina's economy, growing uncertainties in U.S. money markets, and a generalized global market contraction reduced foreign investment and external demand for Brazilian exports. With a stalled economy and few state resources left to sell, it was unclear how Brazil would pay its oppressive $245 billion public debt, stimulate renewed growth, and satisfy popular demands for greater equality. In the October 2002 presidential elections, the Brazilian people offered their authoritative answer and overwhelmingly elected veteran presidential candidate and leader of the leftist Workers' Party, Lula da Silva, who promised to "break with the current economic model" and "suspend or reevaluate the privatization program." Lula's platform sought to unite a broader coalition of leftist parties, ranging from Liberals to Communists. Presenting himself as a more mature, sophisticated candidate, Lula also went out of his way to reassure nervous investors that his government would honor its legitimate obligations, but he also promised to "negotiate new ones with an eye to protecting national interests and without accepting impositions."

Barring a repeat of the electoral enganos that had plagued the nation's past, it seemed as if the future augured a change for Brazil's developmental model. No wonder the George W. Bush administration made clear its displeasure with Brazil's democratic politics and Goldman, Sachs and Co., an influential stock brokerage firm, urged its clients to shift their investments to Mexico!

# Storm over the Andes: The Struggle for Land and Development

16

I N THE SECOND HALF of the twentieth century, reform came at last to three countries whose economic and social structures were among the most archaic in Latin America: the Andean republics of Peru, Bolivia, and Ecuador. Here, as elsewhere on the continent, the movement for reconstruction fused the effort to modernize with the struggle for greater social justice for the masses: economic sovereignty, industrialization, and land reform were the main slogans of the Andean revolutions. But the presence of large, compact indigenous groups, ranging from some 70 percent of the population of Bolivia to about 40 percent of the populations of Peru and Ecuador, gave a distinctive character to the nationalist, reformist movements in these countries.

## Three Andean Revolutions

### BOLIVIA, 1952–2003

Landlocked Bolivia, with the largest indigenous population of the three lands, was the scene of the first true Andean social revolution. This revolution unfolded within the historical context of racial, class, and gender conflicts unleashed by foreign investment, transatlantic market growth, and dependent capitalist development. During the late nineteenth century, highland indigenous commu-

nities had agreed to pay tribute and provide seasonal labor services to Hispanic hacendados in exchange for their recognition of indigenous communal land rights, but the lure of larger profits produced by a growing market demand for exports led them to expand their haciendas at the expense of the indígenas.

In the early twentieth century, the *caciques apoderados*, an armed indigenous movement that spread throughout the Andean highlands, defended their community lands and cultural traditions in violent uprisings like the 1921 Aymara Rebellion, led by Jesús de Machaqa, and the Chayanta Rebellion of 1927, which together mobilized thousands of peasants. This rural ferment, further complicated by growing worker unrest in the mines, factories, and urban centers, where a nascent women's movement also became active, led to greater collaboration among the army, landed oligarchs, and their foreign allies. Against this background, the disastrous results of the Chaco War (1932–1935), economic depression, and the growing domination of foreign mining companies inspired by wartime demand for strategic mineral raw materials all combined to alienate middle-class support for successive military dictatorships that had dominated Bolivian politics before 1940.

The last straw was the army's 1942 Cataví massacre of unarmed striking miners and their

395

families. Fearing greater social unrest, the mobilization of popular sectors, and its implications for their own power and property, middle-class activists organized the National Revolutionary Movement (MNR) and led a massive protest that brought the reformist government of Gualberto Villaroel to power the following year. But Villaroel was assassinated three years later. Thereafter, during a six-year struggle, the MNR mobilized the countryside and urban centers. Women especially played a significant role: the Women Workers' Federation (FOF) and the Barzolas, the MNR's infamous female "secret police" (named for María Barzola, a woman miner who died in the Cataví massacre), organized street demonstrations, hunger strikes, and other political protests.

By 1952 the MNR, led by Victor Paz Estenssoro, finally overthrew the rule of the great landlords and tin barons with the support of armed miners and peasants. The Bolivian land reform, begun by the spontaneous rising of the peasantry and legitimized by the revolutionary government of President Paz Estenssoro, broke the back of the latifundio system in Bolivia. Like the Mexican land reform, however, the Bolivian reform created some new problems even as it solved some old ones. The former latifundia were usually parceled out into very small farms—true minifundia—and the new peasant proprietors received little aid from the government in the form of credit and technical assistance. Yet despite its shortcomings, the Bolivian land reform brought indisputable benefits: some expansion of the internal market, some rise in peasant living standards, and, in the words of Richard W. Patch, "the transformation of a dependent and passive population into an independent and active population."

Women, workers, and indigenous communities became politically energized. Women joined private charitable associations and international organizations like the Inter-American Women's Commission (CIM) to agitate for the right to vote, civil equality, indigenous rights, and greater access to education. Lydia Gueiler Tejada, for example, advocated "the free association of women in legitimate defense of her interests, without distinction of class, race, creed, or even political ideas."

Mineworkers, led by Juan Lechín, demanded nationalization of the tin mines and *control obrero*, workers' control in the management of state-owned mines. Indigenous communities called for immediate, wholesale land reform and greater cultural freedom.

In response, the new government nationalized the principal tin mines, most of which were controlled by three large companies, and recognized its debt to the armed miners by placing the mines under joint labor-government management. It also abolished the literacy and gender restrictions on voting and thus enfranchised women and the indigenous masses. But the new regime inherited a costly, rundown tin industry, while the initial disruptive effect of the agrarian reform on food production added to its economic problems.

Increasingly fearful of the lower classes' revolutionary demands for equality and social justice, and under strong pressure from the United States, which made vitally needed economic aid to the revolutionary government conditional on the adoption of conservative policies, the MNR leadership gradually moved to the right. The government of Paz Estenssoro offered generous compensation to the former owners of expropriated mines, invited new foreign investment on favorable terms, ended labor participation in the management of the government tin company, and reduced welfare benefits to the miners.

Likewise, Paz abandoned any particular interest in women's rights or their social agenda and, instead, cynically manipulated the party's historic support for women's enfranchisement to secure their votes. According to Domitila Barrios de Chungara, a militant activist in the mineworkers' Committee of Housewives (CAC), Paz, who excluded women from leadership positions in the government, nonetheless used the Barzolas women to disrupt radical working-class protests: "the Barzolas would jump in front of them, brandishing razors, penknives, and whips, attacking the demonstrators." But the largely middle-class male movement's patriarchal prejudices clearly limited the political ascendancy of women revolutionaries like Gueiler Tejada, a militant feminist and one-time commander of MNR militias, whose political influence dissipated after she was assigned to a distant diplomatic post in Germany.

Paz also ignored the needs of Bolivia's indigenous peoples, which caused Laureano Machaka, an Aymara peasant leader opposed to the government's policies, to organize a short-lived independent Aymara Republic in 1956. Equally important, Paz agreed to the restoration of a powerful U.S.-trained national army to offset the strength of peasant and worker militias. These retreats broke up the worker–middle class alliance formed during the revolution and facilitated the seizure of power in 1964 by right-wing generals.

In the violent ebb and flow of Bolivian politics since 1964, governments rose and fell, but a persistent theme was the conflict between radical workers, women, students, and nationalist military on the one side and a coalition of elite businessmen, politicians grown wealthy through U.S. aid, and conservative military on the other. The indigenous peasantry, neutralized by the land reform that satisfied its land hunger, initially remained passive or even sided with the government in its struggles with labor, but later unrest began to grow as a result of deteriorating economic conditions.

Major factors in Bolivia's continuing political and economic crisis since 1964 were the collapse in the price of tin, the country's major traditional export, compensated for by the meteoric rise of cocaine as its chief dollar earner; heavy pressure on Bolivia by international lending agencies to adopt neoliberal policies of austerity and privatization; and equally heavy pressure by the United States on Bolivia to take part in a "war on drugs."

The overall rightward direction of Bolivian politics since 1964 was reflected in the important election of July 1985, in which neither former dictator, General Hugo Banzer Suárez, nor Paz Estenssoro, the 78-year-old leader of the 1952 revolution, commanded more than 50 percent of the vote. Disillusioned with politics, two-thirds of the electorate stayed away from the polls.

Although Congress, with the support of leftist deputies, eventually elected Paz president, pressure from Banzer and the International Monetary Fund (IMF), which demanded a severe austerity program as a condition for badly needed new loans, forced him to the right. Accepting the IMF's terms, he slashed government subsidies for basic services and food, froze wages, devalued the currency over 1,000 percent, removed all restrictions on foreign imports and investments, and resumed payments on Bolivia's foreign debt.

In alliance with Banzer, Paz announced a neoliberal plan designed to end hyperinflation and stabilize the economy. The plan, drafted by Harvard economist Jeffrey Sachs, called for closing down as many as eleven unprofitable state-owned mines, laying off thousands of workers, selling other state enterprises to the private sector, making deep cuts in public services, and increasing taxes. Paz's decision to close down Bolivia's largest tin mine in August brought the conflict between the government and the labor movement to a head. The miners' union called a general strike and thousands began a march on the capital of La Paz. The government imposed a state of siege, arresting hundreds of labor and community leaders, and sending troops, tanks, and planes to patrol the mining regions.

The mining crisis added to the tension caused by a 1986 decision to invite U.S. troops to join with the Bolivian military in "Operation Blast Furnace," a campaign to eradicate the country's cocaine laboratories. Ironically, the cocaine trade was the most dynamic sector of Bolivia's economy—despite these well-publicized anti-narcotic raids, this chief source of dollars was compensating for the sharp decline in the country's export earnings. Sale of coca paste generated $600 million annually, one-third more than the nation's legal export earnings of $400 million.

The conflict between the miners and the government took a dramatic turn when some one thousand miners protested government mine-closing plans, the state of siege, and other repressive measures by occupying mine shafts and launching a hunger strike. The miners' plight and the stubborn refusal of the government to negotiate a solution to the conflict caused growing public sympathy and demonstrations of support for the miners. In a momentous show of solidarity, the Bolivian National Federation of Peasant Women led national sympathy strikes and blockades to protest the government's neoliberal policies.

Aware of the unpopularity of its position, the Paz government accepted the offer of church mediation in its dispute with the miners. Eleven days of talks produced an agreement providing for the release of a hundred labor, peasant, and community leaders, a halt to government efforts to close mines, new jobs or compensation for miners who lost jobs, a lifting of the blockade on the flow of supplies to the mining regions, and consultations with the union on further decisions regarding mines.

The miners, the backbone of the *Central Obrera Boliviana* (COB), historically Latin America's strongest labor movement, had beaten off government efforts to destroy their union. But there was no indication of a change in the government's overall economic policy, a neoliberal, free-market policy that sought to eliminate or sell off state-owned industries, remove tariff barriers to foreign imports, and lift all restrictions on foreign investment. The fruits of that policy were apparent in the decline of traditional industries, a drop in consuming power of some 40 percent in 1985–1986, and an unemployment rate of 30 percent.

Paz and Sachs celebrated their program's successful conquest of inflation. However, the resulting high unemployment contradicted their free-market theory that assumed the tens of thousands of displaced miners would find work in the private sector. But the only expanding private-sector economic activity in Bolivia was coca and cocaine production. Thousands of miners, finding no alternative employment, invested the indemnification money they received from the government in land and began to grow coca. Bolivian coca-leaf production increased 60 percent—from 50,000 metric tons before the Sachs plan to 80,000 afterward—making Bolivia the second largest producer of coca. It was also the second largest producer of cocaine. An estimated 500,000 Bolivians were now dependent on the coca economy, which made cocaine "like a cushion that is preventing a social explosion."

The neoliberal policies that made Bolivia dependent on coca cultivation also increased its dependence on U.S. military and financial aid, which ironically was conditioned by an agreement to mobilize the Bolivian army, as an instrument of the U.S. war on drugs, to eradicate coca plantings. Joint U.S.-Bolivian sorties were soon regularly occurring in the Chaparé region, where most of Bolivia's coca was cultivated. But there was no evidence that the sorties, the destruction of access roads, and other military measures won the Bolivian war on drugs. Increasing or declining supplies of coca from the Chaparé region seemed above all to reflect the movement of peasants into and out of coca cultivation according to fluctuations in coca-leaf prices.

Recognition by the Clinton administration that the highly militarized Andean "drug war" approach—after an expenditure of nearly $1 billion—had not achieved its goals, resulted in a sharp reduction in drug war allotments to Bolivia, Colombia, and Peru. Meanwhile, indigenous peasant communities, whose livelihoods increasingly depended on coca-leaf cultivation, fiercely resisted all Bolivian and U.S. military efforts to eradicate it. Under their relentless pressure, the Bolivian government in 1992 sought to decriminalize the coca leaf, as opposed to cocaine. This "coca diplomacy" stressed the coca leaf's alleged medical benefits. Coca had been used for centuries in Bolivia and other Andean countries to alleviate hunger and counter the debilitating effects of living at high altitudes. However, U.S. drug policy sternly opposed any proposal to end the illegal status of the coca leaf.

During the 1990s successive presidential elections provided a forum for populist campaign promises that invariably disguised neoliberal policies. Gonzalo Sánchez de Lozada, a millionaire businessman, won a comfortable victory in 1993, with 36 percent of the vote in a field of four candidates. At his inauguration, attended by Fidel Castro, to whom the new president granted his first formal audience, and by Rigoberta Menchú, the Guatemalan Nobel Peace Prize winner, Sánchez proclaimed his commitment to the country's poor and promised to redistribute income.

But the core of his economic program was the privatization of state enterprises and state restructuring demanded by the IMF and the World Bank

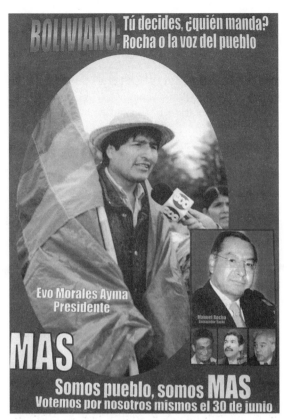

Evo Morales, a leader of Bolivia's indigenous rights movement and defender of peasant coca farmers, emerged as a powerful political force in that nation's 2002 presidential elections. As this poster shows, his campaign, which asked voters to choose between U.S. Ambassador Manuel Rocha and "the voice of the people," focused on the U.S. intervention in Bolivia's internal affairs.
[Reuters NewMedia Inc./Corbis]

as the condition for continued economic aid to Bolivia. One month after the inauguration he fired ten thousand state workers, sparking a wave of strikes and demonstrations, led by the Bolivian Workers' Central (COB), that paralyzed the country for weeks.

The crisis over state restructuring, combined with a renewed crisis in the tin-mining industry, itself the result of falling world market prices, led to the closing of hundreds of small mining cooperatives employing thirty-five thousand workers, and to accumulating losses by the much diminished state-owned Corporación Minera de Bolivia (Comibol). Because tin accounted for almost 49 percent of Bolivia's total exports, the fall in its price had a disastrous impact on the country's trade balance.

By the end of Sánchez's term, Bolivian society remained desperately poor; despite moderately high annual economic growth rates, population increases produced an annual per capita income of only $800—next to Haiti, the lowest in the hemisphere. But even this figure understated the social crisis, because real wealth in Bolivia was so unequally distributed: 78 percent of urban households lived below the poverty line, and of these, 40 percent were classified as "indigent," meaning that their income did not cover their most basic needs.

Moreover, poverty there as elsewhere had a distinctively feminine cast: 10 percent of women were single heads of households, 67 percent of whom were raising one or more children. Two-thirds of rural women were illiterate and therefore limited to extremely low-wage jobs. Thirty-three percent of all children were chronically malnourished. Even Sánchez conceded that "while the economy is going well, what is going poorly are the social problems of the country."

The decade ended with neoliberalism firmly entrenched in the policies of the new president and former dictator Hugo Banzer, who soon resigned for health reasons in favor of Jorge Quiroga. This produced a stable, even impressive, economic growth rate averaging 4 percent annually, as elsewhere in the region largely financed by high interest rates to attract foreign capital, which expanded external debt from $385 to $494 million by 1999. But it also left over 5 million people—60 percent of the nation's population—impoverished, with the second-highest infant mortality rate (57 of 1000) in the hemisphere and the third-lowest life expectancy (64). Underemployment was widespread and unemployment rates hovered around 12 percent. Bolivian women, workers, trade unions, indigenous rights activists, and debtors' organizations increasingly joined together to protest neoliberalism's negative social consequences; they often won modest victories—for example, reversing the privatization of parts of the state-owned Bolivian Mining Company (COMIBOL) in 2002.

As the new millennium opened, it was clear that more than a decade of neoliberalism had brought Bolivia no closer to prosperity or balanced development. Even the *Economist*, the conservative English tribune of free trade, had to acknowledge that Bolivia's experience had sorely tested faith in market forces: "Market economics, whatever its promise for the future, has not brought prosperity to the poor."

This apparently also was a conclusion reached by the declining share of politically active Bolivians. In the 2002 elections, none of the presidential candidates sang the praises of privatization and unfettered markets. Former president and millionaire mine owner Gonzalo Sánchez de Lozada, who won a narrow plurality (22 percent) of the vote, promised to improve the free market by using state revenues to create jobs. But all the others severely criticized neoliberalism and called for its rejection or reform. The candidate of the Movement Toward Socialism (MAS), Evo Morales, a defiant leader of indigenous coca growers, shocked all observers by finishing second in the balloting with 20.94 percent. He advocated indigenous rights, suspension of foreign debt service, renationalization of industries privatized over the previous two decades, and state regulation of the economy to reduce poverty and promote greater social equality. Because no candidate received 50 percent of the vote, the new Congress selected Sánchez. Nonetheless, two things seemed certain: indigenous peoples, whose congressional representation increased from 10 to 30 percent, would play a more influential role in the nation's future, and there would be a change in the reigning neoliberal development model. According to Bolivian political analyst Carlos Toranzo, Evo Morales and Bolivia's newly mobilized indigenous rights movement represented "ideas that are in style all over the world—antiglobalization, antineoliberalism, anti-imperialism."

## ECUADOR, 1972–2003

Ecuador, the smallest of the Andean republics, experienced the faint beginnings of a social revolution in 1972, when a group of nationalist military headed by General Guillermo Rodríguez Lara ousted the aging, demagogic President José María Velasco Ibarra, who had dominated Ecuadorian politics for the previous four decades. Velasco Ibarra had favored a dependent industrialization, shaped by the Alliance for Progress and based on massive importation of foreign capital and goods. This rapid modernization rested on the 1964 Agrarian Reform Act, which abolished the *huasipungo*, the country's serf-like labor system, expropriated church lands and inefficient haciendas, but also promoted colonization of so-called *tierras baldías*, untitled lands most of which had been occupied historically by self-sufficient indigenous communities. The discovery of oil in lowland territories in the late 1960s accelerated incursions into indigenous lands and cultural autonomy, even as petroleum production threatened the environment by contaminating surface and underground water supplies. By the early 1970s, foreign interests controlled some 35 percent of all industrial enterprises, nearly 60 percent of all commercial enterprises, and half of all banking assets in Ecuador.

The new nationalistic military junta promised social reform, including radical land reform, and offered a program of rapid economic development that stressed industrialization and the modernization of agriculture. It also promised to reverse previous official policy that surrendered the country's rich oil resources in the Amazonian lowlands to foreign companies. The new government counted on revenue from oil to finance the planned reforms and program of economic development.

Five years later, however, the advance of the Ecuadorian Revolution appeared to be stalled. Opposition from the still-powerful hacendado class had almost completely paralyzed agrarian and tax reform. Some land had been distributed to the peasants, but big landowners controlled 80 percent of the cultivated area. The military government appeared virtually to have abandoned land redistribution in favor of cooperating with the hacendados to increase production and revenues by mechanization, greater concentration of landownership, and the ouster of peasants from the land. The result was growing peasant agitation for true land reform, accompanied by invasions of estates and clashes between peasants and security forces.

Finally, under pressure from foreign oil companies for lower taxes and wider profit margins—a pressure exerted through a boycott on oil exports—the military regime also retreated from its insistence on tight control over prices, profits, and the volume and rate of oil production. These concessions represented a defeat for the nationalist left wing of the military junta and sharpened the divisions within it.

In Ecuador, as in other Latin American countries under military control, the late 1970s saw a growing popular movement for social justice and a return to civilian rule. But unlike other countries in the region, groups like the Indigenous People's Organization of Pastaza (OPIP), founded in 1979, increasingly played an influential role in these movements, joining with women's rights activists and trade unionists. In addition to a return to democracy, indigenous leaders demanded that the government recognize their communal land titles, cultural identities, and political autonomy.

Aware of its economic failures and especially its failure to relieve the dismal poverty of the Ecuadorian masses—official figures showed that the wage earners' share of the national income had declined from 53 percent in 1960 to less than 46 percent in 1973 and that 7 percent of the population received more than 50 percent of the national income—the military appeared quite willing to abandon the burden of governing the country. In July 1978, Jaime Roldós, a populist candidate, handily won the ensuing presidential election. During the campaign, the young, energetic Roldós promised to revive agrarian reform and end foreign economic control.

Central to this program was the use of large amounts of Ecuador's oil earnings to modernize agriculture, promote industrialization, and construct a network of roads to expand the internal market. Roldós's five-year plan called for investment of $800 million in rural development that would bring some 3 million acres of coastal, highland, and Amazonian farmland into new production. The pace of agrarian reform was to be accelerated, with almost 2 million acres to be distributed to landless peasants by 1984. Roldós's foreign policy stressed greater independence from the United States, reflected in his maintenance of friendly relations with Cuba, expansion of diplomatic and commercial ties with socialist countries, and support for Central American revolutionary movements. But Roldós's ambitious reform and development program had hardly begun when he was killed in a plane crash in May 1981.

His successor inherited deteriorating economic conditions as a result of a developing recession and declining prices for Ecuadorian oil. The economic slump sharpened the social problems created by advances in industrialization and the modernization of agriculture. From 1970 to 1980 the proportion of peasants in the population had fallen from 68 percent to 52 percent. The agrarian reform, stressing mechanization and concentration of landownership rather than distribution of land to the landless, had ended semiservile relations in the countryside but aggravated the problem of landlessness and rural unemployment. The result was to swell the number of rural people fleeing to the cities in search of work that only few found. By the early 1980s the great port city of Guayaquil had a population of 1,000,000; an estimated two-thirds of its inhabitants were unemployed or underemployed and lacked adequate shelter, food, or medical care. Thus, in an atmosphere of economic and political crisis, social problems and tension accumulated with little prospect that solutions would soon be found.

In the mid-1980s, Ecuador, like Bolivia, became the scene of a determined effort to implement the free-market, neoliberal policies for which the United States under the Reagan administration provided a model. In 1984 León Febres Cordero was elected president and signed an agreement with the IMF to defer payment on Ecuador's foreign debt, which stood at about $7 billion and consumed more than 30 percent of Ecuador's export earnings to pay interest. The price exacted was that usually demanded of Third World countries by the IMF: Ecuador must take steps to encourage foreign investment and restrict domestic consumption, lower tariffs on foreign imports, and modify the monetary exchange system in favor of exporters. In this and in other ways, Febres justified the tribute paid to him by President Reagan when he visited Washington in January 1986: Febres, declared Reagan, was "an articulate champion of free enterprise."

A balance sheet of the impact of Febres Cordero's economic and social policies on Ecuadorian living standards made dismal reading. A study by Ecuador's Catholic University disclosed that foreign corporations took three dollars out of the country for every dollar they invested. Between 1981 and 1984 workers' share of national income fell from 32 to 20 percent and employers' profits rose from 60 to 70 percent. Ninety percent of schoolchildren suffered from parasitic diseases, and the infant mortality rate according to various estimates stood at between 150 and 250 per thousand.

In the 1988 general elections, Ecuadorians voiced their displeasure with neoliberalism. The country's trade unions mobilized behind a program calling for the nationalization of the oil industry, the rescinding of price hikes, and a 100 percent increase in the country's $80-per-month minimum wage. They helped elect Rodrigo Borja Cevallos, whose campaign stressed social needs over debt interest payments to foreign banks. But Borja faced what he called "the worst economic crisis" in Ecuador's history. In the last four years food prices had jumped 240 percent and half the labor force was unemployed or underemployed. The crisis sharply limited Borja's options in economic and social policy. A moderate leftist in the social democratic mold, Borja assured businessmen that his government would carry out no nationalizations but would seek to regulate the economy and support the private sector.

His efforts to achieve debt payment relief met with resistance from the foreign banks: Ecuador was forced to accept IMF demands for a devaluation of its currency, a commitment to raise fuel prices, and other austerity measures as a condition for starting debt rescheduling talks with creditor banks. As a result, the Borja regime faced growing opposition both on the right and among its former supporters on the left. Denouncing Borja's economic policies as unjust and dictated by the IMF, the socialist parties joined conservatives in voting censure of the ministers responsible for the austerity measures.

The growing militancy of Ecuadorian labor, reflected in a 1991 general strike, was matched by that of indigenous peoples, who made up more than 40 percent of the country's population. In 1990 organizations like OPIP and the Ecuadorian Confederation of Indigenous Nationalities (CONAIE) spearheaded the Inti Raymi uprising, which mobilized hundreds of thousands of supporters from eight provinces in the sierra and several in the Amazon. The indigenous demands included land redistribution and a constitutional declaration that Ecuador was a multiethnic country. Although the government agreed to dialogue with indigenous leaders, pressure from the great planters and ranchers resulted in the government's abandoning its promises. The new militancy of indigenous peoples, traditionally reputed to be peaceful and docile, caused alarm among the country's landed elite.

By 1992, Ecuadorians had come to distrust Borja's promises and opted instead for the populist pledges of Sixto Durán-Ballén, who campaigned on a program of state reconstruction and privatization. But his plan for the "modernization of the state" called for the dismissal of up to 120,000 employees out of a total state sector of 400,000 over the following four years and the privatization of 160 state companies. Durán-Ballén also announced a structural adjustment package that included a 35 percent devaluation of the national currency, fuel price increases of more than 125 percent, rises in electricity rates of up to 90 percent, and a 190 percent increase in cooking-gas prices.

Received with enthusiasm by international financial institutions, this plan caused an immediate drastic decline in Durán-Ballén's popularity at home. The major trade union, the United Workers' Front (FUT) and CONAIE both opposed him. Two months into his four-year term, a poll showed that half of those who had voted for him would not do so again and 75 percent disapproved of his policies. In mid-1993 the unions claimed that living standards had fallen by 50 percent since Durán-Ballén had taken office. The minimum wage was about

$30 a month, but unofficial estimates put the cost of a shopping basket of basic goods at about $250.

In 1993 this opposition mounted a successful "guerrilla campaign" of strikes and demonstrations to limit the government's neoliberal "modernization" program. Peremptory dismissals of state employees were abandoned, and the privatization of state companies in areas regarded as "strategic," such as oil, telecommunications, and electric power, would require the passage of special laws by Congress.

A nationwide teachers' strike, the longest such strike in Ecuador's history, grew into a major battle in the war between the president and labor. It was provoked when Durán-Ballén pushed through Congress changes in the code governing teachers' salary scales and school administration. The strike became a battle of wills; it ended after Congress passed a new package of changes that restored the status quo and assured the National Educators' Union's participation in school policymaking. The union declared that the strike was a turning point in the grassroots struggle against "the IMF-dictated policies that [the government] is implementing."

Another front in Ecuador's social wars opened when indigenous Huaoranis, who live deep in the Ecuadorian Amazon, traveled to Quito in 1993 to protest the intrusion of oil companies into their territory. The protest was aimed at halting the construction of a highway by the Dallas-based company Maxus that would run through the heart of the Huaorani reserves. The Huaorani complained that the road would bring in thousands of settlers and land speculators, leading to deforestation, loss of animal and plant species, and destruction of the indigenous economy and way of life.

Although President Durán-Ballén met with the Huaorani, he made no promises. But even the state oil company (Petroecuador) admitted that since 1972, when Ecuador began oil production in large quantities, pipeline failures had dumped 450,000 barrels of oil into the Amazon forest. According to a 1993 "Letter from the Amazon" in *The New Yorker*, "a spill filled the Napo [River] with a slick that stretched from bank to bank for forty miles." The Huaorani, wrote reporter Joe Kane,

"were trapped in the path of an American juggernaut, their fate bound up with a culture whose thirst for oil was second to none." "It is likely," Kane noted sardonically, "that the Huaorani will be wiped out for the sake of enough oil to meet United States energy needs for thirteen days."

The Huaorani promised to use force if necessary to prevent construction of the highway. In 1993 other Ecuadorian indigenous groups filed a billion-dollar class action suit in New York against the Texaco oil conglomerate over massive environmental devastation of the Oriente rain forest. According to the suit, Texaco knowingly dumped millions of gallons of crude oil into open pits and lakes in the region at the rate of 3,000 gallons a day for twenty years. A Harvard University study confirmed that most residents of the area suffered severe health problems as a result of the dumping.

By the 1996 presidential elections, Durán-Ballén's popularity had declined from more than 70 percent to less than 10 percent because of his neoliberal economic policies. Simultaneously, indigenous peoples joined with Afro-Ecuadorians, women, students, trade unions, and peasant organizations to form the Movement of National Pluricultural Unity Pachakutik, a political coalition that won many state offices and successfully lobbied for the creation of CONPLADEIN, an independent state agency, to represent the autonomous cultural and economic interests of black and indigenous Ecuadorians. Pachakutik, though a successful and growing political party, still functioned as a powerful social movement that mobilized "pluricultural" opposition to the newly elected President Abdala Bucaram, a wealthy businessman who also violated his 1996 populist presidential campaign promises by privatizing state assets and cutting state spending on social services. By February 1997, outrage over this violation of campaign promises, fueled also by charges of widespread corruption, led directly to Bucaram's ouster, an ensuing political crisis, and economic chaos, exacerbated by devastating El Niño–inspired floods that wiped out whole villages and destroyed basic infrastructure.

In 1998, after campaigning on a populist platform, new president Jamil Mahuad, a Harvard

In 2000, indigenous rights protesters joined with disgruntled army officers and various social movements to denounce the neoliberal polices of Ecuador's President Jamil Mahuad. His subsequent resignation unleashed a national political instability that recently culminated in the 2002 presidential election of Lucio Gutiérrez, a military officer who had supported the populist rebellion. [AFP/Corbis]

graduate, faced an economic crisis aggravated by a steep decline in global oil prices and sought relief by implementing a neoliberal austerity program in exchange for an $800 million IMF loan. His government promptly declared a state of emergency, abolished income taxes, bailed out the nation's private banks, doubled gasoline prices, and reduced spending on social services for the 60 percent of the nation's population classified as poor. Strikes and massive, angry protest marches proliferated. Unemployment grew to more than 50 percent and

Mahuad's popularity fell to 16 percent, prompting even his congressional allies to abandon him.

In January 2000 the United Workers' Front and CONAIE, representing indigenous peoples, together organized massive protests against Mahuad's neoliberal privatization plans and his dramatic increase of the price of bus transportation and cooking gas, all of which targeted the nation's poor majority and curried favor with wealthy Ecuadorian business leaders and foreign bankers. Angered by military budget cuts, elements of Ecuador's army later joined the opposition and effectively forced Mahuad to resign. Fearing the radicalism of this popular rising, especially its indigenous complexion, military officers in this racially and class-stratified nation organized a countercoup to restore Mahuad's vice president, Gustavo Noboa, to power.

Although he initially made concessions, Noboa soon confronted an economic crisis in which inflation surpassed 90 percent, unemployment exceeded 10 percent, and external debt almost equaled the total value of the nation's GDP. To tame inflation and generate revenues to repay foreign bankers, Noboa adopted the U.S. dollar as the nation's currency, slashed social spending, and sought to privatize an array of state resources, prompting domestic business elites to celebrate and popular forces to renew their resistance. Now joined by university students, CONAIE and the popular coalition launched yet another massive demonstration to "combat the neoliberal economic model." But this time, with thousands of indigenous peoples camped out in Quito, they also pressed the Noboa government to end its cooperation with U.S. and Colombian forces seeking to militarize the border and use Ecuadorian military bases to support Plan Colombia, a U.S. proposal for a military solution to neighboring Colombia's decades-long conflict.

Negotiations to end the protest ultimately reinforced the social movement's power and its grassroots democratic structure; the protestors won various concessions, including increased spending on national indigenous health, education, and development projects and a pledge to end "the regionalization of Plan Colombia, and the involvement of Ecuador in foreign conflicts." Emboldened by these gains, the protesters mobilized in support of the 2002 presidential candidacy of Lucio Gutiérrez, a retired colonel who had joined the 2000 rebellion of workers and indigenous people. Gutiérrez promised to reduce poverty, create jobs, and stimulate national production. He pledged to root out business corruption, reform tariffs, and allocate 15 percent of the budget to public works projects.

Notwithstanding these important victories for the popular opposition, the contest over Ecuador's future was far from over. A traditional propertied elite preserved its privileged positions and, dependent upon a foreign debt whose repayment annually consumed 25 percent of export income, Ecuador remained vulnerable to external pressure to ignore the democratic voice of its own citizens in favor of a developmental model that they unambiguously rejected. In fact, "dollarization" of the economy effectively limited the capacity of domestic democratic politics to affect national economic policy and also reinforced the nation's economic dependency on the United States, because it now had to pay for the importation of its circulating currency. Augusto de la Torre, director of the World Bank's Ecuador office, candidly admitted that "politics are now less relevant in Ecuador. If you talk to entrepreneurs now, they look at politics like they look at soap operas." As the importance of electoral politics receded, it was clear that, in the words of a Pachacutik representative, "the struggle will continue in other forms."

## PERU'S "AMBIGUOUS REVOLUTION"

A revolution of a unique kind began in Peru in October 1968. Developments in that country between 1968 and 1975 exposed the fallacy of the common assumption that the Latin American military constitutes one reactionary mass. Moving with greater speed and vigor than any civilian reformist regime in Latin American history, a military junta headed by General Juan Velasco Alvarado decreed nationalization of key industries and natural resources, land reform that transferred great estates to peasant and worker cooperatives, and creation of novel new forms of economic organization that should be "neither capitalist nor communist." In 1975 the Peruvian Revolution halted its advance and began a retreat that threatened even its major conquests—the agrarian reform and the great nationalizations—with erosion and even destruction. Yet it must rank among the more serious recent Latin American efforts to achieve a breakthrough in the struggle against backwardness and dependency. Despite its mistakes and failures, it made an indelible mark on Peruvian society. The study of those mistakes and failures should help Peruvians as they search for new approaches to the solution of their country's great national problems.

Peru's "ambiguous revolution" poses some intriguing questions. Why should a group of military officers, a class commonly regarded as the staunchest defenders of the old order in Latin America, launch a major attack on that order in Peru? What economic and social interests did the Peruvian military reformers represent? In the last analysis, was the Peruvian Revolution a "bourgeois revolution" designed to promote the rise of an autonomous native capitalism? If the military reformers failed to make a clean break with the past, with the model of dependent development and the problems it generates, what were the reasons for that failure? An attempt to answer these questions requires an examination not only of the revolution itself but of its late nineteenth century origins.

## Neocolonial Peru: The English and North American Connections, 1883–1968

The War of the Pacific left a heritage of political and social turbulence as well as economic ruin. Military and civilian leaders disputed one another's claims to be the legitimate president and mobilized *montoneros* (bands of guerrillas and outlaws) for their armed struggles. In some areas, the indigenous peasantry, having acquired arms during the war with Chile, rose in revolt against oppressive hacendados and local officials. Banditry was rife in parts of the sierra; on the coast, factions armed by landowners or their agents fought among themselves for control of irrigation canals or over property boundaries.

From the struggle for power the militarists once again emerged victorious: in 1884 Andrés Cáceres battled his way into Lima and seized the National Palace. Two years later, he was elected president for a four-year term. Under Cáceres, a slow, painful process of economic recovery began. His first concern was the huge foreign debt. In 1886 the Peruvian government negotiated the so-

called Grace Contract with British bondholders. This agreement created a Peruvian Corporation, controlled by the British bondholders, that assumed the servicing of Peru's foreign debt and received in exchange Peru's railways for a period of sixty-six years. The agreement confirmed British financial domination of Peru but also initiated a new flow of investments that hastened the country's economic recovery. Particularly important was the resulting rehabilitation of the railways and their extension to important mining centers, especially into La Oroya, whose rich silver, zinc, and lead mines began to contribute to the economic revival.

Economic recovery strengthened the political hand of the planter aristocracy and the commercial bourgeoisie, who were increasingly impatient with the arbitrary ways of the military caudillos. In 1895 their leader was the flamboyant Nicolás Piérola, who sought to bring the military under civilian control and led a successful revolt against Cáceres. Piérola presided over four years of rapid economic recovery. On the coast, the sugar plantations expanded at the expense of small landholders and indigenous communities and underwent intensive modernization. In the Andes, the economic revival spurred a renewed drive by hacendados to acquire indigenous communal lands, a drive extended to regions hitherto free from land-grabbing. An 1893 law that in effect reenacted Bolívar's decree concerning the division and distribution of communal lands facilitated the process of land acquisition. In this period there also arose a new contract labor system, the *enganche*, designed to solve the labor problem of coastal landlords now that Chinese contract labor was no longer easily available. By this system, indígenas from the sierra were recruited for prolonged periods to labor on coastal haciendas, sometimes under conditions of virtual serfdom.

### INDIGENOUS RESISTANCE

Yet the postwar period also saw the birth of a new sensitivity to the social struggle of indigenous peoples. The rise of this *indigenismo* among intellectuals was closely connected with the crisis of conscience caused by the disastrous War of the Pacific. By exposing the incompetence and irresponsibility of a creole elite that had totally failed to prepare Peru materially and morally for its greatest ordeal, the war led many intellectuals to turn to the indigenous peasantry as a possible source of national regeneration. At the University of San Marcos in Lima there arose a generation of teachers who rejected the traditional positivist tendency to brand Indians as inherently inferior. The alleged apathy, inertia, and alcoholism of indigenous peoples, these scholars claimed, resulted from the narrow, dwarfed world in which they were forced to live. But as a rule these bourgeois reformers ignored the economic conditions of indigenous peoples and focused on a program of education and uplift that would teach them ways to enter the new capitalist society.

The great iconoclast Manuel González Prada (1848–1918) rejected this gradual, reformist approach to the problem. "The Indian question is an economic and social question rather than one of pedagogy," he wrote. Schools and well-intentioned laws could not change a feudal reality based on the economic and political power of the *gamonales* (great landowners), lords of all they surveyed. Elimination of the hacienda system, therefore, was needed to rescue indigenous people. But that change would never come through the benevolence of the ruling class: "The Indian must achieve his redemption through his own efforts, not through the humanity of his oppressors." And González Prada advised them to spend on rifles and cartridges the money they now wasted on drink and fiestas. His powerful indictment of the oppressors of indigenous peoples, his faith in their creative capacity, and his rebellious spirit, expressed in prose that flowed like molten lava, profoundly influenced the next generation of intellectuals.

For their part, indigenous highland communities, whose passive resistance to the gamonales' encroachment on their lands and autonomy the intellectuals had mistaken for laziness and apathy, now openly rebelled. Sparked by indigenous leaders like Teodomiro Gutiérrez Cuevas, the Rumi Maqui movement, a millenarian insurrection that swept like wildfire through southern Peru and the central sierra between 1915 and 1930, proclaimed the restoration of Tawantinsuyu, the fabled empire of the great Inca kings.

## THE RETURN OF PARDO

Integration of indigenous peoples was Peru's gravest social problem, but the rapid economic advance that began under Piérola produced the emergence of a working class whose demands also threatened the peace and security of the ruling class. By 1904 an organized labor movement had arisen, and strikes broke out in Lima's textile mills and other factories. In 1918, during World War I, miners, port workers, and textile workers, responding to a catastrophic inflation of food prices, went on strike. Armed clashes took place between the strikers and the troops sent out to disperse them, and many strikers were arrested. News of the success of the Russian Revolution contributed to the workers' militancy. This movement culminated in a three-day general strike in January 1919; the workers demanded the implementation of currently unenforced social legislation, the reduction of food prices, and the imposition of the eight-hour workday. Under pressure from the workers, President Manuel Pardo granted part of their demands, including the eight-hour day for the manufacturing and extractive industries. The labor struggles of that stormy year merged with the struggle of university students for the reform of an archaic system of higher education that made the university the preserve of a privileged few and denied students any voice in determining policies and faculty appointments.

But sections of the oligarchy were convinced that this new and unstable political and social atmosphere required a different way of ruling. An astute businessman and politician, Augusto B. Leguía, who had served as minister of finance in the early 1900s and as president from 1908 to 1912, offered a new political model that could be called Caesarist: it combined unswerving fidelity to the dominant domestic and foreign interests with severe repression of dissidents and a demagogic program of nationalism and social reform designed to disarm the workers and achieve class peace. In July 1919 he seized power, sent Pardo into exile, and established a personal dictatorship that lasted eleven years (1919–1930).

### THE LEGUÍA REGIME: NORTH AMERICAN INVESTMENT AND PERUVIAN DISILLUSIONMENT

Leguía encouraged by every means at his disposal the influx of foreign—especially North American—capital. This was the cornerstone of his economic policies. Oil and copper were major fields of North American investment in Peru in this period. The fruits of Leguía's policy of opening the doors wide to foreign capital soon became evident; in 1927 a vice president of the First National City Bank wrote that "Peru's principal sources of wealth, the mines and oil-wells, are nearly all foreign-owned, and excepting for wages and taxes, no part of the value of their production remains in the country." Perhaps the most scandalous example of Leguía's policy of giving away Peru's natural resources was his cession of the oil-rich La Brea–Pariñas fields near the northern coastal town of Talara to the International Petroleum Company (IPC), a subsidiary of Standard Oil of New Jersey, in return for a minimal tax of about 71 cents a ton. This cession and a 1922 arbitral award confirming the dubious claims to the area in question of an English oil company, whose rights had passed to the IPC, became an abiding source of Peruvian nationalist resentment.

Peru under Leguía received a plentiful infusion of North American loans, amounting to about $130 million. The bankers were aware of the risks involved, but the prospects of extremely large profits made these transactions very attractive. A trail of corruption, involving Leguía's own family, followed these deals; Leguía's son Juan, acting as agent for Peru, received more than half a million dollars in commissions.

Leguía used the proceeds of these loans and the taxes on foreign trade and foreign investment operations for a massive public works program (including a large road-building program carried out with forced indigenous labor) that contributed to the boom of the 1920s. During those years, Lima was largely rebuilt, provided with modern drinking water and sanitation facilities, and embellished with new parks, avenues, bank buildings, a racetrack, and a military casino. But these amenities did not improve the living conditions of Andean peoples or dwellers in the wretched *barriadas* (shantytowns) that began to ring Lima.

Convinced that the threat of communism required some concessions to the masses, however, Leguía did make some gestures in the direction of reform. The constitution of 1920 had some striking resemblances to the Mexican constitution of 1917. It declared the right of the state to limit property rights in the interest of the nation, vested ownership of natural resources in the state, and committed the state to the construction of hospitals, asylums, and clinics. It empowered the government to set the hours of labor and to insure adequate compensation and safe and sanitary conditions of work. It also offered corporate recognition of indigenous communities, proclaimed their right to land, and promised primary education to their children. But these and other provisions of the constitution were, in the words of Fredrick Pike, a "model for the Peru that never was."

That same contrast between promises and performance marked Leguía's labor policy. During his campaign for the presidency, he denounced "reactionaries" and made lavish promises to the workers. Indeed, on seizing power in July 1919 he immediately freed the labor leaders imprisoned under Pardo. He also permitted a congress of workers to meet in Lima in 1921 and form a Federation of Workers of Lima and Callao. But when the labor movement began to display excessive independence, he intervened to crush it. Workers were forced to accept token reforms and a program of government- and church-sponsored paternalism, crumbs from the well-laden table of the wealthy.

Leguía's performance was especially disillusioning to the university students. Impressed by his promises of educational reform, they had proclaimed him "Mentor of the Youth" and supported his presidential campaign in 1919. But once in power, he sought to drive a wedge between students and workers, jailing student leaders and outlawing the Popular University of González Prada, organized by the students to provide workers with political education. Frequent jailings and deportations of dissident journalists and professors brought Leguía into chronic confrontation with students and faculty, who often went on strike, while the University of San Marcos was repeatedly closed down by the government.

The fledgling women's rights movement also fragmented during the Leguía dictatorship. In 1914, María Jesús Alvarado Rivera had created *Evolución Feminina*, a journal devoted to the cultivation of cross-class, interracial alliances in pursuit of women's liberation and social justice. But patrician women refused to join these mixed-race organizations. According to Carrie Chapman Catt, the U.S. feminist and president of the Pan-American Women's Suffrage Alliance, "the pure castillian woman would die before she moved equally herself with those of color." As a result, an aristocratic Peruvian National Women's Council supported Leguía, resisted broader social reforms, and largely favored enfranchisement of literate women because it would strengthen their conservative cause. Radicals like Alvarado and Magda Portal soon abandoned this feminism dominated by *"damas patrióticas civilistas"* and joined the class struggle against Leguía.

## INDIGENISMO AND SOCIALISM

The traditional oligarchical parties' surrender to the dictator and the weakness of the young Peruvian working class meant that the leadership of the opposition to Leguía fell to middle- and lower-middle-class intellectuals who sought to mobilize the peasantry and the workers for the achievement of their revolutionary aims. Socialism, anti-imperialism, and indigenismo provided the ideological content of the movement that issued from the struggles of the turbulent year of 1919, but indigenismo was the most important ingredient.

Influenced by the revered González Prada, these intellectuals believed that the revolution necessary to regenerate Peru must come from the sierra, from the Andean indigenous peoples, who would destroy age-old systems of oppression and

unify Peru again, restoring the grandeur that had been the Inca Empire. Common to most of the indigenistas was the belief that the Inca Empire had been a model of primitive socialist organization (a thesis rejected by modern scholars) and that the indigenous community had been and still was the "indestructible backbone of Peruvian collectivity" (in fact, by the 1920s almost all land in Peru was individually owned and worked). The mission of the intellectuals, they believed, was to blow life into the coals of indigenous rebellion and link it to the urban revolution of students and workers.

An influential indigenista of this period was Luis E. Valcarcel, author of the widely read *Tempest in the Andes* (1927). In ecstatic prose, Valcarcel hailed indigenous revolts of the sierra as portents of the coming purifying revolution. A more important and systematic thinker, José Carlos Mariátegui (1895–1930), attempted the task of wedding indigenismo to the scientific socialism of Marx and Engels. His major work was the *Seven Interpretive Essays on Peruvian Reality* (1928). Basing his theory on indigenous communal practices and traditions, on the revolutionary experience of other lands, and on his study of history and economics, Mariátegui concluded that socialism offered the only true solution for the indigenous problems.

Like other indigenistas of his time, Mariátegui idealized the Inca Empire, which he regarded as the "most advanced primitive communist organization which history records." But he opposed a "romantic and anti-historical tendency of reconstruction or re-creation of Inca socialism," for only its habits of cooperation and corporate life should be retained by modern scientific socialism. Moreover, he stressed that the coming revolution must be led by the urban proletariat. Before his untimely death, Mariátegui in 1929 founded the Peruvian Communist Party, which affiliated the next year with the Communist International.

Indigenismo was a major plank in the program of the *Alianza Popular Revolucionaria Americana* (APRA), a party founded in Mexico in May 1924 by Victor Raúl Haya de la Torre and Magda Portal, student leaders who had been exiled by Leguía. Haya de la Torre proclaimed that APRA's mission was to lead the indigenous and proletarian masses of Peru and all "Indo-America" in the coming socialist, anti-imperialist revolution. Despite the high-sounding rhetoric of *Aprista* propaganda, the party's first concern was and remained Peru's middle sectors—artisans, small landowners, professionals, and small capitalists. These groups' opportunities for development diminished as a result of the growing concentration of economic power in Peru by foreign firms and a dependent big bourgeoisie.

In a revealing statement in the mid-1920s, Haya de la Torre declared that the Peruvian working class, whether rural or urban, lacked the class consciousness and maturity needed to qualify it for the leadership of the coming revolution. He assigned that role to the middle class. To this opinion he joined a belief in the mission of the great man (himself) who "interprets, intuits, and directs the vague and imprecise aspirations of the multitude." Portal's view of Peruvian women was equally condescending; without APRA's guidance, she insisted, they could not be entrusted with the vote because of their low "cultural level" and "unquestioning dependence on masculine influence."

Haya de la Torre early assumed an ambiguous position on imperialism. Standing on its head Lenin's theory that imperialism was the last stage of capitalism, he argued that in weak, underdeveloped countries like Peru, imperialism was not the last but the first stage of capitalism, for there it provided the capital needed to create industry, a powerful working class, and the middle class that would lead the nation in a socialist revolution. From this to the position that imperialism must be encouraged and defended was an easy step, one that Haya de la Torre eventually took. Mariátegui, who was associated with Haya de la Torre in the student and labor struggles of the early 1920s, soon perceived the inconsistencies and ambiguities of his position and assailed APRA for its "bluff and lies" and its personalism. Despite or precisely because of its opportunism and the vagueness of its ideology, APRA managed to win over an important section of the Peruvian middle class, especially the students, during the three decades after 1920 and to gain great influence over groups of

peasantry and urban workers, whom it organized into unions that were its main political base.

## APRA VERSUS THE MILITARY

The onset of a world economic crisis in 1929, which caused a serious decline of Peruvian exports and dried up the influx of loans, brought the collapse of the Leguía dictatorship. But neither the small Communist party nor the stronger APRA movement was able to take political advantage of Leguía's downfall. An army officer of *cholo* (indigenous) background, Luis Sánchez Cerro, seized power and became the dominant figure in a ruling military junta. In 1931, Sánchez Cerro won the presidency campaigning on a populist platform that proclaimed the primacy of the indigenous problem, the need for agrarian reform through expropriation of uncultivated lands, and the aim of regulating foreign investments in the national interest. In effect, Sánchez Cerro had stolen much of APRA's thunder, to the annoyance of Haya de la Torre.

But the Apristas refused to accept the election results and launched an unsuccessful revolt in 1932 that led to mass executions and the assassination of Sánchez Cerro. This created a vendetta between the army and APRA that helps explain the long, stubborn opposition of the Peruvian armed forces to APRA's assumption of power, whether by force or peaceful means. More important, it enabled the financial and landed oligarchy to consolidate their power. Thereafter, they courted foreign investors like the U.S.-based International Petroleum Company, promoted export production, and presided over a stagnant economy due to low prices for the country's chief exports (copper, cotton, lead, and wool), a situation only temporarily relieved by growing demand and high prices during World War II (1939–1945) and the Korean war (1950–1953).

In the wars' aftermath, however, Peru, despite modest development of its extractive mineral industry, remained a largely agricultural, export-dependent country with a wealthy, powerful landed oligarchy, a weak and fragmented middle class, a marginalized indigenous peasant majority, and a largely unorganized and undeveloped urban working class. Nonetheless, APRA militants continued to agitate for policies designed to restore popular democracy, renew anti-imperialist struggle, and promote social justice. Largely influenced by the *comandos femeninos*, these policies included land reform; civil and political equality irrespective of race, class, or gender; and state regulation of foreign investment. In 1955, at the end of General Manuel Odría's dictatorial rule, Peruvian women finally won the right to vote, but little more. APRA's male leadership, fearful of a growing lower-class power, increasingly abandoned women and their social justice issues to curry favor with conservative elites.

Meanwhile the inequities of Peru's income distribution continued to increase, as did collisions between large landowners and increasingly militant and well-organized indigenous peasants. In some cases, peasants were revolting against precapitalist labor systems (like the yanacona system, which often required personal service); in others, violence arose as a result of the efforts of landowners to evict their tenants and sheep in favor of wage labor and cash rent systems. These evictions increased landlessness and population pressure in indigenous communities and accelerated the flow of highland emigrants to the coast, swelling the population of city slums and shantytowns.

This first generation of indigenous highland migrants, known as *provincianos*, now found themselves in a foreign environment, surrounded by hostile urban elites who ridiculed their rural lifestyles, scorned their racial origins, and limited their social, economic, and political opportunities. For hundreds of years, Peru's *criollo* elite had preserved its cultural authority and political power by institutionalizing a rigid race-based social hierarchy that defined criollos as "white," civilized, and superior; it likewise identified indigenous peoples, mestizos, and blacks as inferior, barbaric, ignorant, and uncivilized. Not surprisingly, the new migrants sought to assimilate into their strange surroundings by publicly emulating criollo culture even as they privately celebrated their various highland traditions. They settled together in *barriadas* (slums) or *pueblos jovenes* (squatter communi-

ties) and often supported their families by opening small businesses in the informal sector, selling a broad range of commodities on street corners or working as domestic servants. By the early 1960s, however, this postwar demographic shift had transformed them into a potentially useful political constituency that successive criollo politicians sought to exploit.

## BELAÚNDE: BROKEN PROMISES

In 1963, Peruvians elected President Fernando Belaúnde Terry, whose campaign had a decided indigenista tinge. Visiting the remotest Andean villages, Belaúnde extolled the Inca grandeur, called on the natives to emulate the energy and hard work of their ancestors, and proclaimed the right of the landless peasantry to land. But his performance in the field of agrarian reform did not match his promises. The agrarian law that issued from Congress the following year stressed technical improvement rather than expropriation and division of latifundia, with the hope that hacendados would adopt modern methods to improve production. As amended in Congress by a coalition of Apristas and rightists, the law exempted from expropriation the highly productive coastal estates, whose workers had been unionized by APRA, reserving for land distribution the archaic haciendas of the sierra. But the loopholes or exceptions were so numerous that the results of the law were very modest.

Meanwhile, Belaúnde's lavish promises had given great impetus to peasant land invasions. By October 1963 invasions had multiplied in the central highlands and were spreading to the whole southern part of the sierra. The land-invasion movement also changed its character; whereas before the peasants had seized only uncultivated lands, they now occupied cultivated land, arguing that they had paid for it with their unpaid or poorly paid labor of several generations. Militant peasant unions under radical leadership appeared, and a guerrilla movement arose in parts of the sierra. Meanwhile, a wave of strikes broke out in the cities, and workers occupied a number of enterprises in Lima and Callao.

These outbreaks took the Belaúnde administration by surprise. The extreme right, supported by APRA, demanded the use of the armed forces to repress the peasant movement. Indeed, APRA—once so "revolutionary"—called for the harshest treatment of the rebellious peasants. At the end of 1963, after some vacillation, the Belaúnde government decided to crush the peasant movement by force, a task the armed forces apparently assumed with reluctance, preferring "civic action" programs of a reformist type. By 1966 the peasant and guerrilla movements had been suppressed, at least for the moment. According to one estimate, the repression left 8,000 peasants dead and 3,500 imprisoned, 14,000 hectares of land burned with fire and napalm, and 19,000 peasants forced to abandon their homes.

Belaúnde had failed to solve the agrarian problem. He also failed to keep his promise to settle the old controversy between Peru and the International Petroleum Company over the La Brea–Pariñas oil fields, claimed by Peru to have been illegally exploited for some forty years. Finally, under strong pressure from U.S. interests, who delayed large planned investments in Peru, Belaúnde's government signed the Pact of Talara, which represented a massive surrender to the IPC. Peru regained the now almost exhausted oil fields, but in return agreed to the cancellation of claims for back taxes and illegal profits amounting to almost $700 million. IPC also received a new concession to exploit a vast area in the Amazon region and was allowed to retain the refinery of Talara, to which the government agreed to sell all the oil produced from the wells it had regained at a fixed price. A scandal rocked the country when the government, forced to publish the document, claimed to have "lost" the page setting the price that the IPC must pay the state oil company for its crude oil. As public indignation grew, the armed forces, opposition parties, and even the Catholic church denounced the agreement.

For Peru's military leaders, this was the last straw. For some years, they had engaged in intense soul-searching over the past and future of their country; now they were convinced that Belaúnde's government and the social forces that supported it had sold out the national interest and were incapable of solving Peru's problems. In October 1968 the armed forces seized the presidential palace, sent Belaúnde into exile, and established a military governing junta that began a swift transformation of Peru's economic and social structures.

## The Rise and Fall of the Peruvian Revolution, 1968–2003

### THE MILITARY ABOUT-FACE

Initially, the military seizure of power appeared to be another in the long series of military coups that punctuate the history of Peru and other Latin American countries—coups that change the occupant of the presidential palace but leave the existing order intact. The error of this opinion became evident as the self-proclaimed "Revolutionary Government of the Armed Forces," under the leadership of General and President Juan Velasco Alvarado, decreed the nationalization of oil, a sweeping agrarian reform law, and a law providing for workers' participation in the ownership and management of industrial concerns.

Observers found these events as startling, in the words of Fidel Castro, "as if a fire had started in the firehouse," for the Latin American military had traditionally been regarded as loyal servants of the area's oligarchies. But in Peru a social and ideological gulf had been developing between the military and civilian elites for decades. Most army officers came from a military family or from the lower-middle class. These officers, fearing the rise of an autonomous, indigenous peasant and working-class radicalism, sought to protect and promote national capitalist development in Peru by shifting power from landed oligarchs, foreign investors, and their government representatives to a socially responsible state controlled by a nationalistic new bourgeoisie.

Within a week, the Velasco junta had nationalized the IPC's oil fields and its refinery at Talara, and soon after it seized all its other assets. Having settled the IPC question, the junta went on to tackle the country's most burning economic and social questions.

## LAND REFORM AND NATIONALIZATION OF RESOURCES

Land reform was the key problem: Peru could not achieve economic independence, modernization, and greater social democracy without liquidating the inefficient, semifeudal latifundio system, the gamonal political system that was its corollary, and the coastal enclaves of foreign oligarchical power. Major specific objectives were to expand agricultural production and to generate capital for investment in the industrial sector; thus landowners were to be compensated for expropriated lands with bonds that could be used as investment capital in industry or mining. On June 24, 1969, President Velasco announced an agrarian reform designed to end the "unjust social and economic structures" of the past. The program deviated from orthodox Latin American reform policies in two respects: first, it did not retain the homestead or family-sized farm as its ideal; second, it did not exempt large estates from expropriation on account of their efficiency and productivity. Indeed, the first lands to be expropriated were the big coastal sugar plantations, largely foreign-owned and constituting highly mechanized agro-industrial complexes. These enterprises were transferred to cooperatives of farm laborers and refinery workers.

Next came the turn of the haciendas of the sierra. The reform applied to most highland estates above 35 to 55 hectares and initially aimed to encourage division of estates into small- or medium-sized commercial farms, but this would have reduced the number of potential beneficiaries. Under pressure from militant, unionized peasants, who were demanding employment and the formation of cooperatives, the junta moved from parcellation toward cooperative forms of organization. Eventually fully 76 percent of the expropriated lands were organized into cooperatives, with the remainder distributed in individual plots.

The agrarian reform produced some undeniable immediate and long-range benefits. To begin with, it ended the various forms of serfdom that still survived in the sierra in 1968. Second, food production increased, though not substantially or to the level required by Peru's growing population. Third, according to a 1982 field study of the agrarian reform, it "proved a major economic and political benefit to a significant sector of the peasantry," at least in the case of cooperatives with an adequate capital endowment. "In such cooperatives, members' wages and quality of life improved, often dramatically."

But these gains were offset by the failure of the agrarian reform to raise the general material and political level of the Peruvian peasantry—a failure stemming from incorrect planning and methods on the part of the well-meaning military reformers.

First, the reform was neither as swift nor as thorough as the dimensions of the problem required. Delays in implementing the program and the ruses employed by landowners to evade it meant that a considerable amount of land escaped expropriation. As a result, the reform made only a slight impact on the problem of landlessness and rural unemployment and underemployment, especially in the sierra.

Second, the military reformers lacked a coherent strategy for the general modernization of the agricultural sector within an overall plan of balanced, inwardly directed national development. Basically, the agricultural sector was viewed as a means of pumping out food and capital to promote development in the urban-industrial area. This was reflected in the military government's food-pricing policy, which was to keep food prices low to check inflation and keep the urban working class and middle class content. In the absence of compensating subsidies for small farmers, this policy "served to perpetuate the long-run unfavorable trend of the rural-urban terms of trade." Within the agricultural sector, the allocation of resources and credit was skewed in favor of the already well endowed and efficient coastal estates producing for export, with the bulk of agricultural investment going into large-scale irrigation projects. The needs of highland small farmers for small-scale irrigation works, fertilizer, and technical assistance were neglected. As a result, the coastal sugar, cotton, and coffee cooperatives tended to become "islands of relative privilege in a sea of peasant poverty and unemployment."

The same lack of a coherent strategy for the development of the agricultural sector as a whole was reflected in the method of distributing hacienda lands. The land was generally transferred to the workers who had been employed full time on the estates. They alone were eligible to be members of the new cooperatives. This left out the temporary laborers and the neighboring peasant villagers who eked out subsistence livings from tiny plots and small herds of sheep. This often led to serious tension and conflict, with the cooperatives defending their privileges and land against invasions by the *comuneros* (peasant villagers). Combined with the failure to distribute all the land subject to expropriation, this pattern of distribution contributed to the continuing flight of campesinos to the coastal cities, where they swelled the ranks of a large unemployed or underemployed population.

Finally, a major flaw of the agrarian reform was that it was a "revolution from above," with little input from below. Despite lip service to participatory ideology, the military technocrats made the final decisions with respect to work conditions, income policy, crop selection, and the like. Because the government's economic policy tended to subordinate peasant interests to the drive for rapid industrial growth, many peasants became disillusioned with the cooperative model. In some cases, particularly after 1975, when the nationalist reformist Velasco wing of the military was ousted from power by a conservative group stressing private enterprise and a free market, the disillusionment led to peasant demands for dismantling the cooperatives and parceling out the land.

After land reform, the nationalization of key foreign-owned natural resources and enterprises and of domestic monopolies that the military regarded as obstacles to development was the most important objective of the junta's program. When the revolution began, foreign firms controlled the commanding heights of the Peruvian economy. Eight years later, state enterprises had taken over most of these firms. The process began with the nationalization of the IPC, whose assets passed into the control of *Petroperu*, the state-owned oil company. Later, the national telephone system, the railroads (the Peruvian Corporation), and Peru's international airline came under state ownership.

The cement, chemical, and paper industries, defined as basic and reserved to the state, were taken over. The important fishmeal industry, in which large amounts of foreign capital were invested, was nationalized. The sugar industry, in large part controlled by the Grace interests, and the cotton industry, dominated by the U.S. firm of Anderson, Clayton, were seized under the agrarian reform law. Nationalization of the giant U.S.-owned mining complex of Cerro de Pasco in 1974 gave the state ownership of four thousand concessions and vested control of the bulk of mining and refining of copper, lead, and zinc in two state companies, *Minoperu* and *Centrominperu*; nationalization of Marcona Mining in 1975 gave the state control of iron ore and steel. In addition to the takeover of these primarily extractive and manufacturing firms, state companies obtained marketing monopolies of all major commodity exports and most food distribution. Through stock purchases, the government nationalized most of the banking and insurance industries. Thus the state came to control decisive sectors of the Peruvian economy.

The original intent of the military reformers was not to substitute the state for local private capital but to promote its formation by removing such impediments as the latifundio and foreign monopolistic firms and by the creation of an industrial infrastructure to be financed through the export of minerals and agricultural exports. But the radical rhetoric of the nationalistic military only frightened the local bourgeoisie, who were generally satisfied with their technological and financial dependence on foreign capital, and they failed to respond to the incentives for industrial investment. As a result, the government itself had to assume the role of the economy's main investor and by 1972 accounted for more than half the total investment in the economy.

But the cost of this investment, added to the large sums expended for compensation for expropriated estates and foreign enterprises, came very high. Tax reform offered one possibility of mobilizing considerable amounts of previously untouched wealth. Such a move, however, would have antagonized the local bourgeoisie, whom the military was wooing, and the middle class, which formed its principal mass base. Because of disputes over expropriation, Peru could not apply for loans to the United States and the multinational agencies it controlled. Accordingly, Peru had to turn to foreign private banks. Encouraged by the high price of copper and other Peruvian exports and by the prospect of rich oil strikes in the Amazon Basin, the banks willingly complied with Peru's requests for loans. They lent $147 million in 1972 and $734 million in 1973, making Peru the largest borrower among Third World countries in the latter year.

Although women's rights issues clearly were not a priority for the military regime, a new women's movement, led by Virginia Vargas, founder of the Flora Tristán Peruvian Women's Center, nonetheless emerged. These women were very active in grassroots neighborhood organizations, unions, teachers' associations, and social work agencies, which provided experience with collective action and heightened their consciousness of gender-based inequality. Under pressure from this women's movement, the military adopted the eighteenth-century Inca revolutionary leaders, Micaela Bastidas and her husband, Tupac Amaru, as the symbols of their 1974 Plan Inca, which demanded civil and political equality for women, laws against discrimination, affirmative action in public employment, and rural education programs.

The military likewise had not intended to unleash a cultural revolution, but its nationalist ideology mobilized popular political participation and reinforced artistic explorations of the country's indigenous and African roots. This led to a dramatic expansion of popular theater and folk music that challenged criollo cultural hegemony and decisively shaped a radically new multiracial Peruvian national identity. In the early 1970s, for example, Yuyachkani, a politically committed theater group that took its name from a Quechua word meaning "thoughts and memories," sought to organize indigenous workers by touring highland mining communities and performing *Fist of Copper*. This was a play that drew on Spanish and European theatrical traditions to extol the virtues

of popular resistance to violent police repression of a miners' strike. During post-performance discussions, the young urban actors, who aimed to raise the consciousness of their indigenous audiences, instead learned about the long tradition of indigenous Andean theater, which integrated dance, music, puppets, masks, and colorful costumes. These elements were later incorporated into plays that shared with highland peoples the "good news" about the 1969 land reform that gave them the legal authority to fight for their land against the landowners and their hired thugs. They also became very popular in the universities, urban slums, and squatter settlements, where provincianos had migrated in search of jobs.

By early 1975, a new cyclical crisis had begun to ravage the capitalist world. Rising prices for oil and imported equipment and technology, combined with falling prices for Peru's raw material exports, undermined the fragile prosperity that had made President Velasco's reforms possible. These circumstances created unmanageable balance-of-trade and debt service problems. The model of development based on export expansion and foreign borrowing had again revealed its inherent contradictions.

The experience of the Peruvian Revolution shows the difficulty of escaping from dependent development without radical structural changes in class and property relationships and income distribution. Like the Mexican Revolution, Peru's experience suggests that the revolution that does not advance risks stagnation and loss of whatever gains have been made.

## THE REVOLUTION UNDER ATTACK, 1975–1983

The economic crisis of 1975 provoked a sharp struggle within the military between radical nationalists, who proposed to extend the social and economic reforms, and those who called for measures that would win the confidence of native and foreign capitalists, thereby making possible a revival of private investments. In August 1975 a peaceful coup replaced President Velasco with his conservative prime minister, Francisco Morales Bermúdez; this was followed by a gradual purge of radical nationalists from the government and the forced resignation of leftist officers from the armed forces.

The so-called First Phase of the revolution had ended. To appease foreign and domestic capitalists, the new government introduced a package of severe austerity measures that called for sharp reductions in government investments in state enterprises, steep increases in consumer prices, and a 44 percent devaluation of the currency, only partly offset by wage increases of from 10 to 14 percent. The government next announced the end of agrarian reform, although only about one-third of the land subject to expropriation had been distributed. In early 1978, after long negotiations, Morales Bermúdez capitulated to the IMF and accepted its conditions for a new loan, including privatization of state enterprises, heavy cuts in budgets and subsidies, large price increases, and severe restraints on wage increases. These measures provoked widespread strikes and rioting, which were crushed by the government with a full-scale military operation.

For the thoroughly discredited military junta, the prime concern was how to make a smooth transfer of power to a civilian regime that could be trusted to continue its conservative policies. A new constitution, remarkably similar to the 1933 document, served this function. It established a bicameral Congress, both elected, like the president, for five years. It contained language ensuring that the foundations of the Peruvian economy would be the free market and the primacy of the private sector. The constitution guaranteed the right to strike and collective bargaining, but those rights were subject to parliamentary regulation. The biggest novelty was the grant of the right to vote to illiterates.

Predictably, Fernando Belaúnde Terry, a master of populist rhetoric who enjoyed an aura of martyrdom thanks to his ouster by the military in 1968, won the 1980 elections. It soon became clear that he intended to continue and extend the "counterreformation" begun by the Morales Bermúdez government. Export expansion and debt repayment were the great priorities, to be achieved with the familiar arsenal of austerity measures and devaluation, combined with wage freezes.

The Belaúnde government also dismantled the major reforms of the Velasco era. A principal objective was to restore a free market in agricultural land by dissolving the cooperative system. A new agricultural promotion and development law gave the government the power to divide cooperative land into small individual plots and turn them over to cooperative members. The plots could then be bought, sold, or mortgaged, which fostered the reconcentration of land in a few hands.

Other legislation empowered the government to sell off state-owned companies and increase private participation in publicly owned firms through stock issues and other programs. The government proposed to ban general and sympathy strikes, and drastically reduce public works spending, and phase out subsidies on basic foods and fuel. These proposals caused bitter wrangling in parliament between the government and the opposition parties, but they caused unprecedented popular protest; for the first time in Peruvian history, all the major labor groups joined in a general strike.

Thus, fifteen years after the military seized power in Peru, the nation again faced a crisis of unprecedented proportions. Its population had doubled between 1960 and 1980, from 10 to 20 million, and its distribution between town and country had changed dramatically. In 1960, 60 percent of the people were rural, but in 1980, 60 percent were urban. Unemployment climbed to new heights; strikes succeeded each other in industry, the railroads, and the banks; and the rural exodus continued to swell the population of the barriadas that ringed Lima.

## POPULAR CULTURE AND RESISTANCE

Second-generation provincianos had played a role in many of the urban protests that helped inaugurate the 1968 Peruvian revolution, and they likewise joined this new popular movement to defend its achievements. Unlike their parents, however, they had become more economically independent of criollo society. They had created their own self-help migrant community associations, usually based upon their region of origin (e.g., Punenos from Puno and Ayacuchanos from Ayacucho),

During the 1980s, migrants from highland communities adapted indigenous musical instruments and folk rhythms to reflect a new urban experience of modernity that they found simultaneously exciting and disturbing. [Alison Wright/Corbis]

joined trade unions, and participated in other grassroots social movements that strengthened their public embrace of indigenous identities. This growing independence of thought and action was clearly reflected in the birth of a new cultural form, a popular urban musical style variously called *cumbia andina* or *chicha*, for the corn beer that was the preferred beverage in highland Andean indigenous communities. No longer interested in assimilating criollo values, these sons and daughters of highland migrants increasingly challenged established social hierarchies based on race, ethnicity, and class power.

Chicha music drew on three radically different sources for its creative inspiration: Colombian cumbia rhythms, whose origins lay in Afro-Colombian cultural traditions; folk melodies indige-nous to the Andean highlands; and the electric instruments commonly associated with U.S. and British rock and roll. Chicha songs typically explored the everyday lives of poor, hard-working urban provincianos. According to ethnomusicologist Thomas Tutino, one of the earliest chicha bands, Los demonios del Mantaro (Mantaro Devils), sold 200,000 copies of "La Chichera," a song that celebrated the life of a street peddler who sold Andean corn beer. Established criollo critics understandably disparaged chicha as crude, amateurish, "mindless" music, and leftist intellectuals either dismissed its lyrical interest in unrequited love as politically disengaged or criticized it for "internalizing criollo values" by promoting upward mobility.

But young provincianos, often feeling unloved, socially marginalized, out of place, and lacking a clear sense of their own identity, thrilled to its "modern" beat and identified with its lyrical lament about their real life experiences. In one very popular song, "Ambulante Soy" ("I Am a Street Vendor"), the lead singer of Los Shapis, perhaps the most famous of the chicha bands, bemoaned "How sad is life, how sad it is to dream" and then proudly announced that "I am a street vendor, I am a proletarian." Similarly, Grupo Alegría's "Pequeño Luchador" ("Little Fighter") described the daily survival struggles of "a small child/Who runs through the city/Hawking advertisements that will sell" and then celebrated the heroism of this "Little boy with dirty face/Little fighter/Your hands now know/What it means to work." Even songs like Los Shapis's "Somos Estudiantes" ("We Are Students"), which some have criticized for its alleged identification with criollo concerns about "occupational status" and social mobility, clearly stressed the value of professional positions as a means of promoting the development of their communities, not their own personal self-aggrandizement. "We are teachers/For our children," Los Shapis sang, "Doctors we will be/For the orphans. We are lawyers/Of the poor."

Chicha music soon outsold all its competitors in Peruvian markets, including internationally renowned artists like Julio Iglesias and Michael Jackson. Initially performed on street corners and in vacant lots in the pueblos jovenes (squatter communities), chicha artists later regularly played to large crowds in "chichadromes" and provided musical entertainment at community religious festivals, weddings, birthday parties, and other social events. Supported by the progressive indigenista policies of Velasco's revolutionary nationalist regime, which had made Quechua an official national language and required radio stations to promote authentic local music, they soon dominated national radio broadcasts, claiming almost 40 percent of airtime by the early 1980s. Chicha music also expanded its popularity from the urban centers of its birth to rural highland communities. As the reformist Velasco dictatorship crumbled and more conservative forces seized control of the nation, chicha artists and their concerts provided young provincianos with useful meeting places to organize popular resistance and promote a return to democracy. Thereafter, they would lend their voice to support reformist state social programs proposed by Aprista and other populist politicians who sought to curry political favor with urban and rural provincianos alike.

## APRA IN POWER, 1985–1990

The Aprista candidate who most benefited from Belaúnde's failure was thirty-six-year-old Alán García Pérez, a disciple of the late Haya de la Torre. García campaigned on a populist, reformist program in 1985, promising to defend the agrarian and industrial reforms of the Velasco era and to reject Belaúnde's free-market policies.

In his inaugural address, García proclaimed that henceforth Peru would not deal with the IMF but directly with the creditor banks. He also announced that he would limit interest payments on Peru's foreign debt of about $14 billion to 10 percent of Peru's export earnings—about $400 million. "Peru," García declared, "has one overwhelming creditor, its own people." Other parts of his economic program included measures to halt capital exports, freeze the price of necessities, and raise the minimum wage by 50 percent—all measures opposed by the IMF and the foreign financial community.

García's restrictions on foreign debt payments and his measures to prevent the flight of capital, prevent luxury imports, and raise wages formed part of a coherent program to revive the sluggish Peruvian economy. The long-term goal was promoting the development of an autonomous Peruvian capitalism based on expanded import-substitution industrialization and reduced dependence on imported raw materials. The restriction on debt repayments and the controls on foreign trade were designed to make capital available for development; the substantial wage increases were expected to expand purchasing power and demand for Peruvian-made goods. In a speech marking the anniversary of his first year in office, he took care to reassure businessmen, declaring that even as he rejected devaluation and new indebtedness as a regression to "the colonial recipes of the IMF," so he rejected nationalization. His path, he said, led to "a strong state redirecting the structure of Peruvian industry toward less import-dependent options."

But economic problems remained. Business's resistance to the price freeze produced shortages of consumer items and forced the government to relax price controls, allowing some prices to rise. Moreover, there was a growing gap between the costs of the recovery program and government income from all sources, including export earnings and the savings obtained by limiting debt payments. García had few options. He could try by tax reform to tap the large wealth of Peruvian elites, left untouched by the military reformers, but this was an unacceptable solution given the moderate nature of his program. Printing money or a slowdown in economic growth was equally unacceptable. There remained the option of going to foreign banks for loans, but García had ruled out "new indebtedness" as a colonial recipe of the IMF, which had in any case declared him ineligible for new credits.

A major obstacle to the sound, balanced economic growth envisaged by García was the continuing cleavage between the sierra and the coast; the contrast between the poverty of the highlands (largely populated by Quechua- and Aymara-speaking peasants) and the relative prosperity of the coast. Landlessness and unemployment or underemployment continued to be the burning problems of the sierra. The result was that the highlands became the scene of a struggle between the landless peasantry and the giant cooperatives, often controlled by elite groups of managers, engineers, and bureaucrats.

Into this struggle over land, with all its potential for violence, entered the Maoist *Sendero Luminoso* (Shining Path). This group was repudiated by other left-wing movements, which viewed it as terrorist and mistaken in its effort to polarize Peruvian society into militarists and *senderistas*. For the most part led by radicalized students and other middle-class individuals, the Sendero Luminoso emerged in May 1980 with a program of terrorist activity against all who supported the existing bourgeois order; it also encouraged peasants to invade, occupy, and loot cooperatives. The García government responded to this threat by continuing Belaúnde's counterinsurgency campaign, which had placed nineteen of Peru's twenty-three provinces under a state of emergency with the military in overall control and suspended most civil rights. García justified this action, claiming that thousands of officials, police, members of other security forces, and uncooperative peasants had been killed by the Sendero Luminoso, but church authorities and other independent observers asserted that the security forces had themselves committed many repressive acts and that many killings of peasants ascribed to the guerrillas were the work of these forces.

As his term of office drew to an end, a balance sheet of García's record in power could point to some positive initiatives and accomplishments, including his decision to limit debt interest payments to a certain proportion of export proceeds, thereby making more funds available for development purposes. García's debt strategy marked an advance over that of the military reformers, but it was not enough. Peru needed a program of structural economic and social change: the creation of a self-sufficient industrial base that would lessen dependency on foreign imports and capital; a more thoroughgoing agrarian reform that would attack the age-old problem of Andean poverty and backwardness, overcome the need for food imports, and expand the domestic market; and a reduction of the immense inequities in income distribution.

But these changes were not made. As a result, by 1987 García's project for creating an autonomous Peruvian capitalism was running out of steam; the country had a serious trade deficit, its foreign reserves were declining, and the business class, despite generous incentives from the government, was not increasing its level of investment. From 1988 to 1989 the per capita gross economic product declined by 20 percent, the biggest decline in the region. As if the economic crisis were not enough, the war with the Maoist Sendero Luminoso movement grew more intense. Moreover, the indigenous struggle to reclaim ancestral lands led to a wave of *tomas de tierras* (land invasions) that produced a new militance among peasant leaders and fueled the rural rebellion.

Amid the economic gloom, the only light and cheer was provided by Peru's illicit coca trade. In Peru, as in Bolivia, the jobs and dollars generated by the coca boom cushioned the impact of a devastating economic crisis. With opportunities for employment in the legal economy shrinking, thousands of migrants joined the "white gold rush" to the Upper Huallaga Valley, the heart of Peru's coca empire. The coca, processed into a white paste, was sold to Colombian dealers, who pocketed most of the profits. But Peru's share came to about $1.2 billion annually, roughly 30 percent of the value of all Peru's legal exports. Without these illicit dollars, according to one Peruvian economist, the exchange rate would have nearly doubled, making vitally needed imports much more expensive. Like Paz in Bolivia, García liberalized Central Bank rules to permit the purchase of coca dollars, no questions asked.

With APRA in total disgrace as a result of García's economic fiasco and failure to end the civil war, the 1990 presidential elections became the site of a new contest between neoliberal free-market philosophy and the populism of an obscure agronomist, Alberto Fujimori, the son of poor Japanese immigrants, who insisted that people's basic needs must be met before any economic adjustment was begun. Surprising most political pundits, Fujimori's populist crusade solidified his base and attracted leftist support, thereby ensuring his electoral triumph.

## BACK TO THE PAST, 1990–2003

Following his election, Fujimori caused consternation among his followers by enacting severe austerity measures akin to those that they had soundly rejected at the polls. "Fujishock," as the program was immediately dubbed, included the removal of customer subsidies. The result was soaring price increases, with the price of such staple foods as milk and bread nearly tripling. The program provoked widespread rioting and looting in Peru's shantytowns. In contradiction of the pledge that he would not privatize major public enterprises,

**EL FISGÓN**

FUJIMORI: A MAN WHO SUITS ALL OCCASIONS.

Peru's President Fujimori quickly learned how to manage democratic capitalism's potentially fatal contradiction: to serve the powerful minority of international bankers and local elites who supported neoliberalism, successful politicians had to deceive their lower-class constituents with populist rhetoric and election-year patronage.
[El Fisgón/NACLA]

Fujimori, hoping to attract foreign capital, offered to sell 232 state-owned companies, including the controlling shares of the state copper mines. Despite their many problems, these firms provided one-half of Peru's foreign exchange earnings.

Fujimori confronted a comatose economy kept alive only with large injections of coca dollars, a fanatical guerrilla movement rampaging in the countryside and gaining ground in the cities, and a Congress that was becoming increasingly restive over his use of the special decree powers it had granted him. Fujimori used those powers to promote his extreme neoliberal program and to give the military absolute control over the counterinsurgency. When Congress finally reacted to his abuse of the decree powers by overturning or amending some of the most offensive decrees in a special session, Fujimori aggressively attacked Congress and the judiciary for their alleged inefficiency and corruption. Then, on April 5, 1992, he carried out his famous *autogolpe* ("self-coup"), closing Congress and the judiciary, suspending the 1979 constitution, and proclaiming a "Government of Emergency and National Reconstruction."

Public support for this coup, revealed in polls that showed approval rates of between 70 and 90 percent, reflected widespread fear of the Shining Path, which played into Fujimori's hands by its merciless killing of popular community leaders who organized communal soup kitchens and glass-of-milk programs. As a result, the public applauded government victories in its fight against the Shining Path and the smaller Tupac Amaru Revolutionary Movement (MRTA), capped in September 1992 by the capture of Shining Path leader Abimael Guzmán.

This terrorism provided a convenient pretext for the security forces' equally indiscriminate repression of those who opposed Fujimori's insidious neoliberal program: popular organizations, leftist parties, and journalists, a number of whom were arrested on charges of promoting terrorism. Fujimori apparently had come to the same conclusion as Carlos Menem in Argentina: neoliberalism worked more efficiently in the context of an authoritarian political system.

In an effort to remove the taint of dictatorship and gain international respectability for his regime, in 1992 Fujimori drafted a new constitution that fully conformed to his authoritarian temper and neoliberal economic views. It concentrated all power in the president by allowing him to dissolve Congress at will, veto laws, and promulgate laws by decree; and it permitted his reelection in 1995. The document provided for a laissez-faire economy with the private sector assigned the dominant role, and for privatization of state enterprises. State activity in education would be reduced, with less support for free education. The constitution established a strongly centralized government, eliminating regional governments, subordinating the provinces to the executive branch, and denying provinces the right to keep a portion of the profits generated by the exploitation of natural resources in their territory. Finally, the document adopted the death penalty for terrorism.

In 1995, Fujimori sought to lower inflation, expand consumption, and guarantee his reelection by opening Peru to a flood of cheap foreign imports. Although this produced short-term benefits, it also doubled the trade deficit, increased the nation's balance-of-payments deficit by 80 percent, and, over time, drove small- and medium-sized industrial manufacturers and agricultural producers into bankruptcy. He also borrowed heavily from foreign bankers to pay for dramatically higher expenditures on poverty relief in poor communities devastated by his neoliberal structural adjustments. External debt grew by 72 percent from 1993 to 1995, and interest payments on that accumulated debt skyrocketed to 31 percent of export revenues.

In addition, the crafty president, dressed in indigenous garb, traveled daily to the *pueblos jovenes* (squatter cities), composed of indigent highland migrants forced off their lands or fleeing the grinding poverty of the countryside, and directly dispensed presidential patronage, agreeing to build schools, roads, or public infrastructure. Government allocations to poverty relief increased by nearly 60 percent in 1994 and another 90 percent in 1995. Social spending more than doubled from 3 percent of gross domestic product (GDP) in 1993 to 7.8 percent in 1995; whereas Fujimori had spent only $12 on the social welfare of each Peruvian in 1990, he paid out $176 in 1995. Despite the long-term risks for national development, the strategy worked and Fujimori captured 60 percent of the vote in the 1995 elections; moreover, according to political scientist Kenneth Roberts, "Fujimori's support in 1995 was highest in Peru's poorest departments, especially in the southern and central Andean highlands, where opposition to the constitution had been strongest in 1993."

However, although backing for Fujimori's economic policies was solid among foreign investors, the IMF, and domestic elites, it remained highly volatile among the impoverished masses. If every year were a presidential election year, the poor majority might be convinced to vote for Fujimori and poverty rates might even be expected to decline from their historic highs in 1993, when 53.6 percent of Peruvians lived in poverty and 21 percent lived in "extreme" poverty. His 1995 reelection effort alone reduced poverty by almost 10 percent, but recent statistics suggest a somewhat darker future.

Despite the dramatic increase in 1995 GDP and Fujimori's effective anti-inflation program, the nation's economy did not expand sufficiently during his tenure to justify the sacrifices that his neoliberal policies imposed on Peru. Growth rates averaged 4.7 percent per year since 1991, but unemployment, averaging almost 9 percent a year, remained stubbornly high and the poorly paid "informal sector," composed of part-time and self-employed street vendors, experienced the most sustained growth. As a result, despite a decade of growth, in 2002, 54 percent of Peruvians were anchored in poverty. External debt, trade deficits, and net outflows of wealth all increased steadily since Fujimori took over in 1991. In 2000, the external debt was a whopping $28 billion, almost twice as large as when he took office; the trade deficit averaged almost $1 billion per year during his administration, almost three times higher than the annual average $500 million surplus accumulated in the two economically depressed years before Fujimori took office; finally, the payments deficit, the measure of wealth which flowed *out* of the nation, also grew, to $3 billion in 1997, and averaged $2.5 billion per year since 1990, double the annual average rate in the last years of García's presidency.

But this economic picture of growing poverty and increased external dependency tells only part of the story. Fujimori's government continued to rely on authoritarian methods to preserve his power and implement his neoliberal agenda. But this weakened his standing among both political elites and popular sectors. After a constitutional tribunal ruled unconstitutional his bid to run for reelection in 2000, he promptly fired the justices. Next, reports surfaced that he had authorized his security forces to tap the telephones of 167 political opponents, including the former secretary-general of the United Nations, Javier Perez de Cuellar. Fujimori's military then virtually declared war on the opposition press, engaging in beating, kidnapping, and torture. When a television reporter criticized the $600,000 salary of the president's intelligence chief, Fujimori revoked the station owner's citizenship and transferred ownership to minority shareholders.

Determined to remain in power, no matter the cost, Fujimori pressed his National Intelligence Service (SIN), the equivalent of the United States's CIA, to intervene boldly in the electoral process to guarantee it. Emboldened by popular opposition to these high-handed, overtly authoritarian tactics, Alejandro Toledo, born to poor indigenous parents, denounced the impending fraud and withdrew from the elections. International observers quickly followed suit and even the U.S. State Department, which had supported Fujimori's neoliberal economic policies, described the 2000 election as "invalid." Popular grassroots movements quickly organized a general strike, and a wave of social protests, some of which became violent, swept the countryside. Suddenly, the issue that galvanized all Peruvians, regardless of their other disagreements, was Fujimori. Toledo, an economist educated in the United States, seized upon this popular mobilization to energize his own presidential ambitions; he now denounced Fujimori's authoritarianism, his "antipopular economic measures," corruption, and failure to reduce poverty among the 55 percent of the nation that earned less than $2 per day. The resulting tumult forced the Congress to dismiss Fujimori, who sought exile in Japan.

Ironically, this messy transition dramatically increased Toledo's popularity, but without requiring him to spell out his vision of a post-Fujimori Peru. Although he supported free trade, his populist campaign called for a review of Fujimori's privatization program, specifically promised not to sell off the state's public utilities, and pledged to reduce unemployment and poverty. As a result, when he assumed the presidency in 2001, public expectations were understandably high. The popular sectors that had supported his candidacy had one agenda, but the Peruvian business elite and foreign bankers urged another. Toledo quickly made clear which program would shape his presidential administration. After meeting with officials of the IMF, he agreed to raise $700 million in 2002 and almost $1 billion in 2003 by selling off state assets, but this required him to break his campaign pledge to the people who had elected him. Thereafter, he announced the privatization of two profitable state-owned electric companies, Egasa (which earned $14 million on sales of $50 million in 2001) and Egesur, to be sold to a Belgian company, Tractebel, for $167 million, one-half their declared value.

This naturally ignited a storm of violent popular protests that led to the declaration of a state of emergency and produced two deaths, hundreds of arrests, and $100 million in damages. Pressed by this "democracy in the streets," Toledo, whose pop-ularity already had plunged from a historic high of 60 percent to 16 percent, was forced, at least temporarily, to abandon his privatization plans and apologize publicly for having violated his campaign promises. But Toledo also had failed to make good on a promise to create 2 million jobs, restore workers' rights usurped by Fujimori, and reduce unemployment and poverty, both of which rose as a result of his neoliberal policies. Greatly weakened by a growing popular clamor to "pay the poor, not the foreign debt," Francisco Toledo's future, like Peru's, seemed especially uncertain. Like the rest of the region, Peru appeared poised to abandon its decade-long experiment with unfettered free enterprise in search of a more socially productive mix of state regulations and market forces.

# 17 The Cuban Revolution

LIKE THE OTHER Latin American nations we have examined, Cuba has suffered from the cyclical nature of world market demand for its products. Moreover, Cuba suffered the additional burden of almost total economic domination by the United States. But in 1959, Cuba—an island ninety miles from Key West and ruled by one of the region's most firmly entrenched dictatorships—became the scene of perhaps the first and certainly the most successful social revolution in Latin America during the twentieth century. Under the banner of Marxism and with the military, economic, and political support of the Soviet Union, until recently the government led by Fidel Castro made great progress toward the elimination of such problems as illiteracy, mass unemployment, and unequal distribution of income and wealth. But the collapse of the Soviet Union and Cuba's other trading partners in the socialist bloc, combined with an intensified effort by the United States to bring about its downfall, produced the most serious crisis in socialist Cuba's history, a crisis it is now struggling to overcome.

## Independence and the Spanish-Cuban-American War

### JOSÉ MARTÍ AND THE REVOLUTIONARY MOVEMENT

By the early 1890s a global economic crisis, compounded by high U.S. tariffs on Cuban sugar imports, reduced external demand for sugar, destroyed sugar planters' profits, swelled unemployment, and inflamed long-simmering class, racial, and gender animosities. Afro-Cubans, workers, women, colonos, creole elites, and U.S. investors in Cuba increasingly identified Spanish imperial authority as the principal source of this injustice and therefore revived the movement for independence.

The spiritual, intellectual, and organizational leader of the revolutionary movement was José Martí (1853–1895). As a lad of sixteen, Martí was arrested on a charge of supporting the 1868 revolt and sentenced to six years in prison at hard labor; but in 1871 he was sent into exile. In 1880, Martí came to New York, his home for the next fourteen years. In the United States, he earned his living in brilliant journalistic and literary activity that won him fame throughout Latin America.

Meanwhile, Martí worked tirelessly to establish and unite Cuban émigré revolutionary groups. In 1892 he founded *El Partido Revolucionario Cubano* (the Cuban Revolutionary Party), which proposed to obtain, "with the united effort of all men of good will, the absolute independence of the island of Cuba, and to foment and aid that of Puerto Rico." He then set about recruiting such military veterans of 1868 as Máximo Gómez and Antonio Maceo, in preparation for an invasion of the island. In April 1895, Martí himself landed on a Cuban beach with a group of insurgents; a little

José Martí (*left*), a brilliant writer and thinker, became a towering figure in Latin American history when he joined with Antonio Maceo (*right*), the Bronze Titan, to lead the revolutionary movement for Cuban independence. [Bettmann/Corbis]

more than a month later, he was killed in a skirmish with a Spanish patrol.

Despite the loss of its charismatic leader, the revolution spread and the National Liberation Army achieved major successes with the aid of time-proven guerrilla tactics. Afro-Cubans played particularly prominent roles in the armed struggle. In every rebellious province except Camaguey, Afro-Cubans constituted a majority of the soldiers, known as *mambises*, and they fought in integrated battalions, often under the command of black officers like Maceo, his brother José, and Agustín Cebrerco. This prompted some Afro-Cubans to conclude that in the army, where "nobody cares about the color of a man," the *Cuba Libre* movement was "putting the principles of democracy

into practice." This wartime experience reaffirmed Afro-Cubans' long-standing commitment to equality and social justice.

Women also shaped the independence struggle in decisive ways. Some, like university graduate Adela Azcuy, distinguished themselves in battle, whereas peasant women, despite Spanish attempts to enclose them in concentration camps, continued to provide food and intelligence information to the liberation army. This "women's war" shaped the consciousness of the revolutionary generation and led to a political demand for women's suffrage, public employment, and educational opportunity.

At the beginning of 1896 a new Spanish commander, General Valeriano Weyler, instituted counterinsurgency measures of the type that

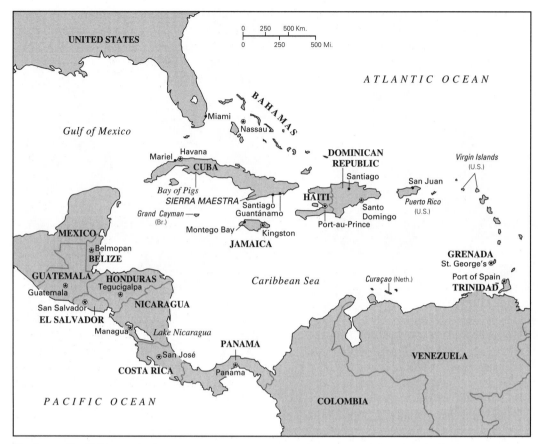

**Modern Caribbean Nations**

would later be employed against twentieth-century rebels in the Philippines, Algeria, and Vietnam. He set up population concentration centers and free-fire zones, which resulted in enormous hardships and losses to the peasantry. But his successes were transient and counterproductive, serving mostly to intensify popular hatred for Spanish rule, and whole provinces remained under the absolute control of the liberating army. The failure of Weyler's military policies and growing pressure from the United States led Spain to promise autonomy to Cuba in late 1897.

### INVOLVEMENT BY THE UNITED STATES

As the rebellion spread over Cuba, it became an increasingly volatile issue in the United States.

Inevitably, property was destroyed or damaged in the fighting, and this brought complaints from powerful U.S. businessmen and financiers with interests in Cuba. These leaders, white supremacists themselves, also feared the possibility that Cuba's "race war," as Spanish propagandists depicted it, might transform the island into another Haiti and simultaneously inflame the African community in the United States. But the Cuban struggle for independence struck a sympathetic chord with some Americans, particularly among the working class. William Randolph Hearst and Joseph Pulitzer, then engaged in a newspaper circulation war in New York City, helped keep popular interest high by running lurid stories of Spanish brutality.

Meanwhile, within the McKinley administration as well as among enthusiastic expansionists like Theodore Roosevelt, there was a growing feeling that the Cuban situation was getting out of control, that the autonomy proposal sponsored by the United States was failing, and that if the United States did not intervene, an unmanageable Cuban revolutionary government might take over from the collapsing Spanish regime. In the midst of this ferment, the USS *Maine* blew up in Havana Harbor on February 15, 1898, with heavy loss of life. This incident helped spur McKinley to a more belligerent stance; he demanded that Spain terminate the concentration camp policy, offer an armistice to the rebels, and accept the United States as a final arbiter between the parties. There was no mention of Cuban independence. When Spain delayed its response to U.S. demands, McKinley sent a message to Congress asking it to authorize military intervention by the United States in Cuba. Congress, after considerable debate, adopted a joint resolution to that effect.

But Cubans did not rejoice: almost every major revolutionary figure—Martí, Maceo, Gómez—opposed U.S. entry into the war, fearing it would result in direct or indirect U.S. political and economic control of Cuba. "The Cuban war," Martí wrote in 1895, "has broken out in America in time to prevent . . . the annexation of Cuba to the United States." All they sought from the United States was recognition of Cuban belligerency and the right to purchase arms in the United States. McKinley, of course, had worked feverishly to defeat the Turpie-Foraker Amendment, recognizing Cuban belligerency, and had unsuccessfully opposed the 1898 Teller Amendment, which prohibited U.S. annexation of Cuba.

The ensuing war was short and nasty. U.S. commanders ignored their Cuban counterparts, excluding Cuban generals from decision making and relegating Cuban soldiers to sentry and cleanup duties. Incompetence was the key feature of both Spanish and U.S. war efforts. U.S. military actions were ill prepared and badly led. Thus, in a bizarre little war, the United States Army— wretchedly led, scandalously provisioned, and ravaged by tropical disease—swiftly defeated a demoralized, dispirited Spanish army and snatched the fruits of victory from the mambises,

who had fought gallantly in a struggle of three years' duration. The exclusion of Cuban leaders from both war councils and peace negotiations foreshadowed the course of U.S.-Cuban relations for the next sixty years.

## THE FIRST U.S. OCCUPATION, 1899–1902

The United States Army occupied Cuba from January 1899 to May 1902. The occupation had three basic goals. First, the United States sought to make Cuba into a self-governing colony, an arrangement designed to achieve political stability without the administrative burdens and costs of an outright colonial occupation. To this end, the U.S. military sought to pacify the island without serious conflict with the Cuban army, which was still intact and in control of much of rural Cuba. The revolutionary army, however, did not resist the U.S. takeover, as did Emilio Aguinaldo and his insurgent forces in the Philippines at the same time. Cuban passivity in part reflected the fact that the years of struggle had taken their toll—the leading Cuban generals, such as Calixto García and Máximo Gómez, were tired old men, and many of the younger men who could have led a resistance movement had died in battle.

In addition, U.S. authorities bought off the army by offering to purchase its arms, an offer that hungry, unemployed soldiers found difficult to refuse. They also offered key rebel leaders well-paid positions and ably manipulated the volatile issue of race to divide and conquer Cuba Libre. At the same time, the occupation government established a Rural Guard, largely devoid of Afro-Cubans, most of whom could not meet eligibility requirements, which included literacy, a recommendation from propertied elites, and sufficient wealth to purchase a uniform, equipment, and horse. The Guard's primary purpose was to eradicate banditry and protect foreign property—in the words of General Leonard Wood, to put down the "agitators who began to grow restive at the presence of the Americans."

After political stability, necessary to attract U.S. capital, the second major goal was to repair the destruction wrought by the war and provide the services needed to sustain the U.S. occupation and promote economic recovery. General Leonard Wood, appointed governor general in 1899, launched a program of public works and sanitation that led to a major achievement of the occupation—the conquest of yellow fever. Taking its lead from a Cuban doctor, Carlos Finlay, whose theory correctly attributed the transmission of the dread disease to the mosquito, the American Sanitary Commission succeeded in eliminating it. Another major accomplishment of the Wood administration was the creation of a Cuban national education system, vastly superior to what had existed under Spain but designed to inculcate U.S. principles; even the textbooks were translations of U.S. textbooks. All these programs and reforms, as well as the expenses of the U.S. troops, were paid for from the Cuban treasury.

Ruling with arbitrary methods and largely ignoring the former revolutionaries, especially the Afro-Cubans, in favor of Spaniards and conservative planters who had opposed independence, Wood imposed a new electoral law that empowered the "better class" by restricting the franchise to literate adult males with property worth $250. Elihu Root, McKinley's secretary of war, especially celebrated the law's impact on Afro-Cubans: "Limited suffrage," he wrote, effectively excluded "so great a proportion of the elements which have brought ruin to Haiti and San Domingo." Elections for a constitutional convention, not surprisingly, produced a conservative assembly which, after several months of bitter debate, adopted a document that, under intense U.S. pressure, included the so-called Platt Amendment. This amendment limited the ability of independent Cuba to conduct foreign policy and to borrow money abroad, gave the United States the right to maintain a naval base at Guantánamo Bay, and most important, gave the United States the right to intervene in Cuba for the "preservation of Cuban independence" and for the "maintenance of a government adequate for the protection of life, property, and individual liberty."

The third goal of the occupation was to absorb Cuba into the United States's economic sphere of influence. Because the Platt Amendment assured U.S. businessmen of protection and a generally favorable investment climate on the island, capital poured into sugar and railroad construction. A reciprocal trade agreement signed by the two nations in 1903 was the final step in bringing Cuba under U.S. hegemony. This treaty cut by 20 percent the tariff on Cuban sugar exported to the United States; in return, Cuba reduced the duties on imported U.S. goods.

The end of Spanish rule and the U.S. occupation also transformed Cuban society by removing the final obstacle to the development of the latifundio in Cuba. Two processes worked hand in hand in the following decades: the concentration of land and mills and the proletarianization of the sugar workers. The two wars of independence had devastated small mills: the total number fell from two thousand in 1860 to one thousand in 1877 to only two hundred in 1899. The rapid and huge influx of foreign—mostly U.S.—investment into sugar enabled the larger mills to buy up surrounding cane land. The colono was reduced to circumstances close to slavery. Ramiro Guerra y Sánchez has estimated that the great mills owned perhaps 20 percent of the island's area in 1927.

The expansion of the latifundio impoverished the rural masses of the island. The colonos were kept at subsistence levels, deeply indebted to the mill and in constant fear of eviction. The wages of rural workers were kept low because the mills imported cheap labor from other Caribbean islands. As a result, a considerable reserve pool of labor was available; even those lucky enough to get work worked only four months of the year during the harvest period. Displaced farmers had two choices. They could remain and work for small wages on a seasonal basis for the sugar mills (*centrales*), or they could emigrate to the cities, where jobs also were scarce. Small independent growers were at a severe disadvantage, for the mills squeezed the price paid for their cane to a minimum. In addition, the mills controlled the transportation network.

The ruin of the small mills and farmers and the low wages paid rural labor, which reduced the purchasing power of the masses, sharply limited the domestic market for manufactured goods and commercial services. There was thus little Cuban industrialization. Sugar companies monopolized the railroads and operated them solely for their own benefit, often without regard to the public interest. Although Cuba's railroad network exceeded that of most Latin American nations, it was inadequate to develop an internal market.

U.S. companies, which had poured money into Cuban sugar during the first occupation, had invested $200 million by 1913, predominantly in sugar. This accounted for nearly one-fifth the total U.S. investment in all of Latin America.

# Dependent Development and Popular Struggle, 1902–1953

### INTERVENTION, CORRUPTION, AND POPULAR RESISTANCE, 1902–1924

Cuba's political life, afflicted by its status as a U.S. protectorate and suffering from interventions, had a weak and stunted growth. Its first president, Tomás Estrada Palma, the aging former head of the government-in-exile during the Ten Years' War, had not even lived in Cuba for twenty-five years and consequently relied heavily on U.S. support to secure his election in 1901. Without a loyal Cuban constituency even among the "better class," Estrada set an enduring pattern in twentieth-century Cuban politics by implementing U.S.-sponsored policies and currying favor among local elites through patronage, graft, fraud, corruption, and intimidation.

Although these tactics served Estrada well in his 1905 reelection bid, they also alienated propertied elites excluded from the public dole; meanwhile, lower-class Cubans—peasant *guajiros*, workers, and Afro-Cubans—seethed at the government's neglect of the national liberation struggle's original goals: independence, equality, and social justice. The combination of elite and popular discontent, always a volatile mix, produced a series of revolts (in 1906, 1912, 1917, and 1921) that caused weak Cuban governments to invite U.S. military intervention.

In 1906 President William Howard Taft responded by sending in the Marines, and shortly

afterward appointed Charles Magoon, a judge from Minnesota, to preside over a U.S. provisional government. Magoon's solution for the problem of factional violence was to divide patronage more equitably among contending Cuban groups. During the second occupation, elite resistance to U.S. domination virtually disappeared, due in large part to this new system of institutionalized corruption, which united all sections of the elite in the eager pursuit of U.S. favor and protection.

Magoon's provisional government also reformed the Cuban Army and reinvigorated the decade-old racist immigration policy of "whitening," which prohibited "races of color" but encouraged Spanish immigrants with travel subsidies and promises of public employment. According to the 1907 census, this had significantly reduced the proportion of Afro-Cubans to less than 30 percent of the total population. Magoon also attacked *brujería, ñáñiguismo,* and *santería,* the cultural centers of Afro-Cuban resistance, purged political partisans from the Rural Guard, reorganized the Cuban Army as a political counterweight to it, and developed both as institutions designed to protect private property and elite rule in Cuba.

Nonetheless, the lower classes remained restive. Workers, irrespective of race and gender, continued to organize trade unions and press their agenda for social justice. Meanwhile, Afro-Cuban mambises like José Isabel Herrera complained that U.S. investors, Spanish immigrants, and loyalist elites "took over the businesses, factories, and public jobs that we had just brought to independence." The case of Quintín Banderas was instructive: an Afro-Cuban who fought for thirty years against Spanish colonialism and rose to the rank of general, he died penniless and propertyless, unable even to secure a janitorial job with the government of independent Cuba.

In 1908, under the leadership of Evaristo Estenoz, a veteran of Cuba Libre, Afro-Cubans organized the Independent Party of Color (PIC) to defend the interests of black Cubans, to promote integration and racial democracy, and to protest against monopolization of the material rewards of independence by white elites and foreigners. The PIC denounced white supremacy

This 1912 cartoon, entitled "Today's Trendy Sport," depicts a U.S. Marine and a white Cuban soldier playing soccer with the heads of Evaristo Estenoz and Pedro Ivonnet, leaders of the Afro-Cuban insurrection in Oriente province. The caption reads, "Is this how 'football' will be played in Oriente?" [Biblioteca Nacional José Martí]

and demanded an end to racial discrimination, expansion of public employment and education programs, establishment of the eight-hour day, agrarian reform, and "Cuba for the Cubans." Despite official efforts to disrupt its activities, the PIC continued to expand until 1912, when, fearing imminent threats to capitalist labor and property relations, U.S. Marines joined the Cuban Army in what historian Aline Helg calls a "racist massacre" that left thousands of blacks dead and thereafter forced Afro-Cubans to pursue social justice through class and anti-imperialist struggles.

## WORLD WAR I AND THE DANCE OF THE MILLIONS

Cuba's greatest sugar boom and bust occurred as a consequence of World War I. The fighting in Europe, which disrupted sugar production on the continent, from the first caused large price increases: prices nearly doubled in the first two months alone. Eventually, the Allies became totally dependent on Cuban sugar production, because they were fighting their major former supplier, Austria-Hungary. This demand spurred further expansion of Cuban sugar production, with planters moving into previously uncultivated land. The last great surge of mill construction also

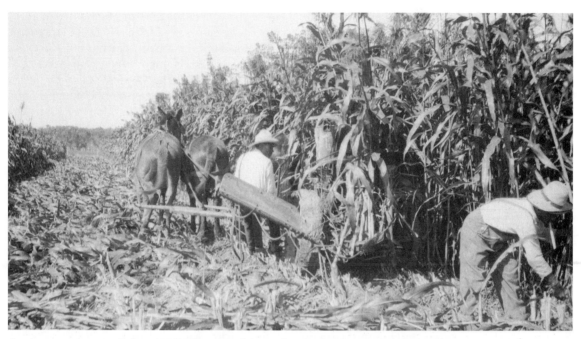

Cutting sugar cane, Cuba, 1920. The end of Spanish rule in 1898 and the onset of U.S. occupation hastened the transformation of the island into a "large sugar plantation producing sugar for the benefit of foreign customers." [Bettmann/Corbis]

occurred. As production spread into virgin land, centrales were built and new towns sprang up.

The Allies attempted to keep commodity prices from skyrocketing by establishing purchasing committees to handle the acquisition of raw materials and food. Nonetheless, Cuban production rose in 1916 to 3 million tons at an average price of 4¢ a pound. Expansion created a severe labor shortage on the island, and laborers were imported from Jamaica and other Caribbean islands to fill the void. The colonos staged a comeback, and a few actually prospered.

The war accelerated the trend toward the concentration of the industry in U.S. hands. By 1919 approximately half the island's mills were owned by U.S. companies, and these controlled more than half the total production. The boom also led to the integration of sugar mills and plantations with distributors and companies that were large sugar users. Giants such as Coca-Cola, Hershey (chocolate), and Hires (root beer) bought up producers to

guarantee their supplies. Producers in turn purchased distributors and refiners.

The postwar years of 1918 to 1920 brought unprecedented prosperity to Cuba as sugar prices soared and Eastern European sugar-producing areas were slow to recover from the war. After the Allied purchasing committees deregulated prices in 1920, they began an incredible upward spiral called the "Dance of the Millions." In February 1920 the price of sugar stood at 9.125¢ per pound. By mid-May the price had climbed to 22.5¢. But soon prices collapsed as a result of a worldwide depression and Europe's agricultural recovery; by December, Cubans were getting 3.75¢ per pound—the prewar price level.

The precipitous rise and equally sudden collapse of sugar prices caused chaos in the Cuban economy. Mills had contracts to buy large quantities of sugar at high prices, prices that were now far higher than the world market. Producers and processors had taken out loans to expand—loans based on anticipated high prices. Banks began to call in these loans. In April 1921 the island's largest bank, the *Banco Nacional*, closed, and others throughout the country followed suit. Simultaneously, the United States raised its tariff on sugar by 1¢, thereby inflicting another blow on the already devastated industry. In 1921 the First National City Bank of New York—long heavily involved with U.S. sugar interests in Cuba—took over nearly sixty bankrupt mills. The harvest reached 4 million tons in 1922, but prices stayed low. The following year, prices rose to 5¢ a pound as a result of the crisis over the French invasion of the Rhineland. Prices were not to reach that level again for three decades.

In 1920, Alfredo Zayas, a former liberal who had participated in an unsuccessful revolt in 1917, won the presidency with conservative support. Troubled over the crash of sugar prices in the second half of 1920 and the resulting political unrest in Cuba, President Warren Harding sent General Enoch Crowder to Cuba in January 1921 as his special representative. In effect, Crowder ruled Cuba from his headquarters on board the battleship *Minnesota* until 1923, when he became U.S. ambassador.

In the last two years of the Zayas administration, Cuban nationalism revived. Crowder's blatant meddling in Cuban politics and the postwar collapse of Cuban sugar revealed the disastrous consequences of foreign domination and monoculture. Searching for solutions to these problems, Cuban university students, one-quarter of whom were women, entered the political arena in the postwar period. Believing that to change society they must change the university, they directed their first attacks against inept and corrupt professors and administrators; in 1922 students at the University of Havana demonstrated for reforms along the lines of the recent university reform in Argentina. Students would henceforth play an important role in Cuban politics until the fall of Batista in 1959.

Women also played increasingly influential roles in Cuba. Economic growth, especially in household services, textiles, and the tobacco and sugar-refining industries, created greater employment for women outside the home. But as they moved "from the house to the streets," in the words of historian Lynn Stoner, women brought to their public activities a communal consciousness forged in family life. Even the Women's Club, organized in 1917 and composed primarily of upper- and middle-class women, insisted that the state, the *pater familias* of Cuban society, should regulate domestic social relations consistent with the common welfare. It therefore supported women's suffrage, equal pay for equal work, greater access to education, and civil equality.

But for Cuban elites and U.S. policymakers, the growing political activism of students and women was not their greatest concern. In the 1920s there emerged a much larger cultural struggle over Cuban national identity that could have had grave implications for the future security of property rights and U.S. hegemony. Historically, Spanish and criollo elites alike had sought to identify the island's culture with Spain and racist doctrines of white supremacy. The various U.S. military occupations, reflecting their own racial and class prejudices, thereafter reinforced these efforts and joined criollo elites in fashioning an image of Cuba as a white Spanish woman menaced by its black population. This image of whiteness was reinforced by a "national music" identified with Spain and the *danzón*, a rigidly structured dance favored by Cuba's upper class, whose origins lay in the French *contredanse*. But popular sectors in Cuba, especially in Oriente province, long a stronghold of Afro-Cuban culture, had contested this elite vision of Cuba's national identity and preferred the multicultural sound of *son*, a musical style that joined traditional Spanish melodies with African rhythms to reimagine a racially diverse Cuban national culture.

Initially denounced by criollo elites like composer Luis Casas Romero as a "true disgrace," and suppressed by the Cuban government, postwar working-class Cubans defiantly resisted the elite's cultural hegemony and thrilled to the pulsating beat of *son* and the *rumba*, the dance it inspired. Together, son and the rumba, which pantomimed sexual intercourse, gave voice to a popular culture that sought to liberate Afro-Cubans and the lower classes from social controls imposed by the dominant class. During the 1920s the development of radio and recording industries soon created a new audience for this music and dance that, according to historian Louis Pérez, previously had been confined to "working class bars, waterfront cafés, and dancehalls." Boaz Long, the U.S. Minister to Cuba, perhaps best expressed elite fears of this spreading cultural rebellion in a 1920 letter that scorned Cubans' growing affection for the "syncopated music of Africa" and specifically deplored the social dangers of the rumba, which "often become indecent" and "have the effect of developing a mob spirit." More to the point, however, Long was especially concerned that "in the case of the negro they may arouse a sense of racial solidarity."

## MACHADO, 1925–1933

Taking advantage of growing nationalistic sentiment and appealing for women's support with promises of enfranchisement, Gerardo Machado y Morales won the 1924 presidential election. Despite his nationalistic declarations, however, Machado had very close links to U.S. economic interests, for he had been until his election vice president of a U.S.-owned utility in Havana. Even before he took office, Machado visited the United States to assure President Calvin Coolidge of his government's good intentions. Likewise, Machado neglected his promise of suffrage for women, although he authorized breaks for working mothers to nurse their children and established some female hiring quotas.

Machado began his term auspiciously. He embarked on an ambitious program of public works and attempted to institute a system of controls for sugar production designed to protect small- and medium-sized producers against severe price declines. Thanks to these and similar efforts, Machado enjoyed unparalleled popularity and faced virtually no opposition for two years.

Already, however, there were disturbing signs of tyranny and economic instability. The number of political assassinations increased alarmingly. A wave of strikes during 1925 was broken by police shooting down strikers. The nation's most prominent Communist leader, Julio Antonio Mella, was murdered in his Mexican exile by a Machado gunman in 1929. Machado's secret police routinely eliminated his opponents by throwing them to the sharks in Havana Harbor.

Meanwhile, the sugar industry entered a long period of stagnation and decline. It became clear that the Cuban economy was painfully vulnerable not only to world-market fluctuations but also to U.S. political conditions. During this decade, Cuba lost much of its U.S. market because it encountered the powerful interests of sugar-beet farmers in the western United States. To make matters worse, sugar consumption stayed constant as international competition increased supply.

Consequently, the 1926 Cuban harvest reached nearly 5 million tons but brought an average of only 2.2¢ per pound. For the rest of the decade, the price of sugar stayed below 3.0¢, and after the U.S. Congress passed the Hawley-Smoot Tariff Act, Cuba's share of the U.S. market shrank steadily, from 49.4 percent in 1930 to 25.3 percent in 1933. By 1932 the price for sugar fell below a penny per pound. Mills closed, and people were thrown out of work all over the island.

Given this growing economic instability, Machado outlawed the party of his main rival, Carlos Mendieta, to secure his reelection in 1928. Until the onset of the world Depression in 1930, Machado maintained an iron grip on Cuba, despite mounting opposition from university students, women, Communists, labor unions, Afro-Cuban "negristas" like Nicolás Guillén, and many old-line politicians led by Mendieta. Because of Cuba's heavy reliance on exports, the Great Depression had particularly catastrophic consequences, fueling greater political unrest, to which Machado responded with increasingly harsh repression that included tightened censorship and stepped-up terror tactics on the part of his secret police, the *Porra*.

By 1933 the U.S. government had become seriously concerned about the spreading violence, which appeared to threaten U.S. economic interests. In April incoming President Franklin Roosevelt dispatched Sumner Welles in an unsuccessful attempt to negotiate agreement between Machado and the "responsible" opposition, which effectively excluded popular organizations like the

Student Directory and the National Confederation of Cuban Workers (CNOC). Then in the summer, a bus drivers' strike in Havana mushroomed into a general strike that nearly paralyzed the city. After the police massacred several demonstrators in August, Machado's position seriously deteriorated, for he had lost the support of Welles and the army, both of whom lacked confidence in his ability to contain the revolutionary storm. On August 12, Machado resigned and fled into exile.

## THE REVOLUTION OF 1933

For the next three weeks, a provisional government headed by Carlos Manuel de Céspedes struggled unsuccessfully to end the escalating violence. But in August two hundred thousand sugar workers, led by Afro-Cuban Communist León Álvarez, joined student protests and seized a sugar mill in Camaguey province, sparking similar actions throughout Cuba; within a month fully 30 percent of Cuban sugar production was controlled by workers organized into rural soviets. With the old regime rapidly unraveling, a group of army sergeants, led by Fulgencio Batista, overthrew the government. The Student Directory immediately allied itself with the sergeants, and together they formed a revolutionary junta.

The new junta had no organized political backing, and its two main components, the non-commissioned officers and the Student Directory, had sharply divergent aims. The sergeants were concerned only with defending their newly won dominant position against any challenge, whereas the students sought genuine reforms but were unsure just how to achieve them. Within a week, the junta turned over the reins of government to Dr. Ramón Grau San Martín, a well-known physician and long-time opponent of Machado. Grau, Antonio Guiteras Holmes, a leader of the Student Directory, and Batista were dominant figures in the new alignment.

The first move of the new government was to abrogate the onerous Platt Amendment. A flurry of decrees produced more social legislation than in all the previous history of independent Cuba: an eight-hour day for labor, a labor department,

an end to the importation of cheap labor from other islands in the Caribbean, and greater access for children from lower-income groups to the university. There were also measures to redistribute land to peasants, eliminate usury, and give women the vote. Thus empowered, seven newly elected women congressional representatives helped expand the revolution's social achievements by legislating protections for working mothers, including a twelve-week maternity leave, mandatory employer-provided child care for infants, and prohibitions against firing women for getting married.

Ultimately, however, the revolutionary coalition soon disintegrated, leaving the Grau government caught in the classic bind of the reformer: the left, which included the Student Directory and Communists, was dissatisfied because the reforms were not sufficiently radical; moderates like the ABC, a group of middle-class intellectuals, opposed Grau because his program had become "too radical"; and the right opposed all reform. Grau also alienated U.S. financial and agricultural interests when he suspended repayment of several loans owed to the Chase National Bank of New York and seized two mills of the Cuban-American Sugar Company. The U.S. government adamantly refused to recognize the Grau government.

The behavior of Sumner Welles throughout the Grau interregnum was extraordinarily similar to the conduct of U.S. Ambassador Henry Lane Wilson in Mexico during the Madero administration. Welles persistently falsified reports and misrepresented the Cuban government to Secretary of State Cordell Hull and President Roosevelt. As Wilson had befriended Huerta and helped him to power, so Welles allied himself with Batista. Eventually (in November 1933), Welles was recalled, but he had seriously undermined the Grau government. As the economic and political situation worsened, Welles's successor, Jefferson Caffery, maneuvered with Batista to form a new government acceptable to the United States. In January 1934, Grau, unable to rule effectively in the face of U.S. opposition, went into exile and was replaced by Carlos Mendieta, but Batista ruled from the shadows.

## POPULIST INTERLUDE, 1938–1952

Fulgencio Batista y Zaldívar, the sergeant-stenographer mulatto son of a sugar worker, dominated Cuban politics for the next decade, ruling the island through puppet presidents from 1934 to 1940 and as elected president from 1940 to 1944. Although Batista alienated many of the "respectable" elements of the middle and upper classes, he was extremely popular among the masses. During the first two years after his successful coup, he endorsed a mild reform program with some effort at land redistribution. In 1937, in preparation for a presidential candidacy, he distanced himself from the United States and moved leftward, openly courting the support of labor unions and the Communists.

In the same year, the world's sugar-producing nations met in London to try to reach an agreement that would divide up the market, limit production, and stabilize prices. They formed an International Sugar Council, which allotted Cuba 29 percent of the U.S. market, half its share in 1929. Moreover, the bulk of the profits generated by Cuba's sugar economy continued to flow out of the country, because foreign companies accounted for 80 percent of Cuban production (U.S. companies controlled 56 percent), whereas Cubans owned barely 20 percent.

At the end of 1939, Batista permitted the election of a constituent assembly to draft the constitution of 1940. Grau and his *Auténtico* Party (founded in 1934) and other moderates won the election to the assembly and produced a liberal document with provisions that protected labor, guaranteed women equal rights, and limited the right of property when it conflicted with the public good. Batista, however, won the presidential election.

World War II brought on another economic boom. In 1944 production reached its highest level since the Depression. In 1946, as part of its efforts to aid European recovery, the United States agreed to purchase the entire sugar harvest for 3.7¢ a pound. During the Korean war, the price of sugar soared to 5.0¢. Inevitably, however, Cuba's competitors, especially the Philippines, expanded production. The market soon became glutted with sugar, and prices fell. But wartime prosperity, while deepening Cuba's trade dependence on sugar and U.S. markets (sugar exports accounted for 80 percent of all Cuban export earnings, 69 percent of which came from U.S. sales), also swelled company profits and government tax receipts, creating a fund to support intra-elite corruption and populist social programs without unduly burdening business, foreign or domestic. These modest reform programs typically aimed to stabilize capitalist labor and property relations.

Grau, elected president in 1944, continued this tradition. A symbol of Cuban regeneration and democracy, he offered hope to Cuban workers, peasants, women, and fledgling industrialists. He especially acknowledged his political debt to Cuban women voters, declaring that "my government is a government of women." But Grau did little to make good on his promises; instead he presided over an unparalleled reign of corruption. True, the Grau government initiated some reforms, the most significant of which was encouragement of trade-union organizing. By the end of his presidential term, 30 to 50 percent of the work force was unionized and represented the key industries of sugar, tobacco, textiles, transportation, and light manufacturing. These workers used their collective bargaining power and the favorable market conditions to demand higher wages and better working conditions. But Grau made no attack on such key problems as agrarian reform and monoculture.

In 1947 a charismatic populist leader, Eddie Chibás, launched a new campaign against government oppression and corruption. A former ardent supporter of the Auténticos, Chibás had become disillusioned and formed the *Ortodoxo* Party, which featured a mild program of social reform and clean politics. Extremely popular, he posed a serious threat to the Auténticos, whose 1948 presidential candidate, Carlos Prío Socorrás, former leader of the Student Directory, nonetheless won easily because he controlled the election machinery. Prío became another in a long line of Cuban country-club presidents who spent much of his time serving his guests daiquiris at his opulent farm in the suburbs of Havana. There was no letup in the corruption, gangsterism, and spoils system characteristic of his predecessor's regime. As under Grau, the prosperity brought on by high sugar prices concealed Prío's mismanagement.

But a dramatic postwar contraction of overseas sugar markets and collapse of international sugar prices, intensified by U.S. laws that reduced the Cuban sugar quota to protect domestic sugar producers, spread economic depression throughout Cuba. This produced growing unrest among the lower class and increasing opposition among foreign and Cuban businesses that could no longer afford to finance the Auténticos' insatiable corruption or expensive populist reforms. Foreign investors especially insisted that the Auténticos rein in militant workers; an executive at the Cuban subsidiary of Bethlehem Steel, for example, noted with obvious displeasure that "the problem during the Grau and Prío Governments was labor strikes."

Still worse, the unorthodox populist Eddie Chibás, a leading candidate for the presidency in 1952, anticipated that either a military coup or fraud would prevent his election. Seeking to ignite a popular uprising against corruption and foreign influence, he killed himself during a nationwide radio broadcast, plunging the nation into political pandemonium. Six months later, Fulgencio Batista, with tacit U.S. support, overthrew the Prío government, outlawed the Cuban Communist Party, violently suppressed labor strikes, abolished recalcitrant unions, and eliminated most earlier populist restrictions on business freedom.

## THE RETURN OF BATISTA AS DICTATOR, 1952–1959

Batista's new minister of labor, Dr. Carlos Saladrigas, seeking to reassure Cuban business elites and U.S. investors, immediately announced that the coup's goal was to "bring about a radical change in labor-employer relations and remove obstacles for investment of national and foreign capital." A week later, the U.S. government officially recognized the Batista regime, and corporate leaders praised his policies: "When Batista took over there were no more strikes," a Bethlehem Steel executive told historian Morris Morley. "I found economic conditions under Batista more

stable." A Merrill-Lynch executive likewise praised Batista for permitting "business, the competitive system, the free enterprise system to operate."

While the policies protected by Batista's political terrorism found much favor among business elites, they remained highly unpopular with most Cubans. Moreover, like his contemporaries, Carlos Ibáñez in Chile, Getúlio Vargas in Brazil, and Juan Perón in Argentina, Batista soon discovered that ruling a second time would prove more difficult than the first. A new generation of revolutionaries rose to replace the discredited leaders of 1933. Unlike Grau or Prío, they would not be bought off or collaborate with the dictator. Several groups opposed Batista, including the Federation of University Students (FEU) and the Auténticos, who plotted from their havens in Florida; the 26th of July Movement, led by Fidel Castro, unsuccessfully tried to overthrow the government in 1953 by assaulting the Moncada army barracks. Despite the activities of the students and Castro's guerrilla group, the dictator seemed to be firmly entrenched, but his greatest vulnerability remained the structural weakness of the economy, produced by reliance on a single crop, sugar.

Meanwhile, Cuba's sugar industry had stagnated, and the resulting malaise had spread throughout the economy. Agriculture had not become diversified because the land was concentrated in a very few hands—twenty-two companies held one-fifth of the island's farmland. Much of the land was kept idle in case sugar prices should ever boom. Industry was almost nonexistent, for a series of reciprocal trade agreements with the United States—which guaranteed Cuba's sugar market—made it impossible to compete with U.S. imports. These same treaties also stunted agriculture by permitting a flow of agricultural products from the United States, the low prices of which barred potential Cuban competition. Because of its stagnant economy and the peculiar nature of the sugar industry, Cuba suffered from structural unemployment and underemployment. Most sugar workers were needed only during the harvest; even if well paid during this four-month period, they went jobless and often hungry during the other eight months. These structural deficiencies and the economic injustices created by them helped lay the foundation for the Cuban Revolution.

## The Revolution: The Odyssey of Fidel Castro

The Cuban Revolution was deeply rooted in the history of the island, for the movement headed by Fidel Castro continued the revolutionary traditions of 1868, 1898, and 1933. By no coincidence, both before and after gaining power, Castro often cited the ideals of José Martí and the principles of the liberal constitution of 1940. Yet profound disillusionment accompanied those traditions, for Cuba's past revolutions had invariably failed—either its leaders had succumbed to the temptations of great wealth, or the United States had intervened to thwart their programs. In large part, the complex development of the Cuban Revolution reflected a combination of loyalty to those revolutionary traditions and a fear of falling into their errors. Castro desperately sought to avoid past mistakes.

Fidel Castro Ruz, the son of a wealthy Spanish farmer in northwest Cuba, was born in 1927. He attended the famous Jesuit school of Belén in Havana and acquired a reputation as a fine athlete. In 1945 he went off to the University of Havana, where he soon became involved in the frequently violent politics that then plagued the university. In 1947 he participated in an ill-fated invasion of the Dominican Republic, sponsored by student political groups that sought to overthrow dictator Rafael Trujillo. Later he became a follower of Eddie Chibás, to whose Ortodoxo Party he belonged from 1947 to 1952.

On July 26, 1953, Castro, in hopes of sparking a rebellion against the Batista dictatorship, led a small band of lower-middle-class and working-class rebels that attacked the Moncada army barracks near Santiago de Cuba. Their program called for a return to the constitution of 1940, land reform, educational reform, and an end to the vast waste caused by government corruption and large weapons expenditures. Although the assault failed, with heavy casualties, and Castro was captured, the drastic acts of repression the government carried out in its wake and Castro's eloquent defense speech at his trial ("History Will Absolve Me") made him a national hero.

Castro spent the next nineteen months in prison on the Isle of Pines. During this period, the leadership of the 26th of July Movement fell largely to women compatriots like Haydée Santamaría, a founding member of the 1952 anti-Batista resistance, and Melba Hernández, the intrepid lawyer who had defended Castro at trial. They forged political alliances with other anti-Batista groups like the Association of United Cuban Women, led by Gloria Cuadras, and the Women's Martí Civic Front, organized by Carmen Castro Porta, whose antidictatorial activities were rooted in struggles against the Machado regime in the 1920s.

Together, they built a network of urban and rural women who served the revolution as lawyers, interpreters, medical aides, grassroots organizers, educators, spies, messengers, and armed combatants. In addition to Celia Sánchez, perhaps Cuba's best-known woman guerrilla, the revolution also spawned a female combat unit known as the Mariana Grajales Brigade, in honor of the "heroic mother" of the Afro-Cuban independence fighter, Antonio Maceo.

By 1955 these women had produced and distributed some ten thousand copies of Castro's *History Will Absolve Me*, which enhanced his reputation. Batista's general amnesty freed him in 1955, and shortly thereafter he went to Mexico to organize a new attack on the dictatorship. While in Mexico, Castro's group received support from ex-president Prío and Venezuelan exile Rómulo Betancourt (later president of Venezuela). Late in 1955, Castro met Ernesto (Che) Guevara, who was to become the revolution's second-in-command and its greatest martyr.

Castro was determined to return to the island to renew the struggle. In 1956 he and his band departed from Mexico aboard a small yacht, the *Granma*, with eighty-two persons aboard. Originally, Castro had planned to coordinate the landing in Oriente Province with an uprising in Santiago. As happened with the Moncada attack, however, the landing encountered logistical and scheduling problems, and Castro and his followers were betrayed. He and a small group of survivors barely escaped to the Sierra Maestra. From these mountains, the rebels carried out guerrilla raids and beat off attacks by vastly superior forces.

In February 1957, with Vilma Espín, wealthy daughter of a Bacardí rum company executive, acting as interpreter, Castro granted an interview in his mountain hide-out to Herbert Matthews, a well-known reporter for the *New York Times.* The resulting articles enhanced Castro's credibility in the United States and also gave notice to the Cuban people that he was still alive, despite government claims to the contrary. The articles overstated the numerical strength and success of the movement and thereby helped win adherents to the rebel cause all over the island. The guerrillas continued to conduct raids throughout the spring of 1957, picking up recruits and gaining increased sympathy and support from the peasants of Oriente, who rendered invaluable assistance in the form of supplies and intelligence information about government forces.

By mid-1957 violence, especially in Havana, had become endemic as various groups, most unaffiliated with Castro's 26th of July Movement, attacked the regime and met with brutal retaliation. Even women revolutionaries, insulated from earlier repression by the regime's sexism, began to experience wholesale arrests, torture, and imprisonment. But they maintained a sense of humor; when their lawyer, Margo Aniceto Rodríguez, was also imprisoned for denouncing Batista's terrorism, other jailed rebels joked that "Margo is such a good lawyer that, if she cannot free us, she at least comes to stay with us in prison."

Life in Santiago and Oriente Province was completely disrupted by terrorism and strikes. Cuba was increasingly gripped by civil war. In the fall there was an abortive uprising of junior naval officers at Cienfuegos. Batista used bombers and other military equipment to crush the revolt; this alienated some of his U.S. support, as the terms of Cuba's military assistance agreement with the United States expressly forbade using this equipment for domestic purposes.

After the new year, the trend of events turned decisively against Batista. The United States suspended arms shipments to the Cuban government in March 1958. The middle class abandoned the dictator. In May, Batista launched a major effort to dislodge Castro from his base in the Sierra Maestra, and the resulting defeat doomed his regime. Rebel forces inflicted heavy losses on the government troops. Withered by corruption and led by incompetent cronies of Batista, the army was no match for the guerrillas.

As Batista's plight grew desperate, frantic negotiations involving the U.S. embassy began with a view to staving off Castro's victory by the creation, through a coup or fraudulent elections, of a new government, which the U.S. government would recognize and assist militarily. Batista actually held presidential elections, printing up filled-in ballots in advance, and readied a president to take office in February. But the strong drive of the rebel forces frustrated these maneuvers; by the end of December 1958 the *barbudos* (bearded revolutionaries) were on the outskirts of Havana. On January 1, 1959, abandoned by his U.S. allies, Batista and his closest aides fled to Miami.

Thus, a rebel band, numbering fewer than three hundred until mid-1958 and scarcely three thousand when the old regime fell, won a great victory because they were persistent and disciplined and gained the sympathy of all the people—peasants, workers, and the middle class. But they also faced an army wracked by favoritism and incompetence. Batista's army, when put to the test, proved able to terrorize unarmed citizens but disintegrated when confronted with a formidable insurgency.

## The Revolution in Power, 1959–2003

During its first four years (1959–1962), the revolution consolidated its domestic political position, began the socialization of the economy, and established a new pattern of foreign relations. In 1959 the revolutionary leaders made a series of decisions that determined the course of the revolution for the next decade. First, they concluded that parliamentary democracy was inappropriate for Cuba at that time. The Fundamental Law of the Republic, decreed in February 1959, concentrated legislative power in the executive. As prime minister and later as first secretary of the Communist Party, Castro held the decisive posts in the government and the ruling party of the Cuban state. Within eighteen months, the revolutionary regime had suppressed the right of free press and the centuries-old autonomy of the University of Havana. The revolutionaries conducted public trials of former *Batistianos*, and a large number of Batista's henchmen were executed.

Second, Castro moved the revolution leftward to consolidate its political support and accomplish its economic goals—land reform, income redistribution, agricultural diversification, and economic independence from the United States. The radicalism of this economic program and the concentration of political power in the hands of the close-knit 26th of July Movement alienated middle-class supporters like Major Huber Matos and President Manuel Urrutía, who resigned in July 1959. In October, Matos, one of the revolution's foremost military leaders and a violent anticommunist, was charged with treason and imprisoned. At the same time, the revolutionaries allied with the Popular Socialist (Communist) Party, seeking its help in administering the country.

In January 1960 moderate elements were purged from the leadership of Cuban labor unions and the Soviet Union was cultivated as an ally to diversify the nation's economic dependence and protect the revolution from U.S. intervention. Soviet deputy premier Anastas Mikoyan agreed that the Soviets would purchase 425,000 tons of Cuban sugar in 1960 and 1,000,000 tons the next year. In May, Cuba resumed diplomatic relations with the Soviet Union.

## UNITED STATES–CUBAN RELATIONS

Meanwhile, Cuban relations with the United States, already suffering from the unfavorable publicity brought by the trials and the expropriation of large estates, reached a crisis in May 1960. The Cuban government requested that the major petroleum refineries, owned by Texaco, Standard Oil, and Royal Dutch Shell, process Soviet crude oil, which the Cubans had obtained at a lower price than the three companies charged for their oil. At the urging of the U.S. State Department, the companies refused, forcing Cuba to expropriate the refineries. The United States retaliated by abolishing the Cuban sugar quota, and Cuba in turn expropriated numerous U.S.-owned properties.[1] In October all U.S. exports to Cuba were banned—an embargo that has not yet been lifted. This action set off a new wave of expropriations of U.S. property, including that of Sears, Roebuck, Coca-Cola, and the enormous U.S. government–owned nickel deposits at Moa Bay.

As relations between the two nations deteriorated, the Central Intelligence Agency (CIA) funneled money to various exile groups for arms and set up a training camp in Guatemala to prepare an invasion force. On January 3, 1961, the outgoing Eisenhower administration severed diplomatic relations with Cuba, and three months later, President John F. Kennedy authorized the exile invasion at the Bay of Pigs on April 15. But the revolutionary army swiftly crushed the attack, which had been poorly planned and executed. Based on the false assumption that the Cuban people would revolt in support of the exile invasion, the Bay of Pigs fiasco immeasurably increased Castro's prestige and gave new impetus for radical reconstruction of the Cuban economy and society.

What had begun as a program of social and political reform within a framework of constitutional democracy and capitalism evolved into a Marxist revolution. One month after the Bay of Pigs, Castro proclaimed allegiance to socialism, and the Soviet Union, pledging to defend Cuba in the event of another U.S. attack, stepped up its flow of arms to the island.

These included missile emplacements and aircraft capable of delivering atomic weapons throughout most of North and South America. Although Cuba and the Soviet Union argued that

---

[1]The government had previously taken over only the operation of these properties.

the missiles had a defensive, deterrent character, the United States claimed that they were offensive weapons, ordered a naval quarantine of Cuba, and demanded the dismantling of the missile sites. For a time it appeared as if Kennedy was losing control of his military, which was pressing to use force against Cuba. After several days, during which the world came close to nuclear war, the two superpowers reached a compromise by which the Soviet Union agreed to remove its missiles from Cuba in return for a pledge from the United States not to invade Cuba and to remove its own missiles from Turkey. However, the United States continued to subvert and harass the Cuban Revolution with the aid of counterrevolutionary Cuban exiles; this included CIA-sponsored raids against refineries and ports, infiltration of enemy agents, and even some bizarre attempts to assassinate Castro.

## REVOLUTIONARY ECONOMICS

The Cuban Revolution benefited from advantages few other socialist revolutions have enjoyed. The guerrilla war (in contrast to that of China or Vietnam) was relatively short and caused little destruction of human life or property. Moreover, Cuba had well-developed communications and transportation systems, including an extensive railroad network and excellent primary roads. The character of Cuba's rural population promised to make the process of socialist land reform easier than it had been in Russia, for example. Because the sugar industry had proletarianized much of the agricultural work force, farm workers did not demand their own land but sought improved working conditions and wages. Cuba also had considerable unused land and industrial capacity, which could be quickly employed to raise living standards and increase productivity. Finally, by 1959 there existed a number of developed socialist states that could offer Cuba substantial assistance, thus offsetting the severe negative effects of the U.S. embargo on exports.

But the revolution also faced serious problems. To begin with, the revolutionaries, inexperienced in economic affairs, made mistakes. The socialist reorientation of the economy inevitably caused disruptions, and the U.S. embargo caused crippling shortages of parts and other difficulties, which the development of new patterns of trade with countries in the socialist camp (and with some capitalist countries) only gradually overcame. Also, many of Cuba's ablest technicians joined the first wave of refugees that fled to the United States. Finally, revolutionary leaders initially spurned material incentives, endorsed by more traditional Marxists as the best spur to production, in favor of moral incentives, which would give rise to the "new socialist man." Application of this theory caused considerable economic damage before it was replaced in 1969 by a more pragmatic mix of material and moral incentives.

The first goal of the revolutionary government was to redistribute income to the rural and urban working class. During the first three years, it met with considerable success, raising wages 40 percent and overall purchasing power 20 percent. Unemployment was virtually wiped out. These benefits accrued predominantly to areas outside Havana, for the revolutionaries were determined to reverse the trend toward the superurbanization characteristic of most of Latin America.[2]

Castro decreed the first Law of Agrarian Reform in May 1959. This law restricted the size of landholdings and gave the government the right to expropriate private holdings in excess of stated limits; the owners would be indemnified depending on the assessed value of the property for tax purposes. The estates of Batistiano government officials were taken over immediately, followed by seizure of the great cattle estates when their owners resisted. The government distributed the expropriated land in small plots or established cooperatives, which the Institute of Agrarian Reform (INRA) administered. Much of the land redistribution took place in Oriente Province, where the peasants had provided early and crucial support for the 26th of July Movement. Eighty-five percent of all Cuban farms fell under the jurisdiction of the reform law because landownership had been so highly concentrated under the old regime.

---

[2]"Superurbanization" is used to describe the vast expansion through internal migration and concentrated industrialization of one city, usually the capital.

During the first year of its rule, the Cuban government experimented with various types of agrarian holdings. Eventually, all became *granjas del pueblo* (state farms). Administered by INRA, they usually employed the same workers who had toiled on them before the revolution, but workers were paid better wages and offered improved working conditions.

The redistribution of income to workers and peasants resulted in some long-range problems. With more money to spend, Cubans demanded more food, especially meat, the consumption of which rose 100 percent. This rising demand led to the overkilling of cattle, which seriously damaged the ability of the government to supply meat in later years. The government lowered rents and utility rates and supplied many services free of charge, which increased disposable income even more. Inevitably, shortages arose because Cuba no longer imported consumer goods and foodstuffs. Rather than limit consumption inequitably by raising prices, the government began rationing in March 1962. The revolutionaries also poured large sums into rural housing, roads, and other improvements, but poor planning wasted scarce resources.

Two other important programs had mixed success during the first three years: agricultural diversification and industrialization. The revolutionary government sought to become more self-sufficient by transferring cane land and idle fields to the production of cotton, vegetable oils, rice, soybeans, and peanuts, which would save badly needed foreign exchange on these previously imported commodities. Industrial reforms began slowly; the government at first took over the management of just one major foreign company, the extremely unpopular telephone company. But U.S. efforts to sabotage the revolution ultimately led to sweeping expropriations of U.S.-owned refineries, factories, utilities, and sugar mills. Next, the government took over the banking system and most urban housing. Finally, the revolutionary regime began to expropriate native-owned businesses. But more ambitious industrial development plans proved too difficult, and the program was officially put off in 1963.

The revolutionaries encountered serious problems in agriculture after 1961 because of their inability to organize, plan, and administer the economy. Although Castro set up a central planning agency, JUCEPLAN, in February 1961, more often than not he ignored or circumvented it with his personal "special" plans. For a long time, the government also ignored the private agricultural sector, a critical oversight because more than half the farmland remained in private hands. In early 1961, in an effort to overcome this neglect, the government established the National Association of Small Farmers (ANAP), which tried to coordinate the production of small farms with national goals. It also furnished credit, set up stores, and organized various associations.

## THE RETURN TO SUGAR, 1963–1970: THE TEN-MILLION-TON HARVEST

Experience had shown that Cuba lacked the resources and the administrative and technical expertise to industrialize. As a consequence, Cubans decided in 1963 to reemphasize agriculture and return to intensive sugar production, while continuing the diversification program. Increased agricultural production, it was hoped, would generate large earnings and eventually underwrite future industrialization.

Unfortunately, agriculture, especially sugar, had suffered enormously from well-intentioned but short-sighted policies. The sugar harvests of 1960 and 1961 had been extraordinarily successful because they benefited from very favorable weather and because the island's cane was at the age of peak yield. Also, for the first time in a decade, the entire crop was harvested. But the sugar harvest of 1962 was the worst since 1955, and subsequent harvests continued to be disappointing. The essential problem was that the revolutionaries, in their fervor to diversify, had ripped up some of the best cane land. They had not replanted cane in two years, and as a result most Cuban cane was well past its peak yield. Moreover, equipment and manpower were badly administered. Transportation and distribution were in chaos. Sugar mills were damaged and left unrepaired for years. As a result, from 1962 to 1969, agricultural production fell 7 percent.

Nonetheless, the government made considerable efforts to correct the situation. The regime decreed the second Law of Agrarian Reform in October 1963; under this law, it expropriated thousands of medium-sized farms. State farms became the dominant form of agriculture, controlling 70 percent of the land and taking responsibility for all the major export crops. The government also forced those small farmers who remained to sell it their crops at low cost. Cuba put a remarkable portion of its gross national product into investment, but that achievement was largely wasted through inefficient administration and poor planning. Many projects were abandoned unfinished, and those that were completed were often improperly maintained and rendered useless.

Thereafter, Cuba launched a new campaign of socialization that centralized the administration of the economy. The most visible symbol of this policy change was the ill-fated, ten-million-ton sugar harvest of 1970. Designed to model the effectiveness of a socialist developmental strategy that stressed "moral" over "material" incentives for workers, it also aimed to produce the largest sugar harvest in Cuba's history and to use the anticipated foreign exchange bonanza to invest in the nation's independent industrial development. Confronted with the reality of a severely damaged and underdeveloped agricultural infrastructure capable of producing at best six million tons of sugar, however, the effort was doomed to fail. Ironically, even revolutionary successes contributed to its failure: the revolution had created considerable employment opportunities outside the sugar industry, but this left it with one-fifth the former number of professional cane cutters in 1959 and required a mobilization of nonagricultural labor that seriously depleted resources and destabilized the national economy.

## Failure, Reassessment, and Institutionalized Revolution, 1970–1990

The ballyhooed "ten-million-ton harvest" of 1970 failed to reach its acclaimed goal and in the process did extensive damage to the Cuban economy as a whole. To get the 8.5 million tons they did eventually harvest, the revolutionaries virtually ruined the sugar industry, and subsequent harvests generally were poor. Resources and labor were siphoned off from other sectors, causing disruption and turmoil.

Even more significantly, however, these disastrous economic policies—and the centralized authoritarian state whose administration they seemed to require—began to separate the revolutionary leadership from its base of popular support. No matter how much U.S.-sponsored counterrevolutionary terrorism may have justified it in these years, the regime's blatant disregard for civil liberties and its authoritarian manner would remain a permanent stain on an otherwise laudable revolutionary record. Many Cubans, especially young people excited by the revolution's democratic promise, refused to accept these practical constraints on their liberty. Slowly, a new popular anti-authoritarian cultural movement emerged around the *canción de protesta* (protest song). This movement attracted youth who believed in the revolution's goal of social justice but increasingly opposed the hierarchical nature of state decision making, especially its personalist association with Fidel Castro. Ironically, it was greatly influenced by African and Asian anticolonial struggles, the celebration of indigenous folk cultures in Chile and Argentina, and especially Brazilian popular resistance to military dictatorship—all of which the Cuban revolutionary regime also promoted.

Protest songs marked a distinctive development in Cuban music and culture. In the early 1960s folk artists like Carlos Puebla and Los Compadres (The Godfathers) had combined *son* and traditional Cuban country music (*música guajira*) with lyrics that sang the praises of the revolution and its guerrilla heroes. Los Compadres's popular song *"Se acabarán los bohíos"* ("The Shacks Will Disappear"), for example, celebrated the revolution's promise of "a living wage, an apartment for every family, hard work," and the eradication of bohíos, except those that "remain as museum pieces." The protest singers of the late 1960s, however, identified with the revolution's idealistic and humanitarian goals but criticized its failures, especially its authoritarianism and restraint of artistic freedom.

Silvio Rodríguez, one of the movement's principal voices, captured this sense of revolutionary patriotism and youthful alienation when he denounced state bureaucrats as "bosses who said one thing and did another, squares, those who didn't trust the young, guys with all the perks, enemies of culture, the establishment cowards who were ruining the revolution that I carried inside of me." For Rodríguez and thousands of other young Cubans, it was hypocritical for the revolutionary leadership to encourage Latin American, Asian, and African peoples to rebel against tradition but simultaneously to restrain youthful Cuban rebels, who expressed their dissatisfaction by wearing long hair, hippie clothing, and tattoos.

Some within the revolutionary state agreed. Haydée Santamaría, a veteran of the Sierra Maestra and the 1953 attack on Moncada, refused to surrender to bureaucratic pressures and sought to protect these young protest artists. As the head of the Casa de las Américas, a revolutionary state institution that coordinated cultural exchanges with the rest of Latin America, she organized a series of international music festivals that gave voice to protest songs and, for a time, secured their access to state radio and television programming. But in general, as sugar harvests failed and protest singers were jailed, these were bleak years for the revolutionary economy, cultural expression, and political freedoms.

The great failure of the 1970 sugar harvest, however, prompted a searching self-criticism and dramatic rethinking of revolutionary policies and process. Castro himself admitted his personal responsibility for this failure and vowed to make changes that would advance the revolution. This led to greater political openness and popular political participation. It also enabled the revolutionary leadership once again to embrace its rebellious youth culture. According to ethnomusicologist Robin Moore, "In the space of only a few years, protest song moved from the margin into the mainstream of socialist music making." Changes in revolutionary state policy, not the surrender of young artists' independence, clearly facilitated this rapid rapprochement.

The Cuban government now increasingly supported this new music, known as *nueva trova* (new ballad), and encouraged its young musicians to represent Cuba at international music festivals organized in Latin America, Spain, and Eastern Europe. It also created the National Movement of the Ballad (MNT), a state organization designed to encourage musical careers and fund the creative arts. Performance centers were established in every province. Although the MNT refused to support particular songs like Pablo Milanés's "La vida no vale nada" ("Life Is Worthless"), the lyrical content of which was deemed to be antisocial, it dramatically expanded the resources available to aspiring young musicians, introduced them to new instruments and electronic technologies like the synthesizer, increased their access to studio time, and helped them distribute their recordings.

During the next five years, Castro depersonalized the government and institutionalized the revolution. He delegated authority to a new executive committee of the Council of Ministers and gave the bureaucracy wider scope of action and more influence. President Osvaldo Dorticós and Carlos Rafael Rodríguez, a veteran Communist who had fought with Castro in the Sierra Maestra, took charge of Cuba's economic development. Castro reorganized the government to draw clear lines of separation between the armed forces, the bureaucracy, and the Communist Party. The militia was disbanded and merged into the army. The military was restructured along traditional hierarchical lines, and Cuba's first revolutionary generals were named. The judicial system was revamped. In addition, an attempt was made to broaden the popular base of the regime and to strengthen the Communist Party. The labor movement was revitalized; a larger role was assigned to the trade unions and the workers' tribunals that saw to the enforcement of labor laws and workers' rights. Steps were taken to involve workers more actively in the formulation of production goals and plans.

The Cuban leadership also drastically overhauled the revolution's policy of economic development. It introduced sophisticated computerized planning techniques and inaugurated a system of material incentives for workers and managers. A work quota system was implemented between 1971 and 1973, resulting in a 20 percent increase in productivity in just one year (1972). The government also began to differentiate between jobs for pay purposes. No longer were people paid according to their need but rather according to the productivity and complexity of their job. These and other economic reforms led to a dramatic rise in productivity. From 1971 to 1975 the gross national product grew at an annual rate of more than 10 percent, compared with an annual growth rate of 3.9 percent for the period from 1966 to 1970.

The first Communist Party congress in December 1975 completed the formal institutionalization of the revolution. The congress adopted Cuba's first socialist constitution, approved by nationwide referendum in February 1976. The constitution, an attempt to make government more responsive to the people, provided for a pyramid of elected bodies. At the bottom were popularly elected members of municipal assemblies, who elected delegates to provincial assemblies and to the National Assembly of People's Power. Most of these representatives were Communist Party members. Castro remained entrenched at the top as first secretary of the Communist Party, head of government, and president of the Council of State (elected from the National Assembly).

Political institutionalization was accompanied by efforts to reorganize and rationalize the economy, whose performance had slowed in the last half of the decade. Still heavily dependent on sugar for its economic well-being, Cuba's economy grew a disappointing 4 percent a year from 1976 to 1980. At the root of the problem was the lack of professional management, quality control, and labor discipline, all of which contributed to poorly manufactured goods, ranging from shoes to televisions.

Persistent economic problems and political disaffection led to a massive emigration of Cubans, primarily to the United States, from April to September 1980. More than 125,000 Cubans left, mostly through the port of Mariel, many aboard dangerously overcrowded, leaky boats. Nonetheless, Cuba's outmigration (a rate of less than 2 percent in 1980) compared favorably to that in the rest of the Caribbean, where émigrés constituted about 20 percent of the population.

Great political and social upheavals historically have caused similar flights of disaffected people; after the American Revolution, 10 percent of the population left for Canada or England rather than live under the new republican rule.

Between 1981 and 1985, Cuba seriously attacked its chronic economic problems, and there was a significant quantitative and qualitative improvement in the economy. The average annual growth rate for the period was 7.6 percent. Export diversification grew, with reexports of Soviet oil accounting for over 40 percent of Cuba's hard-currency earnings in 1985; but in 1988 this share fell to 17 percent because of lower prices on the world market. Despite Cuba's many economic problems, economists Claus Brundenius and Andrew Zimbalist have concluded that Cuba's economic growth between 1960 and 1985 was the second highest in Latin America. Moreover, the distribution of income generated by this growth was far and away the most equitable, both within and outside the region.

### CUBA AND THE WORLD

From its early years, the Cuban revolutionary government sent military aid to other Third World countries. It helped the Algerian independence movement and guerrilla groups in Zaire, the Portuguese African colonies, and Tanzania during the 1960s. In the same period, facing the bitter hostility of most Latin American governments, Castro virtually declared war on them (with the exception of Mexico) in the Second Declaration of Havana (1962), vowing to turn the Andes into the Sierra Maestra of South America.

With the murder of Che Guevara and the economic disasters of the late 1960s, Cuba changed course and sought to reestablish normal diplomatic and trade relations with the other governments of the hemisphere. During the 1970s, as the danger of U.S. invasion diminished and the economy improved, Cuba again took an important role in Africa. Eleven thousand Cuban troops assisted Ethiopia in repelling Somalia's 1978 invasion of the Ogaden region, and fifty thousand Cuban soldiers helped Angolan forces in their fourteen-year

This witty cartoon reminds Americans, who still lack universal health care, that socialist Cuba, against all odds, has transformed itself into a world-class health-care provider. [©1994 Dan Wasserman, *Boston Globe*. Distributed by Tribune Media Services]

struggle against counterrevolutionary rebels supported by the United States and South Africa and in thwarting a South African invasion of Angola across its southern border. At Cuito Cuanavale, in one of the decisive battles of modern African history, a joint Cuban-Angolan army inflicted a crushing defeat on the South African invaders, which led to the signing of an agreement in 1988 between Angola, Cuba, and South Africa for the mutual withdrawal of Cuban and South African troops and for the independence of Namibia.

Cuba sponsored what the *New York Times* called "perhaps the largest Peace Corps–style program of civilian aid in the world," with some 16,000 doctors, teachers, construction engineers, agronomists, economists, and other specialists serving in twenty-two Third World countries. The Cuban international aid program included free education in Cuba. In addition to the motive of "international solidarity," Cuban international aid had the objective of providing the country with much-needed hard currency. Fees were charged on the basis of ability to pay, and poor countries received aid free. Cuba's foreign construction projects were a major income producer.

### ACHIEVEMENTS

Despite its mixed economic record, the revolution's achievements in the areas of employment, equitable distribution of income, public health, and education were remarkable. Until the onset of the

1990 economic crisis, which caused many factories to shut down due to lack of fuel, Cuba had the lowest rate of joblessness in Latin America. But workers who were laid off because of plant closings continued to receive 60 percent of their wages. Inequalities in the standard of living were dramatically reduced from the days of Batista. The working classes in particular benefited from government policies; rents were controlled, limited to no more than 10 percent of income, as were rationed food prices (but the government tolerated an open market in farm products). Eighty percent of Cubans owned their own homes. Agricultural workers on state farms and cooperatives got furnished houses with televisions and community recreational centers. Cuban city streets had virtually no beggars and sidewalk vendors, which set them apart from those in other Latin American countries. Education and health care were free and equally accessible to all.

The revolution had always promised equality and social justice, but these were special goals of the Cuban Women's Federation (FMC), organized in 1960 under Vilma Espín's leadership. The FMC played a crucial role early in the development of revolutionary social services: literacy crusades reduced illiteracy from 24 to 4 percent; a national child-care system freed women, irrespective of class, to pursue their own careers; an innovative rural education program taught vocational skills and provided peasant women with modern health-care information; and schools for maids and prostitutes discouraged exploitation of women and retrained them as professionals in socially productive activities.

Since then, the FMC, Latin America's largest women's organization with a membership of 3 million, has continued to influence Cuban policy regarding health care, education, women's employment, daycare, sexual discrimination, and family life. For example, it secured passage of the 1975 Family Code, which recognized the equal right of both spouses to education and career, required them to share in household duties and child care, and established divorce as a legal remedy for any spouse whose mate refused to comply. Although a 1988 survey showed that men worked only 4.52 hours per week at home whereas women worked 22.28 hours, it also revealed the law's potential: most respondents acknowledged that this inequity was diminishing steadily.

Women gained enormously from the revolution. In 1953, 20 percent of women were illiterate, without hope of either education or rewarding employment; but by the early 1960s the revolution had eradicated illiteracy and established equal access to a free education. After the revolution, higher education, long the redoubt of elite women, who had composed 45 percent of a small university student population in 1956–1957, also opened its doors to women of every class; by 1990 women represented 57 percent of a university population that was ten times larger.

Before the revolution, women composed 13 percent of the work force, one-third of them employed as domestic servants. By 1990, however, women represented 38.6 percent of Cuba's workers and constituted 58 percent of technical, 85 percent of administrative, and 63 percent of service workers. Yet the percentage of women managers, Communist Party leaders, National Assembly members, and People's Power delegates was 27, 16, 33, and 17, respectively. Distressing as these figures might be, they resembled the gender inequality typical of developed countries and represented a vast improvement on the records of Cuba's Latin American and Caribbean neighbors. Nonetheless, Castro, clearly disturbed by this inequality, called for increased women's representation commensurate with "their participation and their important contribution to the building of socialism."

Children were special objects of the government's solicitude. Children aged seven and under and pregnant women received a daily distribution of milk and enjoyed the best medical care in Latin America. With the region's lowest doctor-to-patient ratio, according to a 1990 study in the *Latin American Research Review*, Cuba had "transformed itself into a world-class health-care provider, an extraordinary achievement." Sophisticated medical procedures performed in Cuba included heart transplants, heart-lung transplants, and microsurgery. The educational budget amounted to 7 percent of the nation's GNP, the highest in Latin America. The population had an average ninth-grade education, and illiteracy was wiped out.

For nearly thirty years, the Cuban Revolution's success had derived from a searching self-criticism, careful attention to its mass political base, and an enduring socialist pragmatism. The ongoing effort to correct past mistakes, known as *rectificación*, was renewed in the mid-1980s, even before the dramatic changes in Eastern Europe created economic difficulties for Cuba. In particular, Castro spoke of the need to improve economic efficiency and incorporate more blacks, women, and youth in revolutionary leadership positions.

Castro himself, by calling on Cubans in 1959 "to end racial discrimination at the workplace" and in "cultural centers," raised a public voice against Cuban racism that had long been silenced by the 1912 massacre of Afro-Cubans and white republican elites' insistence thereafter that Cuba was a racial democracy. The structural transformation of Cuban society since 1959 led most scholars to conclude that "the revolution has achieved racial equality" even as a "racist mentality" endured within Cuban culture. This was reflected in a demographic shift of blacks and mulattos from 26.9 percent of the population in 1953 to more than 60 percent recently, and it was confirmed by improvements in such social indices as literacy, employment, fertility, interracial marriage, and mortality rates.

Yet Afro-Cubans, who undeniably have benefited from the revolution and currently hold prestigious positions throughout Cuban society, still remained statistically underrepresented in higher education, professional employment, and leadership positions in both the government and mass organizations; they were also overrepresented in vocational schools, blue-collar jobs, and *solares* (substandard tenement houses). More disturbingly, they made up 58 percent of the *jóvenes desvinculados*, alienated youth who neither work nor study.

Undoubtedly, most Cubans benefited from the revolution, which explains their extraordinary support for it, almost forty years later in the midst of its deepest economic crisis. According to an independent 1994 poll commissioned by the Miami *Herald* and conducted by a Costa Rican affiliate of the Gallup Organization, 69 percent of Cubans identified themselves as revolutionaries, socialists, or communists and 58 percent believed the revolution had produced more achievements than failures.

### RECTIFICACIÓN AND THE "SPECIAL PERIOD," 1990–2003

During the early 1990s, however, the socialist collapse in Europe threatened Cuba's progress in streamlining its economy and creating greater equality. As they transitioned toward a market economy, Cuba's Eastern European trading partners were forced to trade on international prices, conducted in hard currency. But Cuba also needed its limited stock of hard currency to pay interest on its foreign debt and purchase certain vital products from the West. Anticipating increased difficulties with some of its former socialist trading partners, Cuba diversified its trade links, doubling its trade with China and increasing its trade with Latin America by 20 percent.

Nonetheless, the Soviet collapse dealt a devastating blow to the Cuban economy, resulting in a national income decline of approximately 45 percent between 1989 and 1992. Before 1990, Cuba had received 13 million tons of oil annually from the Soviet Union, but this fell sharply to 1.8 million tons in 1992 (from Russia). In addition to routine blackouts and factory shutdowns, the resulting energy crunch led to a revival of horse-drawn carriages, the use of oxen-drawn tractors, and wholesale replacement of cars in transport by bicycles—good for the environment and health, but economically inefficient and uncomfortable. The shortfall in oil dealt a heavy blow to another of Cuba's major hard-currency earners, the nickel industry. Cuba had the world's third-largest nickel reserves, but the Soviet collapse caused production to fall 36 percent, from 46,600 metric tons in 1989 to 29,900 in 1994. To make matters worse, world-market prices for nickel, which had peaked at over $6 per pound in 1989, plummeted more than 50 percent during the next five years to $2.87. Foreign-exchange earnings therefore declined disastrously.

The economic crisis also temporarily reversed the trend of steadily improving social conditions and produced a decline in living standards. During the early years of this "special period," most Cubans lived on a drab diet of white rice and red beans, supplemented by some vegetables and fruit, an occasional chicken, and what they could purchase on the open market. The food rationing system, however, prevented the emergence of the massive hunger and malnutrition so common in the rest of Latin America.

This crisis was aggravated by the United States's intensified effort to strangle socialist Cuba through passage of the 1992 Torricelli Act, which extended the U.S. trade embargo against Cuba to U.S. subsidiaries in third countries and barred any ship docked in Cuba from entering a U.S. port for 180 days. The Helms-Burton Act of 1996 tightened the noose by allowing U.S. citizens to sue foreign corporations whose trade or investment profits derived from properties expropriated more than forty years ago. These laws drew angry protests from Canada and the European Community, which felt the United States had no right to apply its laws extraterritorially. Each year since 1992 the U.N. General Assembly has voted by overwhelming majorities (157 to 2 in 1998) to condemn the embargo, and in July 1993 a summit of the leaders of Latin America, Spain, and Portugal unanimously called for an end to the embargo against Cuba. Pope John Paul II, during a much-celebrated visit to Cuba in 1998, added his voice to those protesting the embargo, as did Nobel laureate and former president Jimmy Carter in 2002.

In the midst of crisis, the socialist government showed its revolutionary pragmatism. In 1992 the National Assembly adopted sweeping changes in the constitution and electoral law, including enhanced constitutional protections for all religious faiths; authorization of 100 percent foreign-owned companies and joint-venture enterprises with foreign capital; and provisions for direct, secret election by voters of deputies of the National Assembly and provincial assemblies. The first direct, competitive elections for deputies of the National Assembly resulted in a lowering of their average age to forty-three—a reflection of the generational change of guard taking place in Cuba. In another sign of the new political atmosphere, candidates for office no longer needed approval by the Communist Party, and other reforms aimed to make the National Assembly "a more independent and effective body for legislation, governmental monitoring and oversight, and economic planning."

According to Cuban Vice President Carlos Lage, the revolutionary government during this "special period" also sought economic reform "without altering its socialist essence." In fact, unlike all the other Latin American countries pressed by their domestic business classes and the IMF to combat economic problems in the 1990s by slashing state social spending to reduce budget deficits, the Cuban government's investment in social services actually increased from an average 17 percent of GDP during the 1980s to 24 percent in 1993, the depth of the national crisis.

The government monitored foreign investment, closely regulated its relations with Cuban labor, and scrutinized its impact on the environment. Ironically, Cuba's socialist infrastructure of national planning, free universal health care, and education may be the most attractive feature to foreign investors, who grudgingly endure inevitable state interventions in exchange for the benefit of a healthy, disciplined, productive, highly educated work force; relative labor peace; and freedom from the extraordinary expense of unemployment and medical insurance payments. In effect, they gain access to scarce resources and First World workers at Third World costs. "It's one of the advantages of a centralized economy," a Cuban economist explained. "We can actually make a company's investment more secure than it would be in an unregulated economy."

As a result, foreign firms were eager to engage in joint ventures in fields ranging from a new overseas telephone system to tourism. In June 1994 a Mexican company signed a $1.5 billion deal to rehabilitate Cuba's telephone system. New hotels built by joint ventures with Spanish companies were rapidly springing up on Cuban beachfronts, with the number of foreign tourists topping 500,000 in 1993 and rising to 1,000,000 annually thereafter. In 2000 tourism earned $1.9 billion in reserves, Cuba's largest source of hard currency. More than three hundred joint ventures with some fifty-seven countries in forty different sectors of the economy attracted investments in excess of $5 billion; domestic investment also increased, rising to 9 percent in 1997. Cuba still depended greatly on sugar, but the economy also had diversified. Income from manufacturing netted $415 million, tobacco and cigars brought in $100 million, a relatively new biotechnology industry earned $100 million, and nickel production grossed $90.8 million. Moreover, the government invested heavily in modernizing the sugar industry. Most cane was harvested by machine and many new mills were built.

After five years of declines, Cuba's gross domestic product (GDP) rose steadily after 1993, averaging 3.3 percent per year between 1994 and 2000. Trade also rose consistently, although it failed to achieve its 1989 levels: the annual average increase in the value of exports and imports since 1993 was almost 20 percent. As a percentage of GDP, budget deficits had grown astronomically to 40 percent in 1993 but thereafter declined to 4 percent in 1996, producing dramatic improvement in consumer confidence and strengthening the Cuban peso by 40 percent. More important, these macroeconomic indices of national recovery were reflected in the experiences of everyday life in Cuba. Ascribing this apparent renaissance to Cuba's "entrepreneurial socialism," one recent visitor concluded that "in Havana some of the new wealth is clearly starting to be felt in the population generally. On almost every block, it seems, is a freshly painted house. The discos are jammed every night with both Cubans and foreigners."

Cuba hoped to overcome its energy crisis through the discovery of large oil reserves off its shoreline. In June 1994 two Canadian firms announced that they had found commercial quantities of oil at wells offshore in Matanzas Province. Utterly dependent on frequently expensive oil imports since its independence, Cuba produced more than 1 million metric tons of oil annually

since 1993, an increase of 400 percent during the decade. This reduced the nation's import bill, lowered its energy costs, improved industrial efficiency, and contributed to greater economic independence.

In addition to promoting such traditional exports as sugar and nickel and expanding tourism, the Castro government made the development of biotechnology and medical exports an essential part of its economic survival strategy. In the 1980s, Havana's center for genetic engineering produced interferon, an important drug in the treatment of cancer. Since then Cuba invested more than $1 billion in biotech research, organized thirty-eight biotech centers, and developed four hundred patents on products ranging from fetal monitors to vaccines against hepatitis B and meningitis B. Ironically, in 2002, Cuba contracted with Glaxo SmithKline, a multinational pharmaceutical company, to market this meningitis B vaccine around the world, including the United States, where annually three thousand cases of meningitis claimed three hundred lives, mostly in impoverished, high-risk areas. But the U.S. government, which usually opposed restraints on private trade and investment, nonetheless prohibited the use of this life-saving vaccine unless Glaxo agreed to pay Cuba its royalties in kind—for example, through the export of medicines—rather than in cash. If Cuba can find sufficient markets for its biotechnological and medical products, the exports could be worth $1 billion a year.

In response to the continuing economic crisis, in 1993 the Cuban government instituted additional reforms. Most important, a reorganization of agriculture replaced large state farms with autonomous cooperatives in land "ceded for an indefinite period by the state." These "Basic Units of Cooperative Production (UBPC)" operated on a profit-sharing basis and administered their own resources. They received from the state credits for purchasing farm equipment, seeds, and other inputs in exchange for a commitment to sell a fixed amount of their harvest to the government; any surplus crops could be sold at prevailing prices in the open market. By 1998 over 1,500 UBPCs controlled 3 million hectares of land and employed almost 122,000 workers, 114,000 of whom were co-op members. This decentralization of agriculture, appealing to the workers' self-interest, led to more efficient use of resources and contributed to a 17.3 percent growth of agricultural production in 1996.

Cuba also launched a vast technological experiment in agriculture that aimed to end dependence on costly foreign agricultural inputs by converting from conventional modern agriculture to large-scale organic farming. The "alternative model," as the Cubans call it, sought "to promote ecologically sustainable production by replacing the dependence on heavy farm machinery and chemical inputs with animal traction, crop and pasture rotations, soil conservation, organic soil inputs, and what the Cubans call biofertilizers and biopesticides—microbial pesticides and fertilizers that are nontoxic to humans." Two agricultural scientists who have studied the program, Peter Rosset and Shea Cunningham, stress its "potentially enormous implications for other countries suffering from the declining sustainability of conventional agricultural production."

A second general reform authorized self-employment in a long list of trades and occupations. In reality these new rules simply legalized long-existing activities, but they also generated tax revenues and provided regulatory controls, inspections, and licenses. This "informal sector" expanded rapidly, averaging between 10,000 and 15,000 self-employed Cubans in 1993 and mushrooming to 180,000 by decade's end. Cuba's informal sector, however, contrasted sharply with the poverty and economic insecurity of its counterparts in the rest of Latin America. Because socialism guaranteed them inexpensive housing, basic subsistence, free health care, and education, self-employed Cubans typically spent their income on discretionary consumer goods; in a 1997 article in *The Atlantic Monthly,* Joy Gordon reports the example of a woman with a *paladar* (private home restaurant), serving dinners for four dollars, who could afford a Sony stereo system, a VCR, and new color television. "Yet," Gordon concludes, "this is possible in Cuba only because and insofar as it has remained socialist."

Finally, in an obvious move to encourage the inflow of dollars through family remittances from the United States, the government announced in July 1993 that it would no longer penalize the holding of foreign currencies and would authorize Cubans to spend U.S. dollars in a network of government stores. These measures eased the government's cash crisis and put a dent in the flourishing black market, but they created a privileged class of people with access to U.S. currency and increased inequality: according to one Cuban economist, "The 4:1 income gap between best-paid and worst-paid has widened in ten years to 25:1." But this still leaves Cuba the most egalitarian society in the hemisphere.

As a result of these reforms and Cuba's growing insertion into the world economy, the new millennium opened with Cuban officials expressing quiet confidence that Cuba had turned the corner, that the worst was over. Some professional economists agreed that, in defiance of neoliberal orthodoxy, this "Cuban miracle" had "confounded its critics," but many problems remained unsolved. Largely due to the U.S. economic blockade, which increased the cost of Cuban imports and limited income from exports, Cuba suffered from massive trade deficits that also increased its reliance on short-term foreign loans at high interest rates. By 2001 its foreign debt was $13 billion.

During the late 1990s the nation had relied upon dollar remittances and a rapidly growing $1.5 billion a year tourism industry to cushion the impact of its trade deficit. An important consequence of the September 11 terrorist attacks on the World Trade Center, however, was a dramatic decline in worldwide tourist travel, which threatened to reduce national revenues. Finally, the rising cost of oil and the fall of sugar prices damaged Cuban prospects for a full economic recovery. Although Cuban socialism guaranteed every citizen free access to health care, education, and a basic subsistence diet, Cubans interested in resurrecting pre-1990 living standards had to access private markets; but this required dollars that could be secured only in the tourist industry or through family remittances from abroad. Naturally, this tended to undermine the revolution's long-standing commitment to social and economic equality.

As a result, it was not surprising that a new debate about racism, civil rights, and equal opportunity emerged among Cuban intellectuals and in popular culture. Historian Alejandro de la Fuentes suggested that a recent proliferation of Cuban scholarly studies of race in its historical and contemporary context reflected concerns about rising inequality in Cuba. To be sure, dollarization immediately privileged families with relatives living in self-imposed exile in the United States, and these overwhelmingly tended to be light-skinned Cubans of Spanish ancestry. But more disconcerting was the virtual invisibility of Afro-Cubans in the tourism industry, the only other source of dollars. In 2000, Castro himself admitted that Cuba was not "a perfect model of equality and justice" and acknowledged that, although "we established the fullest equality before the law and complete intolerance for . . . sexual discrimination in the case of women, or racial discrimination," these racial, gender, and class prejudices persisted.

These prejudices, growing social inequality, and their collective impact on Afro-Cuban identity also became lyrical themes in the rapid emergence of a new hip-hop culture in Cuba. Initially influenced by rap music broadcast by Miami commercial radio stations, young, mostly black males fused hip-hop styles with traditional Afro-Cuban rhythms to deplore injustices associated with the "special period": racism, class inequality, prostitution, and selfishness. According to an official of a Cuban state organization that promoted rap artists, "Cuban rap is criticizing the deficiencies that exist in society, but in a constructive way, educating youth and opening spaces to create a better society." Indeed, Cuban rappers increasingly recognized the nation's enduring cultural identification with "whiteness" as the historical source of its lingering racism; this was reflected in the response of a hip-hop producer to a Cuban reporter's question about whether or not there were any "white" rappers: "Well, let's say there are lighter-skinned rappers," he replied, "because no one in Cuba is white."

Despite all these problems, however, it was still true in 2002 that, in the face of the collapse of its major trading partners a decade earlier and forty years of unremitting, implacable opposition from the United States, including a trade blockade that openly violated international law, Cuba had made a remarkably quick recovery. It ranked fifty-fifth in the United Nation's Human Development Index of 180 countries and fifth in Latin America behind Argentina, Chile, Uruguay, and Costa Rica.[3] Cuba's doctor-patient ratio ranked second in the world, with 530 physicians per 100,000 people. Among eighty-eight developing countries, Cuba had the fourth-lowest poverty index. Its infant mortality rate, at 7 per 1,000 live births, was the lowest in Latin America and equaled that of the United States. Its literacy rate for youth was the highest in Latin America (99.8%) and the second highest for adults (96.7%). It had the largest number of scientists and engineers per capita of any Latin American nation (1,611 per 1,000,000 people), twice that of second-place Argentina. During the 1990s, Cuba's 3.7 percent average annual per capita economic growth rate placed it second only to Chile among Latin American nations. Despite growing inequality, it still had the most egalitarian income distribution in the region, perhaps in the world. With understandable pride, in June 2000, Cuban president Fidel Castro surveyed the devastation wreaked by the early 1990s economic Armageddon and remarked: "In spite of this we did not close down a single health care centre, a single school or daycare center, a single university, or a single sports facility. . . . What little was available we distributed as equitably as possible." No other nation in the region could make a similar claim.

Further Cuban development would of course be greatly facilitated and hastened by a change in U.S. policy that would result in economic advantages for both countries. Unfortunately, the United States continued to harbor cold-war prejudices and illusions about Cuba that it abandoned long ago about a much more powerful communist state,

[3]Cuba's ranking in Latin America likely would have been higher if the calculations had been based upon 2002 data instead of information from 2000, before the Argentine economy collapsed and Uruguay staggered.

the People's Republic of China. The collapse of socialism in a number of Eastern European states, the success of the U.S. invasion of Panama in December 1989, and the victory of the U.S.-supported opposition in the Nicaraguan elections of February 1990 produced gloating in Washington and predictions that Cuba, whose economic collapse was considered imminent, was next.

But reports of the early demise of the Cuban Revolution were greatly exaggerated. Short of a massive U.S. invasion, there was very little prospect that Cuba's socialist regime would be overthrown from within or without. In Cuba, unlike in Eastern Europe, socialism did not arrive in the wake of a victorious Red Army; it was created by an indigenous popular revolution that linked the ideals of socialism and independence, and it still enjoys overwhelming popular support: 98 percent of eligible voters participated in the 1998 National Assembly and People's Power elections and less than 4 percent protested by defacing their ballots. Despite many economic problems, the Cuban Revolution had a record of social achievement without parallel in Latin American history and presented a vivid contrast to the economic and social crises gripping most of the capitalist societies of Latin America.

Until 2003, the process of "rectification" included efforts to democratize still further Cuba's political and economic structures, widening popular participation in decision making and increasing tolerance for expressions of dissidence. This process seemed to culminate with the release of most "prisoners of conscience" in 1998, Pope John Paul's historic January 1998 visit, and the 2002 arrival of former U.S. president Jimmy Carter, who condemned the forty-year U.S. blockade and openly promoted the Cuban dissidents associated with the Varela Project.

But despite this new openness and the Cuban government's agreement to allow Cubans who wish to leave to do so, U.S. government hostility to Cuba remained relentless, in the process violating its own sacred rhetorical commitments to the free movement of people, trade, and investment. The United States denied travel visas to internationally renowned intellectuals like Gabriel García

Márquez; prevented, under terms of the Helms-Burton Act, Canadian, Mexican, and European business executives with Cuban investments from entering the United States; and refused to allow U.S. citizens to travel freely to Cuba.

Moreover, the 1978 Cuban Adjustment Act, which granted immediate legal status to all Cubans arriving in the United States, effectively encouraged Cubans to emigrate illegally aboard dangerous, leaky, makeshift boats and rafts or to hijack planes and ferries, without fear of serious punishment in the United States. Meanwhile, the United States approved fewer than three thousand legal immigration applications per year, even though a 1984 immigration accord permitted annual legal immigration of twenty thousand Cubans and three thousand political prisoners. President Castro accordingly chastised the U.S. government for needlessly endangering Cuban lives through its cynical manipulation of the immigration issue to destabilize Cuba and subvert the revolution. U.S. radio broadcasts routinely urged Cubans to protest and commit terrorist acts of sabotage against their government, reinforcing this lawlessness by refusing to prosecute Cubans who hijacked boats or planes en route to the United States. By contrast, in the 1960s, when several planes were hijacked to Cuba, the Cuban government arrested and convicted the hijackers for their crimes; more recently, it executed Cubans found guilty of hijacking a ferry.

As the new millennium opened, however, Cuba's economic renewal had created additional pressure on the U.S. government to lift its economic blockade. Influential newspapers called for rolling back the embargo. The *New York Times* complained that U.S. policy toward Cuba remained frozen in the past and appeared to be dictated by the most radical factions of the anti-Castro Cuban exile community. Fearing the impact of Asia's economic crisis on U.S. trade and investment, "an exponential increase" of U.S. companies became interested in Cuban markets, according to the May 1998 testimony of the United States–Cuba Trade and Economic Council, a business group that supported a gradual dismantling of the embargo. Eager to claim a share of Cuba's health care market, worth $500 million to $1 billion, and its bulk-food commodity imports, valued at $800 million, influential corporate executives like Dwayne Andreas of Archer Daniels Midland Company, Ted Turner of Time Warner, and Donald Fites of Caterpillar also opposed the embargo. Because removal of the embargo would produce an estimated $3 billion to $7 billion of trade, at least $2 billion worth of exports, and some forty thousand new jobs, doing so clearly would bring substantial economic benefits to both the United States and Cuba, and would undoubtedly contribute to the further liberalization of Cuban life that the Bush administration claimed to desire.

Doubtlessly, this explains why a bipartisan majority in the House of Representatives overcame the truculent opposition of Republican leaders to pass a 2002 bill that foreshadowed the demise of the U.S. embargo by lifting U.S. restrictions on travel, trade, and monetary remittances to Cuba. According to Cuba expert Wayne Smith, "This vote reflects the growing momentum in favor of getting rid of the embargo against Cuba altogether." But before this could occur, there were still powerful obstacles that would have to be overcome, not least of which was the opposition of President Bush, whose election in 2000 had depended upon the votes of a rabidly anti-Castro, antirevolutionary Cuban exile community in Florida. In 2003, perhaps flushed with confidence from his apparent victory in another "splendid little war," this time in Iraq, President Bush once again appeared to ratchet up the political pressure on Cuba. James Cason, head of the United States Interest Section in Cuba, opened a more extensive and aggressive campaign to encourage, organize, and coordinate dissident, anti-Castro groups in Cuba, prompting the Cuban government to respond by arresting, summarily convicting, and sentencing some seventy-five alleged dissidents to long prison sentences. As the United States vainly sought another U.N. resolution condemning Cuba for its alleged human rights abuses and the international community joined Cuba in its annual denunciation of the U.S. trade embargo, the island nation's future remained uncertain, but seemed likely to mirror its turbulent past.

# 18

# Revolution and Counterrevolution in Central America: Twilight of the Tyrants?

THE JULY 1979 VICTORY of the Sandinista Front for National Liberation (FSLN) over one of Latin America's oldest tyrannies—the Somoza family dynasty of Nicaragua—was an extraordinary event that reverberated throughout Latin America and the United States. Like the Cuban Revolution of 1959, this anti-imperialist social revolution challenged U.S. power in a part of the world that for almost a century had been its own secure preserve. In Washington, the Sandinista triumph caused gloom and disarray as to how to deal with the new Nicaragua and prevent the spread of the revolutionary virus to its Central American neighbors. It heartened Latin American revolutionaries, their supporters, and all the democratic forces of the region, ending the discouragement caused by a long series of defeats for radical and progressive causes—from the Brazilian counterrevolution of 1964 to the destruction of Chilean democracy in 1973. Some unique aspects of the Nicaraguan revolution—its blend of Marxism and progressive Catholic thought, its effort to maintain a mix of state and private enterprise—excited the imaginations of those committed to social change in Latin America.

In El Salvador, meanwhile, guerrilla activities against a repressive military-civilian junta had developed into a full-scale civil war by the spring of 1980. The guerrillas had created a revolutionary government (the *Frente Democrático Revolucionario*) with its own army, the *Frente Farabundo Martí de Liberación Nacional* (FMLN). Ten years later, despite massive infusions of U.S. military and economic aid (over $4.5 billion) to the government, rebel forces held much of the country and showed themselves capable of disrupting its economic life and launching powerful offensives at will. By the spring of 1990 popular discontent with the U.S.-supported government, revulsion in the United States at the atrocities committed by the Salvadoran military, and the demonstrated strength of the guerrillas had forced the government to accept rebel proposals for U.N.-sponsored peace talks without preconditions. The resulting peace accords provided for demilitarization and democratic elections in which the FMLN would take part. Less than completely "free and fair," those elections (March–April 1994) gave victory to the entrenched right-wing parties, but the FMLN obtained a strong presence in the national legislature and prepared for a long struggle for the political and social transformation of El Salvador.

Guerrilla movements had risen and waned in Guatemala since 1954, when a counterrevolutionary coup organized and armed by the CIA overthrew a reformist regime and the social changes it had instituted. The guerrilla struggle gained in intensity and popular support in the late 1970s, even as the level of violence on the part of government security forces and death squads reached new heights. After the Guatemalan military government adopted a scorched-earth policy, accompanied by massacres of indigenous villagers thought to have supported the guerrillas, the rebels faded into the mountains and jungles. The roots of revolution—massive poverty, injustice, and repression—remained, however, even after the civilian government of Vinicio Cerezo took office in 1986. By the spring of 1990 the guerrilla war had revived and rebel units maintained a presence only thirty miles from the capital, Guatemala City. Here too, peace talks made slow progress against the bitter resistance of the dominant military, but they finally produced the Peace Accords of 1996.

Why should Central America, a region so richly endowed by nature—where U.S. economic, political, and cultural influence has been so strong—be such a violent land and present such immense contrasts of wealth and poverty? The answer to this question requires a more detailed survey of the twentieth-century history of three countries, Guatemala, Nicaragua, and El Salvador, where revolutionary movements shaped the contours of modern life.

## Guatemala

In Guatemala, the historical sources of political violence and late twentieth century revolution could be found in the nation's growing external dependence, its domination by foreign monopoly, and the collaboration of a rapacious landed oligarchy that supported a series of military dictatorships between 1898 and 1944. The first of these was led by Manuel Estrada Cabrera, a tyrant famous for his cruelty, who ruled ruthlessly for two decades before his own previously obedient Congress declared him insane and sought his removal. During his presidency, Estrada Cabrera began to invest in the national infrastructure, particularly road and port facilities for transporting and shipping coffee.

Although initially funded with Guatemalan resources, the financing and construction contracts for this infrastructure soon passed into the hands of foreign, predominantly U.S., companies.

A U.S. firm, International Railways of Central America (IRCA), which was linked to the United Fruit Company (UFCO) through interlocking directors, acquired monopolistic control over land transport in Guatemala and virtual ownership of the major Atlantic port of Puerto Barrios. The UFCO secured a contract in 1901 to carry Guatemalan mail from Puerto Barrios to the United States in its "Great White Fleet" and to carry bananas, obtained from producers at fixed prices, to the North American market. In time the company acquired vast banana holdings of its own on very favorable terms from the Guatemalan government.

The enormous U.S. economic influence, based on direct investments, loans, and control over Guatemala's chief foreign market, was translated into a growing U.S. tutelage over Guatemala. After World War I, the U.S. embassy became in effect a branch of the Guatemalan government; U.S. ambassadors were approached for favors in return for cooperation with U.S. corporations.

By the end of Estrada Cabrera's brutal regime, Guatemala's economy was utterly dependent upon the export of bananas and its land was concentrated in the hands of a few, but unlike Nicaragua and El Salvador, much of this was owned by a single foreign company, UFCO. During the next decade coffee oligarchs battled each other, sought to renegotiate the state's relationship with UFCO, pursued constitutional limitations on the military, and simultaneously worked to preserve their control over natives, peasants, and workers. The resulting instability provided fertile ground for the emergence of a new military strongman, Jorge Ubico, who seized power in 1930 and dominated Guatemala until a 1944 revolution overthrew him.

During his reign, Ubico consistently supported UFCO and IRCA, but he also cultivated close relations with the nation's coffee oligarchy, whose interests were threatened by the Great Depression. During the 1930s coffee prices declined to less than half the 1929 level. By cutting off European markets, World War II deepened dependence on the U.S. market and further depressed coffee prices. The crisis in foreign trade led to rising unemployment, wage cuts, and business failure for many small producers. The Guatemalan planter oligarchy and associated export-import interests, closely linked to U.S. enterprises, made the masses pay for the Depression through wage cuts, intensified exploitation, and reduced government expenditures. In the 1930s the level of official repression rose; in 1933 alone the government executed some one hundred labor leaders, students, and political dissidents.

Ubico was determined to guarantee the planter class a reliable, cheap source of labor. In 1934 he abolished debt peonage, replacing it with a vagrancy law that required all persons owning less than a stipulated amount of land to carry cards (*libretas*) to show that they had worked at least 150 days a year on the haciendas. Those who failed to comply with this obligation to do "useful work" were jailed. Fearing popular uprisings and peasant land invasions, Ubico also legalized murder for landlords seeking to protect their properties.

The fall of the detested Ubico regime came as a result of popular democratic opposition movements, fostered by the antifascist climate of opinion created by U.S. and Latin American participation in the war against the Axis powers. Although Guatemala, under U.S. pressure, had declared war on the Axis in December 1941, Ubico's profascist views and the ties of many of his close advisers and ministers to German interests were well known. In June 1944 a general strike and antigovernment demonstrations forced Ubico to resign. A triumvirate of two army officers and a civilian took over and organized congressional and presidential elections to be held in December 1944. The overwhelming victory of Juan José Arévalo, a prominent educator and scholar who had spent many years in exile, confirmed the demand of the Guatemalan people for the establishment of a government pledged to democracy and social progress.

## REVOLUTION AND COUNTERREVOLUTION, 1944–1983

The Guatemalan democratic revolution of 1944 was largely the work of a coalition of urban middle-class groups and discontented junior military, with the small working class as junior partner and the indigenous peasantry in a marginal role. The revolutionary leadership favored a capitalist course of development and was friendly to the United States. The program of the Arévalo administration (1945–1951) reflected its desire for a capitalist modernization. An ambitious social welfare program was launched that stressed construction of schools, hospitals, and housing as well as a national literacy campaign.

The 1945 constitution abolished all forms of forced labor, enfranchised literate women, prohibited press censorship, limited presidential power, criminalized racial discrimination, required equal pay for equal work, and established civil equality for men and women. The 1947 labor code guaranteed to workers the right to decent working conditions, social security coverage, and collective bargaining through trade unions of their own choosing; it also provided for compulsory labor-management contracts and mandatory paid maternity leaves. These reforms spurred a rapid organizing drive among urban, banana, and railroad workers, who made a number of limited gains.

Following the example of many Latin American governments in this period, Arévalo began a program of industrial development and diversification, employing the newly created state bank and other agencies for this purpose. As for the existing foreign economic enclaves (chiefly UFCO and IRCA), Arévalo's policy was not to nationalize but to regulate their operations in the national interest. The government insisted, for example, that UFCO submit wage disputes to arbitration. New laws stipulated that in the future the state or predominantly national companies should exploit natural resources; in industry, foreign investors could operate on the same terms as nationals.

Arévalo's agrarian program was equally moderate. Government programs offered state support to cooperatives and provided agricultural credit and technical assistance. A new law protected tenants from arbitrary ouster by landlords, who were required to rent uncultivated lands to landless peasants, but the latifundia remained intact, although the constitution of 1945 permitted expropriation of private property.

Urban, middle-class *ladina* women played an influential role in the Arévalo government. The Democratic Union of Women (UMD), organized in 1946, included former students at the University of San Carlos who had mobilized against Ubico. They agitated for women's rights, participated as teachers in the literacy crusade, and hosted a 1947 Inter-American Women's Conference that advocated greater democracy, human rights, and national industrial development. The Guatemalan Women's Alliance (AFG), founded in 1947 and closely associated with the clandestine Communist Party, championed working-class interests, agrarian reform, and indigenous rights. Its most famous member arguably was María Vilanova de Arbenz, whose husband became Guatemala's president in 1950.

The pace of reform quickened with the election of Major Jacobo Arbenz, who sought to convert Guatemala from a dependent nation with a semicolonial economy into an economically independent country. His major strategy to achieve this objective was import-substitution industrialization, to be accomplished by private enterprise. But the creation of a modern capitalist economy was impossible without an expansion of the internal market—that is, of mass purchasing power—through agrarian reform.

Prompted by indigenous peasant uprisings, the phenomenal growth of the Guatemalan National Peasant Confederation (CNCG), claiming more than 200,000 members, and a 1950 census report showing that 2 percent of Guatemalans controlled 74 percent of the arable land, Arbenz supported a 1952 agrarian reform law. It provided for the expropriation of holdings over 223 acres and their distribution to the landless, with compensation made through twenty-five-year bonds. By June 1954 approximately 100,000 peasant families had received land, together with credit and technical assistance from new state agencies.

The agrarian reform inevitably affected UFCO. No more than 15 percent of its holdings of over 550,000 acres were cultivated; the company claimed that it needed these large reserves against the day when its producing lands were worn out or ruined by banana diseases. The land expropriation, coming on top of a series of clashes between the government and UFCO over its labor and wage policies, brought their relations to the breaking point.

Meanwhile, in its struggle with the landed oligarchy, a weak middle class needed allies, and workers used this situation to expand their demands. They organized independent trade unions like the Guatemalan Confederation of Labor (CTG) and the Guatemalan Syndicalist Federation (FSG) and pressed for higher wages and greater worker autonomy. Their success, reflected in the establishment of the General Confederation of Guatemalan Workers (CGTG), with more than 100,000 members, coupled with the growing politicization of indigenous peasants organized in the CNCG, moved Arbenz to the left, but it frightened his supporters in the agro-industrial middle class, inducing them to seek a modus vivendi with the planter aristocracy and its U.S. associates.

The moderate Arévalo had already been attacked in the U.S. media as being procommunist. Arbenz's deepening of the revolution, threatening the profits and properties of UFCO, evoked a much angrier reaction in the United States and caused UFCO's friends in high places to prepare for direct action against Guatemala. By 1953, President Dwight D. Eisenhower had approved "Operation Success," a CIA–State Department plan to remove Arbenz and replace him with Colonel Carlos Castillo Armas. Deeply involved in the conspiracy against Guatemala were Secretary of State John Foster Dulles and his brother, CIA director Allen Dulles (both former partners in UFCO's legal counsel), United Nations Ambassador Henry Cabot Lodge, and Assistant Secretary of State for Latin America John Moors Cabot, both UFCO stockholders. Headquartered in Miami, a CIA official served as field commander for the operation and funneled guns and ammunition to Castillo Armas's army. The man in charge of psychological warfare was E. Howard Hunt, later of Watergate fame.

Because the United States had imposed an arms embargo against Guatemala, Arbenz purchased a shipment of Czech arms, whose arrival in May 1954 provided a pretext for implementing "Operation Success." In June, Castillo Armas advanced six miles from the Honduras border into Guatemala and waited for his U.S. allies to do the rest. While U.S. pilots in CIA planes dropped propaganda leaflets and incendiary bombs on the capital, Guatemalan army officers refused to arm workers and peasants who wanted to defend the revolution. Instead, they pressured Arbenz to resign, turning over the government to a three-man junta. But the United States insisted on the installation of Castillo Armas, the CIA candidate, as president. On July 3 he arrived in the capital in a U.S. embassy plane and promptly launched a campaign of terror against supporters of the revolution. According to one estimate, eight thousand persons were executed. The land reform of 1952 was revoked, UFCO and other landowners regained holdings that had been expropriated, and Castillo Armas surrounded himself with an entourage that has been described as a gang of "grafters and cutthroats."

The counterrevolution returned power and property to the landed oligarchy, its foreign allies, and their new middle-class partners. The process of land reform was reversed; after 1954 the size of the average peasant landholding decreased, whereas the percentage of land devoted to commercial farming increased. But the Guatemalan economy did not stand still. The new ruling coalition promoted the growth of a small dependent industry and some major shifts in the composition of agricultural exports.

Despite a modest advance of industry, mostly of the maquiladora type controlled by foreigners, Guatemala remained basically a producer of foodstuffs and raw materials. The composition of its exports changed considerably as a result of declining coffee prices. Coffee was still the leading export in 1980, but cotton, sugar, and cardamom ranked second, third, and fourth in value. While commercial agriculture gained, basic grains (wheat and maize) had to be imported from the United States. This reflected the continuing concentration of the best lands in the hands of latifundistas, often by usurpation of the plots of mestizo and indigenous smallholders, with army and security forces present to suppress armed resistance. Because peasant unions were forbidden by law and the minimum-wage laws were ignored, extremely low wages were the rule.

The narrow social base of the post-1954 regimes and the fact that they owed their existence to a flagrant foreign intervention explain their militaristic, repressive character. In the thirty-four years after 1954, there was only one civilian president—Mario Méndez Montenegro, elected in 1966—and he escalated the repression, directing counterinsurgency operations as much against peasants as guerrillas. Aided by U.S. military advisers, an estimated fifteen thousand people were slaughtered in the department of Zacapa alone between 1966 and 1968.

Despite the crushing blows inflicted by this and subsequent counterinsurgency campaigns, the guerrilla movements survived and reached a new height of activity in the mid-1970s with the formation of the Guerrilla Army of the Poor (EGP). The resurgence was marked by growing cooperation among guerrilla movements, trade unions, and peasant organizations. Another significant development was a cleavage in the church between the conservative Archbishop Mario Casariego, firmly loyal to the regime, and some bishops sympathetic to liberation theology and many working clergy active in the Catholic *comunidades de base* (grassroots communities). Their involvement in the daily struggles of the poor brought charges of subversion and attacks by government and paramilitary forces against them; in 1981 alone, twelve priests were killed and many others, including some bishops, were threatened with death.

The guerrilla struggle achieved a high point of organizational unity in 1981 following the decision of the three major guerrilla organizations and the Guatemalan Communist Party to form a unified command to coordinate their military operations. By the end of 1981 they had scored considerable successes. The widespread violence and the growing power of the guerrillas intensified the flight of capital, adding to the economic gloom brought on by low commodity prices and declining industrial activity.

The guerrilla advances produced discord among the military. One group of officers favored a more defensive strategy, controlling what was feasible; others favored an aggressive policy, including "scorched earth" tactics against the areas that were supposed to support the guerrillas. This group gained the upper hand in March 1982 and installed General Efraín Ríos Montt as head of a new three-man junta, whose policy, according to the *Latin America Weekly Report*, was to eradicate the mainly indigenous population: "Troops and militias move into the villages, shoot, burn, or behead the inhabitants they catch; the survivors are machine-gunned from helicopters as they flee. Any survivors are later rounded up and taken to special camps where Church and aid agencies cope as best they can."

These conditions did not deter the Reagan administration from certifying to Congress that the human rights situation in Guatemala had improved, thereby renewing military aid and arms sales to its government. But the United States, carefully avoiding the subversive term *reform*, also continued to pressure the military government to build a broader domestic political constituency by implementing periodic programs of "agrarian transformation." This typically meant that landless indigenous peasants were relocated on inaccessible, uncultivated, relatively infertile, state-owned jungle lands and received minimal credit and technical assistance, all of which increased their dependence on markets and eroded traditional autonomy.

## Return to Democracy, Guatemalan Style, 1983–2003

In August 1983 a military coup toppled Ríos Montt. The desperate state of the economy, the country's international isolation, and growing internal opposition from social movements that overcame traditional racial, ethnic, gender, and class divisions all persuaded the military to withdraw in favor of civilian elites. The domestic opposition particularly frustrated the army. Despite savage repression, hundreds of thousands of indigenous peoples, Catholic activists, homeless people, urban workers, and housewives bravely resisted the government by joining organizations like the Committee of Peasant Unity (CUC), Catholic Action, the National Movement of Shantytown Dwellers (MONAP), the National Committee of Union Solidarity (CNUS), and the Consumers' Defense Committee (CDC). Together these groups organized the Democratic Front Against Repression (FDCR), to demand democracy and social justice. But the return to democracy was hedged with conditions. It was well understood that no future civilian government could hope to survive if it interfered with the military's conduct of the ongoing counterinsurgency war or attacked the oppressive land system.

The first step in the transition to this curious democracy was the election of a constituent assembly. Notable for its repressive atmosphere, a "reactionary pluralism" that severely limited political debate, and the resulting abstention of 57 percent of eligible voters, this constituent assembly enabled basically conservative parties to schedule elections in 1985 and write a new constitution that ignored social problems, institutionalized the military repression, and sanctified the rights of private property.

Despite constitutional provisions that criminalized voter abstention, fewer than 50 percent of eligible Guatemalans voted in successive elections that empowered Vinicio Cerezo Arévalo and José Serrano Elías, both of whom promised to honor the military's autonomy, curb inflation, create jobs, respect human rights, and expand democracy. Although the military distrusted these civilian leaders, it understood that their governments, with connections to powerful sister parties in Europe and patrons in Washington, had the best chance of securing urgently needed foreign aid and overseeing the "recomposition" of the state and civil society.

Under Cerezo and Serrano, the military retained effective control of rural Guatemala, scene of a prolonged counterinsurgency war that transformed 38 percent of urban women and 56 percent of rural wives into widows, and caused an immense flow of indigenous refugees, an estimated 10 percent of the population. In Phase One of the process, the army burned down Maya villages, laid waste fields, and killed over 30,000 villagers, according to estimates. Phase Two, designed to turn the indígenas against the guerrillas, created "model villages" (reservations) in which to resettle surviving indígenas and those who had returned home after fleeing and living like hunted animals in the mountains.

The military also reorganized indigenous society, forcing hundreds of thousands of Mayans to participate in a civil defense patrol program. Israel, a major supplier of arms to Guatemala, provided it with a wide range of sophisticated hardware and also furnished advisers on counterinsurgency.

Meanwhile the guerrilla struggle, after suffering severe defeats that drove the partisans into remote parts of the mountains and jungles, revived. Many model villages were surrounded by guerrilla territory; the guerrilla presence was particularly strong in three zones: the Petén, Quiché and Huehuetenango, and Solola. Despite the increase in guerrilla activities, the *Unidad Revolucionaria Nacional Guatemalteca* (URNG), which led and coordinated the guerrilla movement, sent Cerezo an open letter expressing willingness to discuss peace talks. In April 1989 preliminary talks were held between a reconciliation commission approved by the government and rebel leaders, and the talks continued under Serrano.

Nor were Cerezo and Serrano able to deliver on their economic promises. An economic austerity program reflecting the dominant influence of landowning and business elites kept both unemployment and inflation high. Economic aid from the United States and European countries fell below expectations. The economy continued to stagnate, and poverty skyrocketed. Between 1980 and 1987, according to the United Nations, the proportion of poor people rose from 79 to 87 percent; the percentage of people in "extreme poverty" grew from 52 to 67 percent. Guatemala's historically high income inequality also worsened substantially. Naturally, this led to dramatic declines in the "physical quality of life," measured by infant mortality, literacy, and life expectancy. Still worse, this crushing poverty was disproportionately concentrated among women and indigenous people.

But popular sectors took advantage of greater political freedoms to create a powerful opposition. Guided by the United Guatemalan Workers (UNSITRAGUA), a new independent labor confederation, students, teachers, workers, shantytown dwellers, human rights activists, peasants, women's groups, and indigenous rights organizations joined together to form a cross-class coalition that called for nationwide general strikes to protest neoliberal policies that produced greater unemployment and higher prices for bread, milk, and urban transportation. Although they succeeded in winning some important concessions, these popular social movements still lacked the power of the army, international bankers, and Guatemala's propertied elites; but they functioned effectively, consciously or not, as a civilian front for the rural guerrilla insurgency.

Although Cerezo and Serrano pledged to work for peace and end human rights abuses, their promises were contradicted by a wave of assassinations. The U.S.-based Council on Hemispheric Affairs found that Guatemala, closely followed by El Salvador, was the worst human rights violator in Latin America in 1990. In that year, according to one human rights organization, there were 773 killings, including the murders of dozens of street children, mostly at the hands of the military, the national police, and right-wing civilian death squads.

By 1993 a number of factors combined to produce a crisis for the Serrano regime. One was the public anger caused by a series of drastic electricity rate increases. A second shock was the 1992 award of the Nobel Peace Prize to the Maya activist Rigoberta Menchú, which provided the indigenous masses of Guatemala with an internationally recognized leader in their struggle for political and social rights. Against a background of mounting unrest and popular demonstrations, Serrano announced the dissolution of Congress and the Supreme Court and took all power into his own hands. The move, reminiscent of Fujimori's power grab in Peru, was quickly dubbed the *autogolpe*, or self-coup.

By a certain irony, the United States—which in 1954 had plotted the ouster of the democratic nationalist government of Jacobo Arbenz—now suspended economic assistance to Guatemala in protest against the coup, producing consternation in business circles and wavering within the military, which finally withdrew its support from Serrano. The coup promptly collapsed, and Serrano fled to Panama.

There followed prolonged negotiations among the military, political, and business elite, which searched for a presidential candidate acceptable to them and the United States but hostile to Serrano. They selected Ramiro de León Carpio, a lawyer and human rights critic who also opposed the guerrillas and supported the neoliberal economic policies sponsored by the International Monetary Fund (IMF) and the World Bank.

The military undoubtedly saw in him a figure who could give Guatemala a respectable image but with whom they could live, a judgment that his first presidential acts served to confirm. After firing some members of the military high command who allegedly backed the coup, he promptly replaced them with very similar individuals. Against the advice of human rights groups, León Carpio decided to keep the Presidential Guard, a group implicated in numerous human rights violations, including the assassination of anthropologist/activist Myrna Mack. He reopened negotiations with the guerrillas, but the talks proceeded slowly and haltingly, largely because León Carpio insisted on separating the negotiations for a cease-fire from discussion of the social and economic issues—land, labor, and political reform—that were at the base of the war.

In general, despite his populist rhetoric, León Carpio showed little interest in the problems of the 90 percent of the population who lived in poverty. Even by the low Latin American standards, the dimensions of those problems were staggering: the share of national income received by the poorest 10 percent of the population dropped from 2.4 percent in 1980 to 0.5 percent in 1991. The problems were especially acute for indigenous people (55 to 60 percent of the population). According to official statistics, the indigenous infant mortality rate was 134 per 1,000 live births, twice that of the nonindigenous population. Only 10 percent of the indigenous population was literate; three out of four indigenous children suffered to some degree from malnutrition; and the average life expectancy

of forty-five years represented a sixteen-year gap separating them from other Guatemalans. The root cause of indigenous poverty was lack of access to land. According to a U.S. Agency for International Development (AID) study, 2 percent of the country's farms held two-thirds of the farmland, whereas 70 percent of the farms possessed 17 percent of the land. Government efforts to promote highland production of winter vegetables for export replaced grain production for local consumption, promoted concentration of landownership, and spurred the flight of the indigenous population to the cities.

Many indigenous (and nonindigenous) people found employment in the free-trade zone factories or *maquilas*, the fastest-growing sector of the Guatemalan economy. A 1984 law exempted these factories from import duties and (for ten years) from taxes. The majority were owned by Koreans. The maquilas accounted for 36 percent of Guatemala's exports to the United States. Seventy percent of the workers were women, and they earned about $2.50 a day. "I work from 7:30 in the morning to 10:00 o'clock at night," said one machine operator, "and what I earn doesn't cover what I need to eat." But employers successfully resisted demands for higher wages, shorter hours, and better working conditions.

The repression continued, but it met with growing resistance from thousands of Guatemalan refugees returning from exile in Mexico and from thousands of indigenous people who had lived for a decade in the so-called communities in resistance, refugees in their own country. The award of the Nobel Peace Prize to Rigoberta Menchú gave indigenous people new hope and courage. In November 1993 thousands of indigenous Guatemalans held a protest march in the capital to demand total abolition of the civil defense patrols imposed by the army. The social ferment was accompanied by a renaissance of Maya culture, which included the formation of centers for the study of Maya culture, an association of Maya writers, and a publishing house devoted to the publication of books in the Maya languages.

Álvaro Arzu Irygoyen, whose campaign had stressed a negotiated peace with the guerrillas, won the 1995 election, but even more significant was the surprising success of a newly formed, poorly financed political party, the New Guatemala Democratic Front (FDNG), which won almost 8 percent of the presidential vote and elected six congressional deputies, three of them women: Nineth Montenegro, head of a national organization of women widowed by army violence; Rosalina Tuyuc, a Maya founder of the Guatemalan Widows' Confederation (CONAVIGUA); and Manuela Alvarado, a Maya indigenous rights activist.

Arzu seemed to appreciate the significance of these elections and seized upon his "mandate" to sign peace accords with the URNG that required United Nations verification of compliance with its provisions. These included demobilization of guerrilla forces; promotion of indigenous rights; legislative, judicial, and electoral reforms; state decentralization and public administration reform; increased social spending; rural development; and the restructuring of public security and national defense.

But there remained powerful opposition to the accords within the military, its oligarchical allies, and the international community. First, contrary to the Accord on Socioeconomic and Agrarian Issues, elites supported neoliberal policies designed to secure international loans, encourage foreign private-sector investment, and expand export trade by discouraging business regulation, higher taxes, social spending, and higher wages—none of which benefited the poor majority. Also, foreign financiers made it clear that Guatemala's access to international credit depended on its compliance with IMF prescriptions, not the 1996 peace accords.

Moreover, privatization of public utilities and other neoliberal policies did little to stimulate growth or stem the nation's mushrooming poverty. Per capita gross domestic product (GDP) had grown an anemic 1.3 percent since 1988 but averaged only 0.8 percent since 1996. Although tax revenues in the 1990s grew modestly from 7 to 9 percent of GDP (well below the peace accord's target of 12 percent), government spending fell steadily, even as capital expenditures doubled.

Trade and payments deficits, though alarmingly high, had begun to decline slightly until 1996, when both rose sharply. In Guatemala neoliberalism produced economic stagnation and aggravated social decline, the very situation that earlier had precipitated years of violent civil war.

Second, the elected Congress, notoriously unrepresentative of the nation's politically excluded indigenous majority, was dominated by wealthy propertied elites. Declaring their opposition to the accords, supporters of ex-dictator Efraín Ríos Montt, the second largest political bloc in Congress, defiantly refused to cooperate. In 1997 they used their power to create a new civilian police force, in clear violation of the demilitarization accord.

Last, the military and paramilitary death squads associated with Guatemala's landed oligarchy, shielded by a 1996 amnesty law and a corrupt judicial system, continued to operate with impunity. This was the unmistakable message delivered on April 26, 1998, when Bishop Monsignor Juan Gerardi, a veteran champion of indigenous and human rights, was assassinated, allegedly by the right-wing *Jaguar Justiciero* (Righteous Jaguar). His exhaustive report on human rights abuses had just concluded that the army and its allies were responsible for 90 percent of the two hundred thousand civilians who were killed or "disappeared" during the civil war.

In 2000, Guatemalans elected Alfonso Portillo, a rightist whose presidential campaign had endorsed populist measures like salary increases for workers and an investigation of the Arzu administration's sale of the state-owned telephone company. Although many critics doubted his commitment to reform, he deserved credit for securing convictions of three high-ranking military officers accused of murdering Bishop Gerardi. But an atmosphere of terror and impunity continued to reign in Guatemala. Between November 2000 and February 2002, six judges and lawyers were assassinated, an accountant for the Rigoberta Menchú Foundation was murdered, a prosecutor and ten judges in the Gerardi case were forced into exile, and six Gerardi witnesses were killed.

This menacing atmosphere had become a potent weapon in the Guatemalan oligarchy's struggle to maintain its power in a changing world. In November 2000, the head of a coffee workers' union received a message, signed by "The Gladiators," advising him "to leave the country if you don't want to die." Threats of this kind helped explain the weakness of Guatemalan labor; as of 1997, only 2.9 percent of Guatemalan workers were unionized. But this weakness reflected more than "a history of intense anti-union repression, including firings, threats, kidnappings, and murders of union activists." The cards were stacked against workers in every possible way. They could not legally unionize until they had worked continuously for the same employer for three months, after which they became eligible for social security programs like retirement and disability benefits. To avoid this requirement, plantation owners rarely hired workers for more than ninety consecutive days.

Moreover, conditions in the coffee industry, which employed 2.2 million workers out of the total Guatemalan population of 11 million, had fundamentally changed. Historically most coffee workers had lived full-time on the plantations where they worked. In recent decades, however, owners, seeking to cut costs, replaced these workers with temporary labor. According to a United Nations report, in 1992, 87.5 percent of rural workers had temporary or migratory jobs. This contributed to an appalling rate of poverty: 76 percent of rural Guatemalans lived on an income of less than $2 a day, and 49 percent of this number lived in extreme poverty (defined as income of less than $1 a day).

In addition, racism and prejudice reinforced rural poverty and also prevented the multiethnic masses of Guatemala from uniting in a common struggle for their economic and social liberation. Until the mass of ordinary Guatemalans—Maya, ladinos, former guerrillas, trade unionists, peasants, and the middle class—united to oppose the power of the propertied elite and its foreign allies, Guatemala would remain a savage mix of the sixteenth-century conquistador's brutality and the maquilized society created by modern neoliberalism.

# Nicaragua

## MODERNIZATION, U.S. INTERVENTION, AND SANDINO, 1894–1934

Like Guatemala, Nicaragua's twentieth-century history was shaped by foreign economic dependency and gross inequality in the distribution of land; but unlike its northern neighbor, it also suffered from recurrent U.S. military intervention that weakened progressive local elites and decisively undermined national sovereignty. José Santos Zelaya, the late-nineteenth-century Nicaraguan dictator who had opened his nation to foreign investment and trade, nonetheless had been an ardent nationalist: he successfully asserted Nicaragua's claim to sovereignty over the Atlantic Mosquitia coast in 1894; he was a champion of Central American federation; and he angered the United States by turning down its canal treaty proposal and negotiating with other countries for construction of a Nicaraguan canal that would have competed with the United States–controlled route in Panama. Like Porfirio Díaz in Mexico in the same period, Zelaya had become alarmed over the extent of U.S. economic influence in his country; he sought to reduce that influence by granting concessions to nationals of other countries.

These signs of independence convinced the United States, where imperialist attitudes and policies had flowered since 1898, that Zelaya must go. With U.S. encouragement, a conservative revolt broke out in 1909. The U.S. Marines landed at Bluefields on the Atlantic coast and protected the conservative forces there against government attack. Under military and diplomatic pressure from the United States, Zelaya resigned, and in 1910 the conservatives came to power. Their triumph represented a victory for the traditional landed oligarchy and a defeat for its progressive wing, which sought a capitalist modernization.

The conservatives installed Adolfo Díaz, an obscure bookkeeper in a U.S. mining firm in eastern Nicaragua, as president of a puppet regime that hastened to satisfy all the U.S. demands. A U.S. banking firm made loans to the Nicaraguan government, receiving as security a controlling interest in the national bank and state railways and the revenues from the customhouse.

The servility and unpopularity of Díaz and his puppet regime provoked a liberal revolt in 1912, led by the young liberal Benjamín Zeledón. The rebels were on the brink of victory when U.S. Marines were again sent in at the request of the conservative government. Ordered by U.S. officials to end his revolt, Zeledón fought on, warning the U.S. commander that he and his country would bear "a tremendous responsibility and eternal infamy before history . . . for having employed your arms against the weak who have been struggling to reconquer the sacred rights of their fatherland." Zeledón, fighting to the last, suffered defeat and was executed by the conservatives with the apparent approval of the United States. There followed the first U.S. occupation of Nicaragua, with the United States ruling the country through a series of puppet presidents from 1912 to 1925. In return for U.S. protection, the conservative regimes made a number of important concessions, notably the Bryan-Chamorro treaty of 1916, which gave the United States the exclusive right to construct an interoceanic canal across Nicaragua (because the Panama Canal already existed, its real purpose was to prevent any other country from doing the same).

In August 1925, convinced that the conservatives could maintain themselves in power without U.S. assistance, the United States withdrew the Marines. Two months later fighting again broke out, and in 1926 the Marines returned, ostensibly to protect U.S. and other foreign property. This time they stayed until 1933. The new U.S. strategy was to arrange a peace settlement between cooperative conservative and liberal politicians that would give the latter an opportunity to share in the political spoils. With Henry L. Stimson (President Coolidge's personal representative) as mediator, such a settlement was reached in 1927. Under U.S. supervision, presidential elections held in 1928 and 1932 gave victory to the liberals. But real power remained in the hands of the United States.

Only one liberal officer, Augusto César Sandino, refused to accept the U.S.-sponsored peace treaty of 1927. The mestizo son of a moderately well-to-do, ardently liberal landowner and an indigenous servant girl, Sandino had worked as a mechanic and had lived in postrevolutionary Mexico between 1923 and 1926. There he was exposed to radical nationalist and social revolutionary ideas. He returned to Nicaragua in 1926 to join the liberal struggle against a conservative puppet regime. He met with a cool reception from José María Moncada, the head of the liberal army, who later claimed that he immediately distrusted Sandino because he heard him speak of "the necessity for the workers to struggle against the rich and other things that are the principles of communism." Although no Marxist, Sandino was a revolutionary leader who had profound sympathy with all the disinherited and planned to make far-reaching social and economic changes after achieving his primary goal, the departure of U.S. troops.

Unable to convince the liberal leaders that he should be given an independent command, Sandino organized his own force, consisting mainly of miners, peasants, workers, and indígenas. "I decided," he wrote, "to fight, understanding that I was the one called to protest the betrayal of the Fatherland." For seven years (1927–1933), Sandino's guerrilla army waged war against the U.S. Marines and the U.S.-sponsored Nicaraguan National Guard. Learning from early defeats and heavy losses when he attempted to meet the enemy in frontal combat, Sandino developed a new kind of warfare based on hit-and-run attacks, ambushes, temporary occupation of localities and, most important of all, close ties with the peasantry, who provided a supply base for the guerrillas and gave them accurate information about enemy movements and other assistance.

In the United States, meanwhile, the war was growing increasingly unpopular, and eventually Congress cut off all funding for it. The new Hoover administration decided to extricate itself from the Nicaraguan quagmire, but without loss of control. The instrument of that control would be a powerful National Guard, created by the Marines in 1927 and trained and equipped by them. In February 1932, Secretary of State Stimson announced the withdrawal of one thousand

General Sandino (*second from left*) and his staff. Third from left is Salvadoran Agustín Farabundo Martí. (The soldiers at left and right are unidentified.) [Corbis]

Marines in Nicaragua, the rest of whom were to be recalled after the U.S.-supervised presidential election in November.

The conservative Adolfo Díaz, widely regarded as a U.S. puppet, was pitted against Juan B. Sacasa, generally regarded as a more independent and genuine liberal than his predecessor Moncada. The election results gave Sacasa a substantial majority, and on January 1, 1933, he was sworn in as president. Meanwhile, the U.S. minister to Nicaragua had picked a new director of the National Guard, Anastasio Somoza García, a liberal general who had links to the prominent Moncada and Sacasa clans and who had served as foreign minister under Moncada. After his election, Sacasa wrote Sandino, proposing a peace conference. The election and postelection developments created a

dilemma for Sandino. He had promised to lay down his arms after the Marines left on January 2, 1934. But he profoundly mistrusted Sacasa's entourage, especially Somoza, who demanded that Sacasa order the total disarmament of the Sandinistas. In February 1934, Sacasa invited Sandino to Managua for negotiations, giving assurances for his security. In these negotiations Sandino demanded that the National Guard be disbanded— a demand that angered Somoza—but as the talks ended, the president and Sandino appeared to be moving toward agreement. On February 21 the president held a farewell dinner, but as Sandino, his brother, and two Sandinist officers were leaving, they were arrested by Somoza's officers, taken to the airfield, and shot. Questioned by Sacasa, Somoza protested his innocence; he later assumed full responsibility for the murders. It was his first step toward the establishment of a tyranny that would oppress the Nicaraguan people for well over four decades.

## THE SOMOZA ERA, 1934–1979

Following the assassination of Sandino, Somoza gradually consolidated his political power, more and more openly defying President Sacasa. With the aid of a fascist-type paramilitary force known as the Blue Shirts, Somoza easily secured election to the presidency as the liberal candidate in 1936, taking care to combine the post with that of director of the National Guard. With the Guard at his disposal, Somoza had no difficulty extending his term of office indefinitely, ruling directly as president or indirectly through puppet presidents until 1956, when he was assassinated, or *ajusticiado* (brought to justice) as Nicaraguans saw it, by the young poet Rigoberto López Pérez.

Thoroughly cynical and self-seeking, Somoza represented the total degeneration of the liberal ideology that had inspired the progressive acts of a Barrios or Zelaya. Always obsequiously pro-U.S., he abandoned his admiration for Hitler and Mussolini when the United States moved toward war with the Axis powers in the 1930s. Thereafter, President Franklin D. Roosevelt professed admiration for Somoza's democratic and progressive ideas, which unfortunately were not reflected in Nicaragua's political system. The saying ascribed to Roosevelt, "Somoza is an S.O.B. but he is our S.O.B." may be apocryphal, but it accurately sums up the U.S. official posture toward the Nicaraguan despot. U.S. friendship for Somoza brought him loans and assistance in establishing a military academy to turn out officers for the National Guard. Graduates of the school usually spent their senior year at the School of the Americas, the U.S. military training center in Panama.

Following Somoza's assassination in 1956, his elder legitimate son and vice president, Luis Somoza Debayle, took over. Somoza's younger son, Anastasio Somoza, Jr., a West Point graduate, became director of the National Guard. Luis was president from 1956 to 1963; he then allowed

puppet presidents to rule from 1963 to 1967, when he died. In that year, Anastasio Somoza, Jr., had himself elected president for a term that was to have lasted until 1971. Once in office, however, he amended the constitution to allow himself another year, then retired for two years while a puppet junta presided over the writing of a constitution that permitted him to be reelected for another term, which was supposed to run until 1981.

Differences between the Somozas' ruling styles reflected their adaptations to the changing phases of U.S.–Latin American policy. The relative mildness of Luis's rule appeared to reflect the reformist and developmentalist stress of the Alliance for Progress of the 1960s. In fact, all three dictators ruled Nicaragua as a personal estate for their benefit and that of their domestic and foreign allies. By 1970 the Somoza family controlled about 25 percent of the agricultural production of the country and a large proportion of its industry; the total wealth of the family was estimated to be $500 million. U.S. firms also enjoyed profitable investment opportunities in the food-processing industry and mining. Both foreign and domestic employers benefited from the repressive labor policies of the regime, but Nicaraguan capitalists grew increasingly unhappy with the monopolistic propensities of the Somoza family. The church, originally aligned with the Conservative Party, shifted its support to the first Somoza and generally remained loyal to the family until the 1960s, when it joined the Christian Democratic Party in opposition to Anastasio Jr.'s plans for his perpetual reelection. From first to last, however, the ultimate foundation of the family's power was the National Guard, whose top command always remained in the hands of a Somoza.

While the dynasty and its allies prospered, the economic and social condition of the Nicaraguan people steadily worsened as a result of the unchecked exploitation of rural and urban labor and the developmental programs of the Somoza era. Responding to growing world demand for new products, especially cotton, the Somozas opened up new lands to the planter class. Once again, as during the coffee boom a century earlier, many peasant families were driven from the land and into the cities. Nicaragua under the Somozas had one of the most extreme disparities in income distribution in Latin America; in 1978 the lower 50 percent of the population had an annual per capita income of $256.

Resistance to the Somoza dictatorship had begun in the 1950s, with a series of unsuccessful revolts led by the irrepressible Pedro Joaquín Chamorro, publisher of the highly respected *La Prensa* and son of parents from two of the most powerful conservative clans—a fact that explains why he was pardoned and allowed to return to Managua after each revolt. A more serious threat to the dictatorship arose with the formation in 1961 of the Sandinista Front for National Liberation (FSLN) founded by Carlos Fonseca, Silvio Mayorga, and Tomás Borge and composed largely of students. Its initial efforts to organize guerrilla warfare in the mountains met with defeat, but the rebels gradually improved their tactics and organization, attracting a growing number of recruits, especially among students.

A turning point in Nicaragua's recent history was the devastating earthquake in 1972, which killed ten thousand Nicaraguans and reduced the entire center of Managua to rubble, wiping out almost all businesses. There was immense public indignation over the shameless behavior of the Somozas, who diverted large amounts of foreign international aid into their own pockets and those of the National Guard. The center of Managua remained "an unreconstructed moonscape," for Somoza and his cronies had bought large parcels of land on the periphery of the city where they built new houses and shops, profiting from the disaster.

In January 1978 the Somozas committed an act of folly that largely contributed to their downfall. Stung by a series of articles in *La Prensa* about the commercial blood-plasma operation through which Somoza sold the blood of his people in the United States, the family or one of its supporters ordered Pedro Joaquín Chamorro's liquidation. The murder of a much-loved and courageous journalist provoked an effective general strike that ended only after considerable violence and repression by the National Guard, but its repercussions continued. The crime alienated from the regime

sections of the elite who could tolerate the murder, jailing, and torture of peasants and Sandinistas, but who were shocked at the killing of a member of an old privileged family like Chamorro.

The Chamorro affair, the general strike, and a brutal National Guard attack on an indigenous community that was commemorating the forty-fourth anniversary of Sandino's assassination with a Catholic celebration strengthened the FSLN and contributed to a general broadening of the resistance movement. In August 1978 the Sandinistas launched their most audacious operation to date. Invading the National Palace, twenty-five guerrillas seized as hostages most of the members of the Chamber of Deputies and some two thousand public employees. After frantic negotiations, Somoza agreed to most of the Sandinista demands: the release of fifty-nine Sandinista prisoners, a huge ransom, and a safe flight for the guerrillas and released prisoners to Panama. This development was soon followed by another prolonged general strike and a spontaneous uprising in the city of Matagalpa by *muchachos* (youngsters) who forced the National Guard to retreat to their barracks and hold out for two weeks. On September 8 the FSLN launched uprisings in five cities. With their headquarters surrounded by civilian and FSLN combatants, the Guard called in Somoza's air force for a ferocious bombing of the cities before government ground forces retook the cities one at a time. This was followed by a house-to-house search in a genocidal "Operation Cleanup," with a death toll of some five thousand persons.

Alarmed by the September uprisings, the United States attempted to mediate a compromise between Somoza and his traditional elite opponents through a committee of the Organization of American States (OAS). The U.S. initiative was frustrated by Somoza's obstinate refusal to resign and the withdrawal of liberal factions from the mediation process, charging that the OAS commission wanted "*Somocismo* without Somoza." Meanwhile the FSLN, overcoming the differences over insurrectionary tactics of three groups within it, created a nine-man directorate.

The September uprisings were followed by a mobilization of both sides for a final struggle.

Somoza prepared for the worst by liquidating his vast assets and shipping his capital abroad. Meanwhile the FSLN, aided by the Social Democratic Parties of Western Europe and governments as diverse as those of Costa Rica, Panama, Venezuela, and Cuba, restocked its arms supply with weapons purchased on the international arms market. The regular FSLN army expanded from a few hundred to several thousand. Throughout the country the network of neighborhood defense committees established after the September revolts worked feverishly to prepare for the coming struggle by stockpiling food and medical supplies. Comunidades de base (Catholic grassroots organizations) took an active part in these preparations.

In June 1979 the FSLN announced a general strike and launched a final offensive, infiltrating Managua and occupying barrios on both sides of the central zone. Somoza, retreating into his recently constructed bunker in the fortress of La Loma, ordered a counterattack that included a massive air and artillery bombardment of the city.

By July 5 the Sandinistas had encircled the capital, leaving only one way out via the airport six miles east of the city. The Sandinistas could have taken it at will but allowed it to remain in the government's hands, perhaps to give the Somozas and their entourage an opportunity to leave the capital and thus avoid another bombardment and battle. With victory in sight, the Sandinista directorate named a provisional government—a five-member junta that included three Sandinistas; Alfonso Robelo, the leader of the business opposition to Somoza; and Violeta Chamorro, the widow of the martyred Pedro Joaquín Chamorro.

Meanwhile the United States made last-minute efforts to prevent the coming to power of a radical revolutionary regime. It called on the OAS to send a "peacekeeping" force to Managua but was unanimously rebuffed. Then it sent a special representative to Nicaragua to try to persuade the FSLN to broaden the base of the new junta. But the Sandinistas pointed out that they had already made a large concession by including the conservative Robelo and the moderate Violeta Chamorro in the junta; inclusion of the persons nominated by the United States—one being a general of the National Guard and the other a personal friend of Somoza—would ensure the preservation of "Somocismo without Somoza."

Under intense pressure from Archbishop Miguel Obando y Bravo and people in other influential quarters to accept his inevitable defeat and to spare the capital a new assault, Somoza agreed on July 16, 1979, to go into exile in Florida. The next day he drove to the airport and left Nicaragua forever. Two days later the FSLN and its government entered Managua.

## THE SANDINISTAS IN POWER, 1979–1990

The cost of the Sandinista victory in lives and material destruction was enormous. Estimates of the dead ranged up to fifty thousand, or a loss of 2 percent of Nicaragua's population. The material damage was estimated at $1.3 billion; the national debt, a large part of which represented sums that Somoza had diverted into his foreign bank accounts, stood at $1.6 billion.

The government that presided over the immense task of national reconstruction consisted of four parts. The official government included the five-member junta; its cabinet or ministries of state; and the council of state, a legislative and consultative assembly in which a broad variety of mass and economic organizations were represented. The composition of these bodies reflected the sincere desire of the Sandinista leaders to maintain a pluralistic system and approach to the solution of the country's problems. In the first cabinet, in addition to Marxists like Tomás Borge, minister of the interior, and Jaime Wheelock Román, minister of agriculture, sat two bankers and two Catholic priests, the Maryknoll Father Miguel D'Escoto and the Trappist monk Ernesto Cardenal, "making Nicaragua probably the only country in the world with Catholic priests in the cabinet." From the first, however, it was understood that these formal organs of government were responsible to the nine-member directorate of the FSLN that had created them. The directorate had direct control of the Sandinista armed forces and police. Elections had been promised, but the state of war in which Nicaragua soon found itself as a result of CIA-organized efforts to destabilize and overthrow the Sandinista regime delayed elections until 1984.

Economic problems dominated the agenda of the new government. One immediate problem was that of repairing the ravages of war and the earthquake of 1972, a task mainly entrusted to the municipalities and the Sandinist Defense Committees. It was completed with such speed that visitors to Nicaragua in the fall of 1979 marveled at the relatively normal appearance of the country. Food shortages were another serious problem and required the importation of great quantities of foodstuffs, mostly financed with foreign donations. Meanwhile emergency food crops were sown so that domestic supplies of food would be available by the middle of 1980. The work of repair was combined with food-for-work schemes to provide a temporary solution for the vast unemployment that was a legacy of the war.

What to do about the national debt was a vexing question for the new government, for it knew well that many of the more recent loans had served only to swell the bank accounts of Somoza and his cronies. But it decided to agree to pay all the loans, even the corrupt ones, for both economic and political reasons. The Sandinistas wanted to retain access to Western loans and technology; they also wished to disprove the charge that the new Nicaragua was a Soviet or Cuban "puppet," solely dependent on the socialist bloc for economic and political support. The socialist countries, particularly the Soviet Union and Cuba, in fact did give considerable aid in the form of food shipments and other supplies. Cuba also sent large numbers of teachers and doctors to assist in the work of reconstruction.

The international lending agencies and Western governments hoped financial aid to Nicaragua would enable the private sector of the country to survive and keep the economy pluralistic. The principal difficulty in renegotiation arose with the United States. The Carter administration agreed to make a new loan of $75 million, chiefly for aid to the private sector. When Ronald Reagan came to the presidency, however, he froze the remaining $15 million of the loan, alleging without evidence that Nicaragua was sending arms to the rebels in El Salvador. Thereafter Nicaragua had to rely for aid on the socialist countries, friendly social democratic governments of Western Europe, and Third World countries, including Brazil.

Although some Sandinista leaders viewed socialism as a more or less distant goal, the regime pursued a mixed-economy strategy of national development and recognized that private enterprise had a vital role to play in the reconstruction of the national economy. The state, however, became the most decisive and the most dynamic element in the economy and in the provision of social services, particularly health, education, and housing. The strengthening of the state sector was a direct result of the takeover of the enormous properties of the Somoza dynasty and its allies. These properties became the basis of the People's Property Area, including half the large farms over 500 hectares, a quarter of all industry, large construction firms, hotels, real estate, an airline, a fishing fleet, and more. The expropriation of the holdings of Somoza and his supporters placed approximately 40 percent of the gross national product in the hands of the state. The banking system and foreign trade were completely nationalized.

These expropriations, however, left 60 percent of the gross national product (GNP) in the hands of the Nicaraguan capitalist class, which continued to control 80 percent of agricultural production and 75 percent of manufacturing. Thus, the country remained capitalist, with the state sector no larger than that of France, Mexico, and Peru in the 1970s. The policy of the Sandinista government was to avoid radical changes that might cause a rupture with the "patriotic bourgeoisie," the results of which would be disastrous for the economy. Accordingly, it courted and maintained an alliance with some of the country's largest entrepreneurs. At the same time the government insisted on safeguards with respect to working conditions, wages, hours, and the like that would at least modestly improve the life of Nicaraguan workers. It also encouraged the trade unions to watch over the proper functioning of factories to prevent decapitalization, slowdowns in production, and other sabotage by capitalists hostile to the revolution. The result was a built-in tension between the government and a section of the business class. Partly because of this tension and partly because of objective conditions—lack of foreign exchange to buy inputs, obsolete machinery, and other problems—private businessmen began dropping out of manufacturing or failing to invest.

The growth of the public sector was most marked in agriculture. Land reform was placed under the *Instituto de Reforma Agraria* (INRA), which by the end of 1979 had confiscated without compensation over one-fifth of Nicaragua's cultivable land that belonged to persons or corporations affiliated with the Somoza regime, land that "was almost universally held to be little more than stolen property." The government proposed to maintain these estates as productive units rather than to divide them into small parcels. Most of these lands were large farms that had been operated as capital-intensive enterprises, so parcelization would have resulted in heavy production losses. Consequently, many of these estates were converted into state farms. Others were organized as production cooperatives, called Sandinist agricultural communes. In late 1980 there were about 1,327 of these cooperatives. INRA simultaneously tried to improve the living conditions of state-sector workers through the establishment of clinics, schools, and housing projects. In 1980 more than fifty thousand workers worked full time in the state sector.

Although the government favored state farms and production cooperatives as basic agricultural units, small independent farmers were not neglected. Agricultural credit for small producers was greatly expanded, and they were encouraged to form credit and service cooperatives. In 1979–1980 there were 1,200 of these co-ops organized; they received over 50 percent of the agricultural credit extended by the government in the same period.

Even after the confiscation of Somocista estates, large commercial farms producing such crops as cotton, coffee, cattle, and sugar still held 66.5 percent of Nicaragua's cultivable land. The relationship between this private agricultural sector and the revolutionary government was an uneasy one. Most of the large landowners despised the Somozas, resented their hoggish propensities, and welcomed their overthrow. But the rules of the game had changed, and the new rules were not always to their liking. Landowners could no longer mistreat their workers; they had to comply with reform legislation defining the rights of tenants and workers.

Despite the government's assurances that it wanted to preserve a private sector, large landowners were understandably nervous about their future. The commercial farmers and cattle ranchers defended their interests through their own associations, which negotiated with the government over prices, acreage quotas, and the like. The commercial farmers had access to credit at low interest rates, and a coffee stabilization fund was established to protect growers against fluctuations in the world market. The economic importance of this sector is evident from the fact that in 1979–1980 it accounted for 62 percent of the production of cotton and 55 percent of the production of coffee.

The difficulties of Nicaraguan agriculture were not due primarily to inadequate volume of production but stemmed above all from falling world prices for its major export crops. Sugar, which sold for 24¢ a pound in 1981, sold for 9¢ in 1983. Natural disasters also hurt production of staple foods in 1982. In May flooding destroyed twenty thousand acres of just-planted basic grain crops, destroyed $3.6 million in stored grains, and caused $350 million in damage to the national economic infrastructure, according to a United Nations survey. A drought in July and August caused estimated losses of $47 million. Finally, the greatly increased scale of CIA-organized counterrevolutionary activity that began in 1981, diverting manpower and resources to military purposes, caused serious damage to Nicaraguan agriculture and to the economy in general—a major aim of the U.S. destabilization program.

The implacable pressure of the Reagan administration on Nicaragua represented a threat not only to its economy but to the existence of the revolutionary government. Although the Carter administration's policy was "more than a little schizophrenic," once the FSLN was firmly in power it made a serious effort to come to terms with the revolution, hoping thereby to enable capitalism to survive in Nicaragua. With the election of Reagan, the U.S. attitude changed drastically.

Reagan authorized formation of a paramilitary force of ex-National Guardsmen, with an acknowledged budget of $19 million. In a move recalling the 1954 coup against Guatemala, Honduras was converted into a staging area for Nicaraguan operations. Beginning in 1981, Argentine and U.S. advisers trained the Somocistas (familiarly called the *contras* by both sides) and assisted them in making terrorist raids into Nicaragua, killing hundreds of Nicaraguan soldiers and civilians and destroying bridges and construction equipment.

The "secret war" against Nicaragua quickened its pace when Ambassador John Negroponte arrived in Honduras in 1982 to mastermind the operation. The CIA station in Honduras grew to an admitted fifty employees, plus a large number of secret agents, including many Vietnam veterans who were now mercenaries under contract to the CIA. To secure the Honduran military's cooperation in this "secret war," U.S. military aid to Honduras, under $2 million in 1980, grew to $10 million in 1981, and may have reached as high as $144 million in 1982–1983, with some of it coming from a hidden budget.

In March 1983 the operation moved into high gear when several thousand Somocistas and other mercenaries, supported by Honduran troops, invaded Nicaragua at several points on its northern border with Honduras. Simultaneously, in a gesture of "gunboat diplomacy" several U.S. warships were sent to Nicaragua's Pacific coast, ostensibly to monitor suspected movements of arms from Nicaragua to rebels in El Salvador. By the end of March, despite claims of victory from the invaders' radio, the Nicaraguan armed forces and militia had crushed the counterrevolutionary attacks, although the contras continued to make raids, mostly of the hit-and-run variety.

Under the hardest conditions, Nicaragua's Sandinista leadership continued its difficult struggle to stabilize the economy, expand social reforms, replace the revolutionary government with a parliamentary democracy, and solve long-standing problems like the demand for autonomy from the Miskito and Sumo peoples of Nicaragua's Atlantic coast. In the same period the United States intensified its "covert" war against Nicaragua, provided the contras with supplies and logistical support, mined Nicaraguan harbors, and even issued a manual for use within Nicaragua instructing the contras in terrorist methods—including the liquidation of government officials and progovernment activists. The "covert" war flouted U.S. laws, treaty obligations, and international law. In June 1986 the World Court, acting on a complaint by Nicaragua, ordered the United States to halt all its military and paramilitary actions against Nicaragua, but the Reagan administration, refusing to accept the jurisdiction of the court, disregarded the order.

Despite hundreds of millions of dollars' worth of U.S. financial and military aid to the contras, in early 1986 Nicaraguan President Daniel Ortega celebrated the rebels' "strategic defeat." A major factor in this "victory," despite stepped-up U.S. aid, was growing Sandinista military effectiveness and superior morale.

But the Reagan administration had not sought a contra military victory. The administration's support for the contras aimed to sustain a "low-intensity conflict" designed to wear down the Nicaraguan government, disrupt its economy, create hardships and war weariness to undermine popular support for the regime, force the Sandinistas to divert precious resources from social programs to its army, and thereby eventually to produce an internal collapse.

The war contributed to a sharp decline in the Nicaraguan economy between 1983 and 1990. The GDP fell by 30 percent in 1985 alone and continued to fall until the "covert war" ended; inflation reached an annual rate of 10,000 percent in 1988; and severe shortages of goods of every kind prevailed. But the war was not the sole factor responsible for the economic decline. Other causes included deterioration in the terms of trade for Nicaragua's exports; the U.S. trade embargo of May 1985, which isolated Nicaragua from its traditional export market and from a source of goods and technology difficult to replace; and the unwillingness of some private sector interests to invest in maintaining and expanding Nicaragua's production.

The Nicaraguan government responded to the economic crisis with measures to stimulate production by increasing prices paid for basic grains and other staples, while protecting the real value of salaries and wages by periodic adjustments to compensate for inflation; by expanding trade with the European Economic Community and the socialist bloc to compensate for the loss of the U.S. market; and by redesigning the agrarian reform to make more land available to individual peasants as a means of stimulating production of basic grains.

The Sandinistas had promised in 1979 that elections would be held by 1985, but the need to refute U.S. charges that their regime was undemocratic and illegitimate led to a decision to accelerate the timetable for elections. In November 1984, Nicaraguans went to the polls to vote for a president, a vice president, and a ninety-member national assembly that would frame a constitution for the country. Opposition poll watchers and a large number of foreign observers, including a task force of the Latin American Studies Association (LASA), the major organization of teachers and students of Latin American affairs in the United States, found no evidence of irregularities in the voting or the vote-counting process. The Sandinista Front received 67 percent of the vote, the rest going to opposition parties. In January 1985 Daniel Ortega Saavedra and Sergio Ramírez Mercado took office as president and vice president, respectively.

The new constitution, adopted after intense democratic discussion and debate at mass meetings throughout the country and in the national assembly, established political pluralism, a mixed economy, and nonalignment as its guiding principles, and divided power among the executive, legislative, judicial, and electoral branches. It guaranteed individual and social rights, including the rights to a job, education, and health care; free expression of opinion and association; the right to strike; and the right to a fair trial. The constitution

also sought a definitive solution for the troubled relations between the central government and the indigenous peoples of the Atlantic coast.

## SELF-DETERMINATION FOR THE PEOPLES OF THE ATLANTIC COAST

The Sandinistas inherited a long history of state neglect of coastal peoples, who consequently distrusted government. The Sandinistas acknowledged that they had made serious errors in their effort to integrate indigenous peoples into the revolution because the government failed to take account of their unique culture and traditions. The problem was complicated by the fact that the United States and the contras sought to exploit those errors and misunderstandings and draw the Atlantic coast peoples to the side of counterrevolution.

In 1981 the Nicaraguan government, to prevent their use as a contra military base, forcibly evacuated thousands of Miskitos and Sumos from ancestral lands along the Coco River, destroyed their villages, and resettled the refugees in camps away from the threatened coastal area. Although the camps provided improved health care, food subsidies, education, and improved housing and electricity, the indígenas, who were strongly attached to their villages and lands, viewed the camps as prisons. As a result, several antigovernment native-based guerrilla groups arose on the Atlantic coast. However, U.S. efforts to pressure the Miskitos into an alliance with the major contra groups, as a condition of military and financial aid, also produced splits that the Sandinistas exploited to negotiate cease-fire agreements with individual indigenous commanders.

Two major Nicaraguan government initiatives paved the way for a solution of the Atlantic coast problem. First, in 1984 the government created a commission to define an autonomous status for the Atlantic coast peoples under the new constitution. The ensuing dialogue led to a compromise that recognized the right of the Atlantic coast peoples to autonomy and guaranteed the preservation of their languages, religions, cultures, and social organization. They would elect their own representatives to the national Congress and use their resources to satisfy their own needs, as determined by a regional assembly. Second, in 1985 Interior Minister Tomás Borge announced that the Miskitos living in relocation camps would be allowed to return to the Coco River area.

## WOMEN AND THE REVOLUTION

Women also gained appreciably from the revolution, in which they had played a large role militarily, economically, and politically. Making up one-third of all combatants, many women had been integrated into the guerrilla army; others had organized all-women battalions like the Juana Elena Mendoza Infantry Company; and some, like Doris Tijerino and Dora María Téllez, had become respected field commanders. Although their participation in the regular army after 1979 declined to about 20 percent, women were especially active both in local civil defense committees and the popular militias, where they made up 60 percent of urban contingents.

Most women had always worked both inside and outside the home, but before the revolution, their waged labor (estimated at 48 percent of the labor force) had tended to be relatively invisible and greatly undervalued, concentrated in the informal sector and domestic service. After the revolution, labor legislation guaranteed equal pay for equal work, paid maternity leave, and legal protections against the dismissal of pregnant women. Of course, private employers frequently ignored these laws, and the revolutionary government, due to the contra war, often lacked the necessary financial resources to enforce them. But these laws, instead of providing traditional protections to employers, now placed the state on the side of women, their trade unions, and mass organizations like the Nicaraguan Women's Association (AMNLAE).

Moreover, as the state sector of the economy grew and an escalating contra war absorbed more men, women's waged employment expanded: in 1985 women comprised 50 percent of state employees, 70 percent of coffee harvesters, and 70 percent of textile workers. This naturally raised the issue of the inequitable "double workday," wherein women, in addition to laboring eight hours in the factory or field, worked nine to twelve hours at home whereas their husbands worked less than an hour at household chores. To remedy this injustice, the Sandinistas encouraged men to assume their fair share of domestic responsibilities and by 1988 also funded daycare centers—182 at urban workplaces and 69 on state farms. But once again wartime fiscal demands sabotaged this initiative.

Women made up nearly two-thirds of the *brigadistas* who participated in the Sandinista literacy crusade that between 1979 and 1980 reduced illiteracy from 50 to 12 percent. Thereafter, Popular Education Collectives (CEPs) allowed mostly rural people to select local teachers whose instruction would further develop literacy skills; 95 percent of these teachers were women. Free, universal education for adults and children six to twelve years of age was the Sandinista revolution's commitment; before 1985 nearly four thousand new classrooms were built and the number of primary school teachers, again mostly women, tripled. Here again, however, the contra war intervened; by the late 1980s fewer resources were available for education, and illiteracy rates climbed to 23 percent.

Politically, the revolution facilitated women's participation in the leadership of the FSLN Party, the national government, and grassroots organizations. In the 1984 and 1990 parliamentary elections, women comprised almost 20 percent of the FSLN candidates and almost 22 percent of those Sandinistas elected to the legislature. In 1994 the party decided to allot 30 percent of leadership positions to women, who also made up 34 and 43 percent, respectively, of their department and national legislative candidates in the 1996 elections. By decade's end almost one-third of FSLN legislators were women.

## THE QUEST FOR PEACE AND THE NEOLIBERAL DEBATE, 1990–2003

By the end of 1986 external opposition to the revolution had begun to fragment. The U.S. congressional elections had handed a heavy defeat to President Reagan, and his administration suffered another blow due to the revelation that part of the proceeds of an arms sale to Iran, in a supposed swap for U.S. hostages in Lebanon, had been illegally diverted to the contras through the use of secret Swiss bank accounts. The scandal—with new revelations of CIA involvement in drug smuggling—increased opposition to the additional contra aid that President Reagan requested. By the end of the Reagan presidency, Congress had rejected an administration request for military aid and voted to limit funding to so-called humanitarian aid.

The Iran-contra scandal and its repercussions created a favorable atmosphere for new peace negotiations. An earlier peace initiative by the Contadora group of Latin American nations had produced a draft regional peace treaty, which Nicaragua in September 1984 offered to sign immediately without further modifications. But U.S. pressure on its Central American allies caused them to reject it. The new peace process was initiated by Costa Rica and Guatemala, whose governments had no love for the Sandinistas but feared that the Nicaraguan conflict might provoke a direct U.S. intervention, with unforeseeable consequences for the entire region. In August 1987 all five Central American presidents signed a set of agreements that barred outside assistance to insurgent forces, provided for the release of political prisoners, and called for steps toward democratization and the holding of honest elections in all countries, with particular reference to Nicaragua.

Thanks to the Sandinista government's desire for peace and its full compliance with conditions set by the 1987 agreements, elections were held on schedule in February 1990. The FSLN faced the National Opposition Union (UNO), an unlikely coalition of fourteen small parties, ranging from the far right to the Communist Party (PC de N). The overwhelming majority of foreign observers found that the elections were free and fair, but some noted that they took place "within a climate of U.S.-generated military and economic pressure." For example, on election eve, largely due to the decade-long U.S.-sponsored contra war, the national economy teetered on the verge of collapse: purchasing power had declined 90 percent since 1980; per capita GDP had fallen almost 20

percent since 1988; basic food shortages were epidemic; inflation raged at over 5,000 percent; foreign debt service payments consumed 62 percent of export income; and unemployment had reached a postrevolution high. The Sandinista government reluctantly acceded to a modest program of "structural adjustment," or *compactación*, which meant still more pain for Nicaragua's impoverished majority. As if the deck were not sufficiently stacked against the FSLN, the Bush administration also intervened directly in the election, plowing millions of dollars into the campaign of the UNO presidential candidate Violeta Chamorro, who triumphed with 55 percent of the vote.

What factors caused the UNO victory? Most observers agreed that the election results did not represent a popular repudiation of the Sandinista program of social reforms. There was general agreement that the key factors in the Sandinista defeat were the war and the disastrous state of the economy. In a country of less than 4 million people, the war had left sixty thousand dead, twenty-eight thousand wounded, and thousands of others kidnapped. For years, more than half the national budget had been directed to military needs. UNO campaign literature had concentrated on the war-weariness and opposition to the draft, omitting mention that the contra war was the cause of the draft. UNO campaign rhetoric also blamed the Sandinista government alone for the economic crisis.

Washington's strategy of bringing Nicaragua to its knees by a combination of economic blockade and low-intensity warfare had finally achieved its goal. But the aftermath of the election produced new surprises. In a stinging defeat for the extreme right wing in the UNO coalition, Chamorro announced that General Humberto Ortega, chief of the Sandinista army and brother of the outgoing president, would remain. Moreover, Chamorro loyalists next joined FSLN deputies in electing a slate of National Assembly officers that included two Sandinista deputies. Chamorro's temporary alliance with the FSLN was sealed by her appointment of three Sandinistas to cabinet positions, including the strategic position of agrarian reform. "In a strange twist of events," commented

*Latinamerica Press*, the "coalition that Chamorro led to victory in 1990 has switched places with the Sandinistas and now considers itself the opposition." Chamorro's moderation also irritated Bush administration officials, who warned that $300 million in U.S. aid would be endangered if she made appointments that did not meet with Washington's approval.

But the spirit of amity soon vanished as the Chamorro government began to implement a harsh neoliberal economic austerity program, including periodic devaluations that weakened the earning power of workers, an end to subsidized prices for staple products, massive layoffs of government workers, and efforts to dismantle the agrarian reform and other social conquests of the Sandinista revolution. Although designed to achieve "stabilization," this policy produced political and social conflicts that threatened to end in civil war.

The first major confrontation between the Chamorro government and the Sandinista unions ended in victory for the latter. A ten-day general strike was settled on July 10, 1990, on terms that were very favorable to the strikers, including wage increases and major political concessions like union consultation on economic policies, assurances there would be no large-scale layoffs of government workers, and the abandonment of a program for returning confiscated land to its former owners. The agreement proved to be only a truce in a continuing struggle between the Chamorro government, which sought to dismantle most of the Sandinista reforms, and the unions, which sought to preserve their social and economic gains. But it gave the government a breathing space at least to seek relief from its desperate economic crisis through foreign loans and U.S. aid. Chamorro officials admitted that they needed "the Sandinistas to keep the country from exploding."

Sandinista supporters of this temporary alliance could point to other victories as well as some defeats. If the Sandinistas could not prevent the return of many large properties to their former owners, with Chamorro's support they succeeded in defeating UNO's plan to totally undo the Sandinista agrarian reform. If they could not pre-

vent the privatization of almost all the state enterprises, they succeeded in including a provision for the workers' right to own 25 percent of the privatized firms and in some cases acquire total ownership of such firms.

Meanwhile the Chamorro government had expected Washington and the international financial community to reward its free-market policies of austerity and privatization with the aid and loans it needed to rebuild a shattered economy. But U.S. aid was slow in coming and limited in amount, largely due to the opposition of right-wing Republican Senator Jesse Helms, who contended that the Sandinistas were still in power. Combined foreign aid and loans were clearly insufficient. Between April 1990 and January 1993 the country received about $715 million in donations and about $997 million in new loans, but in the same period the government paid over $1,210 million in debt payments on its foreign debt of more than $11 billion to remain qualified for loans and another $456 million for oil. The country's exports in 1992 were valued at a little more than $250 million, but it imported goods valued at more than $850 million. The resulting deficit left nothing for development.

Internal disputes, the FSLN's temporary collaboration with Doña Violeta, and declining voter turnout weakened the party in the 1996 presidential elections, which Arnoldo Alemán, a wealthy Somocista coffee planter, won decisively with 51 percent of the vote. Assured of solid support from traditional conservative Nicaraguan oligarchs and foreign bankers, Alemán's populist campaign, promising economic growth, lower prices, and more jobs, reached out to middle-income and poor people crushed by years of neoliberal reforms sponsored by Chamorro and reluctant Sandinistas.

Once elected, however, Alemán ignored his promises and embraced the neoliberal faith, fully aware of its devastating impact on the poor majority. "We know that to move forward and confront the future," he arrogantly announced, "we have to take bitter medicine." Thereafter, his regime privatized state-owned industries and banks, fired state workers, reduced protective tariffs, raised interest rates, restricted credit, cut

In 2001, outgoing millionaire President Arnoldo Alemán greatly assisted the election of his successor, Enrique Bolaños, another wealthy businessman, but Bolaños quickly abandoned his mentor, who faced devastating corruption charges in 2002. This cartoon depicts the historical links that bound Bolaños to the portly Alemán, pictured here wallowing in the tar pits, grasping the slimy tail of the Bolaños salamander, and shouting, "Come back here little buddy. We started out together, let's finish together."
[From *Vision Sandinista*, October 2002]

taxes and social spending, created "free-trade zones" to encourage foreign investment by exempting companies from all taxes, and subsidized sugar production on big commercial estates while denying peasants access to alternative credit programs. To secure open access to U.S. markets, Asian *maquilas*—foreign companies that used low-cost Nicaraguan labor to assemble imported raw materials for overseas export markets—eagerly took advantage of these benefits and Central America's lowest average hourly wage of 41¢ to fatten corporate profits.

Alemán's "bitter medicine" kept inflation low and, largely stimulated by foreign loans, increased average per capita GDP by an anemic 2 percent. This left a 1997 external debt three times greater than Nicaragua's national income, and debt service payments consumed 40 percent of foreign-exchange earnings, five times the rate paid in 1988 when the Sandinistas were in power. The largest single component of national income, $300 million, almost equal to total export earnings, came from family remittances paid by Nicaraguans living abroad! High interest rates, designed to lure foreign investment, drove peasants in search of rural survival to mountainside cultivation and forest destruction, decisive factors in the devastation wreaked by Hurricane Mitch (1998), which killed more than three thousand people in Nicaragua. Alemán's government contributed to the scale of the disaster by what can only be called criminal neglect. Three days after Mitch assumed hurricane strength, "Alemán played meteorologist in front of television cameras, assuring everyone that the little drizzle would soon pass."

Still worse, social indicators declined dramatically. Because the Chamorro government had dismantled the literacy program in 1990, illiteracy, reduced to 12 percent in 1980, exceeded 34 percent in 2000. Nicaragua's infant mortality also remained high, vying with Guatemala for the unenviable distinction of having the highest rate in Central America. Ranked eighty-ninth on the U.N. Human Development Index in 1990, Nicaragua plummeted to one hundred eighteenth in 2001, making it the third-poorest country in Latin America after Guatemala and Haiti. Seventy percent of Nicaraguans were unemployed or underemployed, 80 percent were mired in poverty, and half lived on less than $1 a day—one-fifth of the $150 per month that the government conservatively estimated to be the price of a family's basic survival. Health care and education, free and universally available during the revolution, were plagued by material shortages and limited to the wealthy few who could afford the rising fees. "It's very bad now," complained Dr. Manuela Rodríguez of Bluefields' Hospital. "There are often no medications, no analgesia, no sheets. People are dying because they can't afford to pay." According to the Catholic Church, sixty thousand children had abandoned school for the streets, where they begged for coins or sold worthless trinkets to survive. A *Washington Post* correspondent captured the heart-rending scenes that marked the Alemán administration's indifference toward the sea of misery that surrounded it. "In a soccer field in the town of Matagalpa," he wrote in 2001, "100 hungry children begged for some rice or milk—anything. Some just whimpered, unable to muster more of a protest on hollow stomachs."

Nonetheless, a majority of Nicaraguans voted for Alemán's ally, Enrique Bolaños, in the 2001 presidential election. The Bolaños campaign benefited greatly from a massive U.S. intervention that included money, provision of food aid for Bolaños to distribute at rallies, and pressure on other conservative candidates to withdraw from the race. But perhaps most decisive was the full-page ad in *La Prensa* featuring Jeb Bush, the president's brother, denouncing Bolaños' opponent, Daniel Ortega, as "an enemy of everything the United States represents" and "a friend of our enemies." In the aftermath of the September 11 terrorist attacks and the Bush warning that "every nation in every region now has a decision to make: either you are with us or you are with the terrorists," the ad suggested to Nicaraguans that the United States would again make war on Nicaragua if its people elected Ortega, who "has a relationship of more than 30 years with states and individuals who shelter and condone international terrorism." As bad as life was under the neoliberal regimes of the 1990s, many Nicaraguans seemed to be saying that it was better than a nation at war with itself and the United States.

## El Salvador

The history of El Salvador, the smallest and most densely populated country in Central America, presents in exaggerated form all the economic and social problems of the area: an extreme dependence on a single crop, making the economy very vulnerable to fluctuations in price and the demand of outside markets; a marked concentration of land and wealth in a few hands; and intolerable exploitation of the peasantry, accompanied by ferocious repression of all attempts at protest or revolt.

Ironically, however, the early twentieth century bore witness to considerably more political freedoms, at least among the landed aristocracy. Although nineteenth-century liberal reforms had promoted a concentration of land ownership in El Salvador, the coffee oligarchs, largely orchestrated by the Meléndez and Quiñónez families, had developed a political consensus that allowed them to deploy various weapons of social control. Moreover, before World War I, the demand for coffee had not appreciably affected the nation's labor markets and *finqueros* still relied upon a healthy supply of migrant and resident workers. Consequently, in addition to the usual repressive violence of the National Guard and the Casa Salvadoreña, the Salvadoran elite also created mass-based political organizations like the Liga Roja to co-opt and contain urban-middle-class-, peasant, and working-class challenges to its power.

Driven by a postwar international market expansion, however, coffee markets expanded by 50 percent during the 1920s. The coffee oligarchs hastened to respond, both by dedicating more acreage to coffee and by securing new supplies of labor. As a result of these changes, more peasants were deprived of their traditional *milpas*, the subsistence plots that were the bedrock of peasant survival. This transformed them into full-fledged proletarians, propertyless people whose survival depended exclusively upon the sale of their labor.

The economic and social problems generated by the coffee monoculture became more acute with the advent of the Great Depression in 1929. Campesinos who made 50¢ a day before the Depression had their wages reduced to 20¢ a day. The price of coffee was cut in half between July 1929 and the end of the year, ruining many small producers and forcing them to sell their lands. High unemployment and below-subsistence-level wages added to the discontent caused by harsh treatment by overseers and frauds practiced by company stores.

Even before the Depression, there had been scattered peasant revolts in the twentieth century; they were always put down by the National Guard. In the 1920s urban workers and some of the peasantry began to form unions. In 1925 a small Communist Party began to operate underground; its leader was Agustín Farabundo Martí, who had been introduced to Marxism at the national university. Expelled from El Salvador in 1927 for his radical activities, Martí joined Augusto César Sandino, who was fighting the U.S. Marines in Nicaragua. Martí returned to El Salvador in 1930 and again plunged into political activity. Aided by a small group of youths, mostly university students, he carried out propaganda and organizational activity among peasants in the central and western parts of the country. He was soon jailed but was released after going on a hunger strike.

Against this background of depression and growing left-wing agitation, perhaps the first free presidential election in Salvadoran history was held. The winner was the wealthy landowner and civil engineer Arturo Araujo, whose admiration for the British Labour Party led him to conclude that an enduring social peace required class harmony and modest reforms, like improving education, defending the rights of women and workers, and promoting limited land redistribution. His election caused much disquiet among the coffee planters and the military. The new president immediately ran into storms: teachers and other public servants clamored for back pay and peasants demanded land and other reforms, while the coffee oligarchy and the military pressed him to make no concessions.

On December 21, 1931, a military coup ousted Araujo and installed his vice president, General Maximiliano Hernández Martínez, as president. The coup signified the end of direct rule by the oligarchy and the beginning of a long era of military domination. The fall of the liberal Araujo and the rise of Hernández Martínez to power closed the door to popular participation in politics. Convinced that the new regime had no intention of allowing reforms or free elections, Martí and other radical leaders decided on insurrection. Simultaneous uprisings were set to take place in several towns on January 22, 1932. But the authorities got wind of the plot several days in advance, and Martí and two of his aides were seized. Other rebel leaders then tried to call off the revolt, but communications had broken down, and the largely indigenous revolt began without its ladino leadership.

In town after town, these campesinos rose up, often armed only with machetes. Having taken over much of the western area of the country, they attacked the regional center of Sonsonate, where the cacique José Feliciano Ama led a revolt that fused long-standing class, racial, and ethnic grievances. The unequal combat between peasants armed with machetes and the garrison, supported by the Guard and other police units, all armed with modern weapons, ended in total defeat for the insurgents. In a few days the captured towns were retaken. Then the oligarchy began to take its revenge, relentlessly hunting down the "communists," defined as any peasant who was not vouched for by a landowner as not having taken part in the revolt. As many as thirty thousand peasants died in this *matanza* (massacre), which verged on genocide by wiping out indigenous dress, languages, and cultural traditions. Ferocious repression was the coffee oligarchy's way of teaching the peasantry a lesson, of ensuring social stability. The history of El Salvador since 1932 shows how vain that expectation was.

## OLIGARCHS AND GENERALS, 1932–1979

The coup that installed Hernández Martínez in the presidency marked a turning point in modern Salvadoran history. Terrified by the peasant uprising of 1932, the oligarchy struck a bargain with the military that allowed the military to hold the reins of government while the oligarchy directed the economic life of the country. A network of corruption that permitted the officer class to share in the oligarchy's wealth cemented the alliance between the two groups. Nevertheless, the persistence of reformist tendencies among junior officers and a growing faction of agro-industrialists involved in the coffee-processing industry periodically produced tensions within the alliance that threatened its existence.

Hernández Martínez, known as *El Brujo* (the Witch Doctor) because of his dabbling in the occult, maintained a tight rule over the country through his control of the army and the National Guard until 1944. In addition, power and access to wealth were concentrated in a clique of Hernández Martínez's cronies. This created discontent among junior officers, who allied with agro-industrialists and urban professionals, inspired by wartime rhetoric about democracy, to overthrow Martínez and demand political reform, women's suffrage, economic modernization, and agricultural diversification. This "Revolution of 1948," championed by Colonel Oscar Osorio, inaugurated a decade of import-substitution industrialization, expanded cotton cultivation, and greater export dependency, all under the watchful eye of the military and its oligarchical allies. Then in 1961, alienated by the civilian-military junta's increasingly progressive program, its mobilization of popular sectors, and its friendly relations with Cuba, Colonel Julio

Alberto Rivera joined with the U.S. embassy to organize an anticommunist coup d'état that restored the military's monopoly of power.

Rivera established a system, patterned on the Mexican idea of a single dominant party that would perpetuate itself in power, that involved holding elections every five years and employing fraud, coercion, and co-optation to maintain control. This allowed a number of opposition parties to exist. The most important were the Christian Democratic Party (PDC), headed by José Napoleon Duarte, mayor of San Salvador from 1964 to 1970; a Social Democratic Party, *Movimiento Nacional Revolucionario* (MNR), led by Guillermo Manuel Ungo; and the *Unión Democrática Nacionalista* (UDN), a front for the Communist Party, which had been illegal since 1932.

As the economic difficulties of the country multiplied during the 1960s and 1970s, however, the strains within the system grew and it became increasingly unworkable. The roots of the problem lay in the monoculture that made the country dependent on a world market over which it had no control and a system of land tenure and use that progressively reduced the land area available to small landowners and staple food production.

Land monopoly and the prevailing system of land use led to population pressure on land, a problem greatly aggravated by the population explosion. Thanks to the eradication of yellow fever and malaria and to the successes of preventive medicine, the population shot up from 1,443,000 in 1930 to 2,500,000 in 1961 and 3,549,000 in 1969. By 1970 the population density was about 400 per square mile. The swelling population put great pressure on wage levels: the average daily wage for a field hand in the early 1960s was about 62¢ a day, for an overseer or *mayordomo*, a little over $1.00 a day. Because labor on coffee plantations was seasonal and a peon was lucky to get 150 days of work a year, the labor of an entire family for that period might yield a total yearly cash income of $300.

With land reform ruled out as a solution for land hunger and population pressure, Rivera attempted another remedy: industrialization and economic integration through the creation of the

Central American Common Market (CACM) in 1961. The underlying reasoning was that the unrestricted flow of goods and capital throughout the area would stimulate an expansion of markets and industrialization, relieving population pressure and unemployment. Unfortunately, this industrial expansion took place without a corresponding growth in employment, for the new industries were capital intensive and required relatively few workers. Also, much of the new industry was foreign owned and geared to exports; much of it was designed to assemble imported components.

The problem of population pressure on the land grew much more acute as a result of a bitter dispute between El Salvador and Honduras that culminated in a war that took several thousand lives and left at least one hundred thousand Salvadorans homeless. Called the Soccer War because it followed a series of hotly contested games between teams representing the two countries in the qualifying rounds of the 1969 World Cup, the conflict had more pragmatic causes. One was a border dispute of long standing. Another was Honduran resentment over the marked imbalance of trade between the two countries as a result of the operations of CACM, to which both countries belonged. Honduras, an extremely underdeveloped country whose economy was largely based on bananas, lumber, and cattle, felt that it was subsidizing the industrial development of El Salvador. The third and decisive cause of the war was the presence in Honduras of some three hundred thousand illegal Salvadoran settlers. Following adoption of an agrarian reform law, Honduras had ordered the expulsion of some eighty thousand settlers. El Salvador retaliated by invading Honduras and destroying most of its air force on the ground. The war was over in five days, largely due to U.S. pressure on El Salvador in the form of threatened economic sanctions. The war, which was very popular in El Salvador, momentarily diverted popular attention from its great problems, but the effects on the country were entirely negative: El Salvador lost the Honduran market for its manufacturers for over a decade, and the return of Salvadorans from Honduras swelled the number of landless and homeless peasants.

These developments contributed to the ever-growing economic and social crises of the 1970s. Population growth continued to outstrip the food supply; among the Latin American countries, only Haiti's people had a lower caloric intake than El Salvador's. By the early 1970s, unemployment was running at 20 percent and underemployment at 40 percent; in 1974 the annual inflation rate reached 60 percent. The proportion of landless peasantry rose from 11.8 percent in 1950 to 41 percent in 1975. The calamitous economic situation gave the opposition parties hope for victory in the presidential election of 1972; in September of that year the Christian Democratic Party, the MNR, and the Communist UDN formed a united front, the *Unión Nacional Opositora* (UNO). Its candidate for president, José Napoleon Duarte, had clearly won the election by some 72,000 votes, but the electoral commission found that the official candidate, Colonel Arturo Molina, had won by about 100,000 votes. The flagrant electoral fraud provoked a revolt by reformist junior military that ultimately failed. Duarte, the candidate of the united opposition, was arrested, tortured, and exiled to Venezuela.

Clearly, the military and the agrarian wing of the coffee oligarchy had become impatient with the agro-industrialists and their modest reform agenda, which, despite their protests to the contrary, never seemed to pacify the nation, but instead merely provided political space for popular sector mobilization. As a result, the Molina regime increasingly relied on repression to preserve order. In 1975, hoping to promote the emerging tourist industry, Molina hosted the 1975 "Miss Universe" pageant and spent about $30 million on the show. In a country with so many unfilled social needs, this impressed many Salvadorans as a scandalous extravagance. Units of the National Guard—without any provocation—fired on students attending a protest rally in San Salvador. At least thirty-seven died and an unknown number of others "disappeared." The massacre was part of a pattern of growing violence—from the right and from the left. With increasing frequency, guerrilla organizations that had sprung up since 1970 kidnapped and held members of the oligarchy for ransom. In the countryside, the National Guard, aided by right-wing paramilitary organizations like ORDEN *(Organización Democrática Nacionalista)*, conducted sweeps against "subversive" peasants, surrounding and destroying villages, killing many villagers, and abducting others who "disappeared."

Although convinced that the familiar pattern of fraud would be repeated in the 1977 presidential election, the UNO decided to run a symbolic candidate, a hero of the Honduran war, Colonel Ernesto Claramount Rozeville. The election was in fact marked by widespread fraud, with rampant stuffing of the ballot boxes for Carlos Romero and armed ORDEN thugs on hand to discourage close scrutiny by the opposition at the polls. The outcome was never in doubt. A massive protest demonstration held on February 15 in the main square of San Salvador and addressed by Claramount and other speakers was attacked by army and police units and by members of ORDEN. More than two hundred people were killed by machine-gun fire. Claramount was exiled, but as he departed for the airport he uttered a prophetic comment: "This is not the end, it is only the beginning."

Ending all hope of reform via the electoral process, the fraudulent election of 1977 and the spiral of violence that followed it marked the opening of a prerevolutionary stage of Salvadoran political development. On the left, the revolutionary organizations that had emerged since 1970 mobilized their forces and attempted to overcome their ideological and tactical differences. They robbed banks, seized radio stations to broadcast propaganda, kidnapped oligarchs for ransom, and assassinated persons identified with official or unofficial repression. There was a rapid growth of labor and peasant unions and other mass movements, known collectively as *Fuerzas Populares* (Popular Forces), and of umbrella organizations, such as FAPU (Front for United Popular Action), which organized many groups for joint action against the government. On the right, meanwhile, there was increased repressive activity by the National Guard, the National Police, and other security forces as well as by the death squads of ORDEN and another terrorist organization, the White Warrior Union.

A major development of this period was the changing posture of the church toward the Salvadoran crisis. Prior to the Second Vatican Council (1962) and the Medellín Bishops' Conference, the church in El Salvador—as elsewhere in Latin America—had supported the regime and the oligarchy. Although most of the hierarchy maintained that position, Archbishop Luis Chávez y González and his successor Oscar Romero, with Vatican II and Medellín as their guides, committed themselves to what Romero called "the preferential option for the poor." One result of this ferment in the church was the formation in a few short years of hundreds of comunidades de base, which combined Bible study with attention to the economic and social problems of their localities. The messages the priests brought to their parishioners was that God is "a God of justice and love who acts on the side of the poor and oppressed" and that the people "have a basic human right to organize in order to begin taking control of their own lives."

Their social activism inevitably marked the priests as targets of right-wing death squads and security forces. The Jesuit Father Rutilio Grande was murdered by a death squad of the White Warrior Union in March 1977, and three other Jesuits who had been working with him were expelled from the country. By May 1977 leaflets urging Salvadorans to "Be a Patriot! Kill a Priest!" were circulating in San Salvador. Altogether, seven priests were killed by death squads or security forces between 1977 and 1979. The death of Father Grande, three weeks after Romero was installed as archbishop, contributed to what the archbishop referred to as his "transformation." From then on, during his three years and one month as archbishop, Romero used his position to denounce the regime's human rights violations and to plead for social justice. His sermons, transmitted via radio to almost every part of the country, "became the single most listened-to program in the nation."

The church also helped organize human rights groups like COMADRES, mothers of the imprisoned, assassinated, or "disappeared." Created in 1977, COMADRES courageously protested against the repression with public demonstrations, hunger strikes, and sit-ins at government buildings. According to a founding member, Alicia, their objectives were symbolized by their attire: a black dress to mourn the dead, a white scarf to celebrate "peace with justice, not . . . impunity," a red carnation to recall the bloody dictatorship, and its green leaves to represent "the hope for life." In response, military and paramilitary forces bombed their offices five times, threatened to "decapitate" them, and kidnapped, tortured, and raped more than forty members.

As the crisis deepened month after month, divisions began to appear within the military. A group of reformist junior military watched with profound anxiety the revolutionary course of events in Nicaragua in July–August 1979; they became convinced that a coup offered the only alternative to a solution of the Nicaraguan type. After regular consultations with Archbishop Romero, representatives of the Christian Democratic Party, and the U.S. embassy, which indicated it would not oppose such an action, the coup took place on October 15 with virtually no resistance from any garrison. Incumbent President Romero meekly accepted exile, and a military-civilian junta was formed. The civilians included two moderate leftists, Román Mayorga Quiroz, rector of the Central American University, and the Social Democrat Guillermo Ungo; the military representatives were the authentically democratic Colonel Adolfo Majano and the rightist Colonel Jaime Abdul Gutiérrez, head of the Military School, who owed his inclusion to U.S. pressure. The junta's program called for dissolution of the terrorist ORDEN organization, respect for human rights, agrarian reform, freedom for the Popular Forces to operate, and improvement of relations with Nicaragua.

Although Gutiérrez gave his nominal approval to the program, he decided, without consulting his colleagues, to change the balance of forces in the government by appointing another conservative, Colonel José Guillermo García, as defense minister in the cabinet that was to assist the junta. It was a fateful decision.

The left and the Popular Forces, meanwhile, regarded the junta with an intense suspicion that time was to justify. On October 28 a demonstration by several organizations demanding to know the fate of the many persons who had "disappeared" was met with gunfire by the National Guard, leaving twenty-five people dead. In fact, the October 15 coup did not end repression by the security forces; more people were killed by them in the three weeks after the coup than had died in any similar period under Romero. Efforts by civilian junta members Mayorga and Ungo to restrain the official violence were totally ineffective, for the armed forces listened to no one but García.

These events led to the resignation of the civilian members of the junta, followed by the formation of a new government, the product of a secret deal between the military and the Christian Democratic Party. Two Christian Democrats replaced Mayorga and Ungo. The military committed itself to a program of agrarian reform and nationalization of the banks; a cessation of all repression; and a dialogue between the armed forces and the Popular Forces. Barely one week after accepting these conditions, the security forces fired on a massive demonstration of the Popular Forces, the largest in Salvadoran history, killing about twenty persons. This and similar repressive acts that demonstrated the bad faith of the military caused a split in the Christian Democratic Party. One of its representatives, Héctor Dada, resigned from the junta and was replaced by José Napoleón Duarte. At least 60 percent of its membership resigned from the party by November 1981. To add to the junta's problems, a rightist coup led by Roberto d'Aubuisson, head of the White Warrior Union, was barely averted by Defense Minister García and other high military officers. The agrarian reform promulgated with dramatic suddenness by the junta in March 1980 resulted from intense pressure by the United States, eager to give a reformist face to its protégé, even as James Cheek, the U.S. chargé d'affaires, advised the junta to conduct a "clean counterinsurgency war." Typical of its strategy of reform and repression, the junta announced a state of siege on the same day that it promulgated the agrarian reform.

The agrarian reform was to be implemented in three stages. Phase I, promulgated in March 1980, nationalized 376 estates of more than 500 hectares, belonging to 244 owners and consisting largely of pasture and cotton land. The owners were to be compensated with thirty-year bonds, and the estates were to be converted into cooperatives with 29,755 peasant members. As of January 1, 1983, only twenty-two cooperatives had received final title, although 130 of the owners had been paid for their farms. Phase II, which would have affected about 200 farms of between 100 and 500 hectares, including most of the coffee fincas, "died before it was born," postponed for an indefinite period.

Phase III, called "Land to the Tiller," promulgated in April 1980, allowed peasants who rented up to forty-two hectares of land to buy it from the owner. As of January 1983, 58,152 applications had been received, roughly half the number that were possible under Phase III provisions. By June 1982 no permanent titles had been issued to applicants; the number rose to 251 in August of that year, and to 1,050 by January 1983. The Salvadoran Peasants' Union charged that the increase resulted from the need to provide the Reagan administration with proof for certifying to the U.S. Congress that El Salvador was making progress in essential economic reform and had therefore fulfilled the requirements for continued economic and military aid.

This curious land reform was accompanied by a wave of repression directed above all against the peasantry. Responsibility for seizure and distribution of land was assigned to the army and the security forces, who used their authority in several ways. Often they distributed land to members of the terrorist ORDEN organization whether or not they were entitled to it. They also used ORDEN members to identify peasants who belonged to the Popular Forces or to the guerrilla movements; these peasants were then killed by the military. Sometimes they collaborated with landowners who evicted tenants from lands they had recently acquired under land reform provisions.

In December 1981 the Peasants' Union reported to junta President José Napoleón Duarte (he had been named president in a leadership reshuffle in November 1980) that the "failure of the agrarian reform is an immediate and imminent danger." The union claimed that at least ninety of its officials and "a large number of beneficiaries" of the agrarian reform had died during 1981 at the hands of ex-landlords and their allies, who often were members of the local security forces. The report also charged that twenty-five thousand former *aparceros*, or sharecroppers, had been evicted from their plots before they could obtain provisional titles. Duarte's inability to carry out the agrarian reform or to check the terror in the countryside proved that the junta was in fact "a rightist military regime with a civilian façade"; it also showed that Duarte himself was an "ornament," in the words of one observer, needed by the United States to maintain the reformist image of the junta, and accepted by the military to pacify the U.S. State Department.

The most prominent victim of the terror that accompanied the promulgation of the agrarian reform was Monsignor Oscar Romero, archbishop of San Salvador. For years his attacks on the military and the security forces for their violations of human rights had been a thorn in the government's side. Increasingly disillusioned with the role of the Christian Democratic Party in the junta, he gradually moved toward supporting armed struggle as the only remaining resort. In a sermon on February 2, 1980, he proclaimed: "When all peaceful means have been exhausted, the church considers insurrection moral and justified." On March 23, responding to the repression that accompanied the land reform, he appealed to soldiers not to turn their guns on unarmed civilians. The next day, as he celebrated mass in a chapel in San Salvador, he was gunned down, probably by a military officer.

The National Guard celebrated his death with a savage attack on his hometown of Ciudad Barrios that left ten dead. According to the judge appointed to investigate his death—who made these revelations after he had fled for his life to Costa Rica—the assassination was planned by General José Alberto Medrano, founder of ORDEN, and Major Roberto d'Aubuisson. Robert White, former U.S. ambassador to El Salvador, informed a congressional committee that there

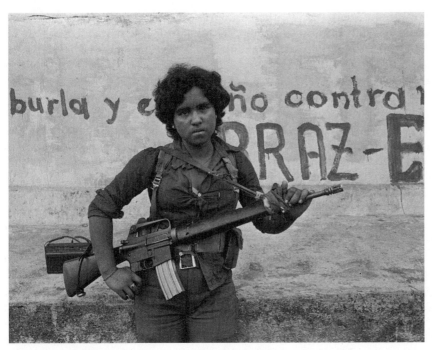

Many women, like the Salvadoran guerrilla shown here, took part in recent Central American revolutionary struggles, and some held high positions in the guerrilla commands. [Bettmann/Corbis]

was "compelling" evidence that d'Aubuisson was involved in the killing. Romero's martyrdom was to have profound political and military repercussions.

### THE SALVADORAN REVOLUTION, 1980–1992

"If I am killed," Archbishop Romero had prophesied shortly before his death, "I shall rise again in the struggle of the Salvadoran people." His death, in fact, served as a powerful catalyst for the growth of that struggle. In particular, it hastened the breakup of the Christian Democratic Party and the unification of its center and left wings with Social Democratic and Marxist-led groups in opposition to the junta. In April 1980 a broad coalition of political parties, professional associations, trade unions, and revolutionary groups formed the Democratic Revolutionary Front (FDR). In January 1981, the FDR set up a government-in-exile, headed by the Social Democratic leader Guillermo Ungo.

As important as achieving the political unity of the opposition was the unification of the various guerrilla movements. By mid-summer of 1980 the five major guerrilla groups had united in a single command, which was given the name *Frente Farabundo Martí de Liberación Nacional* (FMLN), in honor of the leader of the abortive 1932 revolt. In January 1981 the FMLN launched its first general offensive and achieved significant successes, capturing from U.S.-equipped government soldiers, M16s that virtually became the FMLN's standard weapon. Between June and October 1982 alone the rebels captured six hundred fifty firearms; over twenty guns, mortars, and heavy machine guns; and about eighty thousand rounds of ammunition.

Although the guerrillas invariably evacuated the large population centers captured in their offensives, by the spring of 1983 they had considerably expanded the zones of their control. They dominated areas inhabited by some two hundred thousand people; in these areas, political power was based on a self-governing system called the *Poder Popular Local* (PPL). To combat rebel successes, the military leadership changed and pursued a more aggressive strategy that relied on increased military aid from the Reagan administration, but this required it to improve the image of the regime by holding elections to legitimize it and give it a "democratic" face. The elections, it was assumed, would give victory to the Christian Democratic Party and its leader, José Napoleón Duarte. He would then preside over a modest reform and civic action program that would win "hearts and minds" for the government; Duarte's reforms, combined with expanded military aid, were expected to lead to a speedy pacification of the country.

In compliance with U.S. wishes, elections for a sixty-member Constituent Assembly were held in El Salvador in March 1982. Insisting that fair elections were impossible under existing conditions, the left and the guerrillas boycotted them. Less than a year earlier, the entire leadership of the FDR had been assassinated and, more recently, the army had published a hit list of FDR and FMLN members; if the government could not guarantee the security of political leaders, it certainly could not protect grassroots campaign workers! As a result, these "demonstration elections," organized for the benefit of the U.S. government, upon which the Salvadoran military depended, were dominated by right-wing parties.

In any event, the outcome of the elections did not conform to the expectations of the Reagan administration. With only 35 percent of the vote, Duarte and the Christian Democrats proved unable to form a majority government. The Nationalist Republic Alliance (ARENA) of Roberto D'Aubuisson garnered one-fourth of the vote and pressed for a coalition with other right-wing parties that would leave the Christian Democrats out in the cold. Thus, instead of legitimating Duarte and the Christian Democrats, as projected in the Reagan administration scenario, the elections appeared to legitimate D'Aubuisson and ARENA. Undaunted, however, the United States pressured

all parties to sign a pact for cooperation in the transition to a new constitutional government. As part of the deal, the U.S.-supported "moderate" banker Álvaro Magaña was elected provisional president of the republic and D'Aubuisson president of the Constituent Assembly.

The Reagan administration's policy in El Salvador had one overriding purpose: at all costs to prevent the FMLN-FDR from coming to power. To ensure congressional support for the large infusions of military and economic aid needed to achieve this objective, the Reagan administration strongly supported the 1984 presidential candidacy of Duarte, who was identified by many in El Salvador and the United States with social reform. At the same time that it backed this supposed reformer, Washington demanded a more aggressive strategy in the war against the rebels, with massive use of air power and large-scale sweeps into rebel territory to force out the civilian population and to isolate the insurgents, thereby denying them the material and logistical support they needed to survive. This more aggressive strategy was to be combined with civic action programs designed to win the rural population's support.

Soon it became evident that Duarte lacked the power, the resources, and perhaps the will to carry out his promises. He initiated peace talks with the FMLN in late 1984 but broke them off; the talks were probably intended above all to prove his goodwill regarding peace to his domestic supporters and his congressional backers in Washington. Duarte's promises of social and economic reform proved equally illusory. He presided over a moribund economy that survived due only to the immense largesse of the United States. (Between 1981 and 1987, U.S. government military and economic aid to El Salvador totaled $2.7 billion.)

Duarte faced a dilemma. His promises and election had encouraged the labor movement to organize, call strikes, and engage in political activity; the right responded with repression, including a revival of death-squad killings and disappearances. Even if he had the means, Duarte could not satisfy labor's economic and social demands over the opposition of the oligarchy, the army, and even the Reagan administration. On the other hand, he could not openly support repression without losing his base in the labor movement. Duarte solved the problem by denouncing repression in words, while tolerating and even sanctioning it in practice.

In January 1986 the Duarte government announced an economic austerity program to help pay the costs of the war against the FMLN-FDR; the program included a 100 percent devaluation of the currency and large increases in fuel prices, measures that hit workers the hardest. Thousands of angry workers responded by leaving the trade union federation, controlled by the Christian Democrats, and joining a newly organized leftist federation, the National Union of Salvadoran Workers (UNTS). In October, Duarte introduced another economic austerity package that levied steep taxes on basic goods and services and reduced already minimal social services. The package, described as an act of "political suicide" by a rebel leader, set off a fresh wave of strikes and demonstrations that drew ever-larger numbers of workers. Duarte's labor base virtually collapsed. He could not even count on the support of the business sector. Of great significance, the strikes and demonstrations increasingly linked economic demands to calls for an end to the civil war through negotiations; these calls were strongly supported by the head of the Salvadoran church, Archbishop Arturo Rivera y Damas.

But the Reaganites still sought a military victory, and a massive influx of new U.S. military aid, including gunships and helicopters, and a considerable increase in the size of the Salvadoran army undoubtedly changed the balance of forces in the civil war. U.S. reconnaissance flights from Honduras and the Panama Canal Zone helped pinpoint rebel columns and command posts, using infrared tracking systems. Unable to compete with the army in numbers and firepower, the FMLN developed a new strategy. The large battalion-size units were broken up into small units of classic guerrilla warfare; these moved out of the way of the army's sweeps and returned after the army had left. The rebels, however, were still capable of launching major surprise attacks. Other new FMLN tactics included using mines, which caused perhaps as much as 70 percent of the army's casu-

alties; another was economic sabotage through efforts to destroy the country's electrical grid by downing power lines and blowing up installations and dams, and through the destruction of coffee-processing plants.

Believing a military triumph unlikely, the FMLN now aimed to mobilize trade unions, a growing antiwar movement, and other popular forces to create conditions for a "negotiated peace." But success also required a separation of the two oligarchical factions, the hard-line coffee planters, or "agrarians," and the moderate coffee processors, or "agro-industrialists," whose unstable marriage had contributed to the government's historical oscillation between repression and reform. The FMLN sought to encourage negotiations by making the war too expensive for the agro-industrialists, led by Alfredo Cristiani, a wealthy coffee processor and past president of their trade association, ABECAFE. U.S. sources estimated the 1979–1985 loss through economic sabotage at $1.2 billion.

By 1988 the failure of the U.S. counterinsurgency strategy in El Salvador was apparent to all. The economy was in ruins, with industry operating at 40 percent of capacity. Riddled with corruption, the Duarte administration had proved unable to end the war, implement serious reforms, or check the repression. The results of March congressional and local elections, carried out under the guns of the military, represented a repudiation of both Duarte and his U.S. sponsors. Most of El Salvador's eligible voters stayed away from the polls; a majority of those who voted cast their ballots for D'Aubuisson's ARENA, which gained control of parliament and most of the country's local governments.

One year later, Alfredo Cristiani assumed the presidency. He complied with his campaign promise to initiate talks with the FMLN guerrillas following his inauguration but demanded their virtual surrender by insisting they lay down their arms as a condition for a cease-fire. As a result the peace talks were suspended and fighting resumed, accompanied by an escalation of death-squad killings and torture of civilians. Cristiani's intransigent attitude, it was widely believed, reflected the decisive influence of the so-called *Tandona*, an elite group of extreme right-wing military from the cadet class of 1966 that included the defense minister, the army's chief of staff, and the chiefs of the air force, the national police, and the national guard. This tight-knit group regarded D'Aubuisson as its leader. Nonetheless, Cristiani's apparent moderation was sufficient to convince some liberal U.S. senators like Christopher Dodd and John Kerry to vote more money for El Salvador.

Prospects of peace suffered a shattering blow in 1989, when bombings of the headquarters of the National Federation of Salvadoran Workers (FENESTRAS) killed ten persons and wounded many others. In response to the bombings, the FMLN announced that it would not resume talks with the government as long as "guarantees for the labor movement are not achieved"; then it launched its most powerful offensive since 1981, striking at a number of cities, including San Salvador. Its main objective was to take control of the working-class quarters in the city's densely populated northern outskirts, where it enjoyed considerable political support. The government responded with a ferocious aerial bombing of these working-class barrios, but the FMLN held sections of the city for up to two weeks before withdrawing.

The concentrated bombardment of densely populated working-class barrios caused many civilian casualties and provoked an international outcry. The bombardment was accompanied by a new wave of repression directed against church and labor critics of the government. Six Jesuit priests and professors at San Salvador's Central American University, whom the military regarded as the "brains" of the uprising, together with their housekeeper and her daughter, were shot in cold blood.

The FMLN's offensive was designed to prove to the Cristiani government and to the United States that after nine years of war the FMLN was stronger than ever and could not be defeated militarily, and thereby to bring the ARENA regime to the bargaining table for serious negotiations.

Moved by this demonstration of rebel power, and even more, perhaps, by the threat of a congressional halt to U.S. aid to El Salvador in reaction to the murder of the six Jesuits and other human rights abuses, the Cristiani government agreed to resume negotiations with the FMLN without preconditions, with the United Nations as mediator.

In 1992, President Cristiani and delegates of the ruling ARENA party and the FMLN finally signed peace accords that ended the decade-long civil war. Its provisions required the National Guard and Treasury Police to be disbanded and replaced with a new professionally trained National Civil Police, open to both former national police and FMLN guerrillas. The size of the armed forces would be reduced by about 50 percent, and the U.S.-trained Immediate Reaction Infantry Battalions, charged with the commission of numerous atrocities, were to be disbanded. FMLN military structures were to be dismantled under U.N. supervision and their members integrated into the political and institutional life of the country, but the FMLN could form its own party and set up its own radio and TV facilities.

The accords also dealt with economic and social issues. The government agreed to implement the existing agrarian code and respect the de facto land tenancy in "conflictive zones" (zones under FMLN control during the war) while it sought to purchase land from absentee owners. The FMLN conceded the right of the government to press on with its neoliberal "structural adjustment" policies; the government in turn agreed to take measures to alleviate the social cost of those policies. With the support of the U.N. Development Program, the government agreed to develop a National Reconstruction Plan for the conflictive zones, involving infrastructural development as well as employment, education, housing, and health programs. Finally, the accords provided for the creation of a "Truth Commission," to be composed of three foreigners, that would investigate human rights abuses during the war and could recommend prosecutions or other punishment for the responsible parties.

In 1993 the U.N.-sponsored Truth Commission released its long-awaited report. The report was based on the testimony of two thousand persons who had come forward, under promises of confidentiality, to testify as witnesses about the fate of seven thousand victims and on secondary information about the fate of more than eighteen thousand victims. The report found that 85 percent of the nine thousand human rights abuses investigated, and 95 percent of the killings, were committed by government-supported death squads and the military. Government atrocities included the massacre of nearly one thousand civilians— men, women, and children—in the village of El Mozote and nearby hamlets by the U.S.-trained Atlacatl Battalion; the 1980 assassination of Archbishop Romero; and the 1989 murder of the six Jesuit priests, their housekeeper, and her daughter. The report found that the FMLN had also committed human rights violations, such as the killing of right-wing mayors, but on a much smaller scale. The report implicitly pointed a finger of blame at the United States by noting that the majority of the human rights abuses were directly attributable to graduates of the School of the Americas at Fort Benning, Georgia, where many of El Salvador's death-squad leaders received their training in counterinsurgency methods.

The Truth Commission's report and newly declassified documents lifted a veil of deception practiced by the Reagan and Bush administrations to persuade Congress to provide continued military assistance to the Salvadoran armed forces. In 1981, for example, the CIA called ARENA party leader D'Aubuisson "the principal henchman for wealthy landowners and a coordinator of right-wing death squads that have murdered several thousand suspected leftists and leftist sympathizers" and described him as "egocentric, reckless, and perhaps mentally unstable." The CIA also reported that D'Aubuisson trafficked in drugs, smuggled arms, and directed the meeting that planned Romero's assassination. But William Walker, Bush's special envoy to San Salvador and Reagan's deputy assistant secretary of state for inter-American affairs, confronted with the documents, displayed no compunction and responded: "We had to deal with D'Aubuisson."

## THE SALVADORAN REVOLUTION: A RECKONING, 1992–2003

After twelve years of fighting, seventy-five thousand dead, 2 million displaced, an estimated 1 million war refugees, and billions of dollars in economic losses, what was the revolution's legacy? First, it demilitarized Salvadoran society and created space for popular mobilization that had been suppressed since the 1932 matanza. This transformed domestic power relations and produced a new pluralism, reflected in a reorganized national political structure, that contrasted starkly with a political culture that traditionally had limited competition to two factions within the coffee oligarchy: murderous planters and slightly more moderate processors. As a result, an ongoing movement for social justice and national liberation was not only possible, but irrepressible.

Second, it engendered a new male and female consciousness. Women, traditionally consigned to family roles within the household, became active participants in public life, first as defenders of their families in human rights organizations like COMADRES and later in other organized popular movements like the Salvadoran Women's Association (AMES). Her COMADRE activism, for example, taught one woman that "the fight for human rights is all about . . . the rights of workers, the rights of women—before I didn't know this." The war also depleted the male labor force; created new demands for women workers, whose participation in the waged economy increased dramatically to 40 percent by 1992; and expanded women's presence in trade unions.

Lastly, women sought to escape the prison of patriarchy by joining the revolution, where they made up 30 percent of FMLN combatants and 20 percent of the military leadership: "We grew up with a mentality . . . that a woman is no more than a person to look after the house, raise the children," explained María Serrano, a guerrilla mayor. "But with the revolution this stopped; women found that they could do the same things as men." Naturally, this new feminist consciousness also had implications for men; one guerrillero who fought in a predominantly female unit acknowledged the difficult "process of coming to see women as compañeras and not as sex objects." Their shared experiences gave a gendered meaning to the revolution's national liberation struggle, which now included freedom from patriarchal as well as racial, class, and imperialist domination.

These potentially momentous changes, however, while clearly evinced in the peace accords, required a vigilant popular struggle and unflagging international pressure to secure their fullest development. A vigorous participatory democracy was the best guarantor of social justice, without which there could be no enduring peace. But in March 1994, with the infamous Atlacatl Battalion dissolved, a new police force organized, and the FMLN prepared to participate as a political party in its first elections, dark clouds still threatened the fragile peace. On the eve of the elections there was a dramatic escalation of violence against candidates and other leading members of the FMLN. In addition, since the cease-fire there had been some two hundred unresolved cases of former guerrillas who had been killed. Despite these troubling signs, the Clinton administration continued to send both military and economic aid ($140 million a year) to El Salvador and maintained 450 military advisers in the country.

During the early 1990s, ARENA's well-healed political machine elected Armando Calderón Sol to the presidency, and he ruled with an absolute legislative majority. Over spirited FMLN objections, ARENA implemented an IMF-sponsored neoliberal program even as it blocked fulfillment of the peace accord's provisions regarding the transfer of land in the former conflict zones, the development of reinsertion programs for former combatants in the civil war, and the demilitarization of the national police force. By early 1994 only 25 percent of former FMLN fighters had received the land they were promised in the peace accords. The deployment of the new National Police Force (PNC) was behind schedule; more ominous was the infiltration into the PNC, with the government's consent, of many members of the old security services who were known to be torturers and death-squad members.

But 1997 brought a greater flowering of the peace process and seemed to reward the FMLN's determination to continue the civic struggle. Despite rival ARENA's financially well-endowed political patronage machine, a shortage of campaign funds, and the usual electoral fraud (three hundred thousand dead people remained on the voter rolls and four hundred thousand voters did not receive registration cards), the FMLN won a resounding victory in the March legislative and municipal elections. Compared to 1994 its share of the total vote increased from 21 to 33 percent. It elected twenty-seven deputies, one-third of whom were women; captured fifty-three municipalities, including San Salvador; and governed a majority of the population.

Meanwhile, ARENA's vote declined by 35 percent, leaving it with only twenty-eight of eighty-four National Assembly seats. Although ARENA cobbled together a majority coalition, it could no longer ignore the left. More important, the FMLN and its allies had sufficient votes to block legislative approval required of international loan agreements, thereby potentially frustrating ARENA's neoliberal agenda. This had involved privatization of banks and pensions, slashed tariffs, establishment of maquiladora "free-trade zones," and draconian social service budget cuts in areas like education, whose share of the federal budget fell almost a quarter to 13 percent in a nation with a 30 percent illiteracy rate.

In fact the FMLN's success appeared to owe much to its principled opposition to these widely unpopular neoliberal reforms that enriched foreign capital and produced impressive annual per capita economic growth in 1992–1993, before falling thereafter to a dismal 2 percent in 2000 and 2001. But the price for this small growth was high; it deepened external dependency, expanded underemployment, and increased poverty. El Salvador's foreign debt burden increased steadily since 1988, rising to $4 billion in 2001. More troubling still, 48 percent of the population was mired in poverty, 18.5 percent in extreme poverty. Unemployment remained stubbornly high, and real wages fell consistently.

Equally important to the FMLN's electoral success, however, was its strategic decision to nominate women, comprising half of its national candidates, to carry its gendered social justice message, a message that transcended racial and class lines. This reflected the militancy of FMLN feminists and the party's rhetorical commitment to women's rights, but it also showed a keen understanding that ARENA's neoliberal policies had contributed to the "feminization" of poverty; men's participation in the formal economy steadily declined since 1988 from 93 to 83 percent even as women's share of waged employment grew from 38 to 41 percent, but two-thirds of women worked in the "informal economy." Moreover, by the late 1970s, 40 percent of poor Salvadoran households were headed by women, a rate that rose during the war and worsened under the neoliberal regime.

This growing demand for women's labor outside the home, irrespective of class, did not reduce their private household obligations, however, and left them vulnerable to double exploitation—reflected in gendered wage inequalities, unequal access to credit and landownership, and soaring rates of domestic violence. These gender inequalities mirrored injustices produced by domestic class and dependent foreign relations. Under these conditions, the FMLN's campaign theme, *poder femenino* (woman power), resonated with a broad cross-section of Salvadorans and mobilized new, historically ignored voters who thrilled to its slogan: "When a woman enters politics, the woman changes; but . . . when women enter politics, politics changes."

Ten years after the signing of the 1992 peace accords that ended the civil war in El Salvador, the forces struggling for democracy and social justice since the 1970s could point to some major achievements. Their greatest success was the consolidation of Salvadoran democracy. The FMLN, formerly a revolutionary army, was now registered as a political party, competing with some nine other parties for power and influence. It had become the strongest single party in the National Assembly and, having captured fifty-three municipalities, including San Salvador, it now governed a majority of the population. But it was unable to win a national presidential election. In 1999 ARENA's Francisco Flores, promising social reforms that would benefit the entire population and soft-pedaling the neoliberal core of the party's program, was elected.

Once in office, however, Flores, whom critics called the "president of broken promises," displayed an increasingly authoritarian ideology and pushed for adoption of a full-scale neoliberal program that included privatization of health care, education, and other public services. As director of the national police, he appointed someone linked by the Truth Commission to death squad activity. Corruption returned to the reformed police forces. Crime and violence increased, and the per-capita death rate was as high as during the war years.

More hopeful signs came from FMLN-controlled municipalities. According to Sara Stowell, Tecoluca, governed by the FMLN since 1994, "has community roads, potable water for over 85% of the communities, access to education for all its citizens, a woman's health-care clinic, a new market, and flood protection infrastructure. In the wake of the two devastating earthquakes, Tecoluca mayor and council were able to work together with their population to respond rapidly to the need for shelter and food, and have one of the most comprehensive reconstruction plans under way as a result of good planning and excellent mayor-community relations."

Clearly, Tecoluca and other progressive Salvadoran communities had mastered the teaching of the martyred Archbishop Oscar Romero: "Learn about the mechanisms that engender poverty, struggle for a more just world, support the workers and peasants in their demands and in their right to organize, and be very close to the people."

# Lands of Bolívar: Venezuela and Colombia in the Twentieth Century

**M**ODERN VENEZUELA AND COLOMBIA have often been cited as oases of democratic and economic stability in a turbulent, poverty-ridden continent. A closer look at their recent history, however, suggests they have not escaped the general crisis of Latin American dependent capitalism. Its effects are clearly evident in the devastating impact of Venezuela's foreign debt on a country whose oil wealth once made it the envy of the continent. In February 1989, after Venezuelan President Carlos Andrés Pérez announced drastic increases in the prices of basic goods and services to satisfy the requirements of the International Monetary Fund (IMF) for loans to his government, the country exploded into riots that were crushed with the loss of hundreds of lives. Between 1981 and 1987 the number of Venezuelans living in poverty had risen from 22 to 54 percent of the population.

Neighboring Colombia presented an even darker picture. Colombia was the home of the Cali drug cartel, which accounted for most of the refined cocaine smuggled into the United States. Under an ostensibly democratic regime, death squads linked to the army, security forces, and the drug mafia operated with impunity against leftists, trade unionists, and human rights activists. Meanwhile, a guerrilla war—the longest continuing insurgency in Latin America, reflecting the vast accumulation of unsolved social problems in this oligarchical democracy—raged in Colombia's jungles and mountains. As we have seen elsewhere in Latin America, the twentieth-century origins of these problems can be traced to the growth of market forces, external economic dependency, internal social inequality, and an increasingly resolute popular resistance. This pattern began in Venezuela with the rise of Juan Vicente Gómez, a modern dictator in the tradition of Antonio Guzmán Blanco, Manuel Estrada Cabrera, and Porfirio Díaz.

## Venezuela in the Early Twentieth Century, 1908–1958

### THE TYRANNY OF JUAN VICENTE GÓMEZ, 1908–1935

On taking power, Gómez tried to placate his foreign patrons and promote a flow of investments into Venezuela by nullifying Cipriano Castro's nationalistic policies, restoring foreign companies' concessionary rights, and allowing foreign nationals to circumvent Venezuelan courts with appeals to their own national courts or to international tribunals.

Gómez especially favored foreign oil companies. The explosive growth of the oil industry eventually transformed Venezuelan economy and society, but the process began slowly. This

Juan Vicente Gómez, the early-twentieth-century liberal dictator, relied on a powerful military to implement unpopular policies that favored foreign investors and local elites. [Corbis]

modernization. The agricultural crisis contributed to a wave of rural migration to the oil fields of the Maracaibo Basin and other petroleum areas and to the growing cities.

Committed to progress based on private investment and the exploitation of wage labor, Gómez and the generation of intellectuals who served his dictatorship realized that Venezuela's "salvation" could not rely solely on the nineteenth century's failed racist immigration policy of "whitening." This recognition largely reflected Venezuela's growing export dependency and its demand for abundant, cheap labor, which discouraged potential European immigrants even as it attracted Caribbean blacks and Asians. Increasingly, the Gómez regime celebrated race-mixing to erase indigenous and African traditions by submerging them within a dominant European cultural motif, now labeled the "social race," whose unstable compound justified dictatorship.

In the 1920s nationalist resentment of foreign economic domination and hostility toward Gómez began to pervade the growing middle class. Venezuelan professionals and would-be entrepreneurs chafed at the difficulties of operating in an economic climate dominated by monopoly, nepotism, and corruption. They also resented foreigners' racist discrimination against their multiracial origins. In 1928 a celebration of the "Week of the Student" turned into a protest against the dictatorship, as students joined trade unionists and other anti-Gómez political factions.

The student protest inspired a military revolt in April 1928, led by young officers of the Caracas garrison and cadets of the *Escuela Militar*. Grievances over the favoritism shown in pay and promotions to officers of unquestioned loyalty to Gómez, and awareness that the army had become a repressive force designed to maintain internal order, fueled their discontent. An informer revealed the conspiracy to the military authorities, and government troops easily crushed the revolt before it had well begun. Some students who had collaborated with the rebellion cadets including Rómulo Betancourt, future president of Venezuela, managed to escape and make their way abroad.

economic transformation did not reduce Venezuela's dependence or broaden the base of its economy; the monoculture of coffee and cacao was replaced by the monoculture of "black gold." The oil industry pumped vast wealth into the hands of Gómez, a small native elite linked to the oil industry, and the foreign concessionaires, three of whom—Dutch Shell, Standard Oil, and Gulf—controlled 89 percent of the market. But little of this wealth trickled down to the masses, nor did it generate significant industrial progress. Government subsidies failed to stem the decline of agriculture, a sector that traditionally resisted

Although separated by class and racial status, women also played a powerful role in the emerging coalition that opposed Gómez. The Venezuelan Women's Association (AVM) largely represented elite women, who shunned politics and the equal rights struggle. They limited themselves to social advocacy on behalf of issues central to home and family: charity for the poor, childcare, orphanages, prenatal medical care, and sex education. But even these modest reforms typically envisioned an activist role for the state in the regulation of civil society and, in the words of political scientist Elisabeth Friedman, "proved too challenging to accepted notions of gender relations."

Unlike the AVM, the Women's Cultural Association (ACF), whose founding members included Cecelia Núñez Sucre and Mercedes Fermín, was a predominantly middle-class social movement that aimed to improve Venezuelan women's social condition, establish civil equality, and secure political rights. In addition to calls for greater access to jobs and education for women, they demanded limits on women's work day, increased wages, and pre- and post-maternity leave. But they also called for women's suffrage and reform of the Civil Code, which, according to one contemporaneous observer, gave a "woman no rights whatever against her husband, either personal or financial, even no rights to her own child."

Working-class women like Olga Luzardo, however, typically joined trade unions and actively identified with leftist political parties that, although dominated by men, nonetheless advocated "improvement of the entire exploited sector." Eschewing "feminism" as a middle-class idea incapable "of resolving the problems of working women," Luzardo, a Communist and working-class militant, scorned the bourgeois values of a social movement that limited itself to demands for gender equality and the "freedom" to work outside the home: "What would the women comrades of the soap and perfume factories, the polishers, the seamstresses, say [to the idea] that we ought to pull woman from her idleness and push her into work?" Luzardo asked contemptuously. "Wouldn't they laugh at such an unbalanced way of thinking?"

## LIQUIDATING THE GÓMEZ LEGACY, 1936–1945

In 1931, Gómez was at the peak of his power. But in the next few years his health began to decline, and in 1935 the prospect of his early demise led to intense factional maneuvering in his inner circle.

Amid growing signs that Gómez's illness was terminal, his minister of war, Eleazar López Contreras, wove a network of alliances, including the solid support of most army commanders, to ensure his own peaceful coming to power without a civil war or dangerous risings of the masses.

Announcing Gómez's death, López proclaimed two weeks of public mourning, but Venezuelans responded to the announcement with rejoicing; in Caracas angry crowds sacked the palaces of Gómez's most prominent supporters. The jubilation and the demands both for vengeance and for social and political reform provoked by the news of Gómez's death made a mockery of López's eulogy of the dead dictator and foreclosed the possibility of an easy transition to a social order resembling that of the old regime. The entrance of the Venezuelan middle classes and workers onto the political scene opened two decades of complicated struggle, culminating in the victory of a new populist model of capitalist development and its associated political form of representative democracy. Nonetheless, the dead dictator's hand-picked Congress chose López Contreras to replace him.

In an atmosphere of great social and political effervescence, however, many exiles with various ideologies returned home and joined activists emerging from the underground in organizing trade unions, political parties, and professional organizations. López found himself under siege from the right and the left. He sometimes yielded to pressures for reform, then stubbornly resisted demands for change to the undemocratic Gómez political system. For example, he supported a new constitution in 1936 but insisted on retaining a Gómez clause that defined communism and anarchism as treason, effectively outlawing the major opposition parties, the reformist *Partido Democrático Nacional* (PDN) led by Rómulo Betancourt and the Venezuelan Communist Party of Gustavo Machado.

World War II, having created insatiable demand for Venezuela's oil, enabled López's hand-picked successor, General Isaias Medina Angarita, to wrest more favorable terms from the oil companies than had been present in the old inequitable contracts. Moreover, domestic social movements of workers, peasants, women, and industrialists pressured him to support progressive policies like Venezuela's first social security and income-tax legislation. His government also encouraged the formation of trade unions, which gained considerable strength, particularly in the oil industry. Pushed by Mercedes Fermín and the Feminine Cultural Group (ACF), a largely middle-class women's rights organization that had opposed Gómez, Medina viewed favorably a movement toward a more democratic system with enfranchisement of women and direct popular election of the president.

Medina also tackled the country's urgent agrarian problem. Near the end of his administration he asked his minister of agriculture, Angel Biaggini, to draft an agrarian reform bill that would distribute the extensive state landholdings to landless peasants. Congress passed the law, but one month after passage it died stillborn as a result of the overthrow of the Medina administration by a military-civilian revolt headed by two men who would dominate Venezuelan politics for the next two decades, Marcos Pérez Jiménez and Rómulo Betancourt.

Betancourt was the most influential personality among that famous generation of student leaders who in 1928 electrified Caracas by leading a public demonstration against Gómez. Of middle-class background, during his years of exile Betancourt had read widely in the classics of Marxist literature. But the most decisive influence on his thought was a nationalist, reformist ideological current best represented in Latin America by the Peruvian Victor Raúl Haya de la Torre, who argued that in Latin America's specific conditions, characterized by economic backwardness and a small, weak working class, the immediate historical task of social revolutionaries was to complete the unfinished bourgeois revolution.

Betancourt thus appears as the standard-bearer of the Venezuelan bourgeois revolution, which sought to end dependency on oil by diversifying the economy through industrialization, to expand the internal market by improving living standards, and to initiate land reform that would increase the productivity of agriculture. All these goals he hoped to achieve within the framework of parliamentary democracy. Betancourt assigned a decisive role in this process to the state, which should plan, regulate, and assist economic development.

The political instrument Betancourt and his colleagues created to achieve Venezuela's bourgeois, democratic revolution was *Acción Democrática* (AD), a multiclass party and mass organization that enjoyed large growth from 1941 to 1945, gaining a clear superiority in numbers and influence among workers, peasants, women, and the middle class over its closest rival, the Communist Party.

There were four key elements in women's strategy for securing civil and political equality. First, they sought to organize and maintain unity across the seemingly insurmountable dividing lines of class and political party. Reflecting this strategic consensus among middle-class women, Ana Luisa Padra announced in 1941 that "We have different interests, but a common problem: the conquest of our rights for which we ought to [fight] together without rancor or distinctions." Second, rather than seek equality with men, the women's movement in Venezuela sought to mobilize the state's resources to protect children and mothers. Third, women raised the issue of equality without addressing it directly, at least initially by seeking merely to reclaim for married women liberties freely granted to widowed mothers—property rights and custody of their children. Thereafter, they insisted that political rights for women logically should flow directly from the successful attainment of civil equality, rather than vice versa; lacking "voice or vote within the boundaries of her home," a feminist newspaper editorialized, "it would be laughable that [women] would be granted the vote within the boundaries of her country."

This particular strategy also aimed to preserve a gender-based unity, but it fractured later when the women's movement exercised a wartime demand for equal voting rights with men, whose franchise already was limited to literates. This immediately raised issues of class inequality by largely excluding working-class women. Class issues, always lurking in the shadows of the women's movement, took center stage in a 1944 competition to elect the queen of the Amateur Baseball World Series, a cultural event, according to political scientist Friedman, widely viewed as a "primer for universal suffrage." One woman advertised herself as the candidate of the "respectable people," by contrast with her opponent, Yolanda Leal, a poor school teacher, who was "for the common folk." When Leal, "daughter of the people," won overwhelmingly, it created a national furor over the franchise that weakened middle- and upper-class support for universal suffrage.

Even as middle-class women abandoned their working-class counterparts, Acción Democrática, in its populist struggle to fashion a multiclass electoral movement, came to power in 1945 and established universal suffrage two years later. Ironically, after enfranchisement ended women's political segregation and integrated their participation into male-dominated institutions, women's rights organizations lost much of their traditional autonomy, their memberships fragmented, and their political agenda dissipated.

### A STRANGE ALLIANCE: BETANCOURT AND THE MILITARY IN POWER, 1945–1948

After the 1945 military-civilian coup that overthrew the Medina regime, a provisional government headed by Betancourt as president seized power. The motives for this coup, born of an alliance between conservative young military officers and the AD's populist leadership, continue to provoke historical debate. The officers, organized in the *Unión Patriótica Militar* (UPM), were disgruntled over promotion, salary, and appointment policies within the military, displayed little interest in governmental affairs, and appeared content to leave government to the AD. Although Medina's progressive record included support for sweeping constitutional reforms, including universal suffrage, his government, composed almost entirely of white elites, had continued to discriminate against nonwhite immigrants and appeared insensitive to the historical links among race, class, and political order that bound together Venezuela's *café con leche* society. Consequently, it had been totally unprepared for the furor over the racist refusal of three posh Caracas hotels to serve the African American singer Robert Todd Duncan. Eager to use race as a powerful organizing tool, the AD had seized upon public outrage to expand and mobilize its political supporters in a bid to control the state.

However dubious the motives that inspired the 1945 coup, it proved a milestone in Venezuelan history. The AD government between 1945 and 1948—a period Venezuelans call the *Trienio*—represented the first serious effort to transform the country's archaic economic and social structures.

Because Acción Democrática was, in effect, the government and had a large nationwide network of party organizations to mobilize the population, it had a distinct advantage over its political rivals. AD control of the distribution of land and agricultural credits under the agrarian reform enabled it to build a clientele of peasant union leaders that gave it a commanding majority of the peasant vote. AD established a similar relationship of influence and leadership over most of the more than five hundred trade unions organized in this period and affiliated with the Venezuelan Confederation of Workers, which included both trade and peasant unions.

The AD also drafted a new constitution that guaranteed many civil and social rights, including labor's right to organize and strike and the principle that land should belong "to him who works it." The constitution established universal, secret voting for all persons over eighteen, with direct election of the president and both houses of Congress.

Among the economic issues with which the AD government had to deal, oil policy was most important, for it involved fundamental questions of dependency, economic sovereignty, and the revenues needed for economic diversification and modernization. In 1946 the government had imposed a supertax of 26 percent on all company profits over 28 million bolívars; the law was aimed primarily at the oil companies. This tax alone increased government income in 1947 by 230 percent over its income in 1938.

In view of the great importance the AD program attached to agrarian reform, the junta's approach was timid. Evidently fearing the political and economic repercussions of a frontal attack on the latifundio, the government preferred to distribute land to the peasants from the extensive state holdings taken over on the death of Gómez, Venezuela's premier latifundist. Out of a landless peasant population estimated at about 330,000, only between 55,000 and 80,000 received land during the Trienio. Because the average peasant received only 2.2 hectares of land to cultivate, "the problem," as Judith Ewell points out, "then changed from *latifundia* to *minifundia*."

The creation of an independent national economy through industrialization was a major government goal. The Venezuelan Development Corporation (CVF) was formed in 1946 to promote this process through loans to private entrepreneurs and direct investment in state corporations. In three years it lent nearly 50 million bolivars to industrial enterprises. But by the Trienio's end, the program of "sowing the petroleum" to diversify and modernize the economy had achieved only modest results. More impressive progress was made in health and education, whose respective budgets for 1948 quadrupled and tripled by comparison to 1945. Important advances were also made in eliminating the country's principal health scourge, malaria, by spraying with DDT the breeding grounds of mosquitos, which carried the disease.

The principal danger to the regime came from the military. The conservative officers, headed by Colonel Marcos Pérez Jiménez, gradually became disenchanted with what they regarded as the radical excesses of their civilian partners. On November 24 the government was overthrown by a virtually bloodless coup, and Minister of Defense Carlos Delgado Chalbaud took power as president of a military junta. Many of the leading members of the AD regime were arrested and imprisoned. Betancourt escaped and took refuge in the Colombian Embassy; later he and other prominent AD leaders were permitted to go into exile.

## THE MILITARY DICTATORSHIP, 1948–1958

In a proclamation issued on November 25, Delgado Chalbaud, who had personal and political differences with Pérez Jiménez, declared that the junta was a provisional government and did not intend to destroy Venezuelan democracy or prohibit the activities of political parties. But the junta's actions contradicted its claims of democratic intentions. Soon after the coup it dissolved Congress, annulled the 1947 constitution, voided the petroleum law, and abandoned other progressive programs like agrarian reform and school construction. The junta also imposed a strict censorship, forbidding any criticism of the regime. In 1949 the junta launched an offensive against the unions, arresting leaders of the Venezuelan Labor Confederation, forbidding union meetings, and freezing the funds of most of the unions.

Initially resistance to the junta and its repressive policies was largely limited to student protests and the activities of the illegal Communist Party, whose members played a leading role in the organization of the resistance movement. With the Feminine Cultural Group and other women's rights organizations under attack, women activists also quickly joined clandestine opposition movements like the Venezuelan Union of Women and the Communist Women's Organization. In 1949 AD leaders who remained in the country formed an underground organization. Against the objections of the strongly anticommunist Betancourt and other AD leaders in exile, the AD underground cooperated with the Communists and other groups of the resistance movement in the struggle against the dictatorship.

After the assassination of Delgado Chalbaud in 1950, the military regime intensified its repressive activity. By the fall of 1952, the regime, evidently convinced that the repression had intimidated the Venezuelan people into accepting its rule, decided it would be safe to hold elections for a Constituent Assembly.

Despite the repressive conditions and the call issued by the exiled AD leadership to abstain from voting—a position it reversed at the last moment— Venezuelans gave a two-thirds majority of the popular vote to the opposition parties. Furious at this outcome, Pérez Jiménez nullified the election and announced he was taking office as provisional president in the name of the armed forces.

For the next five years (1953–1958) Pérez Jiménez was the absolute ruler of Venezuela. A brutally efficient repression, whose principal instrument was the *Seguridad Nacional*, the secret police, made antigovernment activities very difficult. A resistance movement uniting persons of all political tendencies survived and continued its struggle against the dictatorship, however.

The social and economic policies of the regime generated discontent among ever wider sections of the population. Its limitations on the right to organize and strike contributed to a decline in labor's share of the national income. In place of the AD's focus on education, health, agrarian reform, and balanced economic development, the Pérez Jiménez regime emphasized grand works of infrastructure—highways, urban freeways, and port improvements—and urban constructions, some of little or no social utility, like the Officers Club in Caracas or the many-storied shopping center built on the side of one of Caracas's hills.

Women's roles in Venezuelan society once again changed dramatically in this period. First, as Pérez Jiménez promoted economic growth by offering incentives to private, especially foreign, businesses, there was more demand for low-cost labor, which increased women's participation in the work force, to be sure, mostly concentrated in menial jobs as domestics, laundresses, and waitresses. As a share of the wage-earning work force, women's participation increased from 17 to 22 percent during this period. Second, because the dictator dismissed women as political actors, his brutal repression largely targeted men, the effect of which was to create more opportunities for women in the labor market and in popular resistance movements. One of the more active organizations in the antidictatorial struggle was the Venezuelan Teachers' Federation (FVM), 75 percent of whose membership was female.

Although the movement's public leadership remained overwhelmingly male, women shouldered a large measure of the daily organizational responsibilities, ranging from intelligence collection to communications work. The Women's Committee, arguably the most influential of all the women's groups involved in the resistance, was especially successful at building cross-class alliances and uniting women politically even as it mobilized thousands in their opposition to dictatorship. Women also were effective in organizing cultural foundations, like the Gabriela Mistral Center, that efficiently disguised clandestine political objectives. But once again, when the dictatorship collapsed and a fragile democracy reemerged, the women's movement suffered a decline. In the words of Argelia Laya, a prominent activist, guerrilla leader, and founder of Socialist Women, male domination or machismo "was stronger than a military dictatorship!"

Signs of defection from the regime multiplied in 1957. Especially significant was the increasingly critical attitude of the conservative Catholic hierarchy, which issued statements deploring the government's disregard for the interests of the poor. Disaffection also grew among national capitalists, who complained of the government's neglect. With the end of the oil export boom in the late 1950s, the regime's capacity to generate business activity and employment through public works programs began to run out of steam. Within the armed forces there was growing resentment of Pérez Jiménez's arbitrary ways and his reliance on the secret police to watch over the loyalty of officers.

By mid-1957, an underground organization called the *Junta Patriótica* had been formed to unite the principal political parties. This group became the principal motor of the resistance movement and its preparation for a popular revolt. On January 21, 1958, the Junta Patriótica proclaimed a general strike that was overwhelmingly effective and was accompanied by clashes between the people and the regime's security forces. Barricades appeared in the streets of Caracas. The next day the insurgents seized key strategic points in the capital. The majority of military units refused to obey Pérez Jiménez and fraternized with the rebels. Fearing the radicalism of the popular opposition, a new military junta demanded that Pérez Jiménez resign and shortly thereafter he fled the country for the Dominican Republic.

The military junta became a provisional government: its first decrees proclaimed the restoration of all democratic freedoms, amnesty for all political prisoners and exiles, and legalization of all political parties. Almost ten years of rule by a repressive military dictatorship had ended.

# Venezuela's Representative Democracy, 1958–2003

The military-civilian junta presided over the transition to democratic elections, set for December 1958, and invited the return of political exiles like Betancourt. Chastened by experience, Betancourt had become politically more moderate than he had been during the Trienio. Betancourt's efforts to reassure Venezuela's economic elite about his intentions and his decision to choose moderates as his principal political allies reflected his new caution. So too did his decision to join with the nation's other centrist parties to endorse the Pact of Punto Fijo, which provided that whatever the election results, they would form a coalition government to carry out a program of democratic socioeconomic and political reforms.

The Pact of Punto Fijo was important far beyond its impact on the 1958 elections because it created a unique Venezuelan model of representative democracy. The Venezuelan government was consciously tailored to isolate the Marxist left, making it virtually impossible for Marxists to wield political power. Second, although the Pact of Punto Fijo provided for a three-party coalition, the system evolved toward hegemonic control of political life by two parties, the social democratic AD and the social Christian COPEI, whose reformist programs were broadly similar.

A third distinctive feature of the Venezuelan populist model of representative democracy was the major role that it assigned to the state as regulator and arbiter of relations between the classes and interest groups. The massive influx of petroleum revenues over most of the past three decades had strengthened the state and endowed it with the financial resources to perform this role, which required it to balance and mediate the conflicting demands and interests of all the major classes and pressure groups—labor, the peasantry, capitalists, the middle class, the armed forces, the church, the political parties.

Finally, the architect of this model, Rómulo Betancourt, viewed the state as an instrument for the gradual recapture of the nation's natural resources from foreign control, the reform of its socioeconomic structures, and the promotion of a balanced economic development. Betancourt hoped that, in time, economic development would lead to the rise of an autonomous Venezuelan capitalism capable of providing Venezuelans with a high standard of living and culture. Indeed, over the next three decades Venezuela made large advances in such problem areas as health and literacy. But the vast sums expended in "sowing the petroleum" over those decades did not achieve Betancourt's main goals; poverty did not decline but increased, income distribution remained as inequitable as in Mexico and Brazil, and today's Venezuela, burdened with an unpayable foreign debt, is more deeply dependent than it was in the time of Juan Vicente Gómez.

### A DECADE OF AD RULE, 1959–1969

Although the three centrist parties had approved a common program of economic, social, and political reform broadly similar to the one carried out during the Trienio, there remained considerable disagreements that were aggravated by the continuing economic crisis and Betancourt's own contentious nature. The victory of the Cuban Revolution in January 1959 and Cuba's gradual turn toward socialism created an especially divisive issue. Younger activists hailed the revolution as a model that Venezuela could well emulate. But Betancourt, virulently anticommunist, regarded the Cuban socialist regime as a direct challenge to his own reformist philosophy and program and fully supported U.S. efforts to isolate Castro's regime economically and politically.

In 1961 Betancourt promulgated a new constitution that proclaimed the government's responsibility for its citizens' social well-being, provided for proportional minority representation in Congress, and prohibited the president from succeeding himself. But it also gave him significant powers to suspend constitutional guarantees of personal and civil liberties. Moreover, although he had campaigned on the need for redistribution-of-land reform, which earned him an overwhelming majority of the peasant vote, the results of his agrarian reform were mixed, at best, and fell far short of solving Venezuela's acute agrarian problem.

By 1969 only some 150,000 out of the 350,000 peasant families without land in 1960 had received plots. Combined with the estimated 200,000 new families formed in those eight years, there remained 400,000 families without land. Government investments in irrigation, roads, and credit and technical assistance primarily benefited large- and medium-sized commercial farms, which produced the lion's share of profitable crops and accounted for most of the 150 percent increase in agricultural production during the years between 1959 and 1968.

More significant, perhaps, were the large advances made in health and public education during the Betancourt administration. Nearly 9 percent of the national budget was assigned to the Ministry of Health and Social Assistance. A concerted attack on the problems of endemic disease, infant mortality, and malnutrition resulted in a decline of infant mortality from 64 per 1,000 live births in the 1955–1959 period to 46.5 in 1966. The Betancourt years also saw a significant growth of public education.

A major objective of the Betancourt regime was to increase its share of oil profits to make more funds available for industrial development. A 1958 law therefore raised the tax rate on oil profits to 65 percent. In fact, industrialization was a cornerstone of the new Venezuela Betancourt wished to build. The slogan "Venezuela must industrialize or die" expressed the militant spirit of the AD's new campaign to industrialize. The AD government transferred large resources generated by oil exports to the industrialization process in the form of loans and direct subsidies.

The campaign for "economic independence," however, had a peculiar outcome; it fastened more firmly the chains of dependence on Venezuela. Confronted with high tariff walls, unwilling to lose

the large consumer market created by oil wealth, a growing number of U.S. and other foreign firms chose to establish branches in Venezuela, frequently in association with local capital. The label "made in Venezuela" increasingly came to mean an article made with raw materials and intermediate materials imported from the United States and finished or assembled in Venezuela.

Between 1958 and 1970 the number of plants producing such items as cans, foodstuffs, clothing, automobiles, auto tires, paint, and cigarettes mushroomed. The alliance of foreign and native capital achieved the goal of import substitution, but because the dominant partner in the alliance was foreign capital, most of the profits flowed back to the home offices of foreign firms. By 1971, Venezuela had the largest gross accumulated foreign investment in any Third World country: $5.57 billion. But the export of profits reached an annual average of $672 million. Venezuela, observes one economist, had become a "fiscal paradise of foreign monopoly capital."

The drive for import-substitution industrialization was accompanied by the incorporation of labor as a less-than-equal partner in an alliance with the state and industry. In 1958, labor leaders signed a pact with management that committed the unions to seek conciliation of conflicts with employers. The subordination of labor was completed during the following decade of AD rule.

## POPULIST PROBLEMS IN A PETROLEUM REPUBLIC, 1969–1988

Internal division contributed to the loss of the AD candidate in the election of 1968. Responding to growing nationalist sentiment and charges that the foreign oil companies were withholding further investment in Venezuela in reprisal for higher taxes and increased government control, Rafael Caldera of the Social Christian Party promised to pass a law that provided for the reversion to the state of all existing oil concessions beginning in 1983 and was elected president. The law also stipulated that unexploited concessions be ceded to the state petroleum company, CVP, in 1974. In addition, the oil companies were required to post bonds guaranteeing that their plant and machinery would be turned over in good condition. Also enacted in 1971 were bills nationalizing the foreign-owned natural gas industry and giving the government power to control oil-production levels. Finally, during his last months in office, Caldera issued a decree that forbade foreign interest in radio and television stations and electric companies.

Despite the establishment of representative democracy in 1958 and the reforms initiated by Caldera in 1969, a survey of Venezuela's economic and social conditions made in 1973 gave no cause for satisfaction with either of the country's two ruling parties. No basic change in economic structure had occurred; the government remained heavily dependent on oil income. True, import-substitution industrialization had achieved some economic diversification, but it was a dependent industrialization largely based on foreign capital, inputs, and technology. Despite the agrarian reform, agriculture remained the most backward branch of the national economy. In 1971, Venezuela still imported 46 percent of its basic foodstuffs. The failure of the agrarian reform to correct fundamental problems was also reflected in the continuing high concentration of landownership; 1.4 percent of the large estates held 67 percent of all privately owned land in 1973.

Thanks to improved health care and the eradication of such scourges as malaria, the Venezuelan population had grown rapidly, increasing from 7,524,000 in 1958 to 10,722,000 in 1971. But it is doubtful whether the quality of life for the majority of Venezuelans had improved after fifteen years of democratic rule. Although women's share of the labor force had doubled, they still made up a small percentage of wage workers, mostly employed in low-wage service jobs. Prostitutes typically made more money. In 1974, 30 percent of all Venezuelan children suffered from malnutrition; 12 percent of all adults suffered from mental retardation from the same cause, combined with other difficult living conditions. In the early 1960s a United Nations study described Venezuela's income distribution as one of the most unequal in the world. A decade later the situation had not improved.

The AD candidate, Carlos Andrés Pérez, a Betancourt protégé, emerged an easy winner in the 1973 election. The flamboyant Pérez, a master of populist rhetoric, had promised a "war on poverty" and against "privilege." Despite his rhetoric, his program did not differ substantially from those of his predecessors.

Pérez took office under the most favorable auspices: the Arab oil embargo of 1973 had brought a rapid rise in the price of oil, which had gone from $2.01 a barrel in 1970 to $14.26 in January 1974. The resulting vast increase in state revenues appeared to give Venezuela the means to solve all its major social and economic problems. Pérez promised to "manage abundance with the mentality of scarcity," but the flood of oil riches and the irresistible drive to modernize overwhelmed his administration and frustrated his good intentions.

On August 29, 1975, Pérez signed a law nationalizing the Venezuelan oil industry, to take effect January 1, 1976. A state oil company, *Petroven*, was created to control a sector of the economy whose annual sales volume exceeded $10 billion. In addition to a generous compensation of $1 billion to the foreign companies, the nationalization agreement authorized the state to enter into contracts with those companies for the provision of technological assistance and equipment, as well as marketing agreements for the international transshipment of Venezuelan oil exports.

Pérez's populist economic program called for the creation and expansion of heavy industries, especially petrochemicals, steel, and shipbuilding, that would supply the needs of Venezuela's consumer-goods industry. Gradually other projects—a fishery industry, a national rail system, the Caracas metro, and modernized port facilities—were added to this list.

During his campaign Pérez had pledged he would direct "priority attention to the needs of Venezuelan agriculture as the essential motor of economic development." But like his predecessors, Pérez understood those "needs" as the needs of large commercial farmers. Although Pérez claimed in 1975 to have achieved an "agricultural miracle," the reality was very different. Domestic food production increased, but imports of the country's basic foodstuffs rose from 46 percent in 1971 to almost 70 percent by the close of his administration. The rapid growth of the urban population contributed to this increased food dependence.

The immense oil revenues that flowed to the state from 1974 to 1979 proved inadequate to cover the costs of the government's ambitious development program, and Pérez, fearful of alienating business leaders, refused to undertake serious tax reform. Increasingly Pérez had to resort to foreign loans; between 1974 and 1978 Venezuela's foreign debt grew by almost $10 billion.

Pérez cultivated a populist image that did not correspond to his social policies. As a result of the orgy of state spending during his administration, the economy heated up and inflation cut deeply into workers' living standards. For the business, financial, and political elites, however, the boom created vast opportunities for enrichment resulting in an explosion of conspicuous consumption by these classes as the standard of living for peasants and workers deteriorated. The intimate ties among the state, the ruling party, and the economic elites generated corruption on an unheard-of scale.

Finally, the Pérez economic program had clearly failed to solve the dilemma of dependency that continued to plague Venezuela. Measured by the yardsticks of foreign indebtedness and the degree of its reliance for revenue on a single resource—oil—Venezuela was more dependent in 1980 than it had been in 1974.

Pérez's successors in the presidency—the COPEI leader Luis Herrera Campins, elected in 1978, and the AD leader Jaime Lusinchi, elected in 1983—had to struggle with the devastating combined effects of recurrent drops in oil prices and the massive outflow of funds to service the foreign debt. In a New Year's Eve 1989 address to the nation, Lusinchi, proclaiming that debt "is strangling our country's social and economic development and that of the majority of the world's people," announced a payment moratorium on the principal of all debts accumulated with foreign banks before 1983.

## NEOLIBERALISM AND THE DILEMMAS OF A PETROLEUM REPUBLIC, 1988–2003

The 1988 election saw the return of Carlos Andrés Pérez to the presidency. Despite a populist campaign that denounced subservience to foreign bankers, once in office Pérez inaugurated an economic austerity program in response to conditions demanded by the IMF in exchange for a $4.5 billion loan over a three-year period. The program included a massive currency devaluation; the lifting of controls and subsidies on a wide range of products and services such as gasoline, bread, and electricity; and a rise in interest rates. The price increases were announced in advance of their application; as a result, goods vanished from the shelves as shopkeepers prepared to take advantage of the higher prices.

In February 1989 a popular explosion rocked Caracas when a significant rise in bus fares was announced. For many Venezuelans, whose wage increases were cut in half by this measure alone, it was the last straw. Tens of thousands of people took to the streets, rioting and looting shops; from Caracas the rioting spread to the poor barrios surrounding the city, then to the nearby port of La Guaira, and later to more distant cities and towns.

The Pérez government responded with a display of force that many observers found excessive; in contrast to the officially admitted death toll of around three hundred, unofficial estimates placed the number of dead at between four hundred and one thousand. The shock waves of the explosion soon reached Washington, where the U.S. Treasury hastened to make a $453 million "bridging loan" to the Pérez government in advance of its signing an IMF economic adjustment program. In another apparent reaction to events in Venezuela, U.S. Treasury Secretary Nicholas Brady announced a plan providing for a partial reduction of the Latin American debt. Pérez continued to insist that his "six-month shock" economic program was correct in its essentials and would in time create "a new Venezuela."

In the meantime, however, this neoliberal program deepened the recession. Prices for many basic foods and household items, transport, and electricity rose between 50 and 100 percent. Real wages fell between 20 and 50 percent.

Pérez faced a dilemma. He was caught between the neoliberal demands of the IMF, World Bank, and foreign bankers that he continue his austerity program as a condition for obtaining the new loans needed to reactivate the economy and the counterdemands of labor and the middle class that he change course and relieve the suffering caused by his economic adjustment program and a deepening recession. He decided to continue with his economic adjustment plan, which included the privatization of a large number of state-owned enterprises. Not the least irony was that it was Pérez himself who had nationalized the iron and steel industries and proclaimed "evolutionary socialism" his long-term goal. Pérez even called his IMF-style austerity program *el gran viraje* (the great turnabout). For many suffering Venezuelans, however, it was "the great betrayal."

Pérez's privatization program caused significant loss of jobs in a country already burdened with high unemployment. It also transferred ownership of those enterprises to foreign multinationals. The first privatizations resulted in the sale of 40 percent of the state-owned telephone company to the U.S. telecommunications giant GTE, the national airline to the Spanish Iberia, and several large hotels to various international private interests. The sales prices also grossly undervalued these assets and led to considerable corruption.

A one-time bonanza of $2 billion in government revenues from the sale of state companies and a boom in the import-led commercial sector as a result of a reduction in import duties helped spur a partial revival of the economy from its deep recession. But the recovery was mainly in the realm of stock market speculation; industry and agriculture continued to stagnate. Some economic and social indicators reflected the failure of neoliberal economic policy to improve the life of most Venezuelans. The real minimum wage in 1991 was only 44 percent of its 1987 value; the number of people living below the poverty line jumped from 15 percent at the end of 1988 to 41 percent in 1991; and inflation reached a record high of 80 percent in 1989.

Mounting anger over Pérez's austerity program, the growing gap between rich and poor, and revelations of corruption in official circles sparked a series of strikes and protests demanding Pérez's resignation. The growing discontent reached into the middle and lower echelons of the military, whose members were unhappy with their own deteriorating living conditions and with Pérez's privatization program; in 1992 a coup attempt, led by Lieutenant Colonel Hugo Chávez Frías, involved 10 percent of the nation's armed forces and came perilously close to overthrowing the regime and seizing power. Its program included putting all those engaged in corruption on trial; a reversal of Pérez's neoliberal policies; an emergency program to combat misery and poverty; and a dissolution of government and election of a constitutional assembly. Although defeated, Chávez became a folk hero overnight among the poor in Caracas's "belt of misery."

The foiled coups combined with the unending wave of strikes, protests, and other expressions of seething unrest to place Pérez and his corrupt practices in the dock of Venezuelan public opinion. Responding to this pressure, the Supreme Court indicted Pérez, charging him with misappropriating $17 million from a secret fund earmarked for national security. Congress then voted to remove him from office.

Meanwhile, more than a thousand small- and medium-size companies closed, causing the loss of fifty-nine thousand jobs. High interest rates, inflation approaching 40 percent, an influx of imports, and weak demand caused by low purchasing power were blamed for the increasingly severe recession. Foreign investment fell by more than 40 percent.

The 1993 presidential election represented a crushing repudiation, not only of Pérez and his neoliberal policies, but also of the two-party rule that had prevailed since the fall of General Marcos Pérez Jiménez in 1958. Rafael Caldera, the seventy-seven-year-old populist who had been rejected by his own COPEI party for his opposition to neoliberal policies was elected president. His victory and the large gains made by left-wing parties testified to the strength of the movement for social and economic change.

Although it provoked alarm among Venezuelan business elites and foreign investors, in reality,

Caldera's reform program was quite modest. It called for a new labor law—strongly opposed by big business—the provisions of which would discourage layoffs in a time of deep recession. Other goals included a monthly minimum wage increase, repeal of an IMF-inspired value-added tax that sharply increased prices on items of popular consumption, new taxes on luxury items, and a reform of the income tax system that would improve tax collection by imposing heavy fines on tax evasion, estimated at 70 percent of all taxpayers.

As his program evolved, however, Caldera's response to the desperate economic crisis deviated more and more from the expectations of many of his supporters, who had thought he would make a sharp break with the discredited neoliberal policies. Soon, reform-minded ministers in his government resigned and were replaced with neoliberals who renewed the drive to privatize practically all state companies and bail out eight private banks.

Caldera's return to economic orthodoxy was hailed by the business sector but damaged his image as a crusading populist president among workers and shantytown dwellers. Apparently fearing uprisings like the failed military coups of 1992 and the food riots of 1989, Caldera suspended constitutional guarantees, including the rights to liberty, personal security, and free travel, and to protection against unreasonable search. Security forces searched the homes of activists, former military officials, and politicians on both the left and right; they rounded up hundreds of persons in Caracas's slums. Human rights activists and church leaders condemned the suspensions of constitutional guarantees. Increasingly, it appeared that the Caldera phenomenon represented another example of the sadly familiar tendency of populist politicians to make promises of sweeping social and political change that they did not intend to keep, simply to keep the neoliberal boat afloat.

In 1996 the Caldera who in 1993 had denounced his electoral rivals as "IMF-package candidates" accepted a package agreement with the IMF that lent his government $3.3 billion, cut federal spending, and eased the rules of foreign investment, opening the way for privatization of the economy's crown jewels—the oil industry and the aluminum, steel, and electrical companies operated by the public Venezuelan Corporation of Guyana (CGV).

The Caldera regime's acceptance of neoliberal orthodoxy and especially its privatization proposals provoked bitter debates. Aware of the immense public opposition to the privatization of oil, the neoliberal politicians chose a more indirect route. In 1997, Congress passed the so-called "oil opening," which invited private capital to participate in the exploration for and exploitation of oil reserves, but it limited the state's participation in the development of potentially rich reserves to between 1 percent and 35 percent of the total capital of each joint venture. Despite the circumlocutions of the "opening," it was clear, as an anonymous eight-page advertisement in *Time* magazine explained, that it represented "the backdoor route to privatization" of the state-owned oil industry. "Undoubtedly," says Steve Ellner, "the arrangement generates substantial public revenue, but the state's relinquishment of its status as a major investor points in the direction of the early days of the industry when Shell and Standard ruled the oilfields." Meanwhile, privatization of the steel and aluminum industries was stalled by continuing opposition and debate over its terms and, in the case of aluminum, because foreign investors refused to pay the price asked by Venezuela.

These debates took place against a background of continuing economic crisis, reflected in high inflation and unemployment rates, a crisis worsened in 1998 by depressed oil prices and a resulting decline of 35 percent in the central government's revenues. Poverty nearly doubled during the 1990s. A 1996 study by Mark Ungar noted that "62% of Venezuelans live below the poverty line, while prices for basic foodstuffs have risen beyond the reach of 75% of the population." The growth of poverty was accompanied by a parallel growth of crime. Since 1990 the murder rate grew by 73 percent, the robbery rate by 26 percent. A profile of the prison population showed that it was overwhelmingly poor and young. Caldera's neoliberal remedies of austerity and other "structural adjustments" sharpened the pain but did not remove its causes; indeed, they contributed to the panorama of social devastation in Venezuela.

As the 1998 presidential elections approached, the price of oil had dropped by a third, the stock market had lost 70 percent of its value, foreign reserves dwindled, and fears of devaluation raised lending rates to around 100 percent a year. This did not favor Venezuela's traditional political parties and their free-market, neoliberal programs of privatization and public-spending restraints. "Their political mood," wrote a *New York Times* reporter, "seems to be swinging in precisely the opposite direction, with an overwhelming majority apparently convinced that the oil wealth should guarantee decent salaries, government services, job protection, and retirement benefits."

Despite a last-ditch effort to stop his populist juggernaut, retired Lieutenant Colonel Hugo Chávez Frías, whose abortive coup of February 1992, with a left-wing program to combat poverty and misery, had become a hero to many poor Venezuelans. He scored a decisive victory in the 1998 elections, described by the *New York Times* as "freighted with a sense of history in the making." His electoral program stressed protection of domestic industry, a two-year moratorium on debt payments, a review of concessions that had been made to foreign oil companies, a halt to privatization of state assets, and reform of the constitution.

Chávez swiftly moved to secure from Congress for six months all the powers he needed to enact by decree a package of economic and financial legislation. Venezuelans also were treated to the unfamiliar sight of army teams entering the poor barrios of their towns to sell food at low fixed prices, repair schools, and engage in other public works. By the year 2000 it had become clear that Chávez, fortified by a series of sweeping electoral victories, contemplated nothing less than an economic and social revolution. A new constitution, adopted in 1999 and ratified by an overwhelming majority of voters, swept away the elitist, corruption-ridden political system established by the 1958 Pact of Punto Fijo and cleared the way for the construction of what Chávez called "Bolivarian Democracy." "The fight for justice, the fight for equality and the fight for

liberty," Chávez told a Spanish interviewer in April 2002, "some call socialism, others Christianity; we call it Bolivarianism."

The ambitious program issued by his government spelled out in careful detail the reforms to be made, down to the number of new hospitals to be constructed and the medical care they would provide. But the Chávez revolution was essentially moderate in its goals; it did not threaten to destroy Venezuelan capitalism, seeking rather to make it more functional and socially responsible by reforms that would correct the enormous imbalance in access to goods and culture between Venezuela's haves and have-nots. An early achievement of the Chávez revolution was the sense of dignity that it gave to the popular masses. Proud of his indigenous, African, and Spanish ancestry, Chávez helped to eradicate the social stigma historically attached to the terms *mulatto*, *mestizo*, and *black*. This new sense of dignity, not just the hope for improvement in economic status, helped explain the fierce loyalty of these mixed-race masses toward their leader.

Because Venezuela still imported half of its food supply, agrarian reform was fundamental. Consequently, Chávez passed a law that limited farm size in some regions to 250 acres and permitted the government to expropriate uncultivated land over 5,000 hectares in size. Traditionally, the vast majority of land was in private hands, and this law was directed above all at vast cattle ranches and the great, frequently uncultivated estates called latifundios. "We have to finish off the latifundios," the president proclaimed in 2001, "the latifundio is the enemy of the country." The agrarian reform proposed to give parcels of land to as many peasants as possible, chiefly from public lands. But the government also planned to redistribute private lands that lacked a clear title. The distribution of land that was not in dispute had already begun, benefiting thousands of peasants. This land reform, combined with the construction of housing for poor families and other programs for the development of small- and medium-size industry, aimed to correct the enormous imbalance between rural and urban populations. In 2002, 80 percent of Venezuelans were urban dwellers, and most lived in shantytowns on the hillsides that surround Caracas and a few other large cities.

Improved access to education for children of the poor was another important goal of the Chávez revolution. The educational reform eliminated the fees that students formerly had to pay. More than 1.5 million children were added to the public school rolls, and all children received breakfast, lunch, and an afternoon snack in their school. A massive vaccination program was launched in poverty-ridden areas, and the infant mortality rate, which had stood at 23 per thousand, declined a few points. A special bank was created to provide micro credit to women who wished to start their own enterprises. A new mass organization, the "Bolivarian Circles," neighborhood groups that met to discuss and seek solutions for local problems, was another important component of the Chávez program. They received modest subsidies from the state to carry out local improvements.

The state oil company, *Petroleos de Venezuela* (PDVSA), was the main source of state revenue on which the success of Chávez's reform program in education, housing, health, and other areas depended. Chávez doubled the royalties paid by foreign oil companies operating in Venezuela. In cooperation with other members of OPEC (the oil-producing countries' organization) and independent producers, he sought to keep oil prices at satisfactory levels by reducing production quotas when necessary. Finally, he insisted that the state oil company have a controlling interest in new mixed enterprises with foreign oil companies. His nationalistic positions led to conflicts with the state oil company's established bureaucracy, traditionally dominated by the Democratic Action machine and more favorable to foreign companies.

Oil played an important role in Chávez's foreign policy to strengthen Venezuela's ties with its Latin American neighbors. In 2000 delegates from Venezuela and ten Central American and Caribbean countries met in Caracas to sign a document that lowered oil prices for signatory countries and eased the terms of payment when the international price of crude became too high. Venezuela also contracted to supply Cuba with up to 53,000 barrels a day; in exchange, Cuba, whose health system was famed for its high quality, agreed to provide Venezuela with medical services.

The warming relations between Venezuela and Cuba were not lost on the United States, which was angered by Chávez' political "errors." Chávez recently quoted Simón Bolívar's celebrated remark that "the United States appeared destined by Providence to plague America with misery in the name of liberty." He also defined neoliberalism as "the road to hell for Latin America," urged stopping in its tracks "the savage and irrational cart of globalization that destroys and excludes millions," and flatly rejected the United States's project for a "Free Trade Area of the Americas." His political sins included visits in defiance of the United States to countries like Iraq, Libya, and Iran; his embrace of Mercosur, the South American common market; and his refusal to endorse President George W. Bush's "war on terrorism," especially U.S. military operations in Afghanistan.

Thus, it seemed inevitable that if an opportunity arose to topple this Venezuelan "troublemaker," Washington would not hesitate to seize it. In early 2002 the United States temporarily withdrew its ambassador to Venezuela, and high-ranking U.S. policymakers like Elliot Abrams, Otto Reich, and John Negroponte, all of whom had been active in the covert Reagan wars against revolution in Central America, met regularly with Chávez's Venezuelan opponents. These included large business interests, labor leaders, dissident officials of the state oil company's bureaucracy, and a few active military officers. This was accompanied by a drumbeat of attacks on Chávez and his program by the press, radio, and television. It was widely reported that, in the previous year, the United States also had channeled hundreds of thousands of dollars to opposition business and labor groups, using as a transmission belt the National Endowment for Democracy, a nonprofit agency created and financed by Congress.

This agitation took place against a background of economic decline, the result of falling international prices for oil, which reduced state revenue and compelled Chávez to make budget cuts in all areas except social programs. Chávez also allowed the overpriced bolívar (the national unit of currency) to float, causing a measure of inflation that was bitterly resented by the large middle class. The economic downturn and inflation also fed the racist hostility of many white members of that class toward Chávez, whom they contemptuously dubbed *el Mono* (the monkey) or *el Negro* (the black).

2002

The long-prepared blow fell on April 11. On that day two large demonstrations, one for, the other against Chávez, milled about in the streets of Caracas and marched on the presidential palace of Miraflores. In the resulting melee shooting began and some fifty people, mostly Chávez supporters, died in four days of revolt and counterrevolt. Meanwhile, a group of military plotters had invaded the palace, tried in vain to make the president sign a letter of resignation, and then spirited him away to an island off the coast of Venezuela. In Caracas, a prominent businessman, Pedro Carmona, was installed as president, "with a cabinet of conservative fanatics," in the words of *The Economist*, a British magazine generally known for its neoliberal sympathies. Carmona promptly decreed the immediate closure of the Supreme Court and the National Assembly, while a hunt began for prominent members of the Chávez government. A classic military coup or "Pinochetazo" seemed to be in the making.

But the oligarchy, its military and clerical collaborators, and its allies in Washington had badly miscalculated. The generals and admirals of elite origins who supported the coup did not represent the middle-level commanders and the rank-and-file troops. After the initial reaction of surprise and bewilderment, the presidential guard and loyalist military, spearheaded by the parachute division of which Chávez was a former commander, swiftly crushed the revolt and arrested its leaders. Meanwhile a torrent of Chávez's humble supporters, furious at the conspiracy to topple their leader, poured into Caracas from the surrounding shantytowns and took command of the streets.

Restored to power, Chávez promised a full investigation of the coup and trials for those who orchestrated it, but he also struck a conciliatory note. Stressing that he was president of all the classes of Venezuelan society—upper, middle, and lower—he admitted that he had made mistakes, replaced a number of officials the opposition had sharply criticized, and regretted the harsh language he had used against his critics. Two weeks after the coup, looking relaxed as if he had not just survived a political hurricane, Chávez informed the country in an interview that his peaceful Bolivarian revolution continued on course, with the aim of transforming an oil-dependent, neoliberal economy and channeling funds into social programs to achieve social equality in a country that had been plundered for centuries by the rich. He made tactful reference to charges that the United States was involved in the recent coup, saying it would be "horrible" if the United States was involved. "What I have said is that I ask God that it turns out to be false."

Despite Chávez's conciliatory attitude and gestures to win over some of his enemies, the diehard opposition, centered in the most reactionary sectors of the economic elite, remained sullen and unrelenting. It organized an unsuccessful two-month general strike that crippled the economy in early 2003 and thereafter promised to try to bring Chávez down by a referendum, possible in 2004 under the Constitution. For the present, therefore, Venezuela remained largely divided into two nations, a majority struggling to emerge from poverty and backwardness and a minority determined to hold on to its power and privileges.

# Colombia in the Twentieth Century

## THE CONSERVATIVE REPUBLIC, 1903–1930

For Colombia, the twentieth century began inauspiciously with the War of a Thousand Days, which raged for three years at the cost of thousands of lives and untold damage to the nation's economic infrastructure. The savage civil war slowed economic growth and weakened, at least momentarily, the power of the nation-state. Quick to seize on this vulnerability, Panamanian separatists, who had struggled in vain for years to establish their independence from Colombia, now seized the twin opportunities afforded by both the civil war and a renewed U.S. interest in the construction of a trans-isthmian interoceanic canal through Panama. The Colombians had made clear their refusal to approve the Hay-Herran Treaty, which provided for a $40 million payment to a French concessionary company and a mere $10 million for Colombia, in exchange for Colombia's surrender of its sovereignty over the proposed canal zone. Suddenly, the Panamanian nationalists had a new and powerful ally, and with the assistance of President Theodore Roosevelt, they established Panama's official independence in 1903. Needless to say, this dealt a profound psychological shock to Colombians.

At the war's end, Conservative General Rafael Reyes (1904–1909) dissolved Congress and established his personal dictatorship, ruling by decree through a puppet national assembly. Despite his dictatorial methods, Reyes's policies of enforcing peace and order, construction of railroads and highways, encouragement of export agriculture, and protection and subsidies for industry initially attracted much elite support.

Reyes's downfall came when he attempted to conclude a treaty with the United States under which Colombia was to receive an indemnity in return for its recognition of Panama's independence. Colombia's governing class, aware of the growing importance of the North American market for its coffee and hopeful of attracting North American capital, accepted the new relations. But the wound of Panama was still fresh, and news of the treaty aroused a public fury of which Reyes's enemies took advantage to force his resignation.

Conservatives and Liberals now organized a constituent assembly to reform the constitution of 1886. They agreed to weaken the executive, increase the powers of Congress, and ensure minority representation in elective bodies. Other changes included direct election of the president, establishment of elected departmental assemblies, and abolition of the death penalty. These reforms left intact the privileged position of the church, however, as well as property and literacy qualifications for voting that excluded all women and 90 percent of the adult male population from the suffrage.

Although the constitutional reforms made the total hegemony of one party more difficult, control of the electoral process remained in government hands. The constitutional changes also left intact the *gamonal* system under which landowners, public officials, and priests exerted influence on rural voters.

The characteristic blandness of Colombian politics between 1910 and 1930 contrasted sharply with the sometimes stormy developments in economic and social life. These developments, reflecting the rapid overall growth of Colombian capitalism, included the upsurge of coffee exports, centered in Antioquia, with its system of free labor; the accumulation of capital and its transfer from commerce to industry, with the formation of many new companies; a partial shift from the old semiservile forms of rural labor to free, capitalist wage labor, accompanied by a wave of strikes, land invasions, and clashes between landowners and peasants; adoption of racist immigration policies designed to "whiten" Colombia by prohibiting "the entrance of those elements whose organic and racial conditions may be inappropriate for the nation"; and the emergence in cities and plantation areas of the first true trade union movements, left-wing parties, and struggles between workers and employers.

In this period, U.S. capital began to flow into Colombia, facilitated by the 1914 treaty by which the United States paid Colombia for its loss of Panama. The "dance of the millions" began in 1921–1922 and was fueled initially by the first installment of a $25 million U.S. indemnity. Between 1922 and 1928 the U.S. government and private investors poured $280 million into Colombia, most of which was expended for a vast, chaotic program of public construction. The boom lured workers from agriculture into the cities and created low-wage, unskilled employment opportunities for working-class women, who functioned as a "reserve army" for industry. But it reduced food production and raised living costs, leaving workers worse off than before. Naturally, trade unions, energized by the fiery oratory of labor leaders like María Cano, Colombia's "flor de trabajo," grew more militant, culminating in the 1928 United

Fruit "banana" strike whose savage repression claimed thousands of workers' lives.

The golden shower ended in 1929 with the New York stock market crash and the Great Depression, which soon spread to Colombia. Growing unemployment, food shortages, and the government's severe fiscal problems completely discredited a regime weakened by political scandals, public outrage over the massacre of banana workers, and its own internal divisions. Alarmed by an upsurge of peasant and worker unrest, urban strikes, land invasions by peasants organized in leagues and unions,[1] and the rise of new radical ideologies, the nation's oligarchs temporarily closed ranks to avoid revolution and supported Enrique Olaya Herrera, a man of their own kind, in the 1930 election.

### THE POPULIST INTERREGNUM: "THE REVOLUTION ON THE MARCH," 1934–1946

Olaya's term was spent waiting for the Depression to end and the infusions of U.S. loans and investments to resume. His failure to respond to popular expectations for change caused growing tension. In departments where the problem of latifundismo and landlessness was particularly severe, such as Cundinamarca, Tolima, and Cauca, clashes between peasants and landowners and police were frequent. This growing social instability strengthened the appeal of the left-wing Liberal Alfonso López, who won the 1934 elections. He promptly announced a program called *La Revolución en Marcha* (The Revolution on the March). In 1936 he obtained the congressional majority needed to implement his policies.

López and other Liberal reformers knew that social justice and national economic interest required land reform. The advance of Colombian capitalism was blocked by the backwardness of agriculture, especially the food-producing sector, which could not even provide enough food for the growing urban population. The 1936 agrarian reform law provided for reversion to the state of lands not rationally exploited by their owners but gave the latifundists ten years to make the transition to efficient land exploitation based on wage labor. The law also prohibited payment of rent in labor or in kind; this had the effect of speeding up the spread of wage labor and the rise of a land market. The law confirmed the property titles of the great landowners, but it also gave peasants "squatters' rights" on unused public and private lands that they had improved. The eviction of squatters thus became more difficult and dropped sharply.

Other legislation adopted during López's administration defined the rights of labor. Congress passed a law that established a minimum wage and paid vacations and holidays, forbade the use of strikebreakers, set up the eight-hour day and the forty-eight-hour week, and created a special tribunal to provide arbitration in labor disputes. With López's support, the number of organized workers quadrupled between 1935 and 1947. Equally important was the formation in 1936 of the Colombian Confederation of Labor (CTC), headed by syndicalists, Communists, and liberals.

One of the most revolutionary innovations of the López reform era was a new progressive tax law. Before 1936 tax laws had been ineffectually enforced. The new tax law, effectively enforced, almost doubled the state's revenue-raising capacity.

Despite the moderate character of these reforms, they came under bitter attack from all reactionary elements, and López began to retreat. In 1936 he announced a "pause" in reform. This "pause," accentuated by López's successor, the moderate Liberal Eduardo Santos (1938–1942), created a bitter division within the Liberal ranks between moderates and reformers, the leading advocate for whom was Jorge Eliécer Gaitán. As mayor of Bogotá, he had been regarded as the best the capital ever had.

Conservatives and many moderate Liberals denounced Gaitán as a demogogue. He was in fact a magnetic speaker of burning sincerity, capable of presenting his economic and social ideas to audi-

---

[1]The land invasions were spurred by a 1926 Supreme Court ruling that the only proof of ownership was the original title stating the government had ceded title to the land. Many peasants knew that the estates on which they worked had no such titles and had been formed through illegal acquisition of public lands.

ences of peasants and workers in a clear way, but there was nothing exotic or extravagant about those ideas. Although he used socialist terminology, the essence of Gaitán's program was the need for state intervention in the economy to democratize capitalism, control the great private monopolies, and ensure that peasants owned the land they cultivated. In 1945 he proposed limiting landownership to a maximum of 1,000 hectares and suggested a minimum size of four hectares for landholdings to avoid the low productivity of minifundios.

In the 1946 presidential elections, however, Conservatives took advantage of this Liberal split to elect Mariano Ospina Pérez with only 42 percent of the vote.

## COUNTERREVOLUTION ON THE MARCH, 1946–1958

After his inauguration, in a conciliatory gesture to the Liberal Party, Ospina Pérez invited six Liberals into his cabinet, thus establishing parity in the twelve ministries and implementing his campaign promise to form a National Union government. He made no effort to consult Gaitán. The snubbing of Gaitán suggests a design on the part of Ospina Pérez to isolate him politically, deepen the rift between Liberal moderates and reformists, and form a bipartisan coalition of conservative elements to barricade against Gaitán's program of social and economic change. High inflation, static wages, and growing unemployment in the postwar period added to the anger and frustration of workers as they saw their hopes for change crushed by what they perceived as a conspiracy of the "double oligarchy"—Liberal and Conservative—that controlled government.

The Conservative leadership in 1946 presented two faces. Ospina Pérez represented its conciliatory aspect, the desire for a peaceful coexistence of the two traditional parties and their collaboration in a National Union government of sound conservative views. But this aspect was contradicted by the supreme chief of the Conservative Party, Laureano Gómez, who emerged as the new government's gray eminence, the power behind the throne, and scarcely concealed his scorn for the National Union policy.

Gómez quickly had the Liberal general who commanded the national police force dismissed and then followed with a wholesale purge of Liberal police officers, who were replaced by officers known for their fanatical conservatism. The pace of events quickened in 1947. In an evident effort to gain the advantage in the March congressional elections, armed bands organized by Conservative landowners and officials began to attack and persecute Liberals in many rural areas. The outcome of the elections, however, was a clear victory for the Liberals; equally significant was the predominance of radicals over moderates on the Liberal slate.

Claiming the need to restore law and order, Ospina organized a new security force, the *policía política*, which soon became an extension of the Conservative Party and an additional instrument of terror against Liberals; it was widely known as the "creole Gestapo." Beatings, killings, and outrages of every kind spread throughout the countryside, provoking a growing polarization and armed responses by the Liberal peasantry, middle class, and landowners.

As 1948 opened, the violence in some areas began to assume the proportions of a civil war, with battles taking place between Conservative and Liberal towns. The church, with its immense power, also instigated violence and persecution of Liberals. In March the Liberal convention called on party members to resign from every public office under the Conservative administration. The Conservatives rejoiced; one of their journals exulted: "At last we are alone."

In an atmosphere of growing tension, the government prepared to host the Ninth Inter-American Conference. On April 9, 1948, as Gaitán was on his way to lunch, he was approached by a stranger who fired four bullets into him. Mortally wounded, Gaitán collapsed on the sidewalk. The man regarded by the masses as the sole hope for their liberation, generally expected to run and win the election for president in 1950, died the same day he was shot. The assassin was an obscure figure with a history of mental trouble.

Gaitán's murder unleashed long-suppressed racial, ethnic, and class antagonisms and signaled a formidable popular insurrection that tore Bogotá apart and spread to the provinces before it was put down by the army at the cost of thousands of lives. The spontaneous rising of the masses, accompanied by peasant expropriation of haciendas, establishment of revolutionary committees and workers' control over foreign-owned oil installations, and other radical measures, frightened Conservative and Liberal elites, both of whom blamed the violence on the "genetically imprinted resentments" of blacks and indigenous people. Liberal leaders, faced with the choice of joining the insurrection or accepting Ospina's offer to reconstitute a National Union coalition, chose the latter.

During 1949 the coalition government began to come apart as the official and unofficial violence in the countryside, directed above all at Liberals of all classes, continued and widened; it had become a persistent, widespread phenomenon generically called *la Violencia*.

As the 1950 presidential election drew nearer, the threatening, repressive atmosphere visibly deepened. In the countryside goon squads, backed by the military, compelled Liberal peasants to turn in their voting cards and register as Conservatives. In some areas landowners took revenge for the land invasions of the 1930s, using hired thugs to kill or expel peasant occupants. In this stage of the Violencia, however, the conflict had primarily a political character and was based on the peasants' loyalty to political bosses on each side. Finally, in response to a move by a Liberal congressional majority to impeach him, Ospina issued a series of decrees providing for a state of siege, the dissolution of Congress and all departmental legislatures and municipal councils, the grant of extraordinary powers for the governors, and national censorship of the press and radio. With the suppression of all effective opposition, Laureano Gómez assumed the presidency.

Ideologically, the Gómez regime (1950–1953) appeared "feudal" in its effort to restore the intellectual atmosphere of sixteenth-century Spain. In its economic policies, however, the regime showed itself quite favorable to modern corporate capitalism. In the spirit of economic liberalism, all import and export restrictions were removed and foreign investment was encouraged in all possible ways. But for labor it was the worst of times. Wages lagged behind prices, and the state regularly intervened in labor struggles in favor of employers, permitting the use of strikebreakers and blacklists.

In the Colombian countryside, meanwhile, the Violencia gained in intensity and expanded into new regions. But the conflict now increasingly assumed the nature of a class struggle as peasants resisted the efforts of landowners and their hired thugs to eject them from their parcels and Communist Party activists as well as peasant leaders loyal to the Liberal Party became active in organizing strongholds of self-defense among uprooted peasants. Thus the period between 1949 and 1953, in addition to a growth of landowner and official terrorism and banditry, saw the rise of an extensive, well-organized resistance in guerrilla zones inhabited by peasants and other fugitives from regions marked by anarchy or terror. Some of these zones had an elaborate political, economic, and social organization. These guerrilla enclaves may have held twenty thousand armed men, of whom about half were based in the Llanos region. Each zone had its own commander or commanders, some of whom soon became legends.

The failure of the Conservative dictatorship to achieve a military solution to the guerrilla problem contributed to its gradual weakening and eventual collapse on June 13, 1953, when General Gustavo Rojas Pinilla assumed the presidency with the support of the armed forces and representatives of both parties.

To resolve the social and political crisis, his campaign of "Peace, Justice, Liberty" sought compromise among political elites and peasant radicals. One of his first initiatives was to proclaim an unconditional amnesty to all guerrillas who would return to civilian life.

Several thousand accepted the amnesty, surrendered their weapons, and returned to their old homes, but the leaders of some guerrilla fronts, especially the Communist leadership in southern Tolima and the Sumapaz region of southern Cundinamarca, distrusted Rojas Pinilla's sincerity, recalled his role as army commander in a famous massacre of Liberals in Cali in 1949, and warned their comrades not to "believe the false promises of propaganda thrown from planes of the dictatorship." These guerrilla fronts preferred to maintain an armed truce and await further developments.

Events proved the skeptics right. The honeymoon between Rojas Pinilla and the elites and the nation as a whole began to wane as it became evident that instead of restoring the traditional political arrangements he was moving toward the establishment of a personal dictatorship with some populist features, not unlike Argentina's Peronist system. One of his reformist measures was giving women the vote in 1954.

Despite some reforms, the Rojas Pinilla's policies were essentially reactionary. One sign of this was the revival of the Violencia as the president gave a free hand to notorious *pájaros* (hired assassins), Conservative vigilante gangs, and army-police forces to wreak vengeance on veterans of the guerrilla war who had accepted amnesty. As a result, many former guerrillas left their farms and rejoined the surviving guerrilla fronts. The renewal of the civil war combined with other repressive measures and the effects of a deepening depression to unify all elite elements against Rojas Pinilla, whose military colleagues prevailed on him to resign and surrender power to a five-man caretaker military junta.

In July 1957, Liberal leader Alberto Lleras Camargo and Laureano Gómez met and signed an agreement creating a National Front coalition, which in effect provided for a monopoly of shared power for sixteen years by the two parties. There would be parity in legislative positions on both national and local levels and alternation of the presidency between the two parties. The Colombian experiment in bipartisan rule and "controlled democracy" had begun.

## THE NATIONAL FRONT: REFORM AND REPRESSION, 1958–1974

The constitutional pact creating the Colombian National Front in 1958 bears an obvious resemblance to the pact signed between Venezuela's centrist parties the same year. In both cases the intent was the same: to preserve elite rule and to marginalize or isolate political movements that might threaten its property or power. Both may therefore be considered variants of a type of representative democracy that has been called "controlled democracy" or more correctly, "restricted democracy."

The Colombian power-sharing pact, providing for a monopoly of political power for the Conservative and Liberal Parties, excluded the existing Communist and the Christian Democratic Parties as well as new parties that might be formed later. Thus the electorate was denied the opportunity to reject the policies of the National Front coalition or exercise its sovereign right to change the government. The relative absence of issues between the parties promoted voter apathy and alienation, reflected in low turnout rates; participation in congressional elections fell from a high of 68.9 percent in 1958 to a low of 36.4 percent in 1972.

The rules of the political game established by the National Front, designed to prevent the hegemony of either party, tended to immobilize its governments. Their social policies reflected their fundamentally conservative orientation and did nothing to alter the great inequalities in income distribution. Although the unions gained legal recognition, the government repeatedly intervened in labor conflicts on the employers' side.

In 1958 President Lleras Camargo issued an amnesty—to expire in 1959—for all guerrillas who would return to peaceful life. The establishment of the National Front coalition marked the end of the Violencia, a conflict estimated to have taken between 200,000 and 300,000 lives. Between 1958 and 1965 the army and police hunted down the remaining outlaw bands. But the continued existence of the latifundio, an estimated 1 million landless peasants, and landowner and official repression of land-hungry peasants continued to generate violence in the Colombian countryside.

This violence grew so rapidly that, in 1961, evidently fearing that failure to act might produce a Cuban-style revolution, Congress adopted an agrarian reform law that vested apparently limitless power to expropriate and redistribute inefficiently exploited land in a new state agency (INCORA). In Tolima, the site of the first program, however, only 1,115 out of 90,000 landless agricultural workers

The Colombian army's mobilization of paramilitary violence against unarmed civilians increased the popularity of guerrilla movements like the FARC, whose combatants expanded their power and territorial control. [Wide World Photos]

had received titles to land by 1969. Naturally this failed to satisfy the peasants' hunger for land, and the five-hundred-thousand-member National Association of Peasant Unity (ANUC), originally organized to mobilize rural support for the government, quickly became an outspoken critic.

This innocuous agrarian reform coincided with the launching of a large-scale military effort to destroy the guerrilla zones established under Communist Party leadership in eastern and southern Tolima. Like the agrarian law, this offensive seems to have been inspired by the anticommunist strategy of the Kennedy administration's Alliance for Progress, a program combining reform and repression.

The success of this and many other later offensives can be gauged by the fact that twenty years later the few guerrilla bases had grown into a network of thirty guerrilla fronts in the Colombian backcountry, with their own military organization, the Communist-led Revolutionary Armed Forces of Colombia (FARC). In addition to the FARC—the largest of the guerrilla groups, created in 1966, whose members and leaders were primarily peasants—the 1960s and 1970s saw the emergence of other revolutionary organizations, such as the National Liberation Army (ELN), inspired by the Cuban example, and the April 19 Movement (M-19), both largely composed of radical students and other urban elements. The ELN, led briefly by Father Camilo Torres Restrepo, the radical priest whose 1966 death inspired the 1968 Conference of Latin American Bishops at Medellín to endorse a "preferential option for the poor," advocated agrarian reform, nationalization, social justice, and gender equality. Historian Francesca Miller speculates that the endorsement of women's equality reflected the influence of Torres's feminist mother, Isabel Restrepo Gaviria, who was notorious for her public demonstrations "against her sex's inequalities."

In summary, the National Front's political, economic, and social policies produced basically negative results. Its economic policies successfully promoted the accumulation of foreign and domestic capital but neglected the interests of workers and peasants, whose living standards sharply declined. In 1964, 25 percent of the total labor force, 24.6 percent of the urban labor force, and 25.4 percent of the rural labor force lived below the absolute poverty line. By 1973 those percentages had risen to 50.7 percent, 43.4 percent, and 67.5 percent. Clearly, instead of contributing to the solution of grave socioeconomic problems, the sixteen years of National Front rule sharpened them.

## DRUG LORDS, GUERRILLAS, AND THE QUEST FOR PEACE, 1974–2003

Beginning with the 1974 elections, Colombia returned to the political system of electoral competition; but there were still vestiges of the power-sharing system. Despite the renewal of competition, the political system remained a restricted, oligarchical democracy designed to limit the level of conflict between elites and to "keep the masses in their place" with a system of electoral mobilization based on machine politics and payoffs, known as *clientelismo*.

In addition to their loss of credibility, post–National Front governments faced economic problems of unprecedented proportions. The quadrupling of oil prices in 1974, coming at a time when Colombia had ceased to be self-sufficient in oil production, dealt a very heavy shock to the economy. By 1982, Colombia had not only severe inflation but also its worst recession in fifty years.

In this time of economic gloom, some relief came from an unexpected quarter: the drug traffic with the United States. Until recently that traffic had been negligible, mostly confined to the export of marijuana. It began to mushroom in the 1970s, most likely as a result of antidrug campaigns in Turkey and the Middle East. Skyrocketing prices resulting from effective antidrug efforts and high

transportation costs forced the international drug cartels to seek closer sources of supply for the U.S. market. Colombia, with its access to both U.S. coasts, and cocaine, lower in price than heroin or opium and easier to carry in short plane trips to the Florida coast, provided a solution. An efficient distribution system made the new drug available to the ever-swelling U.S. market. A division of labor and profits emerged between the Colombian producers and exporters, centered in Medellín and Cali, and North American domestic wholesalers, bankers, and money launderers. Contrary to a common misconception, Colombia is not a large grower of coca but rather processes the substance, which comes from Peru, Bolivia, Ecuador, and Brazil. By the mid-1980s, with cocaine prices dropping, a new product—crack—known as *bazuco* in Colombia and packaged in small quantities costing only a fraction of cocaine powder, created a large new class of consumers.

Colombia's Medellín and Cali cartels, it was estimated, made $4 to $6 billion annually in cocaine traffic. Of this amount, according to the economist Salomón Kalmanovitz, between $1 and $1.5 billion entered the Colombian black market. Without this "cushion" for the country's balance of payments, he suggests, an exchange crisis would have broken out in 1983 or 1984 at the latest. This contribution of Colombian narcocapitalism to the country's financial stability and the close ties established between the drug lords and landowners, businessmen, government officials, and members of the police and the armed forces explain the singular immunity that the drug mafias enjoyed until recently.

This situation changed as a result of three developments. First, in 1984, Conservative President Belisario Betancur (1982–1986) negotiated a series of historic truce agreements with three of the four major guerrilla movements that did not require them to surrender their arms. The accord with the FARC, the largest of the insurgent groups, stipulated that the government would adopt an agrarian reform program; legislate improvements in public health, education, and housing; and permit local elections of mayors and city councils to broaden popular participation in government.

Although the armed forces and other factions effectively blocked implementation of the agreement, the peace process survived and made available additional resources to pursue a war on drugs. Second, the U.S. placed increased pressure on the government of Liberal President Virgilio Barco (1986–1990) to wage a more effective war on drug trafficking. This pressure was accompanied by an offer of financial aid that was difficult to refuse.

Finally, there was a growing concern on the part of sectors of the elite that the drug traffickers had gotten out of control and their violence was threatening the monopoly of power the elite had enjoyed since Colombia achieved independence from Spain. For years death squads, 149 of which the government acknowledged, were trained by the drug mafia, in alliance with the police and the armed forces. They had murdered, with complete impunity, thousands of trade-union and peasant leaders, left-wing activists, judges, and others who sought to make Colombia a functioning democracy.

In the course of 1989, however, the mafia went too far and began killing prominent members of the elite, including the governor of Antioquia, the country's attorney general, Medellín's police chief, and presidential candidate Luis Carlos Galán. Within hours after Galán's death the Barco government had already ordered the searches and seizures of dozens of mansions, hundreds of cars, and more than one hundred airplanes and helicopters claimed to belong to the drug traffickers. To give these confiscations a firm legal basis, Barco issued a decree making "illicit enrichment" a crime punishable by five to ten years in prison. He also reinstated, by decree, the extradition of drug traffickers to the United States. This was declared unconstitutional by the Colombian Supreme Court in 1987 and opposed by many Colombians as a surrender of the state's autonomy and an admission of the impotence of its judicial system. By 1989 the government's offensive against the cartels had only made a temporary impact and the basic structure of the paramilitary groups remained intact.

To be sure, without major social and economic reforms in Latin America, the principal supplier of cocaine, and in the United States, its principal consumer, the drug wars could not be won. Without new policies that provided Latin American peasants with a viable alternative to growing coca as a cash crop, its cultivation continued, no matter how many fields were burned or sprayed with defoliants. As laboratories that processed coca were destroyed in one part of the region, they moved to another. In both the United States and Latin America, the cocaine epidemic was growing dangerously, the principal social roots of the drug trade were mass poverty, despair, and frustration. Neither the supply side nor the demand side of the problem, in the last analysis, could be solved by military means alone.

But in a land famous for the illusions of "magical realism," the Colombian war against the drug cartels did provide a perfect cover for the government's thirty-year-old war against the guerrilla insurrection. The drug and guerrilla problems always were indissolubly linked, for it had long been common knowledge that there existed a network linking government agencies, elements of the armed forces and police, landowners, industrialists, and drug lords. The primary target of this alliance was Colombia's left-wing movement—the guerrillas first, but also trade unions, peasant cooperatives, and opposition parties.

The country's greatest writer, Gabriel García Márquez, says: "The Constitution, the laws . . . everything in Colombia is magnificent, everything on paper. It has no connection with reality." Typical of that gap between Colombian form and reality was the new constitution of July 1991. The new charter was designed to open up Colombia's political system, ending the monopoly of power and property long held by a handful of Colombian clans. It provided for the popular election of state governors, limited the president to one term, granted Congress the right to veto cabinet members, established the office of a "people's" defender to investigate human rights abuses, recognized the authority of traditional courts on indigenous *resguardos*, ensured representation for minorities in Congress, and barred the extradition of native-born Colombians. It also recognized the "collective ownership rights" of Afro-Colombians and indigenous peoples in this multiethnic, multicultural nation.

The new constitution provided a splendid façade for a corrupt, arbitrary social order, but it was still a façade. It did away with the "state of siege" in force in Colombia for most of the previous four decades but conveniently replaced it with the *estado de excepción*, utilized to put the country on a war footing and ride roughshod over the rights of workers and others. Popular cynicism concerning the new Colombian democracy was reflected in the voter abstention rate of 70 percent. Colombia's murder rate, with 86 murders per 100,000 inhabitants, probably the highest in the world, exposed the thin democratic veneer that masked a lawless state and society. The militarization of the state under cover of the state of emergency also facilitated the imposition of a neoliberal policy featuring the privatization of state enterprises, elimination of subsidies, and other austerity measures promoted by the IMF and the World Bank. These measures, added to the immense costs of the guerrilla war, sharpened all of Colombia's economic and social problems; more than half of Colombia's 33 million people lived below the poverty line and the official unemployment rate in 1998 was 14.5 percent.

Part of the Colombian "reality" of which García Márquez speaks was that Colombia had been the scene of two wars. One was the drug war. From the official U.S. point of view, this war was waged to stem the tide of cocaine flowing into the United States. For the Colombian elite, however, it was a private quarrel with that section of the "cocaine nouveau riche," centered in Medellín, that sought too aggressively to join it in the seats of power. It is noteworthy that the Cali cartel, which was more discreet in its dealings with the traditional oligarchy, experienced less interference from the government than did the Medellín cartel. "We do not kill politicians," a member of the Cali cartel explained, "we bribe them." Consequently, by the end of 1994 the Medellín cartel was only a shadow of its former self, with most of its leaders dead or in prison, whereas the rival Cali cartel had taken over most of the heroin and cocaine trade to the United States and Europe.

The other Colombian war was the "dirty war" waged by an alliance of the military, the security services, drug lords, great landowners, and businessmen against Colombia's left-wing movement, trade unions, peasant leagues, and ethnic minorities. The military made no secret that it was far more interested in fighting guerrillas than in fighting drugs. It repeatedly thwarted government efforts to achieve a cease-fire with the guerrilla movements and continued its repressive activity— bombardment, disappearances, torture, and murder. The majority of the victims were not guerrillas but peasants, workers, and left-wing activists. Despite official government offers to negotiate, successive administrations accelerated the military's counterinsurgency campaign, with a marked increase in aerial bombardments, by U.S.-supplied planes and helicopters, of rural communities. Ostensibly launched to protect the electoral process from "narcoterrorism," the operation actually targeted rural areas where guerrilla forces were active.

Under the discredited Liberal President Ernesto Samper (1994–1998), the government's military fortunes took a turn for the worse. The FARC, numbering an estimated fifteen thousand fighters, maintained a strong presence in 622 of Colombia's 1,071 municipalities. Its military and political control was strongest in the southern departments of Caquetá, Guaviare, Putumayo, Meta, and the Amazon region, but it expanded its military operations into more densely populated northern and central departments like Antioquia, Santander and North Santander, Cundinamarca, and Bolívar. In 1996 the FARC showed its growing military strength by inflicting a number of humiliating defeats on government forces. In June 1997 the FARC handed over to the military some seventy soldiers captured in these operations, in return for the government's agreement to withdraw the army from 5,000 square miles of territory in southern Colombia.

This expansion of guerrilla power reflected the structural crisis of a corrupt, exclusionary two-party system, or "duopoly," the poor training and morale of government troops, and a continuing economic crisis that brought recruits and support to the guerrillas. In the government's mad rush to expand private commercial development of export-oriented logging, shrimp aquaculture, plantation agriculture, and cattle raising, it trampled on the traditional rights of indigenous people and Afro-Colombians in the northern Pacific coastal department of Chocó, home to 455,000 Afro-Colombians, 49,000 natives, and 36,000 mestizos. By 1997 the previously peaceful region had succumbed to violence with the appearance of the army and popular guerrilla groups like the black "Benkos Biojo" and Revolutionary Indigenous Armed Forces (FARIP).

Guerrilla support also was particularly strong in the long-neglected colonization areas in the southern part of the country, where peasant communities produced coca leaves and poppies as the only alternative to the economic crisis. By compelling "fair" payment by the drug traffickers to the coca growers for their products and by resisting the government's herbicidal spraying of the coca fields, which also destroyed subsistence crops, the guerrillas defended peasants against the government's eradication campaigns and against land-grabbing efforts by the rapacious new narcobourgeoisie. In addition to playing a protective role in the regions under their control, the guerrillas assumed many local-level functions of the state, "maintaining order, officiating at weddings, births, and divorces, organizing education, mediating conflict and administering justice, and marketing agricultural products." To finance their activities, the guerrillas imposed "taxes" on the drug barons, laboratories, roads, and drug shipments.

The FARC and peasant leaders were well aware of the devastating human, social, and environmental effects of drug cultivation and trade. The FARC proposed a program for the eradication of coca, poppy, and marijuana plantations by the substitution of other crops, with government aid to farmers in land, seeds, and equipment. In 1998, according to *The Nation*, FARC spokesmen sounded out U.S. officials with a proposal to sever all drug connections in return for a U.S. crop-substitution plan. But neither the Colombian government nor Washington expressed interest.

The "dirty war" had an unexpected impact on gender balance, family structure, and the labor force. With an average of 79 homicides per 100,000 people, seven times the U.S. rate, some 40 percent of families in the 1990s were headed by women who, in addition to their unpaid household labor, were forced to work outside the home, usually for low wages either in unskilled jobs or as self-employed workers in the "informal sector." Within a generation, the proportion of women in the urban work force rose from approximately 33 percent to 43 percent, but women's wages still lagged 30 percent behind men's. The United States, which generously supplied the Colombian military with arms, bore a heavy responsibility for this carnival of death. In March 1994 an Amnesty International report criticized the United States "for remaining silent when aid destined to combat arms trafficking was diverted to counterinsurgency operations and thence to killing of unarmed peasants." In 1991 the CIA established a new military intelligence network in Colombia, ostensibly to fight drugs. "Instead," says journalist Frank Smyth, "they incorporated illegal paramilitary groups into their ranks and fostered death squads. These death squads killed trade unionists, peasant leaders, human rights monitors, journalists, and other suspected 'subversives.' The evidence, including secret Colombian military documents, suggests that the CIA may be more interested in fighting a leftist resistance movement than in combating drugs."

The killings went on. In February 1998 a death squad murdered another leading human rights activist, Jesús María Valle Jaramillo, who had accused certain politicians and members of the military of sponsoring death squads. In April one of Colombia's leading human rights lawyers, Eduardo Umana Mendoza, was murdered in his office. Before his death he had alerted authorities that state security officers were planning to kill him. Yet there was evidence that the tide in Colombia was turning against the killers and their sponsors. In October 1997, 10 million voters—the largest turnout in Colombian history—approved a mandate for peace that called for a cease-fire, peace talks, and respect for the lives and other human rights of noncombatants. In May 1998, in the first round of the presidential election, Noemi Sanin, seeking to become Colombia's first female president with a platform that stressed the fight against corruption, economic recovery, and the search for peace, jolted the two-party system by getting one-third of the vote, carrying Bogotá and the country's next-largest cities, Cali and Medellín. Although Andres Pastrana won the run-off election, he clearly understood his national mandate and announced that he was ready to begin "the long road toward peace" by meeting with the legendary leader and founder of the FARC, Manuel Marulanda Pérez. The FARC in turn announced that it was ready to resume negotiations.

But many obstacles to peace remained, not the least of which was the uncertain stand of the United States, whose support of or opposition to the Colombian peace process would determine whether these negotiations represented a true turning point in Colombia's tragic modern history. A series of events soon put all doubts to rest. On January 11, 2000, President Bill Clinton announced a $1.3 billion aid package for Colombia to assist "in vital counter-drug efforts aimed at keeping illegal drugs off our shores" and "to help Colombia promote peace and prosperity and deepen its democracy." The measure, which made Colombia the third largest beneficiary of military aid from the United States (after Israel and Egypt), formed part of a $7.3 billion "Plan Colombia" prepared by the two governments; but the hand of Washington showed on every page. Colombia was to contribute $4 billion, though it was unclear where the financially strapped government would find the money; the rest was to come from the United States and countries of the European Union, which showed little enthusiasm for the plan and eventually withdrew from the project, believing that a war against the FARC would only worsen Colombia's social and economic problems. Announced after formal peace talks between the Colombian government and the FARC had begun, it made clear that the United States had chosen war over peace in Colombia.

The ambitious plan had several objectives. Its main goal was the reconquest of the vast area, some 40 percent of the national territory, which the FARC controlled, mostly in southern Colombia. This reconquest would go hand in hand with a coca eradication campaign, and the former coca growers would be assisted with a crop-substitution program. The plan ignored altogether the narco-traffickers and their paramilitary allies in the North. As Garry Leech points out in the *Colombia Report* (May 14, 2001), the plan wielded a huge stick, while offering a tiny carrot. Approximately 80 percent of the U.S. aid would go to the military and the police, 8 percent to the crop substitution program, 6 percent to human rights programs, 4 percent to displaced farmers, and 1 percent to the continuing peace process.

The plan also had an economic component that required Colombia to further restructure its economy along neoliberal lines, cut government social spending, and privatize state-owned enterprises, including banks, utilities, and the state's coal company. These policies, needed to comply with commitments made to the IMF in return for a $2.7 billion loan in 1999, were certain to increase the current Colombian combined unemployment and underemployment figure of over 60 percent.

Colombia's former attorney general, Gustavo de Greiff, sharply questioned the effectiveness of Plan Colombia. In July 2001 he wrote that to claim success for the plan's strategy of drug eradication, one would have to show that it resulted in (1) a decline in the area of cultivation of the plants from which cocaine, heroin, and marijuana were produced; (2) reduced availability of those drugs in the market; (3) higher prices for these drugs; (4) a decline in the number of consumers, habitual and occasional. Greiff demonstrated with data from national and international organizations that none of those results had been obtained. For Colombia he cited satellite photographs showing that after the fumigation of 60,000 hectares the area cultivated in coca had grown 60 percent in the previous year. Greiff bristled at the "arrogance" of a U.S. State Department official who, confronted with evidence of increased coca production in Colombia, said in a press interview that this meant "we have to do more of what we have been doing, not less."

The other official justification for military aid to Colombia, "to help Colombia promote peace and prosperity and deepen its democracy," must sound equally unrealistic to students of Colombia's recent history, because this aid failed to address the historical causes of the civil war and the general crisis of Colombian society, which lay in the land-grabbing of a selfish elite and in the massacres of peasants and workers by death squads in its service half a century ago. The successors to those death squads were the contemporary brutal paramilitary outfits, closely linked to the Colombian armed forces, which provided them with intelligence, transport, and weapons. The military officer class, corrupt and incompetent, commanded a rank-and-file consisting mostly of demoralized young workers and peasants who lacked the high school degree necessary to exempt them from the draft. Stung by successive defeats at the hands of the guerrillas, the military recently chose to "privatize" or "outsource" the war, leaving most of the fighting to the paramilitaries. These gunmen served a variety of masters: drug traffickers, great landowners, especially cattle raisers, and modern capitalists. They served the interests of the old and new elites by murdering militant peasants, workers, indigenous people, blacks, or anyone they suspected of sympathy with the guerrillas. They threatened, kidnapped, and killed progressive lawyers, human rights activists, and journalists too zealous in the exposure of their crimes. According to Human Rights Watch, the paramilitaries were responsible for 78 percent of the human rights violations in Colombia in 1999.

Early in the twenty-first century, corruption still pervaded the political life of Colombia, dominated by the two historical parties, Conservatives and Liberals. A pervasive cynicism regarding politics and politicians was reflected in traditionally high abstention rates; only 46 percent of eligible voters turned out for the May 2002 presidential election. Moreover, electoral fraud, including the purchase of votes, was common; in some regions, like the Atlantic coast, a vote had one price at 8 A.M. and was eight or ten times higher at 3 P.M. "Congress," observed *The Economist* in a piece on the March 2002 congressional election, "has come to be seen as a center of shady deals." This corruption, public distrust of politicians, and resulting high abstention rates meant that in his 2002 "landslide" victory, newly elected president Alvaro Uribe Velez captured only 5.8 million votes—24 percent of the eligible electorate.

If the official justifications for the military aid program for Colombia appeared too glib and unrealistic to be adequate, were other, more pragmatic motives involved? Answers to this question were implied in the financial details of the aid package and the new heightened importance of Colombian oil to multinational companies and the U.S. government. A major beneficiary of the aid package was United Technologies Corporation, the Connecticut company that was to supply Colombia with some 30 Blackhawk helicopters, each costing $12.8 million. Another was Bell Helicopter Textron, a Texas subsidiary of Textron, which produces the Huey II helicopter. Indeed, one reason for the delay in getting final approval for the aid package was pork barrel wrangling between Texas and Connecticut legislators over apportionment of the aid package.

Occidental Petroleum, which operated the Caño-Limón pipeline in northeast Colombia, stood to gain hugely if the hopes invested in the aid package were fulfilled. In 2002, Colombia was the seventh-largest supplier of oil to the United States, and it controlled the largest untapped pool of petroleum in the Western Hemisphere. But guerrilla attacks between 1982 and 1990 spilled 1.6 billion gallons of Occidental oil along the way. Washington's 1997 decision to reduce its dependence on Middle Eastern oil suggests that its principal interest may not have been drugs but oil. Other companies with stakes in the aid package included DynCorp, a defense contractor with a $600 million contract to spray coca crops in Colombia, and Monsanto, producer of the herbicide currently used. Colombia recently at least temporarily shelved plans to use a more deadly herbicide, a fungus spray that kills coca plants, because of evidence that it was harmful to the environment and to humans.

The Republican victory in the 2000 U.S. presidential election brought to power George W. Bush, member of a dynasty that had many close links with the oil industry. But the dramatic events of September 11, 2001, raised the question of continuity of U.S. policy in Colombia. Would Washington, deeply involved in a global "war on terrorism" in Afghanistan and at home, reverse its steep descent into the Colombian quagmire? Or would Colombia become a new active front in that war? Colombia, after being temporarily forgotten, sprang back into the news. The United States, although still professing neutrality toward the peace talks, intervened to assure an outcome in conformity with the warlike logic of Plan Colombia.

But media claims of virtually unanimous support for the drug war and the campaign of defoliation were contradicted by evidence of overwhelming opposition to both in the south of the country, the provinces that were the main targets of Plan Colombia. Six governors of that region, all elected in October 2000, said the *New York Times*, "have organized into a formidable bloc that has harshly criticized the central government for everything from the handling of finances to the drug war." Rather than war, these governors demanded "regional public projects and agricultural development programs seen as alternatives to defoliation." The *New York Times* also noted that the group had "the most unlikely governor in Colombia, Mr. Tunubala, a Guambiano Indian who won office in a province well known for discrimination and social inequality." His political movement, "composed of Indians, union leaders, poor farmers, intellectuals, and outside the province's circle of power—has already angered some people in the province of Cauca and prompted death threats."

Against this background of regional discontent and resistance to Plan Colombia, the Bush team fueled the Colombian fire with its "Andean Regional Initiative," announced in 2001 and developed in budgetary detail in 2002. The program increased funding for the counter-drug effort by $731 million, but it also represented a major qualitative change from the Clinton aid package. The stress on the war against drugs was now joined to a new stress on the terrorist threat allegedly presented by the FARC. The qualitative change was illustrated by the fact that the new program would finance a brigade to protect Occidental's oil pipeline, which of course had nothing to do with drugs.

Two years into Plan Colombia, its Colombian and U.S. authors had failed to eradicate coca or reconquer southern Colombia from the FARC, now boasting an army eighteen thousand strong. The Bush "Andean Initiative" evidently contemplated a deeper involvement in Colombia, including the prospect of armed confrontation with the FARC and a smaller guerrilla movement, the Army of National Liberation (ELN). A 2001 study by the Rand Corporation, financed by the U.S. Air Force, even suggested that "the U.S. program of military assistance to El Salvador during the Reagan Administration could be a relevant model." Commenting on this suggestion in *The NACLA Report on the Americas*, Adam Isacson urged those who might want to repeat this model in Colombia to recall that "the United States spent $2 billion on El Salvador's military over a 12-year period, during which 70,000 people died and over a million were forced into exile. Colombia is fifty-three times larger than El Salvador."

As President Uribe's term began, two new, unforeseen obstacles to the success of Plan Colombia appeared. In early July 2002 the Colombian finance minister announced that the Argentine "fever," having spread to Uruguay, Brazil, and Venezuela, had reached Colombia. In other words, the minister implied that Colombia now lacked the financial means to pay for the massive military mobilization necessary to defeat the FARC. A second blow to the implementation of Plan Colombia came from the FARC itself. In June 2002 it responded to the government's termination of the truce by sending every mayor, provincial governor, and government official in Colombia's 1,098 municipalities an ultimatum to resign in 72 hours or become military targets. Panic set in among some officials, including one who decided, "I am not going to lay my life on the line for a problem that I didn't cause."

Meanwhile, in some parts of the 40 percent of the national territory that it claimed to control, the FARC had created "pilot communities" that suggested the kind of political organization it envisioned to replace the ousted mayors. In Caqueta province, for example, the FARC established "people's committees" composed of peasant, worker, and business representatives to administer local affairs. This model of self-governance was given the name "participatory democracy." "We are handing power back to the people," said one guerrilla political officer in Caqueta. "We will not recognize political authorities, but only the desires of civic organizations. Town hall officials will simply become administrators, but the people will give the orders."

# The Two Americas: United States–Latin American Relations

TWO CONSISTENT THEMES appear when the relations of the United States with Latin America over nearly two centuries are examined. First and foremost, the United States sought to protect and expand its economic and strategic interests in the region. Ever since the administration of James Monroe, the United States attempted to establish and maintain Latin America as an economic appendage. U.S. policymakers displayed resourcefulness and flexibility in pursuit of this goal, adapting their methods to meet the varying domestic political pressures, the changing requirements of U.S. business, and the shifting conditions in Latin America. Thus, U.S. policy never relied exclusively or even primarily on unilateral military conquest and subjugation of Latin America; instead, it sought to establish its hegemony, that is, to "manage" hemispheric events by securing Latin America's consent to a multilateral system of inter-American relations whose "general rules," though expressed in universal, humanitarian terms, nonetheless incorporated its special political, economic, and strategic interests.

Second, U.S. leaders consistently justified U.S. policy by portraying the region as hopelessly backward, desperately in need of beneficent U.S. tutelage to save its people from the ravages of barbarism and promote the development of virtuous, democratic republics modeled on an idealized U.S. experience. In this process, according to Mark T. Berger, the work of historians and social scientists in Latin American studies was complicit. This "discourse" of a U.S. "civilizing mission," rooted in white supremacist ideas in the nineteenth century and the discursive language of modernization theory in the twentieth, facilitated "the creation and maintenance of the national and international organizations, institutions, interstate relations and politico-economic structures that sustain and extend U.S. hegemony in Latin America and around the world."

## U.S. Policy Objectives

U.S. policy toward Latin America changed over time to accommodate its burgeoning economic activities in the region. During the early years of the nineteenth century, U.S. commerce with its southern neighbors demanded little more than policing the Caribbean for marauding pirates. As the United States grew into a commercial, industrial, and, eventually, financial power, its foreign policy broadened in scope. The hunt for new markets brought it into competition with European nations, especially Great Britain. As a result, it became one of the major aims of U.S. policy to check the further penetration of European commerce and capital into Latin America.

By the turn of the century, Latin America had become not only a substantial market for U.S.

**U.S. Territorial Expansion**

Original thirteen states
Territories annexed, 1783
Louisiana Purchase, 1803
Florida annexed, 1819–1821
Texas annexed, 1845
Oregon territory annexed, 1846
Mexican territory annexed, 1848
Gadsden Purchase, 1853

products but also an important source of raw materials and a major area for capital investment. Having recently built a powerful navy, the United States assumed the responsibility of protecting its commerce and investment by forcibly maintaining order in the region. Uninvited, it assumed the role of policeman of the Western Hemisphere. In this capacity, the United States focused its attention on the weak and chaotic nations of the Caribbean and Central America, where U.S. economic activity was concentrated.

At mid-century, South America replaced the Caribbean as the focus of U.S. economic expansion. Geography, logistics, and the anti-imperialist temper of the times required the United States to abandon the old policies of military intervention in favor of more subtle and sophisticated ways of achieving its ends; these new methods included the lure of grants and loans, the threat of economic sanctions, and subversion. When these methods failed, however, as they did in Guatemala in 1954, in Cuba in 1959, and in the Dominican Republic in 1965, the United States did not hesitate to resort to the open or covert use of force.

Ideology always figured in U.S. policy toward Latin America. Thus, Theodore Roosevelt vowed to "civilize," Woodrow Wilson to "democratize," and John F. Kennedy to "reform" Latin America. But ideology always was subordinated to the material needs of United States–Latin American policy, and the presidents who made these pious professions were ready to use force in defense of the U.S. empire in Latin America. They were also ready to support the most oppressive regimes in the area as long as they cooperated with the United States. Highlighting this link between high ideals and capitalist class interests, Wilson, for example, argued in 1912 that "if America is not to have free enterprise, then she can have freedom of no sort whatever."

The two Americas, both born in wars of national liberation, followed very different historical paths. In two centuries, the United States rose to become the industrial and financial giant of the capitalist world; despite its many economic and social problems, it provided the majority of its people with a satisfactory material standard of living. Latin America fell far behind the other America in terms of its capacity to meet the economic needs of its citizens.

Many Latin Americans are convinced that these divergent trends are related, that Latin American underdevelopment is the other side of North American development, that Latin American poverty and misery have accumulated as the economic and political power of foreign (chiefly North American) multinational corporations have grown.

# Prelude to Empire, 1810–1897

## MANIFEST DESTINY, 1810–1865

During the early decades of the nineteenth century, westward expansion and nascent commerce brought the United States into its first contact with its southern neighbors. However, U.S. military and economic weakness, lack of information, and British predominance in the area limited U.S. activities in Latin America. U.S. trade with Latin America began in earnest in 1797, when Spain opened the ports of its New World colonies to foreign trade. By 1811 the Spanish colonies accounted for 16 percent of all U.S. trade. A dozen years later, despite the disruptions of the War of 1812, the figure had increased to 20 percent.

With only a small navy and few funds at its disposal, the U.S. government could offer little aid to the Spanish-American nations during their wars of independence (1810–1826). During the first stage of these wars, the War of 1812 consumed the attention and resources of the United States. From 1817 to 1819, it undertook delicate negotiations with Spain for the purchase of Florida and chose not to jeopardize these dealings by helping the Spanish-American insurgents. However, their victory offered powerful strategic and commercial advantages to the United States. First, with the French retreat from Haiti and the Louisiana territories in 1803 and the British in search of a U.S. alliance in the 1820s, Latin American independence eliminated Spain, the hemisphere's last potential military threat to U.S. security. This enabled the United States to spend less on defense and invest more in the development of its civilian economy.

Second, it meant, in Thomas Jefferson's words, that the United States could absorb "piece by piece" the old Spanish-American empire, "a huge, helpless and profitable whale." Similarly, John Quincy Adams, anticipating U.S. economic relations with a "free" Latin America, expected that the United States would grow wealthy from the region's dependence on it: "As navigators and manufacturers, we are already so far advanced in a career upon which they have yet to enter that we may, for many years after the conclusion of the [independence] war, maintain with them a commercial intercourse, highly beneficial to both parties, as carriers to and for them of numerous articles of manufacture and foreign produce."

When it was clear that the Latin American independence movements had succeeded, the United States accordingly acted to prevent other European nations from acquiring colonies or undue influence in the region, developments that could shut off U.S. access to potentially lucrative markets. In his message to Congress on December 2, 1823, President James Monroe declared that as a matter of principle, "the American continents, by the free and independent condition they have assumed and maintain, are henceforth not to be considered subjects for future colonization by any European powers. . . . We should consider any attempt on their [the European powers'] part to extend their system to any portion of this hemisphere as dangerous to our peace and safety." Monroe went on to say that the United States would not interfere with existing colonies, nor would it meddle in European affairs.

The Monroe Doctrine was ineffective for much of the nineteenth century because the United States had neither the resources nor the inclination to back it up. The doctrine, furthermore, failed to prevent repeated European interventions in Latin America. Following the accepted practice of the time, French and British gunboats regularly bombarded or blockaded Latin American ports to force payment of debts or reparations. The United States, too, adopted this practice, landing troops in the Falkland Islands, Argentina, and Peru during the 1830s, in Argentina, Nicaragua, Uruguay, Panama, Paraguay, and Mexico during the 1850s,

and in Panama, Uruguay, Mexico, and Colombia during the 1860s.

Nineteenth-century westward territorial expansion involved the United States in countless wars against Native Americans and two wars against Mexico. After the purchase of Louisiana (1803) and Florida (1821), the country began to covet Mexico's northern provinces, where U.S. citizens conducted a flourishing commerce. In 1825, President John Quincy Adams authorized the U.S. minister to Mexico to negotiate the purchase of Texas. The Mexican government rejected the proposal. During the early 1830s, U.S. settlers poured into Texas and quickly found themselves at odds with Mexican authorities over the issues of local autonomy and the illegal introduction of slavery into the area. In 1836 the settlers rebelled, defeated Mexico in a short war, and won their independence. Texas remained an independent nation for ten years, for the bitter debate over the extension of slavery prevented its annexation to the United States until 1845.

In 1845 President James Polk sent an emissary, James Slidell, to Mexico to arrange the acquisition of California. Outraged at the annexation of Texas, the Mexicans refused to cede any of their territory. Consequently, Polk trumped up a border incident along the Rio Grande, provoking a military clash that led to the war against Mexico (1846–1848). The victorious United States took the territories of Arizona, New Mexico, and California. Barely some seventy years old, the United States, building upon its conquest of Native American lands, had successfully waged another war of territorial acquisition.

## COMMERCE AND THE CANAL

From 1815 to 1860, U.S. foreign commerce increased dramatically; exports grew by nearly 400 percent and imports by 300 percent. The nature of U.S. trade was transformed, for instead of reexporting foreign-made goods, U.S. merchants exported agricultural commodities and manufactured goods produced in the United States. Because of the increased economic activity in the Caribbean, especially Cuba and Central America, the United States began to pay close attention to the region. Cuba became one of the most important U.S. overseas markets, ranking third behind Great Britain and France in total U.S. trade. Throughout the 1850s, there was a strong sentiment, particularly among southern slave owners, to annex the island. President Millard Fillmore tried unsuccessfully to purchase Cuba from Spain in 1852.

Central America became important because of the prospect of a canal through the Central American isthmus. After discussions began in 1825 the United States signed an 1846 agreement with New Granada (Colombia) that guaranteed U.S. access to any canal built in its province of Panama. This concern over a canal and commercial interests in Central America brought the United States into direct confrontation with Great Britain, which had colonies in the region. Each nation sought to keep the other from dominating the area or controlling any canal that would be built. As a result, in 1850 they agreed to the Clayton-Bulwer Treaty, which provided that neither would try to dominate Central America or any part of it or would acquire exclusive rights to a canal. Thus, they eliminated a potential cause of hostilities.

The gold rush to California in 1849 increased the importance of transportation across the isthmus. U.S. entrepreneurs invested heavily in steamships and railroad construction in the region to satisfy the demand for cheap and fast transport across the isthmus to California. Despite the treaty with Britain and these heavy investments in transportation, U.S. interest in a canal continued.

## THE AWAKENING GIANT, 1865–1887

In the two decades after the Civil War (1861–1865), U.S. policymakers focused their concerns on territorial expansion and increased trade in Latin America, finding little success in either. The major diplomatic triumph of the era came in 1866 when Secretary of State William H. Seward, belatedly invoking the Monroe Doctrine, demanded that France remove its troops from Mexico, where they propped up the rule of the Emperor Maximilian, the Austrian archduke. Emperor Napoleon III of France complied the fol-

lowing year, more because of growing tensions with Prussia in Europe than because of fear of the United States.

A succession of U.S. presidents and secretaries of state attempted to acquire new territories, but they were inevitably thwarted by Congress. There were also major efforts to expand U.S. trade to Latin America through the negotiation of reciprocal trade treaties and establishment of inter-American diplomatic conferences. The United States signed bilateral reciprocal trade agreements with six Latin American nations during the 1880s, but no real benefits accrued. The first Inter-American Conference met in Washington, D.C., in 1889. It resulted in little more than the airing of long-simmering grievances and mistrust.

## ADVENTURES IN LATIN AMERICA, 1888–1896

U.S. adventurism in Latin America in the last years of the nineteenth century stemmed from severe domestic economic and social problems, pervasive racism, and from the country's growing stake in commerce and investment in the region. The United States experienced a deep depression from 1893 to 1898, the third such downturn in twenty-five years (the others had occurred in 1873–1878 and 1882–1885). It became evident that the domestic market could not profitably absorb the rapidly growing output of U.S. agriculture and industry. U.S. leaders unanimously agreed that the answer to the problem was to expand foreign markets. The depression of 1893 created deep-seated social unrest as well, resulting in a series of bitter and bloody strikes. Businessmen and politicians alike feared that continued depression would lead to class warfare.

At the same time, U.S. capitalists increased their investment in Latin America. Paradoxically, despite the depression, U.S. banks had surplus funds to invest. Because investments in the United States were unattractive, the bankers turned to potentially more lucrative foreign enterprises. These investors poured millions of dollars into Cuban sugar and Mexican mining and railroads. By 1900 the U.S. stake in Mexico alone had reached $500 million.

U.S. interest, however, was not limited to areas like Mexico and Cuba, where it already had large investments. The United States was willing to go to great lengths, even at the risk of war, both to protect potential markets and to reinforce its political dominance in the region. This was particularly true of the Caribbean, which leaders tended to view as an "American lake." Thus, in 1888 the United States intervened in a civil war in Haiti to secure a favorable commercial agreement and a naval base at Môle St. Nicolas. The U.S. fleet actually broke a blockade to bring about the victory of the faction it favored. Once entrenched in power, however, this group reneged on its promises to the Harrison administration (1887–1893). Then Secretary of State James G. Blaine also tried unsuccessfully to obtain Samaná Bay from Santo Domingo.

Naturally, the same doctrines of white supremacy that sought to justify a domestic racial apartheid, the lynching of thousands of African Americans, disfranchisement of 8 million southern blacks, the "tribalization" of sovereign Native American nations, and the exclusion of Chinese immigrants also shaped U.S. relations with Latin America. U.S. policymakers increasingly came to share the view of Atlanta's Henry Grady, an influential "New South" publisher, who argued that white supremacy reflected "the right of character, intelligence, and property to rule." This, according to diplomatic historian Walter LaFeber, "anticipated some of the arguments Americans later used to justify their new foreign policies."

As the depression of 1893 deepened, U.S. leaders looked southward with growing anxiety. President Grover Cleveland declared in his annual message to Congress in 1893 that unrest and European meddling had threatened U.S. interests in Nicaragua, Guatemala, Costa Rica, Honduras, and Brazil in 1892; the U.S. fleet was finding it difficult to keep up with its "responsibilities." Markets desperately needed by the United States were threatened by disorders and competition from European nations, particularly Britain.

In 1894 the United States became involved in another revolution when it intervened in Brazil to protect a potentially important market and to check British influence there. The United States had signed a reciprocal trade agreement with the newly proclaimed republic of Brazil in 1891, but the rebels who rose up in 1893 opposed the pact. The main strategy of the rebel forces was to blockade the harbor of Rio de Janeiro, the nation's principal city; they hoped to strangle the government by denying it the all-important customs revenue. The United States helped undermine this strategy by refusing to recognize the blockade. U.S. vessels unloaded their cargoes without interference.

Late in 1894, however, with clandestine aid from the British, the rebellion regained momentum. At this time, important mercantile and oil (Rockefeller) interests, fearing the loss of their Brazilian market, brought pressure on the State Department to intervene. The United States responded by sending most of the Atlantic fleet to the harbor of Rio de Janeiro. By maneuvering to prevent rebel bombardment of the capital, the U.S. warships played a crucial part in the defeat of the revolt.

Shortly thereafter, the United States intervened in Nicaragua to protect its rights to an isthmian canal and the substantial holdings of U.S. investors. In 1893 a nationalist government, headed by General José S. Zelaya, took power in Nicaragua; it threatened to cancel a concession granted by a previous administration to the Maritime Canal Company to build a canal through Nicaraguan territory. Later, Zelaya also threatened the prosperous U.S.-run banana plantations in the indigenous Miskito reservation (an area claimed by Nicaragua but controlled by the British) by invading the reservation in 1894. In response, British troops landed and quickly subdued the Nicaraguan force. U.S. interests, with a $2 million stake in the Miskito region, were unwilling to accept either British or Nicaraguan rule. To protect its property, the United States stationed two warships off the coast and in July dispatched marines to restore order. U.S. troops landed three more times, in 1896, 1898, and 1899, to protect U.S. lives and property.

## THE TURNING POINT: VENEZUELA, 1895–1896

The Venezuelan crisis of 1895–1896 ended in full British recognition of U.S. hegemony in the Western Hemisphere. The United States intervened in a boundary dispute between Venezuela and Great Britain that had festered for over half a century. The controversy concerned the region at the mouth of the Orinoco River, the major commercial artery for northern South America, which was claimed by both Venezuela and the British colony of Guiana (present-day Guyana). In the 1880s, Britain extended its claims, causing Venezuela to break off diplomatic relations.

During 1893 and 1894, the Venezuelan government, confronted with mounting economic difficulties and political unrest, appealed to the United States to help settle the controversy. President Cleveland's entrance into the dispute reflected his deep concern about the apparent resurgence of European intervention in Latin America. Between 1891 and 1895, the British had actively intervened in Chile, Brazil, and Nicaragua. The French had become involved in a dispute with Brazil over the boundary of their colony of Guiana and had threatened intervention in Santo Domingo to obtain satisfaction for the killing of a French citizen. The simultaneous scramble for territories in Africa magnified the threat; what the European rivals did on one continent, they could do on another. Specifically, President Cleveland feared that British control of the mouth of the Orinoco would exclude U.S. commerce from northern South American markets.

In 1895, in an obvious effort to intensify U.S. support, the Venezuelan government granted a lucrative concession to a U.S. syndicate for the exploitation of rich mineral resources located in the disputed zone. In July 1895 Secretary of State Richard Olney spelled out the U.S. attitude toward European meddling in Latin America. Citing the Monroe Doctrine, he declared that the United States would intervene whenever the actions of a European power in the Western Hemisphere posed a "serious and direct menace to its own integrity and welfare." In effect, Olney claimed hegemony for the United States in Latin America.

The British initially responded to Olney's claims with disdain; the English foreign secretary denied the validity of the Monroe Doctrine in international law and brushed aside the U.S. assertion of supremacy in the Western Hemisphere.

President Cleveland, however, firmly supported Olney's position and made it clear that the United States was willing to go to war to uphold it. Meanwhile, international developments worked to soften the British stand; the threat of a war with Germany and British problems in South Africa took precedence. Accordingly, in late 1896 the British agreed to submit the dispute to arbitration. The government of Venezuela neither participated in nor was informed of this agreement.

The Venezuelan affair marked the end of British military predominance in Latin America. Its attention now focused on the growing German power and the competition for territory in Africa, Britain could no longer commit substantial resources to the region. With the growing threat of a general war in Europe, British leaders also could not afford to alienate the United States, a powerful potential ally. Thus, the British formally recognized U.S. hegemony in Latin America with the signing of the Hay-Pauncefote Treaty of 1901, which allowed the United States unilaterally to build, control, and fortify an isthmian canal. In 1906, Britain withdrew its fleet from the Caribbean. Great Britain retained its predominant economic position in southern South America but was fated to lose that also to the United States after World War I.

# An Imperial Power, 1898–1945

By 1898 the United States had emerged as an industrial, financial, and naval power. It surpassed Great Britain as the world's leading manufacturing state. Giant U.S. banks and corporations invested heavily overseas. Increasingly, the nation looked abroad for markets, raw materials, and profits. Recurring economic difficulties and mounting social unrest spurred U.S. leaders to seek solutions in overseas economic expansion and foreign adventures.

## THE WAR WITH SPAIN

The war with Spain in 1898 established the United States as a full-fledged imperial power. The primary goal of its Cuban policy during the 1890s was to protect the very large (over $50 million) U.S. investment in the island by stopping the chronic political disorder there. When Spain proved unable to end the turmoil, and it appeared that ungovernable native rebels might take over, the United States intervened. In declaring war against Spain, the U.S. Congress pledged to free Cuba from Spanish tyranny and in the Teller Resolution disavowed any intention to annex the island. But to the dismay of Cuban rebels, the McKinley administration had opposed the Teller Amendment and defeated the Turpie-Foraker bill, which would have recognized the Cuban government-in-exile. The U.S. government proceeded to conduct the war and negotiate the peace without consulting the Cubans.

The United States occupied and ruled the island from 1898 to 1902, departing only after the Cubans agreed to include in their constitution the notorious Platt Amendment, which made the country a virtual U.S. colony. U.S. forces occupied the island three more times—1906 to 1909, 1912, and 1917 to 1922. As noted in Chapter 17, instead of bringing the Cubans liberty and economic progress, U.S. intervention promoted and perpetuated racism, corruption, violence, and economic stagnation.

### AN "AMERICAN LAKE": THE "BIG STICK" AND "DOLLAR DIPLOMACY" IN THE CARIBBEAN

From 1898 to 1932 the United States intervened militarily in nine Caribbean nations a total of thirty-four times. Its occupation forces ran the governments of the Dominican Republic, Cuba, Nicaragua, Haiti, and Panama for long periods; Honduras, Mexico, Guatemala, and Costa Rica experienced shorter invasions. Military intervention was not the only method employed by the United States to control the region; other effective means included threats, nonrecognition, and economic sanctions.

The U.S. economic stake in the Caribbean was substantial. Moreover, the nature of this investment, which was concentrated primarily in agricultural commodities, mineral extraction, oil production, and government securities, made it particularly vulnerable to political disorders. From 1887 to 1914, U.S. investment in Cuba and the West Indies rose almost sevenfold, from $50 million to $336 million. Investment in Central America more than quadrupled, from $21 million to $93 million. By 1914, U.S. investment in Mexico had risen to over $1 billion. In 1914, 43 percent of this investment was in mining, 18.7 percent in agriculture, and 10 percent in oil. An additional 13 percent was invested in railroads, which were built to transport export products to market. The owners of these enterprises often had considerable influence on U.S. policy.

The United States justified its actions in the Caribbean by the so-called Roosevelt Corollary (1904) to the Monroe Doctrine, so named because President Theodore Roosevelt maintained that the United States, as a "civilized" nation, had the right to end "chronic wrongdoing" and thus could intervene in the Caribbean to maintain order. The Roosevelt Corollary was a logical outgrowth of the increasingly aggressive policies successively advanced by Seward, Grant, Cleveland, and Olney.

### THE PANAMA CANAL

U.S. interest in a canal across Central America to join the Atlantic and Pacific oceans had intensified as the nation filled out its continental boundaries and expanded its commercial activities throughout the Western Hemisphere. But the first to attempt to build a canal was Ferdinand de Lesseps, the Frenchman who had constructed the Suez Canal. He began a project to dig a sea-level canal across Panama in 1878. After eleven years of effort, de Lesseps, thwarted by tropical disease and engineering problems, gave up the project. Throughout this period, the United States pressured France to abandon the undertaking; it asserted its "rightful and long-established claim to priority on the American continent." The growth of a large United States Navy, which had two coasts to defend, added to the urgency of constructing an isthmian passageway.

In the 1880s and 1890s support grew for building a canal through Nicaragua. In 1901 a presidential commission endorsed the Nicaraguan route, despite the more favorable engineering

**U.S. Interventions in the Caribbean and Central America, 1898–1945**

and logistical characteristics of the Panamanian alternative, because the French company that controlled the canal concession in Panama wanted the fantastic sum of $109 million for its rights. At this point, two extraordinary entrepreneurs, William N. Cromwell, an influential New York attorney, and Philippe Bunau-Varilla, chief engineer of the de Lesseps project and an organizer of the New Panama Canal Company (the French company that had rights to the canal), acted to change the course of U.S. policy. Cromwell, as lawyer for the canal company, bribed the Republican Party to end its support of the Nicaraguan route. He and Bunau-Varilla then convinced the company to

lower the price for its concession to a more reasonable $40 million.

The two men were faced with the problem of convincing the United States to purchase their company's concession before it expired in 1904. In 1902, Bunau-Varilla and Cromwell managed to push through Congress the Spooner Amendment, which authorized President Roosevelt to buy the New Panama Canal Company's rights for the asking price of $40 million if he could negotiate a treaty with Colombia. In 1903, Secretary of State John Hay pressured the Colombian ambassador to the United States to sign a pact that gave the United States a 99-year lease on a strip of land across the

The construction of the Panama Canal, as depicted in a postcard from the time.
[The Granger Collection, New York]

isthmus in return for $10 million and an annual payment of $250,000. The Colombian Senate, demanding more money, rejected the proposal.

In the meantime, Bunau-Varilla undertook to exploit the long tradition of Panamanian nationalism and rebelliousness for his own end. From the time that Colombia won its independence from Spain in 1821, it had never been able to establish its rule in Panama. During the nineteenth century, the Panamanians revolted fifty times against their Colombian masters. On two occasions, when the Panamanian rebels seemed near success (1855–1856 and 1885), the United States intervened militarily to protect its interests and end the revolts. After a terrible civil war (1899–1902) had severely weakened Colombia, Panamanian nationalists again prepared to rise in revolt. Working closely with the U.S. State Department and the Panamanians, Bunau-Varilla triggered a successful uprising in early November 1903. With the help of the United States Navy and bribes paid to the Colombian officers who were supposed to crush the revolt, Panama won its independence.

The Panamanians, to their own undoing, entrusted to Bunau-Varilla the subsequent negotiations with the United States over the canal concession. Feverishly working to complete the arrangements before the New Panama Canal Company's rights expired, he produced a treaty that gave the United States control over a ten-mile-wide canal zone "as if it were a sovereign of the territory." The United States was to have "in perpetuity the use, occupation, and control" of the zone. In return, the United States was to pay Panama $10 million and assume a virtual protectorate over the new nation. The Panamanian government indignantly protested the terms of the agreement but eventually accepted the pact, fearing that the United States might either seize the canal with no compensation or build one in Nicaragua instead.

U.S. Marines were stationed in Panama from late 1903 until 1914 to protect U.S. interests while the canal was built, largely by black workers recruited from the West Indies. During this period, the United States disbanded the Panamanian army and assumed the responsibility of defending Panama against any external threat. The United States established its own postal system, custom-houses, and commissaries in the Canal Zone, privileges that seriously undermined the Panamanian economy and badly injured Panamanian pride. The canal was completed in 1914.

### THE DOMINICAN REPUBLIC, HAITI, AND NICARAGUA

The United States occupied and administered the governments of the Dominican Republic (1916–1924), Haiti (1915–1934), and Nicaragua (1912–1925 and 1926–1933) to the detriment of these nations' long-range political and economic development.

President Ulysses S. Grant had sought to annex the Dominican Republic (then known as Santo Domingo) in 1869; only rejection of the agreement by the United States Senate, influenced by fears of mingling with "people of the Latin race mixed with the Indian and African blood," prevented him from acquiring the nation, which shares the island of Hispaniola with Haiti. In the decades that followed, a series of venal and brutal dictators, often supported by loans from U.S. banks, produced a debilitating cycle of repression and rebellion. In 1893 the Santo Domingo Improvement Company, a U.S. firm, purchased the country's heavy foreign debt in return for the right to collect its customs revenue. In both 1903 and 1904, the United States dispatched marines to protect the interests of the influential New York financiers who were principals in the company. In 1905 the U.S. government assumed the administration of Dominican customs.

But unrest persisted. In 1916, President Woodrow Wilson sent in Marines after the Dominican government refused to accept broader U.S. control over the nation's internal affairs, and the U.S. Navy maintained a military dictatorship until 1924. The Marines brutally repressed guer-rilla activities that threatened U.S.-owned sugar plantations. In addition, several U.S. officers were subsequently court-martialed for the commission of atrocities.

The U.S. occupation forces attempted administrative and fiscal reforms and built some roads, but these projects were abandoned when the soldiers departed. One institution that remained intact after the occupation ended was the *Guardia Nacional*, the national police force. Rafael Trujillo, with U.S. support, rose through the ranks of the Guardia to become dictator of the Dominican Republic in 1928. His rapacious rule, extending over three decades (he was assassinated in 1961), was the bitter legacy of U.S. intervention.

Events in Haiti followed a similar course. For a century after winning independence from France in 1804, Haiti experienced ruinous political turmoil. Seizing the opportunity presented by the brutal murder of the Haitian president in 1915, Woodrow Wilson sent in Marines, ostensibly to prevent Germany from taking advantage of the chaos to establish a base on the island, which would endanger U.S. commerce and the access routes to the Panama Canal. A treaty signed the next year placed the United States in full control of the country. Although Haitians held public office, they served only at the pleasure of U.S. authorities. Here, too, U.S. troops committed atrocities while engaged in the suppression of rural guerrillas, and civil liberties were ignored. U.S. control lasted until 1934.

The United States also intervened in Nicaragua to protect the interests of U.S. companies operating there. The U.S. investment totaled only $2.5 million, but the largest company, the United States–Nicaraguan Concession, had considerable influence in the Taft administration (1909–1913); Secretary of State Philander C. Knox had been the company's legal counsel. In 1909, General José Zelaya, an old nemesis of the United States, canceled a concession to one U.S. company and threatened the Nicaraguan Concession. The same year, the United States backed a revolution that overthrew Zelaya. In 1912, at the request of the Nicaraguan government, President William Howard Taft sent in Marines to crush a new rebellion; the Marines remained for thirteen years. In

1916 the United States and Nicaragua agreed to the Bryan-Chamorro Treaty, which gave the United States sole rights to build a canal through Nicaragua in return for payment of $3 million.[1] President Calvin Coolidge withdrew U.S. troops for a short period in 1925 but dispatched them again to subdue yet another revolution the following year; the soldiers stayed until 1933.

## PUERTO RICO

The United States became a colonial power with the conquest and acquisition of the island of Puerto Rico in 1898 during the Spanish-American-Cuban War. From December 1898 until May 1900, U.S. military governors ruled the island. In 1900 the U.S. Congress passed the Foraker Act, which established a new civilian government for the island with a governor and an executive council appointed by the U.S. president. In 1917 this government was modified by replacing the executive council with an elected Senate. But the president maintained the power to veto legislation passed by the Puerto Rican Congress. The same year the U.S. Congress granted Puerto Ricans U.S. citizenship in time to make them eligible for the military draft for World War I.

U.S. occupation cost Puerto Ricans dearly politically. At the time of the Spanish-American War, the island had won a large degree of autonomy from Spain. The new colonial regime stripped that from them and ruled Puerto Rico with tactless, condescending mainlanders who had no experience in dealing with different cultures. When Puerto Ricans protested against unresponsive government, U.S. authorities reacted harshly. In 1909, for example, members of the Puerto Rican House of Delegates refused to pass the year's appropriation bill because of their objections to the indifference shown in the court system to struggling coffee growers. President Taft angrily demanded that the right of appropriations be taken from the House of Delegates, and the U.S. Congress enacted this legislation in the so-called

Olmstead Amendment. Puerto Rico did not have a native-born governor until 1947 or an elected governor until 1948.

Puerto Rico also underwent drastic economic changes as a result of the U.S. occupation. In 1898 its leading crop, coffee, was exported to Europe. U.S. policies transformed the island into a monocrop sugar economy with landownership concentrated in very few hands, mostly absentee foreign corporations. Puerto Ricans became dependent on the U.S. sugar quota. The decline of sugar prices during the 1920s and their collapse during the Depression of the 1930s brought chronic economic problems. By 1929 near starvation prevailed in many parts of the island. New Deal agencies, such as the Puerto Rican Emergency Relief Administration and the Puerto Rican Reconstruction Administration, poured some $230 million into the island from 1933 to 1941.

During the 1930s and for decades thereafter, the influence of two Puerto Ricans, Pedro Albizu Campos and Luis Muñoz Marín, dominated Puerto Rican politics. Harvard-educated Albizu became the foremost spokesman for independence. He formed the Nationalist Party and took an ardently anti-U.S. stand. He spent many years in prison for supporting violent confrontation with the island's colonial master. Muñoz Marín, whose father had led the Unionists in the early years of U.S. rule, was also educated in the United States. He did not live in Puerto Rico permanently until 1931. During the dark Depression days of the 1930s, Muñoz Marín became the star protégé of the New Deal.

The terrible plight of Puerto Rico during the Depression led to a reevaluation of its status by policymakers in the United States in the late 1930s. It was, as historian Arturo Morales Carrión has said, "a crisis of the whole colonial system." North Americanization had brought the "rise of absentee landownership, the collapse of coffee culture, the migration to growing slums, and shocking poverty in rural areas." U.S. rule had been a "mixture of paternalism and neglect, self-righteousness and condescension." The U.S. administrators of the island reacted harshly to such criticism and to nationalist protests. In March 1937 during a parade

---

[1]This treaty gave the United States control over the two best routes for a canal in Central America.

of the Nationalist Party in San Juan, police killed seventeen protesters in an unprovoked attack. In the crisis that followed in the aftermath of the massacre, old political coalitions realigned and Muñoz Marín emerged as the leading political figure. Based on his grassroots organization in the countryside, Muñoz Marín's Popular Democratic Party (PPD) rose meteorically, sweeping elections from 1944 until 1968. With help from Washington, he was able to lead Puerto Rico into a new era of industrialization and economic expansion.

Characteristic of Puerto Rican development was its dependence on the U.S. economy. North American corporations effectively monopolized the key sectors of banking, transport, tourism, and high-tech industrialization. This discouraged native capital formation. For North American corporations, however, the combination of low wages and tax breaks proved a bonanza, with profits in the range of $10 billion a year.

The combination of economic, political, and legal dependency adversely affected Puerto Rican political culture, breeding a colonial psychology that made dependency appear a natural condition and independence an impossible dream.

Accurately summarizing the island's colonial legal status since 1898, Attorney General Richard Thornburg declared that "The Congress of the United States holds full powers over Puerto Rico, a relationship that Puerto Ricans are incapable of altering. . . ." He went on to say that this relationship remained inalterable until changed by an amendment to the U.S. Constitution.

### THE MEXICAN REVOLUTION

We have already discussed some aspects of U.S. policy toward the Mexican Revolution (1910–1920) in Chapter 12. That policy was directed above all at safeguarding the vast U.S. investment below the border and securing the favorable political and economic climate required by U.S. interests in Mexico. The specific policies and tactics employed by the administrations of Presidents Taft and Wilson varied with the shifting conditions in Mexico, political pressures in the United States, and the changing international background. The United States twice resorted to military intervention in Mexico. In 1914, U.S. Marines occupied the gulf ports of Veracruz and Tampico in an effort to bring down General Victoriano Huerta, considered too friendly to British and German investors. The second intervention, General John J. Pershing's incursion into northern Mexico in 1916 in pursuit of Pancho Villa, aimed to pressure the regime of Venustiano Carranza to disavow allegedly radical constitutional constraints on foreign investment.

The United States exerted more decisive influence on the military course of the revolution by regulating the flow of arms and munitions across the United States–Mexican border. Through selective application of its neutrality laws, the U.S. government prevented "undesirable" factions from instigating disruptive activities on the U.S. side of the border. Woodrow Wilson introduced a new tactic in U.S. relations with Mexico by announcing that he would withhold recognition of governments that did not measure up to his standard of "morality." Wilson used this ploy against Huerta, Carranza, and Obregón.

U.S. efforts to control the course of the revolution were diluted by stubborn resistance on the part of nationalist Mexican leaders like Carranza, divisions among U.S. investors in Mexico—some favoring and others opposing military intervention—and finally, growing involvement of the United States in World War I. Its entry into the war in 1917 sharply limited policy alternatives, because the country lacked the military resources to fight in both Mexico and Europe. The threat of a Mexican alliance with Germany—a threat strongly posed by the famous Zimmerman telegram[2]—forced the United States to adopt a more moderate policy toward its neighbor.

---

[2]In this dispatch the German government, not yet at war with the United States, offered to return to Mexico the southwestern part of the United States (lost during the Mexican War, 1846–1848) if Mexico would invade the United States. This telegram was a major factor in President Woodrow Wilson's decision to go to war in 1917.

## QUIET IMPERIALISM: THE GOOD NEIGHBOR IN WORDS AND ACTION, 1921–1945

U.S. investment in Latin America grew rapidly in the period between 1914 and 1929. The world war enabled U.S. entrepreneurs to buy up much of the large British and German investment in the region. Total U.S. investment in Cuba and the West Indies, for example, rose from $336 million in 1914 to $1.2 billion in 1929—nearly a fourfold increase. U.S. capital in Central America more than tripled, while investment in South America increased eightfold. In 1929 total U.S. investment in Latin America had reached the staggering sum of $5.4 billion, or 35 percent of all U.S. foreign investment.

Much of the new investment went into oil: U.S. companies channeled $235 million to Venezuela, $134 million to Colombia, $120 million to Mexico, and $50 million to Peru for oil exploration and production. Another $163 million went to manufacturing enterprises in South America. U.S. companies also invested heavily in Chilean copper and nitrate, Argentine beef, and Cuban sugar.

This period marked the full-fledged involvement of large U.S. corporations, later called multinationals, in Latin America. Such giants as Standard Oil of New Jersey, the American Smelting and Refining Company, International Telephone and Telegraph, American Foreign Power, and Armour established or added to their vast stake in the region.

The basic goal of U.S. policy in Latin America did not change during the postwar period; it remained the protection of U.S. economic interests. But public opinion and realism dictated modifications. U.S. citizens were weary of overseas adventures and crusades. The United States remained dominant in the Caribbean, exerting decisive influence in the affairs of Mexico and Cuba and continuing to occupy the Dominican Republic, Haiti, and Nicaragua during the 1920s, but there was growing opposition to the old-style imperialism.

Makers of foreign policy in the United States also realized that growing popular hostility to U.S. policy in Latin America, primarily a response to U.S. actions in the Caribbean, posed a serious long-term danger to U.S. economic interests. An early sign of a shift in U.S. policy came in 1921, when the Colombian government threatened to cancel the concessions of U.S. companies to explore and drill for oil. The United States responded by paying Colombia $25 million to compensate for the loss of Panama. This had a dual meaning: it served to protect U.S. economic interests, and it symbolized a less aggressive policy toward Latin America. The shift in U.S. tactics became even clearer when the United States removed its troops from Cuba in 1922, from the Dominican Republic in 1924, and from Nicaragua in 1925. Despite these actions, the United States encountered bitter criticism of its role in the hemisphere at the Pan-American conferences in Santiago in 1923 and Havana in 1928.

The most important indication that the United States had largely abandoned military intervention as a major tactic was its restraint in dealing with Mexico, the biggest trouble spot in the hemisphere during the 1920s. The Mexican constitution of 1917 was a most radical document by contemporary standards. The constitution's provisions on landownership and ownership of subsoil rights seriously endangered U.S. investments. U.S. oil companies, in particular, objected to the new laws, which sought to reclaim statutory control of Mexico's rich natural resources even as they confirmed foreign usufruct rights.

Throughout the 1920s, the United States and Mexico haggled over application of the constitution, but the basic disagreement inflamed relations until World War II. The United States did not intervene militarily to protect the very large U.S. investments in Mexico because three circumstances discouraged such action. First, public opinion opposed further foreign adventures. Second, a military invasion would have been prohibitively costly in terms of both manpower and finances. Finally, U.S. entrepreneurs with interests in Mexico disagreed sharply over the proper course of action. The oil companies, which were most threatened by the constitution, favored intervention. The banks and the mining companies, whose interests would have been in greater danger in the event of war between the United States and Mexico, opposed intervention. The controversy abated during the late 1920s, after the U.S. government conceded that Mexico's nationalist regulations did not threaten the oil companies' right to profit from oil production.

President Herbert Hoover and Secretary of State Henry L. Stimson continued to shift toward moderation and stepped up U.S. efforts to win goodwill in Latin America. Hoover abandoned Wilson's policy of denying recognition to "unworthy" governments. The Clark memorandum, a milestone in Hoover's efforts, declared that the Roosevelt Corollary had no support in the Monroe Doctrine; consequently, the United States would no longer interfere militarily in the internal affairs of Latin American nations under the provisions of the doctrine. But the president carefully refrained from rejecting intervention outright. In 1933 he withdrew U.S. troops from Nicaragua and would have removed them from Haiti as well had the Haitians not objected to the withdrawal terms.

Building on these experiences, Franklin D. Roosevelt assumed the presidency in 1933 and, officially proclaiming the United States to be a "good neighbor" to the rest of the world, he rejected "interference in the internal affairs of other nations." The following year, the United States abrogated the Platt Amendment, thus abandoning its protectorate over Cuba; the same year, it withdrew its occupation troops from Haiti.

The nonintervention policy was soon put to the test in Cuba. In 1933 political unrest there threatened the substantial U.S. investment on the island. Roosevelt dispatched Sumner Welles to Havana to try to arrange an accommodation between dictator Gerardo Machado and his opponents. After several months of unsuccessful negotiations, Machado fled, and power fell into the hands of a disorganized and disunited junta. Eventually, Dr. Ramón Grau San Martín emerged as leader of the government. He quickly fell into disfavor with the United States when he suspended loan repayments to a large New York bank and seized two U.S.-owned sugar mills. As a result, the United States refused to recognize the Grau government. With U.S. warships lingering in Havana harbor, Grau was forced to relinquish his leadership. Supported by the United States, Fulgencio Batista emerged as the strongman of Cuba. Despite the protestations of the United States to the contrary, it was evident that it had not entirely abandoned the "big stick."

Nonintervention was tested again in Mexico in 1938. The long dispute between the Mexican government and the oil companies culminated in the expropriation of foreign oil holdings when the oil companies defied an order of the Mexican Supreme Court in a labor dispute. While the oil companies clamored for reprisal, Roosevelt tried to settle matters peacefully. In the face of isolationist sentiment in the United States, intervention was unthinkable. Moreover, with war in Europe on the horizon, the United States did not want to endanger an important source of oil. A settlement was eventually reached during the 1940s.

Roosevelt's "good neighbor" policy toward Latin America also involved efforts to achieve reciprocal trade agreements as a means of increasing U.S. trade and influence in the area. Secretary of State Cordell Hull ardently supported such agreements, believing they would help the United States emerge from the Great Depression. From 1934 to 1941, Hull succeeded in signing reciprocal trade treaties with fifteen Latin American nations. Had those treaties succeeded in significantly increasing U.S. trade, which they did not, they would have adversely affected Latin America's nascent industrialization, which was critically dependent on protective tariffs for its survival. In this area, therefore, United States policy was in direct conflict with the goal of Latin American economic development.

In the 1930s the United States grew increasingly concerned over the spread of German economic and political influence in Latin America. In response to this, the United States pushed for closer cooperation among the nations of the Western Hemisphere by promoting a series of meetings to consider common problems. The participants in successive inter-American conferences agreed to consult in the event of war among themselves or outside the hemisphere, approved a joint declaration of neutrality, proclaimed the existence of a safety zone around the hemisphere and warned belligerents not to wage war within it, and agreed to administer French and Dutch colonies in the Western Hemisphere in the event they were in danger of Nazi takeover. They also proclaimed that an attack on any of the conferring nations would be construed as an attack on all. In early 1942, shortly after the Japanese attack on Pearl Harbor, the conferees agreed to cooperate against the Axis; most Latin American nations severed diplomatic relations with the Axis powers. Every Latin American country but Argentina contributed to the Allied war effort.

The war strengthened the economic links between the United States and Latin America. The United States served as the sole market for the region's exports and the only supplier of its requirements of arms, munitions, industrial equipment, and manufactured goods. A growing proportion of U.S. capital went into manufacturing enterprises instead of raw material extraction. By the end of the war, Argentina accounted for 16 percent of U.S. investment in Latin America, Chile 16 percent, Brazil 13 percent, and Peru 4 percent. For the first time, South America accounted for over half the total U.S. investment in Latin America.

## Defending the Empire and Capitalism, 1945–1981

In the postwar era, four factors determined United States–Latin American relations: the need for the United States to protect U.S. interests in the region, its broader efforts to construct global markets open to trade and investment, the desire of Latin American nations to industrialize and diversify their economies, and the rivalry between the United States and the Soviet Union.

### INVESTMENT AND TRADE

Several important trends characterized U.S. investment in and trade with Latin America after World War II. First, the amount of investment increased enormously. Furthermore, the type of investment changed from mostly extractive industries, such as mining and oil, to manufacturing. Also, this investment became concentrated in the hands of a few large corporations and banks. Last, although the amount of U.S. trade with Latin America grew substantially, the relative importance of this trade to the economies of the United States and individual Latin American nations decreased.

All these trends did not mean that the United States had changed its policies. Its leaders continued to base their decisions on U.S. economic interests in the region, as trade and investment represented huge sums, despite declining importance. Accordingly, the editors of *Fortune*, an influential voice of corporate America, urged postwar U.S. leaders to "to organize the economic resources of the world so as to make possible a return to the system of free enterprise in every country. . . ." Policymakers like then–Assistant Secretary of State Dean Acheson, himself a corporate lawyer, shared this worldview; fearing a replay of the Great Depression, he conceded in 1944 that "it is a problem of markets. The important thing is markets. We have got to see that what the country produces is used and sold under financial arrangements which make its production possible. . . . You must look to foreign markets." Thus, every overt or covert U.S. intervention in Latin America during this period—in Guatemala, Cuba, the Dominican Republic, and Chile, for example—took place in countries where the security of large U.S. investments appeared to have been endangered. Moreover, each of these countries challenged the U.S. vision of a global open-door system.

### POST–WORLD WAR II ADJUSTMENTS

Despite the high degree of wartime cooperation, sharp differences between the United States and Latin America surfaced in the immediate postwar years. These disagreements emerged initially at the Chapultepec Conference in February 1945. Latin American leaders felt they should be rewarded for their contributions and sacrifices during the war. The United States, however, regarded European recovery as its first priority. There were also major disagreements over trade, industrialization, the overall direction of Latin American economic development, and the role of the United States in this development. The United States insisted on an open door to Latin American markets and investment opportunities, but it was unwilling to make any concessions that might injure its own producers. Latin Americans, however, feared that such free access to Latin American markets would destroy much of the industrial progress the region had made in the preceding two decades.

U.S. and Latin American interests were clearly opposed. The major Latin American obstacle to U.S. objectives was the region's nationalism: contrary to the open-door philosophy, according to the State Department's Office of Intelligence Research, in Latin America "the idea that the government has direct responsibility for the welfare of the people has resulted in a phenomenal growth of social and economic legislation designed to protect labor, distribute land more widely . . . and increase opportunities for education." Whereas U.S. leaders regarded private capital investment and free trade as the best routes to development, Latin American nations favored a massive government role in industrialization and restrictions on foreign trade and investment as the only means of modernizing and regaining control over their economies.

After the war, Latin America vainly sought help from the United States to finance industrialization and access to U.S.-manufactured goods, especially capital equipment in order to further industrialization. These efforts were hindered further in the next few years as high prices for manufactured products dissipated the dollar reserves Latin American nations had accumulated during the war; declining prices for raw materials eroded Latin America's terms of trade even further.

There was increasing evidence, moreover, that the United States had reverted to its traditional disregard for Latin American sensitivities and to intervention in the internal affairs of nations of the region. In 1946 the United States interfered in the internal political affairs of three South American nations. It meddled disastrously in the Argentine presidential campaign of that year, assuring the election of Juan Perón; it forced the González Videla government in Chile to oust the Communist members of its coalition cabinet; and it helped undermine a revolutionary regime in Bolivia that had been accused of fascist tendencies.

## THE COLD WAR

Alarm in the United States over the vast expansion of communist influence in Eastern and Central Europe as a result of World War II, the communist victory in the Chinese civil war, and the gains of Communist parties in Western Europe had the effect of pushing Latin America to the back burner. In this initial stage of the cold war, which lasted into the 1950s, the United States focused its attention on checking the further spread of communism in Western Europe and Asia by aiding the revival of the shattered capitalist economy.

During this first stage of the cold war, U.S. leaders tended to view the world as two camps, one committed to the United States and its free enterprise system, the other loyal to communism. Since it regarded the world in such black and white terms, the United States viewed with implacable hostility governments and movements that disagreed with its policy or attempted to institute structural social and economic reforms. On two occasions, in Guatemala and Iran, the United States helped topple such governments through the subversive activities of the CIA.

A second stage of the cold war began in the mid-1950s, when a "Third World" emerged, made up of the many newly independent states of Africa and Asia, which proclaimed themselves unaligned in the struggle between the blocs led by the Soviet Union and the United States. The two superpowers, faced with the unacceptable consequences of nuclear war, fought out the cold war in the Third World. In this second stage, the United States became intensely concerned with Latin America, especially after the 1959 Cuban Revolution led to the establishment of the first socialist state in the Americas. U.S. preoccupation with the threat of more Cubas in the hemisphere produced the Alliance for Progress as an alternative to the Cuban model.

Equally important, however, was the use of military aid to shape the internal policies of recalcitrant Latin American nations. The Military Defense Assistance Act of 1951 appropriated an initial $38.5 million to finance the build-up of Latin American armies for "country missions," that is, internal security rather than global or regional defense. This expanded under successive U.S. presidential administrations such that immediate postwar U.S. military aid amounted to more than half a billion dollars for the circum-Caribbean area alone and included paying for the training of thousands of Latin American military officers. By 1954 this policy had borne substantial fruit: thirteen of twenty countries were ruled by pro-U.S. military dictatorships.

The third stage of the cold war followed the disastrous U.S. experience in Vietnam and lasted until Ronald Reagan took office as president in 1981. Losing the Vietnam War and its tragic cost brought home to the U.S. government and its people the limitations of U.S. power and the dangers involved in trying to prevent social revolutions. Nonetheless, the United States remained determined to maintain its hegemony in the Western Hemisphere and to achieve its goals adapted its methods to suit new conditions.

A fourth stage of the cold war brought to the late 1980s the renewal of provocative anticommunist rhetoric, the simplistic 1950s division of the world into "them" and "us," the return to using force as a policy tool, and a revival of illegal, covert activities. The collapse of the Stalinist-type communist regimes in eastern and central Europe and the resulting demise of the cold war created a problem for the military-industrial complex that had flourished in the cold war's protective shadow and for U.S. Latin American policy by depriving it of its traditional enemy, "international communism." In the 1990s the drug trafficker replaced that traditional enemy as a convenient pretext for intervention in Latin America. After the September 11, 2001, terrorist attacks on the Pentagon and World Trade Center, the "war on terrorism" replaced drugs.

### THE LATIN AMERICAN POLICIES OF TRUMAN AND EISENHOWER

The Truman administration (1945–1953) focused its attention on fighting communism in Europe and the Far East. But, as we have seen, it meddled with mixed success in the political affairs of Chile, Bolivia, and Argentina in 1946. Under Truman, the movement for hemispheric cooperation continued, at least outwardly. The Rio Treaty of 1947 brought Central and South America into a military alliance with the United States. The ninth International Conference of American States, held in Bogotá the following year, resulted in the formation of the Organization of American States (OAS). The OAS was to provide collective security, with an attack against one member being viewed as an attack on all. The OAS also was to be a mediator in disputes between members. Truman and his chief advisers were primarily concerned with maintaining the status quo in the region.

The Eisenhower presidency (1953–1961) marked a revival of strong corporate influence in U.S. foreign policy. Eisenhower took office in the middle of the Korean war and at the height of the McCarthy "Red Scare." His administration, particularly the fanatical anticommunist secretary of state, John Foster Dulles, divided the world into two categories: nations that supported the United States and those that did not. Any foreign government that restricted the activities of U.S. corporations under its jurisdiction was adjudged to be communist and a threat to the security of the United States. During his two terms, Eisenhower faced four challenges of this kind in Latin America: Bolivia, British Guiana, Guatemala, and Cuba. In each case, his administration reacted according to the scale of the U.S. economic interests involved and the prevailing domestic and international conditions.

In Bolivia in 1952, a successful revolution headed by Victor Paz Estenssoro and the National Revolutionary Movement (MNR) ushered in sweeping economic and political reforms. In its first year, the new government nationalized the nation's tin mines, wiped out the latifundio system, replaced the old army with workers' and peasants' militias, and greatly increased the number of eligible voters. The outgoing Truman administration, anxious over the radicalism of the regime, withheld recognition and aid from Bolivia. The middle-class leadership of the MNR eventually managed to convince the Eisenhower administration that it was not communist; as a result, Bolivia received millions of dollars in grants and loans and substantial technical assistance over the next decade. U.S. aid had a significant moderating influence on the MNR reform program. Indeed, U.S. assistance decisively altered the whole course of Bolivian development; the United States reestablished, equipped, and trained the Bolivian army, which overthrew Paz Estenssoro in 1964, ushering in a period of conservative rule that continued almost uninterruptedly until 1981.

The United States employed different tactics to achieve the same general results, to adjust to the differing conditions of another Latin American country. In 1953, Marxist Cheddi Jagan was elected on a program of structural reform to head the government of the British colony of Guiana, an important source of bauxite and other metals. Several large U.S. companies, including Reynolds Metals and Kennecott Copper, had substantial holdings in the colony. Alarmed at the prospect of nationalization of these holdings by a Marxist regime, the United States urged the British to nullify the election; the British government duly sent troops to Guiana and deposed the new government.

The Eisenhower administration employed yet other tactics in Guatemala in 1954: conspiring to overthrow a democratically elected government whose reforms threatened the interests of a large and influential U.S. corporation. In 1944 a revolution toppled the oppressive regime of Jorge Ubico, who had ruled Guatemala since 1931. The victorious middle-class revolutionaries favored a capitalist course of development and were friendly to the United States. However, the reform programs of Presidents Juan José Arévalo (1945–1951) and Jacobo Arbenz (1951–1954) provoked the hostility of the United Fruit Company (UFCO) and Dulles. UFCO had operated in Guatemala since the 1890s, when it acquired a virtual monopoly on banana production and distribution. It was Guatemala's largest employer, with ten thousand workers, and its largest landowner. The company also controlled the nation's main transportation artery, the International Railways of Central America (IRCA), and major port facilities on the Gulf of Mexico.

The Guatemalan government clashed with UFCO over labor and land reform. Arévalo enacted a new labor code in 1947. The company, charging that it was being discriminated against, protested

sharply. The ensuing labor agitation severely hampered banana production for several years. In 1952 the Guatemalan Congress enacted a land reform program, expropriating large tracts of uncultivated land for distribution among landless peasants. Again, UFCO charged the government with discrimination.

Unfortunately for the Guatemalan government, UFCO enjoyed great influence with the U.S. government. It was a client of Dulles's law firm. Also, the company's headquarters were in Boston, which made it a constituent of three of the most powerful men in the United States Congress: Senator Henry Cabot Lodge, Speaker of the House Joseph Martin, and Democratic Party leader John McCormack. What was more, the family of the assistant secretary of state in charge of Guatemalan relations, John Moors Cabot, was a major stockholder in United Fruit.

Seizing on allegations of communist participation in the Arbenz government to justify its actions, the United States trained and outfitted a rebel group under the command of Carlos Castillo Armas. Castillo Armas invaded Guatemala through UFCO property and overthrew Arbenz in June 1954. His repressive regime, which lasted until his assassination in 1957, erased all of the postwar reforms and restored UFCO's privileges.

## THE CUBAN REVOLUTION AND UNITED STATES– LATIN AMERICAN RELATIONS

Eisenhower's successful interventions in Bolivia, British Guiana, and Guatemala produced bitter criticism of the United States in Latin America and contributed to the hostile and violent reception accorded Vice President Richard Nixon on his tour of the region in 1958. No major change in policy, however, occurred until the victory of Fidel Castro in Cuba in 1959.

The United States, a steadfast supporter of Batista's cruel dictatorship, consistently had opposed Castro's revolutionary movement and later embarked on a two-pronged program designed to destroy his government. To avert new Cubas, U.S. policymakers simultaneously sought to placate the rest of Latin America with various concessions. Meanwhile, they imposed economic sanctions on Cuba and began clandestinely to train an invasion force of Cuban exiles. To ensure Latin American backing, the United States committed limited funds to a new Social Trust Fund for the region and agreed to support plans for common markets in the area, such as the Latin American Free Trade Association (LAFTA) and the Central American Common Market, proposals which it had long opposed.

Under the new administration of John F. Kennedy, these economic reforms developed into a comprehensive plan for the region, the Alliance for Progress. The United States pledged to spend $10 billion in the region over ten years, to build badly needed transportation facilities and to buy technology and industrial equipment. In return, Latin American governments were to institute programs of social and political reform. The United States proposed to foster democracy and economic justice in Latin America through a program of incentives. To guard against more radical movements like the Castro-led guerrilla movement in Cuba, the U.S. government also undertook to strengthen the military forces of the region with arms and training.

The Alliance for Progress, however, brought neither economic development nor democracy to Latin America. In the first place, the program was not intended to be philanthropic but rather to foster capitalist, private-sector development and to expand U.S. trade and investments. Much aid to the region was in the form of loans that eventually had to be repaid. Moreover, aid money had to be used to buy U.S. products transported on U.S. ships; by eliminating competition, such restrictions reduced the developmental impact of aid. Although the U.S. government and private sources pumped $10 billion into Latin America during the 1960s, more than that amount of capital flowed out from the area. Debt service payments ate up an increasing share of the budgets of Latin American nations, leaving little for social welfare expenditures and economic development. Often, these nations had to obtain new loans just to pay off their old debts. Unfortunately, too, a significant percentage of aid funds was dissipated through corruption and inefficiency.

U.S. support for the Latin American military was the most effective program of the Alliance. Officers from the region received the most modern training in counterinsurgency tactics against both rural and urban guerrillas and were indoctrinated in the U.S. worldview. Sophisticated torture techniques formed part of the curriculum. One indication of the thoroughness of the training was the success of U.S.-trained and equipped Bolivian rangers in hunting down Che Guevara and his comrades. The United States also urged Latin American military leaders to take a more positive role in their nations' development by participating in civic action programs in which military personnel built roads and other public facilities.

It was clear, however, that despite the Kennedy administration's avowed goal of helping Latin America "strike off the remaining bonds of poverty and ignorance," its major concern was to maintain friendly capitalist regimes in the region. Kennedy continued to interfere in the internal affairs of countries in the area, even after the debacle of the Bay of Pigs. In 1961 he attempted to destroy the regime of Cheddi Jagan in British Guiana for a second time by refusing to grant much-needed aid and pressing the British to overturn the democratically elected premier. The CIA also helped subvert the Jagan government. Kennedy was involved in attempts to rid the Dominican Republic of Rafael Trujillo, and there are allegations that the CIA was responsible for the assassination of the dictator in 1961. In his zeal to get rid of Fidel Castro, Kennedy even planned to enlist the aid of the Mafia to liquidate the Cuban leader.

Like its predecessors, the Kennedy administration supported dictatorial regimes in Latin America when U.S. policymakers considered them the only alternative to disorder and possible revolution. In March 1962 the United States made no protest when the Argentine military overthrew the democratically elected President Arturo Frondizi. Four months later, the U.S.-trained and equipped Peruvian army seized power to prevent a democratically elected president from taking office. For a time, the United States withheld recognition and cut off aid, but it soon reached an understanding with the military regime. Like its predecessors, the

Kennedy administration preferred order, even at the expense of democracy.

President Lyndon Johnson carried on Kennedy's Latin American program, although he increasingly shifted the emphasis of U.S. policy from reform to the maintenance of order. Johnson was determined that he, unlike Kennedy, would not "lose" any nation in any part of the world to communism. In the Dominican Republic in 1965, Johnson faced a rebellion against a reactionary military regime that less than two years before had overthrown the nation's first democratically elected president. Johnson claimed that the United States had the right to intervene unilaterally in Latin America to prevent what he feared would be a Castro-like communist takeover. He dispatched the Marines to suppress the rebellion. Johnson was undoubtedly worried about another Cuba in the Dominican Republic, but there is considerable evidence to indicate that his administration's main concern was to assure Dominican sugar production for several important U.S. firms. Not coincidentally, several of Johnson's key foreign policy advisers, including Ellsworth Bunker and W. Averell Harriman, had close links to the sugar industry.

Under Johnson, the United States also played a major role in the military overthrow of the leftward-leaning regime of João Goulart in Brazil in 1964. Disapproving of Goulart's proposed "radical" reforms—which included a mild land reform and the grant of the vote to illiterates—the United States cut aid to Brazil to a minimum in 1963 and began to channel funds instead to pro-U.S. state governors. In April 1964 the Brazilian military toppled Goulart and instituted fifteen years of brutal, repressive dictatorship. The Johnson administration immediately recognized the new government. In the next five years, the United States poured more than $1.5 billion in economic and military aid into Brazil, one-quarter of all U.S. aid to Latin America.

The lavish aid funneled to the Brazilian military helped persuade the Argentine military that they should overthrow the faltering regime of President Arturo Illia in June 1966. The United States gave the military government $135 million in aid during the three years following the coup.

In political as well as socioeconomic terms, the results of the Alliance under Kennedy and Johnson were dismaying. When Kennedy took office, Alfredo Stroessner in Paraguay was the only dictator in power in South America. By 1968 military dictators ruled in Argentina, Brazil, and Peru, as well as in Paraguay. In Bolivia and Ecuador, civilian-elected governments served as figureheads for the military. In Central America, the record was worse. Rightist military coups overthrew democratically elected governments in Honduras, Guatemala, and El Salvador. The Somozas tightened their grip on Nicaragua. In 1968 a military coup ousted the elected president of Panama. More important, by every measure, the Alliance failed to stimulate economic development or rectify the immense economic and social inequalities of Latin America.

## THE VIETNAM ERA

From the late 1960s until 1981, the repercussions of the disastrous U.S. experience in Vietnam and related developments produced readjustments in U.S. foreign policy toward its southern neighbors. But the main goal of this policy—to protect and expand North American economic interests and maintain capitalism as the dominant economic system in the region—remained constant.

In the aftermath of Vietnam, U.S. policymakers did not regard overt military intervention as a realistic option. They relied on such indirect methods as economic sanctions and subversion. The United States used these methods in Chile from 1970 to 1973 to undermine and ultimately to topple a democratically elected socialist government.

The story began in 1958, when the Socialist Salvador Allende narrowly missed victory in the Chilean presidential election. For the next fifteen years, the U.S. government poured millions of dollars into Chile, first to prevent Allende from winning subsequent elections, and then, after his election in 1970, to subvert his administration. The United States helped Eduardo Frei, a moderate reformer, win the presidency and thereafter sent an average of $130 million a year in aid to Chile. Despite this enormous effort and the injection of more millions of dollars in the 1970 campaign, Allende was elected president in 1970.

The United States then tried to orchestrate a military coup d'état, but when it failed, Nixon imposed economic sanctions on the Allende government, cutting aid by 90 percent and denying credit. Meanwhile, the CIA cooperated with opposition groups to destabilize the Chilean economy. Amid growing economic difficulties and political turmoil, the Chilean military overthrew Allende in a bloody coup in September 1973. The United States promptly recognized the military junta and resumed aid and credit.

The U.S. economic stake in Chile, as we saw in Chapter 14, was large and concentrated primarily in copper mining. The first act of the Allende government, supported by the unanimous vote of the Chilean Congress, had been to expropriate the holdings of the U.S. copper companies without compensation. Later, it expropriated the International Telephone and Telegraph Company, whose president enjoyed considerable influence in the Nixon administration. The United States intervened both to protect these investments and to teach a salutary lesson to other Latin American nations that might wish to construct a socialist society in the future.

Nixon also collaborated with brutal military regimes in Argentina and Brazil that organized an international terrorist network, later known as Operation Condor, designed to destroy leftist, antidictatorial political movements throughout South America. An early example of this cooperation developed in response to popular support for the *Frente Amplio* (Broad Front), a coalition of Socialists, Communists, and Christian Democrats, in the 1971 Uruguayan presidential elections. Determined to reduce "the threat of a political takeover by the Frente," Nixon systematically cultivated Brazilian and Argentine military leaders and, in the words of a U.S. Embassy strategy paper, encouraged them to "collaborate effectively with the Uruguayan security forces" to harass Frente candidates and otherwise intervene in the election to secure their defeat. According to a declassified document recently published by the National Security Archive, Nixon himself told British Prime Minister Edward Heath that he knew "Brazil helped rig the Uruguayan elections."

Nixon and his National Security Adviser Henry Kissinger especially identified with these dictators. After a series of personal meetings with Brazil's Garrastazu Médici, Nixon described him as a "strong" ruler whom he wished "were running the whole continent." Kissinger made clear his growing reliance on Brazil as a proxy for U.S. interests in the region. "In areas of mutual concern such as the situations in Uruguay and Bolivia," Kissinger confided to Médici, referring to Brazilian involvement in a 1971 Bolivian coup, "close cooperation and parallel approaches can be very helpful for our common objectives." But Kissinger also made clear his understanding that massive intervention in the internal affairs of sovereign nations, such as he and Médici were contemplating, would not endear them to Latin American people. "[A]s Brazil plays a stronger leadership role," Kissinger lectured, "it may find itself in a position similar to that of the U.S.—respected and admired, but not liked."

### CARTER'S LATIN AMERICAN POLICY: NATIONALISM, THE CANAL, AND HUMAN RIGHTS

President Jimmy Carter took office in 1977 proclaiming a "new approach" for U.S. foreign policy based on "a high regard for the individuality and sovereignty of each Latin American and Caribbean nation . . . our respect for human rights, . . . [and] our desire to press forward on the great issues which affect the relations between the developed and developing nations." He immediately put these principles into practice in two major initiatives: the reopening of negotiations with Panama over the canal and the beginning of talks with Cuba about normalization of relations.

Periodically since the signing of the original canal treaty, Panamanians violently protested the U.S. presence in the middle of their country; serious anti-U.S. riots erupted in 1931, 1947, 1959, and 1964. These riots occurred in times of economic hardship in Panama and remained a source of tension that Carter and General Omar Torrijos sought to remove. After four years of sometimes bitter negotiations, the United States and Panama agreed to a new treaty that gradually returned control of the Canal Zone to Panama by the year 2000. Although Panamanians were unhappy with a provision that gave the United States the right to intervene to maintain the operation of the canal, it was received with general satisfaction in Panama and throughout Latin America.

Negotiations with Cuba led eventually to the opening of United States and Cuban Interest Sections in Havana and Washington in September 1977. These initiatives were short-lived, however, for the two nations came into conflict early in 1978 over Cuba's extensive military involvement in Africa, particularly in Angola and Ethiopia. The Carter administration strenuously objected to the presence of thirty-five thousand Cuban troops in Africa and broke off further talks as a result. Relations worsened during 1980 as a consequence of the exodus of 125,000 Cuban refugees to the United States.

Carter's pursuit of human rights proved to be the most controversial aspect of his foreign policy. He centered his attention on Chile, Argentina, and Brazil, the harshest practitioners of repression in the region. The United States instituted sanctions against all of these nations, ending or reducing economic and military aid and impeding their ability to obtain credit from international lending agencies. In the last two years of his term, as a result of stepped-up pressure from U.S. business and concern about growing communist influence in Central America, Carter backed off his human rights activism.

Nicaragua proved to be Carter's most difficult and pressing problem in Latin America. The growing insurrection of the Sandinista National Liberation Front, a broad coalition movement against the U.S.-backed dictator Anastasio Somoza, brought Nicaragua to crisis in 1978. Carter, worried about leftist elements in the Sandinista coalition, sought a more moderate alternative, proposing at one point that the Sandinistas include members of the hated National Guard in the postrevolution Nicaraguan government. Following the Sandinista victory in 1979, the United States offered economic aid to rebuild the nation devastated by civil war. After

considerable debate the U.S. Congress approved $75 million, most of which was designed to support private-sector businesses that opposed the Sandinista government.

# The Return to "Gunboat Diplomacy," 1981–2003

Ronald Reagan became president in 1981 determined to turn back "communism" in Latin America and reassert U.S. military power. In the process he openly courted repressive right-wing regimes in Argentina and Chile and committed substantial amounts of U.S. money and military advisers to the antiguerrilla war in Central America. During the next two decades, the U.S. decision to intervene militarily or to refrain from intervention revealed traditional U.S. open-door objectives, perhaps most concisely articulated by John Hay in 1898: "a fair field and no favor."

### GRENADA

On October 25, 1983, the United States invaded the tiny island nation of Grenada in the southern Caribbean to oust its allegedly communist, pro-Cuban government. The Reagan administration proclaimed the invasion its greatest triumph in Latin American policy.

In March 1979 the New Jewel Movement, led by Maurice Bishop, had overthrown the British and U.S.-backed dictatorship of Eric Gairy, who had dominated Grenadan politics since the early 1950s. Bishop's program included a massive literacy campaign, the institution of free medical care, free secondary education, and extensive rehabilitation of housing. He regulated foreign investment and stressed agricultural independence, reducing Grenadan food imports. Bishop began to expand tourism, mainly by building a modern airport. The Reagan administration threatened repeatedly to intervene against the popular Bishop regime, but finally invaded Grenada after a radical faction of Bishop's own party had assassinated him.

The invasion of Grenada showed clearly that the United States was as willing as ever to use force to protect its perceived interests in the Caribbean.

The action also conveyed the message—as did U.S. policies in Central America—that the United States opposed far-reaching economic and social reform in its "back yard." Moreover, Grenada, like so many other "crises" in the region, was not seen as a nation struggling to overcome impoverishment, but as part of a worldwide communist threat or at the very least as "another Cuba."

## HAITI

The United States played a decisive role in the history of Haiti, the poorest country in Latin America and one of the poorest in the world.

During the long U.S. military occupation of Haiti from 1915 to 1934, the Haitian elite's monopoly of property was preserved and its dependence on coffee exports was reinforced. The U.S. also trained a national army "specifically to fight Haitians." This army imposed the rule of the sinister François "Papa Doc" Duvalier on Haiti in 1957. Duvalier in turn used the army to centralize power in his own hands to an unprecedented degree. He could not tolerate the existence of any independent institution; distrusting his own army, he organized two parallel paramilitary organizations, a much-feared militia and the overlapping secret police, the even more dreaded Tontons Macoutes. The United States may not have approved of his methods, but it supported him, and when he died in 1971 U.S. Ambassador Clinton Knox personally supervised the transition to the rule of the dictator's son, eighteen-year-old Jean-Claude Duvalier.

The predatory, repressive rule of the Duvaliers aggravated all of Haiti's economic and social problems. The ruin of Haitian agriculture as a result of long misuse of the land and the exactions of the regime caused many thousands of impoverished peasants to flock into the urban centers, especially the shantytowns of Port-au-Prince and its environs where between 1.2 and 1.8 million people endured unspeakable conditions. Workers' families usually ate only one meal a day, consisting of cornmeal with onions or boiled plantains with beans.

Acting on U.S. advice, Jean-Claude Duvalier tried to promote economic growth by using this vast underclass to establish export-assembly industries, subcontracted to U.S. firms. But this program did not diminish the immense inequalities of Haitian society or the growing anger of the masses. In 1986 an explosion of urban rioting forced Jean-Claude to depart from Haiti; he was whisked away to a luxurious exile in a jet provided by the Reagan administration. The U.S. Agency for International Development (USAID), meanwhile, continued to promote Haiti as a low-wage haven for U.S. firms, expending $100 million in the effort. A delegation of U.S. trade-union leaders, visiting a "model" apparel factory in Haiti's export-assembly sector in 1991, found that the highest-paid workers received the equivalent of $1.47 a day. After paying for transportation and a meager breakfast and lunch they had 71 cents to take home.

Jean-Claude Duvalier's departure created a political vacuum that U.S. policymakers rushed to fill. They supported Marc Bazin, linked to export-assembly industries and agribusinesses, and opposed Jean-Bertrand Aristide, a populist priest influenced by liberation theology. Aristide represented grassroots worker, peasant, and student organizations. He supported a massive literacy campaign, land reform, defense of national industries, and an end to Duvalierist violence and corruption. His program included price controls on basic foodstuffs and raising the minimum hourly wage to fifty cents. Despite U.S. support and a $36 million campaign, Bazin lost to Aristide, who received 67 percent of the vote. But he held power for only eight months; in September 1991 a military coup headed by Lieutenant General Raoul Cédras forced him into exile. The coup unleashed a reign of terror in Haiti, claiming thousands of lives and causing a flood of refugees.

The Bush administration's response to the coup was marked by an ambiguity reflecting the contradictions of U.S. foreign policy. The United States rhetorically claimed to support constitutionally elected civilian regimes like Aristide's, but Aristide's anti-imperialism and opposition to neoliberalism contradicted basic U.S. foreign policy objectives. President Bush denounced the coup and said he wanted Aristide's return to power. But this pro-Aristide rhetoric was contradicted by a policy of limiting sanctions against the coup leaders to a "porous" embargo easily breached by exporters and importers and of permitting open attacks against Aristide by a State Department–driven media campaign and CIA leaks casting doubt on his mental stability. The U.S. government also pressured him to moderate his positions and strike a deal with the coup leaders.

President Clinton continued Bush's Haitian policy, virtually unchanged, when he took office in January 1993. He forced Aristide to negotiate with the coup leaders and sought to impose conditions that would leave Aristide powerless to carry out his program, once returned to power. This was the essence of the 1993 Governors Island Accord, which called for the military rulers to resign, with the promise of amnesty, and for Aristide to return to power under the control of U.N. monitors and "peacekeeping" forces, an arrangement vehemently opposed by Haitian popular organizations. But U.S. and Canadian troops refused to enforce the agreement when about 100 armed anti-Aristide thugs demonstrated at the port and threatened foreign diplomats. The quick pull-back suggested Pentagon and CIA reluctance to be involved in restoring Aristide to power on any terms.

Even after Clinton talked openly of a military intervention to restore Aristide to the presidency, according to *The Nation*, he made it "distressingly clear that Haitian independence is not on their minds, and that if exiled President Jean-Bertrand Aristide is returned at the head of an American expeditionary force, the result will be continued clienthood, not freedom."

In the event, after a barrage of publicity about an impending invasion to oust Haiti's military rulers if they did not leave peacefully, a carefully staged "solution" of the Haitian problem came with startling suddenness. On the evening of September 18, 1994, a U.S. delegation led by ex-president Jimmy Carter and the Haitian military signed an accord that provided "an early and honorable retirement" for "certain military officers," full amnesty for all human rights abuses, the eventual return of President Aristide to serve out his term, which ended in 1996, and new elections in December 1995. The accord envisioned that a U.S. occupation force of some fifteen thousand troops

The role for former president Jimmy Carter, shown here with the Haitian president Jean-Bertrand Aristide, in negotiating the accord with the military junta that restored Aristide to office in October 1994, displeased many Haitians who believed the accord was too favorable to the military and seriously abrogated Aristide's power. [AP/Wide World Photos]

would remain for an indefinite period to retrain the Haitian army and police.

Aristide's return to Haiti in October 1994 was greeted with joyful demonstrations by his adoring followers. It soon became clear, however, that he was not his own man; on issue after issue his U.S. military and political advisers forced him to back down. Aristide wanted to fire the entire army high command and supervise the formation of a new army and police within his government, but the U.S. military vetoed his plan. The new "professionalized" army and police would be "retrained" and "candidates" for "professionalization" would be drawn largely from the old armed forces, many of the officers and specialists of which had been trained at the notorious School of the Americas at Ft. Benning, Georgia.

Aristide's candidate for prime minister, who had served as foreign minister in his previous government, was turned down by the Haitian business sector and U.S. officials, and the president was forced to accept businessman Smarck Michel to head the new twenty-member cabinet. Virtually none of its members represented the grassroots movement that had brought Aristide to power, but the cabinet was full of people who supported and benefited from the coup d'état. U.S. advisers were working in key offices and ministries to advise Haiti in its return to democracy. Critics complained that in addition to pro-coup politicians and U.S. advisers, Aristide's chief allies appeared to be the Haitian business sector (whom he once described as "patriots of the pocketbook") and U.S. Ambassador William Swing, who almost always accompanied him when he left the palace.

Under U.S. pressure, Aristide scrapped his nationalist program for reviving Haiti's state industries and accepted a program of neoliberal "structural readjustment" of the economy, by which those industries would be sold to private capitalists, both Haitian and U.S. As summarized by Allan Nairn, the plan included, among other features, commitments from Haiti "to eliminate the jobs of half of its civil servants, massively privatize public services, 'drastically' slash tariffs and import restrictions, eschew price and foreign exchange controls, grant 'emergency' aid to the export sector, enforce an 'open foreign investment policy' . . . 'limit the scope of state activity' and regulation . . . and diminish the power of Aristide's executive branch in favor of the more conservative Parliament." In return, Haiti would receive $700 million in financial aid, but $80 million of this would immediately go to pay the debt accrued to foreign bankers in the three years since the coup.

Ordinary Haitians were surprised at what had happened to their idol. The Aristide they elected came to power as the representative of a massive grassroots movement, calling itself the *lavalas* (flood), that proposed to attack the country's fundamental social problems and end the traditional monopoly of power by a repressive military allied with a corrupt merchant bourgeoisie and U.S. economic interests. The new Aristide appeared to have

cut a deal with the World Bank and the IMF that sacrificed the popular welfare in exchange for $700 million in aid. Chevannes Jean-Baptiste, leader of Haiti's largest peasant organization, had already warned against premature celebration of Aristide's return in the wake of the U.S. invasion: "Don't celebrate and think that the U.S. army is here to liberate us. Only Haitians can free Haiti!"

## Central America

Ronald Reagan's campaigns against the leftist Sandinista regime in Nicaragua and the leftist Farabundo Martí National Liberation Front (FMLN) in El Salvador took on all the characteristics of a holy crusade against communist forces in Central America. Reagan opposed the nationalistic efforts of both groups to use state power to regulate private property and foreign trade to benefit the nation's poor peasants and urban workers. He sought to overthrow the Sandinistas, employing tactics that included economic sanctions, a campaign of public misinformation, support of rightist counterrevolutionary armies (the contras), and covert terrorist operations aided by the CIA.

One of Reagan's first official acts in 1981 was to cut off the last $15 million in aid appropriated by Congress at President Carter's request. More severe economic sanctions followed. By the end of 1985, the United States had effectively foreclosed any possibility of the Sandinistas obtaining loans from any of the major international lending agencies, such as the World Bank or the Inter-American Development Bank. The U.S. government closed Nicaragua's consulates and even forbade the Nicaraguan airline from landing in the United States. The misinformation campaign included unproven allegations against the Sandinistas of running arms to El Salvador, smuggling illegal drugs, and training terrorists.

By far the most damaging U.S. policy against the Sandinistas was support of the armed opposition to the Nicaraguan government. Predominantly led by ex-Somocista National Guardsmen, the contras were the 1979 creation of the CIA, which recruited ex-guardsman Enrique Bermúdez as their leader. In Reagan's first year in office, he secretly funneled $40 million to support these counterrevolutionaries. The CIA forged the Nicaraguan Democratic Force in late 1981, temporarily unifying the contra factions.

Frustrated with Reagan's policy, the U.S. Congress passed the so-called Boland Amendment, which forbade the use of funds to overthrow the Sandinistas; this legislation was in effect from December 1982 until December 1983, but the Reagan administration, in violation of the law, continued to provide covert support. In early 1984 the CIA mined Nicaraguan harbors and staged several helicopter attacks inside Nicaragua. Later that year a CIA manual became public that advised the contras to employ terrorist tactics, including assassinations. The ensuing furor led the Congress to cut off aid to the contras. Nonetheless, by 1987 the United States had invested $200 million in support of the contras and had little to show for it. The counterrevolutionaries were corrupt and quarrelsome, their civilian and military leaders hopelessly divided, and they had made no military headway in overthrowing the Nicaraguan government.

Evidently fearing that the Sandinistas would win a free and fair election in Nicaragua, the Reagan and Bush administrations obstructed the peace process initiated by the Guatemala City Accords of August 1987 and continued to provide millions in "humanitarian" aid to the contras until February 25, 1990, the date of the elections. The United States also gave millions of dollars in aid to the anti-Sandinista coalition (UNO). Exhausted by almost ten years of U.S.-supported contra war and the U.S. economic blockade, Nicaraguans by a large majority voted in the UNO candidate for president, Violeta Chamorro.

In the process of taking over the counterinsurgency war in El Salvador, the United States took over the nation's economy and politics as well. The United States consistently interfered in Salvadoran politics, successfully keeping the far right, led by Roberto D'Aubuisson, from taking power in 1984 and shoring up the tottering centrist government of President José Napoleon Duarte.

The United States poured some $4.5 billion from 1979 to 1990 into a futile military effort to defeat the FMLN guerrillas. This included massive military assistance in the form of equipment and training. Between fifty and a hundred U.S. advisers planned the counterinsurgency campaign, sometimes accompanying Salvadoran government troops in antiguerrilla forays. For a time, during 1984 and 1985, the Salvadoran army kept the guerrillas at bay because of its advantages in equipment. By early 1987, however, the FMLN was again striking at government forces and installations in almost every part of the country at will. Under domestic and U.S. pressure, both Duarte and his successors initiated peace talks with the guerrillas that led to peace accords in 1992 providing for reform of the armed forces and security services, dismantling of FMLN military structures, and elections in which leftist parties, for the first time in El Salvador's history, could take part.

## THE INVASION OF PANAMA

Upon his election as president in 1988, George Bush vigorously continued Reagan's Latin American policy of maintaining and reinforcing U.S. dominance over the region. The new noninterventionist course pursued by the Soviet Union, which withdrew its troops from Afghanistan and made no effort to prevent the collapse of Stalinist-type regimes in Eastern and central Europe, was interpreted by Washington to mean that its freedom of action was no longer hampered by the possibility of a Soviet response. Most Latin American countries, mired in the greatest depression in the continent's history and heavily indebted to U.S. banks, were unlikely to make more than token protests against U.S. interventionist actions. If the end of the cold war deprived U.S. imperialism of its stock in trade, the bogeyman of "international communism," a new villain, the Latin American *narcotraficante*, the drug trafficker, provided a convenient pretext for an armed intervention that could advance traditional U.S. strategic and economic interests.

Bush justified the December 1989 invasion of Panama by the need to protect U.S. citizens (a U.S. Marine had been killed in a shooting incident), defend democracy, seize dictator Manuel Antonio Noriega on drug charges, and protect the canal.

These arguments convinced few foreign governments; the great majority denounced or deplored the invasion as a violation of the U.N. charter, the Organization of American States, and the Panama Canal Treaty. But they were accepted without questioning by the U.S. press, which "did little more than parrot the Bush administration's transparent legal justifications for the invasion." The press ignored the fact that until he began to display an inconvenient nationalist independence and stopped being "our man in Panama," Noriega was a prized ally of the United States, receiving, by conservative estimates, more than $1.2 million in payoffs from the CIA just during the last ten years of his thirty-year connection with the agency. As regards his drug connections, as recently as February 1987 Noriega had received a letter from the U.S. Drug Enforcement Administration (DEA), expressing its gratitude for his traditional position of support for the DEA and the cooperation of his army. The notion that Bush, the former CIA director, did not know of Noriega's drug links strains one's credulity.

The press overlooked, too, long-standing Republican objections to the Carter-Torrijos canal treaties, which provided that in the year 2000 the canal would become Panamanian territory and the U.S. military bases would be dismantled. A document titled "Santa Fe II: A Strategy for Latin America in the Nineties," issued during the 1988 campaign and reflecting the views of the Republican right, in effect provided a blueprint for the invasion, stressing the need for the replacement of Noriega by a "democratic regime" with which the United States would hold talks concerning "the United States' retention of limited facilities in Panama . . . for proper force projection throughout the Western Hemisphere." These and other recommendations in the Santa Fe document closely conformed to the Bush administration's Panama policies.

The administration proclaimed "Operation Just Cause" a huge success. Panamanian resistance was soon broken by intense bombardment. Twenty-four American soldiers were killed; estimates of the Panamanian death toll ranged from Washington's figure of 516 to the figure given by an independent commission of inquiry of between 3,000 and 4,000, the great majority being civilians. The areas hardest hit by the invasion were the poorest neighborhoods of Panama City, inhabited primarily by black and mixed-race people. Thousands were made homeless and resettled in refugee camps that often lacked medical care, sanitary facilities, and food. It was estimated that the invasion had cost $2 billion in damages and reduced the country's economic life, already moribund as a result of U.S. economic sanctions, to paralysis.

In the midst of the invasion, a new president and two vice presidents were sworn in, fittingly enough at a military base of the U.S. Southern Command. The new president, Guillermo Endara, represented the traditional oligarchy of very wealthy white families (90 percent of Panama's 2,200,000 population is black, mulatto, or mestizo) who lost their political but not their economic power as a result of a reformist, nationalist 1968 revolution led by Omar Torrijos. This handful of families, linked by intermarriage and corporate boards, controlled some 150 of Panama's principal businesses. Once again, U.S. policy had rescued propertied elites and preserved open markets for trade and investment.

## LATIN AMERICA AND THE GULF WAR

Latin America felt the impact of the crisis that began with the Iraqi invasion of Kuwait in August 1990 and erupted into the short but destructive Gulf War in February 1991. For most countries of the region, heavily dependent on oil imports, the economic effects of the dramatic rise in oil prices were profoundly negative. Brazil, the largest oil importer, was particularly hard hit, for it had a barter arrangement with Iraq whereby it paid for oil with manufactured goods, and U.N. sanctions against Iraq forced Brazil to use its limited hard currency to buy oil from other sources at world market prices. The region's oil exporters—Venezuela, Mexico, Ecuador, Colombia, and Trinidad and Tobago—profited by increasing their oil exports to compensate for the loss of Iraqi and Kuwaiti supplies and to take advantage of the sharp rise in crude oil prices. But even they stood to lose in the long run—the unexpectedly quick ending of the war left them with large oil surpluses, forcing prices down to much lower levels.

Although most Latin Americans condemned Iraq's invasion of Kuwait, polls showed that they opposed the war option by equal or even greater majorities. In Argentina, whose government was the only one to give military aid to the coalition led by the United States, 91 percent of those questioned opposed Argentina's participation in the war and demanded the return of the two warships sent to join the multinational force. In general, editorial opinion was strongly critical of President Bush's haste to abandon reliance on sanctions against Iraq in favor of war, his rejection of various peace proposals, and the massive destruction of life and material resources caused by the war. There was widespread skepticism, too, regarding Bush's professions of concern for self-determination by critics who recalled the U.S. invasions of Panama and Grenada and the covert war against Nicaragua. Many regarded Bush's call for a "new world order" as a thin disguise for the vision of a unipolar world dominated by the United States, the only superpower.

## Toward a New World Order?

With the collapse of the Soviet Union, U.S. policy in Latin America focused on promoting free trade. The Clinton administration's stand on a series of issues—economic policy toward Latin America, Cuba, human rights, and the drug problem— reflected this essential continuity in foreign policy.

With the IMF and World Bank as "enforcers," U.S. policy used debt as a powerful coercive weapon to impose on Latin America a neoliberal economic system based on free trade and privatization. That system required Latin American countries to nullify past advances toward economic independence, to sell at bargain prices valuable national enterprises, and to enact austerity programs that helped increase the number of people living in poverty by 39 percent in the course of the 1980s. By the late 1990s, even the World Bank's conservative estimates of Latin American poverty had risen from

31.5 percent of the people in 1989 to 38 percent; worse still, this growing poverty was accompanied by modest economic growth.

The imposition of this system prepared the way for the logical next step, the incorporation of the area into a U.S.-dominated Western Hemisphere common market that would aid the United States in its growing competition with Japan and Europe. The continuity of the Reagan-Bush-Clinton policies in this area was illustrated by the North American Free Trade Agreement with Mexico, negotiated by Bush and pushed through Congress by Clinton over the virtually unanimous opposition of the labor movement that had ensured his election. Similar free-trade agreements were projected with other Latin American countries, beginning with Chile.

Given the absence of strong trade-union movements in many Latin American countries, including some, like Mexico, where democracy was little more than a façade, NAFTA-type agreements in effect placed U.S. and Latin American workers in competition to see who would produce goods for the U.S. and Canadian consumer markets for the lowest possible wages. According to Public Citizen's Trade Watch, although the Clinton administration had promised 200,000 new jobs per year in the United States, after five years it was unable to document any new jobs produced by NAFTA even as it certified that nearly 215,000 U.S. workers were casualties of the agreement. While maquiladoras lured to Mexico by NAFTA grew by 37 percent and employment skyrocketed, Mexican workers' wages fell by 29 percent since 1994. As a result of NAFTA, poverty rates in Mexico in 1999 rose to 60 percent from an annual average of 34 percent between 1984 and 1994.

In conjunction with provisions of the Uruguay round of the General Agreement on Tariffs and Trade (GATT), these free-trade agreements also posed a major threat to environmental standards. The agreements with Canada and Mexico, for example, set up unelected trinational boards, made up of trade experts, as secret and final arbiters in all decisions relating to commerce and trade. Any federal, state, or local law or regulation, no matter how democratically arrived at,

NAFTA, originally touted as a boon to Mexico both by U.S. opponents and proponents, actually has bankrupted many peasant farmers and led to increased pollution, lower wages, less safe working conditions, and greater political unrest. [Jack Kurtz/ Impact Visuals]

could be set aside by a NAFTA disputation board that identified it as an impediment to trade. The "side agreements" added to Clinton's version of the NAFTA package made the process of challenging a labor rights or environmental violation so difficult and time-consuming that a Mexican government official could "assure concerned industrialists that they should never worry about repercussions from NAFTA's labor and environmental enforcement boards." In fact, since 1993, complaints filed against corporations like General Electric and SONY were routinely dismissed, but even when the board certified a complaint against Han Young, a Korean subcontractor for Hyundai, it lacked mechanisms to enforce the decision.

The dangers of environmental pollution posed by NAFTA and GATT were of course much greater to Latin America than to the United States or

Canada. The Third World had already become what Eduardo Galeano calls "a kingdom of impunity" for environmental polluters. In the absence of strong grassroots opposition, NAFTA and GATT enhanced the trend to make the South "the garbage dump of the North."

Cuba provided another test of Clinton's willingness to rethink old and discredited Reagan-Bush policies. The United Nations Assembly three times voted overwhelmingly to condemn the U.S. embargo against Cuba; two summits of Latin American heads of state unanimously voted the same way; and a growing number of Cuban-Americans opposed a policy that inflicted hardships on their relatives on the island and obstructed further liberalization of the Cuban regime. The United States had long maintained normal relations with one great communist power,

China, and in early 1994, in apparent response to pressure from U.S. business circles, President Clinton lifted economic sanctions against communist Vietnam, with which the United States once had fought a long and bloody war. As regards Cuba, however, Clinton appeared frozen in the most hard-line cold war attitude. In part this reflected his political debt to the most powerful and ultra-right Cuban-American leader, Jorge Mas Canosa, son of a Batista official, who, until his death in 1997, controlled the Miami-based Cuban American National Foundation and numerous political action committees whose sole reason for existence was to bring about Fidel Castro's downfall. In what was called "a shameless piece of pandering for the votes of extremist elements of Florida's Cuban exile community," during the election campaign Clinton threatened "to drop the hammer on Cuba." He lost Florida anyway but reportedly received millions of dollars in campaign contributions from Mas Canosa's foundation.

On the subject of human rights, the Clinton administration displayed the opportunism of its predecessors. Clinton claimed to favor civilian regimes and oppose dictatorships and military coups. In practice, however, that position was applied selectively, pragmatically, taking account of the relationship of the country in question to the United States and its acceptance or rejection of U.S.-sponsored economic policies. Thus, the Clinton administration remained silent when the Mexican army and paramilitary organizations ran amuck in Chiapas, carrying out summary executions, torture of prisoners, and aerial attacks on civilian populations. Indeed, U.S. military sales and assistance to Mexico, at a historically low total of $214 million from 1988 to 1992, suddenly skyrocketed to $78 million in 1994 alone and annually averaged well over $100 million thereafter. The number of Mexican officers trained at the U.S. School of the Americas also increased dramatically, from an annual average of 7 to 10 before 1982 to 149 in 1996 and 305 in 1997. With its passage of NAFTA, Mexico, of course, had become a favored U.S. junior partner. The Clinton administration took the same benign attitude toward Peru's President Fujimori's *autogolpe* ("self-

coup") after he proved his firm loyalty to the neoliberal economic doctrine and program. In general, in the words of the *Washington Report on the Hemisphere*, "the Administration seems prepared to wink at moderate human rights violations provided they occur in a 'good cause,' like fighting leftist guerrillas."

Despite rhetoric to the contrary, Clinton continued to militarize the "war on drugs." He inherited from Bush a vast antidrug operation with a heavy stress on military involvement. Bush's 1990 Andean Initiative pledged $2.2 billion in military, legal, and economic assistance over five years to be used in the antidrug campaign. Much of the military assistance was openly employed by the Colombian and Peruvian governments for counterinsurgency campaigns that killed more peasants than insurgents. The United States offered no objection to this misuse of its aid. By Bush's last year in office, the U.S. Southern Command was involved in dozens of operations throughout Latin America. That "messy and unsuccessful engagement" continued under Clinton and involved thousands of soldiers and police and billions of dollars of U.S. taxpayers' money. In fact, Clinton's drug-war budget grew to $16 billion, then the highest in U.S. history. Yet the war failed to reduce the availability or use of drugs in the United States. In September 1993 a Senate Judiciary Committee report concluded: "Regrettably, America's drug epidemic is worse today than it was three years ago."

In the decade after the disintegration of the Soviet Union and its strategic restraints on the unilateral exercise of U.S. power, influential U.S. intellectuals and policymakers struggled to define the appropriate mix of economic, political, diplomatic, and military instruments necessary to govern a "new world order" based upon neoliberal principles of globalization, privatization, state deregulation, and free trade. In this task, they shared a certain sympathy with their British counterparts like Richard Cooper, foreign policy adviser to Britain's Prime Minister Tony Blair, who boldly declared in 2001 that "When dealing with the more old-fashioned kinds of states outside the postmodern continent of Europe, we need to revert to the rougher methods of an earlier era—force, pre-emptive attack, deception." Perhaps more bluntly than others, Cooper alleged, "The opportunity, perhaps even the need, for colonization is as great as it ever was in the 19th century" and called for the mobilization of "a new kind of imperialism."

In the United States, these same ideas emerged less candidly in discussions of "nation-building"— that is, external intervention in the sovereign affairs of underdeveloped nations to create institutions to facilitate the process of globalization and manage the growing popular opposition that its expansion inevitably seemed to produce. To this end, in 1994, under the direction of former U.S. Secretary of State Cyrus Vance, the Carnegie Corporation created the Commission on Preventing Deadly Conflict, the purpose of which, according to its 1997 report, was to promote nation-building through multilateral initiatives, including the use of external force. To identify those disputes in which such intervention was justified, the Commission stressed the need to develop "legal standards," against which it might measure regime legitimacy—that is, the degree to which "the responsibilities of governments to themselves and to their peoples" were carried out. This approach provided the intellectual foundation for many Clinton-era interventions in Latin America.

Also in 1997, however, a conservative organization, the Project for the New American Century (PNAC), founded by William Kristol and Robert Kagan, a Reagan-era deputy in the State Department's Bureau of Inter-American Affairs, took up a similar task, although it emphasized unilateral interference. Supported by many who would become high-ranking policymakers in the Bush administration (including Vice President Cheney), the PNAC openly called for a reassertion of the aggressive imperialist intervention that had characterized early-twentieth-century U.S. foreign affairs. According to its senior fellow, Thomas Donnelly, "American imperialism can bring with it new hopes of liberty, security, and prosperity; its attractions can soften the fear of overweening U.S. military power."

Although candidate George W. Bush in 2000 had denounced "liberal" exercises in nation-

building such as those contemplated by the Carnegie Commission, as president in 2001, he nonetheless continued to support Clinton's global initiatives. Especially after the September 11 terrorist attacks on the Pentagon and World Trade Center, however, the Bush foreign-policy team more vigorously embraced the PNAC's idea, if not the specific language, of unilateral imperialist intervention to protect and promote U.S. interests. "Sovereignty entails obligations," according to Richard Haass, director of policy planning in the Bush State Department. "If a government fails to meet these obligations, then it forfeits some of the normal advantages of sovereignty, including the right to be left alone inside your own territory. Other governments, including the U.S., gain the right to intervene."

Naturally, the key question was: What were the special "obligations" that the Bush administration expected sovereign nations to satisfy to avoid U.S. intervention? First and foremost, the president expected them to oppose terrorists who targeted the United States, but he also insisted that they promote free-market principles and practices. According to one administration spokesperson, U.S. policy stressed "the importance of ruling justly, the importance of investing in one's own people, and the importance of operating in an economic policy framework that creates openings for enterprise and entrepreneurship." This meant "sound economic policies" including "more open markets, sustainable budget policies, and strong support for individual entrepreneurship." Wherever a government or popular forces threatened these values or resisted market reforms, the Bush administration overtly intervened politically and sometimes threatened more serious economic and military intervention.

In Venezuela, for example, in the months prior to and during an ill-fated April 2002 military coup against the democratically elected populist president, Hugo Chávez, high-ranking U.S. government officials met repeatedly with military and civilian coup leaders, including Pedro Carmona, formerly head of the Venezuelan Chamber of Commerce (*Fedecámaras*), who was appointed to replace Chávez. One Venezuelan who attended some of these meetings told *Newsday* that U.S. officials only mildly objected to the idea of a coup, leading him to the inescapable conclusion that "All the United States really cared about was that it was done neatly, with a resignation letter or something to show for it." As the coup unfolded, this seemingly was confirmed by a State Department official who allegedly told a Venezuelan diplomat that, although the United States, as a signatory to "the Inter-American Democratic Charter, which condemns any violation of constitutional rule," officially opposed a military coup, it was nonetheless "necessary that the transition currently under way in Venezuela, which [the United States] understands and sympathizes with, conserve constitutional structures." For this reason, the United States unsuccessfully had counseled Carmona against his planned dismissal of the National Assembly.

Although the Organization of American States and every single Latin American government immediately denounced the coup and called for the restoration of democracy, the Bush administration further embarrassed itself by greeting news of the coup with some measure of enthusiasm. Instead of condemning the coup, officials initially blamed it on the alleged "dictatorial" policies of Chávez, the elected president. Chávez apparently had angered U.S. policymakers by his populist rhetoric, his principled opposition to the U.S. war in Afghanistan, his friendly relations with Cuba and other regimes that the United States opposed, and his resistance to neoliberal policies promoted by the United States, the World Bank, and the IMF.

Similarly, the United States openly intervened in Bolivia. First, under the rubric of fighting a hemispheric war on drugs, it funded a mercenary army known as the Expeditionary Task Force, which was accused of murdering an unarmed peasant union leader and engaging in torture and theft. "These are soldiers with no clearly defined loyalties, and a foreign power is funding them to run around our country with guns," a Bolivian official complained. "The existence of this force is a violation of the Bolivian constitution." More recently, in the summer of 2002, the United States

interfered in Bolivian democratic presidential elections. On election eve, the U.S. ambassador announced to the Bolivian press that the United States would cut off all economic aid to the impoverished nation if it elected Evo Morales, candidate of the Movement Toward Socialism Party and an Aymara indigenous leader who had fiercely resisted a U.S.-sponsored coca eradication program. Morales incurred Bush's wrath with his populist proposals and candid insistence that "capitalism is humanity's worst enemy." Notwithstanding U.S. hostility and covert financial support for his opponents, Morales surprised all political analysts with a second-place finish in the race, with 20 percent of the vote.

The United States also openly intervened in Nicaragua's 2001 presidential elections. After early polls showed that Daniel Ortega, candidate of the leftist Sandinista National Liberation Front, led his nearest rival by almost 10 percentage points, the United States organized a spirited campaign to secure his defeat. The U.S. ambassador pressured a Conservative candidate to drop out of the race to avoid splitting the anti-Ortega vote, vociferously denounced Ortega, loudly supported Enrique Bolaños, and used the distribution of emergency food aid to promote his candidacy. Even Jeb Bush, the president's brother, was enlisted in the campaign, alleging that Ortega associated with those "who shelter and condone international terrorism." In the aftermath of September 11 and President Bush's declaration of a "war on terrorism," this sent a powerful message to Nicaraguans, who a decade earlier already had endured horrendous privations caused by U.S. economic and military intervention.

Meanwhile, in Colombia and Ecuador, the Bush administration expanded the Clinton government's militarization of U.S. policy. Under the guise of interdicting drug smuggling, Plan Colombia, developed during the Clinton years, had authorized billions of dollars to support the Colombian military's counterrevolutionary war against the FARC, a guerrilla insurgency that claimed a popular base in the rural communities that it controlled. Even U.S. Ambassador Myle Frechette privately acknowledged in a confidential 1996 memorandum that the FARC's reputation as drug traffickers "was put together by the Colombian military, who considered it a way to obtain U.S. assistance in the counterinsurgency." Nonetheless, according to one U.S. Special Forces trainer in Colombia, although his mission was "ostensibly to aid the counternarcotics effort," everyone understood "perfectly well" that they were "giving military forces training in infantry counterinsurgency doctrine" and "that narcotics was a flimsy cover story for beefing up the capacity of armed forces, who had lost the confidence of the population through years of abuse."

But U.S. military forces continued to cooperate with Colombian forces accused of human rights violations, despite congressional restrictions on such assistance. In May 2000, according to confidential memoranda released to the National Security Archive, U.S. Ambassador Curtis Kamman alerted the State Department that the U.S. Army's "Bravo Company" was "bedding down" with, and receiving logistical support from, a Colombian infantry brigade, whose authorization to receive U.S. military support had not been approved because of unresolved complaints about its involvement in human rights abuses. The State Department, although it acknowledged that the United States could not legally assist this brigade, nonetheless reassured Kamman that its participation was critical "for the success of Plan Colombia."

Shortly after September 11, however, the Bush administration abandoned even these cursory efforts and shamelessly used the "new war on terrorism" to circumvent congressional controls originally designed to guarantee that U.S. military aid would not support human rights violations. Calling the FARC "the most dangerous international terrorist group based in the Western Hemisphere" and alleging that it "engaged in a campaign of terror against Colombians and U.S. citizens," President Bush authorized an additional $1.3 billion to support the Colombian military in 2001–2002 and requested another $98 million to fund the training of a special Colombian military unit to defend Occidental Petroleum's Cano Limón oil pipeline. The Bush government also dramatically increased military assistance to neighboring Peru, Bolivia, and Ecuador, whose military base at Manta became an especially key strategic asset for the U.S. military. This "Andean Regional Initiative" widened the arena of conflict and promised additional military aid through the Foreign Military Sales program, whose funding for Latin America almost doubled, to $8.7 million in 2001. This not only encouraged these impoverished nations to waste precious resources on more military equipment; it also clearly strengthened a sector of Latin American society that had been a historical enemy of democracy and human rights.

As the new millennium opened, popular movements throughout the region gradually coalesced in their fierce rejection of the neoliberal policies that the United States had promoted relentlessly for two decades. From *piqueteros* in Argentina to the FARC *guerrilleros* in Colombia, Latin America appeared to be in revolt. Although some sought to portray this as the routine chaos characteristic of the continent, others saw it as a natural, almost inevitable, consequence of unregulated markets that created wealth for a few and misery for the many. To be sure, it was unclear just how well-organized and politically disciplined these popular movements were. Likewise, it was uncertain how successful they might be. But one thing was indisputable: they challenged a U.S. foreign policy that historically had prized property rights and free markets over human rights and democratic freedoms.

# Latin American Society in Transition

As Latin America entered a new millennium, it became obvious that conventional neoliberal strategies for promoting the area's development were not working. Little progress had been made toward solving the area's stubborn problems of hunger and poverty. Indeed, it was evident that the remedies prescribed by the International Monetary Fund (IMF) and the World Bank had not only failed to cure the patient, but had aggravated its condition. The figures provided by international agencies spoke for themselves. In 1997 the area's foreign debt stood at $644 billion; by the middle of 2002 it had risen to $818.8 billion, representing 31.2 percent of the total foreign debt of developing countries. The rate of economic growth for Latin America and the Caribbean in 2001 was 1 percent. For 2002 it was not expected to exceed 2 percent, far below the level required to reduce poverty and unemployment. As the third millennium opened, more than 180 million Latin Americans lived in extreme poverty. In a report titled "The State of Food Insecurity 2000," the U.N. Food and Agriculture Organization noted that the number of malnourished Latin Americans stood at 55 million, 11 percent of the total population. It appeared that the 1990s, like the 1980s, had become a "lost" decade. In the absence of bold new policies, Latin America seemed doomed to a permanent, unending crisis.

## Economic Problems: A Permanent Latin American Crisis?

The Latin American crisis formed part of a larger crisis of the Third World. According to a report of Amnesty International, in more than eighty countries per capita income was less in 2000 than in 1990, and at least 1.3 billion people were trying to live on less than $1 a day. Growing opposition to the policies of what had become known as the "Washington Consensus" was reflected in massive demonstrations in Seattle, Geneva, Barcelona, and other cities where the World Trade Organization (WTO), the IMF, and other organizations with neoliberal agendas met. The protests were not directed against "globalization" in itself, generally understood to be the inevitable result of technological progress, but against its misuse for antihuman ends. Increasingly, establishment voices echoed the popular protests. At a forum held in Havana in February 2002 and attended by hundreds of economists, 1980 Nobel Peace Prize winner Adolfo Pérez Esquivel and Joseph Stiglitz, one of former President Clinton's economic advisers, co-winner of the 2001 Nobel Prize in Economics, and former chief economist of the World Bank, sharply criticized economic globalization as currently applied. Stiglitz described U.S. financial prescriptions for developing countries as hypocritical and harmful, noting that although the Bush administration urged U.S. citizens to spend their way out of recession, it gave just the opposite advice to developing countries. Rather than follow the recommendations of the IMF for sharp spending and job cuts as "shock treatments" for developing countries, those countries would do better to focus on the satisfaction of social needs. Stiglitz cited the example of China, noting that China had increased its national income 250 percent in the past decade, largely by focusing on job creation and the promotion of literacy as the means of reducing poverty.

## THE FOREIGN DEBT AND THE ARGENTINE DEBACLE

The immense, unpayable foreign debt was the chief obstacle to the solution of Latin America's problems of poverty and underdevelopment. It weighed like a nightmare on Latin America, draining resources otherwise available for sustainable development and imposing policies that made social justice and economic progress impossible. Recognition that the debt is unpayable would lead to negotiations between debtors and creditors that result in forgiveness of all or the greater part of the debt and the extension of new credits on easier terms, or perhaps in a new system that would put the United Nations in charge of funding development, as suggested by Fidel Castro.

Liberation from the debt was a prior condition for the solution of the food and ecological crises of the area. Freed from the burdens of the debt and the associated transnational corporate control of economic policy, Latin Americans could adopt a new agricultural strategy based on different priorities: they could produce to satisfy the area's nutritional needs rather than promote the production of exportable industrial crops, livestock feed, and luxury fruits and vegetables that enrich agribusinesses and generate foreign exchange to pay interest to foreign bankers. But such a shift of priorities would have to take place within the context of thorough, democratically controlled agrarian reforms to overcome the other major obstacle to regional development: the new capitalistic, highly mechanized *latifundio*. These sharply limited employment and absorbed by legal or illegal means

many small plots previously devoted to staple food production, forcing many small farmers to move into rugged hillsides, rain forests, or other land of poor agricultural quality or to migrate to the cities or plantations in search of employment.

It would be naïve, however, to expect that most Latin American governments, currently controlled by and representing elite interests, would willingly accept such new policies. In addition, these governments likely would be unwilling or unable to strictly monitor and control the activities of foreign corporations that in the past have practiced "garbage imperialism"—that is, using Latin America as a dumping ground for toxic waste by freely polluting its soil and rivers, as they have done in the Mexican-U.S. border zone. Sound environmental policies must recognize the relation between poverty and environmental degradation.

Central America offered a prime example. More than two-thirds of the region's rain forests were destroyed, resulting in the loss of many valuable plants and animal species. Deforestation and watershed destruction caused massive soil erosion, undermining the basis for continued subsistence farming. According to an environmental group's 1998 report, "State of Environment and Natural Resources in Central America," deforestation and soil erosion also made the region much more vulnerable to flash floods and landslides unleashed by natural disasters like Hurricane Mitch. These conditions, not the hurricane's high winds, the report noted, caused thousands of deaths and untold destruction of economic infrastructure. Again, much of the deforestation taking place in the Amazonian rain forest was the result of the exodus of landless peasants to the region, where they made clearings for planting, firewood, and other uses. That is why agrarian reform must occupy a central place in the solution of both the food and the ecological crises.

Recognition that the foreign debt problem is insoluble under existing conditions should be the point of departure in the search for solutions. The roots of the problem lie in the dynamics of foreign debt that spiraled upward from $426 billion in 1987 to more than $812 billion in 2002. To begin with, there was a structural imbalance between the economies of advanced and underdeveloped countries. The former, possessing immense technological and industrial superiority, sold expensive machinery, computer software, and know-how to underdeveloped countries like those of Latin America, which depended for the bulk of their exports on primary products like oil and coffee, subject to wide fluctuations in price and demand. True, in recent decades there was a considerable growth of Latin American industry (the *maquilas* or *maquiladoras*), especially in Mexico, Central America, and the Caribbean, that produced manufactured goods for export. But its benefits to the host countries were limited. This industry was foreign owned and low paid, employing unskilled workers to assemble parts or components made in different places. Mexico assembled computers, for instance; it did not make them. Consequently, it retained only one of every four dollars obtained by the export of these manufactures. Finally, the maquila was a highly mobile industry, easily lured away by the prospect of lower wages in another country.

The unequal terms of trade imposed on Latin America, combined with the tariff barriers and subsidies maintained by countries like the United States to protect their own industries (even as they demanded that the dependent countries open their markets wide to foreign imports and capital) almost ensured that sooner or later an underdeveloped country would develop a balance of payments problem. The volatility of investment flows into and out of dependent countries aggravated the problem, because lenders, fearing a possible currency devaluation and debt default, could initiate a flight of capital that spiraled into a devastating depression. At this point the debtor country would turn for help to the IMF and the World Bank. If the discussions went well and the debtor accepted the stringent "structural adjustment" conditions laid down by the international finance agencies, a rescue operation could restore the country's credit and a new cycle of borrowing could begin. Mexico experienced such an adjustment and its sequel of severe depression in the 1990s. "There is no indication," says Mexican economist Carlos Marichal, "that either Mexico or

any other Latin American nation will soon break out of the boom and bust cycles which have been accompanied by large fluctuations in the flows of capital in and out of the region." The current Argentine crisis, affecting the third largest economy of the region, was another case in point.

As president of Argentina (1989–1999), Carlos Menem implemented a sweeping neoliberal reconstruction of the Argentine economy that the military dictatorships of the 1970s had been unable to achieve. He was the IMF's star pupil, an admirer of Margaret Thatcher, Augusto Pinochet, and Ronald Reagan; so close were his relations with Washington that he described them as *relaciones carnales* (blood relations). The process included privatization of all state-owned industries, often sold at fire-sale prices in an atmosphere of shady deals, elimination of all laws that protected labor, and a plan that tied the peso to fictitious parity with the dollar. The parity plan brought temporary relief from the chronic problem of inflation, but the overpriced peso caused a sharp decline in Argentine exports. By 1998 the country was in a recession that steadily deepened. Per capita income, which was $7,300 in December 2001, had fallen by June 2002 to $2,167, making Argentina the continent's sixth poorest country after Paraguay, El Salvador, Ecuador, Bolivia, and Nicaragua. The economy had been in recession for fourteen consecutive trimesters.

Seeking to avoid default on foreign debt payments, Menem's successor, President Fernando de la Rua and his finance minister Domingo Cavallo decided to limit the payment of salaries, pensions, and bank cash withdrawals, using the money thus saved for interest payments. But those measures could not avert default on the $142 billion foreign debt. Outside the Casa Rosada, the government house in Buenos Aires, huge crowds, banging on pots and pans, gathered to protest denial of access to their money and a brutal police repression that took the lives of twenty-seven young demonstrators. De la Rua's proclamation of a state of siege only added to the public anger. On December 20, 2001, de la Rua resigned, fleeing from the roof of the Casa Rosada in a military helicopter. Three more presidents came and went before a legislative assembly on January 2, 2002, elected the Peronist Eduardo Duhalde to the office, pending new elections.

Duhalde abandoned one-to-one parity of the peso to the dollar, but under pressure from the IMF and the United States agreed to let the peso float. As a result bank accounts lost more than half their value overnight, and the peso continued to sink; by the end of June 2002 the exchange rate was about four pesos to the dollar. Meanwhile Duhalde appealed to the IMF and the United States for approval of new loans. Despite his submission to the IMF's demands for austerity and zero budget deficits and his efforts to placate the United States by pledging to support President Bush's anti-Cuban stance, the IMF moved with extraordinary slowness and countered Duhalde's surrender on various issues with new demands. Some believed the IMF's intent was to teach other dependent countries a lesson in fiscal discipline. Whatever the intent, Duhalde's austerity program required the firing of several hundred thousand public employees, which only aggravated the Argentine economic and social crisis. Assuming the IMF granted new loans, the government's first priority was the resumption of interest payments on the old debt, so fresh loans would be needed to revive the collapsed Argentine economy.

Some economists and sociologists argued for an independent economic policy, free from IMF demands and constraints. An eminent scholar, the sociologist Torcuato di Tella, declared: "We need to find a solution without the help of the IMF, to mobilize our own resources, including state intervention in the financial system and the market place." Argentina, he said, must look to "regional trade blocks like Mercosur," including Brazil, while rejecting U.S.-dominated projects such as the Free Trade Area of the Americas. This independent path, he warned "will not be pretty and it will mean more violence and a decline in the standard of living at first," but it was the only approach that would lead Argentina out of the abyss.

Alongside the shattered old economy and the old politics, in which most Argentines had lost all faith, new ways of living and managing were taking shape. One new phenomenon was a resistance movement whose radical tactics angered conser-vatives. Unemployed workers, called *piqueteros*, blocked traffic on the country's main roads to enforce their demand for food and work, and some-times for land so they could set up cooperatives to raise food for their families. Numerous consumer and producer cooperatives arose to fill many unsatisfied needs. Some took over closed factories and restored them to bustling life. Other groups engaged in barter to satisfy their mutual needs in an increasingly moneyless economy. In Buenos Aires and other cities popular ward assemblies regularly met to discuss and search for solutions to local and national problems. By 2002 this movement had not assumed a political form or issued a program, but its distrust of the traditional parties (and of the Duhalde government) was very evident. There was a growing demand for new elections to replace the existing Congress, president, and courts.

The most alarming aspect of the situation was the rapid growth of extreme poverty and its accompaniment of hunger, malnutrition, and disease. The monthly subsidy provided by the government to unemployed heads of families was 150 pesos, or less than $40. This amount did not cover essential needs, estimated to require 400 pesos a month for a family of four. The cost of all basic foodstuffs doubled. According to the most recent official figures, 51.4 percent of the 37 million Argentines now lived below the poverty threshold. More than 66 percent of them were children or adolescents. The majority no longer attended school, for lack of money, but they could not find work to ensure their survival. It is estimated that each month 30,000 "new poor" joined their ranks. In this "new map of misery," writes a *Le Monde* correspondent, what was most significant was the steady rise of "extreme poverty" (indigence). By June 2002, 42 percent of the population fell into that category. Six million suffered from malnutrition. Until recently, poverty had been a marginal problem for Argentina; in 1970 only 5 percent of all households were "poor."

Another problem was the discovery that the police and security services continued to shelter former operatives of the military dictatorships, specialists in torture and the disappearance of radicals and liberals, practices that the return to democracy had supposedly ended. Evidence that these leopards had not changed their spots and continued to enjoy immunity and official position came on June 26, 2002, a day of massive demonstrations by piqueteros and other protestors in Buenos Aires. Press photographers captured images of a police officer's cold-blooded murder of two young piqueteros. President Duhalde initially blamed the demonstrators, but later he expressed anger and promised a cleansing of the security services. Meanwhile, reporters for the Argentine newspaper, *Página 12*, discovered that the police officers implicated in the affair previously had worked in the concentration camps organized by the military dictatorship two decades ago. But the unanswered question remained: How did former operatives of the concentration camps, known and identified as such, obtain and retain their official positions?

The Argentine "fever," meanwhile, was spreading, with varying degrees of severity, to its immediate neighbors—Brazil, Paraguay, and Uruguay, and even Chile and Mexico; the symptoms included currency devaluations, rising interest rates, some inflation, declining foreign investments, and growing social turmoil. "Everyone is looking at Argentina," wrote one analyst, "and crying 'The pox! The pox!' as if it were a medieval city attacked by the Black Death."

## The Choices Before Latin America: Integrate or Disintegrate

How to escape from the tentacles of a strangling foreign debt and still find the resources needed for development? This was Latin America's major economic problem in 2003, and it daily grew more acute as a global recession spilled over most of the continent and the demand and prices for its staples declined, while the flow of investment capital into the area dried up. Increasingly, Latin Americans seemed determined to abandon, or at least to modify, the current "free-market" or neoliberal economic system and to regain control of their nations' natural resources and use them for the general good. Venezuela, where a military

populist, Hugo Chávez, won a stunning electoral victory on a program of radical reform and then easily triumphed over a botched coup supported and financed by the United States, was one straw in the wind. Another was the Bolivian presidential and congressional election in June 2002. An Aymaran leader of Bolivia's coca farmers, Evo Morales and his party, Movement Toward Socialism, surged forward from 4 percent to 12 percent in pre-election polls and finished second, a hair's breadth behind veteran político and oligarch, Gonzalo Sánchez de Lozada. "Evo Morales doesn't just represent an image of ethnicity," one analyst said. "He also represents ideas that are in style all over the world—anti-globalization, anti-neoliberalism, anti-imperialism." Although Morelos lost the run-off election in the Bolivian Congress, the massive participation of indigenous peoples had forever changed the nation.

A closely related problem waited in the wings, and provoked intense Latin American debate. In the next few years, Latin America must decide to accept or reject President George Bush's proposed Free Trade Area of the Americas (FTAA), an agreement that the Bush administration would like implemented by 2005. Although a majority of Latin American heads of state approved the project in principle at a meeting in Quebec in April 2001, Cuban leader Fidel Castro denounced it as a project for U.S. annexation of the continent, and it was harshly criticized by President Fernando Henrique Cardoso of Brazil and President Hugo Chávez of Venezuela. The lower house of the Brazilian Congress, angered by U.S. protectionist measures against Brazilian products ranging from orange juice to steel, voted unanimously for a nonbinding resolution calling for withdrawal of Brazil from current FTAA negotiations with the United States. The head of the Workers' Party, known to most Brazilians as "Lula," won the 2002 presidential election and joined Castro in regarding FTAA as a policy designed to annex Latin America's wealth rather than promote free trade.

The FTAA had been called NAFTA "on steroids," and was based on the same principles, but went farther than NAFTA in its insistence on ending controls over foreign investment and on limiting the state's economic role. The Bush administration claimed that the new pact would promote prosperity by encouraging the free flow of goods among member countries. Critics argued that the immense disparity in wealth and resources between the United States and its trading partners would inevitably result in a total conquest of Latin American markets by the superpower, eliminating all competition and reducing the Latin American countries to the condition of vassal states. They noted that the new pact, like NAFTA, would allow corporations to sue individual governments over legislation that might diminish private profits, including laws that protect labor, indigenous communities, or the environment. In fact, citing Chapter 11 of NAFTA, a U.S. company had successfully sued Mexico for trying to protect itself against toxic dumping by blocking the company's expansion plan. The FTAA would also bar attempts to restrict the free movement of foreign investment capital into and out of Latin America or prevent the total takeover of Latin American companies by such capital.

Since the FTAA proposal was essentially a vast expansion of NAFTA, a brief review of the latter's impact on the Mexican economy since its adoption in 1994 may be instructive. Mexican observers unanimously agreed that it had resulted in an increase of Mexican economic dependence on the United States, a dependence that was almost absolute in 2002. Mexico sent the United States 90 percent of its manufactured exports and 80 percent of its oil exports. Mexico received from the United States 80 percent of its food, 60 percent of its tourism, and about $8.5 billion a year in direct investment. NAFTA gave a large stimulus to U.S. takeover of Mexican companies. Weakened by the Mexican crisis of 1994–1995, they were frequently sold for half their value. In addition, some of Mexico's principal banks were acquired by U.S., Spanish, and Canadian capital. Mexico's control over its money reached a nadir with Citigroup's purchase of Banamex, Mexico's largest bank, in 2000. In 1997 a Mexican think tank monitoring developments in the private economic sector warned that the Mexican entrepreneurial class was disappearing.

An important result of Mexico's dependence on the United States was that the two countries tended to share good and bad times. But the impact of the bad times on the two countries was very uneven. When the United States sneezes, as the saying goes, Mexico gets pneumonia. Thus the recession that began in the United States in 2001 had a marked negative effect on the Mexican maquiladora export zones along the U.S. border and in the interior. These factories had almost no links to the Mexican economy; they assembled components for U.S. and other multinationals. During 2001 employment in the maquiladora industry declined 12 percent, or more than 170,000 jobs from its peak. The decline was due not only to the U.S. recession but also to the fact that many factories were leaving Mexico, Central America, and the Caribbean for countries like China with even lower wage levels. A Mexican think tank reported in September 2001 that Chinese competition was likely to cost Mexico 42 percent of the volume of its exports. Despite the export sector's pitifully low wages, it produced one-third of Mexico's hard currency income from abroad; so its loss may contribute to a future currency crisis. But the shrinkage of Mexican industry was general, affecting steel, shoes, tires, apparel, and auto parts. In October 2001 Carlos Slim Helu, Mexico's leading entrepreneur, issued a gloomy prognosis and called on the Mexican government to prepare a contingency plan to revive the internal market, stimulate employment, and encourage economic activity to confront a looming global recession.

Mexican agriculture suffered most from NAFTA's progressive reduction of tariffs, however, soon to reach zero. Mexico, the classic land of corn agriculture, had lost much of its domestic market for corn and other basic grains, because Mexican peasants could not compete with the intensive production methods of U.S. farmers, aided by massive government subsidies. Roughly a quarter of the corn consumed in Mexico was produced in the United States. Mexican efforts to raise the issue of subsidies at the U.N. International Conference on Financing for Development in Monterrey, Mexico, in March 2002 produced no concessions by the United States or any other great power. Many Mexican small farmers, no longer able to eke out a living on the *milpa* (corn patch) joined maquiladora workers who had lost their jobs in the desperate, often risky search for work across the border in the United States. The deserted, forlorn appearance of a growing number of Mexican villages reflected the crisis of Mexican agriculture.

The patent failure of NAFTA to promote Mexican development or raise living standards—the number of Mexicans unable to satisfy their basic food needs rose between 1989 and 1998 from 5.2 million to 9.5 million, according to a report of the World Bank—and the general failure of neoliberal strategies to achieve their goals have multiplied opposition to FTAA and U.S. trade policy in general. Posing the problem in terms of a choice between disintegration and integration—between greater economic, political, and cultural independence for Latin America and loss of its independence to a hegemonic United States—Cuba's Fidel Castro, President Cardoso of Brazil, and President Chávez of Venezuela sought to revive Simón Bolívar's broad vision of a united, prosperous, and peaceful Latin America as a model for our time. Supporters of this alternative to FTAA argued that the movement toward Latin American unity should build on the gradual strengthening and expansion of such beginnings as Mercosur (the common market uniting Argentina, Brazil, Uruguay, and Paraguay), slated for destruction if FTAA came to pass. They also favored commercial treaties with the European Union and other groupings in order to diversify trade relations and promote greater competition. FTAA's opponents urged that no Latin American state should approve it without consulting its own people and making sure that its people understood the meaning of the pact. (President Chávez noted that a poll of middle-class people and intellectuals in Venezuela showed that less than 5 percent of them knew what FTAA was.) As the target date of 2005 set by the Bush administration for the pact to go into effect drew nearer, the struggle for approval or rejection promised to grow steadily more heated.

## Social Problems

In August 2001 the London newspaper *The Guardian*, noting that British Prime Minister Tony Blair was taking a much needed holiday in Cancún, Mexico, "a place well endowed with that combination of natural beauty and comfortable surroundings that our leaders favor when they gather to order our lives," suggested that the prime minister might notice that "the benefits of the economic liberalization that most countries of Latin America have pursued over the past fifteen years are less evident to those around him than he might hope." *The Guardian* went on to quote the words of a senior U.N. development official: "For the millions of poor, the slum dwellers, globalization now has the face of cruelty, of unemployment and marginalization." A year later, Mexico's leading novelist, Carlos Fuentes, added his voice to the chorus of celebrities who denounced globalization in its current form and application, comparing its effects to those of the savage, unregulated Industrial Revolution of the early nineteenth century. "That this revolution provokes disruption, pain, and injustice is as certain now as it was in the nineteenth century. That this revolution will not go away because of the demonstrations against it is as true as it was in the nineteenth century. . . . But in the streets of Seattle, Prague, Genoa, there is an impatience that little by little is changing into an understanding that it is not enough to demonize globalization; rather it must be transformed into an instrument of public good, of growing well-being."

What these voices tell us is that the social problems provoked by the neoliberal revolution or globalization had reached gigantic, intolerable proportions early in the twenty-first century. In Latin America, as elsewhere in the Third World, the main causes of the social problems were growing poverty and reductions in social programs (social-sector spending declined by more than 50 percent since 1985). Both developments were linked to the ongoing debt crisis and the "structural-adjustment programs" willingly or unwillingly adopted by most Latin American governments in response to that crisis. At a 2001 summit in Caracas, Social Debt and Latin American Integration, Bernardo

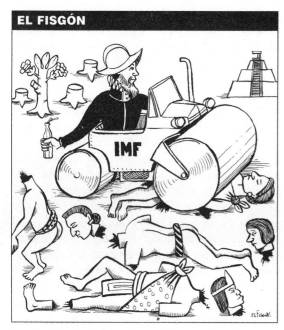

**EL FISGÓN**

Inspired by Pedro de Alvarado's sacking of Tenochtitlán, a famous scene described in the sixteenth-century Florentine Codex, El Fisgón's cartoon depicts the destruction of rain forests and indigenous communities as the second conquest of Latin America. In the 1990s, the conquistadors include the International Monetary Fund, modern technology, and transnational corporations (symbolized by the Coca-Cola bottle). [El Fisgón/NACLA]

These overall figures rightly caused dismay, but they actually diminished the severity of Latin America's social problems because they concealed the much higher levels of poverty and deprivation in those areas of Mexico, Guatemala, Bolivia, Ecuador, Peru, and Haiti heavily populated by indigenous peoples and descendants of enslaved Africans, who suffered the twin indignities of racism and neoliberalism.

### POVERTY, HOUSING, AND HEALTH

The scarcity of safe, secure, affordable housing was one of the area's worst social problems. Much of it lacked proper sanitary facilities and was improvised, ranging from thatched huts and caves to tin and plywood shacks. A few countries like Cuba and, more recently, Venezuela under reformist President Hugo Chávez, attacked the problem with programs of low-cost housing construction. In most countries, however—Mexico being a prime example—access to housing for low-income groups had become more limited and difficult since the adoption of the neoliberal economic model in the 1980s, because there were fewer loans available from government agencies and more stringent conditions for low-income borrowers. The housing problem grew ever more acute because of the vast rural exodus that began in most of the area more than half a century ago as the result of the interplay of two forces: the "pull" of the city, which attracted rural people with the frequently illusory prospect of factory work and a better life, and the "push" of the countryside, where the concentration of landownership and the mechanization of agriculture expelled millions of peasants from their farms and jobs. "Poverty and despair," writes Jorge E. Hardoy, a leading student of urban problems, "are behind many of these massive displacements." Latin America's urban population continued to increase at more than twice the rate of the population as a whole. By the year 2000, Latin America had become the most urbanized region of the world, with 75 percent of its population living in towns or cities.

Kliksberg, research director at the Inter-American Development Bank (IDB), offered some figures that revealed the extent of Latin America's social problems. He reported that 60 out of every 100 Latin Americans lived in poverty; one-third of the population had no potable water, one of every five mothers gave birth without medical assistance, and the average Latin American's education stopped at the fifth grade. Kliksberg linked the growth of urban violence to high unemployment and low education levels among youth and the demoralization produced by misery and hopelessness. Moreover, he noted that the distribution of income in Latin America was the most unequal in the world; the richest ten percent received an income eighty-four times greater than the poorest ten percent.

In Central America the rural exodus was delayed, primarily because of that region's smaller economies and stronger dependence on subsistence agriculture. There the flight to the cities began in earnest during the civil wars of the 1980s, as peasants sought refuge from the fighting and persecution by government forces and paramilitary death squads. Since then a series of natural disasters such as Hurricane Mitch (1998)—which caused floods and landslides that killed thousands—earthquakes, and droughts, combined with plummeting agricultural prices and the inability to wrest a living from their small worn-out plots of land, caused massive peasant migrations. International development groups estimate that by 2010, 55 percent of Central America's population will live in cities.

The border zone between Mexico and the United States offers an example of unplanned internal migration and its social consequences. In the last decade a tidal wave of workers, drawn by the opportunity to work in the rapidly expanding maquiladora industry, washed over the zone. "The overwhelmed Mexican border cities," commented the *New York Times* in February 2001, "lack the means to provide the most basic services. One of the country's powerful drug cartels holds sway here in Juárez and drug-related crime is common. Dozens of women who have come to work in the maquiladoras have been abducted, tortured, raped, and murdered, their bodies tossed like garbage in the desert. . . . All along the border, the land, the water, and the air are thick with industrial and human waste. The National Water Commission reports that the towns and cities, strapped for funds, can adequately treat less than 35 percent of the sewage generated daily. About 12 percent of the people living on the border have no access to clean water. Nearly a third live in homes that are not connected to sewage systems. Only about half the streets are paved." The *Times* reported that the dwellings of families that had worked long enough to save money for conventional building materials were simple structures with walls of concrete blocks and tin roofs. Newer arrivals built homes from crates, old tires, and cardboard. But these Third World conditions were not confined to the Mexican side of the border. "Mirror images of these communities dot parts of the Texas side of the line." Since this report was published, however, the maquiladora boom ended and, in Ciudad Juárez alone, 40,000 maquiladora workers lost their jobs.

In these areas of improvised housing, the absence of adequate drinking water and sewage services contributed to a high incidence of parasitic and infectious diseases. Latin America's rising health problems were clearly related to the continuing economic crisis, the worst since the Great Depression of the 1930s. Purchasing power declined by 40 percent or more in recent years; in some countries half the work force was unemployed or underemployed. Many Latin American governments sharply reduced health services as part of austerity programs designed to meet interest payments on foreign debt. These cutbacks were related to the deterioration of hospital care, decline in pharmaceutical imports, and reduced government support for medical schools.

The relation between economic policy and public health was dramatically illustrated in Argentina where, as a direct result of the debt crisis and economic depression that struck the nation in 1999, the Argentine public health system, once famed for its excellence, collapsed. A correspondent for *Le Monde* visited the Posadas hospital, the most modern in the province of Buenos Aires, in April 2002. He found that hundreds of the hospital's employees had gone on strike because they had not been paid their wages. The hospital had not received the four million pesos that should have come from the Ministry of Health; as a result there were no antibiotics, no syringes, no filters for dialysis, and no radiological plates. Admission to the hospital was limited to the most serious cases, and surgery had been suspended. The reporter found the same critical situation at the children's hospital, the Garrahan. A young pediatrician could not hide his impotent rage. "Cardiovascular surgery has been suspended for a month; nine children have died." The operations were resumed as a result of the doctors' protests and the noisy concerts given by the children's families, banging on pots and pans. *Le Monde*'s correspondent noted that the children came to the hospital with diseases caused by poverty and malnutrition. A few months later, *The Guardian* reported that half of all Argentine infants suffered from anemia and a quarter of all children were suffering from malnutrition. It then pointed to the irony of this happening "in a country so rich in farmland that it produces enough to feed ten times its own population." Meanwhile at Quilmes, a few kilometers from the presidential palace, schoolteachers discovered that hungry children were cooking and eating toads, frogs, and the flesh of sick horses. The massive incidence of malnutrition in Argentina, a "Western" country that until recently was the wealthiest in Latin America, reflected the general deterioration of economic and social conditions in the area.

Children everywhere were the principal victims of malnutrition, the greatest health problem. Recent UNICEF statistics indicated that in Latin America, three thousand children under the age of five died every day; malnutrition was believed to account for half of these deaths. Commercial infant formulas, aggressively promoted in Latin America by such transnational corporations as Nestlé and Bristol Myers, contributed to infant malnutrition because poor women had been persuaded to substitute bottled formula for breast milk. In areas without clean water, the mothers' frequent practice of watering down the milk to save money on formula made bottle feeding especially dangerous for newborns, resulting in repeated epidemics of diarrhea and a vicious cycle of diarrhea and malnutrition that brought early death.

The problem of malnutrition and the associated problem of intestinal disease were most acute in areas heavily populated with indigenous peoples, who typically endured the most severe poverty. In Mexico, for example, 83.6 percent of deaths among indigenous children were caused by intestinal infections, a rate resembling that for African children. In indigenous areas of Mexico, the malnutrition rate approached 60 percent, and 58.12 percent of dwellings lacked clean drinking water, compared with the national rate of 15.7. But the disparity between national rates of poverty and those experienced by indigenous peoples was still broader: 88.3 percent of their dwellings lacked drainage, compared with the national rate of 25

percent; 53 percent of their houses lacked electricity, compared with the national rate of 6.48 percent; their illiteracy rate was 45 percent, compared to the national rate of 10.46 percent; 75 percent of their children failed to complete elementary school, compared to the national rate of 36 percent. Small wonder that Mexico's indigenous peoples, led by their vanguard, the Zapatista Army of National Liberation in Chiapas, demanded autonomy and control of their natural resources.

By June of 2002, Central America, battered in recent years by a succession of natural and manmade disasters, was now the scene of a major health and food crisis, with Guatemala as its epicenter. Even before the worst drought in decades left thousands of subsistence farmers without harvests or food reserves, Guatemala had the highest level of chronic malnutrition in Central America. By the government's own admission, half of all children were chronically malnourished. According to officials, "Nearly 60,000 children under age five now suffer from acute malnutrition, and many of them could perish any day from infections, parasites, and dehydration." In response to this crisis, the U.N. World Food Program organized an emergency feeding project. But this health and food crisis could not be understood in isolation from Guatemala's unjust economic and social structures, marked by a concentration of land and wealth probably unequaled in Latin America. President Alfonso Portillo, himself a member of the elite, conceded that "80 percent of Guatemalans live in misery." That state of misery, we recall, was assured in 1954 when a military revolt, organized and supported by the United States, overthrew the first and only government in Guatemala's history to attempt a serious reform of its economic and social inequalities.

Like earlier Latin American rural migrations, the Central American migration gave rise to a multitude of shantytowns on the edges of cities, often in situations that exposed dwellers to the dangers from which they had fled. In Honduras, which was struck hard by Hurricane Mitch, the hills around Tegucigalpa, the capital, were covered with settlements in landslide zones. In El Salvador, the migrants lived on riverbanks, with makeshift levees of discarded tires their only protection from surging waters. Typical of the improvised construction of these shantytowns was La Nueva Capital, on the edge of Tegucigalpa; here the houses were "cobbled together from scraps of scavenged wood planks and cinder blocks." A government social fund financed new white latrines that "look sturdier than most homes."

"Slums," reflected a *New York Times* correspondent, "have sprung up following a simple rule: where there is space, take it. As a result, the spread of poor communities in high-risk zones is a hallmark of the region's urban growth." The same correspondent ruefully observed: "Development experts said migration had also been pushed along by national governments that had done little to provide sound support for rural communities, often focusing instead on short-term emergency foreign aid, or on attracting foreign-owned factories that offer low-paying jobs."

A striking aspect of Latin American urbanization was the growth in the number of cities with over 1 million inhabitants. Between 1950 and 1970 the number of such cities rose from six to seventeen, and the sum of their populations increased from 15 to 55 million. By 2000 the cities contained about 220 million inhabitants, or about 37 percent of the total Latin American population at that time. In the same period the number of people living below the poverty line increased from 40 percent in 1985 to 60 percent in 2000. Industrialization and the rural exodus together produced the phenomenon of hyperurbanization—the rise of vast urban agglomerations or zones of urban sprawl. About 80 percent of Brazil's industrial production was located in the metropolitan zones of São Paulo, Rio de Janeiro, and Belo Horizonte. Two-thirds of Argentine production was concentrated in the area between Buenos Aires and Rosario. More than half of the industrial production of Chile and Peru was located in the metropolitan zones of Santiago and Lima-Callao, respectively. Caracas accounted for 40 percent of the industrial production of Venezuela. Between 25 and 50 percent of the populations of Uruguay, Mexico, and Argentina lived in the capitals of those countries.

As these vast urban concentrations increased, life became more and more difficult for their inhabitants. All the urban problems—food, housing, drinking water, and transportation—were immensely aggravated. Mexico City was a case in point. In 2002 it had a population of about 20 million. The pollution caused by toxic agents generated by the city's thirty-five thousand industrial establishments and 3 million cars were denounced by medical specialists as a major danger to health and life; half of all infants had unacceptable toxic levels in their blood, which, specialists warned, could reduce IQ levels by as much as 10 percent. (Recently, as a result of more stringent regulation of car use and other measures, the level of air pollution in Mexico City is said to have declined.) Shantytowns covered almost 40 percent of the urban area and housed approximately 4 million people, a large proportion of whom were unemployed or underemployed. In 2001, according to *New York Times* reporter Tim Weiner, nationally some 12 million Mexicans lacked easy access to potable water. "The Latin American metropolis," writes city planner Thomas Angotti, "is characterized by mass poverty and severe environmental pollution on a scale generally unparalleled in the North."

There were important differences between the process of urbanization in the North and the South, leading to different results. In Europe and North America urbanization, industry, and the demand for labor grew at a fairly even pace, but in Latin America industrial growth and the demand for labor lagged far beyond the explosive growth of the urban population. Much of the new industry, especially in foreign-owned sectors, was highly mechanized and automated; it therefore generated little new employment. In a traditional Latin American industry such as textiles, mechanization actually produced a net loss of jobs. The low purchasing power of the masses also hindered the creation of new jobs, for the market for goods was quickly saturated and industry continually operated below capacity. Finally, many of the rural migrants were illiterate and lacked the skills required by modern industry.

Industry's inability to absorb the supply of labor produced an exaggerated growth of the so-called service or informal sector. The growth of this sector considerably exceeded that of the industrial labor force, which grew from 20 to 24 percent of the labor force from 1960 to 1980, while the service sector rose from 33 to 45 percent during the same period. Since the advent of neoliberal reforms in the early 1990s, however, the International Labor Organization estimated that the informal sector accounted for 60 percent of all new jobs and grew by 3.9 percent per year during the decade, compared to an anemic 2.1 percent growth in formal employment. This informal sector included a great number of poorly paid domestic servants and a mass of individuals who eked out a living as lottery vendors, car watchers and washers, shoe shiners, and street vendors of all kinds.

Cuba alone has made a serious effort to check and reverse the hypertrophy of the city. Almost from the day it took power, the revolutionary government undertook to redress the imbalance by shifting the bulk of its investments to the countryside and by raising rural living standards through the provision of adequate medical, educational, and social services, a more rational distribution of the economic infrastructure, and the creation of planned new cities. Despite these efforts, including restrictions on migration to the capital, Havana's population grew to 2,000,000, and the provision of adequate housing to the population remained one of Cuba's most difficult, unsolved problems.

The enormous concentration of poverty, on the one hand, and of wealth, on the other, made the great Latin American city a study in stark contrasts. The Brazilian city of São Paulo, "a city of 18,000,000, populated by the fantastically wealthy and the severely poor with little in between," was a case in point. The alienation inevitably generated by such contrasts was heightened by the new shielded way of life that the very rich chose in response to a surging rate of homicides and kidnappings. São Paulo's homicide rate more than tripled during the 1990s, to some 60 murders per 100,000 residents, compared with 7.8 in New York. "The surge in abductions," reported a *Washington Post* correspondent, "has produced a cottage industry of plastic surgeons who specialize in treating wealthy victims who

return home from their ordeals with sliced ears, severed fingers, and other missing body parts that were sent to family members as threats for ransom payments."

More recently, hundreds of rich Paulistas, accompanied by bodyguards, chose to fly "over their fears" in helicopters to and from their homes to work, business meetings, even to church. Liftoffs were estimated to average 100 per hour, and the city had 240 helipads, compared with 10 in New York City. Home for these Paulistas was a different world from the ever-growing slums, peopled by millions of migrants from the parched, poverty-ridden Northeast, and often ruled by gangs dealing in drugs, kidnapping, and arms. More and more of the wealthy chose to live in walled, guarded communities, like Alphaville, only seven and a half miles from the city center, and home to 30,000 of São Paulo's wealthiest residents. It had three helipads and four entrances and exits, monitored 24 hours a day. Black-clad security guards watched over all communal areas, and at night residents could view their exiting employees as they were patted down and searched in front of a live video feed. São Paulo had more than 300 such communities.

"The elite have made a decision," says Teresa Caldeira, anthropologist and author of the book *City of Walls: Crime, Segregation, and Citizenship in São Paulo*. "Instead of looking to better Brazilian society in general, they are abandoning it and finding their own personal protection behind guarded walls. The rich are retrenching, restricting their lives in incredible ways and living their lives in an increasingly paranoid fashion."

If we assume no basic future change in the Latin American economic and social order, which generated poverty and the associated disorders as part of its normal operation, São Paulo may offer a surreal vision of future life in other great cities of the area. But can such a "paranoid" way of life, based on fear and alienation, long endure?

## CRIME AND PUNISHMENT

Crime in Latin America is above all the child of poverty, and the growth of crime in the area faithfully reflected the ongoing concentration of wealth

The killing of homeless street children by death squads, sometimes hired by businessmen and conservative middle-class groups to "cleanse" the streets, is a fairly common Latin American phenomenon, especially in Brazil and Guatemala. Here a group of Brazilian street children organize their own protest against the killing of some of their number. [Viviane Moos/Corbis]

at one end of the social scale and of poverty at the other. Growing poverty and unemployment drove many young people into crime to survive. Public anxiety abetted an official "get-tough" policy on crime, accompanied by a growth of vigilantism and lynching. There was a frightening indifference on the part of the authorities to the killing of thousands of street urchins by death squads, often composed of off-duty policemen. These "children of chaos" had been forced into the streets to fend for themselves or as street vendors to help out their parents. Some became petty criminals and a source of annoyance to businessmen and conservative middle-class groups, some of whom hired off-duty policemen to assassinate the offending children to "cleanse" the streets. Violence against

children was most common in Brazil and Guatemala, but also occurred elsewhere.

The Latin American prison system was marked by vast overcrowding, inhumane conditions, brutal treatment of inmates, and long delays—sometimes four to eight years—before prisoners were brought to trial. Until recently, at least, in Colombia and Peru defendants were often brought before "faceless courts" and anonymous witnesses, ostensibly to protect judges and witnesses against reprisals by narcotraffickers and subversives—with an obvious chilling effect on the defense process. Brazil offered a dramatic example of an area-wide trend. The rate of incarceration tripled from 30 prisoners per 100,000 inhabitants in 1969 to 95 per 100,000 in 1995, and then soared again to almost 135 in 2000—an increase in the rate of incarceration of 41 percent over a period of five years, reflecting not only a growth in the crime rate but an all-too-willing acceptance by the public of the notion that more prison sentences for longer terms would halt the crime wave. As of December 2000, Brazil's prisoner population numbered 212,000 inmates.

As a consequence of overcrowding, conditions in Brazil's prisons routinely violated prisoners' rights and state laws (the federal government did not have its own prison system, and the states had charge of the police and the penitentiary system). Torture to obtain information and summary execution of prisoners were common practices. Riots by prisoners protesting intolerable conditions were also common and were put down with ferocity. In a case that broke with the usual pattern of tolerance for police brutality, however, in June 2001 a jury found a former police commander guilty of presiding over the worst prison massacre in Brazilian history and handed down a symbolic sentence of 612 years (six years for each death), although 30 years was the maximum sentence under Brazilian law. To put down a riot the commander had stormed Latin America's largest prison, a rundown structure in São Paulo containing 7,000 inmates and massacred 102 prisoners with machine guns, rifles, and pistols. Many of the corpses were naked, interpreted by human rights defenders as a sign of an inmate's surrender. These defenders hoped that the case marked a turning point in the fight against immunity for brutal police officers.

In Mexico City, another metropolis where crime had skyrocketed and the police were notoriously corrupt (police and former police were believed responsible for 60 percent of the crime), two successive elected mayors of the left-wing PRD launched a reform program that stressed improved pay for police officers and a crackdown on corruption. Although handicapped by inadequate financial aid from the federal government, the program appeared to have achieved some initial success.

In Latin America, the official and unofficial violence against real or suspected lower-class criminals contrasted with the impunity often enjoyed by powerful individuals charged with white-collar crime and great landowners or their gunmen who murdered trade unionists or labor organizers. As a result, according to Brazilian political scientist Paulo Pinheiro, "in almost all Latin American countries the poor see the law as an instrument of oppression at the service of the wealthy and powerful."

## EDUCATION

In recent years Latin American leaders like Brazil's president, Fernando Henrique Cardoso, and Mexico's president, Vicente Fox, pledged to make improvement of public education in quantity and quality their primary goal, and a number of countries launched schemes that promised to make regular welfare payments to poor families who kept their children in school. In Brazil, for example, the governor of the capital, Brasilia, introduced a plan in 1996 that paid a minimum wage to poor families who kept all their children in school. The impact of the plan was said to have been "extraordinary," and it was thereafter introduced into other cities in Brazil. It enabled Brazil to claim that it had achieved "near-universal primary education for the first time in its history." A similar Mexican scheme, Progresa, was said to have been so successful in raising and retaining enrollments that some economists urged its adoption in the United States.

But the figures that supported this educational triumphalism must be viewed with caution. As noted earlier, the average Latin American still ended her education at the fifth grade, and the dropout rate remained very high. Overall figures that seemed to reflect victories actually concealed some dismal facts. In Mexico the illiteracy rate in some rural areas was as high as 21 percent, double the national rate, and as we have seen, it was 45 percent among indigenous peoples. Researcher John Scott points out that although Mexico's richest 10 percent usually spent twelve years in school, the poorest 10 percent had on average just two years of education.

There were several reasons for the very high dropout rate in Latin American public schools. One was the economic crisis caused by neoliberal policies and its accompanied cuts in social spending. Part of the burden of educational costs was shifted to parents in the form of "user fees" and other charges; given that most Latin American families lived below the poverty line, this burden was often impossible to carry. A second reason, also linked to the economic crisis, was the lack of decent jobs. As one mother in a Chilean shantytown remarked, "Why should kids read Neruda or go to the theater if they're just going to end up picking oranges?" Often schoolchildren were alienated by formal subject matter and teaching methods that had little relevance to their interests and needs. Finally, rising poverty and the strains it imposed were perhaps the most urgent reasons for parents to take their children out of school and send them to work, sometimes as "street children" who cleaned windshields, sold Chiclets, shined shoes, or worked in microenterprises (sometimes their own parents'), making shoes or other commodities. Other children, like those on Ecuador's banana plantations, some as young as eight years old, were forced to work twelve-hour days in agriculture, where they were exposed to toxic chemicals and sexual harassment.

But the regional crisis in education was not inevitable; it merely reflected the misplaced priorities of local policymakers and international organizations like the IMF, whose decisions all too frequently shaped educational policies in Latin America. By contrast, revolutionary Cuba, which launched its campaign to abolish illiteracy in 1961 with the aid of thousands of young volunteers, quickly achieved its goal. Despite the economic hard times associated with the collapse of its major trading partners in 1990, a decade later Cuba still led all Latin American nations in the quality of the education it offered its people. In 1998, UNESCO conducted tests on primary school students in thirteen Latin American countries. The best performers were Cuba's fourth-graders, who scored the most points by far, 350. They were followed by Chile, Argentina, and Brazil, in that order. Cuba's most recent new departure in education was the creation of the Latin American School of Medicine, which offers free medical training to qualified applicants from the Americas who will commit themselves to return to practice in areas sorely in need of medical care. The student body recently was joined by a number of young people from the United States.

## The New Class Structure

Naturally, Latin America's contemporary class structure was very much a product of its historical evolution. Although the capitalist mode of production, based on free contractual labor, was dominant since about 1880, the area still had not made a clean break with its precapitalist past. This was reflected in the survival of slavery, debt peonage, and other forms of forced labor in various parts of the continent. Such servile or feudal forms of labor were usually associated with primary industries like agriculture, cattle-raising, and logging; these typically were located in politically and socially backward regions dominated by great landowners or powerful companies, where the state was weak and its representatives often corrupt and ready to make deals with the dominant elite.

By the middle decades of the twentieth century, meanwhile, industrialization, urbanization, and the commercialization of agriculture had significantly altered the Latin American social structure and the relative weight of the various classes. These changes included the transformation of the old landed elite into a new latifundista class with a capitalist character, the emergence of a big industrial and financial bourgeoisie with close ties to foreign capital, an enormous growth of the so-called urban middle sectors, and the rise of a small but militant industrial working class.

In the early twenty-first century such quasi-feudal conditions still existed in Brazil's "Wild West," its Amazon frontier, where defenders of the rain forest, indigenous peoples, and small farmers were threatened with death and murdered with impunity. Here thousands of peasants, lured from other parts of the country by promises of good jobs, free housing, and plenty of good food, often found themselves reduced to slavery, felling trees and tending cattle deep in the jungle. One who managed to escape said that "particularly troublesome workers, especially those who kept asking for their wages, were sometimes simply killed." Government authorities admitted that "contemporary forms of slavery," in which workers were held in unpaid, coerced labor, continued to flourish. "The reasons range from ranchers in cahoots with corrupt local authorities to ineffective land-reform policies and high unemployment." Slave-like conditions of labor existed in other regions of Brazil, in the sugar cane factories of Bahia, for example.

Child labor, in violation of the law, flourished among the one million Mexican migrants—*jornaleros* (day laborers)—and their families, who abandoned their homes for part of the year to move north with the harvests. They did not leave their homes, observed a sympathetic *New York Times* reporter, because they were looking for better wages; "they are looking for any wages." There were no jobs at home, and their only means of subsistence was the growing of beans and corn on their little milpas. The $1,500 that he and his family hoped to take home at the end of the harvest, one migrant said, was just about all the money they would see for the year. "If the whole family," including his three children aged 8, 10, and 11, "does not work," he explained, "we all starve."

Mexico's President Vicente Fox, who urged the United States to improve the condition of Mexican laborers who crossed the border, appeared to know little of the problem that migrant laborers faced at home. Informed that children as young as 11 worked packing vegetables in the Fox family's plants, he sheepishly surmised that some other person named Fox was involved. When the claim was verified, more than twenty minors were dismissed and the president admitted that the violations were "a sad reality of Mexican life." But this was increasingly prevalent throughout the region, where it was estimated that in 1999 there were 17.5 million working children between the ages of 5 and 14. In a time of growing unemployment and general instability of labor, illegal forced labor and child labor obviously exerted considerable downward pressure on wages, living standards, and efforts to organize unions.

The neoliberal economic policies adopted by most Latin American governments, favoring multinationals and their local allies, also caused a sharp decline in the number and influence of small- and medium-sized national manufacturers; they caused growing impoverishment and unemployment among the middle class and the working class as a result of the privatization or dismantling of many state enterprises, reduction of social services, and a general downsizing of the state as part of "structural adjustment" programs demanded by the IMF and the World Bank. A survey of these and other developments suggests the complexity of modern Latin American class alignments and the possible direction of future social and political change.

## THE GREAT LANDOWNERS

Although they had to yield first place economically and politically to the new bourgeoisie, with which they maintained close links, the great landowners, Latin America's oldest ruling class, retained immense power, thanks to their control over the land and water resources of the area. Over the last few decades, as earlier chapters have shown, there was a major expansion of the latifundio, especially of the new agribusiness type, which produced industrial and export crops with the aid of improved technology and wage labor. More recently, the dominant policies of free trade and open doors to foreign investment further spurred the trend toward concentration of landownership and penetration of Latin American agriculture by foreign capital. Chile, whose civilian government made no effort to restore the agrarian reform destroyed by the Pinochet dictatorship, and Mexico, where Congress recently approved an agrarian law that ended land redistribution and legalized the sale or rental of communally owned ejido land, illustrate the shift toward policies favoring the rise of a new latifundio.

The traditional hacendado was a vanishing breed. His successor was often a cosmopolitan, university-trained type who combined agribusiness with industrial and financial interests. But the arbitrary and predatory spirit of the old hacendados survived in the new latifundistas. The great landowners continued to be the most reactionary class in Latin American society.

## THE NEW BOURGEOISIE

A native commercial bourgeoisie arose in Latin America after independence and consolidated its position with the rise of the neocolonial order after mid-century. In the second half of the nineteenth century, an industrialist class, largely of immigrant stock, appeared in response to the demand of a growing urban population for consumer goods. World War I further stimulated the movement for export/import-substitution industrialization. But the day of the industrial entrepreneur did not arrive until the great economic crisis of 1930 disrupted the trading patterns of the area. Aided by favorable international and domestic background conditions and massive state intervention, the native industrial bourgeoisie quickly gained strength and in many countries displaced the landed elite as the dominant social and economic force. As a rule, however, the new bourgeoisie avoided frontal collision with the latifundistas, preferring to form bonds of kinship and interest with the landed elite.

Meanwhile, foreign capital, attracted by the potential of the growing Latin American market, began to pour into the area, particularly after 1945. Possessing immensely superior capital and technological resources, foreign firms absorbed many small- and middle-sized national companies and came to dominate key sectors of the economy of the host countries. Aware, however, that the survival of a national bourgeoisie was essential to their own security, foreign capitalists endeavored to form close ties with the largest, most powerful national firms through the formation of mixed companies and other devices. This dependence on and linkage with foreign corporations explains why the Latin American new bourgeoisie often lacked nationalist sentiment.

In its youth, some sections of the Latin American national bourgeoisie supported the efforts of such nationalist, populist chieftains as Cárdenas, Perón, and Vargas to restrict foreign economic influence and accepted, though with misgivings, their concessions to labor. But soon the new bourgeoisie adopted the hostility of its foreign allies to restrictions on foreign capital and independent trade unionism. With rare exceptions, these capital-ists supported repressive military regimes in such countries as Brazil, Argentina, Uruguay, and Chile until, convinced that the policies of those regimes threatened the stability of capitalism itself, they became converts to democracy.

Neoliberal policies during the 1990s gave an immense stimulus to the alliance of foreign multi-nationals and local capitalists, an alliance in which foreign capital played the dominant role. The process was under way in many countries, but particularly in Brazil, Argentina, Mexico, Chile, and Venezuela. Privatization became a major instrument for denationalizing the Latin American economy through auctions and debt-equity swaps that virtually donated valuable state companies to foreign firms.

Small groups of local capitalists linked to foreign capital and with "crony" connections to the ruling parties also benefited by the privatization process. In Mexico, for example, after the 1992 privatization of the banking system, "a mere 224 investors held effective control of the Mexican banks. . . . This oligarchy controls the fundamental instruments of economic—and indirectly—political power in Mexico today." Typical of these aggressive new entrepreneurs was Carlos Slim Helú, included in the *Forbes* 1994 ranking of the richest men in the world. With a fortune estimated to be more than $6 billion, Slim, in partnership with two associates and two foreign firms, bought the Mexican telephone giant Telmex during the administration of his friend and business associate Carlos Salinas. Paying little cash and using credit advanced by a number of banks, he paid a mere $1.7 billion for a company whose worth was estimated to be close to $12 billion. After the sale, the price of the company stock "went through the roof." Slim also owned the Denny's and Sanborn's restaurant chains and Mexico's most profitable investment firm in 1996, Carso-Imbursa, in addition to having a monopoly on cigarette manufacturing. His cousin Alfredo Harper Helú was one of a group of billionaires who controlled Banamex, one of Mexico's three largest banks.

Narcorevenues produced another crop of Latin American "new rich." For obvious reasons the membership of the group and the extent of its wealth cannot be stated with certainty. (U.N. agencies put the annual revenue generated by the illegal drug industry at $460 billion, roughly the equivalent of 8 percent of total international trade.) What is certain is that its wealth was vast and that its activity—as revealed in May 1998 by a U.S. money-laundering sting that led to the arrests of about two dozen Mexican bankers—often intersected with the legitimate operations of Latin American entrepreneurs. The drug traffic, the neoliberal policies pushed by the IMF, the World Bank, and other agencies, and the drug war pushed by the United States "have all intersected in an explosive way." By imposing austerity and privatization measures, and by dismantling the Latin American state, neoliberalism created massive unemployment that "generates thousands of recruits for the drug trade—coca growers, day laborers, smugglers, enforcers." By "freeing up" financial markets, neoliberalism also made it easier to launder drug profits and invest them in "legitimate" activities. And by making international borders more porous, trade liberalization created insuperable obstacles to effective interdiction. Between 1993 and 1994, the year NAFTA took effect, the number of trucks entering the United States from Mexico increased 50 percent to 2.8 million, making the problem of locating the odd vehicle with a few hundred kilos of cocaine among its other cargo "more and more akin to finding a needle in a haystack with each passing year." In 1996, 3.55 million commercial trucks and railroad boxcars entered the United States from Mexico; perhaps 5 to 10 percent of them were inspected. The kingdom of the cocaine mafia actually expanded in recent years from Peru, Bolivia, and Colombia to Mexico (now a major transshipment point), Brazil, and Venezuela, with Colombia and Peru branching off into poppy production for heroin as well. The rise of coca capitalism was accompanied by the spread of unprecedented violence (Colombia had one of the highest homicide rates on earth) and a corruption that involved Latin American presidents, generals, and bankers.

## THE URBAN MIDDLE SECTORS

The urban middle sectors occupied an intermediate position between the new bourgeoisie and the landed elite, on the one hand, and the peasantry and the industrial working class, on the other. The boundaries of this intermediate group with other classes were vague and overlapping. At one end, for example, the group included highly paid business managers whose lifestyles and attitudes identified them with the new bourgeoisie; at the other, it included store clerks and lower-echelon government servants whose incomes were often lower than those of skilled workers.

The longest-established urban middle sector consisted of self-employed artisans, shopkeepers, and owners of innumerable small enterprises. White-collar employees formed another large urban intermediate sector. Urbanization, the growth of commercial capitalism, and the vast expansion of the state in the middle decades of the century contributed to the growth of both public and private bureaucracies. Until recently, public employees made up about one-fifth of the economically active population of the area.

University students composed a sizable urban middle sector. Between 1960 and 1970 their number rose from 250,000 to over 1 million. The great majority came from middle-class backgrounds, and many combined work and study. Student discontent with inadequate curricula and teaching methods and the injustices of the social and political order made the university a focal point of dissidence and protest. But the students were in the end transients, in Latin America as elsewhere; their radical or reformist zeal often subsided after they entered a professional career.

Because of their great size, the ideology of the urban middle sectors and their actual and potential role in social change were issues of crucial importance. Following World War II, many foreign experts on Latin America, especially in the United States, pinned great hopes on the "emerging middle sectors" (to which they assigned the new industrialist class) as agents of progressive social and economic change. The history of the following decades did not confirm these expectations. The urban middle sectors mushroomed, but with the exception of many students and intellectual workers—teachers, writers, scientists—they were not a force for progressive social change.

But the urban middle sectors should not be written off as hopeless reactionaries. By their very intermediate nature, they were capable of strong political oscillations, especially in response to the movement of the economy. The "savage capitalism" implanted in many Latin American countries in recent decades by both military and civilian governments played havoc with middle-class living standards and expectations. In the process it also transformed the traditionally conservative, complacent thought patterns of the urban middle sectors.

A good example of such a transformation was *El Barzón*, a Mexican middle-class debtors' union that took its name from the leather strap that held the oxen to the plow on the great haciendas of prerevolutionary times. With a membership of half a million to a million Mexicans in thirty-one states and the Federal District, El Barzón became the largest, most militant resistance movement formed in the wake of the peso's crash in December 1994, which sent interest rates up over 100 percent and threatened thousands of farmers, small businesses, and assorted members of the middle class with financial ruin. With a combination of direct action that included the public burning of credit cards and the blocking of entrances to bank branches to shut down their operations, El Barzón was able to stop the foreclosures and impose a moratorium on the banks. El Barzón also formed links with domestic and foreign trade unions, the Catholic church, debtors' unions in other Latin American countries, and the Zapatistas of Chiapas. Its national director, Juan José Quirino, became a senator of the left-center Partido Revolucionario Democrático (PRD). "It's not just personal debt that we are talking about now—the foreign debt is the mechanism by which the IMF keeps us chained up," says Quirino. "Latin American debtor nations missed the opportunity to unite after 1982. This time we must be ready to fight for a continental moratorium."

## THE PEASANTRY

The term *peasantry* refers here to all small landowners, tenants, and landless rural laborers. As documented in previous chapters, the expansion of the new type of latifundio created an unparalleled crisis for the Latin American peasantry. The increased use of tractors and other kinds of mechanized farm equipment had already displaced millions of farm workers and the process was accelerating. The removal of trade barriers, opening national markets to competition with more efficient foreign grain producers, threatened the existence of small farmers. Meanwhile, the neoliberal trend reversed land reforms; in Mexico, for example, the passage of legislation making communally owned ejido land alienable removed the last obstacles to the concentration of land in a few hands. The result was a growing exodus of impoverished peasants to the overcrowded cities or, in the case of Mexican and Central American campesinos, a sometimes dangerous and unsuccessful effort to make it across the border into an increasingly inhospitable United States. Behind these desperate migrations were sharply declining standards of living. In January 1998, *El Financiero*, Mexico's leading financial newspaper, reported that 67 percent of households in rural zones were "extremely poor"—meaning that they could not satisfy minimal basic requirements.

## THE INDUSTRIAL WORKING CLASS

The rapid growth of capitalism in Latin America since about 1930 was accompanied by a parallel growth of the industrial working class. Although miners and factory workers formed the best-organized and most class-conscious detachments of the army of labor, they were a minority of the labor force. Artisans, self-employed or working in shops employing less than five persons, constituted the largest group. The predominance of the artisan shop, whose labor relations were marked by paternalism and individual bargaining, hindered the development of workers' class consciousness and solidarity.

Despite its small size, the industrial working class played a key role in major movements for social and political democracy in Latin America. Armed Bolivian tin miners helped achieve the victory of the 1952 revolution and its program of land reform and nationalization of mines. Cuban workers gave decisive support to the guerrilla struggle against the Batista dictatorship, and their general strike in 1959 helped topple it. The working class of Buenos Aires intervened at a critical moment in 1945 to save Juan Perón from being overthrown by a reactionary coup, and its pressure broadened his reform program. In Chile the working class led the Popular Unity coalition that brought Salvador Allende to the presidency, ushering in a three-year effort (1970–1973) to achieve socialism by peaceful democratic means.

These advances—particularly the Cuban and Chilean revolutions—provoked a counter-revolutionary reaction that until recently was still ascendant. In many countries under personal or military dictatorships, all working-class parties were banned, trade unions were abolished or placed under strict government control, and many labor leaders were murdered or forced into exile.

The gradual restoration of formal democracy in the region, accompanied by the imposition of the neoliberal economic model, did not bring full recognition of labor's right to organize and other basic rights. In Chile, for example, the new civilian government retained many features of the Pinochet labor code. In Mexico, workers could not freely join unions of their choice, and most union members were forced to join unions affiliated with the ruling Partido Revolucionario Institucional (PRI). In the export-processing areas, like Mexico's maquila sector or the Central American and Caribbean free-trade zones, union rights were routinely ignored. In Argentina, with the election of Carlos Menem in 1989, "a vicious labor counterreform was set in motion" that gutted the traditional Labor Contracting Law, with the result that nearly 90 percent of new hires were temporary rather than permanent. The changes in workplace accident legislation also caused health and safety conditions to deteriorate dramatically. The stated objective of the law was to create more jobs, but the result was just the opposite, with

Argentine unemployment and underemployment estimated at 40 percent of the economically active population.

But Latin American workers still continued the struggle for equality and social justice. In Mexico the Mexican Confederation of Labor (CTM), which held wages to levels decreed by the government and collaborated with the security forces to repress independent unionists, was challenged by a new federation, the National Workers' Union, led by Francisco Hernández Suárez, head of the telephone workers' union; it represented 1.5 million members and was growing fast. In Mexico's maquila sector and the Central American garment sweatshop zone, some breakthroughs in trade-union organization and improvement of working conditions occurred as a result of cooperation between independent local unions and unions and labor rights groups in the United States. The struggle for free-trade unionism and labor's rights was often linked to the struggle against the neoliberal economic model, whose downsizing of the state and other "structural adjustment" policies led to the virtual disappearance of some national industries, a rapid expansion of the informal economy, and the massive unemployment and atomization of labor.

## THE SERVICE OR INFORMAL SECTOR

This sector, the largest of all,[1] arose as a result of industry's inability to absorb the supply of labor; it included "a great number of poorly paid domestic servants and a mass of individuals who eke out a precarious living as lottery ticket vendors, car watchers and washers, shoeshiners, and street peddlers." But the meaning of "informal sector" was extremely elastic and the list of occupations that fit the category almost endless. Its main defining elements were self-employment and the irregular and precarious nature of the work. " 'Informal

---

[1]According to the International Labor Organization, from 1980 to 1992 informal-sector employment rose from 40.2 percent to 54.4 percent of total employment and grew 3.9 percent per year thereafter.

sector,' " observes sociologist Tessa Cubitt, "implies a dualist interpretation of the urban economy, since it proposes a dichotomy between a formal modern capitalist sector in which big businesses and multinationals flourish, and the mass of the poor who are unable to benefit from participation in this sector."

In fact, many of the activities of the informal sector were integrated into the modern capitalist sector, and the links between them were exploitative. The garbage pickers of Cali, Colombia, collected wastepaper, which they sold to warehouses, which in turn sold it to the giant paper company Cartón de Colombia, whose main shareholder was the Mobil Oil Company. "Why," asks Cubitt, "does Cartón de Colombia not directly employ the garbage pickers? Clearly, it is cheaper for them to operate like this because they do not have regular wage bills to pay. The income the garbage pickers receive for each item is extremely low and reduced even further by the competition between them, which is encouraged by the system that is very much a buyer's market." In effect, the low income of the garbage pickers subsidized the multinational Cartón de Colombia. Similar exploitive relations existed between manufacturers and workers who subcontracted to do work in their own homes and were paid for each completed piece. In all such cases the companies saved on wages and the costs of social security benefits; there was the additional benefit of keeping workers weak and divided, unable to present a common front to employers.

# Attitudes and Mentalities: Change and Resistance to Change

Change was in the air of Latin America as it entered the last quarter of the twentieth century. Economic modernization demanded changes in family life, race relations, education, and the whole superstructure of society, but the old attitudes and mentalities struggled hard to survive. As a result, Latin America presented dramatic contrasts between customs and mores that were as new as the Space Age and others that recalled the age of Cortés and Pizarro.

## WOMEN'S PLACE

The status of women was a case in point. In some ways that status had improved; the struggle to obtain the vote, for example, began around World War I and ended successfully when Paraguay granted women suffrage in 1961. More and more Latin American women held appointive and electoral offices, and in increasing numbers they entered factories, offices, and the professions. By 1970, in some countries, notably Brazil and Argentina, the percentage of women classified as professionals was higher than that percentage for men, a significant fact because the proportion of economically active women was much lower than that of men. In Brazil, out of every 100 women working in nonagricultural services in 1970, 18 were engaged in professional and technical operations, whereas for men the figure was only 6 out of every 100. The ratios were reversed, however, for positions of higher responsibility, reflecting the persistence of discriminatory attitudes.

The movement for women's rights could claim much less progress in such areas as family patterns, divorce laws, and sexual codes. The traditions of the patriarchal family, of closely supervised courtship and marriage, continued strong among the upper and middle classes. The ideology of machismo, the cult of male superiority with its corollary of a sexual double standard, continued to reign almost everywhere in the continent. "The Mexican family," wrote sociologist Rogelio Díaz-Guerrero, "is founded upon two fundamental propositions: (a) the unquestioned and absolute supremacy of the father and (b) the necessary and absolute self-sacrifice of the mother." The flood of economic, political, and social change of almost three decades weakened the force of this statement, but with some qualifications it still held for most Latin American republics.

Socialist Cuba made great advances in abolishing sexual discrimination in law and practice, however; in 1975 it introduced the Family Code, which gave the force of law to the division of household labor. Working men and women were required to share housework and child care equally, and a recalcitrant spouse could be taken by the other to court. But Vilma Espín, head of the Cuban women's movement, admitted that the law was one thing and the way people lived was another: "Tradition is very strong. But we have advanced. Before, the machismo was terrible. Before, the men on the streets would brag about how their wives took care of them and did all the work at home. They were very proud of that. At least now we have reached the point where they don't dare say that. That's an advance. And now with young people you can see the difference."

Nicaragua was another country where a liberating revolution transformed the lives and roles of many women. Women, both rural and urban, took part in the struggle against the Somoza tyranny and made an immense contribution to its final triumph in July 1979. Women prepared for the final offensive by stockpiling food, gathering medical supplies, and organizing communications networks to send messages to Sandinista fighters and their families. By the time of the final victory, from one-quarter to one-third of the Sandinista People's Army was female—some as young as thirteen. Three women were guerrilla commanders; two served on the general staff of the People's Army. Following the triumph of the revolution, women assumed responsible positions at all levels of the Sandinista government. A similar process of women's liberation took place as part of the revolutionary struggle in neighboring El Salvador.

In the Southern Cone, women took the lead in the struggle against the military dictatorships that arose in Chile (1973), Uruguay (1973), and Argentina (1976). That role was thrust upon them as a result of the repressive policies of the dictatorships, the banning of trade unions and political parties, and the murder or disappearance of thousands of activists. Women paid a price for their sacrifices. Thirteen members of the Argentine human rights movement, including the president of the Mothers of the Plaza de Mayo, who demanded an accounting for their disappeared children, vanished into the death camps.

Despite their services, women in Cuba, Nicaragua, and the countries of the Southern Cone had not achieved full recognition of their equality. Gioconda Belli, a former Nicaraguan guerrilla leader, complained: "We'd led troops into battle, we'd done all sorts of things, and then as soon as the Sandinistas took office we were displaced from the important posts. We'd had to content ourselves with intermediate-level positions for the most part." Her complaint was echoed by an Uruguayan trade unionist who had taken part in the struggle against the military dictatorship: "When the men came out of prison or returned from exile, they took up all the spaces, sat down in the same chairs, and expected the women to go back home." And Rosa, one of the Chilean working-class women who played key roles in the resistance to the military dictatorship, wryly remembered: "When the democratic government took over, the men around here said, 'It's okay, Rosa, you can leave it to us now.' We thought, 'Have they forgotten everything we did during the dictatorship?'" Consciously or unconsciously, the old prejudices persisted in the thought patterns of men—even radicals and revolutionaries—from one end of the area to the other.

Women responded to the continuing challenge of machismo by forming a multitude of groups that, whether or not they called themselves feminist, had as their essential goal the end of the old unequal relations between the sexes. One *encuentro*, or meeting, in Nicaragua in March 1992 brought together some five hundred Central American women "who talked about the power Central American women have in their 'public' and 'private' lives, the kind of power they would like to have, and how to go about getting that power." But women were divided among themselves by class, and Latin American working-class women often criticized traditional feminist organizations as middle-class and indifferent to their own practical needs. "We have things in common with middle class women, but we also have other problems that middle class women don't have, like the housing shortage, debt problems, unemployment," said one Chilean woman activist, "and we're not going to advance as women if the two things aren't closely linked."

Economic forces, in particular the disastrous impact of neoliberal economic policies on household incomes and living standards, were silently helping transform gender and familial relations in many parts of the area. It was becoming increasingly difficult for one wage to support a family. From sheer necessity, women were entering industry in record numbers. According to the InterAmerican Development Bank, the proportion of women in the labor force rose 50 percent, from almost 18 percent in 1950 to just under 27 percent in 1990.

The results were particularly evident in an area like the Caribbean Basin, where declining traditional exports such as sugar, coffee, and bananas, industries that employed a predominantly male labor force gave way to export manufacturing, typically employing poorly paid woman workers. Similar economic trends, challenging male dominance in the household, were under way in other countries of the region.

As Latin America entered the twenty-first century, however, a growing gulf appeared between women's legal and social equality. A major legal achievement was the passage of national legislation to prevent and punish violence against women, modeled on the United Nations' Convention on the Elimination of All Forms of Discrimination Against Women. Still another was the creation of state bureaucracies to advance women's interests, sometimes linked to larger agencies responsible for the areas of culture, education, or the family. Finally, in country after country during the 1990s, laws were adopted that established quotas for women in each party's list of candidates. During Fujimori's ten-year rule in Peru, for example, Congress required political parties to field women candidates in at least 30 percent of local and congressional races, enacted laws against domestic violence, and authorized both a Ministry of Women and a Public Defender for Women. Indeed, during Fujimori's last, brief, and chaotic administration, Congress was run by a governing council composed entirely of women.

But, as Maruja Barrig points out, the cause of women's legal equality often advanced without improving their deteriorating social and economic conditions. "In the 1990s, for example, 70% of the Bolivian population was considered poor, climbing to 90% in rural areas. In Peru, close to 50% of the population is classified as poor. The literacy rate among the female indigenous population, as a group, is the lowest in Latin America. The 1991 national census in Bolivia found that 50% of rural women could not read. In Peru, according to the 1993 National Census, the figure was 43%." And the health statistics, Barrig notes, "are no less alarming. . . . In Bolivia, there are 300 maternal deaths for every 100,000 births, but in Potosí the number of maternal deaths per 100,000 could reach 600." Noting that, after Haiti, Bolivia and Peru had the highest rates of maternal death in Latin America, the United Nations Population Fund described this as "one of the most dramatic representations of social injustice and the inequality among women."

Meanwhile, Salvadoran lawmakers, responding to pressure from pro-life groups, eliminated the four legal options for abortion from the country's 1997 legal code. In Chile conservative forces defeated a divorce law and retained in the civil code the statutory definition of the husband as the "head" of the family. In response to these defeats and "internal cracks in the institutional structures created for women," Barrig notes that "in the search for the possible, a subtle pragmatism appears to have become lodged in the strategies of feminists playing by the rules proposed by others." The women's movements of Ecuador and Chile, for example, decided to give priority to lobbying and negotiation "over mobilization and denunciation."

### RACE PREJUDICE

Notions of the inferiority of blacks and indigenous peoples were everywhere officially disapproved, but race prejudice remained strong, especially among upper- and middle-class people who identified themselves as white. In Brazil, often touted as a model of racial democracy, sociologist Florestan Fernandes found that these people clung to "the *prejudice of having no prejudice*, limiting themselves to treating blacks with tolerance, maintaining the old ceremonial politeness in inter-racial relationships, and excluding from this tolerance any true egalitarian feeling or content." In 2002 Brazilian newspapers carried advertisements from private companies that called for a "good appearance," a code phrase understood to mean that blacks should not apply. In a 2000 census, only 6 percent of the population of 170 million identified themselves as black, a low figure that proponents of reform attributed to discrimination and a poor racial self-image. A DNA study by Brazilian scientists suggested that as many as 80 percent of Brazilians had African ancestry. But only 2.2 percent of Brazil's 1.6 million college students were black, and blacks were almost invisible on television except in menial or exotic roles. In 2003 the Brazilian Congress had before it a measure that would reserve 20 percent of university admissions for blacks and apply the same figure to Civil Service jobs; the plan would also require black or mixed-race actors to compose 25 percent of the cast of any theatrical or television production. The measure stirred up much debate, for and against.

In Brazil, Venezuela, Colombia, and other Latin American countries with large black populations, unlike the situation in the United States, where people were categorized as either white or black, there was a kind of "sliding scale" of prejudice and discrimination against blacks that tended to vary according to the shade of skin color. Mulattos were usually favored over blacks. As a rule the higher occupations such as medicine, law, upper-level governments posts, and the officer and diplomatic corps were closed to both categories. But mulattos could aspire to become schoolteachers, journalists, bank tellers, low-level municipal officials, and the like. The lowest-paid jobs were reserved for dark-skinned people. The virulent opposition attacks on populist President Hugo Chávez of Venezuela, who boasted of his black and indigenous ancestry, had a clear racist component.

Even in black Haiti, a vast economic and social gulf separated an urban mulatto elite from the rural black masses of poor people and the "black ghetto" of downtown Port-au-Prince. In the neighboring Dominican Republic, the late President Joaquín Balaguer had preached an overt racism, claiming that his "white and Christian" country was threatened by the "biological imperialism" of Haitian immigrants. In fact, the Dominican Republic has been described as the only true mulatto country in the world. A pervasive Dominican racism, based on a rejection of African ancestry and darkness and on supposed links with a superior indigenous Spanish racial heritage, led to a pattern of mistreatment of the large Haitian immigrant community and periodic waves of immigrant expulsion, the latest taking place in 1999. Meanwhile, only revolutionary Cuba had largely eliminated racism in both theory and practice; here, blacks held high positions in government, the armed forces, and the professions. But the roots of racism in a country with Cuba's history were deep and strong, and Castro himself recognized that racial, gender, and class prejudices persisted.

The indigenous peoples of Latin America remained the principal victims of racist exploitation and violence. In Brazil, according to one recent estimate, the number of indigenous people had dropped from 1,000,000 to 180,000 since the beginning of the twentieth century. This process of cultural destruction in the interests of economic progress continued unabated. Since 1975 some 1,000 Yanomamis, of the 9,000 living in Brazil and 12,000 in Venezuela, had been murdered, mostly by gold miners. Similar wanton killings were reported in the jungle lowlands of Colombia, and murderers of natives by land-grabbing hacendados or their *pistoleros* (gunmen) occurred in Mexico, Guatemala, and other countries with sizable indigenous populations. In Guatemala military regimes practiced systematic genocide against the Maya and attempted to eradicate their culture.

In some countries the native peasantry was subjected to a many-sided economic, social, and cultural exploitation. "The Indian problem," writes Mexican sociologist Pablo González Casanova, "is essentially one of internal colonialism. The Indian communities are Mexico's internal colonies. . . . Here we find prejudice, discrimination, colonial forms of exploitation, dictatorial forms, and the separation of a different population, with a different race and culture." Some Mexican social scientists claimed that Mexicans had long been blind to their own racism and discrimination. One cited a paragraph written in 1985 by a leading historian,

Enrique Krauze: "Mexico constructed a tradition of natural liberty and equality that was rooted in the culture of the people and freed us very early from slavery, servitude, and racism."

These revisionist scholars assigned much of the blame for this blindness to an indigenous policy that dated from the time of independence, and that gave native peoples (and people of African descent) the option of abandoning their cultures or becoming wax figures in a historical museum. The framers of this integrationist policy, whose good intentions were not questioned, included such illustrious names in scholarship or politics as Manuel Gamio, Gonzalo Aguirre Beltrán, Alfonso Caso, and the revered Lázaro Cárdenas. Adding a touch of humor, the ethnologist Luz María Martínez Montiel declared that the anthropologists themselves had made the important Instituto Nacional Indigenista "the last *encomienda* in Mexico." For Martínez, integration of the indigenous peoples consisted not in despoiling them of their identities and cultures but in assuring their equal rights in the process of production, education, and expression. And it is they, she stressed, who must decide.

In the spring of 2001 the Zapatista Army of National Liberation, led by Subcomandante Marcos, staged an impressive march from Chiapas to Mexico City to demand that President Fox comply with campaign promises to quickly solve indigenous demands for autonomy and control of their resources. On the way north the Zapatista caravan was greeted by thousands of supporters and received petitions and memorials like the Declaration of the Indigenous Peoples of Morelos: "What do we want and demand? To be treated with respect as indigenous peoples. That we should not be jailed for defending our land. That there should be true justice. An end to industrial and commercial megaprojects in communal and ejido land. An end to the destruction of our forests, waters, and natural resources. An end to the neoliberal modernization that is causing the disappearance of the indigenous peoples. That we be taken into account when decisions are made. We want to be part of development, not a simple rung on which others step up for their development."

But in the capital disillusionment awaited the rebels. Congress left the implementation of a list of native "rights" to the state legislatures, effectively leaving matters as they were. The Zapatista reply was swift and decisive: "If this reform deserves any name, it should be 'the Constitutional Recognition of the Rights and Culture of the Latifundists and Racists.'" Returning to Chiapas, the rebels and their communities faced the same problems of military encirclement and harassment by paramilitary bands in the service of great landowners and reactionary politicians. In a struggle that had now lasted more than eight years, the Zapatistas avoided a suicidal armed project to seize power. But they also refused to limit their demands to conditions in Chiapas, focusing instead on principles of indigenous self-determination and national democratic reform. By adroit use of the most modern means of communication and a series of national and international meetings, they made their struggle known and won sympathy throughout the world, achieving a front-line place in the battle against globalization and neoliberalism, and making the name of Subcomandante Marcos as well known as that of Che Guevara.

The indigenous peoples of America were on the march, forming broad coalitions with unions, middle-class groups, and international organizations, and they were winning victories. In 2001, grassroots movements from all over the world came to Cochabamba, the third-largest city in Bolivia. "Cochabamba," writes Sophia Style, "became a key symbol of the struggle against global capitalism, when thousands of local people took to the streets against the privatization of their water supply by the U.S. transnational Bechtel—and won." The victory had its costs. After a mobilization of 30,000 people had shut down the city center for five days, President Hugo Banzer (former dictator of Bolivia) sent in troops, including a sharpshooter trained at the School of the Americas, who gunned down a 17-year-old protestor.

One milestone in the struggle of the indigenous peoples of America against old and new forms of exploitation was the decision of the United Nations to declare 1993 the International

The 1992 awarding of the Nobel Peace Prize to the Maya activist Rigoberta Menchú gave a large boost to the struggle against genocide of indígenas and for indigenous political and social rights in her native Guatemala and throughout Latin America. [Reuters Newmedia Inc./Corbis]

Year of the Indigenous Peoples of the World. Another was the award of the Nobel Peace Prize to the Guatemalan indigenous leader Rigoberta Menchú (October 1992), in recognition of her work on behalf of the native peoples of America. More recently indigenous-rights organizations in Ecuador and Bolivia successfully mobilized their members to challenge neoliberal agendas; in 2001 they unseated an unpopular president in Ecuador, and the following year they became a dominant force in Bolivian electoral politics.

## THE CATHOLIC CHURCH

The ideological crisis of Latin America was illustrated by the rifts that emerged in two of the area's oldest and most conservative institutions, the Catholic Church and the armed forces.

The new reformist and revolutionary currents that emerged within the Catholic Church since about 1960 had different sources. One was a more liberal climate of opinion within the church brought about by the Second Vatican Council, convened in 1962 under Pope John XXIII. Another was concern on the part of some elements of the hierarchy that the church's traditional collusion with the elites risked a loss of the masses to Marxism. Still another was a crisis of conscience on the part of some clergy, especially working clergy whose experiences convinced them that the area's desperate dilemmas required drastic solutions.

The new ferment within the Latin American church found dramatic expression in the life and death of the famous Colombian priest and sociologist Camilo Torres. Born into an aristocratic Colombian family, a brilliant scholar and teacher, Torres, who became convinced of the futility of seeking to achieve reform by peaceful means, joined the communist-led guerrilla National Liberation Army. He was killed in a clash with counterinsurgency forces in February 1966.

The proper stand for the church to take in the face of Latin America's structural crisis was hotly debated at the second conference of Latin American bishops, held at Medellín, Colombia, in 1968. The presence of Pope Paul VI at its opening session underlined the meeting's importance. Reflecting the leftward shift of portions of the clergy, the bishops at Medellín affirmed the commitment of the church to the task of liberating the people of Latin America from neocolonialism and "institutionalized violence." This violence, declared the bishops, was inherent in the economic, social, and political structures of the continent, dependent on what Pope Paul called "the international imperialism of money."

Even before Medellín, a group of Latin American bishops had taken a position in favor of socialism. Their leader was Helder Câmara, archbishop of Recife (Brazil). He and seven other Brazilian bishops had signed a pastoral letter issued by seventeen bishops of the Third World that called on the church to avoid identification of religion "with the oppression of the poor and the workers, with feudalism, capitalism, imperialism." Himself rejecting violence as an instrument of revolutionary change, Helder Câmara expressed sympathy and understanding for those who felt that violence was the only effective tactic.

These developments were accompanied by the emergence and growing acceptance by many clergy of the so-called theology of liberation, the product of the study and reflection of leading church scholars in various Latin American countries. This doctrine taught that the church, returning to its roots, must again become a Church of the Poor. It must cease to be an ally of the rich and powerful and commit itself to the struggle for social justice, to raising the consciousness of the masses, to making them aware of the abuses from which they suffered and of the need to unite to change an oppressive economic and political system. Liberation theology rejected Marxism's atheist world view but drew heavily on the Marxist analysis of the causes of the poverty and oppression in the Third World. On the subject of revolution, though deploring all violence, liberation theologians taught that revolution, or counterviolence, was justified as a last resort against the greater violence of tyrants, an orthodox Catholic teaching that went back to St. Thomas Aquinas. It was in this spirit that Archbishop Oscar Arnulfo Romero of San Salvador, in one of the last sermons he gave before he was murdered by a right-wing assassin in March 1980, declared: "When all peaceful means have been exhausted, the Church considers insurrection moral and justified."

To implement the teachings of liberation theology, progressive clergy set about developing a new type of Christian organization, the *comunidad de base,* or Christian grassroots organization. Composed of poor people in the countryside and the barrios of cities, assisted and advised by priests and students, these communities combined religious study and reflection with efforts to define and solve the practical social problems of their localities. The great landowners and the authorities frequently branded their activities as subversive, and both laity and priests were subjected to severe repression. This led to a growing politicization and radicalization of many communities and their involvement in revolutionary movements.

In Nicaragua the Christian communities were integrated into the revolutionary struggle led by the Sandinista Front for National Liberation to a degree not found elsewhere in Latin America. This unity of rank-and-file Catholic clergy and laity with the revolution continued after the Sandinista triumph in July 1979. Five priests held high office in the revolutionary government and defied a 1980 Vatican ruling barring direct priestly involvement in political life. Many priests and nuns enthusiastically supported and participated in the literacy campaign and other reconstruction projects of the new regime.

But conflict between this progressive faction and conservatives in the church hierarchy soon emerged at the third conference of Latin American bishops, convened at Puebla, Mexico, in March 1979. Unlike Medellín, where the progressives had the upper hand, conservatives controlled the agenda and clearly intended to put down the troublesome liberation theology. They prepared a working paper that urged resignation on the part of the poor in the hope of a better hereafter and placed their trust for the solution of Latin America's great social problems in the failed reformist models of the 1960s. This document raised a storm of criticism among progressive bishops and other clergy.

The unknown element in the equation at Puebla was the position of Pope John Paul II, who was to inaugurate the conference. Despite their ambiguity, the pope's statements in general tended to reinforce the position of progressives and moderates at the Puebla conference. Its final document continued the line of Medellín, especially in its expression of overwhelming concern for the poor: "We identify as the most devastating and humiliating scourge, the situation of inhuman poverty in which millions of Latin Americans live, with starvation wages, unemployment and underemployment, malnutrition, infant mortality, lack of adequate housing, health problems, and labor unrest."

Later the pope's opposition to liberation theology and the so-called popular church appeared to harden. He expressed this opposition during his visit to Nicaragua in 1983, a visit that produced an extraordinary confrontation between the pope and the mass of the faithful who came to hear his homily.

Brazil—where many bishops accepted the basic tenets of liberation theology, actively engaged in the struggle for land reform, and enjoyed the support of many thousands of grassroots communities—became another target of the pope's attack on the supposed subversive or heretical teachings of liberation theology. This attack took the form of sanctions against a very popular theologian, Leonardo Boff, and of efforts to weaken the majority of progressive Brazilian bishops by naming more conservative bishops.

The Vatican also joined the Mexican government in efforts to force Bishop Samuel Ruiz of San Cristóbal de las Casas, in Chiapas, to resign. Ruiz, a champion of the poor Maya campesinos of his diocese, was accused of having a Marxist interpretation of the Gospel and "incorrect theological reflection." The effort apparently collapsed when the Salinas administration asked Ruiz to mediate between the government and the indigenous rebels after the outbreak of a revolt in Chiapas in January 1994.

But in the course of a historic January 1999 visit to Cuba, the pontiff seemed to signal some change of course. Although he called on the Castro government to grant greater religious, civil, and political liberties to Cubans, he praised the social achievements of the Cuban Revolution and, in what appeared to be a thinly veiled reference to the United States, urged Cubans to reject the neoliberal capitalist policies of Western nations because such policies led to the creation of a small wealthy upper class and a large impoverished underclass. Most striking of all, he repeatedly criticized the U.S. embargo against Cuba as unjust.

The recent rapid growth in membership and influence of Protestant evangelical or fundamentalist sects posed a major challenge to the religious supremacy of the Catholic Church in Latin America. Between 1981 and 1987 the membership of these sects had doubled to 50 million. In Guatemala they claimed 30 percent of the population; the most recent figures for Chile and Brazil were 15 and 10 percent of the population. The dramatic economic and social changes taking place throughout the continent had much to do with the phenomenal growth of these new churches. Their revivalist preaching and "pie-in-the-sky" message brought color, excitement, and hope to the lives of the uprooted rural immigrants of the shantytowns that ringed every Latin American city. The churches' support networks often provided these "marginal" people with material assistance as well.

Despite the current pope's ambiguous attitude toward progressive Catholic social thought, liberation theology still strongly influenced the theory and practice of Latin American Catholic clergy. Their continuing activism was reflected in a statement issued by four bishops of dioceses on the Colombian-Ecuadorian border, meeting in

Esmeraldas, Ecuador, June 18–22, 2001. These bishops denounced Plan Colombia, the Free Trade Area of the Americas, and President George W. Bush's Andean Initiative as part of an unjust system that would aggravate instead of solve the area's problems of poverty and violence. Poverty, they declared, was the primary evil and the principal cause of violence in the area. The bishops were responding to a request by priests, religious and lay church workers, and representatives of nongovernmental organizations working on the border that they speak out on the effects of Plan Colombia in their dioceses. "What is happening now in Colombia," declared Bishop Arturo Correa of Ipiales, Colombia, "will happen in Ecuador, Peru, Venezuela, Brazil, and all of poor America."

Interestingly, the bishops' statement directly opposed the official Colombian and Ecuadorian governments' support of Plan Colombia, which included permission for the U.S. government to install a military base at the port of Manta to carry out surveillance of drug cultivation and trafficking in Colombia, Peru, Bolivia, and the Caribbean. But the bishops went farther and rejected "the imposition of an unjust economic system that fails to respect human dignity and attacks the most elemental human rights." They viewed Plan Colombia, the FTAA, and the Andean Initiative as part of the neoliberal economic model, reflecting the ambition of wealthy countries for a redistribution of areas of influence. Ecuadorian Bishop Gonzalo López of Sucumbios saw a connection between the militarization of the drug war and these free-trade initiatives. "One is a military attempt to control the region, while the others will be used to ensure open markets and access to our countries' resources." The bishops stressed that they favored the eradication of illicit crops, but demanded "procedures that respect the ecosystem, biodiversity, and especially human life" and called for a different economic plan "based on sustainability and economic solidarity."

## THE MILITARY

Within the Latin American armed forces, as within the church, a differentiation was taking place. The phenomenon of the reformist or even social revolutionary military officer was older than is sometimes supposed. In Brazil the tenente revolts of the 1920s paved the way for the triumph of Getúlio Vargas's reformist revolution of 1930. Juan Perón and other members of the Group of United Officers exemplified a similar tendency within the Argentine officer corps in the 1930s. In Guatemala in 1944 a group of progressive officers led by Colonel Jacobo Arbenz overthrew the Ubico dictatorship and installed a government that enacted a sweeping land reform and other democratic changes. Although the military regimes in Peru (1968), Panama (1968), and Ecuador (1972) differed considerably in the scope and depth of their reforms, they demonstrated the existence of a reformist or even revolutionary officer class.

The massive influx of North American capital into Latin America after 1945, accompanied by the growing political influence of the United States in the area, altered the balance of forces between conservatives and progressives within the Latin American military. Many high-ranking officers became fervent converts to the North American system of free enterprise and accepted the inevitability of a mortal struggle between "atheistical communism" and the "free world." By the Treaty of Rio de Janeiro (1947), the Latin American republics committed themselves to join the United States in the defense of the Western Hemisphere. In the context of the cold war, this commitment entailed collaboration with the United States in a global anticommunist strategy, to the extent of justifying military intervention in any country threatened or conquered by "communist penetration." Under the cover of this doctrine, in 1965 Brazilian troops joined U.S. forces in intervening in the Dominican Republic to crush the progressive revolutionary government of Colonel Francisco Caamaño. The integration of Latin American armies into the strategic plans of the Pentagon converted many into appendages of the North American military machine.

This integration was accompanied by the establishment of the technical and ideological tutelage of the Pentagon over the Latin American military, aimed particularly at the destruction of Latin American revolutionary movements. After the victory of the Cuban Revolution in 1959, this program of training and indoctrination was greatly expanded. Thousands of Latin American officers were sent to take courses in counterinsurgency warfare at Fort Bragg, Fort Knox, Fort Monmouth, and other installations in the United States and in the Panama Canal Zone. An especially important role continued to be played by the School of the Americas (SOA), run by the United States Army for the training of Latin American officers. Founded in 1946 in Panama, it was moved in 1984 to Fort Benning, Georgia, when the Panama Canal Zone Treaty forced its removal from Panama. Since its inception more than 56,000 Latin American personnel received training at the SOA in the art of waging a "dirty little war."

Dubbed by *Newsweek* "a school for dictators," SOA's graduates included General Augusto Pinochet, former head of the Chilean fascist junta; Manuel Noriega, dictator of Panama and U.S. protégé until an imprudent display of independence caused his downfall; and the late Roberto D'Aubuisson, organizer of death-squad activities and charged with responsibility for the assassination of Archbishop Oscar Romero in El Salvador. According to the United Nations Truth Commission in El Salvador, SOA graduates directed many of the massacres and atrocities committed by the military in that country; nineteen of the twenty-seven officers implicated in the Jesuit priest killings in 1989 were SOA alumni, as were eight of the twelve officers charged with responsibility for the El Mozote massacre. Among documents recently discovered in Paraguay's so-called Horror Archives was a folder labeled "Confidential" containing a torture manual used at the SOA. The manual taught "interrogators" how to keep electric shock victims alive and responsive by methods that included dousing their heads and bodies with salt water. In 1997 the number of Mexican military personnel trained at the SOA more than doubled, rising to 305. U.S. Congressperson Joseph Kennedy, a harsh critic of the school, claimed that SOA graduates planned the massacre of 45 indígenas at Acteal, Chiapas. More recently, the U.S. mil-

itary sought to sanitize the SOA by bestowing on it a new name: The Western Hemisphere Institute of Security Cooperation.

The formation of close ties between high-ranking officers and large foreign and domestic firms contributed to the making of a reactionary military mentality. In Argentina in the 1960s, 143 retired officers of the highest ranks held 177 of the leading posts in the country's largest industrial and financial enterprises, mostly foreign-controlled. Latin America thus developed its own military-industrial complex. Through all these means, the United States acquired an enormous influence over the Latin American military.

The CIA's close links with Latin American right-wing military and their counterrevolutionary projects are well known. The CIA's 1954 role in the destruction of the government of Jacobo Arbenz Guzmán, Guatemala's democratically elected reformist president, offers the classic example. Not until May 1997 did the CIA make public the classified records bearing on that intervention. Perhaps the "most chilling document" in the collection, writes Kate Doyle, is an unsigned "Study of Assassination," in which the agency laid out "in excruciating detail" its proposals to murder leading members of the Arbenz government and military. The CIA also compiled hit lists in preparation for the coup. The success of the operation convinced President Eisenhower that such clandestine operations were "a safe, inexpensive substitute for [the use of] armed force." Not until 1995 did the Clinton administration finally cut off CIA counterinsurgency aid to Guatemala after revelations that an "agency asset," Guatemalan Army Colonel Julio Roberto Alpiréz, had been involved in the murders of U.S. citizen Michael DeVine and Efraín Bámaca Velásquez, a guerrilla leader who was married to the Harvard-educated lawyer Jennifer Harbury. But the Clinton administration still provided counter-drug aid to Guatemala, even though most of the major syndicates uncovered by the Drug Enforcement Agency (DEA) had direct links to Guatemalan military officers.

Revolutionary Cuba was next in line after Guatemala; in 1960 President Eisenhower signed a directive authorizing the CIA "to get rid of

Castro." The Bay of Pigs disaster of April 1961 was "a direct descendant" of the Guatemalan operation, based on the assumption that Castro would suffer the same "loss of nerve" that Arbenz had in 1954. When that failed, the agency launched a series of sabotage efforts against Cuba and unsuccessful assassination attempts against Castro. In July 1998 the *New York Times* published two sensational reports based on interviews with the anti-Castro Cuban exile Luis Posada Carriles as well as declassified CIA files. In the interviews, Posada claimed credit for a series of terrorist activities, including a wave of bombings of Cuban hotels and restaurants in 1997 that killed one tourist and alarmed the Cuban government. "The CIA," he said, "taught us everything—everything. They taught us explosives, how to kill, bomb, trained us in sabotage." The CIA, for its part, commended Posada in one document as "of good character, very reliable, security-conscious," and in another said his "performance in all assigned tasks has been excellent." Posada also claimed that he had received considerable financial support for his terrorist activities from the late Jorge Mas Canosa, the millionaire founder of the anti-Castro Cuban American National Foundation and a close political ally of successive U.S. presidents, including President Clinton; his claim was backed by evidence in the intelligence files.

In Chile, after the election of Socialist Salvador Allende as president in 1970, the CIA desperately tried to prevent his inauguration. According to a recently declassified report on the CIA's Chilean Task Force Activities, the agency "focused on provoking a military coup," the principal obstacle to which was the "apolitical, constitutional-oriented inertia of the Chilean military." To overcome this obstacle, President Nixon ordered CIA chief Richard Helms to "make the economy scream" and pursued a two-track policy combining economic destabilization with shipments of arms and money to right-wing army officers. This eventually led to the overthrow and death of Allende and the establishment of a repressive military dictatorship that ruled for two decades and still casts its long shadow over a supposedly "democratic" Chile.

In 2001 the sons of former Chilean Commander-in-Chief René Schneider, killed in 1970 in a failed attempt to kidnap him, filed suit in a U.S. federal court seeking more than $3 million in damages from Henry Kissinger, President Nixon's national security adviser at the time; Richard Helms, former CIA director; and the U.S. government, for "summary execution," assault, and civil-rights violations. Citing recently declassified CIA documents, the suit charged that U.S. authorities conspired to remove Schneider because he stood in the way of their planned military coup to prevent Salvador Allende from taking office as Chile's elected president. Judges in Chile and Argentina unsuccessfully sought to secure Kissinger's testimony regarding his knowledge of Operation Condor, a vast operation organized between 1970 and 1980 by the dictatorships of Latin America's Southern Cone to aid each other in the elimination of their political opponents, without regard for national borders.

In 1981 in Honduras, turned into a base for the secret war against Sandinist Nicaragua with the cooperation of the Honduran army, the CIA helped create a new army intelligence unit called Battalion 316 to counter subversion. Recently declassified documents reveal that the CIA trained the unit in surveillance, interrogation, and torture. The Battalion learned well, torturing hundreds of Honduran citizens and "disappearing" many others.

In March 1998, attempting to refute charges that the CIA knowingly had cooperated with Nicaraguan contras who ran drugs into the United States, CIA Inspector General Frederick R. Hitz admitted in a curiously roundabout way that, at the very least, there had been instances "where the CIA did not, in an expeditious or consistent fashion, cut off relationships with individuals supporting the contra program who were alleged to have engaged in drug trafficking activity, or take action to resolve the allegations."

# The Flowering of Latin American Culture

By mid-century, Latin American culture had attained maturity in a number of fields. Art and scholarship drew closer to the people and their problems and at the same time displayed a growing mastery of the refinements of technique. The swelling output of Latin American art and scholarship grew into a torrent; we can only note some major trends in each field, with special attention to literature, a faithful mirror of Latin American history and problems.

## THE SOCIAL SCIENCES

Latin American social scientists, continuing the tradition of such nineteenth-century enlighteners as Sarmiento, Alberdi, and Lastarria, have for the most part rejected an impossible neutrality and have openly taken sides in the political and social struggles of the area. In Latin America even history, the most aristocratic of the social sciences, has walked hand in hand with politics. The liberal current, which dominated nineteenth-century historiography, was represented in the twentieth century by such major figures as the Mexican Daniel Cosío Villegas, who directed and took part in the writing of the monumental *Modern History of Mexico*, and the Argentine Ricardo Levene, who founded a historical school stressing archival research, rigorous critical method, and economic factors.

But there also existed a conservative current whose hallmarks were nostalgia for the colonial period and enthusiasm for such right-wing nineteenth-century caudillos as Alamán and Rosas. In Mexico this tendency was typified by José Vasconcelos, who proclaimed that Cortés was the creator of Mexican nationality; in Argentina it was represented by a group of revisionist historians who sought to rehabilitate the federalist caudillo Juan Manuel Rosas and bitterly criticized such fathers of Argentine liberalism as Mitre and Sarmiento.

Less involved in such historical quarrels were younger scholars who applied the new methods of social and quantitative history to the study of history, especially the colonial period. In Mexico this new school was represented by Enrique Florescano, in Chile by Mario Góngora, Alvaro Jara, and Rolando Mellafe. The Marxist historical method also had its able practitioners, such as

Germán Carrera Damas in Venezuela, Caio Prado Júnior in Brazil, and Enrique Semo in Mexico.

The rise of Latin American anthropology was linked to that of nationalist, reformist movements whose programs stressed the redemption of indigenous peoples and their integration in the national society. The triumph of the Mexican Revolution of 1910 gave a large impetus to such indigenismo. With modest official support and in an atmosphere of widespread and sometimes emotional interest in Mexico's indigenous past, Mexican anthropology made large quantitative and qualitative advances after 1920. The long roster of its distinguished names includes Manuel Gamio, Alfonso Caso, Wigberto Jiménez Moreno, and Miguel Covarrubias. In Peru the pro-indigenista propaganda of the Alianza Popular Revolucionaria Americana (APRA) and other reformist or revolutionary movements stimulated a revival of interest in the study of indigenous peoples, past and present; two pioneers of Peruvian anthropology were Julio Tello and Luis Valcárcel. In the same period, Gilberto Freyre and Arturo Ramos in Brazil and Fernando Ortiz in Cuba began to explore the contributions made by blacks and attack racial myths. In recent decades, Latin American anthropology has combined a strong interest in the social, economic, and political structures of the ancient indigenous peoples with much attention to the problems of contemporary indigenous groups.

The first task of modern Latin American sociology was to rid itself of its nineteenth-century Spencerian heritage, which attributed the area's disorder and backwardness to the racial inferiority of indigenous and other nonwhite groups. Since about 1960 there arose a "new sociology" that rejected the "impartial," empirical sociology in vogue in the United States. The new school openly identified itself with the struggle for radical social change. A Marxist perspective illuminated the writings of such scholars as Fals Borda, Rodolfo Stavenhagen, Pablo González Casanova (Mexico), Octavio Ianni, and Florestan Fernandes (Brazil). The new school made contributions to the understanding of such problems as the causes of rural violence, internal colonialism, the social basis of Latin American populism, and race relations in Brazil.

Economics was a relatively young science in Latin America. Its rise was largely connected with the great crisis of 1930 and its disastrous impact on the economy of the area. In the 1940s the U.N.'s Economic Commission for Latin America (ECLA), led by the Argentine economist Raúl Prebisch, advanced a series of propositions, collectively given the name "structuralism," which attempted to explain Latin America's economic stagnation. Prebisch argued that countries of the "periphery," like those of Latin America, were at a permanent disadvantage in their terms of trade with the "center," the industrialized lands of Europe and North America. Two other alleged obstacles to growth were the traditional structure of agriculture, which led to the stagnation of agricultural output, and the excessive concentration of wealth and power in a few hands, which hampered social mobility, capital formation, and industrial development. The theories of the ECLA and of Prebisch gave an important rationale and stimulus to the movement for Latin American industrialization, economic integration, agrarian reform, and social reform in general. A Brazilian economist, Celso Furtado, applied the structuralist thesis to Brazil in his scholarly *Economic Formation of Brazil* (1963).

Prebisch (who died in 1985) and Furtado believed that Latin America could achieve economic independence and balanced development within a capitalist framework. Disappointment with the ECLA reform program and the Latin American economic performance in the 1960s and 1970s, however, produced a progressive radicalization of Latin American economists, whose writings increasingly stressed Latin America's structural dependence on multinational corporations. Pointing to the deformed, dependent character of Latin American capitalist industrialization and the persistence of such problems as the latifundio, Marxist economists like Theotonio dos Santos argued that socialism alone could cure the area's economic ills.

Variants of economic dependency theory flowered in the 1970s. One of the most influential was advanced by the Brazilian scholar Fernando Henrique Cardoso. Impressed by Brazil's rapid economic growth under a military regime that relied heavily on foreign loans and investment, Cardoso argued that development was not incompatible with foreign monopoly penetration of dependent economies. To this development, based on collaboration among international capital, the national bourgeoisie, and the state, he gave the name "dependent capitalist development" or "associated dependent development." The collapse of the Brazilian "economic miracle" and incontrovertible evidence that foreign debt represented the greatest single obstacle to Latin American development cast serious doubt on the validity of Cardoso's thesis, at least as far as a long-range solution for the problem of underdevelopment was concerned. Whatever the particular variants to which social scientists subscribed, dependency theory remained a potent analytical force for all who wish to understand contemporary Latin America's problems.

## THE ARTS

The arts, like the social sciences, combined mastery of modern technical resources with increased use of national subject matter and local folk traditions. National schools of music arose that achieved a synthesis of those traditions with advanced European techniques and styles; examples of such synthesis were the compositions of Heitor Villa-Lobos in Brazil, Carlos Chávez in Mexico, and Alberto Ginastera in Argentina, the first three Latin American composers to achieve world renown. In painting, the Mexican school, led by Diego Rivera, José Clemente Orozco, and David Alfaro Siqueiros, won acclaim with their bold, socially conscious art. Almost equally famous were the monumental murals of the Brazilian Candido Portinari, which portrayed with moving simplicity and sympathy the bleak lives of Brazilian workers and peasants.

In recent decades, however, there has been a movement in the plastic arts toward a more cosmopolitan aesthetic, illustrated by the magical paintings of the Mexican Rufino Tamayo, very different from the art of Rivera, Orozco, and

Frida Kahlo, *Self-Portrait with Changuito*, 1945.
[Frida Kahlo, *Self-Portrait with Changuito*, 1945, Fundáçion Dólores Olmedo, Mexico City, D.F., Mexico, © Banco de México Trust. Schalkwijk/Art Resource, NY]

Siqueiros in theme and technique yet as intensely Mexican in their own way. The same could be said of the work of Frida Kahlo, whose paintings achieved world renown in the 1990s and catapulted her to cult status in the twenty-first century. According to her husband, Diego Rivera, her work "exalted the feminine qualities of endurance and of truth, reality, cruelty, and suffering." But cultural critic, John Berger, associated the growing popularity of her art with the social trauma produced by a decade of neoliberal globalization: "under the new world order, the sharing of pain is one of the essential preconditions for a refinding of dignity and hope."

The sardonic, biting portrayal of the Latin American elite by the Colombian painter Fernando

Botero and the tragic vision of Latin America in the powerful work of the Ecuadorian painter Oswaldo Guayasamín continued the great tradition of socially conscious, critical art. Modern Brazilian architecture impressed foreign observers with its audacity and its skillful solutions of problems of light and air, as evidenced by the work of the architect Oscar Niemeyer, who planned and directed the building of the city of Brasilia.

It is in the field of literature, however, that Latin American culture burned with the most brilliant flame. It may appear surprising that poor countries with masses of illiterates and therefore very small literary markets should produce such a multitude of distinguished poets and novelists, including five Nobel Prize winners in literature,[2] but the phenomenon has its reasons. In the first place, by the early decades of the twentieth century, the advance of the export-import economy had created the necessary economic and social conditions for the rise of literary circles whose members closely followed European artistic developments, plus a small reading public. Second, since colonial times literary culture enjoyed much greater prestige in Latin America than in the United States, illustrated by the fact that many of Latin America's greatest men of letters were rewarded with diplomatic posts, which were often sinecures. Finally, the dramatic contrasts of Latin American life—the extremes of wealth and poverty, the barbarous dictatorships, the rich variety of regional types, the still untamed nature—stimulated the creative imagination of Latin American writers to an extent that did not occur in happier countries. To a very considerable degree, Latin American literature was a literature of protest and struggle. In this, it continued the tradition established by such great nineteenth-century romantic writers as Sarmiento, Echeverría, Martí, and Montalvo.

---

[2]They are the Chilean poet Gabriela Mistral (1945), the Guatemalan novelist Miguel Angel Asturias (1967), the Chilean poet Pablo Neruda (1971), the Colombian novelist Gabriel García Márquez (1982), and the Mexican poet Octavio Paz.

## LITERATURE AND SOCIETY, 1910–1930:
### THE SEARCH FOR SELF-EXPRESSION

After 1900 the art-for-art's-sake creed, of which Rubén Darío had given the supreme example, came under growing attack. Latin American intellectuals, increasingly concerned with backwardness, weakness, and disunity of their continent vis-à-vis its powerful neighbor, the United States, began to descend from Parnassus. In 1899, José Enrique Rodó had already argued that Darío, despite his great technical virtuosity, was not "the poet of America." In a famous poem, "Wring the Neck of the Swan" (1910), the Mexican poet Enrique González Martínez (1871–1952) attacked Darío's proud swan, symbol of beauty as an end in itself. This poem foreshadowed the rise of a new spirit of sincerity, realism, and social consciousness in Latin American literature. By this time, Darío himself had turned away from escapism and had begun to write such powerful public poetry as his "To Roosevelt" (1905).

The intellectuals' concern about the destiny of the continent, about the growing gap in economic and political power between Latin America and the Colossus of the North, inspired numerous essays that probed the causes of the area's problems and suggested solutions. Particularly influential—no doubt because it expressed views Latin Americans wanted to hear—was the essay "Ariel" (1900) by José Enrique Rodó. One of its key themes was the opposition between Latin American spirituality and the materialism of the United States. However, contrary to a common misreading of Rodó, he did not wholly condemn North American utilitarianism; instead, he urged a fruitful fusion of Latin American spirituality and the practical, energetic spirit of the United States. Another important work of stocktaking was *Les democraties latines de l'Amérique* (1912) by the Peruvian Francisco García Calderón, published in France to inform Europeans about Latin America. The book deplores Latin American disunity and anticipates a modern complaint of Latin Americans by its statement that the "new continent, politically free, is economically a vassal." In the same period, there appeared a large number of books that analyzed the problems of individual countries and often found the origins of their malaise in the alleged racial inferiority of indigenous peoples or mixed races; typical of such primitive sociological analysis was Alcides Arguedas's study of Bolivia, *A Sick People* (1909).

The essayists sometimes also stressed the need for artistic originality. García Calderón, for example, claimed that originality in art was as important as economic independence. In the 1920s, a time of preliminary skirmishes in some countries between traditional elites and emerging bourgeois groups, Latin American writers began to try to express the essence of their lands in an original and truly native way. Struggle against an untamed nature, the indígenas, the various regional forms of creole life, and the problems of the peon and the worker were among the varied topics of the new literature. Writers received guidance from one of Latin America's most eminent men of letters, Pedro Henríquez-Ureña, who pointed out in his *Seven Essays in Search of Our Expression* (1928) that every formula of literary Americanism could be useful but that there was only one secret of expression: "To work for it profoundly, to seek to purify it, going to the roots of the things we wish to say, to polish, to refine, with a desire for perfection."

Two postmodernist poets, the Peruvian José Santos Chocano (1875–1934) and the Mexican Ramón López Velarde (1888–1921), illustrate the turning away of the new generation of writers from swans, eighteenth-century palaces, and princesses reclining on velvet divans to the reality of their own lands. Santos Chocano used a wide range of subject matter. He had a certain taste for exotic pre-Columbian and colonial themes: one of his finest poems evokes the ancient city of Cartagena de las Indias, dreaming behind her great walls. Pirates disturb her sleep, but she awakes serene, then softly closes her eyes; fanned by her palm trees and rocked in the hammock of the waves, she falls asleep again. But Santos Chocano could also sound a note of social protest:

> Indian who toils without rest
> on the lands that others own,
> Do you not know that they are yours
> by right of your blood and sweat?[3]

---

[3]"Quién sabe," quoted in Jean Franco, *The Modern Culture of Latin America* (New York: Praeger, 1967), p. 49.

The intensely personal poems of López Velarde celebrated the provincial scenes of his youth in verse free from sentimentality. His most famous poem, however, is "Suave Patria" (1921), a poem in two tender, teasing "acts" in which the poet expresses his love for Mexico with complete freedom from rhetoric. In the "intermezzo" between the acts, the poet invokes the hero Cuauhtemoc, an early illustration of the indigenismo that is a major aspect of twentieth-century Mexican culture. The intermezzo opens: "Young forebear: hear me praise you, the only hero of artistic stature." But there are no heroics: the mood is subdued, tragic, compassionate. Upon the poet's spirit weigh the terrible losses and sufferings of the Mexican Revolution. His Cuauhtemoc is a Man of Sorrows; he is also an instrument for the fusion of Spanish and indigenous elements into a Mexican synthesis.

The Mexican Revolution, which subtly colors "Suave Patria," also pervades the somber novels of Mariano Azuela (1873–1952). Their main theme is the betrayal by middle-class leaders and cynical intellectuals of the peasants and workers whose ignorance and valor they exploit. Azuela's best novel, *The Underdogs* (1916), tells the story of a peasant, Demetrio Macías, who organizes a guerrilla band, rises to the rank of general, and is killed fighting for Villa. He is the victim of blind forces he does not understand and over which he has no control. His simplicity and naiveté contrast with the cunning of the demagogic medical student Luis Cervantes, who carefully keeps out of harm's way and uses looted diamonds to lay the foundation of his future professional career.

The new cultural nationalism also found expression in the novels of the Colombian José Eustasio Rivera (1888–1928) and the Venezuelan Rómulo Gallegos (1884–1969). In Rivera's best work, *The Vortex* (1924), a violent tale of rubber collectors in the Amazonian jungle, the implacable wilderness joins the "rubber lords" in debasing men, in shattering their hopes and bodies. A novel of protest against the barbarism of his country, it is also a truly national novel, the first Colombian novel to depict the difficult lives of the cowboys of the plains and the rubber collectors of the jungle.

The novels of Rómulo Gallegos, an active opponent of long-time dictator Juan Vicente Gómez, depicted the hitherto-neglected life of Venezuela's llanos (plains and jungles) and suggested that the country's destructive regional conflicts could be solved by the fusion of the antagonistic elements: whites and blacks, indigenous and European cultures, barbarism and civilization. In *Doña Bárbara* (1929) the mulatta heroine whose name the novel bears embodies the barbaric vigor and lawless spirit of the people of the plains. Santos Luzardo, on whose land she has encroached, is a city-educated lawyer who finds that he himself must resort to violence to defeat her. Their duel is finally ended by Santos Luzardo's marriage to Doña Bárbara's daughter, a child of nature whom he carefully educates, with particular care that she drop the plebeian dialect of the llanos and learn to speak and act like the "exquisite young ladies of Caracas." The patent artificiality of the civilization-barbarism dichotomy, reflecting Gallegos's middle-class liberalism, weakens his works.

A different viewpoint on the quarrel between civilization and barbarism emerged in the gaucho novel *Don Segundo Sombra* (1926) by Ricardo Guiraldes (1886–1927). One of the most perfect Latin American novels, it evokes with incomparable skill a regional type rapidly receding into the past, but the portrait is clearly touched with nostalgia. The gaucho hero emerges as a dignified and rounded individual, perfectly adapted to his milieu; he needs no transformation from without, for he is already a completely civilized human being.

## LITERATURE AND SOCIETY, 1930–2003: A SOCIAL CONSCIOUSNESS

In the 1930s, a time of growing economic difficulties accompanied by the sharpening of class struggles in mines, factories, and plantations, the radicalization of Latin American writers gave rise to the novel of social protest, frequently influenced by Marxist ideology. Because the principal victims of capitalist exploitation in Latin America were indígenas, the new novels of social protest were usually "Indianist" novels as well. Leading representatives of this genre were Jorge Icaza (b. 1906) in Ecuador, Ciro Alegría (1909–1967) and José M. Arguedas (1901–1969) in Peru, and Miguel A. Asturias (1899–1974) in Guatemala.

The early "Indianist" novels, like *Birds Without a Nest* (1889) by Clorinda Matto de Turner or *Race of Bronze* (1919) by Alcides Arguedas, had found the roots of indigenous misery and exploitation in the personal vices or weaknesses of the ruling classes or of the indígenas themselves. In these indígenas novels, the destruction of the indígenas flows inexorably from the operation of blind economic forces, of which the grasping landlord or exploitive foreign company (these novels often explored anti-imperialist themes as well) are mere instruments. These novels also made a more serious effort to enter the indigenous mind and sometimes prepared themselves for their task by living with the indígenas to learn their speech and customs.

Icaza's *Huasipungo* (1934) reports with blazing anger the brutal exploitation of a group of native Ecuadorians, which culminates in an effort to expel them from their parcels of land (*huasipungos*) to make way for the exploitation of the area by foreign oil companies. But the natives are shown as so degraded by their servitude, so brutish even in dealing with one another, that it is difficult to sympathize with them. More successful in this respect is Ciro Alegría's *Broad and Alien Is the World* (1941), which also relates the destruction of an indigenous community by a landowner bent on acquiring its lands. Alegría's idealized portrayal of indigenous life and virtues borders on the sentimental, yet he convincingly portrays a communal society whose driving force is mutual aid, and therefore engages the reader's sympathy with the indígenas.

Land and labor struggles also characterize the novels of José M. Arguedas, who knew Quechua before he knew Spanish and had a profound mastery of native culture and customs. His novels achieve an unusual penetration of the indigenous mentality through his effort to reproduce the rhythm and syntax of Quechua and evoke the religious world view of the native peoples.

The Guatemalan writer Miguel A. Asturias was one of the founders of the school of magical realism, which attempted to depict indigenous life as the indígenas themselves experienced it, in terms of myth. In *Men of Maize* (1949), he records from this mythic perspective the losing struggle of the natives to retain their land and way of life, using a style whose language and rhythms resemble those of the Maya language. The blend of fantasy and reality in Asturias's novels is far removed from the documentary tone of such regional novelists as Rivera, Gallegos, and Icaza.

In Brazil in the 1920s and 1930s there arose a "northeastern school" that portrayed the varied social types and struggles of the drought-ridden sertão and the coastal sugar plantations. This group included Graciliano Ramos (1892–1953), José Lins do Rego (1901–1957), and Jorge Amado (b. 1912). In *Barren Lives* (1938), Ramos deals with the struggle of a cowherder against drought and starvation and his eventual flight to the city. The "sugar-cane cycle" of Lins do Rego (1932–1943) chronicles the decline and fall of the old sugar aristocracy—the rise of the great *usina* (sugar mill) and the impact of economic change on planters, slaves, and their descendants. Partly based on Lins do Rego's own childhood and adult experiences, these novels reconstruct the social history of Brazilian sugar. In his *Cacao* (1933) Amado describes the life of the workers on the cacao plantations south of Bahia; in *The Violent Land* (1943) he records the bloody struggles for economic and political power of the cacao planters.

Cuban novelist Alejo Carpentier applied the method of magical realism to West Indian blacks in *The Kingdom of This World* (1949); set in Haiti in the time of the French Revolution, it presents the rise and fall of the black dictator Henri Christophe and the emergence of a new mulatto ruling class as seen through the eyes of a house slave. Revolution and the corruption of revolutionaries are major themes of Carpentier's *The Age of Enlightenment* (1962), which is also set in the period of the French Revolution but deals with the Caribbean as a whole.

Poetry, like prose, revealed a new social consciousness. At the same time, Latin American poets struggled to free their verse from rhetoric and the tyranny of old forms. The difficult poetry of Peruvian Cesar Vallejo (1892–1938), though concerned from first to last with human anguish, with the inherently tragic human condition, reveals in its later phase a compassion for the victims of war and exploitation, a vision of a possible better life, that reflects his new socialist ideology. For the Chilean poet Pablo Neruda (1904–1973), as for Vallejo, the Spanish Civil War was a turning point; in a poem written at the beginning of the war he declares that henceforth he will unite his "lone wolf's walk" to the "walk of man." At the end of the war, he joined the Communist Party and combined his poetic career with political activism until his death. His major work is *Canto general* (1950), an epic attempt to tell the history of the Latin American continent from the point of view of figures neglected by textbooks—workers, peasants, and fighters for freedom. Another major poet of left-wing tendencies, the Cuban Nicolás Guillén (b. 1902), founded the Afro-Cuban poetry movement, based on the rhythms and images of Cuban black folk poetry. With the passage of time, his poetry acquired strong social revolutionary and anti-imperialist tones.

The period since 1940 saw a continuing revolution in the technique of the novel. This technical revolution was marked by intensive use of such devices as stream of consciousness, flashbacks, symbolism, and fantasy. Some writers, like Argentina's Jorge Luis Borges in his *Ficciones* (1944), employ fantasy and other avant-garde techniques to demonstrate the absurdity and senselessness of life. Others employ them to heighten awareness of an abhorrent social and political order. To one degree or another, these writers continue the Latin American tradition of employing literature as an instrument of social protest and change. Typical of such novelists is Mario Vargas Llosa, author of *Conversations in the Cathedral* (1970), whose structural and verbal disorder appears to reenact the disorder of Peruvian life and geography.

Guatemala's Miguel Asturias also penned powerful social protest novels. His *Mr. President* (1941) deals with a sinister dictator who rules with a vast apparatus of repression. In it dreams, memories, and imaginings replace the truth the characters cannot speak. Fantasy and reality blend in Asturias's anti-imperialist trilogy, *Strong Wind* (1950), *The Green Pope* (1954), and *The Eyes of the Buried* (1960), which deal with the formation of a monopolistic banana company and the struggles of small farmers and workers against it. In *Strong Wind*, when those struggles fail, a hurricane summoned by a native witch doctor destroys the company's plantations.

Fantasy is the means employed by Gabriel García Márquez to attack a monstrous social and political order in *One Hundred Years of Solitude* (1967), which records the history of an imaginary town set in the remote Colombian *ciénaga* (swampland) where García Márquez grew up. The book describes extraordinary people and events in deadpan fashion; in this magical world, miracles occur in the most natural way. Many of the fantastic situations "are absurd but logical exaggerations of real situations." The fantasies are a parody of Colombian history itself. Indeed, no event depicted in the book is as fantastic as history's la Violencia, the civil war unleashed in the Colombian countryside by conservative repression in 1949, a war that took perhaps 300,000 lives in the course of a few years.

Accelerated urbanization and industrialization placed their stamp on the new novel; frequently, it was set in the great city and dealt with the psychological problems of the urban middle class. In the urban novels of the Mexican Carlos Fuentes (b. 1929), a major theme is the betrayal of revolutionary ideals by the men who made the revolution. In *Where the Air Is Clearer* (1958), *The Clear Consciences* (1959), and *The Death of Armemio Cruz* (1962), Fuentes skillfully depicts the life of a cynical, cosmopolitan society. Alienation and the emptiness of middle- and upper-class life are also common themes in the Argentine urban novel; a good example is *A November Party* (1938) by Eduardo Mallea (1903–1982).

A significant recent development is the emergence of a "testimonial literature" that depicts the struggle of lower-class Latin American women and their families to survive under the most difficult, intolerable conditions. In her diary, *Child of the Dark* (1962), Carolina Maria de Jesus, a black *favela* (shantytown) dweller, records the violence and squalor of favela life. Its publication in Brazil brought Carolina immediate fame, and the book was later translated into many languages. In *Let Me Speak! Testimony of Domitila, A Woman of the Bolivian Mines* (1978), Domitila Barrios de Chungara portrays the bleak lives of a Bolivian miner and his family. In *I, Rigoberta Menchú: An Indian Woman in Guatemala* (1982), the Nobel Peace Prize winner and pro-indigenista activist records the cruelties inflicted by the Guatemalan military on her own family and community. These books testify to the intellectual maturity and talent for self-expression of some Latin American peasant and working-class women with little or no formal education.

Although the beginnings of the Latin American film go back to the first decades of this century, its emergence as a major art form dates from the 1960s, when a group of Latin American filmmakers initiated a reaction against the dominant commercial Hollywood model. Revolutionary Cuba took the lead in this process, producing a large number of excellent films in a variety of styles and relatively free from political constraints. Two such works were Tomás Gutiérrez Alea's *Memories of Underdevelopment* (1968) and Humberto Solas's *Lucía* (1968). Working under difficult, sometimes clandestine or semiclandestine conditions, Argentine, Bolivian, Brazilian, and Central American filmmakers have produced first-class films that explore the history and the social and political problems of their nations. A number of recent Latin American films have won international awards and distinctions. Particularly valuable for an understanding of some episodes of Latin American history are the Argentine filmmaker María Luisa Bemberg's *I, The Worst of All* (1991), a sensitive reconstruction of the life of the poetess Sor Juana de la Cruz, and two Mexican films, Nicolás Echevarría's *Cabeza de Vaca* (1991), which captures the essence of the conquistador's pro-indigenous message, and Alfonso Arau's delightful mix of Mexican twentieth-century history and fantasy, *Like Water for Chocolate* (1992), which broke all foreign-film records for popularity in the United States.

Continuing a tradition established by the founders of Latin American culture, modern Latin American scholars, writers, and artists often tended to view their work not only as a means of self-expression but as an act and instrument of social and political protest. To be sure, in Latin America as elsewhere, there were poets who write very private verse, novelists who deal with intensely personal themes, and painters whose abstract or surrealist art conveys no explicit social message. But to a greater extent than elsewhere, perhaps, the Latin American poet, novelist, painter, and filmmaker have also been the voice and the conscience of the people.

# GLOSSARY

**Adelantado**   Commander of a conquering expedition with governing powers in a frontier or newly conquered province.

**Alcabala**   Spanish sales tax imposed by the crown.

**Alcalde**   Member of a *cabildo* who in addition to administrative duties served as a judge of first instance.

**Alcalde mayor**   Royal governor of a district. See *Corregidor.*

**Aldeia**   An indigenous community in colonial Brazil, governed and controlled by the Catholic church until the Bourbon crown reasserted its authority in the mid-eighteenth century.

**Arpilleras**   A folk art tradition that engaged mostly women in communal activities to produce embroidered quilts that communicated the everyday, lived experiences of ordinary people and, especially in Chile, their resistance against social injustice and the brutal repression of a military dictatorship.

**Audiencia**   A colonial high court and council of state under a viceroy or captain general, or the area of its jurisdiction.

**Auto-da-fé** or **auto-de-fé**   The church's public ceremony of pronouncing judgment during the Inquisition, followed by execution of the sentence by secular authorities.

**Ayllu**   A kinship and territorial unit of social organization, originally Inca, in the Andean region.

**Bandeirante**   Brazilian frontiersmen, usually of mixed racial background, who scoured the interior in search of gold, indigenous slaves, and runaway black slaves.

*Note:* Terms repeatedly defined or glossed in the text are not included in the Glossary.

**Barriadas**   Slum neighborhoods.

**Bohíos**   The traditional thatched-roof shacks in which the vast majority of impoverished Cuban rural workers lived before the 1959 Revolution.

**Brujería**   Witchcraft, especially as practiced by women of African and indigenous American descent, whose knowledge of native cultural traditions offered a refuge from, and served as a source of resistance to, Spanish cultural domination.

**Cabildo**   A municipal council in the Spanish colonies.

**Cacique**   (1) An indigenous chief or local ruler. (2) A tyrannical local boss.

**Calpulli**   A kinship and territorial unit of social organization in ancient and colonial Mexico.

**Campesinos**   Usually poor, powerless rural residents, including farm workers, peasants, sharecroppers, and small farmers.

**Candomblé**   Popular among Afro-Brazilians, a religious sect that worships Ogun, the African god of birth and death, and preserves the cultural traditions of Africa's western Yorubaland, home of many Africans enslaved by the Portuguese and sold to Brazilian fazendeiros.

**Capitão mor**   The commander in chief of the military forces of a province in colonial Brazil.

**Capitulación**   The contract between the Spanish monarch and the leader of an expedition of conquest or discovery.

**Caudillo**   A powerful political boss whose authority is unassailable.

**Cédula**   A royal decree issued by the Spanish crown.

**Charanga**   A traditional musical instrument similar to a guitar, combining the technologies of Spanish and indigenous peoples, who originally used the shell of an armadillo to construct it.

**Chicha** Originally a type of beer made from corn and common among Andean indigenous communities; later became the slang name for a new musical genre pioneered by recent migrants who combined highland indigenous sounds with urban electronic instruments and rock-and-roll rhythms.

**Chinampa** A garden or piece of arable land reclaimed from a lake or pond by dredging up soil from the bottom and piling it on a bed of wickerwork (Mexico).

**Científico** A policy maker in the government of Mexico's Porfirio Díaz (1876–1911) who believed in the "science" of positivism, racist doctrines of white supremacy, and national economic modernization based on private property and foreign investment.

**Cofradía** A religious brotherhood, originally indigenous; sodality.

**Colegio** A college or school.

**Compadrazco** Spanish cultural institution of godparents, which expanded aristocrats' patriarchal power by establishing dependent kinship relationships with lower-class families.

**Compadrio** Portuguese version of *compadrazgo.*

**Composición** A settlement legalizing title to usurped land through payment of a fee to the king.

**Congregación** Resettlement of scattered indigenous populations to facilitate Christianization and the collection of tribute.

**Consulado** A merchant guild and a tribunal of commerce during the colonial period.

**Conversos** Converted Spanish Jews or their descendants.

**Corregidor** A royal governor of a district. A *corregidor de indios* administered indigenous pueblos.

**Cortes** The Spanish parliament.

**Côrtes** The Portuguese parliament.

**Creole** An American-born Spaniard in the Spanish colonies.

**Cumbe** In Spanish America, the name given to communities composed of African peoples who had escaped enslavement and established settlements independent of Spanish royal control.

**Cumbia** An influential musical genre born of Colombia's Atlantic Coast, drawing upon the traditional West African *cumbe* dance and combining Spanish melodies with African rhythms and indigenous American harmonies.

**Curaca** A hereditary chief or ruler in ancient or colonial Peru.

**Ejidatarios** A member of a community that owned lands in common.

**Ejido** Commonly owned lands, customarily farmed collectively by indigenous communities.

**Encomendero** The holder of an *encomienda.*

**Encomienda** An assignment of indígenas who were to serve the Spanish grantee with tribute and labor; also, the area belonging to indigenous people so granted.

**Enganchador** Literally "one who hooks or ensnares," referring to individuals who act as labor contractors to recruit desperate workers by coercion or deceit.

**Fazenda** A large estate (Brazil).

**Fazendeiro** The owner of a *fazenda.*

**Fueros** Special privileges granted to military officers, church officials, and others that exempted them from civil legal proceedings.

**Guachibales** Indigenous religious brotherhoods that aimed to maintain cultural identities; defend their autonomy; and preserve communal customs, ancestral languages, and religious rituals.

**Hacendado** The owner of a *hacienda.*

**Hacienda** A large landed estate.

**Hidalgo** A member of the lower nobility of Spain.

**Indígenas** Individuals whose customs, traditions, dress, or physical features identified them as peoples indigenous to the Americas before the arrival of Europeans.

**Inquilino** A Chilean tenant farmer.

**Jipitecos** Mexican or foreign youth who identified with "hippie" counterculture, rejected the commercialism associated with modernity, and emulated the traditional lifestyles of impoverished indigenous peoples.

**Ladino**   Generally, any person who adopts customs and traditions alien to his own cultural birthright. Depending upon the context, this may refer to (1) Hispanicized people of Jewish, indigenous American, or African descent who embraced Christianity; (2) landless free laborers, born of mixed-race parentage, who embraced the cultural traditions of creole aristocrats; or (3) especially in contemporary Central America, mixed-race peoples who identify as "white" to distinguish themselves from indigenous peoples.

**Latifundio**   The system of large landholdings, feudal in its origins, that has dominated Latin America since the colonial period.

**Mambises**   Nineteenth-century Cuban guerrilla soldiers who fought for political independence and racial justice in integrated battalions, often under the command of black officers.

**Mandamiento**   A system of coerced indigenous labor.

**Mayeque**   A tenant farmer or serf on the estate of a noble family in ancient Mexico.

**Mayorazgo**   An entailed estate.

**Mazombo**   A person born of Portuguese parents in the Americas, similar to the Spanish *creole*.

**Mestizo**   A person of mixed indigenous and Spanish descent.

**Minga**   A free indigenous miner in colonial Peru.

**Mita**   In colonial Peru, the periodic conscription of *indígenas* for labor useful to the Spanish community. See *Repartimiento*.

**Moderados**   Individuals comprising the moderate wing of the Liberal party in nineteenth-century Mexico.

**Ñañiguismo**   The practice, common among Afro-Cubans, of organizing religious brotherhoods, under church protection, to resist racism and preserve African cultural traditions.

**Negrista**   An intellectual who participated in the early-twentieth-century philosophical and literary movement that celebrated African cultural contributions to Latin American societies.

**Nueva Canción**   Literally "New Song," a cultural movement that swept across Latin America in the 1960s, rejected the marketplace values of modernity, and drew inspiration instead from communal traditions linked to folk arts, music, and crafts.

**Obraje**   A primitive factory or workshop, especially for textile manufacture, often employing convict or debt labor.

**Oidor**   A judge of an *audiencia*.

**Ouvidor**   A royal judge who usually combined judicial and administrative duties (Brazil).

**Patria**   The fatherland.

**Patrón**   Master.

**Patronato real**   The right of the Spanish crown to dispose of all ecclesiastical offices.

**Peninsular**   A person born of Spanish parents in Spain and temporarily residing in the Americas.

**Peso**   A monetary unit of eight *reales*.

**Piqueteros**   Unemployed workers in Argentina who joined together to protest against neoliberal policies that produced poverty and social injustice.

**Pitucos**   The derisive and derogatory term used by ordinary folk to describe wealthy people accustomed to privilege and power.

**Porteño**   In Argentina, an inhabitant of Buenos Aires.

**Pueblos jovenes**   Poor "squatter" communities (literally "young towns") constructed on vacant lands by homeless men and women who lacked proprietary rights, but who insisted that their right to survive superseded all other legal claims.

**Quilombo**   In Brazil, the name given to communities composed of African peoples who had escaped enslavement and established settlements independent of Portuguese royal control.

**Quinto**   One-fifth; the royal share or tax on all mine production or spoils of a conquest.

**Rancheros**   People, usually of mixed race, who owned and operated small farms interspersed among indigenous villages and large commercial estates.

**Real**    A monetary unit; one-eighth of a *peso*.

**Rectificación**    The process of searching self-criticism and economic reform designed to make socialism more efficient in Cuba.

**Regidor**    A councilman in a *cabildo*.

**Relacão, *pl.* relaçoes**    A high court in colonial Brazil that combined judicial and administrative functions.

**Repartimiento**    (1) An assignment of indígenas or land to a Spanish settler during the first years of the Conquest. (2) The periodic conscription of indígenas for labor useful to the Spanish community. (3) The mandatory purchase of merchandise by indígenas from royal officials; also *repartimiento de mercancías.*

**Repartimiento de mercancías**    See *Repartimiento* (sense 3).

**Residencia**    A judicial review of a colonial official's conduct at the end of his term of office.

**Santería**    A religion, popular in Cuba and the Caribbean more generally, that combines Spanish Catholic and African traditions and ritual celebrations.

**Senado de câmara**    A municipal council in colonial Brazil.

**Seringueiros**    Independent rubber tappers whose survival depends on the preservation of Brazilian rain forests threatened by commercial ranchers and mining companies.

**Sertão**    Underdeveloped backlands of Brazil, especially in the impoverished northeastern region.

**Soldaderas**    Women who often fought, gathered military intelligence, fed insurgent troops, and provided medical care to those wounded in the Mexican Revolution.

**Son**    First developed among rural Afro-Cuban workers, a musical genre that combined Spanish melodies and the syncopated rhythms of West Africa and that, by the middle of the twentieth century, became the dominant musical form identified with Cuban popular culture.

**Tenente**    A Brazilian army lieutenant, usually associated with junior army officers who sought political, economic, and social reforms in the 1920s.

**Tienda de raya**    A hacienda's company store, which typically exploited its commercial monopoly to coerce a stable labor supply through debt peonage.

**Visita**    A judicial investigation of a colonial official's conduct; a tour of inspection, or other official visit, usually made unannounced.

**Visitador**    An official entrusted by the crown or the viceroy with the conduct of a *visita.*

**Yanacona**    (1) A servant or retainer of the Inca in ancient Peru. (2) An indigenous laborer or tenant farmer of semiservile status attached to a Spanish master or estate in colonial Peru.

**Zambos**    The offspring of sexual liaisons between Africans and indigenous Americans.

# Suggestions for Further Reading

The indispensable *Handbook of Latin American Studies*, published annually since 1936 and now available on-line through the Library of Congress Web site (http://lcweb2.loc.gov/hlas), attempts to digest published material on Latin America in the social sciences and humanities. C. C. Griffin, ed., *Latin America: A Guide to the Historical Literature* (1971), "provides a selective scholarly bibliography, covering the entire field of Latin American history."

Students can keep abreast of the most recent writing in the field by consulting the review sections of *The American Historical Review* (1895–), *The Hispanic American Historical Review* (1918–1922, 1926–), *Revista de Historia de America* (1938–), *The Americas: A Quarterly Review of Inter-American Cultural History* (1944–), *The Review of Inter-American Bibliography* (1951–), *Latin American Research Review* (1965–), the British *Journal of Latin American Studies* (1969–), and the *Colonial Latin American Historical Review* (1993–).

The LANIC Web site at the University of Texas (http://www.lanic.utexas.edu) has abundant information, organized by country and subject directories, with extraordinarily useful electronic links to other relevant Web sites. Molly Molloy's *Internet Resources for Latin America* (http://lib.nmsu.edu/subject/bord/laguia) is also a useful tool for locating reliable electronic sources on Latin America.

For well-informed coverage of current events in the area, see *Latinamerica Press* (Lima, Peru, 1969–) and the *Latin American Weekly Report* and the *Latin American Regional Reports*, published by Latin American Newsletters Ltd. (London). For more extended coverage of particular topics and events, see the bimonthly *NACLA Report on the Americas*, published by the North American Congress on Latin America (1967–) and focusing on the political economy of the area. The articles in *Latin American Perspectives* (1973–) offer scholarly Marxist interpretations of past and present problems of the area.

## General Works

James Lockhart and S. B. Schwartz, *Early Latin America: A History of Colonial Spanish America and Brazil* (1983). L. N. McAlister, *Spain and Portugal in the New World* (1984). M. A. Burkholder and L. L. Johnson, *Colonial Latin America*, 3rd ed. (1997). S. J. and B. H. Stein, *The Colonial Heritage of Latin America: Essays on Economic Dependence in Perspective* (1966). David Bushnell and Neill Macaulay, *The Emergence of Latin America in the Nineteenth Century* (1988). Leslie Bethell, ed., *The Cambridge History of Latin America*, 8 vols. (1985–1991). Benjamin Keen, ed., *Latin American Civilization: History and Society, 1492 to the Present*, 6th ed. (1995), provides a compact but comprehensive collection of source materials.

## Chapter 9
## Dictators and Revolutions

David Bushnell and Neill Macaulay, *The Emergence of Latin America in the Nineteenth Century* (1992). Tulio Halperin-Donghi, *The Aftermath of Revolution in Latin America* (1973). E. B. Burns, *The Poverty of Progress: Latin America in the Nineteenth Century* (1980). H. M. Hamill, ed., *Caudillos: Dictators in Spanish America* (1992).

C. A. Hale, *Mexican Liberalism in the Age of Mora, 1821–1853* (1968). Barbara Tenenbaum, *The Politics of Penury: Debts and Taxes in Mexico, 1821–1856* (1986). R. N. Sinkin, *The Mexican Reform, 1855–1876: A Study in Liberal Nation-Building* (1979). Jan Bazant, *Alienation of Church Wealth: Social and Economic Aspects of the Liberal Revolution, 1856–1875* (1971). Nelson Reed, *The Caste War of Yucatan* (1964). Florencia Mallon, *Peasant and Nation: The Making of Postcolonial Mexico and Peru* (1994); Peter F. Guardino, *Peasants, Politics, and the Formation of Mexico's National State: Guerrero, 1800–1857* (1996).

Miron Burgin, *The Economic Aspects of Argentine Federalism, 1820–1852* (1946). John Lynch, *Argentine Dictator: Juan Manuel Rosas, 1829–1853* (1981). David Bushnell, *Reform and Reaction in the Platine Provinces* (1983). J. C. Brown, *A Socioeconomic History of Argentina, 1776–1860* (1979). R. A. White, *Paraguay's Autonomous Revolution* (1978). Thomas Whigham, *The Politics of River Trade: Tradition and Development in the Upper Plata* (1994).

Brian Loveman, *Chile: The Legacy of Hispanic Capitalism* (1979). Simon Collier, *Ideas and Politics of Chilean Independence, 1808–1833* (1969). Arnold Bauer, *Chilean Rural Society from the Spanish Conquest to 1930* (1975).

R. S. Schneider, *"Order and Progress": A Political History of Brazil* (1991). Leslie Bethell, *The Abolition of the Brazilian Slave Trade* (1971). Gilberto Freyre, *The Mansions and the Shanties*, tr. Harriet de Onis (1963). Robert Conrad, *The Destruction of Brazilian Slavery, 1850–1888* (1973). Katia M. de Queiros Mattos, *To Be a Slave in Brazil, 1550–1888* (1986). Stanley Stein, *Vassouras: A Brazilian Coffee County* (1957). Harry Bernstein, *Dom Pedro II* (1973). Peter Blanchard, *Slavery and Abolition in Early Republican Peru* (1992).

## Chapter 10
# The Triumph of Neocolonialism

Celso Furtado, *The Economic Development of Latin America*, tr. Suzette Macedo (1970). Roberto Cortes Conde, *The First Stages of Modernization in Spanish America* (1974). Florencia Mallon, *The Defense of Community in Peru's Central Highlands: Peasant Struggle and Capitalist Transformation, 1860–1910* (1983).

M. C. Meyer and W. L. Sherman, *The Course of Mexican History*, 4th ed. (1990). J. K. Turner, *Barbarous Mexico* (1910). J. M. Hart, *The Coming and Process of the Mexican Revolution* (1987). R. J. Knowlton, *Church Property and the Mexican Reform, 1856–1910* (1976). R. D. Anderson, *Outcasts in Their Own Land: Mexican Industrial Workers, 1906–1911* (1976). L. B. Perry, *Juarez and Diaz, Machine Politics in Porfirian Mexico* (1979). J. H. Coatsworth, *Growth and Development: The Economic Impact of Railroads on Porfirian Mexico* (1981). J. D. Cockcroft, *Intellectual Precursors of the Mexican Revolution, 1900–1913* (1968). Charles Hale, *The Transformation of Liberalism in Late Nineteenth-Century Mexico* (1990). Mark

Wasserman, *Capitalists, Caciques, and Revolution: The Native Elite and Foreign Enterprise in Chihuahua, Mexico, 1854–1911* (1984). Allen Wells, *Yucatán's Gilded Age: Haciendas, Henequen, and International Harvester, 1860–1915* (1985).

Nicolas Shumway, *The Invention of Argentina* (1992). Thomas McGann, *Argentina, the United States, and the Inter-American System, 1880–1914* (1957). H. S. Ferns, *Britain and Argentina in the Nineteenth Century* (1960). James Scobie, *Argentina: A City and a Nation* (1971). James Scobie, *Revolution on the Pampas: A Social History of Argentine Wheat* (1964). David Rock, *Politics in Argentina, 1890–1930: The Rise and Fall of Radicalism* (1975).

Brian Loveman, *Chile: The Legacy of Hispanic Capitalism* (1979). A. J. Bauer, *Chilean Rural Society from the Spanish Conquest to 1930* (1979). William Sater, *Chile and the War of the Pacific* (1986). Harold Blakemore, *British Nitrates and Chilean Politics, 1886–1896* (1974). Maurice Zeitlin, *The Civil Wars in Chile (or the Bourgeois Revolutions That Never Were)* (1984).

R. M. Schneider, *"Order and Progress": A Political History of Brazil* (1991). Euclides da Cunha, *Rebellion in the Backlands*, tr. Samuel Putnam (1957). P. L. Eisenberg, *The Sugar Industry in Pernambuco, 1840–1910* (1974). Richard Graham, *Britain and the Onset of Industrialization in Brazil, 1850–1914* (1968). Warren Dean, *The Industrialization of São Paulo, 1880–1945* (1969). June Hahner, *Poverty and Politics: The Urban Poor in Brazil, 1870–1920* (1986). Jeffrey D. Needell, *A Tropical Belle Epoque: The Elite Culture of Turn-of-the-Century Rio de Janeiro* (1986). Sandra Lauderdale Graham, *House and Street: Domestic World of Servants and Masters in 19th Century Rio de Janeiro* (1992). María Odila Silva Dias, *Power and Everyday Life: The Lives of Working Women in Nineteenth-Century Brazil* (1995).

## Chapter 11
# Society and Culture in the Nineteenth Century

Tulio Halperin-Donghi, *The Aftermath of Revolution in Latin America* (1973). Richard Graham, *Britain and the Onset of Modernization in Brazil* (1968). Frank Safford, *The Ideal of the Practical: Colombia's Struggle to Form a Technical Elite* (1976). Silvia Arrom, *The*

Women of Mexico City, 1790–1857 (1985). June Hahner, Emancipating the Female Sex: The Struggle for Women's Rights in Brazil, 1850–1940 (1991). Francesca Miller, Latin American Women and the Search for Social Justice (1992).

J. L. Mecham, Church and State in Latin America: A History of Politico-Ecclesiastical Relations, rev. ed. (1966). Leopoldo Zea, The Latin American Mind (1963). Leopoldo Zea, Positivism in Mexico, tr. Josephine Schulte (1974). Charles Hale, The Transformation of Liberalism in Late Nineteenth-Century Mexico (1990). Richard Graham, ed., The Idea of Race in Latin America, (1990). Jean Franco, An Introduction to Spanish American Literature (1969). Allen Woll, A Functional Past: The Uses of History in Nineteenth-Century Chile (1982).

## Chapter 12
# The Mexican Revolution—and After

R. E. Ruiz, The Great Rebellion: Mexico, 1905–1924 (1980). Friedrich Katz, The Secret War in Mexico: Europe, the United States, and the Mexican Revolution (1981). Alan Knight, The Mexican Revolution, 2 vols. (1986). J. M. Hart, The Coming and Process of the Mexican Revolution (1987).

Thomas Benjamin and Mark Wasserman, eds., The Mexican Revolution: Essays in Regional Mexican History, 1910–1929 (1990). G. M. Joseph, Revolution from Without: Yucatán, Mexico, and the United States, 1880–1924 (1988). H. F. Salamini, Agrarian Radicalism in Veracruz, 1920–1938 (1971).

James Cockcroft, Intellectual Precursors of the Mexican Revolution, 1900–1913 (1968). John Womack, Zapata and the Mexican Revolution (1968). M. C. Meyer, Huerta: A Political Portrait (1972). Friedrich Katz, ed., Riot, Rebellion, and Revolution: Rural Social Conflict in Mexico (1988). Gilbert M. Joseph and Daniel Nugent, eds., Everyday Forms of State Formation: Revolution and the Negotiation of Rule in Modern Mexico (1994).

Ana Macias, Against All Odds: The Feminist Movement in Mexico to 1940 (1982). Maria Patricia Fernández-Kelly, For We Are Sold, I and My People: Women and Industry in Mexico's Frontier (1983). Shirlene Soto, Emergence of the Modern Mexican Woman: Her Participation in Revolution and Struggle for Equality, 1910–1940 (1990). Heather Fowler-

Salamini and Mary Kay Vaughan, eds., Women of the Mexican Countryside, 1850–1990: Creating Spaces, Shaping Transitions (1994).

William H. Beezley, William E. French, and Cheryl E. Martin, eds., Rituals of Rule, Rituals of Resistance: Public Celebrations and Popular Culture in Mexico (1994). Nestor Garcia Canclini, Transforming Modernity: Popular Culture in Mexico (1993). Gilbert M. Joseph, Anne Rubenstein, Eric Zolov, Elena Poniatowska, eds., Fragments of a Golden Age: The Politics of Culture in Mexico Since 1940 (2001). Eric Zolov, Refried Elvis: The Rise of the Mexican Counterculture (1999).

J. D. Cockcroft, Mexico: Class Formation, Capital Accumulation, and the State (1983). J. M. Cypher, State and Capital in Mexico: Development Policy Since 1940 (1990). David Barkin, Distorted Development: Mexico in the World Economy (1990). Susan Tiano, Patriarchy on the Line: Labor, Gender, and Ideology in the Mexican Maquila Industry (1994).

## Chapter 13
# Argentina: The Failure of Democracy

David Rock, Argentina, 1516–1982: From Spanish Colonization to the Falklands War (1985). C. F. Diaz Alejandro, Essays on the Economic History of the Argentine Republic (1970). Laura Randall, An Economic History of Argentina in the Twentieth Century (1978).

J. A. Page, Perón: A Biography (1983). Roland Crassweller, Perón and the Enigma of Argentina (1987). Daniel James, Resistance and Integration: Peronism and the Argentine Working Class, 1946–1976 (1994). Peter Ranis, Argentine Workers: Peronism and Contemporary Class Consciousness (1992).

Asunción Lavrin, Women, Feminism, and Social Change in Argentina, Chile, and Uruguay, 1890–1940 (1995). Marifran Carlson, Feminismo!: The Woman's Movement in Argentina from Its Beginnings to Eva Perón (1988). Nicholas Fraser and Marysa Navarro, Evita: The Real Life of Eva Peron (1996). Donna J. Guy, Sex and Danger in Buenos Aires: Prostitution, Family, and Nation in Argentina (1991).

David Rock, Authoritarian Argentina: The Nationalist Movement, Its History and Impact (1993). D. C. Hodges, Argentina, 1943–1976: The National Revolution and Resistance (1976). Carlos Waisman,

*Reversal of Development in Argentina* (1987). M. E. Andersen, *Dossier Secreto. Argentina's Desaparecidos and the Myths of the "Dirty War"* (1993). Monica Peralta-Ramos. *The Political Economy of Argentina: Power and Class Since 1930* (1991). Marguerite Guzman Bouvard, *Revolutionizing Motherhood: The Mothers of the Plaza de Mayo* (1994). J. Patrice McSherry, *Incomplete Transition: Military Power and Democracy in Argentina* (1997).

Laura Podalsky, *Specular City: The Transformation of Culture, Consumption, and Space After Perón* (2002). Donald S. Castro, *The Argentine Tango as Social History, 1880–1955: The Soul of the People* (1991). James P. Brennan, *The Labor Wars in Córdoba, 1955–1976: Ideology, Work, and Labor Politics in an Argentine Industrial City* (1995). Luis Alberto Romero, *A History of Argentina in the Twentieth Century* (2002). Donna J. Guy, *White Slavery and Mothers Alive and Dead: The Troubled Meeting of Sex, Gender, Public Health, and Progress in Latin America* (2000).

## Chapter 14
# The Chilean Way

Brian Loveman, *Chile: The Legacy of Hispanic Capitalism* (1979). M. J. Mamalakis, *The Growth and Structure of the Chilean Economy from Independence to Allende* (1976). Maurice Zeitlin and R. E. Ratcliff, *Landlords and Capitalists: The Dominant Class of Chile* (1988).

Brian Loveman, *Struggle in the Countryside: Politics and Rural Labor in Chile, 1919–1973* (1976). Peter Deshazo, *Urban Workers and Labor Unions in Chile, 1902–1927* (1983). Thomas Miller Klubock, *Contested Communities: Class, Gender, and Politics in Chile's El Teniente Copper Mine, 1904–1948* (1998). Elizabeth Quay Hutchison, *Labors Appropriate to Their Sex: Gender, Labor, and Politics in Urban Chile, 1900–1930* (2001). Heidi Tinsman, *Partners in Conflict: The Politics of Gender, Sexuality, and Labor in the Chilean Agrarian Reform, 1950–1973* (2002). Peter Winn, *Weavers of Revolution: The Yarur Workers and Chile's Road to Socialism* (1989). Edy Kaufman, *Crises in Allende's Chile* (1988). Barbara Stallings, *Class Conflict and Economic Development in Chile, 1958–1973* (1978). James Petras and Morris Morley, *The United States and Chile* (1976). Margaret Power, *Right-Wing Women in Chile: Feminine Power and the Struggle Against Allende, 1964–1973* (2002).

J. S. Valenzuela and Arturo Valenzuela, eds., *Military Rule in Chile: Dictatorship and Oppositions* (1986). J. R. Ramos, *Neo-Conservative Economics in the Southern Cone of Latin America, 1973–1983* (1986). L. H. Oppenheim, *Politics in Chile: Democracy, Authoritarianism, and the Search for Development* (1993). James Petras and F. I. Leiva, with Henry Veltmeyer, *Democracy and Poverty in Chile* (1994). Annie G. Dandavati, *The Women's Movement and the Transition to Democracy in Chile* (1996). Marjorie Agosin, *Tapestries of Hope, Threads of Love: The Arpillera Movement in Chile, 1974–1994* (1996). Joseph Collins et al., *Chile's Free Market Miracle: A Second Look* (1995). Eduardo Silva, *The State and Capital in Chile: Business Elites, Technocrats, and Market Economics* (1996).

## Chapter 15
# Republican Brazil

R. M. Schneider, *"Order and Progress": A Political History of Brazil* (1991). June E. Hahner, *Emancipating the Female Sex: The Struggle for Women's Rights in Brazil, 1850–1940* (1990). Susan Kent Besse, *Restructuring Patriarchy: The Modernization of Gender Inequality in Brazil, 1914–1940* (1996). George Reid Andrews, *Blacks and Whites in Sao Paulo, Brazil, 1888–1988* (1991). Kim D. Butler, *Freedoms Given, Freedoms Won: Afro-Brazilians in Post-Abolition Sao Paulo and Salvador* (1998). Joel Wolfe, *Working Women, Working Men: Sao Paulo and the Rise of Brazil's Industrial Working Class, 1900–1955* (1993). John D. French, *The Brazilian Workers' ABC: Class Conflict and Alliances in Modern Sao Paulo* (1992). Barbara Weinstein, *For Social Peace in Brazil: Industrialists and the Remaking of the Working Class in Sao Paulo, 1920–1964* (1996). Teresa A. Meade, *"Civilizing" Rio: Reform and Resistance in a Brazilian City, 1889–1930* (1997).

Cliff Welch, *The Seed Was Planted: The Sao Paulo Roots of Brazil's Rural Labor Movement, 1924–1964* (1999). Biorn Maybury-Lewis, *The Politics of the Possible: The Brazilian Rural Workers' Trade Union Movement, 1964–1985* (1994). Christopher Dunn, *Brutality Garden: Tropicália and the Emergence of a Brazilian Counterculture* (2001). Hermano Vianna, *The Mystery of Samba: Popular Music and National Identity in Brazil* (1999). John Wirth, ed., *State and Society in Brazil: Continuity and Change* (1987). M. E. Keck, *The Workers' Party and Democratization in Brazil*

(1992). S. A. M. Sandoval, *Social Change and Labor Unrest in Brazil Since 1945* (1994).

Sonia E. Alvarez, *Engendering Democracy in Brazil: Women's Movements in Transition Politics* (1990). Nancy Scheper-Hughes, *Death Without Weeping: The Violence of Everyday Life in Brazil* (1992). Michael George Hanchard, *Orpheus and Power: The Movimento Negro of Rio De Janeiro and Sao Paulo, Brazil, 1945–1988* (1994). Warren Dean, *With Broadax and Firebrand: The Destruction of the Brazilian Atlantic Forest* (1997).

## Chapter 16
# Storm over the Andes: The Struggle for Land and Development

C. M. Conaghan and J. S. Malloy, *Unsettling Statecraft: Democracy and Neoliberalism in the Central Andes* (1994). H. S. Klein, *Bolivia: The Evolution of a Multi-Ethnic Society* (1982). James Malloy and Eduardo Gamarra, *Revolution and Reaction: Bolivia, 1964–1985* (1988). June Nash, *We Eat the Mines and the Mines Eat Us: Dependency and Exploitation in Bolivian Tin Mines* (1979). Lesley Gill, *Precarious Dependencies: Gender, Class, and Domestic Service in Bolivia* (1994). W. Q. Morales, *Bolivia, Land of Struggle* (1994).

Anita Isaacs, *Military Rule and Transition in Ecuador* (1994). C. M. Conaghan, *Restructuring Domination: Industrialists and the State in Ecuador* (1988). N. E. Whitten, Jr., *Cultural Transformations and Ethnicity in Ecuador* (1981).

Paul Gootenberg, *Between Silver and Guano: Commercial Policy and the State in Postrevolutionary Peru* (1991). David G. Becker, *The New Bourgeoisie and the Limits of Dependency: Mining, Class, and Power in Revolutionary Peru* (1983). Nils Jacobsen, *Mirages of Transition: The Peruvian Altiplano, 1780–1930* (1994). J. C. Mariategui, *Seven Interpretive Essays on Peruvian Reality* (1971). R. F. Watters, *Poverty and Peasantry in Peru's Southern Andes* (1993).

Thomas Turino, *Moving Away from Silence: Music of the Peruvian Altiplano and the Experience of Urban Migration* (1993). Raul R. Romero, *Debating the Past: Music, Memory, and Identity in the Andes* (2001). Vincent C. Peloso, *Peasants on Plantations: Subaltern Strategies of Labor and Resistance in the Pisco Valley, Peru* (1998). Jorge Parodi Solari, *To Be a Worker: Identity and Politics in Peru* (2000).

Tom Alberts, *Agrarian Reform and Rural Poverty: A Case Study of Peru* (1983). Rosemary Thorp and Geoffrey Bertram, *Peru, 1890–1977: Growth and Policy in an Open Economy* (1978). J. D. Rudolph, *Peru: The Evolution of a Crisis* (1992). Elsa Chaney and Ximena Bunster, *Sellers and Servants: Working Women in Lima, Peru* (1988). Carol Andreas, *When Women Rebel: The Rise of Popular Feminism in Peru* (1986). Susan C. Stokes, *Cultures in Conflict: Social Movements and the State in Peru* (1995). D. S. Palmer, ed., *Shining Path of Peru* (1992).

## Chapter 17
# The Cuban Revolution

Hugh Thomas, *Cuba: The Pursuit of Freedom* (1971). Ramiro Guerra y Sanchez, *Sugar and Society in the Caribbean* (1964). F. W. Knight, *Slave Society in Nineteenth Century Cuba* (1970). R. J. Scott, *Slave Emancipation in Cuba: The Transition to Free Labor* (1985).

P. S. Foner, *The Spanish-American-Cuban War, 1895–1906* (1972). L. A. Pérez, *Cuba Under the Platt Amendment, 1902–1934* (1984). Louis A. Pérez, *Cuba: Between Reform and Revolution* (1995). K. Lynn Stoner, *From the House to the Streets: The Cuban Woman's Movement for Legal Reform, 1898–1940* (1991). Aline Helg, *Our Rightful Share: The Afro-Cuban Struggle for Equality, 1886–1912* (1995). Robin Moore, *Nationalizing Blackness: Afrocubanismo and Artistic Revolution in Havana, 1920–1940* (1997). Louis A. Pérez, Jr., *On Becoming Cuban: Identity, Nationality, and Culture* (2001). Alejandro de la Fuente, *A Nation for All: Race, Inequality, and Politics in Twentieth-Century Cuba* (2001).

J. R. O'Connor, *The Origins of Socialism in Cuba* (1970). Lee Lockwood, *Castro's Cuba, Cuba's Fidel*, 2nd ed. (1990). S. B. Liss, *Fidel! Castro's Political and Social Thought* (1994). Marifeli Pérez-Stable, *The Cuban Revolution: Origins, Course, and Legacy* (1993). Lois M. Smith, *Sex and Revolution: Women in Socialist Cuba* (1996). Susan Eckstein, *Back from the Future: Cuba Under Castro* (1994). Carollee Bengelsdorf, *The Problem of Democracy in Cuba: Between Vision and Reality* (1994). Mona Rosendahl, *Inside the Revolution: Everyday Life in Socialist Cuba* (1998).

Andrew Zimbalist and Claes Brundenius, *The Cuban Economy: Measurement and Analysis of Socialist*

*Performance* (1989). Sandor Halebsky and J. M. Kirk, eds., *Cuba: Twenty-Five Years of Revolution, 1959–1984* (1985). Jorge Domínguez, *To Make the World Safe for Revolution* (1988). T. C. Dalton, *"Everything Within the Revolution": Cuban Strategies for Development Since 1960* (1993).

## Chapter 18
# Revolution and Counterrevolution in Central America: Twilight of the Tyrants?

R. L. Woodward, Jr., *Central America: A Nation Divided* (1976). James Dunkerley, *Power in the Isthmus: A Political History of Modern Central America* (1988). F. S. Weaver, *Inside the Volcano. The History and Political Economy of Central America* (1994). William Roseberry, Lowell Gudmundson, and Mario Samper Kutschback, eds., *Coffee, Society, and Power in Latin America* (1995). Jeffrey M. Paige, *Coffee and Power: Revolution and the Rise of Democracy in Central America* (1998). Aldo Lauria-Santiago and Aviva Chomsky, eds., *At the Margins of the Nation State: Identity and Struggle in the Making of the Laboring Peoples of Central America and the Hispanic Caribbean* (1998).

R. L. Woodward, Jr., *Rafael Carrera and the Emergence of the Republic of Guatemala, 1821–1871* (1993). W. H. Clegern, *The Origins of Liberal Dictatorship in Central America. Guatemala, 1865–1973* (1994). Suzanne Jonas, *The Battle for Guatemala: Rebels, Death Squads, and U.S. Power* (1991). P. J. Dosal, *Doing Business with the Dictators: A Political History of United Fruit in Guatemala, 1899–1944* (1993). Deborah J. Yashar, *Demanding Democracy: Reform and Reaction in Costa Rica and Guatemala, 1870s–1950s* (1997). Deborah Levenson-Estrada, *Trade Unionists Against Terror: Guatemala City 1954–1985* (1994). Tracy Bachrach Ehlers, *Silent Looms: Women and Production in a Guatemalan Town* (1990). Robert M. Carmack, *Rebels of Highland Guatemala: The Quiché-Mayas of Momostenango* (1995). C. A. Smith, ed., *Guatemalan Indians and the State* (1990). Ricardo Falla, *Massacre in the Jungle: Ixcan, Guatemala, 1975–1982*, tr. Julia Howland (1994).

E. B. Burns, *Patriarch and Folk: The Emergence of Nicaragua, 1798–1858* (1991). Jeffrey L. Gould, *To Die in This Way: Nicaraguan Indians and the Myth of the Mestizaje, 1880–1960* (1998). Charles R. Hale, *Resistance and Contradiction: Miskitu Indians and the Nicaraguan State, 1894–1987* (1994). T. W. Walker, *Nicaragua: The Land of Sandino*, 3rd ed. (1991). Gregorio Selser, *Sandino*, tr. Cedric Belfrage (1981). D. C. Hodges, *The Intellectual Foundation of the Nicaraguan Revolution* (1986). Gary Prevost and Harry E. Vanden, eds., *The Undermining of the Sandinista Revolution* (1997). Thomas W. Walker, ed., *Nicaragua Without Illusions: Regime Transition and Structural Adjustment in the 1990s* (1997). Laura J. Enríquez, *Agrarian Reform and Class Consciousness in Nicaragua* (1997). Margaret Randall, *Sandino's Daughters Revisited: Feminism in Nicaragua* (1994). Carlos M. Vilas, *State, Class, and Ethnicity in Nicaragua: Capitalist Modernization and Revolutionary Change on the Atlantic Coast* (1989). Hazel Smith, *The Nicaraguan Revolution: Self-Determination and Survival* (1993).

T. P. Anderson, *Matanza: El Salvador's Revolt of 1932* (1971). T. S. Montgomery, *Revolution in El Salvador, Origins and Evolution*, 2nd ed. (1994). Marilyn Thomson, *Women of El Salvador: The Price of Freedom* (1986). Maria Teresa Tula and Lynn Stephen, *Hear My Testimony: The Story of Maria Teresa Tula, Human Rights Activist of El Salvador* (1994). Leigh Binford, *The El Mozote Massacre: Anthropology and Human Rights* (1996). Philip J. Williams and Knut Walter, *In the Shadow of the Barracks: Militarization and Demilitarization in El Salvador's Transition to Democracy* (1998).

## Chapter 19
# Lands of Bolívar: Venezuela and Colombia in the Twentieth Century

Judith Ewell, *Venezuela, A Century of Change* (1984). D. C. Hellinger, *Venezuela: Tarnished Democracy* (1991). Winthrop R. Wright, *Cafe Con Leche: Race, Class, and National Image in Venezuela* (1993). Judith Ewell, *Venezuela and the United States: From Monroe's Hemisphere to Petroleum's Empire* (1996).

B. S. McBeth, *Juan Vicente Gomez and the Oil Companies in Venezuela* (1983). Douglas Yarrington, *A Coffee Frontier: Land, Society, and Politics in Duaca, Venezuela, 1830–1936* (1997). Steve Ellner, *Organized Labor in Venezuela 1958–1991* (1993). Terry Lynn Karl, *The Paradox of Plenty: Oil Booms and Petro-States* (1997). Jennifer McCoy et al., *Venezuelan Democracy Under Stress* (1995). Elisabeth J. Friedman, *Unfinished*

Transitions: Women and the Gendered Development of Democracy in Venezuela, 1936–1996 (2000).

David Bushnell, The Making of Modern Colombia: A Nation in Spite of Itself (1993). Jonathan Hartlyn, Politics of Coalition Rule in Colombia (1988). Jenny Pearce, Colombia: Inside the Labyrinth (1990). Michael Taussig, Shamanism, Colonialism, and the Wild Man: A Study in Terror and Healing (1991). Peter Wade, Blackness and Race Mixture: The Dynamics of Racial Identity in Colombia (1993). Ann Farnsworth-Alvear, Dulcinea in the Factory: Myths, Morals, Men and Women in Colombia's Industrial Experiment, 1905–1960 (2000). Peter Wade, Music, Race, and Nation: Música Tropical in Colombia (2000).

David Sowell, The Early Colombian Labor Movement: Artisans and Politics in Bogotá, 1832–1919 (1992). Marco Palacios, Coffee in Colombia, 1850–1870: An Economic, Social, and Political History (1980). Charles Bergquist, Coffee and Conflict in Colombia (1976). James Park, Rafael Núñez and the Politics of Colombian Regionalism (1985). Catherine LeGrand, Frontier Expansion and Peasant Protest in Colombia (1986). Herbert Braun, The Assassination of Gaitan: Public Life and Urban Violence in Colombia (1986). James Henderson, When Colombia Bled: A History of the Violencia in Tolima (1985). Charles Bergquist et al., Violence in Colombia: The Contemporary Crisis in Historical Perspective (1992).

# Chapter 20
# The Two Americas: United States—Latin American Relations

Harold Molineu, U.S. Policy Toward Latin America: From Regionalism to Globalism (1986). Michael L. Krenn, Race and U.S. Foreign Policy from the Colonial Period to the Present (1998). Walter LaFeber, The Cambridge History of American Foreign Relations: The American Search for Opportunity, 1865–1913 (1993). Michael L. Krenn, U.S. Policy Toward Economic Nationalism in Latin America, 1917–1929 (1990). Thomas J. McCormick, America's Half-Century: United States Foreign Policy in the Cold War and After (1995). Frank Niess, A Hemisphere to Itself: A History of U.S.-Latin American Relations (1990). Dean B. Mahin, Olive Branch and Sword: The United States and Mexico, 1845–1848 (1997). J. W. Park, Latin American Underdevelopment: A History of Perspectives in the United States, 1870–1965 (1995).

L. D. Langley, The Banana Wars: An Inner History of American Empire, 1900–1934 (1983). J. R. Benjamin, The United States and Cuba: Hegemony and Dependent Development, 1880–1934 (1974). J. R. Benjamin, The United States and the Origins of the Cuban Revolution: An Empire of Liberty in an Age of National Liberation (1990). Morris Morley, Imperial State and Revolution: The U.S. and Cuba, 1952–86 (1987). Piero Gleijeses, Conflicting Missions: Havana, Washington, and Africa, 1959–1976 (2002). Peter Kornbluh, ed., Bay of Pigs Declassified: The Secret CIA Report on the Invasion of Cuba (1998).

J. L. Dietz, The Economic History of Puerto Rico (1986). A. Morales Carrion, Puerto Rico: A Political and Cultural History (1983). Richard Weiskoff, Factories and Foodstamps: The Puerto Rican Model of Development (1985). Pedro Cabán, Constructing a Colonial People: Puerto Rico and the United States, 1898–1932 (2000).

S. L. Baily, The United States and the Development of South America, 1845–1975 (1976). David Green, The Containment of Latin America: A History of the Myths and Realities of the Good Neighbor Policy (1971). Bryce Wood, The Dismantling of the Good Neighbor Policy (1985). Cole Blasier, The Hovering Giant (1986).

Ruth Leacock, Requiem for Revolution: The United States and Brazil, 1961–1969 (1990). Ariel C. Armony, Argentina, the United States, and the Anti-Communist Crusade in Central America, 1977–1984 (1997). Stephen G. Rabe, The Road to OPEC: United States Relations with Venezuela, 1919–1976 (1982). Stephen J. Randall, Colombia and the United States: Hegemony and Interdependence (1992). Sewall H. Menzel, Fire in the Andes: U.S. Foreign Policy and Cocaine Politics in Bolivia and Peru (1996). Jon V. Kofas, Foreign Debt and Underdevelopment: U.S.–Peru Economic Relations, 1930–1970 (1996). G. K. Lewis, Grenada: The Jewel Despoiled (1986). Michel-Rolph Trouillot, Haiti: State Against Nation: The Origin and Legacy of Duvalierism (1990). Amy Wilentz, The Rainy Season: Haiti Since Duvalier (1990). Alex Dupuy, Haiti in the New World Order: The Limits of the Democratic Revolution (1997). J. Zoraida Vasquez and Lorenzo Meyer, The United States and Mexico (1986).

Walter LaFeber, Inevitable Revolutions: The United States in Central America (1993). Walter LaFeber, The Panama Canal (1990). Luis E. Murillo, The Noriega Mess: The Drugs, the Canal, and Why America Invaded

(1995). Piero Gleijeses, *Shattered Hope: The Guatemalan Revolution and the United States, 1944–1954* (1991). Morris H. Morley, *Washington, Somoza, and the Sandinistas: State and Regime in U.S. Policy Toward Nicaragua, 1969–1981* (1994). E. B. Burns, *At War in Nicaragua: The Reagan Doctrine and the Politics of Nostalgia* (1987). W. L. Robinson, *A Faustian Bargain: U.S. Intervention in the Nicaraguan Elections and American Foreign Policy in the Post–Cold War Era* (1992). P. D. Scott and Jonathan Marshall, *Cocaine Politics: Drugs, Armies, and the CIA in Central America* (1991).

Eldon Kenworthy, *America/Americas: Myth in the Making of U.S. Policy Toward Latin America* (1995). Mark T. Berger, *Under Northern Eyes: Latin American Studies and U.S. Hegemony in the Americas, 1898–1990* (1995). Lars Schoultz, *Beneath the United States: A History of U.S. Policy Toward Latin America* (1998). William I. Robinson, *Promoting Polyarchy: Globalization, U.S. Intervention, and Hegemony* (1996). Philip Oxhorn and Graciela Ducatenzeiler, eds., *What Kind of Democracy? What Kind of Market? Latin America in the Age of Neoliberalism* (1998).

## Chapter 21
# Latin American Society in Transition

Suzanne Jonas and E. J. McCaughan, eds., *Latin America Faces the Twenty-First Century: Reconstructing a Social Justice Agenda* (1994). M. S. Grindle, *State and Countryside: Development Policy and Agrarian Politics in Latin America* (1986). Rachel Garst and Tom Barry, *Feeding the Crisis: U.S. Food and Farm Policy in Central America* (1990). David Goodman and Michael Redclift, *Environment and Development in Latin America: The Politics of Sustainability* (1991). Alan Gilbert and P. M. Ward, *Housing: The State and the Poor: Policy and Practice in Three Latin American Cities* (1984). Alan Gilbert, *The Latin American City* (1994).

F. H. Cardoso and Enzo Faletto, *Dependency and Development in Latin America* (1979). Peter Evans, *Dependent Development: The Alliance of Multinational, State, and Local Capital in Brazil* (1979). Richard Farmer, ed., *Profits, Progress, and Poverty: Case Studies of International Industries in Latin America* (1985). D. C. Betts and D. J. Slottje, *Crisis on the Rio Grande: Poverty, Unemployment, and Economic Development on the Texas-Mexico Border* (1993). Duncan Green, *Silent Revolution: The Rise of Market Economies in Latin America* (1995).

J. J. Johnson, *Political Change in Latin America: The Emergence of the Middle Sectors* (1958). S. M. Lipset and Aldo Solari, eds., *Elites in Latin America* (1967). I. L. Horowitz, ed., *Masses in Latin America* (1970). Andrew Pearse, *The Latin American Peasantry* (1975). Alain de Janvry, *The Agrarian Question and Reformism in Latin America* (1981). H. A. Spalding, *Organized Labor in Latin America: Historical Case Studies of Workers in Dependent Societies* (1977). Charles Bergquist, *Labor in Latin America: Comparative Studies on Chile, Argentina, Venezuela, and Colombia* (1986). S. B. Liss, *Marxist Thought in Latin America* (1984).

J. S. Jaquette, ed., *The Women's Movement in Latin America: Participation and Democracy*, 2nd ed. (1994). H. I. Safa, *The Myth of the Male Breadwinner: Women and Industrialization in the Caribbean* (1994). Florestan Fernandes, *The Negro in Brazilian Society* (1969). G. R. Andrews, *Blacks and Whites in São Paulo, Brazil, 1888–1988* (1991). Francesca Miller, *Latin American Women and the Search for Social Justice* (1991). John D. French, ed., *The Gendered Worlds of Latin American Women Workers* (1997). Peter Wade, *Race and Ethnicity in Latin America* (1997).

Philip Berryman, *The Religious Roots of Rebellion* (1984). Rowan Ireland, *Kingdom Come: Religion and Politics in Brazil* (1992). E. L. and Hannah Stewart-Gambino, *Conflict and Competition: The Latin American Church in a Changing Environment* (1992). F. M. Nunn, *Yesterday's Soldiers: European Military Professionalism in South America, 1890–1940* (1983). J. K. Black, *Sentinels of Empire: The United States and Latin American Militarism* (1986).

Jean Franco, *An Introduction to Spanish-American Literature* (1969). John King, ed., *Modern Latin American Fiction* (1987). Cristobal Kay, *Latin American Theories of Development and Underdevelopment* (1989). William Rowe and Vivian Schelling, *Memory and Modernity: Popular Culture in Latin America* (1992). E. B. Burns, *Latin American Cinema: Film and History* (1978). Julianne Burton, *Cinema and Social Change in Latin America: Conversations with Filmmakers* (1986).

# INDEX

Abertura policy (Brazil), 387
Abolition and abolitionism: in Brazil, 204, 235–236; in United States, 205; in Cuba, 208; in Venezuela, 213
Abortion: in Chile, 348; in El Salvador, 577
Abrams, Elliot, 505
Academy of Letrán (Mexico), 261
Acción Democrática (AD, Venezuela), 494, 495, 496; rule by, 498–499
Acculturation: of indigenous peoples, 252–253
Adams, John Quincy, 524
Additional Act (1834, Brazil), 203
"Adiciones": to Plan of Guadalupe, 292
Administration, *see* Government
Advanced countries: foreign debt and, 557. *See also* Developed countries
Afonso Arinos Act (Brazil), 375
Africa: Battle of Cuito Cuanavale in, 445; Cuban involvement in, 543. *See also* Slaves and slavery; Slave trade
Afro-Brazilians, 365, 370, 375; rights in World War II, 374; prejudice against, 578
Afro-Colombians, 514, 516
Afro-Cubans, 425, 428, 451; discrimination against, 209; in Cuban Rural Guard, 427; U.S. and, 429; insurrection by, 430 (illus.); culture of, 432–433; status of, 447; poetry of, 592
Afro-Ecuadorians, 403
*Age of Enlightenment, The* (Carpentier), 591
Agrarian law: in Peru, 411
Agrarian provisions: in Constitution of 1917 (Mexico), 294
Agrarian reform: in Guatemala, 244, 456, 457; in Mexico, 285, 288, 292, 296, 298, 300, 301–302, 313; in Chile, 350–351; in Brazil, 372, 385, 388; in Ecuador, 401; in Cuba, 440–441; in Nicaragua, 474–475; in El Salvador, 482–483; in Venezuela, 494, 504–505; in Colombia, 511–512. *See also* Land reform

Agrarian Reform Act (1964, Ecuador), 400
Agrarian unrest: in Mexico, 224–226
Agribusiness: in Chile, 361
Agricultural communes: in Nicaragua, 470
Agriculture: large estates in, 180; in Mexico, 185, 223, 560–561; Juárez policy and, 192; labor for, 219; in Brazil, 240, 241, 366, 387; in Peru, 242, 243, 413; in Guatemala, 244, 458; in El Salvador, 245; in Nicaragua, 245, 470; modernization and, 255–257; ejido sector in Mexico, 312; in Argentina, 333; in Chile, 350, 358, 361; in Ecuador, 401; in Cuba, 433, 441–442, 449–450; in Venezuela, 492, 500–501; in Colombia, 508; child labor in, 570; economists on, 587. *See also* Farmers and farming; Haciendas (estates); Landowners; Latifundio (great estate)
"Agriculture of the Torrid Zone, The" (Bello), 260
Aguascalientes: convention at, 290–291
Aguinaldo, Emilio, 427
Aguirre Beltrán, Gonzalo, 579
Alamán, Lucas, 186, 188, 586
Alberdi, Juan Bautista, 195, 586
Albizu Campos, Pedro, 532
Alcohol: as fuel in Brazil, 387n
Alcoholism: in Mexico, 224
Alegría, Ciro, 591
Além, Leandro, 228
Alemán, Arnoldo, 475–476, 476 (illus.)
Alemán, Miguel, 304
Alencar, José de, 263
Alencar Caselo Branco, Humberto de, 275
Alessandri, Arturo, 345; return to presidency, 345, 346–347
Alessandri, Jorge, 352
Alfonsín, Raul, 336, 338
Alianza Popular Revolucionaria Americana (APRA), 409–412, 418–420, 586

*Allegory of the Departure of Dom Pedro II for Europe After the Declaration of the Republic* (illus.), 237
Allende Gossens, Salvador, 275, 342, 349, 350, 353 (illus.), 541–542; socialism of, 274; as president of Chile, 352–356; overthrow of, 356; responsibility for death of, 362; CIA and, 585
Alliance for Progress, 273, 540; Ecuador and, 400; Nicaragua and, 466; Colombian Communist Party and, 512; results of, 541
Almacenes del Pueblo (People's Grocery Cooperatives): in Chile, 355
Alpiréz, Julio Roberto, 584
Altamirano, Ignacio, 261
Aluminum industry: in Venezuela, 503
Alvarado, Pedro de, 562 (illus.)
Alvarado Rivera, María Jesús, 409
Alvarez, Juan, 188, 253
Álvarez, León, 434
Alvear, Marcelo de, 326–327
Amado, Jorge, 591
*Amalia* (Marmol), 260
Amazon Development Agency (Brazil), 387
Amazon region: Huaorani people in, 403
*America in Danger* (Bilbao), 262
*American Gospel, The* (Bilbao), 262
American Indians, *see* Indigenous peoples
*American Poems* (Gonçalves Dias), 263
American Sanitary Commission: yellow fever and, 428
Amigas del Pueblo (AP), 284
Amnesty: for Colombian guerrillas, 511
Amnesty International: on Colombia, 516
Anaconda Copper Co., 343, 349
Anarchism: in Chile, 234
Ancón, Treaty of, 231, 243
Andean Initiative: bishops' denunciation of, 583
Andean region: Colombia and, 214; land in, 218; tenant farmers in, 252; Bolivia and, 395–400;